T0296273

Strategy, Leadership, and AI in the Cyber Ecosystem

Strategy, Leadership, and AI in the Cyber Ecosystem
The role of digital societies in information governance and decision making

Edited by

Hamid Jahankhani
Northumbria University, London, United Kingdom

Liam M. O'Dell
Senior Project Manager, Member of the Association for Project
Management (MAPM); Associate of the Chartered Institute for Building
(ACIOB), London, United Kingdom

Gordon Bowen
Northumbria University, London, United Kingdom

Daniel Hagan
Northumbria University, London, United Kingdom

Arshad Jamal
Northumbria University, London, United Kingdom

Academic Press is an imprint of Elsevier
125 London Wall, London EC2Y 5AS, United Kingdom
525 B Street, Suite 1650, San Diego, CA 92101, United States
50 Hampshire Street, 5th Floor, Cambridge, MA 02139, United States
The Boulevard, Langford Lane, Kidlington, Oxford OX5 1GB, United Kingdom

© 2021 Elsevier Inc. All rights reserved.

No part of this publication may be reproduced or transmitted in any form or by any means, electronic or
mechanical, including photocopying, recording, or any information storage and retrieval system, without
permission in writing from the publisher. Details on how to seek permission, further information about the
Publisher's permissions policies and our arrangements with organizations such as the Copyright Clearance
Center and the Copyright Licensing Agency, can be found at our website: www.elsevier.com/permissions.

This book and the individual contributions contained in it are protected under copyright by the Publisher (other
than as may be noted herein).

Notices
Knowledge and best practice in this field are constantly changing. As new research and experience broaden our
understanding, changes in research methods, professional practices, or medical treatment may become
necessary.

Practitioners and researchers must always rely on their own experience and knowledge in evaluating and using
any information, methods, compounds, or experiments described herein. In using such information or methods
they should be mindful of their own safety and the safety of others, including parties for whom they have a
professional responsibility.

To the fullest extent of the law, neither the Publisher nor the authors, contributors, or editors, assume any liability
for any injury and/or damage to persons or property as a matter of products liability, negligence or otherwise, or
from any use or operation of any methods, products, instructions, or ideas contained in the material herein.

Library of Congress Cataloging-in-Publication Data
A catalog record for this book is available from the Library of Congress

British Library Cataloguing-in-Publication Data
A catalogue record for this book is available from the British Library

ISBN: 978-0-12-821442-8

For information on all Academic Press publications
visit our website at https://www.elsevier.com/books-and-journals

Publisher: Mara Conner
Editorial Project Manager: Rafael G. Trombaco
Production Project Manager: Punithavathy Govindaradjane
Cover Designer: Miles Hitchen

Typeset by SPi Global, India

Working together
to grow libraries in
developing countries

www.elsevier.com • www.bookaid.org

Contents

Contributors   xv

Foreword   xvii

Section 1   Strategic leadership in the digital age

1. The evolution of AI and the human-machine interface as a manager in Industry 4.0   3
Liam M. O'Dell and Hamid Jahankhani

   1 Introduction   3
   2 Artificial intelligence (AI)   5
   3 Data emerging into big data   7
   4 Artificial intelligence technology and the workplace   8
   5 Artificial intelligence and the workforce   8
   6 The digital twin   10
   7 Artificial intelligence ethics and governance   11
   8 Artificial intelligence in project management   13
   9 Research findings and critical discussion   14
   10 Conclusions   17
   References   17

2. Digital leadership, ethics, and challenges   23
Gordon Bowen

   1 Introduction   23
   2 Ethics and consent   24
   3 Ethical dimensions and leadership   26
   4 Risk and vulnerability assessment—Reputation   31

    5 Regulatory challenges   32

    6 Implications   34

    7 Conclusion   37

    References   37

3. **Integrating social media and warranty data for fault
    identification in the cyber ecosystem: A cloud-based
    collaborative framework**   **41**
    Syed Imran Ali, Farooq Habib, Abdilahi Ali, Abdul Ali,
    Murtaza F. Khan, and Arshad Jamal
    1 Introduction   41
    2 Literature review for fault identification   43
    3 Research questions and contributions   46
    4 Use of social media data   46
    5 Methodology   50
    6 Results and evaluation   51
    7 Cloud-based framework   56
    8 An illustrative cloud-based framework   63
    9 Managerial implications   66
   10 Concluding remarks   66
    References   67

4. **Getting it right: Systems Understanding of Risk
    Framework (SURF)**   **71**
    Simon M. Wilson and John McCarthy
    1 Introduction   71
    2 Systems Understanding of Risk Framework   74
    3 SURF methodology   80
    References   88
    Further reading   89

Section 2   AI: The cyber-physical management professional

5. **Blockchain as a tool for transparency and governance in the delivery of development aid**   93
   Hamid Jahankhani, Stefan Kendzierskyj, and Anita Colin

   1 Background to blockchain and relevance to development aid   93
   2 Viability of cryptocurrency and smart contracts in development aid   96
   3 Blockchain application to development aid   101
   4 Construction of a conceptual framework: A blockchain and development aid synergy   107
   5 Conclusions   108
   References   109

6. **A proposed OKR-based framework for cyber effective services in the GDPR era**   113
   David Wilson and Hamid Jahankhani

   1 General data protection regulation and data breaches   113
   2 Data breach, identity theft, and impact on organisations   118
   3 Research methodology   124
   4 Data analysis and critical discussions   126
   5 A proposed framework for delivery of cyber effective services in the GDPR era   129
   6 Conclusions and future work   133
   References   134

7. **Balancing privacy and public benefit to detect and prevent fraud**   137
   Sudhir Gautam and Hamid Jahankhani

   1 Introduction   137
   2 Data sharing and fraud detection   139

3 Data privacy   142

4 The General Data Protection Regulation (GDPR) landscape   143

5 Use of public task as data sharing function to combat fraud   144

6 Research findings   149

7 Critical discussions   149

8 Digital Economy Act 2017   154

9 Conclusions   154

References   155

8. Securing the digital witness identity using blockchain
    and zero-knowledge proofs   **159**
    Lynton Lourinho, Stefan Kendzierskyj, and Hamid Jahankhani

1 Introduction   159

2 Blockchain   170

3 Threat model: Digital witness concept   175

4 Conclusion and future work   192

References   192

9. Zero Trust networks, the concepts, the strategies,
    and the reality   **195**
    David Allan Eric Haddon

1 Introduction   195

2 What is Zero Trust?   196

3 What are the key principles of a Zero Trust network?   196

4 Are there variations on the Zero Trust concept?   197

5 Let's examine Zero Trust core concepts?   198

6 So what products that can assist with a Zero Trust
   network monitoring?   199

7 The Cloud, Dev-Ops, and Zero Trust   201

8 The on-premise environment and Zero Trust   202

9 Authentication mechanisms for Zero Trust networks   203

10 Zero Trust and the threat of data theft   207

11 Wireless and mobile networks and Zero Trust   207

12 DHCP and Zero Trust   207

13 How do network security auditing standards align
    with Zero Trust?   208

14 Implementing Zero Trust concepts starts with the data   208

15 Developing a Zero Trust network strategy   208

16 How a future on-premise Zero Trust network might look   210

17 Practical limitations of the Zero Trust model   212

18 Conclusion   212

    References   213

Section 3   Digital 'hand-shake' of business

10. An analysis of the perceptions of the role of social
    media marketing in shaping the preferences of the
    electorate: A case study of the 2018 Colombian
    presidential election   219
    Natalia Gomez Arteaga and Lillian Clark

    1 Introduction   219

    2 Literature review   220

    3 Research methodology   226

    4 Findings and analysis   232

    5 Synthesis and conclusion   234

    References   237

11. Will the new security trends achieve the skin in the game?
    (Lesson learned from recent IOCs)   243
    Giovanni Bottazzi, Gianluigi Me, Giuseppe Giulio Rutigliano,
    Pierluigi Perrone, and Luciano Capone

    1 Introduction   243

    2 Most widespread cybersecurity threats   244

3 The attackers' perspective   245

4 The defenders' perspective   249

5 The security frameworks' perspective   253

6 Did we forget anything on the way?   256

7 Conclusions   262

   References   263

12. The role of social media, digitisation of marketing,
    and AI on brand awareness   265
    Daniel Hagan, Hamid Jahankhani, Lea Broc, and Arshad Jamal
    1 Introduction   265
    2 Social media   266
    3 Advertising and the hierarchy of effects   269
    4 Customers and smart retail interactions   270
    5 Categorising social media influencers   272
    6 Instagram as the most effective platform/audience   272
    7 Branding   273
    8 Artificial intelligence and brand awareness   276
    9 Customer information processing   278
    10 Conclusion   279
    References   279

13. The marketing situation of music public relation agencies
    in the United Kingdom in relation to client acquisition
    methods and client search behaviour   285
    Karsyn Robb and Lillian Clark
    1 Introduction   285
    2 Literature review   286
    3 Methodology   288
    4 Results and analysis   289
    5 Conclusions   298
    References   301

Section 4   Future digital landscape

14. The application of Industry 4.0 in continuous professional development (CPD)   307
Eustathios Sainidis and Guy Brown

    1 Introduction   307

    2 Higher education in the Industry 4.0 era   308

    3 Career development in emerging technologies: The need for effective and transformational leadership   309

    4 Career leadership   311

    5 Transformational leadership   311

    6 The role of the transformational leader in engaging in continual learning   313

    7 Off-the-job learning   317

    8 Summary   318

    References   318

15. A regulatory investigation into the legal and ethical protections for digital citizens in a holographic and mixed reality world   321
Russell Watkins and Hamid Jahankhani

    1 Introduction   321

    2 Biometrics: The de facto standard   323

    3 Future direction of mixed technologies   325

    4 Holographic reality   326

    5 One-to-many communications   327

    6 Privacy challenges for holographic communications   328

    7 Research methodology   330

    8 Critical discussions   333

    References   335

16. The implication of big data analytics on competitive
    intelligence: A qualitative case study of a real estate
    developer in the UAE   339
    Eman Reda AlBahsh and Amin Hosseinian-Far

    1 Introduction   339
    2 Literature review   340
    3 Research methodology   346
    4 Findings   349
    5 Discussion   354
    6 Implications   355
    7 Conclusion   356
    References   356

17. Commodification of consumer privacy and the risk of data
    mining exposure   361
    John Bridge, Stefan Kendzierskyj, John McCarthy, and
    Hamid Jahankhani

    1 Data brokerage background   361
    2 Tracking and targeted ads   366
    3 Location tracking   369
    4 Data leakage   371
    5 Conclusion   375
    References   377

18. Value of data as a currency and a marketing tool   381
    Sumesh Dadwal, Anwar Haq, Arshad Jamal, and Imad Nawaz

    1 Introduction   381
    2 Concept of data and concept of currency   382
    3 The utility of data and value as a currency   383
    4 Why data is currency?   384

5 How organisations are monetising data as currency 385

6 Role of government and public policy in data as currency 390

7 Data literacy and data value 393

8 Models to calculate the monetary value of data as a currency 394

9 Conclusion 397

References 397

Index 399

Contributors

Eman Reda AlBahsh University of Northampton, Northampton, United Kingdom

Abdilahi Ali University of Salford, Salford, United Kingdom

Abdul Ali Northumbria University, London, United Kingdom

Syed Imran Ali University of Huddersfield, Huddersfield, United Kingdom

Natalia Gomez Arteaga Northumbria University, Newcastle upon Tyne, United Kingdom

Giovanni Bottazzi LUISS Guido Carli University, Rome, Italy

Gordon Bowen Northumbria University, London, United Kingdom

John Bridge Northumbria University, London, United Kingdom

Lea Broc Northumbria University, London, United Kingdom

Guy Brown Northumbria University, London, United Kingdom

Luciano Capone Arma dei Carabinieri, Rome, Italy

Lillian Clark QA Higher Education, London, United Kingdom

Anita Colin Amnesty International, London, United Kingdom

Sumesh Dadwal Northumbria University, London, United Kingdom

Sudhir Gautam Northumbria University, London, United Kingdom

Farooq Habib Cranfield University, Cranfield, United Kingdom

David Allan Eric Haddon Imperial College, London, United Kingdom

Daniel Hagan Northumbria University, London, United Kingdom

Anwar Haq Northumbria University, London, United Kingdom

Amin Hosseinian-Far University of Northampton, Northampton, United Kingdom

Hamid Jahankhani Northumbria University, London, United Kingdom

Arshad Jamal Northumbria University, London, United Kingdom

Stefan Kendzierskyj Cyfortis, Surrey, United Kingdom

Murtaza F. Khan University of Law, London, United Kingdom

Lynton Lourinho Northumbria University, London, United Kingdom

John McCarthy Oxford Systems, Bicester, United Kingdom

Gianluigi Me LUISS Guido Carli University, Rome, Italy

Imad Nawaz Northumbria University, London, United Kingdom

Liam M. O'Dell Senior Project Manager, Member of the Association for Project Management (MAPM); Associate of the Chartered Institute for Building (ACIOB), London, United Kingdom

Pierluigi Perrone University of Rome 'Tor Vergata', Rome, Italy

Karsyn Robb Northumbria University, Newcastle upon Tyne, United Kingdom

Giuseppe Giulio Rutigliano University of Rome 'Tor Vergata', Rome, Italy

Eustathios Sainidis Northumbria University, London, United Kingdom

Russell Watkins Hiscox Insurance, London, United Kingdom

David Wilson Northumbria University, London, United Kingdom

Simon M. Wilson Northumbria University, London, United Kingdom

Foreword

I think we can safely say we have never seen so much technological change in such a short time and nor has society been so challenged by the individual empowerment by personal computing and mobility. Perhaps the most surprising aspect has been the rise of social networks and the almost universal willingness to sacrifice personal privacy in the interest of greater apparent advantage. The impact on the world of work, play, retail, entertainment, and services has been profound—and so has the mutation of the media and politics! Everyone is now a voter with a public voice, and everyone can be an influencer or be influenced.

These changes are fundamental indicators of a much wider and deeper transition from the world of the 'slow, simple, linear, and comfortable' where plentiful solutions are obvious, to a faster world of the 'complex, nonlinear, disquieting, and discomforting' where solutions are not obvious or evident. In turn, this is invisibly fuelled by a growing automation that sees robotics and AI providing and managing the production and supply of all our basic goods and commodities whilst also powering our services and utilities.

Mention AI and robotics to most people and it tends to conjure some ScFi-Spectre such as Terminator, but at the same time, people embrace Amazon Alexa and Apple's Siri and trust highly automated vehicles designed by AI tools and manufactured by robots. But there is perhaps no more a contentious arena than that of self-driving cars and who is to blame when there is an accident, and how many driving jobs will they destroy? At the same time, governments and institutions suffer members, managers, and boards sustained by the 'simple world model' and thinking that inevitably results in less than ideal outcomes.

Managing a 21^{st}C Economy using processes founded in the 17^{th}C, or management models from the 19^{th}C always sees sub-optimal results, and often promotes decline.

So, at last, I am pleased to say that I have found a book that addresses this landscape to paint a picture of change to date and change to come and troubles to explain the why's where's, needs, and advantages. It also proffers solutions to various conundrums posed by the inability of peoples, institutions, and companies to embrace the new and change. This then make a most compelling and comprehensive text that deserves a space in every manager and politician's office.

Professor Peter Cochrane OBE
UNIVERSITY OF SUFFOLK, IPSWICH, UNITED KINGDOM

Strategic leadership in the digital age

1

The evolution of AI and the human-machine interface as a manager in Industry 4.0

Liam M. O'Dell[a] and Hamid Jahankhani[b]

[a]SENIOR PROJECT MANAGER, MEMBER OF THE ASSOCIATION FOR PROJECT MANAGEMENT (MAPM); ASSOCIATE OF THE CHARTERED INSTITUTE FOR BUILDING (ACIOB), LONDON, UNITED KINGDOM [b]NORTHUMBRIA UNIVERSITY, LONDON, UNITED KINGDOM

1 Introduction

It was artificial intelligence (AI) leader and investor Andrew Ng who said, 'Data is the new oil, AI is the new electricity, IoT is the new nervous system' (Leonhard, 2015). Presently, the industry as a whole is undergoing a fourth industrial revolution—Industry 4.0 (Schwab, 2016). This revolution is bringing with it a digital age and the emergence of AI. In addition, in recent times the workforce has been evolving from one of a 'digital nomad' to that of a 'digital native' (Prensky, 2001), with some arguing that we are merely 'digital refugees' (Coombes, 2009). This shift in workforce demographics has resulted in the exponential growth of the amount of data that is being produced by the workforce, which is known as 'big data' (Boyd and Crawford, 2011). This is supported by innovations in machine learning (ML). These 'intelligence explosion' (Muehlhauser, 2013) characteristics of the fourth industrial revolution are referred to generally as the 'AI revolution'. Just as the first industrial revolution saw the invention of steam- and water-powered machinery that developed transportation, driving change in the workplace, so too will the innovations in technologies such as AI and ML be the powerhouse of the future.

The term 'artificial intelligence' first come into existence in 1955, when McCarthy et al. (1955) prepared a research proposal for what is now known as the 1956 Dartmouth summer research project. This proposal stated:

> ...to proceed on the basis of the conjecture that every aspect of learning or any other feature of intelligence can in principle be so precisely described that a machine can be made to simulate it.

In 2018, Hao argued that due to the constantly evolving nature of AI technology, so too does the definition of AI change. Moreover, Mitchell (1997) defined ML as the basis of composing computer algorithms that automatically evolve with experience. Mitchell (1997) asserted that the further development of ML technology might lead to a better understanding of human learning abilities and even more so disabilities.

Whilst both AI and ML technology can be treated as individual industries by themselves, in combining both these technologies, they become a powerhouse for the evolution of the way we think, create, and work. Similarly, the authors of this research study, like any experienced project managers over the past 20 years, may have experienced the third industrial revolution of computerisation, having sat in front of a new computer for the first time and been amazed by the new technology.

There has almost certainly been a time when a project manager has wished for an expansive team with all the knowledge at their disposal and all possible experience to guide them through an issue or assist in making an informed decision. Until now, though, this has perhaps not been possible or indeed feasible (Johnsonbabu, 2017).

However, with the universal innovations in AI and ML technology being experienced, these new emerging tools of today and into the future will impact and change the way project managers deliver projects by applying big data to evaluate how to undertake complex tasks more quickly, efficiently, and with better quality (The Economist, 2018).

As the fourth industrial revolution ensues (Schwab, 2016), the emergence of technology and especially innovation within AI and ML are seen as potential major disruptors in the way projects will be managed in the future as well as the progress of project management knowledge and the required skills. The main competence areas (Project Management Institute, Inc., 2017) within project management already experiencing some influence of AI and ML technology innovation are primarily estimating, planning, health and safety, risk management, and commercial dispute management. In addition, there are several other early innovator industries that, with the development of AI and ML technologies, are already starting to see significant advancement such as in healthcare to assist doctors in making earlier and more robust diagnoses and in the insurance industry for expediting claims management (Twentyman, 2018).

The research has recognised innovation in AI and ML technologies as an emerging theme within the project management professional services domain. These technologies have perhaps even taken some leaders in industry by surprise (Clement-Jones, 2018). With the advancement of AI and ML technologies, businesses are starting to transform. Though, how project management is undertaken and the powerfully important provision of day-to-day insights or data a project manager may rely upon when working, in addition to the potential for developing new cognitive process intelligence and different skills of project managers, is yet to be fully explored.

Nonetheless, just as Henry Ford revolutionised the manufacturing industry with the introduction of the assembly line (Daugherty and Wilson, 2018), with the emergence of technologies such as AI and ML, the project management profession will start to see a revolution of these sometimes complex day-to-day management tasks, potentially leading to efficiencies in time, consistency, and quality outcomes or decisions (Johnsonbabu, 2017).

2 Artificial intelligence (AI)

AI itself is multifaceted and perhaps ever evolving, depending on where the industry is in the timeline of the discovery of new technology. By explanation, AI is a wide-ranging and constantly evolving collection of technologies. Luger (2009) further argues that the definition for AI is based on the principles of science and that the development of AI as a science is far from being anywhere near as mature as physics, for example. There is a thought that AI technologies discovered in the past, including developments of recent times, are merely aspirational (Hao, 2018). Therefore, a more general definition is seen as possible.

> *Artificial intelligence (AI) may be defined as the branch of computer science that is concerned with the automation of intelligent behaviour.*
>
> *Luger (2009, p. 2)*

As a pioneer in AI research, scientist Alan Turing wrote several papers on machinery and computing capabilities. Turing went on to devise a test to determine if a machine had the same capabilities as a human, known as the Turing test (Turing, 1950). After the inception of AI in the 1950s, the scientific community has been working extensively on AI technologies to replicate human intelligence and have now developed certain applications that can replace it.

With these significant advancements and the development of AI, it may be feasible that machines will undertake human tasks and computing technology that has never been seen before will be developed (Nikolaus, 2018). At the dawn of the fourth industrial revolution (Schwab, 2016), AI innovation is potentially as disruptive as the first industrial 19th century revolution and the invention of the steam engine (Goldin and Katz, 1998), both in terms of technology in industry and the world economic impact (World Economic Forum, 2018).

Satell in 2018 argued that the rise of the digital age has yet to have any real impact at the stage of development and innovation we are seeing compared to the industrial revolution of water, steam, power, and the internal combustion engine. With emerging AI technologies, research indicates that AI is ubiquitous across all of industry. AI is fast becoming the focal point for many industry sectors and has impacted the economy in recent years. The development and application of AI technology is rapidly changing the global economy (Brynjolfsson and Mitchell, 2017). These developments are further evidenced by the United Kingdom (UK) government (HM Government, 2017) identifying the potential economic opportunities associated with Industry 4.0 and the next digital era supported by the UK government launching a digital strategy underwritten by considerable funding for the development and innovation of digital technologies (Government Office for Science, 2017).

Consequently, the UK is perhaps seen as a global leader (HM Government, 2017) in AI and in 2017 established the All-Party Parliamentary Group on Artificial Intelligence (Big Innovation Center, 2017). The UK government is further strengthening its position as a leader in AI by creating several cross-industry initiatives and funding programs with a commitment to investing about £725M in the Industrial Strategy Challenge Fund and a further £64M in digital and construction training schemes (HM Government, 2017). In a wider context, the European Union is also funding nearly €80 billion (European Commission, 2018a,b) for innovation and research and at a global level all other countries of the world are also starting to realise the predominance of AI (Dutton, 2017).

Whilst the term AI has been around for nearly 63 years (McCarthy et al., 1955), the uptake by industry has been predominantly driven by advances in computer technology (Theis and Philip Wong, 2017) and the speed at which processors are able to combine, analyse, and create reliability in outcomes (Wu et al., 2014).

When developing AI technology, most research is based around two principles of application: knowledge representation or language and the problem-solving process or search technique (Luger, 2009). Most innovation in AI is focused on a person's ability to problem solve (Newell and Simon, 1976). Although, Newell and Simon (1976) argued that in order for a person to be able to solve a problem, certain characteristics form the basis for problem solving: a level of knowledge within a subject matter or discipline together with a problem to solve. A search for possible alternative solutions to the problem identified within the confines of the subject matter or discipline knowledge is then undertaken. An example may be a doctor who specialises in cancer and is researching alternative treatment solutions within their existing knowledge base.

Innovation in AI is about stepping away from the industrial era and moving towards a new era of digital technology innovation. That is, a transformation within technology from what professionals have known and interacted with in the beginning such as steam, the advent of electricity, and more recently the breakthrough of digital technology such as computers. Furthermore, it is possible that no one would have predicted that when the early pioneers of computer technology such as Moore's Law were being established, that one day the computer would have the same ability as humans and even start to become redundant (Theis and Philip Wong, 2017). In this respect, it is argued that we are no longer working within an industrial age, but rather a digital age of technology innovation (Satell, 2018) using AI and ML.

2.1 Machine learning (ML)

Early innovation in ML was challenging (Luger, 2009), as the AI tool kit being used was not capable of learning when being used, in contrast to a human that learns from the problems encountered. Conversely, current research within ML has focused on algorithms and on the analysis of larger volumes of big data, which is also known as data mining (Bilal et al., 2016). A literature review has revealed that research in ML predominantly addresses the use of ML databases within industries such as plant and machine maintenance (Bloem et al., 2014), financial services (Trippi and Turban, 1992), and medical services (Peek et al., 2015), to name a few.

However, Hart (2017) argues that the development of similar technology will be implemented to discover improved working practices, enhance commercial propositions, and solve complex problems quickly, evolving the way businesses utilise project management.

Nonetheless, developments in ML are further supported by research conducted as part of the Technologies and Innovation Futures (TIF) of the UK government (Government Office for Science, 2017). The TIF report identified that vast amounts of data are now being gathered in such a manner that it is automated in a free and undefined manner. The TIF report also argues that search and decision-making algorithms are the catalysts for innovation in AI and ML technologies (Government Office for Science, 2017). At an industry level, developments such as automated decision making and operations are coming to the forefront of the way we work (HM Government, 2017). A significant factor in these developments is the way data are collected and used (Daugherty and Wilson, 2018).

3 Data emerging into big data

As a consequence of the rapid innovation of AI technologies, we are also seeing the steady increase of data production and its use (Bilal et al., 2016); project management will clearly be included in this revolution. Interestingly, from 2003 to 2011, the production and storage of data increased almost three times (Bounie and Gille, 2012; Lyman et al., 2003). It has been recognised that in addition to the advancement of AI technologies, the ways people and businesses collect and use data will also evolve. Generally, the data gathered by business practices and operations are structured forms of data such as forms, documents, and even reports. However, Boyd and Crawford (2011) contend that businesses produce far more unstructured data, calling this development in data gathering 'big data'.

Similarly, Frankel and Reid (2008) contend that big data may be defined by its characteristics of volume, velocity, and variety. Research by Bilal et al. (2016) concluded that these characteristics manifest themselves within construction/project management data and are the emerging innovation in the industry. Nevertheless, as the use of data shifts from the structured form and towards deeper and wider use of data (Williams et al., 2014), it is possible that this shift in data use will create opportunities for a broader and richer use of data. However, in doing so, project managers will be faced with certain challenges. DalleMule and Davenport (2017) make the assertion that if companies are not building a strategy for the management of the data they have or are collecting, they either need to start to catch up with the expansion of data growth or perhaps consider starting to even exit the market. This argument is supported by the fact that the proliferation of data over an approximate period of 40 years highlights that Internet traffic has surpassed the one zettabyte threshold (1021). Furthermore, DalleMule and Davenport (2017) cite a calculation by Cisco Systems that estimates that this volume will possibly double in an exponentially shorter period of time than it took to reach this previous threshold, which was only 4 years.

By comparison, big data might remove the present limitations enabling users to access information the data creator might not have first envisaged when doing so (Wu et al., 2014). It is highlighted that a project manager will start to have available to them an autonomous way of collecting wider and deeper unstructured data combined with the possibility of real-time working never seen before. Research by Williams et al. (2014) concludes that the way in which a project manager uses these technological advancements must be undertaken so as to ensure that privacy is not compromised. Equally, whilst the benefits for the use of big data are becoming more apparent over time, the use of data is manifesting within project management in what is known as knowledge discovery databases (Bilal et al., 2016). The realisation of these benefits is supported by research on the use of big data, including the use of data mining and learning from past projects to improve the delivery of future projects (Carrillo et al., 2011). This combined with the identification of the causes within projects for issues such as delays, cost increases, and quality control (Soibelman and Kim, 2002) leading to direct impacts within the workplace and workforce alike.

4 Artificial intelligence technology and the workplace

The benefits of AI technology innovation are perhaps ubiquitous in equal measure for both the employer and employee. The Economist (2018) argues that just as employers can develop technology to track employees to increase productivity or even detect fraud, the benefits to the employees may be working smarter than before with improved insights or innovation in the way you are hired, given a salary increase, or even promoted. Similarly, Mitchell (1997) asserts that there is the potential for AI technology to develop unruly characteristics in the way the technology is used or performs in the digital age. In recent times, these characteristics have been evident in several AI innovation projects conducted by companies, including the development by Microsoft of a chatbot 'Tay' (Schlesinger et al., 2018) with racist and sexist overtones and other AI technologies that develop other biases such as gender and even the postcode used (Sharkey, 2018). Just as, the workplace collaboration tool called Slack which is an acronym for, 'searchable log of all communication and knowledge' that is being used in the workplaces of today and is using AI and ML capabilities (Dewnarain et al., 2017).

Furthermore, Crouch (2018) highlights the advancement in AI technology innovation that might be seen to only serve to strengthen an employer's control over its employees whilst the utilisation of AI technology may be perceived by workers as archaic and draconian. The Economist (2018) argues that the lower represented job roles such as retail or manufacturing may face the dilemma of accepting that AI technology will be used in the workplace, for example monitoring productivity, or simply be replaced by the new technology itself such as robots to create a workforce.

5 Artificial intelligence and the workforce

Undoubtedly, as with any past industrial revolution or digital revolution, as the present experience of never seen before capability in technological advances within the Industry 4.0 (Schwab, 2016) revolution is becoming known and unveiled, our way of work and live will adapt and change too. As innovation in AI becomes prolific within industry, it is perhaps expected that cynicism towards future ways of working will also arise (Zistl, 2018). This from the threat of being made redundant due to the rise of new technology through to emerging companies that will possibly dominate industry and the way we work, learn, and even live tomorrow.

Nevertheless, Wilson and Daugherty (2018) argued that, rather than actually making workers redundant, the workplace will simply evolve with the use of AI technology in a collaborative way to augment human capabilities, resulting in the possibility of changing the way we work and how we work. There has been a lot of speculation (Goldin and Katz, 1998) as to what the future of the present workforce may be or look like in regard to discoveries made in correlation with innovation and skills. The Economist (2018) argues that the dominance of AI technology may have an impact on the number of workers required within the workforce as it is known today. Conversely, Daugherty and Wilson (2018) argue that emerging AI technology is an enabler to different workplaces, and that the types of jobs will simply change.

Wilson and Daugherty (2018) argue from a viewpoint of efficiency and assert that the real benefit of AI technology within the workforce is to be able to develop capacity. This would allow to undertake processes presently that take time and requiring vast resources by offering scalability within areas such as data analysis.

Whilst the business benefits of speed, competitive edge, and potential cost savings are possible strengths of AI technology (PwC, 2007), a little more than a third of companies are seemingly working towards addressing the human-to-machine ways of working (Daugherty and Wilson, 2018). Petter (2017) argued that the present ways of working must be adapted to make the workforce of today fit for purpose.

Twentyman (2018) supports this argument by highlighting that the type of work presently being undertaken will shift from a structured data type environment to one with an analytic style of working, where employees will be more analytic-focused rather than seeking out data. Conversely, Wilson and Daugherty (2018) also believe that the natural humanistic skills such as socialisation, leadership, creativity, and teamwork will still be required. In this respect, several of the management consultancies (Daugherty and Wilson, 2018; PwC, 2007) also argue that several key aspects to employee hiring and training must be looked at closely. This includes how to train and develop the current workforce to keep pace with innovation and how to focus on recruitment with a particular emphasis on automation and human capabilities.

In Zistl (2018), the AI expert Rolf Heuer argues that there are always reservations towards any new technology, likening it to when the steam engine was first introduced into industry. Heuer asserts that any possible dangers with the application of AI technology and job roles must be evaluated using facts and robust information. Similarly, whilst the current general consensus within industry is that the way we work will change, Frey and Osbourne (2013) predict that up to 47% of jobs may be susceptible to the impacts of technological developments and automation.

Furthermore, Petter (2017) states that a majority of today's businesses are finding that the data they hold are becoming more valuable than their employees. Nonetheless,

Daugherty and Wilson (2018) contend that whilst there will be the possibility of redundancies in certain job roles, there will be a shortage of the required alternative skilled workers to deploy and manage AI technologies.

The traditional evolution of the workforce should see the 'digital immigrants' (Prensky, 2001) starting to decrease as this generation is approaching their expected retirement period and 'digital natives' (Prensky, 2001) rise through to become the norm. Nevertheless, research by Coombes (2009) suggests that as the innovation in digital technology becomes more complicated, complex 'digital natives' (Prensky, 2001) will merely become 'digital refugees' due to the natural level of confidence in use, even if they do not like using it and often accept a digital technology as the norm rather than exploring its real capacity or learning its real ability.

According to Shah (2015), there is the real possibility of there being up to seven generations within the future workforce. Hannay and Fretwell (2011) further argue that this situation is possible due to the need for the digital immigrant population to rely more on their retirement savings, so they have to retain their jobs longer. This will cause generational diversity in the workplace to exist longer. With this shift, the expectations of a digital experience of using or being exposed to AI technology will also increase (Hart, 2017). Similarly, the Association for Project Management (Hart, 2017) states that this movement will see a decline in the requirements for training in digital technology. Also, the need to learn how to implement and work in tandem with digital technologies will become the normal way of working, therefore gaining a digital twin.

6 The digital twin

The term 'digital twin' (DT) first appeared in the early 2000s (Grieves, 2014) and was more recently used by NASA (Shafto et al., 2010) in describing virtual vehicles or systems that could not be accessed once launched into space (Boschert et al., 2018). A simple definition of a DT could be the physical and functional connection of a system, component, or product together with all available operational data; therefore, it is cyberphysical (Uhlemann et al., 2017).

The connection between physical information and a virtual space supported by the use of big data is known as the DT (Tao et al., 2018). However, as AI technology develops, there is a propensity for further issues with the combining of the physical and cyber elements. Research by Tao et al. (2018) determined that the marriage of physical information and data has the potential for isolated working and disjointed data to arise when attempting to link these into the cyberphysical state. Similarly, research undertaken by Uhlemann et al. (2017) highlights the evaluation of big data used to maintain a digital twin with a robust connection between the physical and cyberphysical environment.

Conversely, Bentley Systems (2018) argues that the issues highlighted may be overcome when digital twins are coupled with a consistent big data source thread. This results in creating consistent project control workflows that generate quality project outcomes within the project management triple constraint triangle of time, cost, and quality. This is further supported by Lee et al. (2014), who discuss that the evolution of Industry 4.0 is giving rise to an awareness of the benefits of interconnected systems whilst motivating companies to develop methodologies for combination cyberphysical systems; big data will be likely to achieve further profitability and business success. Likewise, in Gilchrist (2016), DT is identified as an emerging AI technology that has been primarily built within the manufacturing, aerospace, and technology sectors with the next generation of DT now starting to emerge across a wider range of industries facilitated by the advancement of Industry 4.0. The innovation of DT in Industry 4.0 and applications are widely discussed, highlighting the propensity of the use of big data as the enabling factor. In doing so, this poses some further ethical questions around how big data may be gathered, stored, and used for the evolution of the project management profession.

7 Artificial intelligence ethics and governance

The speed at which digital innovation is taking place, predominately due to the competitive market of industry, brings with it a certain increase in risks and issues primarily involving ethics and governance (Turcin and Denkenberger, 2018). Seen as a foundation to AI technology development, as data transforms into 'big data' (Boyd and Crawford, 2011), it is set to become a key driver in the application of AI technology. The way in which data will be used creates certain ethical issues. AI technology is allowing data to become widely accessible, and the way people will use data will pose ethical issues (Bostrom and Yudkowsky, 2014). These issues are especially around the change in data use from a previously structured type of environment to more of a broader and deeper use that was not necessarily envisaged by the creator of the data (Wu et al., 2014). Boyd and Crawford (2011) maintain that as access to data increases, data may be further susceptible to unethical use.

Research indicates that the implications of the ethical gathering and use of data are becoming widespread. The most prevalent examples of these challenges are the recent events such as the Facebook/Kogan/Cambridge Analytica scandal (Cadwalladr and Graham-Harrison, 2018) in the use of AI and the practice of data mining, together with Google having had their AI technology challenged for the military contract to develop AI technology to enable the algorithmic analysis of drone footage (Conger and Dell, 2018). These events and data use call into question the potential dangers of the unregulated use of AI technologies.

In this respect, several key AI leaders such as Elon Musk, Bill Gates, and Stephen Hawking have emphasised AI's potential negative impacts and questionable aspects (Sainato, 2015). These leaders have advocated for further examination of potential AI technologies and suggested the need to regulate and govern how AI is developed around core principals (Smith, 2018) focused around bias, ethical purposes, human-centric AI (Goodman, 2018), and trustworthy AI (High Level Expert Group on Artificial Intelligence, 2018), albeit with a word of caution. Similarly, the cofounder of Google-DeepMind (DeepMind Technologies, 2018) Mustafa Suleyman including another circa 100 plus other AI leaders have signed an open letter (Walsh, 2017) to the United Nations encouraging the management of the risks associated with the development and ethical use of AI technology and to engage the leaders in AI industry to act to prevent the potential for destabilisation and misuse of AI.

Formal governance is where industry may have to now relearn to become more focused and a little slower in development. This is to ensure that adequate governance frameworks for these ethical factors can be developed alongside the technology. In the same way with the focus on AI improving industry, the workplace and the advancement in the way people work; all gained from the application of AI technologies balanced in terms of global interoperability and standard operating procedures (Datta, 2017), other industry leaders appear to be supporting the benefits and expansion of AI technology (OpenAI, 2018).

The Economist (2018) argues that to develop and use AI technology in the workplace, three key principles of data regulation should be established and implemented. Initially, any data used should be made anonymous. The workforce should be made aware of the AI technology being used within the workplace (where) together with the collection of data (what) and subsequent use (how). Lastly, there should be provisions for an individual to access the data held on them.

Leonhard (2015) argues that the development of AI could be as important as the developments in nuclear technology. He proposes that a digital ethics treaty to manage the impact of AI technology and the ethical and governance themes should be established in the same vein as the nuclear nonproliferation treaties were created to manage that technology. Furthermore, research into the behaviours seen in technology innovation within the digital revolution would indicate that pace, agility, and disruption are prevalent. Cath (2018) argues that the mainstay of the AI governance framework should be threefold, grounded in the ethical, legal, and technical aspects of the use for which the technology is developed such as healthcare and diagnostic analysis or fintech support for trading. Given these characteristics, AI technology leader Robbie Stamp states that an AI development tool should be able to manage the human/machine relationship and evolve whilst accounting for the ethical and governance aspects of the business (Bioss, 2018).

In addition, Cath (2018) further argues that each aspect identified should have robust governance themes, particularly around accountability, fairness, and transparency. These principals have recently been recognised with the introduction of the General Data Protection Regulations (GDPR) in the UK (Goddard, 2017). Similarly, technology leader Tim Cook has called for similar regulations in the United States (Allen, 2018). However, with the introduction of the GDPR, the framework for these regulations is unclear and it is still uncertain as to how these regulations will be essentially used and governed, both in the UK (Watcher et al., 2017) and in a wider global sense (Cath et al., 2018).

These recent events where AI ethics have been called into question and observations around governance for the use and development of AI are made by the author. This suggests that it still remains unclear as to how the ethical development and governed use of AI technology will influence the project management profession.

8 Artificial intelligence in project management

The author has undertaken an in-depth review of diverse sources of academic literature using the PMI PMBOK (Project Management Institute, Inc., 2017) as a basis to evaluate those areas of practice where AI innovation may be present and to determine what aspect of AI innovation is being used or developed. Initially, it was difficult to determine the present-day use of AI technology within the project management profession.

Hall and Pesenti (2018), in their report on the growth of the AI industry in the UK, made recommendations for the development of specialist knowledge dedicated to AI. More specific to project management, Floyd (2016) argued that project managers will have to become familiar with the dynamics generated by AI and human interactions. Nevertheless, as AI technology becomes ubiquitous as a part of Industry 4.0 (Bloem et al., 2014), the author as a project manager acknowledges as a profession having to deal with interpersonal relationships, the human/machine interface (Bioss, 2018) that should develop as AI technology evolves and may possibly become an essential aspect of project management. Furthermore, Hart (2017) states that if a project manager is to remain relevant or be effective, an amount of familiarisation and interaction along with an understanding of how to work in tandem with AI may be required. This will be seen as a resource to better manage the time, cost, and quality aspect of project management.

Nevertheless, Floyd (2016) issues a cautionary statement that whilst project managers may gravitate towards the use of AI, there may be bottlenecks between AI and humans. This is due to the attraction of the AI resource being easily manageable as well as possible labour efficiencies and cost savings. However, Floyd (2016) further argues that whilst AI might seem an attractive resource, project managers will have to be prepared for the human/machine interface by offering creativity, judgment, and intuition and supported in professional development.

There are several government agencies (Big Innovation Center, 2017) established to take an active role in the development and funding of AI technology in UK industry (HM Government, 2017). This is further supported by the European Commission Digital Single Market (European Commission, 2018a,b) and the AI4EU Project (AI4EU, 2018). Similarly, when evaluating the project management professional organisations such as the Association for Project Management (APM) and Project Management Institute (PMI) for specific AI and technology special interest groups (SIG) within each of these organisations, it was found at time of researching whilst each organisation has several SIG's all based around the traditional knowledge competence areas there were no specific SIG's for AI and Digital Innovation. The PMI/APM have finally caught up in the last 8–12 months and have formed AI task groups.

8.1 Project management knowledge competence areas and frameworks

With a further critical review of each of the knowledge competence areas within the Project Management Body Of Knowledge, PMBOK (Project Management Institute, Inc., 2017) with the application of AI technology in project management as the primary factors for review, it has been determined that within each knowledge area, there is limited advancement and opportunity for ML to be developed alongside human systems. Moreover, upon critically reviewing the various sources of literature available, the mainstay of project management professional frameworks identified seemingly also have a limited narrative on the aspects of emerging AI technologies such as data analytics, predictive planning, and risk management in practice.

9 Research findings and critical discussion

The principal objective of this study using a synthesis of the available information in a critical literature review was to establish the key themes of innovation in AI technology. This research study helps to further analyse and determine the level of awareness and the attitudes towards the key themes within the project management profession.

A research methodology and survey were designed and circulated via the Internet to engage project management professional organisations, including the Association for Project Management (APM) and the Project Management Institute (PMI), together with the authors own professional network and organisation project management office (PMO).

The age ranges in this research are varied, with the average age range of the sample population between 40 and 49. The average age suggests that the sample population is perhaps considered on the cusp of being digital native (Prensky, 2001). Nonetheless, Coombes (2009) argued that the workforce is perhaps more likely to be digital refugees rather than digital natives. This would seem to stem from innovation in ML and the exponential growth of the amount of data being produced by the workforce, known as big data (Boyd and Crawford, 2011).

During research on the utilisation of AI technology in today's workplace, a research question was used to test the work of The Economist (2018) which suggests that companies are becoming increasingly smarter in the use of AI with just over a quarter (26%) of the workforce stating that the organisation they work for has already incorporated AI technology into their service offering. By comparison, this study would indicate that nearly half (45%) of the sample population has no awareness of the organisation they work for utilising AI technology in the workplace. Variances between The Economist (2018) and this study can probably be accounted for by the sample population significance and the attitude towards technology such as social media.

As AI technology advances within the workplace, the uses for this technology may mean that both employers and employees alike will have to adapt to current working practices. This study also investigates research by Crouch (2018), highlighting that AI technology may be seen to only serve to strengthen the employer control over its employees and the attitudes towards the workplace being monitored (The Economist, 2018). The range of data from this survey indicates that the general response is there is likely to be less concern with the use of AI technology if it is related to the welfare of the employee, such as fatigue risk and health and safety, as opposed to workplace mobility and break times.

As organisations look to innovate in AI technology, the literature review identifies the propensity for businesses to start to develop a digital strategy (DalleMule and Davenport, 2017) or risk being at a disadvantage in their professional arena. Likewise, with jobs being susceptible to the impacts of AI technology (Frey and Osbourne, 2013), the fluctuation in the workforce between the requirement for new skill sets and the potential for job losses (Daugherty and Wilson, 2018) may be a conceivable issue to be addressed. This survey considers the potential impact over the next 5 years that AI technology may have on project management within the workforce. The data show that whilst there is an argument for workplace change with new roles being created and potential increases in productivity, it may present problems and be counterproductive due to organisations not having the ability to implement new innovations with AI together with the lack of integration. Similarly, it is suggested that a matrix of the required skill set for a project manager in the future to be effective may be equally as important, and it is considered to be focused around those core skills identified.

The human/machine interface has the potential to further develop as the use of AI technology in the workplace becomes prevalent (Bioss, 2018). Therefore, creating the potential for a cyberphysical relationship (Uhlemann et al., 2017) as well as a digital twin relationship (Tao et al., 2018). As this style of relationship evolves, the need to ensure the humanistic characteristics such as creativity, judgment, and intuition are supported (Floyd, 2016). This research tests the relationships and awareness of the key themes of AI technology, particularly the digital twin. The data indicate that there is a relatively low awareness of the use of digital twin technology within project management. This may be attributed to the significance of the data collected.

Subsequently, this survey investigates the utilisation of the identified AI technology in the workplace by the sample population. The data indicate that the likely primary focus of AI use is centred on the more commonly adopted forms of AI technology such as cloud computing and collaboration tools. This might be attributed to the focus within industry at present to build a digital strategy (DalleMule and Davenport, 2017) as well as a relatively low awareness and uptake on the use of digital twin technology as a potential emerging theme over time.

With big data as a likely foundation and emerging key driver of innovation in AI technology (Boyd and Crawford, 2011), there is a possibility that as AI technology is being developed and used, AI may acquire unruly characteristics (Mitchell, 1997).

Furthermore, it is exceedingly possible, given the series of recent occurrences where data has been misused (Cadwalladr and Graham-Harrison, 2018), that AI innovation may pose further ethical issues (Bostrom and Yudkowsky, 2014). Cath (2018) argued that a threefold AI governance framework should be established around the ethical, legal, and technical properties of the AI technology being developed and used. Therefore, the key ethics and governance themes for the construct and AI technology questions are used to investigate how each theme is believed to be important to a project management professional. The data obtained suggest that it still remains uncertain as to how the ethical development and governed use of AI technology will influence the project management profession.

As the AI industry grows within the UK (Hall and Pesenti, 2018), addressing the training, development, and skills for project managers in the utilisation of AI technology should come to the forefront of the profession. This study explores the current activity and level of learning and development over the last 2 years by asking the sample population to provide data on what training and development has been undertaken. The survey probes research by Hart (2017), who argued that a certain amount of familiarisation and interaction to gain an understanding of how to work in tandem with AI will be key for a project manager to remain present and effective within the profession in the context of Industry 4.0 (Schwab, 2016).

Furthermore, this question supports the call by Hall and Pesenti (2018) for the active establishment of learning and development programs in AI technology. The data indicate a little over half (56%) of those surveyed had undertaken some form of skill development in project management. However, this survey indicates that possibly only a small fraction (7%) of the skill development included any modules on AI technology. This may be due to the report by Hall and Pesenti (2018) not having taken affect or the assertion for the project management professional organisations to begin to promote AI technology and skill development within the project management community. Moreover, the Economist (2018) asserted that a risk to the workforce is that organisations are not ready for the implementation or use of new AI technology.

Similarly, this survey gathered data on the knowledge and competences of project management using the APM (Association for Project Management, 2012) and PMI (Project Management Institute, Inc., 2017) bodies of knowledge (Johnsonbabu, 2017). Questions within the survey examined the correlation of both the APM and PMI knowledge and competencies for a project manager. The range of results of this survey were shown to overlap, indicating the possibility for development in AI technology with the propensity to have an impact focused around the knowledge and competencies of time and cost management, followed closely by procurement. Ethics compliance and professionalism are also included within this scope.

Research indicates that the emergence of AI technology is arguably the biggest disruptor within the workplace. A possible conclusion may be using the digital age to share innovations equally so as to ensure that a balanced approach is achieved with a productive yet highly effective workforce. Nonetheless, this should not be at the expense of humanity.

It remains evident from this study that innovation in AI technology is constantly evolving and may well present a number of significant challenges. The possible impacts this may have on the project management profession are presently immeasurable. However, it is important that both business and project managers of the future are prepared to address the advancement of AI technology in the workplace as well as the associated characteristics of human/machine relationship management, the utilisation of AI technology, and the governance and ethical perspectives. For a project manager to remain relevant, it would be important to ensure that their skills are adaptable whilst embracing the emerging ideas. Also, a business should develop a robust business strategy to assist in managing any further developments that may arise in the advancement of this emerging digital era.

10 Conclusions

The purpose of this study was to provide useful initial insight whilst assisting the project management professional to gain further understanding of how AI innovation and technology are entering the workplace and how to potentially engage with AI. In addition, this study is expected to stimulate future researchers to develop ideas for innovation in the use of AI within the project management profession. Similarly, as the research was developed, it also aimed to be a significant part of the restructuring of the project management profession in the future with the aid of AI and the cyberphysical digital twin interrelationships. The profession is believed to be undertaking an exciting transformation in the next few years whilst embracing AI technology into the body of the knowledge competencies.

This was achieved by the completion of three objectives. Objective 1 was to undertake a critical review of the literature relating to the emergence of AI technology innovation in the backdrop of Industry 4.0, identifying the key aspects. Similarly, Objective 2 was achieved through a critical review of current research where a further in-depth review of the realisation of key aspects of AI technology within project management have been presented. Objective 3 was to prepare a research methodology to gather data using a survey presented in the findings and discussion.

Several limitations of this research study were identified. The literature review has identified several key themes within AI technology. Whilst this study looks largely at all the key themes, further research would benefit from looking especially at one theme applied in further depth to the project management context.

Additionally, there was a vast amount of research and data collated as this research was progressing. However, due to the limitations of space and resources, this presentation only addresses a fraction of the research landscape on innovations in AI technology.

It is hoped that this study provides useful initial insight whilst assisting the project management professional to gain further understanding of how AI innovation is entering the workplace and how to potentially engage with AI.

References

Allen, T., October 24, 2018. Computing. Retrieved November 2018, from Tim Cook Calls for GDPR-Like Law for US: https://www.computing.co.uk/ctg/news/3065071/tim-cook-calls-for-gdpr-like-law-for-usa (Viewed on 12th December 2019).

Association for Project Management, 2012. APM Body of Knowledge, sixth ed. Association for Project Management, Princes Risborough, Buckinghamshire, UK.

Bentley Systems Inc., August 27, 2018. Siemens and Bentley Partner in New Digital Solution to Optimize Capital Project Delivery. Retrieved September 2018, from Bentley Systems—Newsroom: https://www.

bentley.com/en/about-us/news/2018/august/27/siemens-and-bentley-partner-in-new-digital-solution-to-optimize-capital-project-delivery (Viewed on 8th January 2020).

Big Innovation Center, January 2017. APPG AI. Retrieved June 2018, from All Party Parliamentary Group on Artificial Intelligence: http://www.appg-ai.org (Viewed on 17th November 2019).

Bilal, M., Oyedele, L.O., Qadir, J., Munir, K., Ajayi, S.O., Akinade, O.O., et al., 2016. Big Data in the construction industry: a review of present status, opportunities, and future trends. Adv. Eng. Inform. 30, 501–519.

Bioss, 2018. The Bioss AI Protocol. Retrieved November 2018, from Bioss International Limited: http://www.bioss.com/ai/ (Viewed on 23rd November 2019).

Bloem, J., Van Doorn, M., Duivestein, S., Excoffier, D., Maas, R., Van Ommeren, E., 2014. The Fourth Industrial Revolution. Issy-les-Moulineaux, Sogeti VINT.

Boschert, S., Heinrich, C., Rosen, R., 2018. Next generation digital twin. In: Horvath, I., Rivero, J.P.S., Castellano, P.M.H. (Eds.), Proceedings of TMCE 2018, May 7–11. Organizing Committee of TMCE, Las Palmas de Gran Canaria, pp. 209–218.

Bostrom, N., Yudkowsky, E., 2014. The ethics of artificial intelligence. In: Frankish, K., Ramsey, W.M. (Eds.), The Cambridge Handbook of Artificial Intelligence. Cambridge University Press, Cambridge, UK, p. 334.

Bounie, D., Gille, L., 2012. Info capacity: international production and dissemination of information: results, methodological issues and statistical perspectives. Int. J. Commun.. 6(21).

Boyd, D., Crawford, K., 2011. Six provocations for big data. In: A Decade in Internet Time: Symposium on the Dynamics of the Internet and Society.

Brynjolfsson, E., Mitchell, T., December 22, 2017. What can machine learning do? Workforce implications. Science 358 (6370), 1530–1534.

Cadwalladr, C., Graham-Harrison, E., March 17, 2018. Revealed: 50 Million Facebook Profiles Harvested for Cambridge Analytica in Major Data Breach. Retrieved July 2018, from The Guardian: https://www.theguardian.com/news/2018/mar/17/cambridge-analytica-facebook-influence-us-election (Viewed on 3rd November 2019).

Carrillo, P., Harding, A., Choudary, A., 2011. Knowledge discovery from post-project reviews. Construct. Manage. Econ. 29 (7), 713–723.

Cath, C., August 28, 2018. Governing artificial intelligence: ethical, legal and technical opportunities and challenges. Philos. Trans. A 376 (20180080), 1–8.

Cath, C., Wachter, S., Mittelstadt, B., Taddeo, M., Floridi, L., 2018. Artificial intelligence and the 'Good Society': the US, EU, and UK approach. Sci. Eng. Ethics 24 (2), 505–528.

Clement-Jones, L., 2018. AI in the UK: Ready, Willing and Able? Select Committee on Artificial Intelligence. House of Lords, London.

Conger, K., Dell, C., June 3, 2018. Google is Helping the Pentagon Build AI for Drones. Retrieved August 2018, from Gizmodo: https://gizmodo.com/google-is-helping-the-pentagon-build-ai-for-drones-1823464533 (Viewed on 18th December 2019).

Coombes, B., 2009. Generation Y: are they really digital natives or more like digital refugees. Synergy 7 (1), 31–40.

Crouch, C., 2018. Redefining labour relations and capital in the digital age. In: Neufeind, M., O'Reilly, J., Ranft, F. (Eds.), WORK IN THE DIGITAL AGE: Challenges of the Fourth Industrial Revolution. Rowman & Littlefield International Ltd., London, pp. 187–197 (May–June 1).

DalleMule, L., Davenport, T., 2017. What's you data strategy? Harv. Bus. Rev, 1–11.

Datta, S.P., 2017. Emergence of digital twins. J. Innov. Manage. 5, 14–34.

Daugherty, P., Wilson, H.J., 2018. Process Reimagined. Research. Accenture, New York.

DeepMind Technologies Limited, 2018. About Us. Retrieved November 2018, from DeepMind Health: https://deepmind.com/applied/deepmind-health/about-deepmind-health/ (Viewed on 3rd November 2019).

Dewnarain, G., O'Connell, D., Gotta, M., October 6, 2017. SWOT: Slack, Worldwide. Retrieved November 2018, from Gartner: https://www.gartner.com/doc/reprints?id=1-4K5I75Fandct=171108andst=sb (Viewed on 28th November 2019).

Dutton, T., July 2017. Medium. (A Medium Corporation). Retrieved November 2018, from Politics + AI: https://medium.com/politics-ai/an-overview-of-national-ai-strategies-2a70ec6edfd (Viewed on 28th November 2019).

European Commission, 2018a. European Commission. (November). Retrieved from Digital Single Market: https://ec.europa.eu/commission/priorities/digital-single-market_en.

European Commission, 2018b. FET Open—European Commission. Retrieved 2018 November, from Horizon 2020: https://ec.europa.eu/programmes/horizon2020/en/h2020-section/fet-open (Viewed on 28th November 2019).

Floyd, S.A., 2016. Do machines hold a key to business? PM World J. 5 (10), 1–10.

Frankel, F., Reid, R., September 4, 2008. Big data: distilling meaning from data. Nature 455 (7209), 30.

Frey, C.B., Osbourne, M.A., September 17, 2013. The Future of Employment: How Susceptible are Jobs to Computerisation? University of Oxford, Oxford, Oxfordshire, UK.

Gilchrist, A., 2016. Smart factories. In: Industry 4.0—The Industrial Internet of Things. Apress Media LLC, New York, NY, pp. 218–230 (Chapter 14).

Goddard, M., 2017. The EU General Data Protection Regulation (GDPR): European regulation that has a global impact. Int. J. Mark. Res. 59 (6), 703–705.

Goldin, C., Katz, L.F., August 1, 1998. The origins of technology—skill complementarity. Q. J. Econ. 113 (3), 693–732.

Goodman, J., March 22, 2018. Internet of Business. (Vinelake). Retrieved June 2018, from AI Regulation & Ethics: How to Build More Human-Focused AI: https://internetofbusiness.com/ai-regulation-and-ethics-how-to-build-human-centric-ai/.

Government Office for Science, 2017. Technology and Innovation Futures 2017. Office of Science. OGL-Crown, London (Viewed on 18th December 2019).

Grieves, M., 2014. Digital Twin: Manufacturing Excellence Through Virtual Factory Replication, White Paper. Retrieved November 2018, from Apriso: http://www.apriso.com/library/Whitepaper_Dr_Grieves_DigitalTwin_ManufacturingExcellence.php (Viewed on 10th December 2019).

Hall, W., Pesenti, J., 2018. Growing the Artificial Intelligence Industry in the UK. Department for Digital, Culture, Media & Sport and Department for Business, Energy & Industrial Strategy. HM Government, London.

Hannay, M., Fretwell, C., 2011. The higher education workplace: Meeting the needs of multiple generations. Res. High. Educ. J. 10, 1.

Hao, K., November 10, 2018. MIT Technology Review. Retrieved November 2018, from Is this AI? We Drew You a Flowchart to Work It Out: https://www.technologyreview.com/s/612404/is-this-ai-we-drew-you-a-flowchart-to-work-it-out/ (Viewed on 18th December 2019).

Hart, B., 2017. The Robot Professional? The Role of Project Professionals in the Digital Future. Association for Project Management, Princes Risborough.

High Level Expert Group on Artificial Intelligence, December 18, 2018. Have Your Say: European Expert Group Seeks Feedback on Draft Ethics Guidelines for Trustworthy Artificial Intelligence. Retrieved December 2018, from European Commission—Digital Single Market—News: https://ec.europa.eu/digital-single-market/en/news/have-your-say-european-expert-group-seeks-feedback-draft-ethics-guidelines-trustworthy (Viewed on 18th December 2019).

HM Government, November 2017. Industrial Strategy. Building a Britain Fit for the Future. Controller of Her Majesty's Stationery Office, London, UK.

Johnsonbabu, A., 2017. Reinventing the role of project manager in the artificial intelligence era. In: Project Management National Conference, India. Project Management Institute, Inc., Chennai, pp. 1–11.

Lee, J., Bagheri, B., Kao, H.A., 2014. Recent advances and trends of cyber-physical systems and big data analytics in industrial informatics. In: International Proceeding of Int. Conference on Industrial Informatics (INDIN), pp. 1–6.

Leonhard, G., 2015. Redefining the relationship of man and machine. In: Talwar, R. (Ed.), The Future of Business. Fast Future Publishing Ltd., London, UK, pp. 82–93.

Luger, G.F., 2009. Artificial Intelligence: Structures and Strategies for Complex Problem Solving. Pearson Education, Inc., Boston, MA

Lyman, P., Varian, H.R., Swearingen, K., Charles, P., Good, N., Jordan, L., et al., 2003. Retrieved May 2018, from How Much Information: http://groups.ischool.berkeley.edu/archive/how-much-info-2003/ (Viewed on 9th December 2019).

McCarthy, J., Minsky, M.L., Rochester, N., Shannon, C.E., 1955. A Proposal for the Dartmouth Summer Research Project on Artificial Intelligence. Retrieved May 2018, from Stanford University: http://www-formal.stanford.edu/jmc/history/dartmouth/dartmouth.html (Viewed on 10th December 2019).

Mitchell, T., 1997. Machine Learning. McGraw Hill, Ohio, USA.

Muehlhauser, L., 2013. Machine Intelligence Research Institute. Retrieved November 2018, from Intelligence Explosion FAQ: https://intelligence.org/files/IE-FAQ.pdf (Viewed on 10th November 2019).

Newell, A., Simon, H.A., 1976. Computer science as empirical inquiry: symbols and search. In: Communications of the ACM. vol. 19. Association for Computing Machinery, Inc., Pittsburgh, pp. 113–126.

Nikolaus, K., 2018. Five Things That You Need to Know About Artificial Intelligence. Retrieved July 2018, from Pictures of the Future: https://www.siemens.com/innovation/en/home/pictures-of-the-future/digitalization-and-software/artificial-intelligence-5-things-to-know.html (Viewed on 11th January 2020).

OpenAI, 2018. OpenAI Charter. Retrieved September 2018, from OpenAI: https://blog.openai.com/openai-charter/ (Viewed on 11th January 2020).

Peek, N., Combi, C., Marin, R., Bellazzi, R., 2015. Thirty years of artificial intelligence in medicine (AIME) conferences: a review of research themes. Artif. Intell. Med. 65, 61–73.

Petter, J., October 4, 2017. Is Your Greatest Asset People, or Data? City A.M., p. 23.

Prensky, M., October 2001. Digital natives, digital immigrants. On the Horizon 9 (5), 1–6.

Project Management Institute, Inc., 2017. A Guide to the Project Management Body of Knowledge (PMBOK Guide), sixth ed. Project Management Institute, Inc., Newtown Square, Pennsylvania, USA.

PwC, 2007. Preparing for Tomorrow's Workforce, Today. Retrieved November 2018, from Workforce of the Future: The Competing Forces Shaping 2030: https://www.pwc.com/gx/en/services/people-organisation/publications/workforce-of-the-future.html (Viewed on 21st January 2020).

Sainato, M., August 19, 2015. Observer. Retrieved September 2018, from Stephen Hawking, Elon Musk, and Bill Gates Warn About Artificial Intelligence: https://observer.com/2015/08/stephen-hawking-elon-musk-and-bill-gates-warn-about-artificial-intelligence/ (Viewed on 21st January 2020).

Satell, G., 2018. The industrial era ended, and so will the digital era. Harv. Bus. Rev. https://hbr.org/2018/07/the-industrial-era-ended-and-so-will-the-digital-era (Viewed on 18th January 2020).

Schlesinger, A., O'Hara, K.P., Taylor, A.S., 2018. Let's talk about race: identity, chatbots, and AI. In: Proceedings of the 2018 CHI Conference on Human Factors in Computing Systems. ACM, Montréal, p. 315.

Schwab, K., 2016. Global Agenda: The Fourth Industrial Revolution. World Economic Forum. https://www.weforum.org/agenda/2016/01/the-fourth-industrial-revolution-what-it-means-and-how-to-respond/ (Viewed on 18th January 2020).

Shafto, M., Conroy, M., Doyle, R., Glaessgen, E., Kemp, C., LeMoigne, J., et al., November 2010. NASA Technology Roadmap—DRAFT Modeling, Simulation, Information Technology & Processing Roadmap Technology Area 11. Retrieved November 2018, from NASA: https://www.nasa.gov/pdf/501321main_TA11-MSITP-DRAFT-Nov2010-A1.pdf.

Shah, R., February 23, 2015. Working beyond five generations in the workplace. Forbes. https://www.forbes.com/sites/rawnshah/2015/02/23/working-beyond-five-generations-in-the-workplace/#71f31ce7296e (Viewed on 18th January 2020).

Sharkey, N., 2018. The impact of gender and race bias in AI. In: International Committee of the Red Cross—Humanitarian Law & Policy Blog. http://blogs.icrc.org/law-and-policy/2018/08/28/impact-gender-race-bias-ai/ (Viewed on 26th January 2020).

Smith, R., 2018. 5 Core Principles to Keep AI Ethical. Retrieved November 2018, from World Economic Forum: https://www.weforum.org/agenda/2018/04/keep-calm-and-make-ai-ethical/ (Viewed on 7th December 2019).

Soibelman, L., Kim, H., 2002. Data preparation processes for construction knowledge generation through knowledge discovery databases. J. Comput. Civ. Eng.. 16(1).

Tao, F., Cheng, J., Qi, Q., Zhang, M., Zhang, H., Sui, F., 2018. Digital twin- driven product design, manufacturing and service with big data. Int. J. Adv. Manuf. Technol. 94 (9–12), 3563–3576.

The Economist, March 28, 2018. The Workplace of the Future—AI-spy. Retrieved April 2018, from The Economist: https://www.economist.com/leaders/2018/03/28/the-workplace-of-the-future (Viewed on 12th December 2019).

Theis, T.N., Philip Wong, H.-S., March 2017. The end of Moore's law: a new beginning for information technology. Comput. Sci. Eng. 19 (2), 41–50.

Trippi, R., Turban, E., 1992. Neural Networks in Finance and Investing: Using Artificial Intelligence to Improve Real World Performance. McGraw-Hill, Inc., New York.

Turcin, A., Denkenberger, D., 2018. Classification of global catastrophic risks connected with artificial intelligence. AI & Soc. 1–17.

Turing, A., 1950. Computing machinery and intelligence. Mind LIX (236), 433–460.

Twentyman, J., 2018. Intelligent Economies: AI's Transformation of Industries and Society. The Economist Intelligence Unit, London.

Uhlemann, T.H., Lehmann, C., Stienhilper, R., 2017. The digital twin: realizing the cyber-physical production system for Industry 4.0. Procedia CIRP 61, 335–340.

Walsh, T., August 21, 2017. An Open Letter to the United Nations Convention on Certain Conventional Weapons. Retrieved September 2018, from Future of Life: https://futureoflife.org/autonomous-weapons-open-letter-2017/?cn-reloaded=1 (Viewed on October 2019).

Watcher, S., Mittelstadt, B., Russell, C., 2017. Counterfactual explanations without opening the black box: automated decisions and the GDPR. Harv. J. Law Technol.. 31(2).

Williams, N., Ferdinand, N.P., Croft, R., 2014. Project management maturity in the age of big data. Int. J. Manag. Proj. Bus. 7 (2), 311–317.

Wilson, J., Daugherty, P., 2018. Collaborative Intelligence: Humans and AI Are Joining Forces. Retrieved October 2018, from Harvard Business Review: https://hbr.org/2018/07/collaborative-intelligence-humans-and-ai-are-joining-forces (July–August 1).

World Economic Forum, November 2018. Mapping Global Transformations. Retrieved November 2018, from Future of Economic Progress:https://toplink.weforum.org/knowledge/insight/a1Gb0000001hXcwEAE/explore/summary (Viewed on 8th January 2020).

Wu, X., Zhu, X., Wu, G., Ding, W., 2014. Data mining with big data. IEEE Trans. Knowl. Data Eng. 26 (1), 97–107.

Zistl, S., 2018. Artificial Intelligence: Interview With Rolf Heuer. Retrieved June 2018, from Pictures of the Future: https://www.siemens.com/innovation/en/home/pictures-of-the-future/digitalization-and-software/artificial-intelligence-interview.html (Viewed on October 2019).

2

Digital leadership, ethics, and challenges

Gordon Bowen

NORTHUMBRIA UNIVERSITY, LONDON, UNITED KINGDOM

1 Introduction

In 2014 IBM stated that the top five industries that reported the most cyberattacks were manufacturing 26.5%, finance and insurance 20.9%, information and communication 18.7%, health and social services 7.3%, and, lastly, retail and wholesale 6.6% (Risks and Compliance by Number, 2015). The statistics paint a clear picture of the danger that cyberspace has for personal data. Related to the problem earlier, Kroll identified that 67% of wire fraud originated from social media and that in 100% of the cases of wire fraud that originated from social media, the social media users were duped into believing the transactions were authorised and genuine (Risks and Compliance by Number, 2015). To meet the challenges demonstrated by the earlier data, a study from Forrester Research suggested that 89% of firms intend to invest more in information governance programmes in the next 2 years and 64% are planning to introduce governance initiatives relating to tablets (Risks and Compliance by Number, 2015). The rate of suspicious cyber-related activities has grown to 80,000 per year according to the Financial Crimes Enforcement Network in the US Treasury Department; included in the number are 13,500 reports per year of suspicious business emails, which is up by 95% from 2016 (Reisinger, 2019).

The scale of the problem of cyber-related activities requires digital leadership and information governance to safeguard personal and business data, and these should be implemented based on ethical behaviour. It is now evident from the statistics presented that a regulatory environment should be set up that underpins information governance and digital leadership. A focus of this paper is to discuss what the regulatory environment should look like and what constitutes digital leadership and information governance. However, all these areas must be strongly linked to ethics and ethical behaviour.

This paper will use concepts and models from strategy, ethics, and leadership from the academic literature but evaluate them in the context of artificial intelligence (AI) and cybersecurity.

Strategy, Leadership, and AI in the Cyber Ecosystem. https://doi.org/10.1016/B978-0-12-821442-8.00013-6
© 2021 Elsevier Inc. All rights reserved.

2 Ethics and consent

Decision making in management and business is expected to adhere to ethical standards, and failure to comply can be relatively easily identified. Firms are exposed to various governance processes from documented company governance policies to external intervention from agencies such as accounts and auditors. These governance structures are not perfect, and transgressions of a serious nature do occur, but they give a degree of transparency and thus oversight and have an ethical context. However, because activities in cyberspace are less transparent, the question is how to improve transparency.

Consent has been fundamental to ethics for many years or even centuries. Moral responsibility requires consent and is central to any interaction from a personal or business perspective. The process of consent requires two actors: the consentee who gives the consent and the consenter who requests consent from the consentee (Jones et al., 2018). Without consent, actions are not permissible and are thus deemed impermissible. This necessitates the consentee to give permission to the consenter and transforms their relationship positively to give a clearly defined action, such as the use of personal data. Without permission, any action is considered an invasion of privacy. The outcome can be negative or positive; a negative outcome may encourage the consenter to invade the privacy of the consentee or abide by a moral code. The challenge is to ensure as much as possible that negative outcomes in relation to personal data exchange are underpinned by a moral ethical foundation. However, AI programs manipulate data, and the permission consent process may not always be enacted. It is easier to implement the consent process in the case of personal data permission than in AI in particular or cyberspace in general.

Applying the consent process to AI has its own challenges, but one approach is documented in this paper. Consent is a transfer of rights in every respect, unless conditions and terms are applied. The transfer of rights makes consent a transformation process that alters the moral landscape between the parties agreeing to the transfer of rights; thus actions become permissible or otherwise impermissible (Miller and Wertheimer, 2010). Because of the transformational nature of consent, agreements must be clearly written, and the consentee must have all the relevant information. When consent is given under the conditions described, then informed consent is achieved. However, after consent has been given, things can go wrong, and the consentee must have the option to withdraw from the transaction, which has parallels with the doctor-patient relationship. The patient can withdraw anytime in their interaction with the doctor, which is during the interaction or even after the interaction has ended. However, codified informed consent does not always protect the consentee and does not always convey the moral value expected. On occasions, medical practitioners will want patients to sign a disclosure before medical treatment can go ahead; this accomplishes less than expected, because the patient will have very little option but to sign, to allow the treatment to go ahead, and a loss of liability (Jones et al., 2018). Digital consent is often seen as an empty gesture. Digital consent can be legally appropriate but morally lacking, which is similar to the patient-doctor relationship that required a disclosure signature.

Barocas and Nissenbaum (2014) suggested that digital consent is unworkable and an empty procedural gesture. This criticism has not prevented researchers from creating digital tools to improve digital consent; for example, Miller and Wertheimer (2010) suggested improvements such as continual consent and cooperative consent. Continual consent requires fair and predictable standards, so that consent is a bilateral relationship that necessitates the transactional agreement of the consentee and consenter. Another proposed change to consent is transactional consent that requires communication and cooperation. The notion is that this type of consent is not a one-off. Transactions that extend over a period of time require ongoing interaction between the consentee and consenter. When the period is extended, such as for days, weeks, or years, then the consentee should have the right to withdraw consent. The different extensions of consent could be a useful way to apply digital consent (Jones et al., 2018). The different models of consent are ways of dealing with personal data capture; personal data are normally held over an extended period. They also have relevance for applications of AI in which data are held and acted upon to detect trends and to personalise data based on existing data. AI is applied to personal data to manipulate or change the data to create information intelligence.

Following the discussion on consent, one can now address digital consent. The challenge is to make digital consent morally binding, and given the situation discussed in the introduction, it is very necessary. Online notices of consent rely on clicking 'OK' in a cookie banner or pop up setting. The most common approach is to stay on the site and not change any settings. These approaches to obtaining binding consent are legally correct, but are they morally acceptable? Solove (2013) identified several issues with digital consent to manage information. Firstly, users cannot be expected to read all the terms and conditions and privacy policies. Secondly, to write binding consent in a language that is easy to understand and not ambiguous is difficult to achieve. Finally, even if users could read the terms and conditions and privacy policies and comprehend the action to take, it is challenging to quantify risk. Barocas and Nissenbaum (2014) suggested that even if digital consent were possible, it would not be effective because of the wide usage and purposes of information. Barocas and Nissenbaum (2014) turned to a paternalistic approach that makes certain actions with data permissible. Schermer et al. (2014) agreed with Barocas and Nissenbaum (2014) and made a further point that the information overload and an absence of meaningful choice leads to consent overload or 'consent desensitisation'.

Continual consent is more appropriate than conclusive consent because it gives the option to withdraw. Tools that support continual consent use a privacy dashboard approach such as Google and Facebook. Normally, data and information are given to third parties and then are not visible to the public or users. Consequently the most effective privacy consent is one that rejects or limits data collection. However, the aforementioned types of consent do not support cooperative partnership consent (Jones et al., 2018).

An early attempt at privacy consent, before the prevalence of AI and big data analysis, was to allow users to set their own privacy settings (Cranor, 2012). A privacy preference platform was developed by the Internet Privacy Working Group in the mid-1900s, namely, the Platform for Privacy Preferences (P3P). The platform developed for P3P enabled more standardisation and understandable settings; thus it enabled users to understand the privacy practices and policies of the website, which allowed them to make comparisons. Further improvements included visualisation of data collection practices and a standardised template, which was easily adaptable for privacy policies, to convey the most important policies (Jones et al., 2018). The shortened template and the setting of one's own privacy settings continued to overwhelm users, and they wanted more detail (Cranor, 2012).

Why not use AI to develop information privacy systems? Leveraging the benefits of machine learning is a distinct possibility and could be used to build trust, informed recommendations, and relevant information. AI can now evaluate the behaviour of apps; for example, AI was used to analyse the privacy policies of 18,000 free Android apps and revealed widespread discrepancies in privacy policies. Users and designers would benefit from an AI-generated consent, because the user would now be able to give informed consent, and the designer could limit liabilities (Zimmeck et al., 2017). Regulatory oversight does little to prevent users accidently or unwittingly violating privacy policies. Users inadvertently give data in plain sight that pose a risk to their privacy, and they do not understand the associated risks. Exposure still occurs even if the user has a setting that restricts public information flow, but common sense would dictate that information sharing such as photographs of homes, usernames, and new credit cards would violate their privacy. The application of AI could help to minimise these self-inflicted privacy violations (Orekondy et al., 2017; Jones et al., 2018). This is another opportunity to leverage machine learning to prevent unintended consequences originating from human behaviour.

Automating privacy consent would facilitate improved notice and choice but might be able to grant consent to agents or third parties. Machine learning would be able to understand the behaviour of the user and deduce if passing the information would draw privacy objections from the user. Furthermore a machine learning tool could offer predictability of users' privacy settings, leading to 'privacy profiles'. Liu et al. (2016) used AI to design privacy profiles to predict users' permission settings behaviour with a 79% success rate. Pascalev (2017) suggested an alternative approach to automating consent: AI as proxy consent. The proxy approach would convey the user profile as the initial initiation and would not require privacy profile, which are approximation to the users' privacy profile. AI could take the role of the doctor in a doctor-patient relationship and explain and provide information to the user. Building on these different privacy consent models may lead to AI systems that are be able to more accurately and consistently understand informational context (Barocas and Nissenbaum, 2014). Consent changes the moral behavioural landscape, and one needs to consider if some aspects of automated consent enable consent or simulate consent. Overautomation could undermine basic trust and the control required for consent to function (Jones et al., 2018).

3 Ethical dimensions and leadership

The discussion on privacy consent introduces the idea of ethics and morality, which links nicely to the type of leadership style digital organisations need to aspire to and reach. A fitting model as a starting point to discuss leadership in the digital environment is the attribution model. The attribution model states that people interpret the behaviour of others (Kelley and Michela, 1980). Their interpretations will influence their decision-making process. Hence the application of machine learning without noticeable links to moral consent would influence the perception of the firm. How firms treat personal data and information privacy in particular in the digital environment could have a profound impact on how users and consumers interpret the behaviour. In 2007 Fischer and Reuder (as cited in Ogunfowora et al., 2015) suggested that when consumers know about a firm, they form impressions, which are interpreted to respond to markets. Information flow, thus, influences the attribution model. Drivers of the inferences are information or signals from the firm, such as marketing campaigns or leadership structure and composition (Bear et al., 2010). Ogunfowora et al. (2015) proposed that the ethical stance of the executive leadership serves as a signal or source of information that influences consumer attributions towards the firm's corporate social responsibility (CSR) motives. A signal from an ethical CEO could be that the company is driven by moral CSR (Aguilera et al., 2007). Ogunfowora et al. (2015) found a correlation between the ethical behaviour of a CEO and the attributions afforded to the organisation by consumers. If CEOs are morally questionable, then consumers interpret the behaviour of the firm negatively (i.e. the firm has questionable moral values). CEO leadership ethics has an impact on organisational outcomes (Sharif and Scandura, 2014). A theme of this paper is that the behaviour of leadership (e.g. the moral behaviour of the CEO) has a positive or negative influence on the organisation. This has striking implications for consent in the digital landscape. Given the scandals that retrieval and use of personal data has caused, which has affected firms such as Google and Facebook, the need for ethical leadership is ever more pressing.

Before ethical leadership can be discussed, one needs to understand what antecedents are associated with effective leadership. Cohen's (2008) critique of Drucker's writing on leadership is discussed in the succeeding text.

The first attribute of effective leadership is to *build on strategic planning*—Drucker stated that the future cannot be predicted, but it can be created. Creation of the future requires strategic planning, but it is risky and challenging. Strategy is about taking decisions that affect the future to create a desired position for the firm. Strategic planning overcomes the actions in the environment to reach the desired position in the future. As a starting point the objectives of the leader underpin the strategic planning process. Given that the data and information landscape can be transformational in the digital environment, leaders need to use a strategic lens.

The second attribute is the requirement for *business ethics and personal integrity*—strategic planning forms the foundation for business, but ethics and personal integrity are the necessary conditions for effective leadership. Although Drucker concluded business ethics and personal integrity are requirements for effective leadership, he would not be drawn on what this means in absolute terms. Ethical behaviour is driven by culture; what is acceptable in one culture may not be appropriate in another. The legal process (i.e. the law) is not the same as integrity. When Drucker examined different cultures, he found them all wanting. How we deal with information consent will be dependent on the cultural conditions prevailing at the time.

The third attribute is that effective leadership requires a *model military leadership*—although this inclusion was surprising, Drucker did make reference to Xenophon, a Greek general, and he wrote about leadership in battle. Drucker postulated that good leadership in battles is required to win wars; by extension, 'business is a war'. To reinforce the point that good leadership is a necessary condition to win wars, he stated that the Army trains and develops many more leaders than other institutions—with a lower casualty rate. Organisations need to outperform their competitors in the leadership of information consent, and leadership techniques used by the military have a role to play. To sustain a competitive advantage in information consent management, organisation needs to continually improve.

The fourth attribute for effective leadership is for leaders to *motivate in the correct way*—Drucker stated that the role of workers is a sensitive issue, and he thought that firms were dependent on 'worker knowledge'; this is typically known nowadays as human capital. From Drucker's perspective, all workers make a valued contribution or have the potential to make a valued contribution and not just those that use their 'brains'. The *cost of labour* undermines the value of employees from Drucker's perspective. Labour from Drucker's viewpoint is not an expense but added value; it is the greatest resource a firm has. Workers are led and not managed. Thus the workplace is a participatory environment, but not laissez faire. Workers have different motivational needs, and money is not the only one. Motivation depends on needs and the situation. Drucker made the point that all workers should be treated as volunteers and with respect. Workers are mobile volunteers, and when economic conditions are right, they could move. To ensure the information privacy consent process is effective, workers have to be motivated because of the sensitive nature of dealing with personal data, from financial to health data. Hacking and fraud can occur because of inside worker cooperation; with the right motivation and tools, the information privacy process would be more secure and robust.

The final attribute is to *apply marketing concept to leadership*—Drucker called workers 'partner', who cannot be ordered, but persuaded; this is a change in paradigm from workers being 'knowledge workers'. Fundamentally, marketing is about understanding the needs and wants of customers and then satisfying them. This is not just about convincing customers to purchase products or services. Drucker reflected that if marketing was done perfectly, then selling would not be required. In practice, selling works in conjunction with marketing. However, to approach customers in a manner that demonstrates an understanding of their requirements and in a way they can relate to, modern day marketing requires an understanding of customer segments and their values and behaviour. Leaders need to approach workers in the same way.

Drucker (as cited in Cohen, 2008) summarised leadership as 'the lifting of a man's vision to higher sights, the raising of a man's performance to a higher standard, the building of a man's personality beyond its normal limitations'.

After the exploration of effective leadership based on Drucker, the management guru, it is now appropriate to visit ethical leadership. Spitzer (2000, p. 7) stated: 'Good ethics are good for business'. However, ethics depends on the moral position of the firm; ethics could be applied from a moral belief or due to expediency. Over time, users of a firm's privacy information process and consumers will judge the organisation's behaviour (attribution model), and any lack of consistency could have a negative outcome. Spitzer (2000, p. 4) suggested firms should move to a 'principle-based ethics'. Alternative approaches, such as ethical reflection, do not work because business environments change rapidly and privacy information consent is a rapidly evolving space. The law was never meant to replace conscience, but if a firm has standards, then 'uncrossable lines' (Spitzer, 2000, p. 4) are established. Spitzer (2000, p. 4) suggested that the consequences of not following principle-based ethical leadership are as follows:

1. increasing lawsuits and legal costs;
2. employees trying to get a 'fair deal' by missing work or stealing;
3. a rapid deacceleration in trust;
4. a rapid increase in fear, passive aggression, and anger;
5. a loss of integrity and moral rectitude.

Ethics appears to be in a 'perpetual state of ambiguity'; to break this trend, firms need to develop a 'backbone', that is, to move beyond ambiguity and subjectivity towards principled-based ethics. Firms need to develop a 'quasi-inviolable' principle that leads to 'a moral objective that will not be forsaken unless it causes us to violate a higher principle' (Spitzer, 2000, p. 4). Inviolable principles create collective responsibility and foster intrinsic goodness in the individual and organisation (Spitzer, 2000, p. 4).

Principles and challenges are well documented, and it is worthwhile to focus on some of these issues. A consistent theme that runs through this paper is morals and ethics and how these can be adopted to address leadership in the digital era. It is fitting that discussions on ethical and moral leadership are further developed. The digital leadership spectrum needs to embrace technology (creating technical solutions, i.e. problem solving) in the privacy information process. The implementation of technology should include not only the people involved in the implementation but also those who interact or communicate with the outcomes; for example, the privacy information process will require universal (internal and external) access in the organisation. Leadership becomes a holistic activity, which crosses all internal and external borders and gains alignment between people and organisational values. The paper is suggesting that ethical and moral leadership is an approach to address the requirements and challenges.

Ethics and leadership are actively intertwined, and for ethical leadership to succeed, a philosophical approach is necessary (Ciulla, 1995). The challenges of ethical leadership have been widely discussed and range from leader's self-interest and interest of the followers, the dirty hand principle (least bad of several bad options), and the need for leaders to be effective and ethical. Ethical leadership may not be the outcome of conscious intentions, but down to moral luck (Ciulla et al., 2018).

There are a range of ethical leadership approaches, and these will be discussed with a focus on those that are a 'better fit' to leadership in the digital era. Themes on ethical leadership are discussed in the succeeding text (Ciulla et al., 2018).

Plato wrote about the importance of self-knowledge and self-development for the understanding of 'good' or things that matter. Foucault was interested in the relationship between ethics and self, which is at one with Socrates and Plato. Confucius wrote: 'To practice humanity depends on oneself' (Chan, 1963). There is a majority of opinion that ethical leadership requires understanding and knowing oneself.

Machiavelli understood the need for social order against corruption and lawlessness. This is not a rejection of morality entirely, but ethics depends on the situation (i.e. selecting the less bad outcome). Leaders are guided by pragmatism and thus situational leadership. Soft and hard power is associated with situational leadership; thus leadership is grounded in context. The digital environment is fast moving, dynamic, proactive, and evolving; consequently the context can be considered a continuous variable. The development of holistic leadership skills in this kind of environment requires an ability to apply hard or soft skills and identify which type is appropriate within the context of ethical leadership, which is built on moral foundations.

Foucault drew on ethical leadership as a process of self-constitution (Ladkin, 2018). Understanding the interrelationship of power, knowledge, resistance, and freedom is important in ethical leadership (Ladkin, 2018). The challenge is to make oneself into an ethical subject to act ethically (Ciulla et al., 2018).

The other strand of ethical leadership is the ability to be inclusive (i.e. stakeholder management). The ethical leader needs to be a responsible leader (Patzer et al., 2018). In this theme, ethical leadership and business ethics are reconciled with society and corporate interests. Responsible leadership is the realisation of the changes in society and the business environment, such as increased globalisation, multiculturalism, mass migration and diversity, and a hardening of national and religious ideologies and identities (Ciulla et al., 2018).

What are the attributes of future digital leadership? The digital era requires leaders who practise ethical leadership, built on the foundation of morality. They need to be effective leaders with the attributes identified by Drucker, and they need to engage across different junctures internally and externally (customers, users, and consumers), enabling a 'deeper' holistic approach to digital leadership. Digital leaders need to understand technical trends that are evolving and established and demonstrate end-to-end leadership (product-process-people). Moreover, they need skills to work tactically (problem solving), strategically (future looking), and in differing cultures, as well as people management skills (engaging with stakeholders), and to apply an ethical situational leadership style. Situational leadership requires making judgements based on less than ideal situations, which will require digital leaders to make risk assessments (which actions are least bad and how will they impact the organisation, people and reputation in the marketplace). Ethical leaders need to understand vulnerability and risks and their likely impact holistically. This is particularly important because situational leadership means there will be consequences, which make for winners and losers. Continual engagement with employees, users, customers, consumers, and other stakeholders is an approach to mitigate the outcomes of situational leadership. Decision making in situational leadership must be seen to be fair and that the decision maker has a 'moral backbone'.

4 Risk and vulnerability assessment—Reputation

Organisations' worries about reputational risks are not new. The reputational risk report Reputational@Risk surveyed more than 300 executives on the importance of reputational risk to their business and found that 87% of the respondents rated reputational risk as 'important' or 'very important'. Furthermore, 25% of a firm's market value is linked to reputation. In the succeeding text are the hidden reputational risks (Ristuccia and Rossen, 2015, p. 7).

A firm's reputation is affected by the following:

Financial performance—shareholders, investors, lenders, and many other stakeholders.

Quality—willingness to adhere to quality standards. Product recall has an adverse effect on reputation.

Innovation—firms that differentiate themselves from their competitors through innovative processes, and unique/niche products tend to have strong name recognition and high reputation value.

Ethics and integrity—firms with strong ethical policies are considered more trustworthy in the eyes of stakeholders.

Crisis response—stakeholders keep a close eye on how a company responds to difficult situations. Any action during a crisis ultimately affects a company's reputation.

Safety—strong safety policies affirm that safety and risk management are top strategic priorities for the company, which builds trust and value creation.

CSR—actively promoting sound environmental management and social responsibility programmes helps create a reputation 'safety net'.

Security—strong infrastructure to defend against physical and cybersecurity threats helps avoid security breaches that could damage a company's reputation.

Ristuccia and Rossen (2015, p. 10) suggested that companies should invest in risk-sensing technologies. The capabilities of this type of technology are listed as follows:

Real-time analysis—efficiently processing and synthesising real-time data. Tools such as pattern detection and recognition enable real-time problem identification and reporting.

Text analytics—using natural language processing, sentiment analysis, and computational linguistics to identify and extract subjective information.

Big data—cost-effectively monitoring a vast array of internal and external data sources.

Forward-looking and outward-facing view—assessing future strategic, operational, and tactical business drivers, supplemented with an outside-in view of emerging risks.

Early warnings and triggers—improving the signal-to-noise ratio to detect faint early warning signs and avoid surprises.

Actionable insights—delivering operational insights that can be easily integrated into the business, delivering a direct and positive impact on performance.

Investing in risk-sensing technology gives companies additional assistance in decision making, by providing timely and deep insights that could influence reputational risks.

The factors that influence corporate reputation are prominent in the digital environment. Improvement in e-privacy information flow requires innovation, cybersecurity, and the application of machine learning; the application of AI requires innovation, ethics, integrity, and security. All are factors in reputational risk. To minimise reputational risk, stakeholder engagement and communication are important ways to gain agreement and consensus. The diffusion of reputational risks is tied to ethical leadership.

5 Regulatory challenges

The previous section discussed the impact of the digital environment on the nature and properties of weak or improper implementation of e-privacy policies on a firm. However, this is not the only challenge; one also needs to consider the regulatory landscape.

5.1 Risk and vulnerability assessment—General data protection regulation

The EU General Data Protection Regulation (GDPR) was created to protect rights to access data, data portability, and automated decision making (Esayas and Daly, 2018). The current GDPR framework is about preventing bad behaviour and reinforcing good behaviour. Hijmans (2010, 2016) stated that GDPR moved data protection from a market-oriented framework to one that embraces fundamental rights and freedoms. Meese et al. (2019) suggested that the Australian version, Consumer Data Right (CDR), was developed on a much narrower base of economic development and efficiency (i.e. the consumer and the market). Is there a case for reviewing the economic impact of GDPR and incorporating some aspects of the Australian CDR approach? A central focus of GDPR is the regulation of personal data, and it defines what is meant by data and information and is any information that can be linked to an identifiable person or identified natural person. CDR does not clearly define personal data and focuses on the protection of personal information. Personal data and information are not defined, and the legal process ruled that personal data are only related to the individual, but not metadata (Meese et al., 2019). Personal data protection is a global phenomenon and cannot be legislated piecemeal (i.e. country by country). This is a challenge for regulatory bodies in the post-GDPR era. To develop a global integrated 'GDPR' framework requires that the foundation and approach start from a common point so that any departure from an implementation will not impact the fundamentals of the framework. The strategy for a global 'GDPR' framework needs to be global or universal, but the tactical aspects (i.e. implementations) should be left to individual countries, regions, or blocks. However, the different implementation approaches should give consumers the same level of personal data protection. The global 'GPDR' framework must be integrated and not made up of several legal acts that are not integrated (Australia's approach to CDR; Meese et al., 2019). GDPR has become a default framework for many countries, but a truly global framework is required that integrates everyone's interests on data privacy. Thus GDPR is a good starting point to develop a global data protection framework.

In the succeeding text is a summary of the points made in a *Financial Times* editorial on the 27 December 2019 (Financial Times, 2019):

1. GDPR takes a tick-box approach, and firms have not internalised the spirit, and this is also possible for data protection policies developed by firms. There is too much lip service to GDPR, and it is not intertwined in the culture of the organisation.
2. The 28 national regulatory bodies involved in the implementation of GDPR make the process uneven and patchy. Flouting the law is not problematic, and firms are prepared to pay the fines, which can be more than taxes. It is an irritant to doing business, but it is not changing behaviour. How can the regulatory bodies enforce GPDR so that it has a 'real' impact on doing business and not seen as an irritant?
3. There should be a move from making bad companies do good things to a post-GDPR environment in which good companies are encouraged to do good things. There are more good companies than bad ones! The EU needs to rethinks the use of data collection to reshape data markets and not just regulate them.
4. The premise of the GPDR framework is meaningful consent, but consumers without choice cannot be said to have genuine consent. Impenetrable legalese is not a substitute for greater consumer rights and service, given the biased nature of online contracts. PayPal's terms and conditions are 36,275 words, which is greater in word count than Shakespeare's *Hamlet*.
5. The concept of individual data owner is not a helpful approach, because data in isolation generally have little value, as they cannot be sold or traded. Value comes from the combination of others' data. The value of the data is differential, which is dependent on the intended use.
6. Sometimes an individual's data can reveal a lot about others (e.g. blood relatives), especially if it is of a sensitive nature. Post-GDPR needs to encourage research on how to protect collective or group privacy.
7. Processing of data that stay encrypted in the analysis and manipulation stages is 'privacy by design'. Privacy is maintained throughout the process.
8. Improvement in data governance based on a decentralised ecosystem. Data are regarded as a public good that could benefit the local community. The Open Data Institute is pioneering the use of data trusts, creating a legal structure to provide independent stewardship of data. Just having data only goes so far; technology also needs the smartest engineers and algorithms to win.

5.2 Risk and vulnerability assessment—Other challenges

The aforementioned discusses pressing issues in the post-GDPR era, but other challenges are going to emerge. The other challenges are identified as follows:

1. Risk assessment process to rigorously verify the privacy process developed by firms from a governance and individual or collective perspective.

2. Will public liability insurance cover privacy breaches or will companies need cybersecurity insurance?
3. Are financial auditors or forensic accountants qualified to carry out cybersecurity auditing?
4. Service level agreements may need rethinking to incorporate third parties in the privacy information process (i.e. controllers of the data), who are likely to be external to the organisation.
5. Knowledge and awareness of e-privacy and cybersecurity need to be raised. Is this a government versus firm issue, because firms may not want to make the necessary investment?
6. Certification and qualification are issues to guarantee quality and level of expertise of data privacy personnel that are involved in the process.
7. Personnel who can report and repair GDPR security breaches.
8. The business security policy of firms will need shaping so that it is fit for purpose.
9. Ethics concepts and frameworks may require revisiting to encompass the new developments in e-privacy (e.g. collective or group ecosystems).

6 Implications

The advent of personal data collection and AI challenge information systems to guarantee the privacy of user data; in addition, companies seek access to data and information, which are malleable and can yield trends and events, to gain a competitive advantage and improve their competitive position and profitability. Consent has moral and ethical connotations, which clearly requires a regulatory framework to protect the consentee (user) and the consenter (acquirer and user of the information), but the consenter could use an agent (could be external to the acquirer's organisation). Rules of informational engagement require privacy policy documentation to cover the three parties to the information privacy interaction. From an ethical and legal perspective, documenting the rules of engagement is a good thing. However, moral privacy does not follow from ethical or legal privacy. There is also the danger of accidental or unintentional exposure of private information, which no amount of regulation can stop. Human interaction makes a failsafe system of privacy consent challenging. Thus consentees might withdraw consent, which means information data flow could be poorer in quality (more challenging to spot trends from data) and thus the benefits of data mining would be reduced; this would have a knock-on effect on the firm's competitive advantage and competitive position. The privacy information process and policies must keep the consentees engaged, and this suggests an interactive privacy consent approach. Automation of consent is an attractive proposition, but this does lead to a loss of control by the actors involved in the information privacy consent process. People like to have some control over situations and do not generally like to be beholden to systems. This suggests that a compromise approach to privacy information will be needed: semiautomated in some circumstances and users can intervene when they deem it necessary. It may be necessary to integrate aspects of the various privacy information models to move the debate forward. The insecurity that the privacy information consent process causes requires moral integrity of the highest level from the leadership of an organisation.

We discussed the need for effective leadership to underpin the privacy information process. Drucker defined five attributes relating to leadership that are relevant in managing digital environments. Information and the analysis of data can lead to new business opportunities; therefore the integrity of the data from a moral and ethical perspective requires leadership skills that empower employees to behave with integrity so that their behaviour does not impact organisational outcomes negatively. The need for governance structures on the handling of information processes is mentioned in the introduction of this paper, including privacy, but these can only be effective with motivated employees and effective leadership. Drucker noted that leadership is not absolute, but depends on the culture. Another important point is that leadership must set the culture to implement effective leadership, because organisational cultures will vary; thus what is effective leadership in one organisation may not work in another. O'Toole (2009) commented on the difficulty in changing company culture, and he made several points. There are few examples in which a change to a large established organisation that involves its strategy, structure, systems, and behaviours have succeeded. The main problem is that leaders in large and established firms use a centralised approach to change management, because of the centralised and bureaucratic structures in the organisation. Today, leaders in large organisations need to apply shared values, decentralisation, mission, and purpose to gain alignment of the corporate goals, embed adaptive processes for change, and gain commitment to innovation. Implementing a privacy information process will require an organisation to be more dynamic, proactive, and organic. This will be a challenge for all organisations and not just large and established ones.

Effective leadership is effective in discrete environments, but in continuous environments (drivers are globalisation, i.e. connectiveness and integration, as well as cultural identification and religion enforcement) a different leadership style is necessary, which is digital leadership. Digital leadership is transformative leadership, because change must occur within the organisation, and involves the engagement of users, customers, consumers, and external agents and includes the type of interaction through digital privacy processes. Different stances of ethical leadership are helpful in deciding the types of ethical leadership that will fit comfortably in the digital era. Consent, e-privacy, AI, and cybersecurity are just a sample of the challenges digital leaders will face and how these will evolve, and their impact is another major challenge. Needless to say the digital environment is continuous, changeable (disruptive), proactive, complex, and dynamic; these characteristics all affect the window of opportunity and thus sustainability of a firm's competitive advantage. The discussion suggests that to lead in the environment described requires ethical leaders with a moral perspective and that the meeting of ethical standards is not sufficient. Ethical leadership needs to link to corporate values and behaviour; however, values are not standard; they are influenced by culture (country and organisational) and society. It is incumbent on ethical leaders to set standards that are grounded in the corporate values and culture. Spitzer (2000) used the term 'uncrossable' standards that ground decision making so that ethical and moral standards are not breached. Are the values sustainable? The environment in the digital era is continuous and dynamic, which implies corporate values and standards will evolve. A change in CEO may necessitate a change in corporate values causing a shift in the company's 'moral backbone'. Analysis suggests that a situational leadership approach would be an appropriate ethical leadership style. Sometimes, ethical leaders cannot have all positive outcomes (there are no risks or vulnerabilities), but they have to choose from the least bad solutions. This means collateral damage may impact the organisation, including employees, customers, users, and consumers. Is a standardisation of the moral compass suitable in these circumstances? Ethical leadership is an approach to build trust, but this may lead to conflict and erode trust. Another aspect of ethical leadership is stakeholder representation or responsible leadership. Leaders need to engage in dialogue and engage continuously with stakeholders to build communication bridges. Even within responsible leadership, there could be miscommunications, and the outcome suggested may be good for the organisation as a whole but less so for stakeholders. Ethical leadership has many facets and is difficult to achieve without continuous application and moral fortitude. The practice of ethical leadership is effective if leaders know themselves; 'Plato writes about the importance of self-knowledge and self-development for the understanding of "good" or things that matter' (Ciulla et al., 2018, p. 246). Morality is dependent on how well you know yourself and on if you are willing to contemplate self-development, but this depends on the character of the person and their willingness to learn and take on board constructive feedback. What has not been considered is the psychology of the digital leader—personality and ability to learn. Are there particular personality types that would make better digital leaders? Given the scope and challenges required in digital leadership these areas need to be explored.

The e-privacy debate has created more risks and vulnerabilities, including reputational risks, and the need to review the GDPR framework in a post-GDPR era. Issues on reputational risks will galvanise firms to do more on e-privacy, because it will have an impact on their business. The safeguarding of personal data and information requires firms to move beyond a tick-box approach and to make it become embedded in the culture and well-being of the organisation. Financial penalties alone will not bring about this change, because it is profound and transformational. Ensnaring the corporate culture in this new world will require accountability at the top of the organisation, and this might require a legal process that holds the CEO and senior management accountable and legally responsible for the data protection. Fines alone could just be judged to be the price of doing business, and in isolation, they would be unlikely to change behaviour organisation-wide. This is particularly important in the post-GDPR era, when decentralised ecosystems may require revisiting ethics concepts and principles and changes to the GDPR framework. Stakeholder involvement will need to become the norm in the post-GDPR era to ensure business policies and GDPR processes are transparent and that accountability acceptance is ingrained in the organisational culture. Digital leaders need to embrace the post-GDPR era with vigour, commitment, and with a moral compass or 'backbone' that is fit for purpose. CEOs may be required to relearn or modify current ethical thinking, which will affect their moral philosophy. Technology companies are moving the consent debate forward by ensuring that third parties (internal or external to the firm) cannot identify individual personal data, because the e-privacy process maintains the encryption during analysis and manipulation of the data. The 'strength' of the encryption process will determine the credibility of the collective or group e-privacy process. Technology in the future could eavesdrop on the data without breaking the encryption process. Such acts will need building into the post-GDPR era. Different skills in personnel will be required in the post-GDPR era, such as business cybersecurity auditors who will probably have a grounding in finance and IT; assurance of the quality of these new personnel will require recognised qualifications and certification. Who should develop and be the keeper of standards and quality of these qualifications? Does this need regulating by government or will external quality control be sufficient? Should risk assessment be only an internal company matter or is government intervention required to ensure compliance? Is a default GDPR framework (EU framework) adequate to represent a world that is driven by globalisation? These are just a flavour of the type of regulatory issues that will need addressing in the post-GDPR era.

7 Conclusion

One can state with certainty that becoming a digital leader is challenging, because of the scope and skills required. The challenge is for leaders to build a moral philosophy for themselves and the firm (values) that meets the needs of the organisation. The digital era is driven by globalisation, proactiveness, and culture, which requires an ethical leadership style that will have to evolve to meet the new challenges in the post-GDPR era. Leaders who fail to develop an ethical leadership style and use it to embed the necessary and fitting corporate values could impact the privacy environment by inviting government regulatory intervention to ingrain accountability and legal responsibility for ensuring personal data processes are robust and fit for purpose. Leaders need to develop a moral philosophy that is in alignment with the company culture and values to develop a sustainable competitive advantage.

References

Aguilera, R.V., Ganapathi, J., Rupp, D.E., Williams, C.A., 2007. Putting the S Back in corporate social responsibility: a multilevel theory of social change in organizations. Acad. Manage. Rev. 32 (3), 836–863.

Barocas, S., Nissenbaum, H., 2014. Big data's end run around procedural privacy protections. Commun. ACM 57 (11), 31–33.

Bear, S., Rahman, N., Post, C., 2010. The impact of board diversity and gender composition on corporate social responsibility and firm reputation. J. Bus. Ethics 97 (2), 207–221.

Chan, W.-T., 1963. Selections from the *Analects*. In: A Source Book in Chinese Philosophy. Translated and Edited by Wing-Tsit ChanPrinceton University Press, Princeton, NJ, p. 38.

Ciulla, J.B., 1995. Leadership ethics: mapping the territory. Bus. Ethics Q. 5 (1), 5–24.

Ciulla, J.B., Knights, D., Mabey, C., Tomkins, L., 2018. Philosophical approaches to leadership ethics: perspectives on self and responsibility to others. Bus. Ethics Q. 28 (3), 245–250.

Cohen, W.A., 2008. Effective leadership: let's revisit Drucker's model. Leadership Excellence 25 (8), 7.

Cranor, L.F., 2012. Necessary but not sufficient: standardized mechanisms for privacy notice and choice. J. Telecommun. High Technol. Law 10 (2), 273–307.

Esayas, S.Y., Daly, A., 2018. The proposed Australian consumer data right: a European comparison. Eur. Compet. Regul. Law Rev. 2 (3), 187–202.

Financial Times, 2019. December 27. Protecting data privacy needs constant evolution (Editorial comments). Financial Times 20.

Hijmans, H., 2010. Recent developments in data protection at European Union level. ERA Forum 11, 219–231. https://doi.org/10.1007/s12027-010-0166-8. 2.

Hijmans, H., 2016. The European Union as a Constitutional Guardian of Internet Privacy and Data Protection. PhD Thesis, University of Amsterdam. Retrieved from: https://hdl.handle.net/11245/1.511969.

Jones, M.L., Kaufman, E., Edenberg, E., 2018. AI and the ethics of automating consent. IEEE Security & Privacy (May/June), 64–72.

Kelley, H.H., Michela, J.L., 1980. Attribution theory and research. Ann. Rev. Psychol. 31, 457–501.

Ladkin, D., 2018. Self constitution as the foundation for leading ethically: a Foucauldian possibility. Bus. Ethics Q. 28 (3), 301–323.

Liu, B., Andersen, M.S., Schaub, F., Zhang, H.A.S., Sadeh, N., Acquisti, A., Agarwal, Y., 2016. Follow my recommendations: a personalized privacy assistant for mobile app permissions. In: Twelfth Symp. Usable Privacy and Security (SOUPS 16), pp. 27–41.

Meese, J., Jagasia, P., Arvanitakis, J., 2019. Citizen or consumer? Contrasting Australia and Europe's data protection policies. Internet Pol. Rev. J. Internet Regul. 8 (2), 1–16.

Miller, F.G., Wertheimer, A. (Eds.), 2010. The Ethics of Consent: Theory and Practice. Oxford University Press.

O'Toole, J., 2009. Connecting the dots between leadership, ethics and corporate culture. Ivey Business Journal September/October. 1–8.

Ogunfowora, B., Stackhouse, M., Oh, W.-Y., 2015. CSR motive attributions: the roles of executive leadership ethics and consumer cynicism. Academy of Management Annual Review Meeting Proceedings 188, 1–6.

Orekondy, T., Schiele, B., Fritz, M., 2017. Towards a visual privacy advisor: understanding and predicting privacy risks in images. In: Proc. International Conf. Computer Vision (ICCV), pp. 1–22.

Pascalev, M., 2017. Privacy exchanges: restoring consent in privacy self-management. Ethics Inf. Technol. 19 (1), 39–48.

Patzer, M., Voegtlin, C., Scherer, A.G., 2018. The normative justification of integrative stakeholder engagement: a Habermasian view on responsible leadership. Bus. Ethics Q. 28 (3), 325–354.

Reisinger, S., 2019. As Cyberattacks on Business Grow, General Counsel Are 'Thirsty' for More Details. [online] Available from: https://www.law.com/corpcounsel/2019/06/14/as-cyberattacks-on-business-grow-general-counsel-are-thirsty-for-more-details/. (Accessed 23 December 2019).

Risks & Compliance by Number, 2015. [online] Available from: Insidecounsel.com. February/March 2015 (Accessed 23 December 2019).

Ristuccia, H., Rossen, M., 2015. Reputation risk as a board concern. The Corporate Board (January/February), 6–10.

Schermer, B.W., Custers, B., van der Hof, S., 2014. The crisis of consent: how stronger legal protection may lead to weaker consent in data protection. Ethics Inf. Technol. 16 (2), 171–182.

Sharif, M.M., Scandura, T.A., 2014. Do perceptions of ethical conduct matter during organizational change? Ethical leadership and employee involvement. J. Bus. Ethics 124 (2), 185–196.

Solove, D.J., 2013. Privacy self-management and the consent dilemma. Harv. Law Rev. 126 (7), 1880–1903.

Spitzer, R.J., 2000. The ethical leadership. Executive Excellence (May), 4.

Zimmeck, S., Wang, Z., Zou, L., Ivyengar, R., Liu, B., Schaub, F., Wilson, S., Sadeh, N., Bellovin, S.M., Reidenberg, J., 2017. Automated analysis of privacy requirements for mobile apps. In: Proc. Network and Distributed System Security (NDSS) Symp, pp. 1–15.

3

Integrating social media and warranty data for fault identification in the cyber ecosystem: A cloud-based collaborative framework

Syed Imran Ali[a], Farooq Habib[b], Abdilahi Ali[c], Abdul Ali[d],
Murtaza F. Khan[e], and Arshad Jamal[d]

[a]UNIVERSITY OF HUDDERSFIELD, HUDDERSFIELD, UNITED KINGDOM [b]CRANFIELD
UNIVERSITY, CRANFIELD, UNITED KINGDOM [c]UNIVERSITY OF SALFORD, SALFORD,
UNITED KINGDOM [d]NORTHUMBRIA UNIVERSITY, LONDON, UNITED KINGDOM
[e]UNIVERSITY OF LAW, LONDON, UNITED KINGDOM

1 Introduction

Vehicle faults are of major concern to consumers and automotive manufacturers. In the UK automobile industry, which is the focus of this chapter, the Driver and Vehicle Standards Agency (DVSA) has issued over 8400 recalls due to faults in the last decade, resulting in multimillion pound of expense to vehicle manufacturers (DVSA, 2016). These faults usually relate to safety, performance, engine, security, and quality. The identification of faults by automotive manufacturers is mostly done by their own diagnostics tests, vehicle road tests, inspection, and customer feedback (Abrahams et al., 2012). Manufacturers also review warranty claims, dealer reported faults, and customer-filled complaints in agencies like DVSA. However, we believe that, because of the emergence of social media, a large amount of fault-related information is also hidden in social media. Consumers increasingly engage in information sharing on weblogs, forums, Facebook, and Twitter, among others. This valuable information is mostly untapped by the automotive manufacturers cyber ecosystem.

In the existing literature, social media has been used for business intelligence to, for example, predict stock market volatility (Antweiler and Frank, 2004), movie sales (Duan et al., 2008), and power tool equipment faults (Finch, 1999). Researches have explored online forums using manual tagging for product quality information (Finch, 1999). Vehicle defect discovery has been done by, for instance, (Abrahams et al., 2012). However, the use of social media for fault analysis in the context of distributed supply chain management

Strategy, Leadership, and AI in the Cyber Ecosystem. https://doi.org/10.1016/B978-0-12-821442-8.00012-4
© 2021 Elsevier Inc. All rights reserved.

41

has gained less attention. Even when social media is used, the existing literature usually applies a single dataset (e.g. twitter, Facebook, and weblogs), neglecting the fault information which is scattered across the distributed supply chain.

Hence, data from social media can facilitate initial fault identification. These useful data should then be integrated with supply chain data for detailed and prompt fault analysis. Product lifecycle management (PLM) is a 'strategic business approach' which is normally used for managing and integrating the life cycle from design, manufacture, and service till disposal. It is an information and communication technology–driven method which integrates processes, people, and business systems. This technological solution could be used to streamline the flow of information across the supply chain (Terzi et al., 2010; Park et al., 2016). PLM architecture is basically built on the philosophy of delivering the right information at the right time. Until now, PLM has played a 'holistic' role of integrating product knowledge because of nonstandardised systems (Stark, 2005). But recently, due to the emergence of standardised open business information systems, the sharing of information and collaboration across the supply chain has become easier. Srinivasan (2011) summarises some of the key IT developments that might aid data sharing:

1. standardised product development engineering models such as computer-aided design (CAD), computer-aided manufacturing (CAM), computer-aided engineering (CAE), and product data management (PDM);
2. standardised business process systems such as manufacturing execution system (MES), enterprise resource planning (ERP), customer relationship management (CRM), and enterprise asset management (EAM);
3. standardised and mature product data and metadata models by STEP (Standard for the Exchange of Product model data);
4. service-oriented architecture (SOA), that is, principles of service for information sharing that are independent of any software and technology;
5. open-source middleware to connect software components or enterprise level applications.

IT developments and standardised protocols pave a way for easy integration of various business information systems from manufacturing design, modelling, and execution. Although the PLM concept provides a centralised access to product metadata, it is still fragmented across the supply chain. Warranty data (which are important for fault identification in manufacturing) are dispersed across the supply chain. All models and techniques proposed in warranty data analysis (WDA) literature are mostly applied on a single database. Therefore there is a need to integrate warranty data from multiple datasets across supply chain into fault identification system. This will enable the utilisation of product knowledge to support internal decisions and the improvement of fault identification across the supply chain. The availability of integrated models for fault identification in distributed manufacturing industry is very rare. In this study, we propose principles of PLM that can be used for the integration of warranty data across the supply chain.

In the past, cloud computing technology (CCT) was used to integrate various segments of the supply chain with minimum resources (Bruque-Cámara et al., 2016). CCT has shown remarkable results in industries such as banking, healthcare, IT, and logistics (Al-Hudhaif and Alkubeyyer, 2011). It is an emerging technology which is built on service-oriented architecture (SOA) with layers of open standards. CCT can be used to share information across complex networks. CCT's modular structure allows business functions and processes to be provided as services using pay-as-you-go concept. Several service delivery models of cloud such as software as a service (SaaS), platform as a service (PaaS), and infrastructure as a service (IaaS) have led to easier and real-time information availability. Keeping these attributes of wider cooperation and collaboration in mind, this chapter proposes a cloud-based PLM framework.

In light of these preliminaries, the main aim of this chapter is to integrate data from multiple datasets of distributed supply chain for detailed and quick fault identification. The proposed cloud-based PLM framework focusses on integration of faults data from social media and manufacturing supply chain. Multiagent system (MAS) is used for task accomplishment by mutual coordination of autonomous smart agents. The framework is composed of 21 autonomous software agents. These agents are capable of decision-making at various levels without or with minimum human interaction. Three of the agents, that is, supply chain facilitator agent (SCF), fault learning and rectification agent (FLR), and design agent (Di) play a key role in fault analysis. The cloud-based PLM framework facilitates in quick fault identification in short life cycle of products. We evaluate the effectiveness of the cloud framework using fault data from multiple datasets.

In our analysis, we find that social media is very useful for production of fault information related to vehicles. The detailed fault analysis is done using sentiment and content analysis (CA). But in our analysis, we also find that the results may not give a full representation of the population of faults and thus may be biased as per customer sentiments. To overcome this a cloud-based PLM framework is proposed to integrate the warranty data across supply chain for full representation. The warranty management process described here is to simplify the gathering of warranty data from multiple datasets. The combined data can then be used for detailed expert analysis by fault learning and rectification agent. Finally the execution of the framework is demonstrated using an illustrative execution process.

The reminder of the chapter is organised as follows. Section 2 briefly reviews the existing studies on fault identification. Section 3 contains the research questions and contributions, while Section 4 explains the use of social media for initial fault identification. Methodology, results, and evaluation are discussed in Sections 5 and 6. Section 7 discusses in detail cloud-based framework. Section 8 illustrates the execution of framework. Section 9 identifies a number of managerial implications which emanate from the research. Finally, Section 10 ends with concluding remarks.

2 Literature review for fault identification

Over the last decade, extensive research has been done on fault identification in failed products during warranty (Abrahams et al., 2015; Khan et al., 2014). The traditional life cycle of failed products is illustrated in Fig. 1. Here the manufacturer first procures various components of the product from multiple suppliers and assembles them in assembly

FIG. 1 Life cycle of failed products.

units. The products are then distributed to customers through various regional retailers and distributors. Often, it is only when the customer receives the product that the faults are identified and returned to service centres (Wu and Meeker, 2002).

The returned faulty products are checked as per warranty for claims. Generally the reliability literature assumes that warranty claims can be gauged using a single dataset. However, this assumption might not hold in today's distributed manufacturing where complex product data are stored in multiple datasets. In this distributed scenario, there is a need for extensive warranty data analysis from multiple datasets of distributed manufacturing to find the main cause of the fault.

2.1 Warranty data analysis

Blischke et al. (2011) analysed warranty from the reliability viewpoint. They use warranty data and prediction methodologies to identify component failures. Thomas and Rao (1999) develop a complete framework for analysing warranty cost and warranty policy. Wu and Meeker (2002) and Shafiee and Chukova (2013) have categorised WDA into five areas:

(1) Early detection of faults. Here, several techniques and methods have been developed. Karim et al. (2001) use nonparametric estimation for the mean number of failures in repairable and nonrepairable products. Wu and Meeker (2002) apply statistics and statistical detection rules by Poisson distribution estimation. Honari and Donovan (2007) use control charts using artificially generated data and warranty claim data.

(2) Design modification. This is very important for improving the reliability of products. Yang and Cekecek (2004) devise a design improvement method on the basis of warranty claim data and design susceptibility. Buddhakulsomsiri et al. (2006) and Buddhakulsomsiri and Zakarian (2009) use warranty databases. Both of these studies apply rule-based reasoning on warranty data to identify warranty problems.

(3) Field reliability estimation. This is done on the basis of the manufacturer's warranty policy. Warranty policies are categorised as one-dimensional (1D) on the basis of age or usage only and two-dimensional (2D) on the basis of region in the 2D plane, that is, one dimension depicts age and the other, usage. Researchers have analysed 1D approach for warranty policy using mixed distribution, Weibull distribution, mixed-Weibull regression, nonhomogeneous Poisson process, parametric and nonparametric pseudo-likelihood, covariate and lifetime distribution (Majeske, 2003; Ion et al., 2007; Wilson et al., 2009; Suzuki, 1985; Oh and Bai, 2005; Attardi et al., 2005). Methods used to analyse 2D approach to consider failure models in 2D warranty policy include marginal, bivariate, and composite scale (Baik and Murthy, 2008; Chukova and Robinson, 2005; Jung and Bai, 2007).

(4) Warranty claim prediction. This is used to analyse warranty claim cost during warranty coverage time. The techniques that have been developed to predict warranty claims are lifetime distribution, stochastic processes, artificial neural networks, and time series models (Kleyner and Sandborn, 2005; Majeske, 2007; Kleyner and Sanborn, 2008; Rai and Singh, 2005).

(5) Warranty claim estimation. Kalbfleisch et al. (1991) use a log-linear Poisson model, where the Poisson parameter is considered as a function of time in service; Lawless et al. (1992) use a moment estimator for counting warranty claims in single product; Suzuki et al. (2001) and Karim et al. (2001) use nonhomogeneous Poisson process (NHPP) to calculate warranty claims in repairable products, and Hu and Lawless (1996) use nonparametric analysis on warranty claims when observation period of a product is unknown.

The literature review shows that fault identification in complex products is difficult and complicated because of the distributed nature of warranty data. WDA techniques and the statistical methods mentioned earlier use single dataset which is not that much successful in distributed manufacturing. The complexity of today's products and interrelated components (subsystems) make the identification of faults difficult (Khan et al., 2014).

Our central argument in this chapter is that there is a great need of integrating data from multiple datasets of supply chain for quick fault identification. Combined knowledge/data should be used by designers and engineers when using already developed warranty identification methods, engineering techniques, and tools to identify and solve complex product design/technical faults. Cloud computing technology (CCT) is a relatively new technology that can be adopted to integrate the whole manufacturing supply chain data on a manufacturing company's own private cloud. Various deployment and service delivery models make the adoption easier for big and for small- and medium-sized enterprises (SME).

3 Research questions and contributions

In this chapter, two main research questions are tackled:

(1) Do social media contain substantial information related to faults during warranty?
(2) Is the integration of warranty data from multiple datasets important for detailed fault analysis in a complex distributed manufacturing supply chain?

The four objectives of the chapter are as follows:

Obj 1 Extract large volume of social media data for fault identification (Section 5)
Obj 2 Evaluate the data for fault identification using sentiment and content analyses (Section 6)
Obj 3 Design a cloud-based framework to integrate warranty data from multiple datasets of supply chain (Section 7)
Obj 4 Elucidate the whole fault identification process using an illustrative step-by-step execution procedure (Section 8)

4 Use of social media data

To identify faults during warranty, social media data are explored in the UK automobile industry. The selection of the automobile industry for testing the framework is based on following criteria. First an attempt is made to elucidate initial identification of faults during warranty. Second the cost implications of faults during warranty period is scrutinised. Third, customer perception about the fault rectification process is explored during warranty. Fourth the competence of dealers is gauged with respect to fault identification and rectification. It should be emphasised that this is currently not feasible in light of the fact that fault identification data tend to be scattered on different segments of the supply chain (Wiengarten et al., 2013; Thun and Hoenig, 2011). The research in this chapter argue that this issue is important as it can have implications for both customer satisfaction in terms of prompt fault identification and manufacturer's profitability.[a] Unfortunately, attaining access to warranty/fault data is challenging. More specifically, vehicle dealers and manufacturers are not willing to provide access to their warranty data because of commercial sensitivities. In addition, there is the issue of the Data Protection Act 1998 (DPA) in the United Kingdom, which governs how personal information is handled by, among others, firms.

---

[a] For example, there is evidence that Volkswagen's revenues and customer satisfaction dropped as a result of the recent emissions scandal (see Ewing, 2016).

The research in this chapter sidestep the lack of availability of warranty data by utilising social media sources (Abrahams et al., 2012, 2013; Mostafa, 2013). Social media is defined as a group of Internet-based applications build on the ideological and technological foundations of Web 2.0 that allows the communication exchange of user-generated content (Kaplan and Haenlein, 2010). Increasingly, social media such as Facebook, weblogs, microblogging, and Twitter play a key role in shaping business analysis and decisions. Social media have shown a drastic growth in user counts, comments, and tweets in scientific analysis (Stieglitz and Dang-Xuan, 2013). As a result, huge volume of user-generated data is available for business analytics. However, navigating through these huge volumes of scattered and unstructured data requires various approaches including, filtering, sentiment and content analyses, tagging, and text mining (Stieglitz and Dang-Xuan, 2013; Chae, 2015; He et al., 2015).

4.1 Social media analytics framework for fault identification

Collecting data from Facebook requires application programming interface (API). The most frequently used API for Facebook is 'Graph API'. Secret API key is used as access token to extract Facebook data. It provides easy tracking of wall postings (i.e. comments). Weblogs do not have standardised method such as API for extracting data. However most of the blogs offer Rich Site Summary (RSS) for extracting metadata. If RSS is not available, then manual web crawling can be done, which requires HTML parsing (Stieglitz and Dang-Xuan, 2013). The collected data could be unstructured (texts, expressions, etc.) and enriched metadata with user profiles, URLs, or 'likes' (Daniel et al., 2010). In this chapter, graph API and web crawling is used to extract the data from (i) the complaint department (CD) weblog website[b] and (ii) vehicle companies' official UK Facebook (FB)[c] pages. Using these two sources, fault data are extracted during warranty for a period of 1 year, that is, July 2015–July 2016.

As highlighted earlier, navigating through this rich and unstructured social media data requires various research methods and intelligence techniques (Fan and Gordon, 2014; Abrahams et al., 2015). With this in mind the following methods—business intelligence (BI), CA, and sentiment analysis (SA)—are employed. The results of the analyses help us to identify faults in vehicles. The framework is shown in Fig. 2.

4.2 Business intelligence

Business intelligence techniques are valuable to harness product or process information from multiple perspectives: customers, competitors, suppliers, markets, acquisitions, and services to achieve success in competitive global business (Vedder et al., 1999). To gain understanding about products, firms gather intelligence from consumer complaints (Sampson, 1996). The Internet or Web 2.0 is an online information technology that can

---

[b] http://www.complaintsdepartment.com/companies/.

[c] As data are unsolicited, it does not invoke ethical issues, but nonetheless, we have secured ethical clearance.

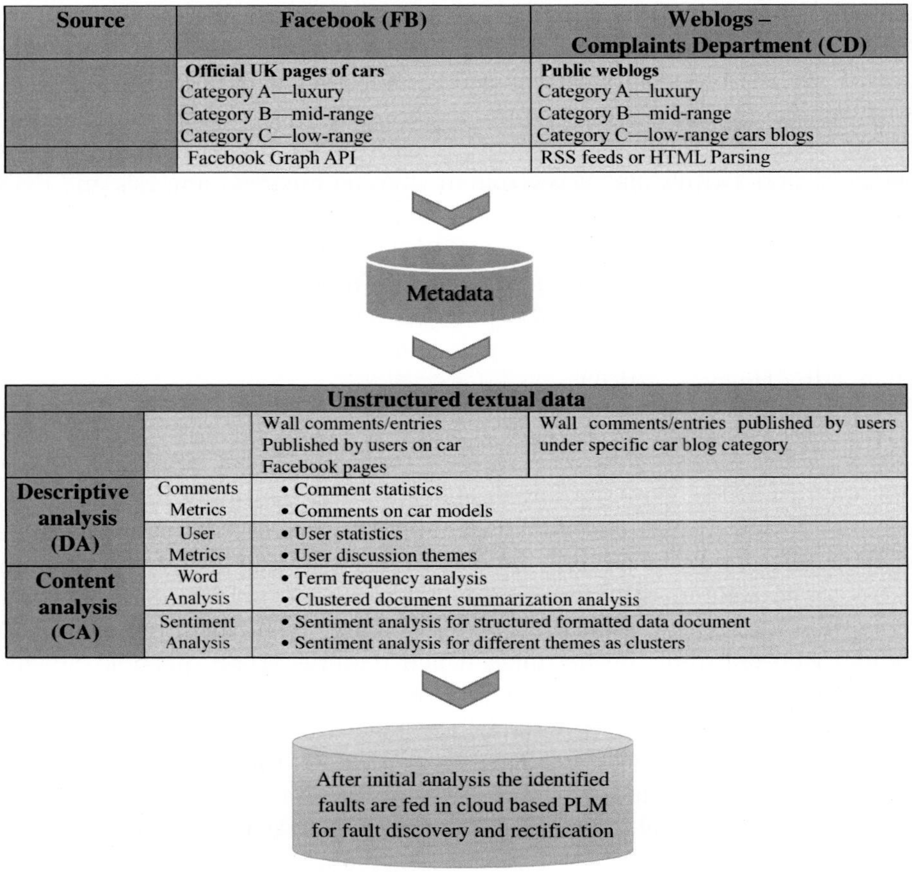

Source	Facebook (FB)	Weblogs – Complaints Department (CD)
	Official UK pages of cars Category A—luxury Category B—mid-range Category C—low-range	**Public weblogs** Category A—luxury Category B—mid-range Category C—low-range cars blogs
	Facebook Graph API	RSS feeds or HTML Parsing

Metadata

Unstructured textual data			
		Wall comments/entries Published by users on car Facebook pages	Wall comments/entries published by users under specific car blog category
Descriptive analysis (DA)	Comments Metrics	• Comment statistics • Comments on car models	
	User Metrics	• User statistics • User discussion themes	
Content analysis (CA)	Word Analysis	• Term frequency analysis • Clustered document summarization analysis	
	Sentiment Analysis	• Sentiment analysis for structured formatted data document • Sentiment analysis for different themes as clusters	

After initial analysis the identified faults are fed in cloud based PLM for fault discovery and rectification

FIG. 2 Analytics framework for fault identification.

enrich business intelligence (Chau and Xu, 2012). Given the magnitude of available information and data, it is important to apply appropriate approaches (e.g. CA) to extract meaning (Stieglitz and Dang-Xuan, 2013; Chae, 2015).

4.3 Content analysis

Social media data is 'unstructured' which is composed of texts and expressions. CA can be adopted using various text mining techniques to extract intelligence from large volume of textual data of Web 2.0 (Chae, 2015). Comments from Facebook and weblogs are composed of short list of words, URL, images, and some other information. Text mining applications are mostly used for extraction, theme tracking, concept linkage, information visualisation, and content filtering (Abrahams et al., 2012). Text mining is an important component of CA to analyse textual data and extract business intelligence (Abrahams et al., 2012). Text mining transforms unstructured textual data into structured formatted data using text capturing techniques of tokenisation, n-grams, and the removal of unnecessary words (Chae, 2015). The structured formatted data are then used for word frequency analysis and keyword analysis using machine learning algorithms like association and clustering analysis (Chae, 2015). Word analysis is the first step in CA. Word analysis includes term frequency analysis (TF), document summarisation, and clustering (Chae, 2015). For information retrieval, TF is combined with n-grams to extract key phrases from the structured formatted data. The unsupervised machine learning algorithms such as clustering assists in analysing the topic of interest from the structured formatted data.

4.4 Sentiment analysis

SA is the detection and analysis of subjective information such as opinions, sentiments, emotions, products, problems, faults, complains, and services (Pang and Lee, 2004; Li and Wu, 2010; Liu, 2010). In SA, polarity of positive, neutral, and negative text is extracted from structured formatted data (Pang and Lee, 2004). A dictionary such as WordNet is a powerful tool to analyse the strength of the sentiments expressed with synonyms and antonyms (Miller et al., 1990). SA can be performed either on the whole structured formatted data document, or the document can be divided into different themes as clusters. Some small number of sentiment words are collected as seeds manually from the structured formatted data. Synonyms and antonyms of these words then are searched in the online WordNet dictionary. The words are combined as a word set with repeated iterations until no new words are found. SA is done by giving a score to the sentiment in a sentence (Hu and Liu, 2004).

4.5 Summary

So far, very few studies have been done with particular focus on fault identification in vehicles for business intelligence using social media. Previous studies have explored online forums by manual tagging for product quality information (Finch and Luebbe, 1997). Others, such as Abrahams et al. (2012), examine vehicle defect discovery using text mining approach on online forums. In particular, they use vehicle expert feedback for defect discovery and remedy planning. However, in today's distributed manufacturing, vehicle fault is not just fixed by analysing data from social media. It needs to be analysed in the context of warranty data from the whole vehicle manufacturing supply chain. Social media data, therefore, can help in initial fault identification process during the warranty period. These data can then be integrated with the supply chain data for detailed fault analysis.

5 Methodology

The ideal approach to better understand the reporting of vehicle faults is to undertake empirical study of social media (Flynn et al., 1990), that is, Facebook and weblogs. In this chapter, data pertaining to July 2015–July 2016 are extracted from Facebook and weblogs (such as complaints department). The original raw dataset includes 51,467 comments and their metadata.

5.1 Data sampling

In sampling a range of criteria is employed to classify the data. First the vehicles discussed in social media are classified into three categories. Category A is luxury, category B is mid-range, and category C is low-range vehicle. Next the data are coded under five themes as inclusion criteria:

- *Types of faults during warranty:* Vehicle is sold with particular warranty. The customer experiences some faults during the warranty period which they then report to the dealer or main manufacturer. An example of fault during warranty was as follows:

  Comment: *the brake squeal issue on our last one had the brakes stripped, cleaned and bedded ok but didn't make a difference so further sound bites were taken and it's been ruled new callipers are needed. This was after 2 months/900 miles.*

- *Faults and cost implications:* Some faults during warranty are covered, but some are charged as service, depending on the liability. An example of fault with cost implications was as follows:

  Comment: *fuse box where it is prone to moisture and water penetration due to its position? The cost of a replacement can cost anything up to £600!*

- *Customer perception about fault rectification:* Customers express certain 'feelings' about their vehicle after having experienced faults and rectified during a specified period. An example of customer perception was as follows:

  Comment: *like other German manufacturers, living on name and past reputation. Cars are too complex and costly when they go wrong and manufacturers ought to stand by their products if they fail prematurely. Not fit for purpose. Is there any recall issues on this Audi in question?*

- *Customer's perception about dealer competence:* Perception of customers depends largely on the service they get from the dealer. Proper and cost-effective fault diagnosis plays a key role in shaping the customers' perceptions about dealer competence. An example of dealer competence was as follows:

Comment: *had disgraceful customer service experience at Audi Epsom. Complained to Audi UK who I thought would resolve the issue quickly as it was a new car however Audi UK's customer service is just as bad as the Dealership, I will never buy an Audi ever again and warn you not to use Audi Epsom.*

- *Junk (i.e. expressions with no faults reporting):* It includes the expressions of vehicle enthusiast, joy, photos, requesting new vehicle model information, general vehicle service questions, vehicle customisation, and modifications questions. An example of junk comment was as follows:

Comment: *myself and quite a few fellow Ford enthusiasts are looking into the availability of repair panels for the Ford Sierra (all variants).*

6 Results and evaluation

Eight hundred ninety-eight useful comments were filtered out of a total of 51,467 comments from the two sources, CD and FB, respectively. In what follows, first the data are elaborated (Section 7.1). Following this, SA is done (Section 7.2).

6.1 Descriptive analysis

The selected comments discuss some 29 unique vehicle models. A total of 3189 users mention vehicle faults and perceptions about their vehicle or dealer. The average comment contains 617 words expressed in 27 sentences. One hundred seventy-nine (37%) of the words are unique, and most of them contain, on average, five characters.

6.2 Content analysis

In this chapter, two types of CA are applied such as word analysis and SA. Word analysis includes term frequency analysis (TF), document summarisation, and clustering (Chae, 2015).

Word analysis: Most popular words in CD comments are change (3306), active (2560), instrument (2543), going (2523), take (1866), and events (1759). On the other hand, popular words in FB comments are change (30,943), act (19,577), get (17,795), move (16,443), make (15,673), and transport (12,587). The other common words in both datasets are shown in Fig. 3.

6.2.1 Types of faults during warranty

A close inspection of both data sources reveals that there are 233 faults which customers point out during the warranty period. The most common 25 faults mentioned are summarised in Table 1. Across both data sources, category A vehicles (i.e. luxury) account

FIG. 3 Word analysis from CD and FB datasets.

for the bulk of reported faults (61.42%) followed by category C (21%), while category B vehicles have the lowest figures (17.42%). So in terms of engine design, complexity, and reliability, category A vehicles are more prone to common faults (during warranty) as compared with the other two categories. This is consistent without a priori expectation.

6.2.2 Fault and cost implications

The two data sources also capture the costs incurred by customers as a result of the faults. A total of 53 faults with costs reported during the warranty period. The combined average costs reported from both sources are as follows: £1534 (category A), £2203 (category B), and £613 (category C).

Thus the data suggest that the repair costs of mid-range vehicles (i.e. category B) are, on average, higher than the two other categories. As expected, low-range vehicles (i.e. category C) are the cheapest to repair (see Table 2).

6.3 Sentiment analysis

In this section the link between (reported) faults and customer satisfaction is explored. There are various tools and techniques of SA that could enable us to capture customer sentiment. For the study purposes the algorithm suggested by Thelwall et al. (2011) is used to cluster the sentiments on the basis of time period. The broad objective is to solicit information regarding customer perception about fault rectification and customer perception about dealer competence.

6.3.1 Customer perception about fault rectification

The comments on customer perception about fault rectification during warranty are clustered on the basis of time period for fault rectification. The criteria for clustering are as follows:

Very good (+2): Fault rectified within a week

Table 1   Cross tabulation of faults in CD and FR datasets.

Sr. no.	Fault type	CD Category A (%)	CD Category B (%)	CD Category C (%)	FB Category A (%)	FB Category B (%)	FB Category C (%)
1	Engine management light	3.65	0.84	2.25	1.12	0.28	0.84
2	Gearbox	1.69	0	0.28	1.40	1.69	0.28
3	Fuel injector	1.69	0	0	0.28	0.28	0
4	Clutch	1.69	0	0.56	2.25	1.40	0.28
5	Coil pack	1.40	0	0	0	0.56	0
6	Suspension	1.40	0	0.28	1.12	0	0
7	Fuel pump	1.40	0	0	0	0	0
8	Wheel alloy cracking	1.12	0	0	0.28	0	0
9	Turbo	1.12	0	0.56	0.84	1.12	0.28
10	Timing chain snapped	1.12	0.28	0.28	1.12	0.56	0
11	Fly wheel	0.84	0	0	0.28	0.56	0
12	Tyre	0.84	0.28	0.28	0	0	0
13	Breaks	0.84	0.28	0	1.69	0.56	0.56
14	Steering failure	0.84	0	0.28	0.28	0	0
15	Triptronic gear box	0.56	0	0	0	0	0
16	Intermittently loss of power	0.56	0.28	0.84	0	0	0
17	Amplifier	0.56	0	0	0.28	0	0
18	Alternator	0.56	0	0.84	0.28	0	0
19	Rattling noise	0.28	0	0	0	0	0.28
20	Cracked windscreen	0.28	0	0.28	0	0	0
21	DPF system	0.28	0	0	0.28	0.28	0
22	Cam chain snapped	0.28	0	0.56	0	0	0
23	Cylinder	0.28	0.28	0	0	0	0
24	Oil leak in the main gasket	0.28	0.56	0	0.28	0	0
25	Others	14.04	1.69	7	12.00	6	4
	Total	**37.64**	**4.49**	**15**	**23.78**	**13**	**7**

Table 2   Fault versus average cost.

	Category A	Category B	Category C
Average cost CD	£1668	£1675	£627
Average cost FB	£1400	£2731	£600
Combined average cost	£1534	£2203	£613

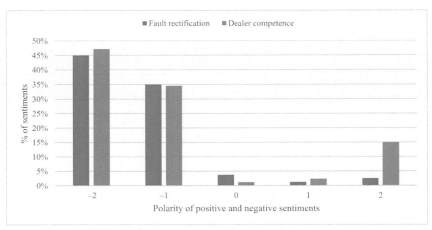

FIG. 4 Sentiments of customers about fault rectification.

Good (+1): Fault rectified within 1 month
Average (0): Fault rectified within 1–2 months
Bad (−1): Fault rectified within 2–3 months
Very bad (−2): Fault rectified in more than 3 months

After the clustering process the sentiment words in WordNet (Section 1.4) are used. Fig. 4 shows customer sentiments about fault rectification at the (aggregated) dataset level (i.e. both sources).

6.3.2 Customer perception about dealer competence

The comments on customer perception about dealer competence during warranty are also clustered on the basis of time period. The criteria for clustering are as follows:

Very good (+2): Dealer was very competent
Good (+1): Dealer was very competent
Average (0): Dealer was ok
Bad (−1): Dealer was bad
Very bad (−2): Dealer was very bad

After the clustering process the sentiment words were used in WordNet (Section 4.4). Fig. 4 shows the customer sentiments about dealer competence at the entire dataset level (CD and FB).

6.4 Summary of key lessons and current practices

The aforementioned simple data exercise underlines some important issues in fault identification during warranty. First, faults do occur during warranty, and these faults tend to affect all types of vehicle categories (Table 1). Category A vehicles are more prone to faults, while category B are least prone to faults. Second, both fault identification and rectification have cost implications for customers. In particular, category C vehicles are cheaper to repair as compared with other two categories (Table 2). Third, fault identification and rectification can be a tedious and lengthy process. The longer the time period it takes to rectify the faults, the more costumers become unhappy (Fig. 4). Finally, he competence of the dealer in identifying and rectifying faults is crucially important. The least competent dealers tend to receive higher negative sentiments (Fig. 4).

The key lesson emanating from the earlier data exercise is that a lot of vehicle fault data is hidden in social media. But the data fail to represent full population of faults. Also the customer sentiments for vehicles and faults stand biased. To overcome this issue, integration of warranty data from multiple datasets of supply chain data is important for full representation. The integrated data will enrich manufacturers in quick identification of faults. Integration of warranty data has been studied in detail by González-Prida and Márquez (2012). They proposed a framework for industrial company after-sales services. Dai et al. (2012) have explored warranty management in the context of centralised and decentralised supply chain for maximising profit.

However, to the best of researcher's knowledge, there are very few integrated warranty data systems or frameworks that integrate data from distributed supply chain. High-tech industries are the hardest hit industries because of distributed manufacturing. The cost of warranty management is on the rise (Chakraborty, 2015). Fault claims can consume a sizeable portion of their revenues. The main factor in the identification process is that it is complex and time consuming to find the root cause of fault in distributed manufacturing. The fault which occurs in one component of a product may be linked with other components which are procured and manufactured in other segments of the distributed manufacturing supply chain. The nonavailability of supply chain warranty data results in slow processing of fault claims. Recently, Madenas et al. (2016) have proposed a system architecture for automotive industry by integrating PLM systems. They designed the system using Unified Modelling Language (UML). The main aim of the system is to find the root cause of fault by integrating warranty data across the supply chain. But the system fails to have full representation of warranty data as semistructured expert interview method was used as a data source.

To overcome these issues a cloud-based framework is proposed to manage the warranty data from supply chain systems, namely, design, manufacture, and service. A private cloud deployment model is used because of confidentiality and the need for greater control of data. Thus, within the framework, the infrastructure is hosted on manufacturer's own private cloud. SaaS delivery model is used to provide services to supply chain stakeholders across the distributed manufacturing. The stakeholders access and retrieve centrally available data from the private cloud. They also upload data through the usage of SaaS. These centrally stored data from multiple datasets are then used for fault identification and decision-making.

7 Cloud-based framework

The conceptual model is shown in Fig. 5. The manufacturer hosts the entire infrastructure over its cloud. Due to data confidentiality and security reasons, the manufacturer employs a private cloud deployment model. This framework is composed of two multiagent-based subsystems, that is, supply chain and manufacturing, which are integrated through interface agent (IA). Both subsystems are explained in detail in Sections 7.1 and 7.2, respectively. These two subsystems access product-related data and warranty data from cluster of cloud databases through discovery agent (DA). SaaS delivery model is adopted. SaaS provides easier access to resources as it uses thin client or a web browser. All the needed software and subsystems are installed over the cloud. SaaS provides access to manufacturing private cloud for sharing, retrieving, and updating product-related data.

The proposed framework provides supporting structure to the distributed manufacturing industry with sophisticated technological requirements and scattered standardised product data. It could help in WDA via integration of warranty data, field data, service data, and customer feedback, manufacturing measurements from supplier, manufacturer, assembly, distributor, retailer, field testing centre, and service centre level. The subsystems are designed in general context so that they could be applied to any industry, for example, aircraft, defence, automotive, and high-tech electronics.

7.1 Multiagent-based supply chain subsystem

The multiagent-based supply chain subsystem provides access to supply chain stakeholders (service centre, field testing centre, customer, distributor, and retailers) as show in Fig. 6. The subsystem is composed of multiple software agents that can solve problems in a distributed and decentralised global manufacturing environment (Akkermans et al., 2003; Mizgier et al., 2012; He et al., 2013).

These software agents are intelligent computers or machines that work autonomously to solve complex problems. In the supply chain subsystem, these software agents facilitate interaction among stakeholders, that is, service centre, field testing centre, customer, distributor, and retailer. The main purpose of having cloud-based multiagent supply chain subsystem is to provide collaboration, interaction, exchange, and sharing of product data among all stakeholders. The private cloud of the manufacturer provides access to stakeholders by using SaaS. Software agents and their respective functionalities as services are briefly summarised in Table 3.

7.2 Multiagent-based manufacturing subsystem

The multiagent-based manufacturing subsystem is shown in Table 4. The multiple software agent concept (as in supply chain subsystem) is also applied in manufacturing subsystem. Agents with dynamic roles and responsibilities have been designed to do relevant

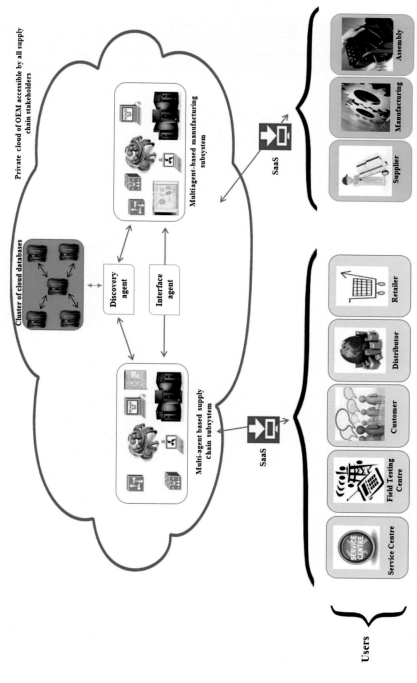

FIG. 5 Conceptual cloud-based framework.

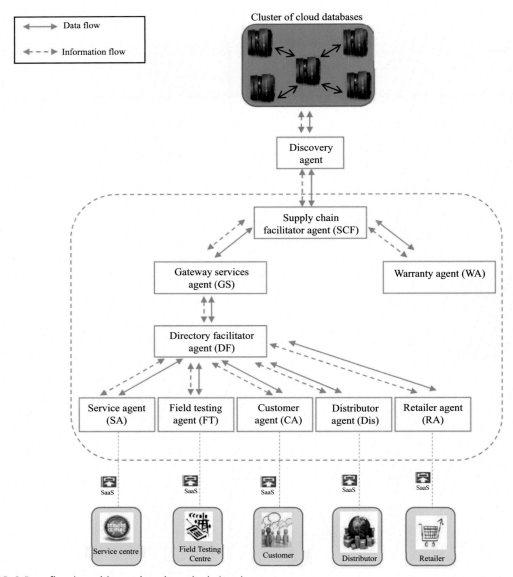

FIG. 6 Data flow in multiagent-based supply chain subsystem.

jobs. The private cloud of manufacturer provides access to stakeholders using SaaS. Software agents and their respective functionalities as services are briefly summarised in Table 4.

Design agent (Di) and fault learning and rectification agent (FLR) are the key agents for fault identification in the proposed framework. These two agents will be discussed here in more detail.

Table 3   Supply chain subsystem agents.

Agent name	Functionality
Supply chain facilitator agent (SCF)	SCF is the main entry agent in supply chain subsystem for services. It is used to facilitate services in manufacturing. Specifically, SCF provides services to all stakeholders of supply chain, that is, distributors, retailers, customers, field testing centres, and service centres
Gateway service agent (GS)	GS agent acts as a coordination agent for services in manufacturer service centres and field testing centres. GS agent communicates with service agents (SA) and field performance (PF) agents for services
Warranty agent (WA)	WA is responsible for maintaining warranty information as per unique product/part number or RFID. The faults and problems that occur in products/parts during warranty period are updated through warranty agent in warranty database. This information is useful for designers and engineers in designing new products and fixing complex problems in existing products/parts. WA retrieves, updates all the warranty information, and updates it through discovery agent (DA). DA helps in locating, retrieving, and updating data in warranty database located over private cloud of manufacturer
Directory facilitator agent (DF)	DF agent provides registration services to all services and field testing centre agents in supply chain subsystem. It helps in keeping proper record of active service and field testing centres. DF agent updates the registry if some changes in status of centres occurs
Service agent (SA)	SA helps in providing services to service centres. Warranty faults that occur during warranty period are reported from service centres. After initial screening of unique product/part number or RFID, warranty validity check is done from manufacturer cloud databases, the services are then offered. All the faults during warranty are updated in warranty database by using DA. This warranty data facilitate designers and engineers in designing of new products by analysing previous history. It also helps them to address warranty faults and fix them at the time of manufacturing
Field testing agent (FT)	FT agent monitors performance of products in field testing centres. The field performance data are entered in field performance databases during performance testing phase. The data are stored by using DA. Field performance data are useful for designers and engineers in early design phase
Customer agent (CA)	CA agents provide customer access to manufacturing systems for logging complaints and review about products
Distribution agent (Dis)	Dis helps in monitoring and tracking distributor network for ready products. It holds stock/inventory data for distribution centres. Dis uses DA to update and retrieve information from inventory database
Retailer agent (RA)	RA is used for maintaining and tracking retailer network for products. It holds product's knowledge on shelves of retail centres and updates that in sales and inventory database. That information is used by distribution agent (Dis) to maintain proper stock/inventory for retailers. DA helps in updating and retrieving data in relevant databases
Software as a service (SaaS)	SaaS is a software application that is designed for accessing cloud resources. The main purpose of SaaS is to access, share, exchange, and manage required product's data from a pool of servers over the cloud. Stakeholders can update and retrieve information from cloud. Cloud access also helps diversely located departments to work in a collaborative and interactive environment

7.2.1 Design agent

Di agent holds product designs in various design formats, that is, CAD, CAM, and CAE. Di agent converts CAD, CAM, and CAE into standardised format, that is, Extensible Markup Language (XML). The XML-based design files are then stored in cluster of cloud databases. Di agent is shown in Fig. 7.

Table 4   Manufacturing subsystem agent functionalities.

Agent name	Functionality
Manufacturing server agent (MS)	MS agent is the main agent in manufacturing subsystem. The job of MS agent is designing of new products/parts, improvement in existing product by analysing warranty data, and fault identification in products under manufacturing. All product's design, workflows, manufacturing processes, product checking, early design stage analysis, inter- and intrarelated parameter checking in products is done through the facilitation of MS agent. MS agent updates and retrieves data files by using DA. DA helps in storing data in specific databases over the private cloud of manufacturer
Marketing agent (MK)	MK agent is responsible for deciding the design marketing strategy. It makes the marketing strategy by analysing warranty, services, and customer feedback data. MK agent retrieves the relevant data through DA. Based on data for products/parts, the marketing strategy is made for designing of new products/parts. The extracted data are helpful in making effective design marketing strategy which fulfils customer requirements
Product development agent (PD)	PD agent maintains product development requirements. PD agent creates a new PD for start of new product requirement and closes it on finishing of product development
Design agent (Di)	Di agent holds product design knowledge. It assures making of product/part as per the specifications and customer demand. Main job of Di agent is to keep record of all design related data, that is, material requirement specification (MRS), bill of quantities (BOQ), process plan, part function-means tree diagrams, and axiomatic diagrams. All data for aforementioned design items are stored in relevant databases which are updated and retrieved by using DA
Design agent for improvement (DAI)	DAI task is to monitor the improvement in existing products. If products/parts have some faults during warranty period then DAI gets recommendations from FLR agent, marketing agent, and manufacturing agent. These recommendations are taken into consideration on the basis of criteria, that is, production cost and manufacturing resource availability. After detailed analysis the faults are rectified, and design data are updated in relevant databases of design and knowledge with the help of DA
Design agent for NPD (DAN)	DAN takes care of new product development (NPD). In design of new products/parts, DAN gets recommendations from FLR agent, marketing agent, and manufacturing agent. These recommendation are then taken into consideration again on the basis of criteria, that is, production cost and manufacturing resource availability. After detailed analysis of previous similar products and their faults, new robust products are designed, and data are updated in product databases with the help of DA
Supplier agent (SA)	SA provides access to all selected supplier of products. DA helps suppliers to acquire standardised product designs from STEP-NC product database
Manufacturer agent (MU)	The main job of MU agent is to monitor manufacturing processes. Whenever a request comes to make product/part, MU agent first checks its STEP-NC product database. If the manufacturing design requirements are met, then particular resources are allocated for manufacturing. MU agent also monitors functional and process design faults during manufacturing. This knowledge is categorised as per products/parts and stored in design and knowledge database of manufacturer. These data are useful for designer and manufacturing engineers to rectify the faults
Assembler agent (AA)	AA provides access to all selected assembler of products. DA grants access to assemblers to STEP-NC product database for accessing designs for assembly

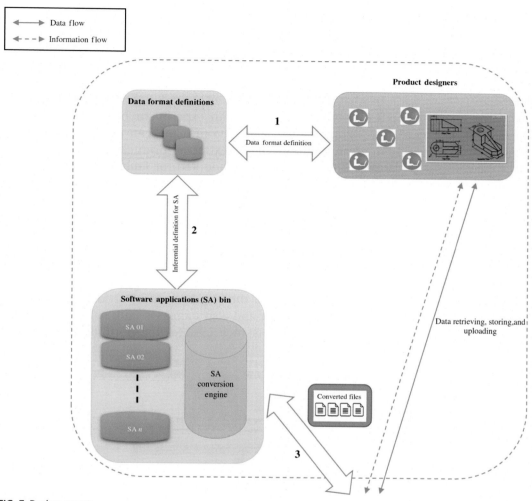

FIG. 7 Design agent.

In step one, designers send design files in CAD, CAM, or CAE format to data format definition databases. After getting the required data format definitions, the appropriate files with inferential definitions are forwarded to a software application (SA) bin in step 2. The software application bin is composed of databases of various software applications like CAD, CAM, and CAE. The application engine, which is in software application (SA) bin, converts the design files as per rules laid down in engine. The converted files are then sent to cluster of cloud databases in step 3 through DA. If the designs or data formats for products/parts are required by stakeholders, then the XML files are compiled and formatted in sequence. The formatted files are then transmitted to supply chain stakeholders, that is, supplier, manufacturer, assembler, service centre, and filed testing centre through DA.

7.2.2 Fault learning and rectification agent

FLR is the main agent for identification of faults in existing/new products (Fig. 8). FLR retrieves data from cluster of cloud databases such as warranty database, extended warranty database, filed performance database, service centre and customer feedback database, parameter database, manufacturing measurement database, and knowledge database. It combines the gained knowledge, background knowledge, design, and manufacturing engineer's expert knowledge to plan experiment by adopting 13 step approach of Coleman and Montgomery (1993). The problem can properly be defined by adopting 13 steps, and relevant information is extracted from cluster of cloud databases. Various methods and algorithms could be adopted for fault solutions. Some of the salient ones in the literature are 0–1 mathematical traditional integer program solver, heuristic approaches such as genetic algorithms (GAs), tabu search (TS), bean search (BS) and hybridised genetic algorithm (HGAs). According to the literature, there is no specific search algorithm which can be regarded as best suited for a particular problem. The selection of a specific algorithm depends on the nature and type of the problem. Keeping this in mind, FLR uses a portfolio of algorithms (Gomes and Selman, 2001). It is a collection of different algorithms or copies of them which run on different processors. The main point is to select the algorithm that meets most of the requirements. Portfolio of algorithm approach minimises the computational cost and also increases fault solving capability (Kumar and Mishra, 2011). New problem instance initiates the portfolio of algorithm

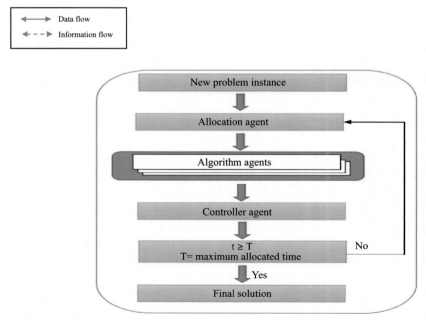

FIG. 8 FLR agent with portfolio of algorithm.

system. Time limit is allocated to provide the solution to the fault with priority. As a first step, allocation agent assigns an experimentation time to various algorithm agents and accordingly decides priority order to algorithm agents (Kumar and Mishra, 2011). The experimentation data collected by algorithm agent will be brought back to selector agent. Selector agent will decide about the algorithm in portfolio to solve the problem (Kumar and Mishra, 2011). In the specified time limit, multiple iterations are made to make a decision about the final selection of an algorithm agent solution (Kumar and Mishra, 2011). The workflow of the portfolio algorithm, as shown in Fig. 8, is adopted from Gomes and Selman (2001), Kumar and Mishra (2011), Mishra et al. (2012). The sorted list of recommendations for fault solution is then forwarded to design agent.

There are two common agents between two subsystems, that is, DA and IA. Functionalities of these agents are as follows:

7.2.3 Discovery agent

DA provides all agents access to cluster of databases over the cloud. DA holds detailed information about location of databases. It helps in updating and retrieving data from relevant databases.

7.2.4 Interface agent

IA facilitates interaction of two subsystems, that is, manufacturing subsystem and supply chain subsystem. Both subsystems interact with each other using agent communication language (ACL).

Section 8 contains a step-by-step execution of the cloud-based framework.

8 An illustrative cloud-based framework

In this section the execution of the framework described in Section 7 is illustrated. The framework could be applied to any complex distributed manufacturing industry. An illustrative process (Fig. 9) is used for fault identification in the automobile industry. It is assumed that the company has global service and field test centres for fault identification.

Steps of multiagent interaction for fault identification in the framework are explained as follows:

Step 1: The customer agent (CA) reports a fault to the GS agent through social media.
Step 2: The GS agent forwards the fault to the regional service agent (SA) through DF agent.
Step 3: The service agent (SA) contacts the customer and does initial identification of the fault and uploads the fault in framework through SaaS. The fault report is then forwarded from service agent (SA) to gateway service (GS) agent through directory facilitator (DF) agent.
Step 4: Gateway service agent (GS) receives SA fault report and checks through warranty agent (WA) for validity of warranty. If warranty is valid, then the request is

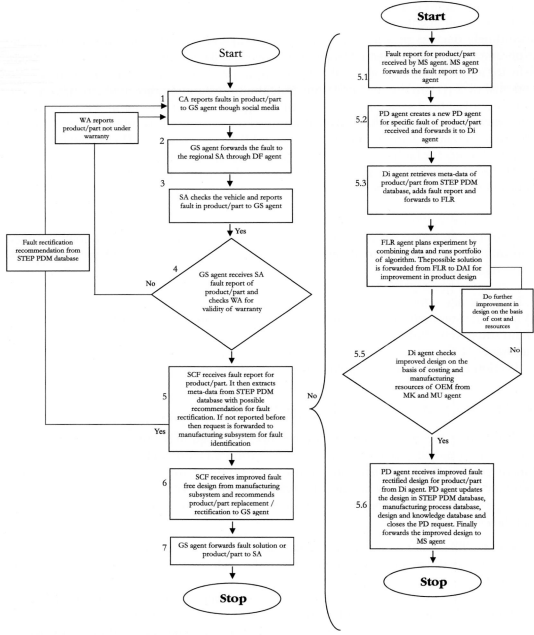

FIG. 9 Flowchart for fault identification in product/part.

forwarded to the supply chain facilitator agent (SCF), otherwise reported back to SA that the product/part is not under warranty.

Step 5: Supply chain facilitator agent (SCF), after receiving the request, extracts metadata from cloud-based STEP PDM database and forwards the same to service agent (SA) via SCF. The service centre repairs the faulty part as per recommendation in the metadata. If the fault is not reported before, then it is forwarded to manufacturing subsystem via SCF.

Fault identification in manufacturing subsystem involves a number of substeps as explained in the succeeding text:

Substep 5.1: Fault report for product/part in manufacturing subsystem is received by manufacturing server agent (MS) through IA. MS agent then forwards the fault report of product/part to product development agent (PD).

Substep 5.2: PD agent creates a new PD agent for the fault received for specific product/part and then sends it to the design agent (Di).

Substep 5.3: Di agent receives the product/part fault report from PD agent. Di agent retrieves product/part details, that is, metadata from STEP PDM database through DA. The product/part metadata and fault report is then forwarded to design agent for improvement (DAI).

Substep 5.4: DAI forwards fault report to fault learning and recommendation agent (FLR). FLR agent extracts all data relating to fault from cluster of cloud databases. The gained knowledge, background knowledge, and design and manufacturing engineers expert knowledge are combined together to plan experiment. On the basis of planned experiment, portfolio of algorithms (see Section 7.2.2) finds possible solution to the fault by running collection of different algorithms. On the basis of recommendations from FLR, DAI does improvement in product/part design and forwards the updated fault free designs to Di agent.

Substep 5.5: Di agent rechecks the improved design in coordination with MK and MU agent. Di agent also seeks recommendations on the basis of costing and manufacturing resource availability. If the costing is ok as per marketing and availability of resources, then manufacturer forwards the updated designs to PD agent; otherwise, it is sent back to DAI for further improvement in design on the basis of costing and manufacturer resource availability.

Substep 5.6: PD agent then updates the improved design of product/part in STEP PDM database, manufacturing process database, and design and knowledge database. Finally, closes PD request for product/part and forwards the same to MS agent.

The procedure for fault identification in product/part by interaction in manufacturing subsystem ends here.

Step 6: SCF receives improved fault free design from manufacturing subsystem. The recommendations of product/part replacement/rectification is sent to GS agent.

Step 7: GS agent forwards fault solution or product/part to SA.

9 Managerial implications

This chapter proposes a framework that integrates data from multiple datasets for the identification of faults during warranty. The whole supply chain is integrated through the central platform of the manufacturer by utilising services of CCT. The proposed framework can be very useful for managers of large and for small- and medium-sized enterprises who have limited resources, infrastructure, IT awareness, and operational experience (Yeboah-Boateng and Essandoh, 2014). This framework not only saves money in implementation but also provides easy and prompt real-time access to any form of data by utilising SaaS from manufacturer's private cloud (Guo et al., 2014). The manufacturer's private cloud maps all supply chain stakeholders. Stakeholders can use SaaS to upload customer feedback, service centre data, field test data, manufacturing data such as order details, production/manufacturing data, threshold limit checks data, and quality control checks data. This can help in mitigating fault identification. In addition, it leads to a lesser dependency on requesting related data in distributed manufacturing. For example, the framework can help managers in tracing the relevant faulty component provided by specific stakeholder across the distributed supply chain. The integrated data facilitate detailed fault analysis. This study can improve the conventional method of fault identification where the faults are analysed using a single dataset. The integration of data from multidatasets concerning the whole supply chain can help managers in effective fault identification. For example, it is demonstrated in this chapter how the social media data can help in prompt start of the fault identification process. Thus the framework has the potential to promptly identify faults and improve customer satisfaction and performance of the industry. The traceability of faults also becomes easier because of the information visibility aspect of CCT. This will help not only the customer to have feedback about the fault in their product but also the managers in tracing the fault.

It is argued in this chapter that proposed framework makes fault identification easier by effective integration of warranty data. Moreover, managers can continuously monitor the progress of faults and their remedy. The fault data stored in the cloud repository could assist engineers, designers, and decision-makers in making robust products in the future.

10 Concluding remarks

Currently, there is some interesting literature and models available for fault identification during warranty. However, the business world is getting more and more agile, competitive, and dynamic, so the emergence of new frameworks with technological improvements and management theories can make a difference. Hence, to address this, the aim of the chapter is to explore how cloud computing technology can be used as a vehicle to integrate data from multiple sources (e.g. social media and supply chain) to aid fault identification. The proposed framework in the chapter uses the PLM concept which is technology solution that could be used to streamline the flow of information across the supply chain.

The following objectives have been attained. First, large volume of social data is extracted for fault analysis in vehicles. Second, for fault identification, the data are evaluated using sentiments and content analyses. Third a cloud-based framework is designed to integrate warranty data from multiple datasets of supply chain. Private cloud deployment model is adopted by manufacturer because of confidentiality and greater control of data. Infrastructure is hosted on manufacturer's own private cloud. SaaS delivery model is used to provide services to supply chain stakeholders across the distributed manufacturing. Social media is utilised for initial fault identification and finally fault recovery by integrating the data with framework. Finally the whole fault identification process is elucidated using an illustrative step-by-step execution procedure. As shown throughout the framework facilitates the mapping of the entire supply chain using CCT through autonomous smart agents, real-time information visibility, prompt fault identification, and collaborative decision-making. It is posited in this chapter that proposed cloud-based framework can boost coordination and make business processes more efficient. The framework is designed in a general context so that it can be applied to any distributed industry. Future research is required, however, to develop automated business intelligence tools and effective algorithms to analyse data in a cluster of cloud databases for fault identification and effective warranty management. This can help in further exploring the vast and valuable amount of datasets which are growing at an exponential level because of the emergence of integrated systems and social media.

Declaration

A rough concept of the chapter was presented in International Conference on Business, Economics, Management and Marketing (ICBEMM 2016), Oxford University, Oxford, 15–17 August 2016.

References

Abrahams, A.S., Jiao, J., Wang, G.A., Fan, W., 2012. Vehicle defect discovery from social media. Decis. Support. Syst. 54 (1), 87–97.

Abrahams, A.S., Jiao, J., Fan, W., Wang, G.A., Zhang, Z., 2013. What's buzzing in the blizzard of buzz? Automotive component isolation in social media postings. Decis. Support. Syst. 55 (4), 871–882.

Abrahams, A.S., Fan, W., Wang, G.A., Zhang, Z.J., Jiao, J., 2015. An integrated text analytic framework for product defect discovery. Prod. Oper. Manage. 24 (6), 975–990.

Akkermans, H., Bogerd, P., Yücesan, E., van Wassenhove, L.N., 2003. The impact of ERP on supply chain management: exploratory findings from a European Delphi study. Eur. J. Oper. Res. 146 (2), 284–301.

Al-Hudhaif, S., Alkubeyyer, A., 2011. E-commerce adoption factors in Saudi Arabia. Int. J. Bus. Manage. 6 (9), 122.

Antweiler, W., Frank, M.Z., 2004. Is all that talk just noise? The information content of internet stock message boards. J. Finance 59 (3), 1259–1294.

Attardi, L., Guida, M., Pulcini, G., 2005. A mixed-Weibull regression model for the analysis of automotive warranty data. Reliab. Eng. Syst. Saf. 87 (2), 265–273.

Baik, J., Murthy, D.N.P., 2008. Reliability assessment based on two-dimensional warranty data and an accelerated failure time model. Int. J. Reliab. Saf. 2 (3), 190–208.

Blischke, W.R., Karim, M.R., Murthy, D.P., 2011. Warranty Data Collection and Analysis. Springer Science & Business Media.

Bruque-Cámara, S., Moyano-Fuentes, J., Maqueira-Marín, J.M., 2016. Supply chain integration through community cloud: effects on operational performance. J. Purch. Supply Manage. 22 (2), 141–153.

Buddhakulsomsiri, J., Zakarian, A., 2009. Sequential pattern mining algorithm for automotive warranty data. Comput. Ind. Eng. 57 (1), 137–147.

Buddhakulsomsiri, J., Siradeghyan, Y., Zakarian, A., Li, X., 2006. Association rule-generation algorithm for mining automotive warranty data. Int. J. Prod. Res. 44 (14), 2749–2770.

Chae, B.K., 2015. Insights from hashtag# supply chain and twitter analytics: considering twitter and twitter data for supply chain practice and research. Int. J. Prod. Econ. 165, 247–259.

Chakraborty, S., 2015. A Next-Generation Approach to Integrated Warranty Management. Retrieved on 4 January 2015 from: https://www.cognizant.com/whitepapers/a-next-generation-approach-to-integrated-warranty-management-codex1231.pdf.

Chau, M., Xu, J., 2012. Business intelligence in blogs: understanding consumer interactions and communities. MIS Q. 36, 1189–1216.

Chukova, S., Robinson, J., 2005. Estimating Mean Cumulative Functions from Truncated Automotive Warranty Data. Mathematical and Statistical Methods in Reliability. World Scientific Publishing Co., Singapore, pp. 121–135

Coleman, D.E., Montgomery, D.C., 1993. A systematic approach to planning for a designed industrial experiment. Technometrics 35 (1), 1–14.

Dai, Y., Zhou, S.X., Xu, Y., 2012. Competitive and collaborative quality and warranty management in supply chains. Prod. Oper. Manage. 21 (1), 129–144.

Daniel, Z., Hsinchun, C., Lusch, R., Shu-Hsing, L., 2010. Social media analytics and intelligence. IEEE Intell. Syst. 25, 13–16.

Duan, W., Gu, B., Whinston, A.B., 2008. Do online reviews matter?—An empirical investigation of panel data. Decis. Support. Syst. 45 (4), 1007–1016.

DVSA, 2016. Search for Vehicle Recalls on Driver and Vehicle Standard Agency, UK. Retrieved on 5 October 2016 from: https://www.dft.gov.uk/vosa/apps/recalls/default.asp?tx.

Ewing, J., 2016. Volkswagen Reports Profit Drop as It Grapples With Emissions Scandal. Retrieved 31 May 2016 from: http://www.nytimes.com/2016/06/01/business/international/volkswagen-q1-earnings.html?_r=0.

Fan, W., Gordon, M.D., 2014. The power of social media analytics. Commun. ACM 57, 74–81.

Finch, B.J., 1999. Internet discussions as a source for consumer product customer involvement and quality information: an exploratory study. J. Oper. Manage. 17 (5), 535–556.

Finch, B.J., Luebbe, R.L., 1997. Using Internet conversations to improve product quality: an exploratory study. Int. J. Qual. Reliab. Manage.

Flynn, B.B., Sakakibara, S., Schroeder, R.G., Bates, K.A., Flynn, E.J., 1990. Empirical research methods in operations management. J. Oper. Manage. 9 (2), 250–284.

Gomes, C.P., Selman, B., 2001. Algorithm portfolios. Artif. Intell. 126 (1), 43–62.

González-Prida, V., Márquez, A.C., 2012. A framework for warranty management in industrial assets. Comput. Ind. 63 (9), 960–971.

Guo, Z.X., Wong, W.K., Guo, C., 2014. A cloud-based intelligent decision-making system for order tracking and allocation in apparel manufacturing. Int. J. Prod. Res. 52 (4), 1100–1115.

He, Z., Wang, S., Cheng, T.C.E., 2013. Competition and evolution in multi-product supply chains: an agent-based retailer model. Int. J. Prod. Econ. 146 (1), 325–336.

He, W., Wu, H., Yan, G., Akula, V., Shen, J., 2015. A novel social media competitive analytics framework with sentiment benchmarks. Inf. Manage. 52 (7), 801–812.

Honari, B., Donovan, J., 2007. Early detection of reliability changes for a non-Poisson life model using field failure data. In: Proceedings of Annual Reliability and Maintainability Symposium, RAMS pp. 346–349.

Hu, X.J., Lawless, J.F., 1996. Estimation of rate and mean functions from truncated recurrent event data. J. Am. Stat. Assoc. 91 (433), 300–310.

Hu, M., Liu, B., 2004. Mining and summarizing customer reviews. In: Proceedings of the Tenth ACM SIGKDD International Conference on Knowledge Discovery and Data Mining, pp. 168–177.

Ion, R.A., Petkova, V.T., Peeters, B.H.J., Sander, P.C., 2007. Field reliability prediction in consumer electronics using warranty data. Qual. Reliab. Eng. Int. 23 (4), 401–414.

Jung, M., Bai, D.S., 2007. Analysis of field data under two-dimensional warranty. Reliab. Eng. Syst. Saf. 92 (2), 135–143.

Kalbfleisch, J.D., Lawless, J.F., Robinson, J.A., 1991. Methods for the analysis and prediction of warranty claims. Technometrics 33, 273–285.

Kaplan, A.M., Haenlein, M., 2010. Users of the world, unite! The challenges and opportunities of Social Media. Bus. Horiz. 53 (1), 59–68.

Karim, M.R., Yamamoto, W., Suzuki, K., 2001. Statistical analysis of marginal count failure data. Lifetime Data Anal. 7 (2), 173–186.

Khan, S., Phillips, P., Jennions, I., Hockley, C., 2014. No Fault Found events in maintenance engineering part 1: current trends, implications and organizational practices. Reliab. Eng. Syst. Saf. 123, 183–195.

Kleyner, A., Sanborn, K., 2008. Modelling automotive warranty claims with build-to-sale data uncertainty. Int. J. Reliab. Saf. 2 (3), 179–189.

Kleyner, A., Sandborn, P., 2005. A warranty forecasting model based on piecewise statistical distributions and stochastic simulation. Reliab. Eng. Syst. Saf. 88 (3), 207–214.

Kumar, V., Mishra, N., 2011. A multi-agent self-correcting architecture for distributed manufacturing supply chain. IEEE Syst. J. 5 (1), 6–15.

Lawless, J.F., Kalbfleisch, J.D., Blumenthal, S., 1992. Some issues in the collection and analysis of field reliability data. In: Survival Analysis: State of the Art. Springer, Dordrecht, pp. 141–152.

Li, N., Wu, D.D., 2010. Using text mining and sentiment analysis for online forums hotspot detection and forecast. Decis. Support. Syst. 48 (2), 354–368.

Liu, B., 2010. Sentiment analysis and subjectivity. In: Handbook of Natural Language Processing. vol. 2. CRC Press, Taylor and Francis Group, pp. 627–666.

Madenas, N., Tiwari, A., Turner, C.J., Peachey, S., Broome, S., 2016. Improving root cause analysis through the integration of PLM systems with cross supply chain maintenance data. Int. J. Adv. Manuf. Technol. 84, 1679–1695.

Majeske, K.D., 2003. A mixture model for automobile warranty data. Reliab. Eng. Syst. Saf. 81 (1), 71–77.

Majeske, K.D., 2007. A non-homogeneous poisson process predictive model for automobile warranty claims. Reliab. Eng. Syst. Saf. 92 (2), 243–251.

Miller, G.A., Beckwith, R., Fellbaum, C.D., Gross, D., Miller, K., 1990. WordNet: an online lexical database. Int. J. Lexicogr. 3 (4), 235–244.

Mishra, N., Kumar, V., Chan, F.T.S., 2012. A multi-agent architecture for reverse logistics in a green supply chain. Int. J. Prod. Res. 50 (9), 2396–2406.

Mizgier, K.J., Wagner, S.M., Holyst, J.A., 2012. Modelling defaults of companies in multi-stage supply chain networks. Int. J. Prod. Econ. 135 (1), 14–23.

Mostafa, M.M., 2013. More than words: social networks' text mining for consumer brand sentiments. Expert Syst. Appl. 40 (10), 4241–4251.

Oh, Y.S., Bai, D.S., 2005. Field data analyses with additional after-warranty failure data. Reliab. Eng. Syst. Saf. 72 (1), 1–8.

Pang, B., Lee, L., 2004. A sentimental education: sentiment analysis using subjectivity summarization based on minimum cuts. In: Proceedings of the 42nd Annual Meeting on Association for Computational Linguisticsp. 271.

Park, K., Min, H., Min, S., 2016. Inter-relationship among risk taking propensity, supply chain security practices, and supply chain disruption occurrence. J. Purch. Supply Manage. 22 (2), 120–130.

Rai, B., Singh, N., 2005. Forecasting warranty performance in the presence of the 'maturing data' phenomenon. Int. J. Syst. Sci. 36 (7), 381–394.

Sampson, S.E., 1996. Ramifications of monitoring service quality through passively solicited customer feedback. Decis. Sci. 27 (4), 601–622.

Shafiee, M., Chukova, S., 2013. Maintenance models in warranty: a literature review. Eur. J. Oper. Res. 229 (3), 561–572.

Srinivasan, V., 2011. An integration framework for product lifecycle management. Comput. Aided Des. 43 (5), 464–478.

Stark, J., 2005. Product Lifecycle Management—21st Century Paradigm for Product Realization. Springer-Verlag, USA.

Stieglitz, S., Dang-Xuan, L., 2013. Social media and political communication: a social media analytics framework. Soc. Netw. Anal. Min. 3 (4), 1277–1291.

Suzuki, K., 1985. Nonparametric estimation of lifetime distributions from a record of failures and follow-ups. J. Am. Stat. Assoc. 80 (389), 68–72.

Suzuki, K., Karim, M.R., Wang, L., 2001. Statistical analysis of reliability warranty data. Chapter 21In: Handbook of Statistics. 20, Elsevier Science B.V., pp. 585–609.

Terzi, S., Bouras, A., Dutta, D., Garetti, M., Kiritsis, D., 2010. Product lifecycle management-from its history to its new role. Int. J. Prod. Lifecycle Manage. 4 (4), 360–389.

Thelwall, M., Buckley, K., Paltoglou, G., 2011. Sentiment in Twitter events. J. Am. Soc. Inf. Sci. Technol. 62 (2), 406–418.

Thomas, M.U., Rao, S.S., 1999. Warranty economic decision models: a summary and some suggested directions for future research. Oper. Res. 47 (6), 807–820.

Thun, J.H., Hoenig, D., 2011. An empirical analysis of supply chain risk management in the German automotive industry. Int. J. Prod. Econ. 131 (1), 242–249.

Vedder, R.G., Vanecek, M.T., Guynes, C.S., Cappel, J.J., 1999. CEO and CIO perspectives on competitive intelligence. Commun. ACM 42 (8), 108–116.

Wiengarten, F., Humphreys, P., McKittrick, A., Fynes, B., 2013. Investigating the impact of e-business applications on supply chain collaboration in the German automotive industry. Int. J. Oper. Prod. Manage. 33 (1), 25–48.

Wilson, S., Joyce, T., Lisay, E., 2009. Reliability estimation from field return data. Lifetime Data Anal. 15 (3), 397–410.

Wu, H., Meeker, W.Q., 2002. Early detection of reliability problems using information from warranty databases. Technometrics 44 (2), 120–133.

Yang, K., Cekecek, E., 2004. Design vulnerability analysis and design improvement by using warranty data. Qual. Reliab. Eng. Int. 20, 121–133.

Yeboah-Boateng, E.O., Essandoh, K.A., 2014. Factors influencing the adoption of cloud computing by small and medium enterprises in developing economies. Int. J. Emerg. Sci. Eng. 2 (4), 13–20.

4

Getting it right: Systems Understanding of Risk Framework (SURF)

Simon M. Wilson[a] and John McCarthy[b]

[a]NORTHUMBRIA UNIVERSITY, LONDON, UNITED KINGDOM [b]OXFORD SYSTEMS, BICESTER, UNITED KINGDOM

1 Introduction

Once upon a time, in the bad old days, if you needed a computer, you went out and bought it. You got the company credit card and went down to the store and picked one up. Then, companies started buying them in bulk to give to more staff. Back then, they were replacing typewriters and in some companies going as far as doing the accounts.

Computers in most places were stand-alone, a tool on a desk, and not seen as much more than a glorified typewriter and/or calculator. No one was particularly worried if it was 'up to spec' or met business requirements, and very little regard was given to thinking about security. Then things started advancing.

Academia was pushing technology, as were the military. The space programmes were also getting more and more from the tech. Places were connected. Computers could do more. IT departments sprang up in organisations where they had never existed before. People started to produce programmes to do 'stuff', and we were all playing games on them too.

As more and more money was being spent on these tools, more controls were put in place, and buying 'a computer' became more complex, but we were still in the bad old days. 'We need it because we do' was a good enough reason. But things improved, and a valid reason was sought before something could be bought, but it wasn't particularly arduous.

The end user would state what they wanted; the IT department and Finance would ask for justification and possibly the impact of not purchasing it, developing, or allocating what is being asked for to them. Very often, back in those days, when something was being developed, if the IT department wasn't developing it, then they didn't get involved, and the developer worked with the end users directly. This is generalising of course and was not

Strategy, Leadership, and AI in the Cyber Ecosystem. https://doi.org/10.1016/B978-0-12-821442-8.00007-0
© 2021 Elsevier Inc. All rights reserved.

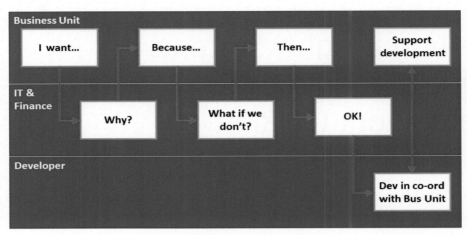

Low governance approval model

the picture everywhere, but scrutiny, governance, and assurance were not terms that many people back in those days would have had on the tips of their tongues. In government departments, IT was often bought out of their unspent budget surpluses, getting rid of the leftover cash at the end of the financial year, so as not to have their budget cut for the following year because they hadn't needed to or been able to spend the previous financial year's allocation. It was not an uncommon picture to hear of companies buying a few more large colour laser printers just to get another few thousand spent.

As computers could do more and more, organisations were finding more and more functions for them to support in roles right across business, government, and academia. As the demand for using technology ran ahead of delivery, many bespoke applications appeared, each meeting a specific need in a specific environment, delivered mainly in stovepipes, causing massive duplication of functionality across individual organisations.

These organisations have attempted to address this stovepipe delivery and duplication of functionality by introducing controls on procurement, requirements management, change approval boards, rationalisation and convergence projects, service-orientated architecture, and more latterly cloud-based services. This has gone a long way to improve the situation, but problems persist.

Poor requirements meant that projects were not fulfilling the business need and rework is expensive, contract change is expensive, cancelling projects is expensive, and delivering something that doesn't work is expensive, especially if it meets the requirements given to the developer and delivery organisation. If so the customer then bears the cost!

This is why so much effort has gone in to improving requirements. 'SMART' requirements that mean scalable, manageable, achievable, realistic, and timely became familiar. Testable requirements were best practice, and if a requirement was viewed to be untestable, it was rejected. Traceability was needed to show where a requirement had come from, who was its owner, who was its sponsor, and who was its manager? We now had accountability!

However, projects still over-run, both on time and cost. Projects also are viewed as falling short of meeting customer expectations.

The Mott-MacDonald Optimism Bias (Supplementary Green Book Guidance—Optimism Bias, 2020) is broadly applied to cost and time and should be continued to be. Why projects fail to deliver to cost or time may be due to truly 'optimistic' estimates, but in reality, competition pushes companies to write hard delivery targets and challenging costings to try to win the work.

Optimism bias recommends that that equipment and development projects[a] adjust project delivery timelines upwards by between 10% and 54% and that capital expenditure[b] (not Resource Expenditure[c]) be adjusted upwards by between 10% and 200%. These upper figures are based on the mean historic optimism bias relative to the outline business case stage of a project, so they can be adjusted further upwards if earlier in a project's life cycle.

This being said, requirements are still a major cause of cost and time estimates and/or quotes being exceeded, which leave the customer to pick up the excess. Ensuring the requirements is good, sufficient, testable, and stable and as early as possible will minimise this risk.

There are various stages of decomposing the concept and requirements through to the end solution and its ultimate design and delivery. The detail required and the necessary scale will of course depend upon the nature and size of the project or programme. There will, however, be commonality in the need to assess that the need has been captured and addressed.

Assessment is a vital activity in the development and delivery of a system. However, there is not just one manner of assessment that can be employed. There are numerous options, dependent upon the aspect of the project that is being assessed and by whom.

The various assessments conducted throughout the system development life cycle can be categorised as follows:

- **Strategic assessment:** High level and dependent upon the current priorities, enterprise vision, mission objectives, and capability goals.
- **Functional assessment:** Bespoke and concerned with how what is required, proposed or delivered operates, and uses and manipulates data.

[a] Equipment and development projects: Projects that are concerned with the provision of equipment and/or development of software and systems (i.e. manufactured equipment, information, and communication technology (ICT) development projects) or leading-edge projects (Supplementary Green Book Guidance—Optimism Bias, 2020).

[b] Capital expenditure comprises major purchases that will be used in the future (Investopedia, 2020).

[c] Resource (or operating) expenditure represents day-to-day costs that are necessary to keep a system or business running (Investopedia, 2020).

- **Nonfunctional/technical assessment:** Concerned with the supporting requirements that enable the functionality of the system.

The criteria for conducting nonfunctional/technical assessment are more stable, supporting and enabling the functional and strategic requirements.

A 'nonfunctional requirement (NFR)' is one that stipulates criteria that can be used to measure the operation of a system, or system of systems, rather than any specific behavioural properties. So, whilst most projects tend to have good functional requirements documented, nonfunctional requirements are not always considered to the degree needed to mitigate requirements and solution risk.

An approach to tackle this is the Systems Understanding of Risk Framework (SURF). SURF originated from the 'strategic intelligence architecture' (Wilson et al. 2009) research project for the intelligence, surveillance, target acquisition, and reconnaissance (ISTAR) domain in the UK Ministry of Defence (MOD) and its follow-on project, 'prioritised future information and intelligence services' (Wilson et al., 2010). These produced a taxonomy for effective information and intelligence exchange, which one of the original authors has taken forward to produce SURF.

Although not well known in the public domain, the predecessors to SURF have been utilised in a number of projects in the defence and security domains.

2 Systems Understanding of Risk Framework

SURF provides a framework that addresses a common and fixed set of attributes that can be applied to requirements, solutions, and designs. It does, of course, not have to be applied out of the box, and different organisations may 'slice the cake' a little differently than others, so they may wish to change SURF to fit their needs. It does, however, give a usable framework and approach, especially where such an approach is new, or an alternative view does not exist.

SURF can be used simply as an assurance check that these areas have been covered in the requirement documentation, proposed solutions, and subsequent designs produced with projects. However, it comes with a more formulated methodology which can be employed. This is assessing the level of risk in requirements, solutions, and designs and also directly comparing different solutions and designs.

The following provides a breakdown of the various sections of SURF.

Assured	Assurance Regime	Governance	Policy			
Connected	With who	With what	Where			
Interoperable	With who	With what	Level			
Secure	Confidentiality	Integrity	Availability	Authentication	Non repudiation	
Safe	Prevent accidental harm to asset	Prevent safety incidents/accidents	Prevent hazards	Prevent safety risk	Detect violation of prevention	React to violation of prevention
Supported	Available	Reliable	Maintainable			
Timely	Capacity	Latency	Responsiveness	Utility		

Systems Understanding of Risk Framework (SURF)

2.1 Assured

'Assured' in this context means to have confidence in the meeting the rest of the nonfunctional requirements meeting the rules, regulations, and strategies in place within the department or wider government.

Assured

The assurance regime is required to give this confidence, whether this is an organisational body or the adherence to a methodology of meeting policy and/or strategy. This needs to be identified and documented so that both the project team and the provider are aware of the process, including the actioning of any waivers with regard to policy and/or strategy.

The governance is with regard to who has the authority to state that the project has the authority to proceed or not in respect of meeting policy and/or strategy. The project team need to be cognisant of whom this is and to ensure any required interactions take place.

Policy as a term should not be limited to standards and rules but also include strategy, such as sharing and reusing systems and technology, and legal requirements such as data protection and privacy legislation.

2.2 Connected

'Connected' refers to the physical connection of organisations, systems, and locations and does not imply interoperability, which is covered in the framework separately for that reason. In the same way, being on the same network does not imply connected systems, as they may be on the same or interconnected infrastructures but have no level of interaction.

Additionally, organisations may be based across a number of different locations but may or may not share systems and may or may not have connectivity. This will have an impact on new implementations, both in opportunities of reuse and with regard to additional implementations.

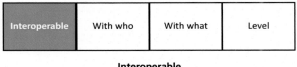

Interoperable

In summary: who are the organisational elements that are to be connected, what are the systems that are to be connected, and where they?

2.3 Interoperable

Interoperability (IO) is a vital consideration in procurement requirements. However, this is often traded out, which results is delivering suboptimal services. It is also the case that many confuse interoperability with connectivity, as stated earlier. Connectivity does not imply interoperability. Interoperability needs to be considered in terms of the organisations and systems employed and to what level.

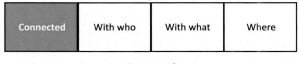

Connected

Organisations need to analyse their requirements, as in who needs to be interoperable with whom and in using what systems (both hardware and software). However, it is additionally of great importance the understanding of what level of interoperability.

The level of interoperability can be assessed using different criteria. In perhaps the simplest but extremely useful sense, this can be stated as three levels, but this can be seen as more if as a guide to a minimum. These are at the highest level where an integrated 'system of systems' (SoS) operates, where there is an intimate dependency between them (**integrated**); where there is a need to exchange data, requiring compatibility (**compatible**); and where resources are shared, that that one does not have a negative impact on the other and result in a resource conflict (**deconfliction**).

However, there are numerous ways to assess this. For example, the North Atlantic Treaty Organisation (NATO) defines technical interoperability (Whitehall Papers, 2003) over six levels, which are actually not confined to system interoperability. These are as follows:

- exchange of documents
- exchange of liaison officers
- exchange of equipment
- electronic message exchange
- direct, controlled access
- direct—no constraints

Whatever method is used needs to be justifiable as applicable to the circumstances it is being applied.

2.4 Secure

Protection of the system, system of systems and/or service, and the information it receives, stores, processes, and/or disseminates is of great importance. The impact of an attack or any malicious action must be assessed to investigate the level of security that is required. This is divided into the following categories, which are commonly accepted to be the core principles.

Secure

These are discussed at great depth elsewhere but are included here for completeness.

Confidentiality: The prevention of the disclosure of information to unauthorised persons or systems. This is a necessity but is by itself insufficient to maintain the security of information.

Integrity: Ensuring that data cannot be covertly modified. Examples of violating the integrity of data (and hence the system) is the modification of data in transit or storage by covert means.

Availability: In terms of the core principles, this refers to the fact that information must be available when needed, which is covered elsewhere in the framework, but in this sense would include denial of service attacks. This concept is thought of in terms of who the system, SoS, service, and/or data are available to, which include the prevention of malicious activity. This can be thought of as restricting access in terms of electronic security but should also be cognisant of factors such as physical access to hardware, employing measures like entry to the locality.

Authentication: Ensuring that all data, communications, and transactions are genuine by authenticating entities (prover) to prove identity to another entity (verifier) to validate that both parties are who they say they are.

Nonrepudiation: This is the personal responsibility of someone to fulfil their obligation to a contract, which is enforced by making it undeniable that a certain action took place and ensuring that it is attributed to the person who undertook it.

2.5 Safe

Safety requirements are often relatively reusable, especially within an application domain and across members of a product line. As quality requirements, safety requirements are typically of the form of a system-specific quality criterion together with a minimum or maximum required amount of an associated quality measure. This structure, taken from Donald Firesmith's 'A Taxonomy of Safety-Related Requirements' (Firesmith, 2004), means that safety requirements can often be written as instances of parameterised generic safety requirement templates.

Safe	Prevent accidental harm to asset	Prevent safety incidents/ accidents	Prevent hazards	Prevent safety risk	Detect violation of prevention	React to violation of prevention

Safe

Prevention of accidental harm to valuable asset: The system design needs to ensure that it shall not cause, or permit to occur, a predefined amount of a type of harm to a type of asset, no more than a predefined measurable threshold. It may seem counterintuitive to accept damage to an asset within a tolerated limit, but, for example, tools may cause wear and tear on equipment, but not render them unusable.

Prevention of safety incidents/accidents: The system design needs to ensure that it shall not cause, or permit to occur, specific types of safety incidents within a measurable threshold of occurrence and possibly within a measurable level of severity. Whereas we would want to eliminate all safety incidents and provide completely safe systems and working environments, this is not always possible. Some activities will inevitably involve risk.

Prevention of hazards: The system design needs to ensure that it shall not cause, or permit to occur, specific types of hazards, no more than a predefined measurable threshold of occurrence. Again, these are unavoidable in some activities, so a level of acceptable danger or hazard needs to be defined, where a hazard is something that presents a danger or risk but does not necessarily result in such an incident.

Prevention of safety risk: The system design needs to ensure that it shall not cause, or permit to occur, any accident/incident or hazard which may cause harm at or above a defined level of severity (categorised, such as under the 'Reporting of Injuries, Diseases and Dangerous Occurrences Regulations' (RIDDOR) (Health and Safety Executive, 2013)), with likelihood greater than a defined level of probability or accident likelihood category. It should cover the need that no credible system accident/incident or hazard shall represent a measurement of safety risk above a defined threshold. Note that risk is a product of both the likelihood of an occurrence and the impact of an occurrence.

Detection of violation of prevention: The system shall detect intentional or unintentional bypassing or disabling of any precautionary system, measure, or procedure, such as when workers may cut corners in carrying out tasks.

Reaction to violation of prevention: When the system detects intentional or unintentional bypassing or disabling of any precautionary system, measure, or procedure, then the system shall respond in a predetermined manner to avoid any accident/incident or hazard.

2.6 Supported

Integrated logistic support (ILS) is a disciplined approach to managing whole-life costs that affect both the customer organisation and its suppliers. It aims to optimise whole-life costs by minimising the support system required for assets; by influencing their requirements, solutions, and designs for supportability; and by determining the optimum support requirements. An asset is defined as an equipment, service, system, or system of systems.

The end result is supportable and supported assets at an optimised cost. In sufficiently scoping the attributes required for supported systems confidence in the delivered solution, its delivery timescale and cost can be assessed as higher and as such risk assessed as lower.

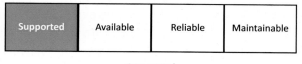

Supported

In this context, 'available' is related to when and where the system, system of systems, and/or services are required to operate, in terms of working hours and locations. There may be no direct connectivity; however, business process may not require this (e.g. remote or stand-alone working), yet location of where the delivered system, system of systems, and/or service are available must be considered. Additionally, ensuring that they are available during the hours they are required is also vitally important—a 24-h operations centre cannot function effectively if it loses service and cannot respond to urgent requests.

As such the downtime that can be tolerated must be determined, as must the restoration time in the event of a failure. Hence the reliability and maintainability of the system, system of systems, and/or service should be sufficiently defined to ensure it will be able to support these requirements.

2.7 Timely

Timeliness is a necessary consideration in the requirement documentation to ensure that essential operations occur within the timescale needed, for either full optimality or to achieve an acceptable level. This is dependent on the following factors.

Timely

Capacity refers to numerous aspects of delivery, which include such aspects as bandwidth provision and storage requirements, but is not limited to a system-orientated approach. Considerations such as numbers of operators and with regard to the estate are also important.

Latency is in terms of what time delay within an operation can be tolerated, such as the sending of the message, and how long it takes for the message to be received.

Responsiveness is how quickly an operation is enacted after it is requested, such as how long it is before the message is sent after the operation is requested.

Utility (as in the quality or condition of being useful) has two distinct types—hard and soft. Hard utility is defined as the output of an operation being regarded as fully optimal until a predefined deadline is reached, after which the optimality is regarded as zero or negative (if it passes the deadline, it is useless, harmful, or disruptive). Soft utility can be defined as where the optimality of the output changes with time, decreasing the longer the output takes (the sooner the better). This measure of 'utility' is of great importance, and care should be taken not to dilute this in using terms such as 'real time', which merely implies a delay, or worse 'near real time'.

3 SURF methodology

3.1 SURF minimal application

The various elements of SURF described within the framework are in the form of a taxonomy, which seeks to give a prescribed set of nonfunctional requirements for addressing within project documentation, split into the top level categories of assured, connected, interoperable, secure, safe, supported, and timely, as described earlier.

In the simplest sense, these can be used as a checklist to assure project governance that the requirements have considered the required nonfunctional aspects of the business's need; in turn the solution has been checked to cover the same aspects, and the design has been verified to ensure it meets these nonfunctional requirements.

This is most suitable on small procurement and development projects, showing that a proportionate amount of diligence has been applied, which should help to manage and mitigate any risk without expending excessive effort on the task but be auditable and accountable.

3.2 SURF risk assessment method

The requirement set will have a level of risk associated with it in not sufficiently conveying the full business's requirements. In turn, it represents 'what' is being asked for within the procurement process, and potential providers will return proposals with a solution to say 'how' they would meet the requirements, which also has a level of risk associated with it in not sufficiently meeting the full business's requirements. Further on down the line, the design will also have the similar risk.

This method works like a combination of a standard risk assessment and a Multicriteria Decision Analysis (MCDA) approach. This would take the form of judgement panels scoring the requirement, solution, and/or design against the SURF.

The concept follows a standard risk assessment criteria and scoring system and is to assess for each of the lowest level SURF elements in the framework (e.g. 'capacity') for what the impact is of each of these not being achieved, giving a suggested score of 3 for high impact, 2 for medium, and 1 for low, using conventional red, amber, and green (RAG) markings, respectively.

The same needs to be carried out in assessing the fitness of the requirements, with respect to the perceived likelihood that the associated requirements would result in that consideration not being achieved, again scored out of 3 as above. It is, of course, of vital importance to record the factors regarding the scoring of the consideration elements for scrutiny and audit purposes.

The same process for solutions and designs is followed.

Both of the scores for each of the elements (impact and likelihood) are multiplied to give a score out of 9—the 'risk' score—and for the respective SURF element above in the framework (e.g. 'timely'), the mean of the scores below each is calculated. For the overall 'requirements risk' score, the mean for all the higher-level considerations is calculated.

The same process for solutions and designs is followed.

Assessments on each SURF element can be made individually for both their 'impact' and 'likelihood', allowing judgement to be made on investment and/or risk mitigation. To aid this the methodology followed allows the analysis of the contributory factors and whether it is needed to look at how to reduce impact, refine requirements, or both.

Again the same is applied to the various solutions that are received from the prospective providers and the ultimate design to give their overall solution and design risk scores.

This gives an auditable assessment of the overall risk to the project as various stages, plus a mapping of where the risk actually lies within the framework. The results of the requirement, solution, and design risk assessments can hence advise and inform the writing of good requirements; risk mitigation strategies; option selection (Multicriteria Decision Analysis); solution downselect; and test, evaluation, and acceptance.

An example of the outputs of the judgement panels is shown in the succeeding text using figures that are for purely demonstratable purposes only.

Assured 2.7	Assurance regime 2	Governance 3	Policy 3		
Connected 3	With who 3	With what 3	Where 3		
Interoperable 2.7	With who 3	With what 3	Level 2		
Secure 2.6	Confidentiality 2	Integrity 3	Availability 2	Authentication 2	Non-repudiation 3
Safe 2.3	Prevent accidental harm to asset 1	Prevent safety incidents/accidents 3	Prevent hazards 3	Prevent safety risk 3	Detect violation of prevention 2	React to violation of prevention 2
Supported 2	Available 2	Reliable 2	Maintainable 2		
Timely 2.5	Capacity 3	Latency 2	Responsiveness 2	Utility 3	

Example likelihood score mapping— overall likelihood score: 2.7

Assured (2)	Assurance regime 2	Governance 3	Policy 1		
Connected (2)	With who 1	With what 3	Where 2		
Interoperable (2)	With who 1	With what 3	Level 2		
Secure (1.6)	Confidentiality 2	Integrity 2	Availability 2	Authentication 1	Non repudiation 1
Safe (1.7)	Prevent accidental harm to asset 1	Prevent safety incidents/accidents 1	Prevent hazards 1	Prevent safety risk 3	Detect violation of prevention 2 / React to violation of prevention 2
Supported (2)	Available 1	Reliable 2	Maintainable 3		
Timely (1.5)	Capacity 1	Latency 1	Responsiveness 1	Utility 3	

Example impact score mapping—overall impact score: 1.8

Assured (5.3)	Assurance regime 4	Governance 9	Policy 3		
Connected (6)	With who 3	With what 9	Where 6		
Interoperable (5.3)	With who 3	With what 9	Level 4		
Secure (3.8)	Confidentiality 4	Integrity 6	Availability 4	Authentication 2	Non repudiation 3
Safe (4)	Prevent accidental harm to asset 1	Prevent safety incidents/accidents 3	Prevent hazards 3	Prevent safety risk 9	Detect violation of prevention 4 / React to violation of prevention 4
Supported (4)	Available 2	Reliable 4	Maintainable 6		
Timely (4)	Capacity 3	Latency 2	Responsiveness 2	Utility 9	

Example risk score mapping—overall risk score: 3.9

3.3 SURF Combined Risk and Investment Appraisal

This is the big assessment method and will be familiar to those who have worked in operational analysis/operational research (OA/OR). The Combined Risk and Investment Appraisal (CRIA) is basically replacing the operational effectiveness in a Combined Operational Effectiveness and Investment Appraisal (COEIA) with the overall risk score for the Y-Axis but inverted to maintain the 'top left best' bias.

The risk score is defined earlier, taking individual assessments separately, using the mean as the point score, then having discarded the outlying high and low scores (if the sample rate is deemed high enough to do), and then using the remaining high and low scores as the range limits for the error bars.

The investment scoring is the estimated or quoted costs for an option as the point score, with the assessed optimism bias applied to provide the error bars.

In the example that follows, the results of three options (A–C) are shown for what may be solutions or designs, allowing them to be assessed for systems risk, alongside other criteria–capability and functionality.

The concept with SURF is to keep it standard and keep it simple. That being said, nothing is fixed, and organisations may wish to customise either the framework or methodology or both.

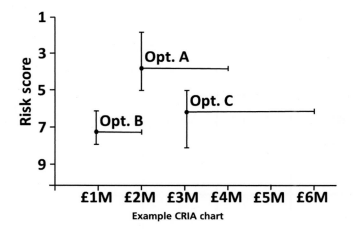

Example CRIA chart

4 Impact on cybersecurity

Cybersecurity of our systems is a sad fact of life and needs to be considered from the start. Security/secure by design (SbD) leads us to ensure that systems are designed and built securely. This needs security to be at the heart of the requirements from the very start, following guidance from one of the many sources available, such as that from the UK Government.

Risk needs to be assessed within the context that it is to be applied, whether that would be service delivery, cybersecurity, or a balance of equities between them. In the cybersecurity context, this needs to be assessed in terms of what the threat is and where it is coming from, and then the level of impact and its likelihood are assessed.

This requires projects and programmes to have an understanding of this risk. So within the cybersecurity domain, the risk landscape can be assessed by considering the sources of those risks and the risk types. The sources are those actors that the threat originates from, which can be categorised as follows:

- Cyber criminals—to make money through fraud or the sale of information
- Foreign intelligence—to gain an advantage for their country
- Hackers—who find it an enjoyable challenge
- Hacktivists—for political or ideological motives
- Users—either by accident or deliberate misuse

The types of cyber threats are as described in the 'STRIDE' acronym.

STRIDE (Shostack, n.d.)

Threat	Property violated	Definition	Example
Spoofing	Authentication	Impersonating something or someone else	Pretending to be any of Bill Gates, Paypal.com or ntdll.dll
Tampering	Integrity	Modifying data or code	Modifying a DLL on disk or DVD, or a packet as it traverses the network
Repudiation	Nonrepudiation	Claiming to have not performed an action	'I didn't send that email', 'I didn't modify that file', or 'I certainly didn't visit that web site, dear!'
Information disclosure	Confidentiality	Exposing information to someone not authorised to see it	Allowing someone to read the Windows source code; publishing a list of customers to a web site
Denial of service	Availability	Deny or degrade service to users	Crashing windows or a web site, sending a packet and absorbing seconds of CPU time, or routing packets into a black hole
Elevation of privilege	Authorisation	Gain capabilities without proper authorisation	Allowing a remote Internet user to run commands is the classic example, but going from a limited user to admin is also elevation of privilege

There are different impacts and likelihoods for each of the threats, dependent upon the actor in question. These can be assessed, considering each actor and threat as shown in the threat landscape that follows, with an example assessment.

In this example assessment, hackers will be very likely to disclose information that they have extracted from their target, but more as proof of having hacked them than to cause intentional harm, whereas a foreign intelligence agent would be looking to have as much impact as possible.

Risk assessment Impact X Likelihood (1 2 3) (1 2 3) = Risk (1 2 3 4 6 9)	Spoofing	Tampering	Repudiation	Information disclosure/ privacy breach	Denial of service	Elevation of privilege
Cyber criminals	2 2 4	2 2 4	3 3 9	3 3 9	3 3 9	3 3 9
Foreign intelligence	3 2 6	2 2 4	3 3 9	3 3 9	3 3 9	3 3 9
Hackers	1 2 2	2 2 4	3 3 9	2 3 6	3 3 9	2 2 6
Hacktivists	1 2 2	3 3 9	3 3 9	3 3 9	3 3 9	3 3 9
Users	2 2 4	2 2 4	2 1 2	3 2 6	3 2 6	1 2 2

Example threat landscape assessment

This risk landscape assessment can then be used to see the areas of higher risk which in turn can inform the prioritisation when producing an action plan to address the problem space. The actual prioritisation will be dependent upon the current policies and protections in place. The status of these has not been conveyed in this scenario. This will need to be added into the risk landscape assessment.

In addition, the risk appetite of the organisation will have an impact. Some organisations choose to be open and operate with a higher level of usability and less hard security, with the ability to rapidly recover from any incident. Other organisations are more risk averse, with higher security, but in turn accepting the impact of service delivery and usability that this results in. Organisations with good cyber situational awareness can vary their stance between these two extremes, managing the balance of equities of cybersecurity and service delivery based on the perceived level of threat as it currently assessed.

The severity of threat can be further derived using the DREAD acronym (Wikipedia.org, 2018):

- Damage—how bad would an attack be?
- Reproducibility—how easy is it to reproduce the attack?
- Exploitability—how much work is it to launch the attack?
- Affected users—how many people will be impacted?
- Discoverability—how easy is it to discover the threat?

When the threat landscape has been properly understood and the requirements fully informed, SURF should be used to ensure completeness and provide assessment throughout the life of the project or programme.

The various parts of SURF apply across STRIDE as in the following matrix and as explained in the following.

Assured and Secure naturally apply across all of STRIDE. Policy, legislation, and strategy need to cover all aspects, and security is at the core of STRIDE.

SURF to STRIDE mapping	Spoofing	Tampering	Nonrepudiation	Information disclosure / privacy breach	Denial of service	Elevation of privilege
Assured	X	X	X	X	X	X
Connected		X		X	X	X
Interoperable	X	X	X	X	X	
Secure	X	X	X	X	X	X
Safe	X	X	X	X	X	X
Supported		X		X	X	
Timely		X	X	X	X	

SURF to STRIDE

Connected applies to who can access your systems. What gateways exist and what protection is in place on those gateways. The systems are also vulnerable through legitimately connected systems and are therefore dependent on the security in place on them. Should those systems be attacked what access could an attacker have?

Similarly, those with sufficient access to interoperable systems could impact your systems through spoofing their system, changing their system to impact yours, acting covertly, stealing your data from their system, and blocking your access to their system in a denial of service (DoS) attack. This falls primarily under the insider threat[d] category.

---

[d] An insider is someone who (knowingly or unknowingly) misuses legitimate access to commit a malicious act or damage their employer (Insider risk | Public Website, 2020).

Safety is a concern across all of STRIDE, as any attack could render a system unsafe, disabling safety measures or changing them to show they are in place when they are not. Additionally, the theft of data can put people at great risk, such as terrorist stealing personal information like names, roles, and addresses.

Supporting the system, in terms of availability, reliability, and maintainability (ARM), is impacted in the main related to availability. Tampering with the system to make it unavailable, stealing data or, as seen in many attacks, encrypting it through ransomware,[e] or carrying out DoS attack. Additionally, tampering with the system in sophisticated attacks can impact the reliability and maintainability, with unfound code that frequently degrades a system and is difficult to find.

Finally the timeliness of the system can be critical in systems where the speed of moving data is a priority. The impact of data being delayed not only does lie in the late arrival but also makes the data vulnerable and should cause data at rest[f] in the system.

Hence, we need to get it right and understand the risk to the system, and SURF is a good framework and methodology to do so.

References

Cpni.gov.uk, 2020. Insider Risk | Public Website. [online] Available at: https://www.cpni.gov.uk/insider-threat.

Firesmith, D., 2004. A Taxonomy of Safety-Related Requirements. [online]. Available from: https://resources.sei.cmu.edu/asset_files/WhitePaper/2004_019_001_29423.pdf.

Health and Safety Executive, 2013. Reporting of Injuries, Diseases and Dangerous Occurrences Regulations – RIDDOR. [Online]. Available from: https://www.hse.gov.uk/riddor/.

Her Majesty's Treasury, UK, 2020. Supplementary Green Book Guidance – Optimism Bias. [Online]. Available from: https://assets.publishing.service.gov.uk/government/uploads/system/uploads/attachment_data/file/191507/Optimism_bias.pdf.

Investopedia, 2020. Investopedia. [Online]. Available from: https://www.investopedia.com/.

Ncsc.gov.uk, 2020a. Mitigating Malware and Ransomware Attacks. [online] Available at: https://www.ncsc.gov.uk/guidance/mitigating-malware-and-ransomware-attacks.

Shostack, A., n.d. Threat Modeling with STRIDE. [online] Users.encs.concordia.ca. Available at: https://users.encs.concordia.ca/~clark/courses/1601-6150/scribe/L04c.pdf.

Thalesesecurity.com, 2020. Thales Esecurity: Cloud And Data Security | Encryption | Key Management | Digital Payment Security Solutions. [online] Available at: https://www.thalesesecurity.com/faq/encryption/what-data-rest.

---

[e] Ransomware is a type of malware that prevents you from accessing your computer (or the data that are stored on it). The computer itself may become locked, or the data on it might be stolen, deleted, or encrypted. Some ransomware will also try to spread to other machines on the network, such as the Wannacry malware that impacted the NHS in May 2017 (Mitigating malware and ransomware attacks, 2020).

[f] When data are collected in one place, it is called data at rest. For a hacker, these data at rest—data in databases, file systems, and storage infrastructure—are probably much more attractive than the individual data packets crossing the network (Thales eSecurity: Cloud and Data Security | Encryption | Key Management | Digital Payment Security Solutions, 2020).

Whitehall Papers, 2003. Technical Interoperability. [Online]. Available from: https://doi.org/10.1080/02681300309414760.

Wilson, S., Shay, W., Miles, J., 2009. Strategic Intelligence Architecture. Dstl, MOD.

Wilson, S., Shay, W., Miles, J., 2010. Prioritised Future Information and Intelligence Services. Dstl, MOD.

Further reading

Logicworks, 2020. What Is Security By Design? [online] Available at: https://www.logicworks.com/blog/2017/01/what-is-security-by-design/.

Ncsc.gov.uk, 2020b. Secure Design Principles. [online] Available at: https://www.ncsc.gov.uk/collection/cyber-security-design-principles.

AI: The cyber-physical management professional

5

Blockchain as a tool for transparency and governance in the delivery of development aid

Hamid Jahankhani[a], Stefan Kendzierskyj[b], and Anita Colin[c]

[a]NORTHUMBRIA UNIVERSITY, LONDON, UNITED KINGDOM [b]CYFORTIS, SURREY, UNITED KINGDOM [c]AMNESTY INTERNATIONAL, LONDON, UNITED KINGDOM

1 Background to blockchain and relevance to development aid

The development aid sector spends over $600 billion annually to support efforts towards ending global poverty and achieving the United Nations (UN) Sustainable Development Goals (SDGs). Long-term effectiveness is generally still a challenge since monitoring tools fall short of budget data evaluation and accountability of funds (ICAI, 2018). The utilisation of technology presents enormous opportunities for a technological solution like blockchain—as a monitoring and evaluation tool for transparency in the delivery of development aid.

As a decentralised technology, blockchain maintains a continuous list of data records and peer-to-peer transactions in a distributed public ledger without any third-party involvement (Christidis and Devetsiokiotis, 2016; Zheng et al., 2018). Cryptography, a feature of blockchain, not only allows for secure public control and ledger access to data and transactions but also is extremely difficult—if not impossible—to change or remove data recorded on a ledger. This has already successfully improved service delivery in sectors such as healthcare, where the use of electronic medical data sharing has reshaped modern practices in medicine (Patel, 2018).

Development aid contracts are mostly paper based, with lengthy aid cash transfers that endure bank transfer charges and the politics of government and aid officials. Smart contracts are a prominent feature of blockchain that can hasten the assessment of, for example, the magnitude of potential disaster and consequently determine the types and quantity of goods and services needed; thus blockchain can provide higher value for both development aid donors and recipients.

Currently, one of the most significant discussions in international development, as an area of practice and field of study, is that tools for monitoring development aid are flawed. Aid budget data, studies, and official development reports on aid effectiveness do not give

Strategy, Leadership, and AI in the Cyber Ecosystem. https://doi.org/10.1016/B978-0-12-821442-8.00006-9
© 2021 Elsevier Inc. All rights reserved.

a clear picture of expenditure, which makes it impossible for performance-based assessments to evaluate achievement of project outcomes. Mostly, development aid systems are faced with allegations of fraud, resource misappropriation, and reliance on 'concocted' progress reports. So the chain of custody becomes 'contaminated', and at the end of the supply chain, intended recipients get (if at all) only a little of what is meant for them. The absence of tools that prohibit mismanagement of aid money and exclusion of beneficiaries from aid initiatives is a cause and consequence of both external and internal variations (Ghosh and Kharas, 2011).

There is a growing body of literature especially from computing and technology disciplines that offers a range of different accounts on blockchain technology. Paynter (2017), Patel (2018), and He et al. (2018) maintain that blockchain is a technological advancement that comes from finance although it is lately being applied to other sectors. It is the founding technology for the Bitcoin cryptocurrency (Yli-Huumo et al., 2016) which its creator defines as a system of electronic payments based on cryptographic proof that permits anyone to conduct transactions directly to another person without the need for a trusted third party (Nakamoto, 2008). Built on this principle, blockchain omits the need for the broker, such as government bodies and financial institutions during transactions (Christidis and Devetsiokiotis, 2016; Yli-Huumo et al., 2016; Miraz and Ali, 2018), and serves as an immutable distribution public ledger where all data and transactions are managed in a decentralised manner in contrast to a general database.

With groundbreaking potential, equivalent to that of the Internet (Swan, 2015), blockchain has been loosely referred to as the technology that is going to change the world. Riani (2018) defines blockchain as a decentralised technology that maintains a continuous list of data records and peer-to-peer transactions in a distributed public ledger without any third-party involvement (Christidis and Devetsiokiotis, 2016; Zheng et al., 2018; Kshetri and Voas, 2018; Morse, 2018). Without regulation of information and transacting, anyone in the blockchain can use and share data across places and people. In their comprehensive overview on blockchain, Zheng et al. (2017) revealed that beyond key characteristics of decentralisation, persistency, immutability, anonymity, and auditability, blockchain is highly reliable and honest, can save costs, and improve efficiency. In the same vein, Yli-Huumo et al. (2016) accentuates blockchain's aim to provide transparency, security, and privacy to all its users.

Distinctively a permanent feature of blockchain is its eternal purpose to connect people and allow user verification although it is impossible to tamper with records (Christidis and Devetsiokiotis, 2016; Miraz and Ali, 2018; Zheng et al., 2018), so the term immutability is used. Thus, for what is increasingly becoming a seamlessly connected world of multi-device computing, blockchain could be adopted quicker than the Internet was, according to current global Internet and cellular connectivity (Swan, 2015). Although numerous studies have established technological challenges and limitations in the application of blockchain, the practicality of blockchain goes beyond finance to health, education, supply chain management, data storage, identity and personal management, economic and social structures, governance and law, environmental sustainability, and development aid projects (Swan, 2015; Morse, 2018; Patel, 2018; Riani, 2018).

With over $600 billion spent on development aid per year to support the achievement of the SDGs, development aid is intended to reduce the gap between the developed and developing worlds (ICAI, 2018). Although development aid is tagged to issues such as donor politics and economic conditionalities, in this chapter, the term is used in its broadest sense to refer to financial aid given for development and humanitarian projects and how it flows from donors to intended recipients. Here the terms 'recipients' and 'beneficiaries' are used interchangeably to mean individuals that development aid is intended for.

Much of the research that focusses on development aid's long-term effectiveness has not been able to convincingly show that evaluation and monitoring tools give donors and beneficiaries real value (Anholt, 2010; Ghosh and Kharas, 2011; Raudino, 2016). Slow progress has provoked high-level discussions among top aid contributors to commit to global monitoring campaigns (Sustainia et al., 2018).

The UN's target for each country to give 0.7% of their gross national income has barely been met, partly owing to aid withdrawal by donors because existing development aid systems are faced with allegations of fraud and resource misappropriation. This is evident in the case of refugee assistance where reports indicate that approximately 30% of aid funds do not reach beneficiaries due to mismanagement, theft, and other challenges (Publish What You Fund, 2018). Likewise, it is reported that almost 40% of UN aid is lost to corruption (Dufief, 2018; Kenny, 2017). A notable example is that of the recent case for Uganda's aid officials being suspended over alleged refugee aid fraud worth $350 million of donations from the 2017 UN Refugee Summit (LSE, 2018) and under investigation by the EU, UN, the United States, and the United Kingdom who threatened to stop and withdraw aid programmes (The Guardian, 2018).

Such cases challenge the misconception that the more aid given, the greater the change. There is some evidence to suggest that monitoring tools fall short of development aid budget data evaluation. Raudino (2016) illustrates this point clearly using the 2013 EU—South Africa case of 'direct budget support' where the EU country office carried out a net transfer of 980 million euros in cash to the South African government in efforts to meet budgetary deadlines. Thus the absence of tools that prohibit aid mismanagement and exclusion of beneficiaries from the aid chain is a cause and consequence of both external and internal variations (Anholt, 2010).

Studies that evaluate development aid show that progress reports do not indeed reflect what exactly happened and how aid money was spent despite other factors (ICAI, 2018; Kshetri and Voas, 2018; Publish What You Fund, 2018). Marshall et al. (2016) recommend using interactive financial systems with set data standards and requirements for donors to show evidence of their work. However, this would still be inefficient because if performance data received from recipient countries are concocted, it means nothing if intended beneficiaries do not receive aid transparently.

Official reports indicate that the procedure of aid and its allocation is more transparent than it was a decade ago. The provision of information and dissemination of country reports on development programmes is seen as an aid transparency indicator

(Dufief, 2018). Although 75% of countries in the 2018 Aid Transparency Index are clustered as transparent in the way they handle aid activities through quarterly or monthly reports (Publish What You Fund, 2018), there is less evidence to show beneficiaries' aid receipt.

Recent studies that report a decline of donor confidence in recipient countries are almost certainly due to low transparency levels in aid. What this means is that a high percentage of compliance levels are not being addressed from a financial transparency point of view and that existing record storage and management procedures are flawed (Anholt, 2010). It is postulated that there are slow efforts to institutionalise transparency through flexible government policies that go beyond statute focus of implementation of aid programmes. This is a probable explanation for studies that have suggested the use of digital tools to ensure transparency (Transparency International, 2014; Zwitter and Boisse-Despiaux, 2018). Dufief (2018) recommends doing this along reforms that support coordination of open societies with institutionally designed digital platforms, to sustain greater transparency in aid disbursements.

A broadly similar point has been made by other studies on the absence of technology in evaluating development aid effectiveness, pointing out the significance of utilising technology in promoting democratic formations based on components of a distributed database. Ko and Verity (2016) advocate for inclusion of communities and permission of public access to data which also relate to current development aid contracts, as they do not account for accessibility to aid data and budgets. For the most part the absence of financial breakdowns of individual aid activities when donors publish financial aid budgets presents challenges when tracking aid (Publish What You Fund, 2018). Without donors publishing sector codes that are mappable to partner country budgets, it remains a challenge to produce accurate budgeting, accounting, and auditing of both external and domestic resources (Easterly, 2007; Kenny, 2017).

2 Viability of cryptocurrency and smart contracts in development aid

As explained in the previous section, blockchain is the foundation upon which Bitcoin cryptocurrency system operates, with enhanced features that have already been applied in the public sector to exchange value safely and transparently around the world as shown in Fig. 1. Likewise, blockchain's prominent features of cryptocurrency and smart contracts have enormous potential for accountability and transparency in the development aid supply chain.

Several studies have shown that a vital feature of blockchain is that it eliminates integrity violations such as fraud whilst reducing transaction costs (Paynter, 2017; Christidis and Devetsiokiotis, 2016). This view is supported by Zheng et al. (2017) whose study explored the nature and prospective trends of blockchain as a cryptography and reports that cryptocurrency transactions allow for secure ledger access, highlighting that is

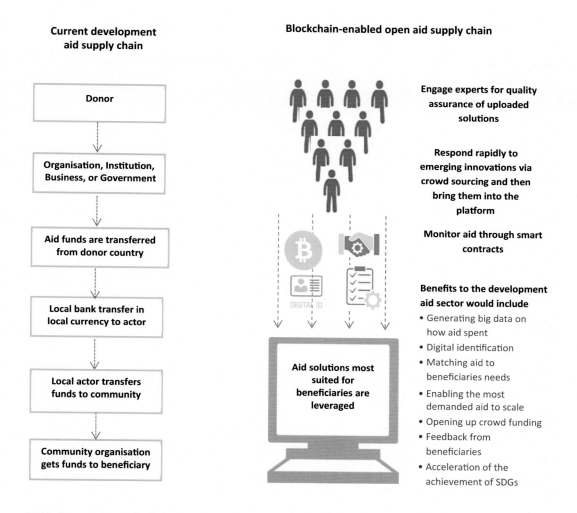

FIG. 1 Current aid supply chain compared with the potential blockchain-enabled aid platform.

extremely difficult—if not impossible—to change or remove data recorded on a ledger. Here the potential for the aid sector lies in a more reliable and transparent ecosystem by utilising blockchain attributes such as immutability (Zwitter and Boisse-Despiaux, 2018).

Cryptography has successfully improved service delivery in various sectors. Patel (2018) gives a good illustration on the use of electronic medical data sharing in the healthcare sector and how it has reshaped modern practices by removing third-party handling of information, hence instilling trust in sharing patient data. In the global food supply chain, origins of food sold to a buyer can be traced back to the farmer to ensure that producers at the beginning of the food chain get a fair wage (Zwitter and Boisse-Despiaux, 2018) and brings about a sense of ethics to validate what all are signed up to in supply chains. Additionally, elimination of a single authority or centralised organisation has enabled parties in fields such as accounts and real estate to have a positive impact, hence guaranteeing transparency (Karamitsos et al., 2018; Zheng et al., 2018). In developing countries, pilot projects have mainly covered land title registry and electronic voting (Zambrano, 2017).

The aforementioned examples support the view that establishment of consensus without any central party intervention makes cryptocurrency transactions attractive to different sectors. For the development aid sector, the efficacy of blockchain is probably not to be limited to cryptocurrency but shows potential in informational infrastructures and smart contracts as well as atomising many logistical processes such as timely provision of humanitarian relief during crises and disasters—by connecting suppliers of, for example, food and water with airliners and planning deliveries at particular locations within certain timeframes (Zwitter and Boisse-Despiaux, 2018; Zambrano, 2017). The idea of smart contracts was first noted by Nicholas Szabo in 1994 as the computerised execution of contracts that does not require intermediaries and reduces unfair exceptions (Christidis and Devetsiokiotis, 2016). Smart contracts have been given due attention in the wake of blockchain because they are self-executing, surpass common send-receive or buy-sell cryptocurrency transactions, and operate distinctively using trust protocol and Bitcoin to write agreements based on the three elements shown in Table 1. Execution of smart contracts is automatic as it is fragmented by codes through computerised transactions (Swan, 2015).

Smart contracts can transform various aspects of supply chain management and atomise contract execution beyond the finance sector (Zheng et al., 2018). In development aid, significance lies in the ability to facilitate management of information and aid delivery coordination, crowd funding control, supply chain tracking, cash-transfer programming, boosting development finance, and generating big data (Ko and Verity, 2016). Here, blockchain's proof-of-work feature ensures that aid funds are held based on agreed rules by all stakeholders to enhance accountability and disbursed once project agreed criteria is met to enhance effectiveness.

Fig. 1 gives an illustration of how blockchain can potentially change the current development aid supply chain by regulating development aid flow.

The use of big data to forecast the onset of natural and man-made crisis to implementing partners using objective indicators can trigger smart contract transactions that facilitate engagement in disaster risk reduction and conflict management (Zwitter and

Table 1 The distinctive features of smart contracts.

Autonomy	There is no need for the agent who initiated the contract to be in further contact with contract after it is launched
Self-sufficiency	Ability to marshal sources through raising funds by providing services or issuing equity and in turn spending them on needed resources
Decentralisation	Contracts are distributed and self-executory across all network

Boisse-Despiaux, 2018). Furthermore, international organisations that push for direct aid cash transfers to vulnerable communities in emergencies and crises can utilise smart contracts since all interactions throughout the whole process are verified and digitally signed. Donations to such programmes would be digitally assigned to intended individuals who must use them to access defined services (Zheng et al., 2018; Ko and Verity, 2016). With this the ability to predict events and identify project outcomes, for example, the magnitude of potential disasters and number of victims, can enable organisations to determine the types and quantity of goods and services needed and when and how to deliver them. Zwitter and Herman (2018) provide valuable insight into the emergence of digital identities in the aid sector as part of blockchain's ability to drive big data and the digital future. This presents the opportunity not only to create digital representations of people without identification such as refugees but also to determine and deliver aid to communities based on known identification and need. Organisations such as WFP have explored possibilities of delivering cash-based aid using digital identities. However, nongovernmental agencies are critical of the creation of immutable identity data. Since contracts are automatically executed, this could lead to inflexible processes that ignore the sensitivity that is always vital when dealing with humanitarian emergencies (Sustainia et al., 2018).

2.1 Blockchain concerns and smart contract

Other research on blockchain has raised concerns on security, privacy, and matters around the EU's GDPR—such as data misuse and rights over personal information (Christidis and Devetsiokiotis, 2016; He et al., 2018; Miraz and Ali, 2018). In development aid, if beneficiaries' data are to be recorded and identifiable without clear clarification on data ownership, then blockchain is subjected to severe criticism. In their comprehensive review, Zwitter and Boisse-Despiaux (2018) concluded that using a cloud or virtual interface could be a better alternative and recommended the use of zero-knowledge proofs. Using some types of hybrid blockchain can also facilitate handling the data questions and where data are kept off-chain and blockchain used as authentication mechanism and smart contract and time stamping. The absence of critical data makes it impossible for stakeholders to monitor, evaluate, and measure aid impact. Audits on development aid projects indicate missing information which makes attainment of goals, through strict budget implementation, impossible. Fifty-nine percent of aid recipient nations avail data during budget implementation, but only 45% make their final expenditure available. Additionally, 74% of the 155 nations that were surveyed could not provide specific details on age, gender, and location of how aid funds were spent to demonstrate the impact of fiscal aid policies (The Open Budget Survey, 2017).

Kshetri and Voas (2018) suggest that the auditability feature of smart contracts can provide higher value for development aid in terms of addressing insecurity, fraud, and misuse of information. Supporting this view, Christidis and Devetsiokiotis (2016) maintain that attempts at fraudulent activities are immediately rejected since all network participants can review contract activities and get a cryptographically provable trace of the actions of the contract.

Regarding environmental development aid programmes, smart contracts can positively impact SDGs through vital real estate since the global concern on climate change has directed aid efforts towards the evolution of smart cities. This involves control of fixed and nonfixed assets, networking, and integration of transactions into forecasting future neighbourhoods whilst connecting people and organisations. This would not only ensure accountability based on data from smart contracts but also improve environments for sustainable livelihoods (Karamitsos et al., 2018). He et al. (2018) and Zheng et al. (2017) looked at establishing and implementing control policies through smart contracts. These authors maintain that the smart contract policy of access control of transaction-based management will extend workflow standards through the attribute-based access control (ABAC) model. Although this makes smart contracts a valuable replacement of traditional access control of data with relational database access control, there's a need for development of a model that is specific to the development aid sector, considering ethical issues, identity protection, human rights, and dignified service delivery to aid beneficiaries.

There is no doubt that the application of cryptocurrency and smart contracts in development aid accentuate blockchain's potential for the sector. However, there has been wide criticism on the ability of smart contracts to retain large amounts of data indicating that time taken to confirm a transaction can be long, thereby making approval of requests and action on key decisions collectively impossible in real time (Christidis and Devetsiokiotis, 2016; He et al., 2018; Morse, 2018). Depending to how heavy data are, there may be available ways to solution on how blockchain should work at optimum levels. As well as data considerations, depending on type of consensus algorithm used on blockchain, it does use extreme energy; critics such as Paynter (2017) and Zwitter and Herman (2018) raise concerns on the delivery of aid to remote areas where there is often no electricity, Internet, or markets that facilitate cash-based transfers. It is also believed that some countries are illegalising cryptocurrency transactions with aid beneficiaries; this could greatly hinder blockchain's progressive application in achieving the Sustainable Development Goals (SDGs). However, such actions could be due to the lack of a knowledge-sharing platform among those that have already applied blockchain and prospective users.

Although donors have access to records and can trace transactions through smart contracts and big data, Zwitter and Boisse-Despiaux (2018) are clearly right to draw our attention to issues around big data and humanitarianism, ethics, norms, and codes of conduct, which remain more important in relation to immutability. In addition, strict technological investments and measures ought to be taken to avoid hacks in development aid digital systems and to ensure that funds are accessed by intended recipients and their privacy is protected.

It appears that anticipated challenges are outweighed by the empirical and conceptual possibilities of using blockchain. The most relevant perspectives to this study incline to focus on the general direction towards blockchain's potential for the development aid sector. For instance, Zheng et al. (2017), Zwitter and Herman (2018), and Dufief (2018) show that the practicability of smart contracts in the context of this study's objectives is based on public access, budget participation, and project monitoring. Similarly, Miraz and Ali (2018), Swan (2015), and Morse (2018) adequately explain that smart contracts can facilitate performance-based resource disbursement since all network participants can review contract activities and get a cryptographically provable trace of the actions of the contract, thus promoting accountability and transparency. Paynter (2017), Kshetri and Voas (2018), and Zwitter and Herman (2018) support this view that since most development aid programmes are aimed at crises, disasters, and emergencies, smart contracts have the potential of presenting real impact, thus identifying beneficiaries and facilitating timely interventions. In contrast, others offer valid counterarguments that blockchain is flawed in various attributes; hence, its applicability in development aid will be faced with challenges of energy costs, market access, and scalability (Riani, 2018; Zambrano, 2017; Zwitter and Boisse-Despiaux, 2018). Additionally, it is important to address issues relating to humanitarian ethics, security, and data privacy and find effective ways to apply blockchain whilst upholding the humanitarian principle of 'do no harm'.

3 Blockchain application to development aid

The central question is how blockchain can enhance the achievement of transparency in development aid and facilitate long-term aid effectiveness for beneficiaries. In epistemology, positivism and realism are critiqued for the view that reality can be externally understood independently from social actors. Hence, this research adopted the interpretivist approach as it is about creating new or richer understanding and interpretations of social worlds and contexts. With this, it's possible to look at the value of aid and get a conceptual assessment of how aid is viewed and understand the differences between blockchain technology and the role of human agencies as social actors (Saunders et al., 2016; Bryman, 2016).

On the contrary, taking an interpretivist stance may lead to findings that are outside the study objectives. Although this might be considered a weakness, it has the potential to uncover relevant findings that would enrich the research outcome and direct areas for further research. For this study an empathetic stance was adopted to enter the social world of how blockchain technology is understood in the development aid sector, from participants' point of view.

3.1 Blockchain case studies in development aid

The following in this section looked at four case studies that have delivered development aid using blockchain. It presents themes in the first part and gives a critical discussion of findings, proposing a conceptual framework in the second part. The summary of this section establishes that blockchain and smart contracts can successfully deliver transparency in development aid despite limitations. The selection of cases for this study was dominantly revelatory. This is because cases cited here had the potential of elucidating more insights on the applicability, viability, and limitations of blockchain in development aid. Although these were relevant to the research topic and produced significant data that addressed the research question, case studies are criticised for replication of data, which diminishes the methodological rigour of making theoretical predictions (Matthews and Ross, 2010). In the same vein, using either single or many cases does not guarantee production of concrete evidence that support hypothesis, and if the unit of analysis sought after in the cases is not explicitly identified, it can be difficult to sieve data from many variables of interest (Bryman, 2016).

3.2 Development aid blockchain

To examine viability of blockchain utilised in development aid programmes, the following highlight the specific areas of interest and why blockchain as the chosen technology.

As illustrated in case study one, it is clear that digital vouchers were successfully delivered to refugees. Personal details attached to vouchers provided identification for each intended recipient. However, voucher replication attempts were identified at point of transaction—attributable to blockchain's immutability features (Christidis and Devetsiokiotis, 2016). Refugees were 100% satisfied, although linking personal details to network activities could reveal identities should private keys get lost (Tables 2–5).

In case study two, we see efficient food aid delivery to Syrian refugees in Jordan. Blockchain facilitated the reduction of costs incurred when transferring money from donors, thus using surplus to increase supplies. In the earlier extract, we see how digital identification can afford refugee employment, banking, and immigration verification through accessible digital wallets. An unreported challenge is privacy and protection of refugee identities. This is articulated in the quote: 'It's a major success, (…) It reduces costs and the risks of sharing refugees' data, while simultaneously improving the WFP's control, flexibility, and accountability. Now if we get a call that 20,000 people are coming in the night, we can have everything ready for them in the morning', he says. 'The old way would have taken two weeks and required paper vouchers'—UN Executive Official at World Food Programme's aid relief project in Jordan.

Table 2   Case study one: aid delivery to Syrian refugees in Lebanon.

Organisation	Project description
AID: Tech	• Syrian refugees and local Lebanese people from surveyed by six Lebanese-based academics
Donor Irish Red Cross	• Irish Red Cross donated $10,000–100 Syrian refugee families
Date December 2015	• Distributed 500 intelligent vouchers worth $20 each
Country Lebanon	• Partnered with a local supermarket in Tripoli, North Lebanon • It took 10 min to train cashiers to understand how it works
Project Syrian War Refugees in Tripoli, Beirut and Aker Refugee Camp	**Project results** • All 500 intelligent vouchers redeemed
Objective Ensure refugees receive aid while preserving their dignity and humanity	• 20 fraudulent vouchers created—all failed at point of sale • All transactions were monitored in real time by IRC • Participating refugee families expressed great satisfaction • Irish Red Cross reported project effectiveness and transparency compared to previous or similar projects

Source: IFRC, 2017. Using Blockchain Technology to Assist Refugees in Lebanon. [Online] Available from: http://media.ifrc.org/innovation/2017/01/04/using-blockchain-technology-to-assist-refugees-in-lebanon/ [Accessed 18 November 2018].

Table 3 Case study two: food aid distribution to Syrian refugees in Jordan.

Organisation	Project description
World Food Programme (WFP)	• 106,000 Syrian refugees redeemed their cash transfers using the building blocks blockchain system
Donor	• Partnered with local supermarket Tazweeed
United Nations	• Supermarket cashiers to identify refugees using an iris scanner called 'EyePay'
Date	• Individual aid entitlements verified against internal databases
February 2017	**Project results**
Country	• 98% reduction in transaction and transfer fees
Jordan	• Feed more people
Project	• Improve local economy
Food-aid solution in Zaatari refugee camp	• Monthly savings of about US$40,000
	• Recipients and aid personnel reported a more secure, efficient, and transparent process
Objective	• WFP expressed great satisfaction in benefiting their work, donors, and recipients
Conduct food-aid distribution through transactions using the WFP building block blockchain system	• Recipients have transaction history and government IDs access to financial accounts, all in one

Source: Juskalian, R., 2018. Inside the Jordan Refugee Camp That Runs on Blockchain. [Online] Available from: https://www.technologyreview.com/s/610806/inside-the-jordan-refugee-camp-that-runs-on-blockchain/ [Accessed 18 November 2018].

Table 4 Case study three: early childhood development aid delivery through secure data systems in South Africa.

Organisation	Project description
TrustLab and ixo Foundation	• Accredited nonstate preschool providers to create registries to get funding and track school attendance
Donor	• Reduce administrative costs, boost performance
UNICEF	• Generate and record verifiable proofs of service delivery
Date	• Exchange cryptographic tokens for funding
November 2016	
Country	• Individual aid entitlements verified against internal databases
South Africa	
Project	**Project results**
Enable early childhood development service providers to receive funding for early learning programs, nutrition, and childcare	• Increased effectiveness of matching funding and services with children's needs
	• Transparency and accountability for funding
	• Generation of genuine child identifiable data which are encrypted and stores a personal record
	• Tracked 3327 children and 81,168 attendances
Objective	• 87 centres and 122 nonstate preschool providers able to access funding
Replace existing paper-based systems to register children for a government funded preschool subsidy and ensure accurate and secure data storage	• Valuable data assets on children's nutrition, social protection, health, education, parent support, and poverty can be derived to benefit the child, and official population-based data analysis

Source: UNICEF, 2018. Trustlab: Proof of Impact for Early Childhood Development. [Online] Available from: http://unicefstories.org/2018/04/11/unicef-innovation-fund-graduate-trustlab/ [Accessed 18 November 2018].

Table 5 Case study four: digital data to support pregnant women to health entitlements.

Organisation	Project description
AID: Tech	• Protect women's data and give them access and control of their antenatal health records
Donor	• Assign a digital ID to each pregnant woman to be entitled to treatments and pregnancy vitamins
Dutch PharmaAccess Foundation	
Date	• Track pregnant women's progress from first hospital visit at 16 weeks, throughout antenatal care, delivery, and postnatal care
April 2017	
Country	• Provide access to postnatal care, medication, and follow up appointments
Tanzania	• Trace entitlements securely and deliver them efficiently
Project	**Project results**
Support 100 pregnant women's health entitlements	• Transparent, efficient, performance-based financing model for healthcare
Objective	• Pregnant women received medical entitlements in an efficient and transparent way
Support the collection, identification, and verification of digital health data to make women's antenatal care a safer and more efficient process	• Care providers were supported to gather patient data quickly and manage appointments
	• Provided proof of concept in assembling, tagging, and verifying digital health data
	• Welcomed world's first blockchain technology born baby on 13 July 2018

Source: AID:Tech, 2018. Transforming Healthcare in Tanzania for Data Transparency. [Online] Available from: https://aid.technology/tanzania/ [Accessed 18 November 2018].

Case study three explores delivering education aid. The project aimed to track children's school attendance in South Africa. Donors are able to access proof of impact and see challenges faced through peer-to-peer logs from parents, health workers, teachers, and the government—which can derive accurate data on children's socioeconomic status for official country data analysis.

Case study four looks at utilising blockchain in the health sector to identify, verify, and deliver maternal healthcare in Tanzania, where pregnant women die due to preventable maternal complications. Here, women received medical entitlements transparently, and staff managed appointments easily, giving prenatal and postnatal care and child immunisation. Although this pilot case was successful, it may have faced challenges with some women not having access to mobile gadgets that are compatible to the AID:Tech blockchain application or not literate enough to understand maternal records.

3.3 Effectiveness and relevance of blockchain

The subsequent section critically discusses emergent themes from case studies, and key themes include development aid effectiveness, technology, and digital data trends.

3.3.1 Theme 1: Development aid effectiveness

This study shows a high recognition of low achievement in development aid efforts. In earlier sections, we see that aid is significant in the pursuit of SDGs. Although most studies focus on aid's long-term effectiveness (Ghosh and Kharas, 2011; Raudino, 2016), the general observation from these results is that long-term aid effectiveness is constrained by power imbalance among stakeholders. Donors and governments have more power in formulating and implementing aid programmes, excluding beneficiaries in decision-making processes—especially on how aid should be spent (Dufief, 2018; Easterly, 2007). However, what we see in *case studies one and two* is that the involvement of beneficiaries in making decisions on how to spend aid money through 'intelligent voucher' issuance and creation of 'digital wallets' enabled refugees to purchase supplies as needed without the need of a middleman. Similarly, data creation, access, and traceability play major roles in aid effectiveness. This study has revealed that development aid data are often restricted and incomparable. Prior studies that have noted the importance of credible data in achieving developing aid effectiveness suggest that monitoring tools fall short of development aid budget data evaluation (Raudino, 2016) and do not reflect what exactly happened and how aid money was spent (Kshetri and Voas, 2018; ICAI, 2018). However, *case study three* illustrates the role of data integrity—generating an effective way of matching funding with children's needs based on school attendance data recorded on an immutable platform. This in turn derived valuable data on children's socioeconomic status, which benefits not only the child but also official national data analyses.

It is interesting to see that aid effectiveness is constrained by grand and petty corruption. Existing development aid systems are faced with allegations of fraud and resource misappropriation. Evidence has proven that, for instance, in refugee assistance, approximately 30% of aid funds do not reach its beneficiaries due to mismanagement, theft, and data falsification (Dufief, 2018; Kenny, 2017). In *case study one*, 20 fraudulent vouchers were created although they all failed at point of sale because intelligent vouchers were issued on a blockchain-enabled platform, which is virtually impossible to alter but ensures that aid gets to intended recipients transparently.

On the topic of transparency, this research found that development aid has failed due to lack of transparency in access to data by all stakeholders. These factors may explain the relatively good correlation between studies that have noted the importance of provision of open information (Dufief, 2018; Publish What You Fund, 2018) and those that have acknowledged it as transparency indicator (Anholt, 2010; Transparency International, 2014; ICAI, 2018). The results also raise intriguing questions for current development aid practice regarding the allocation of money. The proposal that aid should be directly channelled to beneficiaries and grassroots organisations for it to be effective is a probable explanation for suggestions that have been made on the use of digital tools to ensure transparency in development (ICAI, 2018; Transparency International, 2014).

As noted in the *case studies*, blockchain was used to identify aid recipients and directly disburse aid money (*case studies one and two*) as well as match funding directly with intended recipients (*case studies three and four*), thus facilitating transparency. This is supported by Dufief (2018) who suggests that reforms that support coordination of open societies with institutionally designed digital platforms should be used sustain greater transparency in aid disbursements. Nonetheless, it might appear less significant that aid should go directly to beneficiaries due to concerns about social exclusion of beneficiaries that might not be able to plan for their aid money due to illiteracy.

3.3.2 Theme 2: Technology—Applicability of smart contracts and blockchain in development aid

Current findings show that smart contracts verify, facilitate, and enforce the performance, negotiation, and execution of any contract. In development aid, projects can be tied to funding agreements to ensure accountability and transparency (Ko and Verity, 2016). This is evidenced in *case study one*, where all 500 intelligent vouchers were redeemed and fraudulent activities were identified and blocked at point of sale; in *case study two*, where individual aid entitlements were verified using an iris scanner; in case study three, where funding is matched with children's needs upon recording attendance; and in case study four, where pregnant women were matched with medication, hospital visits, and antenatal and postnatal care.

In spite of the success seen in the *case studies*, general agreement among respondents that users in developing countries will find it difficult to use cryptographic tools is consistent with other research that point to challenges such as poor public key infrastructure, legislation, Internet connectivity, and electricity problems in recipient countries (Zwitter and Boisse-Despiaux, 2018). In addition, the lack of political will by governments to adopt blockchain was highly noted and may be explained by the fact that blockchain has the potential to remove the middleman—in this case the government—and allow transfer of aid funds directly from donors to recipients, transparently. Since there were no reports of such problems in the case studies, it is thought that positive results could be attributed to operation of pilot projects in areas where populations had access to electricity and smart devices and were able to use the application. Additional uncertainty arises from the lack of detail in case study four on whether all expectant mothers had access to smart phones and could read and understand content related to their entitlements.

To ascertain the viability of cryptocurrency and smart contracts in development aid, the theme of technology provides certainty that smart contracts can facilitate transparent aid distribution. The general agreement among respondents that smart contracts are capable of facilitating the achievement of aid effectiveness could be explained by the fact that it requires proof of work, upon which automatic triggering of particular payments can only be done when certain conditions are met (He et al., 2018). This is evident in *case study three* where preschool providers are able to generate and record verifiable proofs of service delivery and exchange cryptographic tokens for funding.

Smart contracts manage size and demand according to findings in this study. However, lack of confidence in their scalability by some respondents could be because the technology is still in its infancy and there are questions raised about who decides the algorithmic transactions that implement predefined contractual agreements and whether all stakeholders are indeed included. Zambrano (2017) suggests that actual relevance to specific development aid recipients should be assessed on a case-by-case basis because it would be complex to meet size and demand if the level of human development is low. Although this raises an alarm, we see, for example, in case study three that the early childhood development program reached 800,000 children, which exceeded the anticipated 100,000 at project initiation.

4 Construction of a conceptual framework: A blockchain and development aid synergy

To help visualise the next-generation application of blockchain to development aid a four-fold suggestion of a 'development aid blockchain enabled' conceptual framework is presented in Fig. 2. It represents the transparent flow of development aid from donors to beneficiaries, through the use of smart contracts and cryptocurrencies on blockchain. Humanitarian aid logistics can be handled efficiently through smart contracts with partners and service providers, thus monitoring supply chain management. Creation of digital identities and linking them to projects and available funding would ultimately have a higher impact on the achievement of SGDs by getting aid to those that need it the most without 'leaving anyone behind'.

Although the applicability of blockchain in various sectors is still in the proof-of-concept stage, there's a widely held view that it will thrive. Likewise, for the development aid sector, it is possible that we shall see an intensification of the achievement of SDGs if these four proposed concepts are incorporated in blockchain-based operations:

1. scalability in terms of interoperability of blockchain when handling large donor funds and millions of aid beneficiaries,
2. usability of cryptographic tools that will be a challenge for the poorest and illiterate,
3. structural functionalism in terms of regulations and policies for big data and digital migration,
4. ethical operations to observe humanitarian codes of conduct and preserve the security, privacy, and dignity of powerless and vulnerable populations.

Based on the critical and descriptive discussion earlier, the development aid sector can rely on blockchain for evaluation and monitoring to achieve ultimate accountability and transparency. The outcomes of blockchain and smart contracts in other sectors such as health and education should be used as a linchpin to promote blockchain's potential in development aid as well as major institutions such as the UN. Like any similar system the question is whether it will put ownership of digital identification and a networked system into the hands of those represented or they will become an easier way for corporations and states to control people's digital existence. With the suggested conceptual framework in the succeeding text and full sensitisation of end users, it is unlikely that these fears for blockchain will materialise.

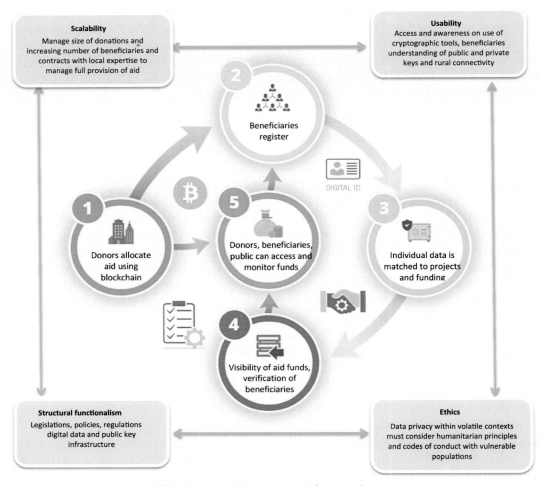

FIG. 2 Proposed development aid blockchain-enabled conceptual framework.

5 Conclusions

This chapter sets out to review current development aid contract models and monitoring and evaluation tools to determine how viable blockchain is in delivering development aid in a transparent and secure manner whilst respecting privacy. Findings clearly indicate that current and traditional models have, overall, been ineffective to development aid and its issues of potential corruption and misuse. Some of the key findings show that existing monitoring and evaluation tools in development aid are weak, aid projects do not mostly achieve project outcomes, official aid data are inaccurate and inadequate, and beneficiaries are not involved in decision making processes. Blockchain, with its attributes and some proven capabilities, can ultimately resolve these traditional issues and enable the development aid sector to achieve the SDGs.

A clear finding to emerge from this research study is that smart contracts and blockchain are feasible in development aid but not devoid of challenges to adoption in recipient countries where governments are reluctant to legalise cryptocurrency transactions, operating costs are high, and there is absence of markets, key infrastructure, and Internet connectivity. However, it has been described here and in other scholarly works that donors appreciate blockchain's potential to deliver aid transparently. Implications from survey results show huge interest from aid personnel in deploying blockchain in the sector. This is because it would allow traceability, evidence-based and cyclic disbursement of aid, efficient delivery, and tracking of supplies; give beneficiaries access to aid data and funds; and ensure transparency and accountability through smart contracts.

This study has raised important questions about the future of digital data in development aid. Ethical issues around data safety, protection of vulnerable populations, and upholding humanitarian principles arise in the era of transformative technology and big data revolutions as this could be interpreted as experimenting with powerless and desperate populations. There is no clarification on who is accountable in case of breaches of privacy and GDPR.

Conclusions drawn from this study are that blockchain and smart contracts' bypasses of centralised epicentres of power mean more transparency and integrity in development aid delivery. It has extended our knowledge of the viability of blockchain in development aid and contributes to our understanding of issues that would challenge its application as stated earlier. In line with general operation principles in the development aid sector, the study has questioned blockchain's ethical ability to protect and serve beneficiaries' needs before the interests of corporations. Potential in blockchains' features are there, although concerns such as the inability to revoke immutable transactions raise questions on whether people will have the freedom to delete themselves completely without trace. As millions of aid beneficiaries get digital identities in the future, there is lack of clarity on the possibility of abusing anonymity to manipulate data, hack the system, or undertake fraud. Additionally, current blockchain platforms in development aid operations are either pilots or small scale, and nothing is known about the maximum size of stakeholders or transactions they can take on; so, it presents a scalability question. However, if AI technologies are employed and connected to smart governments, they could enhance the functionality and intelligence of smart contracts and blockchain.

References

Anholt, S., 2010. The Double-Edged Blade of Aid. Butterworth-Heinemann, Oxford.

Bryman, A., 2016. Social Research Methods, fourth ed. Oxford University Press, Oxford.

Christidis, K., Devetsiokiotis, M., 2016. Blockchains and Smart Contracts for the Internet of Things. IEEE, Raleigh.

Dufief, E., 2018. How Can Development Organisations Improve Their Open Data for Aid Transparency? 17, Publish What You Fund, p. 10.

Easterly, W., 2007. Are aid agencies improving? Econ. Policy 22 (52), 633–678.

Ghosh, A., Kharas, H., 2011. The money trail: ranking donor transparency in foreign aid. World Dev. 39 (11), 1918–1929.

He, Q., Liu, Z., Xu, Y., Zhang, R., 2018. A privacy-preserving Internet of Things device management scheme based on blockchain. Int. J. Distrib. Sens. Netw. 14 (11), 1–13.

ICAI, 2018. DFID's Approach to Value for Money in Programme and Portfolio Management. Independent Commission on Aid Impact, London.

Karamitsos, I., Papadaki, M., Al Barghuthi, N., 2018. Design of the blockchain smart contract: a use case for real estate. J. Inf. Secur. 9 (3), 177–190.

Kenny, C., 2017. How Much Aid Is Really Lost to Corruption? [Online] Available from: https://www.cgdev.org/blog/how-much-aid-really-lost-corruption. (Accessed 8 December 2018).

Ko, V., Verity, A., 2016. Blockchain for the Humanitarian Sector: Future Opportunities. UN-OCHA Digital Humanitarian Network, New York.

Kshetri, N., Voas, J., 2018. Blockchain in developing countries. IT Professional (March/April), 11–15.

LSE, 2018. The Illegal Economy of Refugee Registration: Insights into the Ugandan Refugee Scandal. London School of Economics, London.

Marshall, M., Kirk, D., Vines, J., 2016. Accountable: exploring the inadequacies of transparent financial practice in the non-profit sector. In: Association for Computing Machinery.Proceedings of the 2016 CHI Conference on Human Factors in Computing Systems—CHI '16. ISBN 978-1-4503-3362-7pp. 1620–1631. https://doi.org/10.1145/2858036.2858301. (Accessed 25 May 2020).

Matthews, B., Ross, L., 2010. Research Methods: A Practical Guide for the Social Sciences, first ed. Pearson Education Limited, Harlow.

Miraz, M.H., Ali, M., 2018. Applications of blockchain technology beyond cryptocurrency. Ann. Emerg. Technol. Comput. 2 (1), 1–6.

Morse, E.A., 2018. From Rai stones to blockchains: the transformation of payments. Comput. Law Secur. Rev. 34, 946–953.

Nakamoto, S., 2008. Bitcoin: A Peer-to-Peer Electronic Cash System. [Online] Available from: https://bitcoin.org/bitcoin.pdf. (Accessed 6 December 2018).

Patel, V., 2018. A framework for secure and decentralised sharing of medical imaging data via blockchain consensus. Health Informatics J. 25, 1–14.

Paynter, B., 2017. How Blockchain Could Transform the Way International Aid Is Distributed. [Online] Available from: https://fastcompany.com/40457354/howblockchain-could-transform-the-way-international-aid-is-distributed. (Accessed 7 December 2018).

Publish What You Fund, 2018. Aid Transparency Index 2018. Publish Waht You Fund, London.

Raudino, S., 2016. Development Aid and Sustainable Economic Growth in Africa. Springer International Publishing AG, Cham.

Riani, T., 2018. Blockchain for Social Impact in Aid and Development. [Online] Available from: https://humanitarianadvisorygroup.org/blockchain-forsocial-impact-in-aid-and-development/. (Accessed 6 December 2018).

Saunders, M., Lewis, P., Thornhill, A., 2016. Research Methods for Business Students, second ed. Pearson Education Limited, Harlow.

Sustainia, Danida & Coinify, 2018. Hack the Future of Development Aid. Ministry of Foreign Affairs of Denmark, Copenhagen.

Swan, M., 2015. Blockchain: Blueprint for a New Economy. O'Reilly, Sebastopol.

The Guardian, 2018. 'They Exagerrated Figures': Ugandan Aid Officials Suspended Over Alleged Fraud. The Guardian Press, London.

The Open Budget Survey, 2017. Progress Toward Global Budget Transparency Stalls for the First Time in a Decade. International Budget Partnership.

Transparency International, 2014. Handbook of Good Practices: Preventing Corruption in Humanitarian Operations, second ed. Transparency International, Berlin.

Yli-Huumo, J., et al., 2016. Where is current research on blockchain technology?—A systematic review. PLoS One 11 (10), 1–27.

Zambrano, R., 2017. Blockchain: Unpacking the Disruptive Potential of Blockchain Technology for Human Development. International Development Research Centre, Ottawa.

Zheng, Z., et al., 2017. An overview of blockchain technology: architecture, consensus, and future trends. In: BigData Congress 2017, Honolulu.

Zheng, Z., et al., 2018. Blockchain challenges and opportunities: a survey. Int. J. Web. Grid. Serv. 14 (4), 352–375.

Zwitter, A., Boisse-Despiaux, M., 2018. Blockchain for humanitarian action and development aid. J. Int. Humanit. Action 3 (16), 1–7.

Zwitter, A., Herman, J., 2018. Blockchain for Sustainable Development Goals. University of Groningen, Groningen.

6

A proposed OKR-based framework for cyber effective services in the GDPR era

David Wilson and Hamid Jahankhani
NORTHUMBRIA UNIVERSITY, LONDON, UNITED KINGDOM

1 General data protection regulation and data breaches

The European general data protection regulation (GDPR) came into law in May 2018 and was a follow-up law to the 'EU Protection Directive (95/46/EC)' (EU, 2019). With the digitisation of the economy throughout the early 2000s and the expected explosion in the growth of data in the first half of the century, it was realised that new laws were required to protect the privacy of the individual. Therefore GDPR was conceived and later made law in all European States by May 2018. GDPR has brought about both strengths and weaknesses; Hoofnagle et al. (2019) stated "The GDPR brings personal data into a complex and protective regulatory regime." Whilst referencing the 'protective regulatory regime', they go on highlight the some of the issues.

The main disadvantage of the GDPR is its length and complexity: 99 detailed provisions. Whether the GDPR will actually improve fairness and respect for fundamental rights can, of course, only be assessed when it has been applicable for some time.

Hoofnagle et al. (2019)

Institutions across Europe have had to implement the regulations in a relatively short period of time, embedding processes into mature organisational structures which aren't necessarily a good fit. This has caused conflict and hidden costs with regard to implementation of the laws.

Sullivan (2018) contrasted the GDPR regulation with that of the Asia Pacific Economic Countries Cross-Border Privacy Rules (APEC CBPR) highlighting the concerns that GDPR is a bad fit for business stating "APEC CBP is viewed by many in the United States of America (US) as preferable to the EU approach because CBPR is considered more conducive to business than its counterpart schemes under the GDPR, and therefore is regarded as the scheme most likely to prevail."

Strategy, Leadership, and AI in the Cyber Ecosystem. https://doi.org/10.1016/B978-0-12-821442-8.00005-7
© 2021 Elsevier Inc. All rights reserved.

Breitbarth (2019) also made a similar point referencing countries not in the EU: "In Europe, countries not in the EU, including Norway, Switzerland, Liechtenstein and Iceland, have all aligned their respective regulations almost identically with the GDPR to facilitate access to the internal market." If the European Union is to maintain a competitive advantage in world economics, it is going to have to give this viewpoint thorough consideration. Sullivan goes on to say "Some aspects of the GDPR are concerning, such as the technical and legal implications of reliance on data anonymization and pseudonymization when they are not yet capable of providing the necessary protection from identification or re-identification of data subjects." (Sullivan, 2018).

Li et al. (2019) have recognised that US and Chinese companies have a duty to comply with GDPR so as to maintain a 'competitive advantage', writing "Chinese and US companies should seize the opportunity to enhance their capabilities for protecting personal data so that they can not only minimize the legal liability of GDPR but also win the trust of consumers and create a unique competitive advantage over those who cannot be in full compliance of GDPR."

McDowell (2019) writes about the increasing costs of institutions to put in place the necessary controls to be GDPR compliant: "The article demands companies put in place measures to ensure the ongoing confidentiality, integrity, availability and resilience of processing systems and services, while simultaneously making sure such protections are commensurate with the relevant risks." McDowell also goes on to comment about the complexity on processing different classifications of data: "What complicates the processing of biometric data even more is that the new regulation also gives it a special status, where any of the 28 EU member states may maintain or introduce further conditions, including limitations with regard to processing of biometric data." (McDowell, 2019).

However, Sullivan (2018) summarises the positive effects of GDPR for its impact on the future writing "Just as its predecessor set the global standard for data protection, the GDPR can be expected can be expected to set the standard for the new era, particularly for IoT data processing, and to inform law reform outside Europe." This is an important point to make in that the precedent that the EU has set for previous data protection laws have been followed on a global scale and that they are likely to do the same again with GDPR.

Choi et al. (2019) have made a salient point with regard to the need for new legislation focussing on digital trails of our Internet activities that will leave behind and how these data require treating with care: "As our lifestyle becomes increasingly reliant on the Internet, our daily activities through all kinds of computer and mobile devices leave digital trails, constantly producing up-to-date information about our activities." Should this digital 'footprint' containing personal identifiable data not be subject to data processing regulations, it could lead to considerable issues to the individual and the wider society at large.

As it has been more than a year since the inception of the GDPR regulation, commentators wide and far have been able to view statistics and comment on the performance of the new regulation. MacMillan (2019) made reference to a study undertaken by 'Hiscox' insurance specialists stating "nearly 40% of UK firms still don't understand which organisations are affected by the GDPR (hint: nearly all of them)." The author has noted the number of complaints and fines being made: "In the first nine months of the regulation being in force, 90,000 complaints led to fines totalling EU 56m." It appears that the GDPR regulation for institutions to self-report breaches into DPO's has had an effect on exposing the extent of data breaches throughout Europe. Breitbarth (2019) referencing the European Data Protection Board was also able to publish statistics on reporting in the first 9 months since GDPR was implemented. This is highlighted in Fig. 1.

The statistics show that half the cases reported to DPAs were complaints, just over a quarter were due to data breaches and the rest were classified as 'other'.

Further issues have also been highlighted by Wilson (2018) in the definition of GDPR in law and how institutions decide to implement it and thus report any data breaches: "GDPR 'compliance' is not fully defined by the law and will be determined in part by rapidly advancing security technology capabilities and evolving best practices." Wilson highlights how technology can be brought in to help close the gap between what the law says and how it is executed.

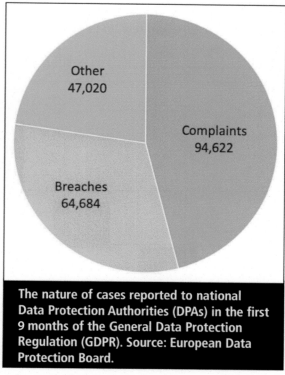

The nature of cases reported to national Data Protection Authorities (DPAs) in the first 9 months of the General Data Protection Regulation (GDPR). Source: European Data Protection Board.

FIG. 1 Nature of cases reported to national DPAs. *Source Breitbarth, P., 2019. The impact of GDPR one year on. Netw. Secur. 2019, 11-13.*

GDPR has led to some significant data breaches that have attracted widespread publicity; these have become ever more evident since the 1-year anniversary in May 2019 most notably the British Airways breach reported in 2018. There have also been other notable breaches and subsequent fines noted. Roberts (2019) has undertaken a study on average cost of a data breach focussing on the loss of customers to an organisation. This is shown in Fig. 2.

Roberts noted the significant loss of customers: "The average customer loss following a data breach is 3.4%, representing a cost of $2.05m to the organisation." With this in mind, CISOs in organisations should also take note of the most popular source of how breaches are undertaken. The 2018 Data Breaches Investigations Report published by Verizon (Verizon, 2019) as found in Fig. 3 has stated that 48% of all breaches are due to hacking.

They noted that the hacking was due to the spread of ransomware and was something that criminal groups saw as a lucrative occupation; it was quoted (Verizon, 2019) "Ransomware has taken centre stage from a malware perspective, and for good reason – it provides criminal groups with a good return on their investment in an industry that has matured quite a bit." The 11th edition of Verizon's annual Data Breach Investigations Report (DBIR) noted: "Looking at actions involved in breaches, stolen credentials tops the list, with phishing third."

One of the most notable attacks in recent years has been the attack on Equifax in the United States. Bates and Ul Hassan (2019) stated "In September 2017, the world awoke to

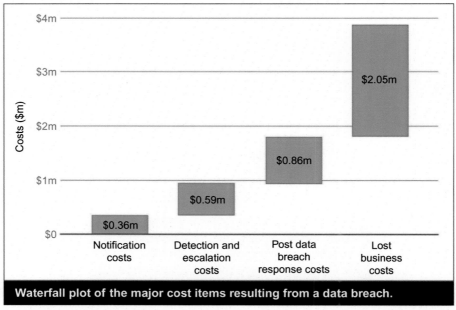

Waterfall plot of the major cost items resulting from a data breach.

FIG. 2 Average cost to an organisation following a data breach. *Source Roberts, S., 2019. Learning lessons from data breaches. Netw. Secur., 2018 (11), 8–11.*

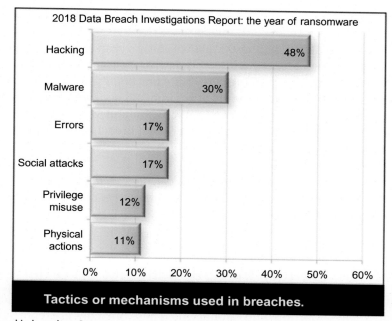

FIG. 3 Tactics used in breaches. *Source Verizon, 2019. 2018 Data Breaches Report. Available from: https://enterprise. verizon.com/resources/reports/DBIR_2018_Report.pdf (Accessed 9 March 2019).*

the news that Equifax, a consumer reporting agency and one of the pillars of the American credit system, fell prey to a data breach that led to the exposure of 147 million individuals' personal information." They discussed how following the first infiltration of the company network they were able to target other parts of the network accessing customer information: "Moving laterally through the network, the attackers would eventually come to access 51 Equifax databases, many of which included personally identifying consumer information."

Data breaches were targeting user identities and that there had been a significant increase in this type of activity: "There were 12,449 data breaches that compromised user identities in 2018 – a 424% increase compared to the previous year, according to figures just released by identity intelligence firm 4iQ." They commented on the results released by 4iQ and how this information was able to be collated "4iQ uses automated crawling of Internet accessible sources – including social media, deep websites and the dark web – as well as analysis by subject matter experts who authenticate and verify the data."

Another concerning trend that was observed was that organisations were failing to report data breaches to the Information Commissioner's Office (ICO) in the year leading up to GDPR; this should sound alarm bells on a global scale with the recent implementation of GDPR "Data from the Information Commissioner's Office has revealed that businesses routinely delayed data breach disclosure and failed to provide important details to the ICO in the year prior to the enactment of the General Data Protection Regulation (GDPR)."

Holm and Mackenzie (2014) had undertaken a study 5 years previous to GDPR looking at the relationship between identity crime and data breaches, and they noted "The relationship between data breaches and identity crime has been scarcely explored in current literature." It is surprising that industry and academia had not given much thought to why data breaches occurred only 5 years before GDPR. Holm and Mackenzie (2014) were able to conclude in detailing the relationship between data breaches, personal identification information (PII), and identity crime:

> *Data breaches are one of the ways in which this personal identification information is obtained by identity criminals, and thereby any response to data breaches is likely to impact the incidence of identity crime.*

2 Data breach, identity theft, and impact on organisations

Since the launch of GDPR, many multinational companies have been breached. These include British Airways, Marriott, and Capital One. These breaches are reported in the succeeding text:

- **British Airways**

The British Airways breach has been one of the most impactful data breaches since GDPR began and has been fined considerably.

The New York Times (2019) noted "The British authorities said on Monday that they intended to order British Airways to pay a fine of nearly $230 million for a data breach last year, the largest penalty against a company for privacy lapses under a new European data protection law." With such a hit to British Airways brand and reputation, it is surprising that the company does not have a 'director of technology' or chief information security officer (CISO) based in the United Kingdom, preferring to manage operations from Spain under the umbrella of the International Airlines Group (IAG). It could be argued that this shows lack of respect to the respective regulator that they don't have 'in country' oversight of data security.

- **Marriott**

The Marriott hotel chain also suffered a significant data breach in 2018 affecting half a billion customers; an article in Forbes (2019) noted: "Marriott first revealed it had suffered a massive data breach affecting the records of up to 500 million customers on 30 November last year." Forbes commented on how the initial breach was uncovered: "The investigation continued and in October, a penetration tool called Mimikatz was discovered by the third-party investigators. This raised suspicions because the tool is also used by hackers to search a device memory for usernames and passwords and could have been used by attackers to move from Starwood to other parts of the network." From an observers' view, we can see how the breach can be linked with identity crime as the attackers went in search of usernames and passwords to traverse the network.

- **Capital One**

Capital One has been one of the most significant data breaches; CNN reported on how this data breach started.

> *Paige Thompson is accused of breaking into a Capital One server and gaining access to 140,000 Social Security numbers, 1 million Canadian Social Insurance numbers and 80,000 bank account numbers, in addition to an undisclosed number of people's names, addresses, credit scores, credit limits, balances, and other information, according to the bank and the US Department of Justice. The breach affected around 100 million people in the United States and about 6 million people in Canada, according to Capital One.*
>
> *CNN (2019)*

Again the attacker could be observed trying to obtain personal information to potentially commit further identity crimes.

2.1 Data breaches

An article on the Health IT Security website (Data Breach, 2019) gave the following definition of a data breach: "A data breach is a confirmed incident of unlawful access/disclosure of sensitive, confidential or otherwise protected data, including personal health or personally identifiable information, trade secrets, or intellectual property." Further to this definition of a data breach, it is interesting to see the impact that a data breach has on customers who pay for or use the services of a breached organisation. Chatterjee et al. (2019) discussed this stating "The news of a data breach can evoke a variety of affective reactions among consumers, including surprise, frustration, anxiety, anger, and fear."

They also discussed how organisations could lessen the impact of a data breach by starting the conversation early with its customers on how they would deal with a data breach: "We propose that a company can do this over time by starting a dialogue with its consumers from the first day." They also recommended where further investigative work could be focussed to further improve customer retention and satisfaction: "Future studies may wish to use stronger, but equivalent, forms of priming anger and fear (e.g., showing graphic videos) and then examine how the judgments of these two groups change with the scope of the data breach incident."

Solove and Citron (2018) also commented on the anxiety that customers suffer due to data breaches and how the legal system should be used to protect them: "Data-breach harms often result in victims experiencing anxiety about the increased risk of future harm."

Our legal system needs to confront data-breach harms because real costs are borne by individuals and society and because ignoring them results in inefficient deterrence.

Roberts (2019) looked at how organisations could avoid data breaches altogether through use of encryption and measuring how much investment should be made by a CISO.

The benefit of employing end-to end encryption and establishing a response team is quite simple to calculate and can be thought of as the chance of any one organisation being breached in the next 12 months multiplied by the average number of breached records times the cost benefit for one breached record – or 50% x 25,000 x $27/record = $337,500. In this hypothetical scenario, the CSO now has an annual benefit of over $300,000 to justify a security investment.

Roberts (2019)

Hammouchi et al. (2019) undertook a study on which kinds of organisations were most at risk from malicious activities: "We found that the most targeted type of organisation are medical organisations and BSO's since they possess the most sensitive personal data."

The direct impact on the organizations is mainly financial and is reflected in the means put in place to implement legal procedures or the implementation of services to protect the identity of victims.

Burn and Johnson (2018) looked at how data breaches have become inevitable due to the Internet and converging of personal and professional lives.

"The Internet is increasingly becoming a conduit for individuals' personal and professional lives worldwide." This digital ecosystem often requires the transmission of personal information across secure and insecure networks, introducing novel information security and privacy issues and a complex chain of custody for personally identifiable information (PII).

Sherstobitoff (2008) was able to surmise of what he saw was the prime reason for data breaches as being based on monetary gain "Hackers target information that is considered valuable and important to the black-market, anything that consists of personally identifiable information, corporate financial records or engineering plans that can be translated into a dollar figure will be stolen."

Newman (2017) also examined how vast amounts of data were being stored in reservoirs and hence an increasingly large target "The number of people affected by data breaches continues to rise as companies collect more and more personal data in inadequately secured data reservoirs." This could be linked back to the British Airways and Marriott breaches where vast amounts of data were targeted having been hosted in storage silos with penetrable defence.

2.2 Digital identity theft

As part of this study, it is important to understand the impact on the victim of identity theft to understand emotional and behavioural responses that a victim may suffer. Li et al. (2019) undertook a survey of 197 self-reported identity theft victims to understand the consequences. Li stated "We show that perceived victimization severity, driven by the amount of financial loss, misuse of personal information, as well as time spent addressing the incident, is a major determinant of perceived distress, and perceived distress is an important antecedent of behavioural responses ranging from refraining from online transactions and information disclosure, emotional adjustment, to more proactive engagement in self-protection such as subscribing to identity theft protection services." It therefore highlights the importance for organisations to address identity theft if it is something that eventually would stop people from using their services.

Aımeur and Schőnfeld (2011) in their articulation of identity theft address the scope that it extends further than use of payment mechanisms: "People must understand that identity theft not only affects people using their credit card or debit card, it also includes people who use their name, their Social Insurance/Security Number, online passwords and even their address."

They make an important observation that the malicious actors often stealing the information in the first place are infrequently the perpetrators who may carry out a subsequent fraud: "Data collected by hackers may not be used directly. They are sold by batch on private forums or protected IRC channels, called *carding forum*."

Aımeur and Schőnfeld (2011) also gave a concise classification of the different types of identity theft as being "Financial, Medical, Criminal, Drivers Licence, Social Security, Synthetic, Child Identity and Business."

The issue with trying to classify identity theft is that the digital world moves quickly and the categories soon become out of date and obsolete or additional categories need to be added. It is evident that social media less prevalent in 2011 is such a big source of identity theft in 2019.

2.2.1 Digital identity schemes

There have been many schemes on a national basis whereby governments have introduced a single digital identity for their citizens. Most notably is the 'Aadhaar' digital identity scheme in India which was launched in 2009. 'Aadhaar' issued a 12-digit unique identity number to all of its citizens. Kotwal et al. (2017) made the following observation.

Aadhaar, meaning foundation, refers to a 12-digit random identification number issued by the Unique Identification Authority of India (UIDAI). The project currently holds a biometric database of more than 1150 million individuals. Covering over 85% of India's population, it is the largest national biometric database in the world.

Kotwal et al. (2017)

They also commented on the issues with the Aadhaar scheme and its potential conflict of interests: "The Supreme Court of India is currently hearing a series of petitions challenging the constitutionality of Aadhaar, its compulsory linkage for the delivery of government benefits, potential for exclusion of beneficiaries; and impact on privacy, among others."

Aadhaar has been criticised in that the government of India failed to have a 'legal framework' in place to support the scheme and had no credible institutions of governance. Data breaches have been a common occurrence. Dixon (2017) observed the following:

> *In early 2017, a spate of articles were published about the ease of locating Excel files that had been posted online erroneously, originating from various Indian government offices, replete with Aadhaar numbers and demographic data, retrievable through a simple Google search; one breach resulting from a programming error led to the publication of the bank details of a million Aadhaar pension beneficiaries on a government website.*
>
> *Dixon (2017)*

Researchers from the Sardar Patel Institute of Technology (Mudliar et al., 2018) commented on how Blockchain could be adopted to aid digital identity schemes.

> *In general, many of the countries have different national identification. For instance, in India, there are several ways to identify an individual such as Aadhar, passport, driving license, etc. With the possibilities of the blockchain technology, all such identities can be consolidated and only one identification can be used for the endless applications.*
>
> *(Mudliar et al., 2018)*

Another scheme of particular interest introducing the concept of 'smart cities' is based in Singapore; Curzon et al. (2019) refer to the 'Intelligent Nation Plan' which provisions 'digital government services' to citizens including contactless payment for transport and 'mobility on demand services'.

Chalaemwongwan and Kurutach (2018) made reference to the Thai national ID database commenting on the fragmentation of the scheme in real life: "Thai national ID still segmented and distributed between government agencies and has no centralization, and it brings bad experience to the users because each service must be registered and the users have to remember the username and password for every service."

Al-Khouri (2014) also commented on digital identity schemes flourishing in Gulf Cooperation Council (GCC) and how additional focus is being made to improve the effectiveness in the public sector before it is extended to the private sector: "The government is currently working to improve promptness of access by service providers to information from the new identity card before extending its use from the public to the private sector." He commented on how GCC countries use smart cards and how they are intrinsically linked to biological features of a citizen, a form of two-factor authentication: "GCC smart identity cards serve as secure documents that uniquely identify individuals and link personal data to their own biological features, such as fingerprints and facial recognition."

Al-Khouri (2014) makes an important point on how GCC schemes differ from EU schemes whereby there is a distinction between national ID programs and digital identity: "An important difference is in the basis for the provision of the digital identity. While GCC countries are issuing digital identities as part of a national ID program, EU countries seem to distinguish between national ID programs and the digital identity, although both serve the same purpose. EU countries are driving the digital identity initiative with a clear goal of promoting the development of the digital economy."

Tammpuu and Masso (2019) have undertaken extensive analysis of the Estonian digital identity schemes. They focus on how Estonia has used digital identity schemes to pull investment into the country by way of virtual residency. This gives access to nonresidents of the country to well-established digital infrastructure.

> *The aim of electronic residency or virtual residency enabled by this programme is to give non-residents of the country, independent of their citizenship and place of residence, remote access to Estonia's well advanced digital infrastructure and e-services via government supported digital identity issued in the form of a smart identity card (the e-resident's ID).*
>
> *Tammpuu and Masso (2019)*

Also in that region, Denmark makes use of digital identity scheme to connect the population to banking services; "Denmark's Nem ID system was launched in 2010 and has grown at a similar rate to Sweden's BankID, with banks and government working together, even to the extent of inviting tenders for technology upgrades together."

As referenced by Deloitte (2019), China is also undergoing somewhat of a renaissance in respect to digital identity schemes; the South China Morning Post made comment on the project:

> *China is issuing digital versions of the national ID card as an alternative to the physical cards in use. The project is backed by the Ministry of Public Security's Research Institute and other bodies such as major Chinese banks.*
>
> *SCMP (2019)*

A scheme in Malaysia has also drawn comment from observers at the Malaya Mail.

> *Putrajaya's plan to implement a National Digital Identity (ID) is a good idea to make digital transactions seamless, but several tech observers are questioning its security and viability.*
>
> *While agreeing that the initiative is a good move, especially with the country moving towards a digital economy and Industry Revolution 4.0, Fong warned that a digital ID is more vulnerable to identity theft. Tan even went as far as saying that a well-*

designed system can even improve personal privacy, with respect to the third-parties relying on the system.

Malayamail (2019)

The McKinsey and Company back such schemes up articulating how the concept of Digital ID increases economic value; "Digital ID holds the promise of enabling economic value creation for each of these three groups by fostering increased inclusion, which provides greater access to goods and services; by increasing formalization, which helps reduce fraud, protects rights, and increases transparency; and by promoting digitization, which drives efficiencies and ease of use." (McKinsey, 2019). An important point to note is how they also make the point of reducing fraud, which again emphasises how important digital identity schemes when implemented well can prevent such negative consequences on an individual.

McKinsey in their study go on to study the general adoption of digital ID.

So far, the state of adoption of digital ID is mixed, indicating room for improvement and growth. Forty or more national or non-national digital identity programs exist today. Roughly 1.2 billion people with digital IDs live in India alone, registered in the Aadhaar program, which began in 2009.

McKinsey (2019)

They noted that the adoption of the eID in Nigeria stalled in 2017 "amid issues with public-private partnerships used to launch the program and difficulty integrating uses and functionality of more than 13 separate identification systems run by separate government agencies." This is in contrast to GCC countries as stated earlier in this study who are using the public sector as a proof of concept. McKinsey also comment on the economic value of digital identity schemes: "Our analysis of Brazil, China, Ethiopia, India, Nigeria, the United Kingdom, and the United States indicates that individual countries could unlock economic value equivalent to between 3 and 13 percent of GDP in 2030 from the implementation of digital ID programs." With growth in many countries stalled due to globalisation, the concept of a digital identity could prove to be a vote winner for governments worldwide.

3 Research methodology

It was decided that the most appropriate method to collect empirical data would be by way of online survey. An online survey was constructed consisting of five questions utilising the 'Likert' scale whereby respondents would rate their feeling/sentiment with regard to an answer by way of 1–10. These data could then be easily harvested and analysed using mathematical techniques to quantify responses. The survey was designed in such a way to generate as many responses as possible from the target audience to harvest as many results as possible. Questions were kept to a minimum so as not to lose the attention of the respondent. The author having received many requests in his commercial role to respond to surveys was well aware of how to get engagement from the survey audience. Questions were written in such a style and technique so as not to alienate the target audience or expose their lack of knowledge.

The survey consisted of the following questions:

(1) Thinking about your interaction with large organisations since the introduction of GDPR, has your perception of their cybersecurity effectiveness improved or deteriorated?

Question 1 was designed to understand the respondents' perception around the effectiveness of cybersecurity controls since the introduction of GDPR. This question would give valuable insight to institutions on the weighting of investment on GDPR as opposed to cybersecurity investment.

Scale 1 (deteriorated) to 10 (improved)

(2) How likely are you to subscribe to services from companies certified as GDPR compliant rather than those that are not?

Question 2 follows on from Question 1 and focusses on GDPR compliance itself without the thought of cybersecurity. The response could then be used to evaluate the response to question 1 to give true context and qualification of the answer.

Scale 1 (less likely) to 10 (more likely)

(3) Would you continue to use the services of an institution affected by a serious data breach?

Question 3 was constructed whereby the concepts of GDPR and cybersecurity had already been introduced and focussed on serious data breaches. The assumption that if an institution had good GDPR compliance and cybersecurity controls in place, how would be business be affected if they suffered a serious data breach.

Scale 1 (less likely) to 10 (more likely)

(4) Thinking about your own digital identity that you may use to submit tax returns or apply for government benefits online, would you be happy for the government to share this (federation) with commercial organisations to provision services to you online?

Question 4 brings in one of the key research objectives around digital identity and the federation of public identities with commercial organisations.

Scale 1 (not happy) to 10 (very happy)

(5) Over the next 5 years, would you be prepared to pay more for a digital service whereby the provider has demonstrated cybersecurity effectiveness (i.e. no data breaches)?

Question 5 builds on all previous questions and interrogates the respondent on their spending inclination with regard to cybersecurity spending by the institution.

Scale 1 (less happy) to 10 (very happy).

4 Data analysis and critical discussions

4.1 Question 1: Thinking about your interaction with large organisations since the introduction of GDPR, has your perception of their cybersecurity effectiveness improved or deteriorated?

The responses from the survey group indicated overwhelmingly that cybersecurity effectiveness had improved since the introduction of GDPR. Ninety-eight percent of the survey group indicated that effectiveness had at least stayed the same or improved. Seven percent of respondents had responded with the maximum perception of improvement. Twenty-eight percent of respondents had said that effectiveness had stayed the same, whilst only 1% said there had been a deterioration.

The research reflects well on the introduction of the GDPR regulation that users of those services perceive that cybersecurity has improved. Very few respondents indicated that cybersecurity had actually deteriorated which is positive news for the European Regulators. With the European Union bringing in this regulation in 2018, they could acclaim that it has forced institutions to improve their cybersecurity as one of the methods for becoming GDPR compliant. Whilst the costs for introducing the GDPR regulation would have been substantial both for the European Union and institutions operating within it, it could be argued that billions of Euros have been saved as a result of improved cybersecurity effectiveness. This in turn makes the European Union attractive to investors who wish to operate their businesses from the jurisdiction. This can be evidenced in Estonia as referenced in the literature review, Estonia has a digital identity scheme which attracts individuals to acquire residency in the country and hence consequential investment can or may follow.

4.2 Question 2: How likely are you to subscribe to services from companies certified as GDPR compliant rather than those that are not?

Ninety-seven percent of those surveyed indicated that their likelihood to subscribe to services from companies certified as GDPR compliant either stayed the same as previous or they were more likely inclined to subscribe. Thirty-two percent of respondents indicated the highest likelihood of choosing a GDPR compliant company. Only 1% of respondents indicated that they were least likely to subscribe to GDPR compliant services. Interestingly, 15% of respondents indicated that their likelihood had remain unchanged.

Following on from the first question in the survey, the results from those surveyed show a positive feeling to organisations compliant with GDPR. The executives from public and commercial institutions can utilise this information when making decisions about cybersecurity investments. It could be used as a negotiating pitch that investment in cybersecurity inherently brings about improved GDPR compliance resulting in greater customer retention and attraction. This reflects in an improved balance sheet for commercial organisations and potentially increased funding for public organisations from central governments. This could also be argued that this reflects well on governments in that they are managing the data of its populous well which results in increased share of the vote at the ballot box.

4.3 Question 3: Would you continue to use the services of an institution affected by a serious data breach?

Ninety-five percent of respondents reacted in a manner that they were either less likely or that there was no change in their attitude to continuing to use services of a company that had experienced a data breach. Twenty-five percent of respondents reacted by indicating they were least likely to using services of such a company. Two percent of respondents indicated that they were more likely to use services. Eight percent responded that there was no change with regard to how they thought about using a company affected by a data breach.

Following on from the first two questions of the survey, it is clear that from the response to this question that population were less likely to use services from a company or institution that had suffered a data breach. With compliance to GDPR being mandatory in the European Union, it could be assumed that users of services assume that their data are being managed securely and effectively. If and when there is a data breach, it could be argued that the perception for the cause of data breach is the ineffectiveness of cybersecurity controls that an institution demonstrates. This in turn leads to trust and confidence in the organisation reducing and potentially loss of customer share or engagement in using institution services. This could potentially result in the failure of the institution, so the executive of the institutions must consider investment in cyber effectiveness very carefully. This aligns with what Roberts (2019) commented on that following a data breach customer loss is at 3.4% which for a US equivalent company results in $2.05 million in costs. Equifax which suffered a data breach affecting 147 million individuals would have attracted costs that may have crippled the company financially. The same could have been applied to Marriott following the data breach in 2018 that affected a billion customers. As Chatterjee et al. (2019) stated "a data breach instils' fear, anger and anxiety in those affected resulting in their loss of patronage." These results from this survey appear to backup this sentiment to companies experiencing a data breach. Li et al. (2019) also commented on the impact on victims of identity theft, potentially caused by a data breach at a larger institution. This caused distress as a result of financial loss and misuse of information. Again, this filters through to the lack of trust in an institution by the user and loss of patronage.

4.4 Question 4: Thinking about your own digital identity that you may use to submit tax returns or apply for government benefits online, would you be happy for the government to share this (federation) with commercial organisations to provision services to you online?

The responses to this question indicated that 92% of respondents were not happy or their feelings remain unchanged with regard to their identities being shared between public and commercial entities. Overwhelmingly, 48% of respondents indicated they were not happy by choosing the most negative rating from the scale. Twelve percent of respondents remained unchanged with regard to their feelings about the concept. Two percent of respondents indicated they were very happy about credentials being federated by choosing the most positive rating.

In previous questions the answers have illustrated that companies that are not GDPR compliant or those that do not evidence cyber effectiveness will lose market share or patronage. This question looks at the relationship between public and private organisations with regard to federation of services through utilisation of digital identity schemes. Again the overwhelming sentiment is that users would not want their digital identity to be shared between public and private institutions. This is a surprising response following earlier responses to questions in the survey that regardless of GDPR they still view federation in a negative manner. There were a significant number of data breaches resulting in stolen identities from public institutions, these results back up the results that users are not ready for federated services, even after the introduction of GDPR. Also, from the commercial sector, the data breach at Capital One whereby 140,000 social security numbers were exposed, the weakness could be attributed to the commercial sector cyber controls. Of particular concern, federation would be seen as an issue between organisations in the health sector as they host the most sensitive data they are prone to attack as discussed previously by Hammouchi et al. (2019). Simmonds (2015) had also discussed the trust necessary between two entities for a digital transaction to take place securely and effectively. If this trust is not in place, the service is subject to failure. This sentiment appears to back up the results with regard to answers on this question regard to federation. In India, where the Aadhaar digital identity scheme is prevalent, there had been a spate of breaches reported in 2017 as a result of data been extrapolated into Excel spreadsheets and exposed on the Internet. Applying the sentiment from the response to this survey to that country would definitely appear to backup that they would not want their digital identities federated between public and private entities.

GCC countries have recognised the sentiment of its population and identifies with the response from this survey. They recognise that they must improve their effectiveness of cybersecurity control in the public sector before federating with the private sector as discussed previously by Al-Khouri (2014). Denmark had already taken the step by federating its national digital identity scheme with banking services. Since the introduction of GDPR in 2018, it would make an interesting piece of further research to survey the users of these services to see how secure they feel their data are and how successful the scheme has become.

4.5 Question 5: Over the next 5 years, would you be prepared to pay more for a digital service whereby the provider has demonstrated cyber security effectiveness (i.e. no data breaches)?

Ninety percent of respondents reacted that they would pay the same or more with regard to companies demonstrating cybersecurity effectiveness. Fifteen percent indicated with the maximum rating on the scale that they would be prepared to pay more. Four percent indicated that they would wish to pay less even though companies had been more cyber secure. Sixteen percent of the respondents' remained in different that their preparedness remained 'about the same'.

It has been established the sentiment with regard to GDPR compliance, cybersecurity effectiveness, and the federation of services between public and private sectors. This question illustrates the sentiment with regard to users of services and whether they would be prepared to pay more or less for these services. From the results the responses have indicated that the majority of users would be prepared to pay more for effective cybersecurity controls over the next 5 years. Sherstobitoff (2008) commented that the prime reason for data breaches was monetary gain. With this being a potential fear of the respondents that they could directly or indirectly lose money through a data breach, it would explain the sentiments on why those who responded would want to pay more. It could be argued that by an individual paying more for a service, they would in effect save money by protecting their data and consequently not experiencing digital identity theft that could result in financial loss. The 'executive' of institutions may also consider what Roberts (2019) outlined that the level of investment in cyber controls, that is, encryption has a direct link to the number of records exposed through a data breach. If an executive invests more to protects its data, it could theoretically pass on the costs to its user base without too much challenge. This makes the investment much easier to justify and implement with this knowledge known.

5 A proposed framework for delivery of cyber effective services in the GDPR era

The previous sections focussed on social attitudes to cyber effectiveness in the GDPR era. The general perception was that as a result of GDPR compliance that cyber effectiveness had improved and that consumers were willing to spend more on services to ensure that their personal information was protected. However, delivering cyber effective services is a complex matter for any executive to master and deliver. Often the underlying factor on investment in cyber defences is available budget finely balanced and attuned to the risk appetite of the board. There are also other factors that have to be considered with regard to delivery of cyber effectiveness services, and this is often determined goals set by the board. The goals need to be measurable so that performance can be measured and evidenced to key stakeholders involving shareholders in the private sector and the general public in the public sector. Throughout the literature review, it became evident that there were no frameworks discussed with regard to delivery of cyber effective services in the GDPR era. As GDPR is such a new legislation, there has been a vacuum with regard to academic writing on the subject. Therefore objectives and key result (OKR) framework was applied to guide to delivering effective services through the lens of a commercial entity.

5.1 OKR framework

Many larger companies including the likes of Google, Facebook, and Netflix have adopted OKRs (outcomes/objectives and key results) as a way of delivering services effectively.

OKR is a framework for defining and tracking objectives and their outcomes. OKRs were the concept of Andy Grove who first discussed the concept in his book "High Output Management" (Grove, 1983). OKRs as shown in Fig. 4, drive teams to deliver output in short periods of time (quarter years). OKRs are supported by having a plan or initiative.

This study looks at the delivery of cyber effective services in the GDPR era through the lens of a commercial organisation utilising the OKR framework. Commercial organisations are increasingly 'customer obsessed' whereby the customer may be an internal stakeholder or external service user. This study has adopted eight OKRs that an executive may wish to adopt and deliver services against. These are 'scalability, delivery, adoption by design, risk, workforce, establish trust, verification, and executive'. As part of this research, we will also look at the environmental factors affecting the delivery of OKRs as a whole through adoption of the PESTLE framework. The strength of OKRs is that they focus on short-term planning whereby the initiatives supporting the goals are achievable and agreed by supporting stakeholders. Table 1 illustrates the OKRs that an executive board may consider for the delivery of a 'Zero Trust' cybersecurity programme in its infancy (Q1 in the next financial year).

Following the agreement and adoptions of OKRs, the executive may wish to detail a 90-day plan. Often, using tooling and techniques may be adopted to aid this process, that is, agile scrum.

Having adopted the OKR framework, it is recommended that environmental factors are considered by the executive with oversight of delivery of the programme of works, by adopting 'PESTLE' as a critical framework for evaluating environmental factors.

5.1.1 Political

When considering political factors influencing cybersecurity delivery, there is one political issue of note in the European Union. Brexit is a key factor within the European Union. At time of writing the United Kingdom is scheduled to leave the EU on 31 January 2020. The Conservative and Unionist Party (a pro Brexit political party) in the United Kingdom have just won a general election on 13 December 2019 with a convincing majority of 80 seats. This gave them a large mandate to effect leaving the European Union in a timely manner.

Objectives	Key results	Plans
• Aspirational • Qualitative • Time bound	• Measurable • Quantitative • Difficult	• Actions/initiatives • High level • Important

FIG. 4 OKRs—constituent parts (OKR's, 2019).

Table 1 OKRs to deliver cybersecurity effectiveness in Q1.

Objective (Q1)	Key results	Initiative
Ensure scalability	Adopted methodology signed off by board	Adopt methodology, way of working that allows cyber solutions to be delivered at scale, that is, review methodology agile/waterfall
Delivery	Deliver solution in timely manner	Assemble diverse team and adopt methodology that allows to deliver at pace
Adoption by design	Deliver solutions that have undergone security due diligence	Ensure security requirements are documented for all projects. Develop threat modelling techniques. Agree SLAs on stability of solutions
Risk	Establish risk programme	Adopt and publish risk framework to assess cyber risk
Workforce	Establish diverse talented team to deliver security initiative	Assemble talented 'diverse' team to oversee delivery of security initiatives Document job profiles, review internal talent, and publish recruitment budget
Establish trust	Gain trust of internal and external stakeholders	Establish communications plan which incorporate 'security and awareness training plan'
Verification	Establish programme to verify access and allowable activities	Establish processes and technologies to constantly verify activities and access. Establish multifactor authentication to verify access of users
Executive	Establish ownership of cybersecurity by executive	Establish policies and embed governance in executive committees with oversight

Brexit would have a big impact with regard to the implementation of GDPR in the United Kingdom and if they continue to align themselves with compliance of the legislation. Plans may also be affected for UK companies subject to which political party has been elected. Institutions in the public sector would be particularly affected that rely on government funding and grants to fund their cyber schemes.

5.1.2 Economical
Economic factors that must be assessed include exchange rates, consumer spending, and interest rates. Interest rates are currently very low in the European Union allowing companies to borrow more to invest in their cyber schemes; however, particular attention must be paid to other environmental factors which could cause interest rates to increase which may be due to globalisation and fear of recession in world economies. It has happened before most notably after the 2008 Global financial crisis and years of recession and austerity that followed. Institutions should factor in enough budgetary contingency to deal with a financial crisis.

5.1.3 Social
Social environmental factors are also very important to institutions delivering services. An ageing population is one factor that will have a considerable effect on how services are delivered and consumed. Ageing populations are less likely to engage with technically delivered services due to their perceived complexity and distrust of having their data looked after by a third party. Organisations must engage with their stakeholders to ensure

that trust is established through awareness campaigns and articulation of the safeguards they have in place to protect personal data. As the survey showed, a data breach can critically damage an organisation potentially leading to extinction. Social demographics within countries also needs to have paid attention to it. Socially deprived sectors of the population may not have access to services delivered by technology as those from more affluent parts of the population. Services should be targeted at all parts of the population in an equal manner.

5.1.4 Technological

From a technological perspective, there has been momentous change evidenced over the past decade with regard to provisioning of services in the digital arena. Most notable is the advancement of blockchain and artificial intelligence deployed via technologies to detect and prevent malicious intent. These technologies often referred to as 'disruptive' can be adopted to replace manual processes often undertaken by a static workforce. The technologies through machine learning can trace disruptive patterns of network traffic and social behaviours to prevent data breaches and subsequent lateral malicious activities.

5.1.5 Legal

Legal factors must also be taken into consideration when planning and provisioning services especially from a digital privacy perspective. An example in the United States is a new bill being discussed at Senate level to protect digital consumer rights (CNBC, 2019). The bill known as 'Miranda' rights looks to "grant citizens the right to request their information from companies and ask for data to be deleted or corrected." The bill's objective is to "provide consumers with foundational data privacy rights, create strong oversight mechanisms, and establish meaningful enforcement" (Cantwell, 2019). This is very similar to the GDPR regulation in the European Union. If the bill gets approved, it will add an additional overhead onto companies in the United States to provision their services in a compliant manner or be subject to large fines similar to the EU. This will reduce the competitive advantage that US companies may have over EU companies causing consumers to potentially move away investment from US to EU companies. The bill was put forward by a Democratic Senator 'Maria Cantwell'. The bill is disputed by the Republican party and large technical companies, and there is a lack of clarity about how it should be applied, be it either federal or state level. Mark Zuckerberg has been in conversation with other technology leaders with regard to bringing in the legislation at federal level, so there is a common approach to digital privacy across the United States.

5.1.6 Ethical

Ethical and environmental factors include sustainability, tax practices, supply chain, and pollution/carbon emissions. With regard to ethical considerations that most affect cybersecurity effectiveness may be the about the amount of data institutions are harvesting on individuals. Ethan Cowan a masters student at the Harvard Extension School made the following point: "The technology has far outpaced the public policy and political knowledge and I don't think that we have – not just in the United States, but as a species – come to terms with the radical effects of the amounts of data that we're generating and what it can tell us about ourselves and about individuals." (Gonzalez, 2019). Organisations must consider the confidentiality, integrity, and availability of these data in addition protect the consumer as to how it should be used.

6 Conclusions and future work

The overall objective of this research was to understand the correlation between digital identities, national identity schemes, GDPR, and data breaches. The critical review looked at each research objective in isolation to understand the latest news and concepts about the survey matter. A detailed study of each concept was undertaken referencing leading academic journals. Following the study a survey was published to help understand the correlation between the four research objectives to gain vital knowledge which would influence public and private leaders on their investment decisions with regard to cyber spend. A subsequent analysis of the OKR framework was adopted with application to a commercial case study looking to provision digital services securely. This was followed by a critical discussion of the approach adopting the PESTLE framework to steer conversation.

The research referenced many leading commentators on the subject matters. Leading subject matter experts commented that GDPR was costly and difficult to implement. It was also mentioned that GDPR was also not fully defined in law which also led to the difficulty in implementing and understanding. However, GDPR was a force for good in that it forced institutions to report on data breaches that previously may have not been revealed, take, for instance, the data breaches at British Airways and Marriott.

Commentary was made that a leading cause for an actual data breach was caused by the 21st century plague of ransomware-type viruses. It was also commented upon that some institutions were still failing to report data breaches. If this was the case, with the knowledge that the respondents from the survey gave with regard to not using services from impacted institutions by data breach, it gives a worrying sentiment that executives are not investing enough in GDPR compliance and cyber defences.

It is recommended that further study be focussed on 'digital identity' and the issues that have arisen around security and privacy. For instance, if an individual with malicious intent gained access to someone's digital identity, what mechanisms are institutions putting in place to prevent them being used? Also, with the harvesting of individuals private data by institutions, that is, credit card information and login credentials, what are institutions doing to protect the privacy of these data and ensuring it does not fall into the wrong hands. Further study could focus on the compliance of the company with 'privacy' laws in addition to GDPR. Privacy and trust building must be at the heart of any institution's objectives and customers when provisioning services to users and customers.

References

Aïmeur, E., Schönfeld, D., 2011. The ultimate invasion of privacy: Identity theft. s.l., s.n.

Al-Khouri, A.M., 2014. Digital identity: transforming GCC economies. Innovation 16 (2), 184–194.

Bates, A., Ul Hassan, W., 2019. Can data provenance put an end to the data breach? In: Systems Attacks and Defences, July/August. IEEE Security & Privacy, pp. 88–93.

Breitbarth, P., 2019. The impact of GDPR one year on. Netw. Secur. 2019, 11–13.

Burn, A.J., Johnson, A., 2018. The evolving cyberthreat to privacy. IT Prof. 20 (3), 64–72. https://ieeexplore. ieee.org/document/8378980 Cited on 18 June 20.

Cantwell, M., 2019. Consumer Online Privacy Rights. Available from: https://www.cantwell.senate.gov/ imo/media/doc/COPRA%20Bill%20Text.pdf. (Accessed 7 December 2019).

Chalaemwongwan, N., Kurutach, W., 2018. A Practical National Digital ID Framework on Blockchain (NIDBC). s.l., s.n.

Chatterjee, S., Gao, X., Sarka, S., Uzmanoglu, C., 2019. Reacting to the scope of a data breach: the differential role of fear and anger. J. Bus. Res. 101, 183–193

Choi, J.P., Jean, D., Kim, B., 2019. Privacy and personal data collection with information externalities. J. Public Econ. 173, 113–124.

CNBC, 2019. CNBC. Available from: https://www.cnbc.com/2019/11/26/senate-democrats-reveal-new-copra-digital-privacy-bill.html. (Accessed 7 December 2019).

CNN, 2019. Capital One data breach: a hacker gained access to 100 million credit card applications and accounts. CNN.   Available from: https://www.cnn.com/2019/07/29/business/capital-one-data-breach/index.html. (Accessed 7 September 2019).

Curzon, J., Almehmadi, A., El-Khatib, K., 2019. A survey of privacy enhancing technologies for smart cities. Pervasive Mob. Comput. 55, 76–95.

Data Breach, 2019. AMCA Files Chapter 11 After Data Breach Impacting Quest, LabCorp. Available from: https://healthitsecurity.com/news/amca-files-chapter-11-after-data-breach-impacting-quest-labcorp. (Accessed 24 May 2019).

Deloitte, 2019. Digital Citizen. Available from: https://www2.deloitte.com/us/en/insights/industry/public-sector/government-trends/2020/government-digital-identity.html. (Accessed 24 June 2019).

Dixon, P., 2017. A failure to "do no harm"—India's Aadhaar biometric ID program and its inability to protect privacy in relation to measures in Europe and the US. Heal. Technol. 7 (4), 539–567.

EU, 2019. Available from: https://eur-lex.europa.eu/legal-content/en/TXT/?uri=CELEX%3A31995L0046. (Accessed 16 June 2019).

Forbes, 2019. Marriott CEO Reveals New Details About Mega Breach. Available from: https://www.forbes.com/sites/kateoflahertyuk/2019/03/11/marriott-ceo-reveals-new-details-about-mega-breach/#5e137d7155c0. (Accessed 7 July 2019).

Gonzalez, M.G., 2019. Radcliffe Felllow Talks Technological Advancement, Privacy and Ethics. Available from: https://www.thecrimson.com/article/2019/12/6/berman-iot-talk/. (Accessed 7 December 2019).

Grove, A., 1983. High Output Management. Random House, New York.

Hammouchi, H., Cherqi, O., Ghogho, M., El Koutbi, M., 2019. Digging deeper into data breaches: an exploratory data analysis of hacking breaches over time. Procedia Comput. Sci. 151, 1004–1009.

Holm, E., Mackenzie, G., 2014. The Importance of Mandatory Data Breach Notification to Identity Crime. IEEE.

Hoofnagle, C.J., van der Sloot, B., Borgesius, F.Z., 2019. The European Union general data protection regulation: what it is and what it means. Inf. Commun. Technol. Law 28 (1), 65–98.

Kotwal, V., Parsheera, S., Kak, A., 2017. Open Data & Digital Identity: Lessons for Aadhaar.

Li, H., Yu, L., Wu, H., 2019. The impact of GDPR on global technology development. J. Glob. Inf. Technol. Manag. 22 (1), 1–6.

MacMillan, K., 2019. Struggling with the GDPR. Comput. Fraud Secur. 2019 (8), 14–19.

Malayamail, 2019. Malyamail. Available from: https://www.malaymail.com/news/malaysia/2019/08/29/the-good-the-bad-the-id-tech-experts-weigh-in-on-putrajayas-new-national-di/1785254. (Accessed 29 October 2019).

McDowell, B., 2019. Three ways in which GDPR impacts authentication. Comput. Fraud Secur. 2019 (2), 9–12

McKinsey, 2019. Digital Identification: A Key to Inclusive Growth. Available from: https://www.mckinsey.com/business-functions/mckinsey-digital/our-insights/digital-identification-a-key-to-inclusive-growth. (Accessed 7 July 2019).

Mudliar, K., Harshal Parekh, H., Bhavathankar, P., 2018. A comprehensive integration of national identity with blockchain technology. In: International Conference on Communication. Information & Comp, Mumbai.

Newman, L.H., 2017. If You Want to Stop Big Data Breaches, Start With Databases. Available from: https://www.wired.com/2017/03/want-stop-big-data-breaches-startdatabases. (Accessed 17 July 2019).

OKR's, 2019. Objectives Key Results. Available from: https://objectives-key-results.com/.

Roberts, S., 2019. Learning lessons from data breaches. Netw. Secur. 2018 (11), 8–11.

SCMP, 2019. A Look at China's Push for Digital National ID Cards. Available from: https://www.scmp.com/tech/article/2129957/look-chinas-push-national-digital-id-cards. (Accessed 19 October 2019).

Sherstobitoff, R., 2008. Anatomy of a data breach. Inf. Secur. J. 17 (5–6), 247–252.

Simmonds, P., 2015. The digital identity issue. Netw. Secur. 2015 (8), 8–13.

Solove, D., Citron, D.K., 2018. Risk and anxiety: a theory of data-breach harms. Tex. Law Rev.. https://texaslawreview.org/wp-content/uploads/2018/03/Solove.pdf Cited on 18 June 20.

Sullivan, C., 2018. Digital identity—from emergent legal concept to new reality. Comput. Law Secur. Rev. 34, 723–731.

Tammpuu, P., Masso, A., 2019. Transnational digital identity as an instrument for global digital, citizenship: the case of Estonia's E-residency. Inf. Syst. Front. 21, 621–634.

The New York Times, 2019. The New York Times. Available from: https://www.nytimes.com/2019/07/08/business/british-airways-data-breach-fine.html. (Accessed 7 July 2019).

Verizon, 2019. 2018 Data Breaches Report. Available from: https://enterprise.verizon.com/resources/reports/DBIR_2018_Report.pdf. (Accessed 9 March 2019).

Wilson, S., 2018. A framework for security technology cohesion in the era of the GDPR. Comput. Fraud Soc. 2018 (12), 8–11.

7

Balancing privacy and public benefit to detect and prevent fraud

Sudhir Gautam and Hamid Jahankhani
NORTHUMBRIA UNIVERSITY, LONDON, UNITED KINGDOM

1 Introduction

In 2016 the then UK prime minister asked permanent secretary to tackle all fraud that affects the public sector. He asked for a collaborative approach to stop fraud and ensure a common defence against it across the public sector. For this to materialise, there needs to be a much more effective data sharing to tackle fraud, but clarity around when data sharing between public bodies can be exercised continues to be a challenge.

The scale of fraud is alarming HM Revenue and Customs (HMRC) estimation, which is at least £15 billion is lost due to tax evasion. The Annual Fraud Indicator values the collective loss to the UK economy from identified and hidden fraud at £193 billion per annum, with much of this being undetected. Fraud losses to public are estimated to be 40.3 billion (Annual Figure Indicator, 2013).

Although different public bodies operate different frameworks and have different structures, the threats faced by fraudsters are similar. Loss to taxpayer, reputational risk, and trust erosion in public sector are some of risks that public sector may face as a result of fraud.

Fraudsters do not recognise organisational boundaries and may make multiple attacks across government, so there is a great benefit in coming together of public bodies to tackle the issue of fraud. Through bringing together of different parts of the puzzle across various departments, only then the cross organisational fraud be detected and managed well.

It has been widely accepted for some time that data sharing can be a very important tool towards fraud prevention, but public bodies continue to face dilemmas on whether to share or not, with who, under what circumstances and how far is the sharing justified.

There is a strong evidence that suggests legal uncertainty of what is lawfully permissible may be hindering data sharing. The resulting outcome of this uncertainty could lead to department reluctance and unwillingness to not pursue data sharing. It is apparent that these doubts are over legal powers and not so much the data protection act or the GDPR, but the data protection regulation is often cited as a failure to effectively share.

Strategy, Leadership, and AI in the Cyber Ecosystem. https://doi.org/10.1016/B978-0-12-821442-8.00002-1
© 2021 Elsevier Inc. All rights reserved.

This issue has been made worse due to recent high-profile data breaches. Data sharing has become a thorny issue as legal implications of inadequate data sharing can range from criminal prosecution, through reputational damage, to civil penalties.

'There is little dispute that the targeted use of government-held personal data, shared between the bodies that can make best use of it, has the power to fuel smarter public services and improve lives' (Pope and Blake, 2019), and 'the government is set on using data more effectively to help deliver better public services'.

Whilst data sharing is inevitable to better service delivery such as fraud detection, it is also of equal importance that the respective body that carries out the sharing meets the relevant regulatory and legal requirements.

> *Public authorities hold many databases with rich datasets that could be used to identify patterns of fraud or known fraudsters. For example, when fraud is identified within one dataset, may be possible to highlight frauds which may not yet have come to light, or to confirm patterns of fraud if these results can be shared with other data sets.*
>
> *Fraud Review (2019, p. 96)*

Despite the quantity of data, the landscape to utilise this remains complex and fragmented.

> *UK legal framework around data sharing is often described as highly complex. New legislation, such as the EU General Data Protection Regulation (GDPR) and Data Protection Act 2018 can create a nebulous system for public-sector organisations to navigate.*
>
> *(Data in the Public Sector, p. 7)*

Ensuring the processing and sharing of personal data is lawful and may be a challenge when the legal framework is not clear, especially if the process to create new information sharing legal powers between entities can take years. This could create a fog of confusion over what can and cannot be shared.

This chapter analyses the data sharing between public bodies to better understand whether there are indeed legal challenges that hinder data sharing in government to combat fraud, what they are and whether and how they can be overcome.

Wells (2011) defines fraud as 'any crime which uses deception as its main modus operandi'. The oxford dictionary defines "'Fraud' as wrongful or criminal deception intended to result in financial or personal gain."

The Fraud Act 2006 provides legislation on the offence and defines three main 'elements': 'fraud by false representation', 'fraud by failing to disclose information', and 'fraud by abuse of position'. In a similar vein, Farrell quotes 'fraud can be perpetrated in three clearly defined ways)'. These are 'by false representation', 'by abuse of position', or 'by failure to disclose' (Farrell et al., 2005).

In 2014 government introduced fraud definitions and typologies to provide a consistent approach for the reporting of fraud and error in the public sector. To ensure a consistent approach, in 2014, the government introduced legal definition of fraud (as set out in the Fraud Act 2006).

'The making of a false representation or failing to disclose relevant information, or the abuse of position, in order to make a financial gain or misappropriate assets'. The true scale of fraud will never be measured due to the nature of deception that goes undetected. 'National Fraud Authority (NFA), which estimated that fraud costs the UK economy around £52 billion annually, of which £21.3 billion is lost by the private sector, £20.6 billion by public sector, £9.1 billion by individuals' (Fraud Review, 2019). 'The Annual Fraud Indicator 2013 indicated the loss to the UK economy from fraud at £52 billion'. In a report issued by Association of Chief Police Officers (ACPO) in 2006, a minimum figure for the direct costs of fraud was almost £13 billion (Annual Figure Indicator, 2013).

> *According to NHS's latest estimate, fraud and other similar crimes cost NHS 1.29 billion a year and has set a target of 2018 to establish an information sharing framework with appropriate partner bodies to enable the detection and identification of fraud using data matching.*
>
> *Counter Fraud Authority (2019)*

Gee and Button (2015), in their review of the financial cost of fraud, estimated losses to the UK economy to be £98.6 billion annually; this is also highlighted in the attorney general conclusion that 'fraud is second only to drug trafficking in the economic harm that it causes to the UK'.

In a report the Cabinet Office and the National Fraud Authority state that 'the theft of taxpayers' money on such a huge scale has a direct impact on reducing the resources that can be spent on frontline services. 'Every pound stolen from government means that there is less to spend on health, education, policing and defence' (Gee et al., 2011; Kemp, 2010).

2 Data sharing and fraud detection

For some time now, there has been a desire to transform public services and enable effective data sharing culture to deliver a joined-up service.

'A great deal of work is already being carried out to improve best practice and understanding of systemic data sharing issues': by the Information Commissioner's Office through the creation of the Data Sharing Code, by the Independent Information Governance Oversight Panel led by Dame Fiona Caldicott, and through the creation of the National Health Service Information Governance Toolkit (Department of Health, 2013).

But information sharing can be a complex task (Yang and Maxwell, 2011) because whenever personal data are collected, accessed, or analysed, there is some degree of risks associated with individual's privacy. Furthermore, sharing of this information introduces additional risks for, for example, the data holders may delete the data after a defined period, but once shared, they may lose control and may remain elsewhere, whereas the data loss risk may still reside with the data owner. This is also coupled with uncertainty over what information and under what circumstances can this be shared. After all, there is no explicit one-size-fits-all power to share information. And 'the legislative infrastructure surrounding personal data sharing in the UK is complex and not widely understood. This greatly complicates the prospects for, and process of, greater collaboration for combating economic crime' (Watson, 2019).

The current government has had similar aims to harness data effectively in the public sector. In 2016 it published a consultation on the better use of data in government. This formed the basis of the data-sharing principles found in the Digital Economy Act, which was meant to facilitate the creation of data-sharing gateways between public bodies for much more efficient data sharing to detect fraud.

In 2011 a report was published by The Counter Fraud Taskforce Interim Report, recommending 'collaborative approach to share in order to combat fraud' (Gee et al., 2011), and as part of the national fraud strategy, the then prime minister asked Francis Maude, the then cabinet secretary, to tackle all types of fraud affecting the entire public sector (Cabinet office, 2015).

The strategic plan to reduce fraud, Fighting Fraud Together, was published in 2019, and it recognised the benefits of working together to tackle fraud and indicated the loss of 38bn (Cabinet Office, 2019) placed a significant focus on awareness and prevention as previously endorsed by the Home Office.

These claims are validated by National Fraud Authority in 2013 that 'it costs £0.15 billion by the voluntary sector and £0.9 million, although there have been some reservations about the data quality' (Annual Figure Indicator, 2013).

Aforementioned points demonstrate substantial losses to the UK economy due to fraud. In an inspection carried out by HMICFRS under the mandate of then home secretary between March and July 2018, it was reported that there is no national strategy for tackling fraud. In the same report, it was reported by one analyst that 'everything is against fraud. It is not a priority, not sexy, people don't report it and it is difficult to prove, which takes time, resources and money' and as such is not a national policing priority (HMICFRS, 2019, p. 50).

Yang and Maxwell (2011) stated that organisations have shifted from a model that emphasised information protection to one where cross-organisational information sharing is the new goal, and there have been few notable moments in the past 20 years that have given rise to the importance of data sharing:

- The Soham case in 2002 has given rise to importance of data sharing in the United Kingdom after the murder of two school girls in Cambridgeshire. From the serious case, review conclusion was that, although not the fault of the police forces, 'better use of information might have prevented the Soham murders' (Thomas and Walport, 2008, p. 2).

- Lack of information sharing was highlighted on 11 September 2001 terrorist attacks in New York that led to numerous reviews and changes in the way American federal, local policing, and intelligence agencies share information.
- The high-profile case to date in the United Kingdom remains the (alleged) loss of 25 million child benefit records by HMRC in 2007. This resulted in the Poynter Report of 2008 (The Review of Information Security at HM Revenue and Customs).

These high-profile cases highlight the importance and benefits of timely information sharing and call for a wider sharing, thus enabling prevention and detection in a timely manner.

Data sharing can mean different things to different people, and for the purpose of this research, the definition as described by Yang and Maxwell (2011) is adopted. The author defines two distinct types:

1. interorganisational information sharing, which focusses on sharing information amongst two or more organisations,
2. interagency/department information sharing, which focusses on sharing information within the organisation and across its departments.

And to make it more relevant and current, the definition is coined by the Information Commissioner 'the disclosure of data from one or more organisations to a third party organisation or organisations, or the sharing of data between different parts of an organisation'.

In 2016 the Cabinet Office urged councils and other public sector bodies to join the Cabinet Office's National Fraud Initiative after a review found it had saved almost £200 m in 2 years. The scheme is based on matching 'within and between public and private sector bodies to prevent and detect fraud' (Public Finance, 2016). More recently, Laura Hough, CIPFA's head of research and development for counter fraud, told delegates that government departments must work together to tackle the issue (Hough, 2019).

From some of the examples earlier, few initiatives have grown piecemeal over time since the National Fraud Authority was established in 2008 to improve the way fraud was managed. One example is National Fraud Initiative (NFI) led by the Cabinet Office (2015) 'a scheme for data matching to identify fraud. This includes collection and matching of participating organisations, over 1300 and most from public sector. Data source includes taxation, benefits, residence employment. This is centrally collected, and cross referenced across the entire data set; details of matches which may indicate potential fraud are returned to the providing organisation for further investigation' (Petraşcu and Tieanub, 2014).

There are few other cases where large public sectors such as HMRC and DWP for some time have been leading the way in combating fraud through effective data sharing. For example HM Revenue and Customs (HMRC) shares real-time PAYE information (known as RTI) with the Department for Work and Pensions (DWP) so that DWP can calculate entitlement to universal credit and have worked on complex projects that took several years to make the data systems compatible. This shows how policy imperatives, collaborative working, and continued commitment despite the difficulties and complexities can achieve results. But it is clear that more needs to be done. The current and past governments have been attempting for some considerable time to get fully committed. Whilst there is handful of such initiatives, the stark reality is that more needs to be done to improve a culture of sharing, and as indicated by The National Audit Office in its report, 'Government lacks a clear understanding of the scale of the fraud problem and departments vary in their ability to identify and address fraud risks'.

3 Data privacy

The public sector data sharing consultation review by the National Archives stated 'There are many myths surrounding the Data Protection - it appears to be one of the most frequently cited yet least understood pieces of legislation', and for this reason, what is and is not permissible may be inhibiting data sharing in some departments. 'Some government departments decide not to pursue new data sharing initiatives because of doubts over what their legal powers allow them to do' (Ministry of Justice, 2011).

To add to already complex data protection law, the advent of GDPR adds extra layers of complexities with its far-reaching requirements, increased data subjects' rights, and significant increase in penalty and fines. Peter Carey puts it 'the dawn of new era in the context of new regulation, the GDPR' (Carey, 2019).

At the surface the GDPR seems straightforward and easy to understand, but due to its overarching scope, for example, what constitutes personal information and its breadth, it has become subject of misinterpretation, impressing on organisations that they seek to protect information from other organisations or use of this information from other organisations or for any other additional purposes. And as a result the requirements are interpreted over cautiously due to uncertainty about its provisions.

The authors believe that due to the lack of clear legal advice for those with day-to-day operational duties, to make better use of data often hinders information sharing. The resulting impact is either noncompliance or defer the decisions to share data.

With new obligations such as mandatory:

(a) Data Privacy Impact Assessment (ICO, 2018; DPIA, 2018),
(b) Maintain and demonstrate a record of all processing activities,
(c) Increased data subject rights, GDPR, are often quoted as 'death of innovation'.

But at the same time, this can be seen a flip side of the coin because through increased transparency and demonstrating better accountabilities, GDPR can provide a fresh opportunity towards effective data sharing across departments and help restore public confidence.

4 The General Data Protection Regulation (GDPR) landscape

Purpose specification is the GDPR fundamental principle. It says that personal data may only be 'collected for specified, explicit and legitimate purposes and not further processed in a way incompatible with those purposes' and that they should be 'adequate, relevant and not excessive in relation to the purposes for which they are collected and/or further processed' and 'accurate and, where necessary, kept up to date' (Legal, social, economic and ethical conceptualisations of privacy and data protection).

For fraud detection purposes a fraud offence must exist against public bodies, for example, to disclose information to take action against that fraud, offence must be listed as a 'specified person' in Schedule 8 of the Digital Economy Bill. And all such sharing must also comply with the requirements of the Digital Economy Act 2017 and the data protection legislation.

First and foremost, GDPR rules set out by the Data Protection Directive are only applicable to data concerning natural persons and define personal data as.

> *Any information relating to an identified or identifiable natural person ('data subject'); an identifiable natural person is one who can be identified, directly or indirectly, in particular by reference to an identifier such as a name, an identification number, location data, an online identifier or to one or more factors specific to the physical, physiological, genetic, mental, economic, cultural or social identity of that natural person.*
>
> *(Art. 4)*

In addition, GDPR Article 6 sets out the requirements for personal data sharing to be lawful, the following conditions must be met. These are as follows:

(a) **Consent**: the individual has given clear consent for you to process their personal data for a specific purpose.
(b) **Contract**: the processing is necessary for a contract you have with the individual or because they have asked you to take specific steps before entering into a contract.
(c) **Legal obligation**: the processing is necessary for you to comply with the law (not including contractual obligations).
(d) **Vital interests**: the processing is necessary to protect someone's life.
(e) **Public task**: the processing is necessary for you to perform a task in the public interest or for your official functions, and the task or function has a clear basis in law.
(f) **Legitimate interests**: the processing is necessary for your legitimate interests or the legitimate interests of a third party, unless there is a good reason to protect the individual's personal data which overrides those legitimate interests. (This cannot apply if you are a public authority processing data to perform your official tasks.)

It is no doubt that GDPR places an increased right to individuals and increased control over how their data are processed, but there is often a misnomer that the data processing relies on individuals' consent (a) and that they may withdraw this consent any time. This is correct, but this does not apply in each case. A vast majority of public sector personal data processing will be carried out under (e) public task function (the ICO, lawful basis for processing). For example, processing and registering a birth are legal requirements or collection and administration of tax or information disclosure for fraud prevention purposes, and this is not dependent on individuals' consent. But for public bodies to rely on public task function, the underlying task, function, or power must have a clear basis in law.

For example, for fraud detection purposes, a fraud offence must exist against public bodies, for example, to disclose information to take action against that fraud offence must be listed as a 'specified person' in Schedule 8 of the Digital Economy Bill. And all such sharing must also comply with the requirements of the Digital Economy Act 2017 and the data protection legislation.

Digital Economy Act (DEA) 2017 is a good example of government initiative to fight fraud through data sharing. It provides a legal framework to share in relation to fraud data provided the overarching UK laws are complied with. These are (a) the data protection legislation, (b) Parts 1–7 or Chapter 1 of Part 9 of the Investigatory Powers Act 2016 (and, until that Act comes fully into force, Part 1 of the Regulation of Investigatory Powers Act 2000), and (c) GDPR and the Human Rights Act 1998.

5 Use of public task as data sharing function to combat fraud

'The power of a government department to share data with other departments comes from laws, regulations, polices or its administrative functions' (Wang, 2018), and the processing of personal data is prohibited but might be permissible if conditions set out in previous section are met. This means a lawful basis in primary legislation is required to share data to combat fraud if public task as a function is to be relied upon.

Processing personal data under any other conditions could constitute unlawful, unless consent is sought and granted of those subjects whose data you would be processing, but this adds whole loads of nuances, for example, getting data subjects' explicit consent, flip side to this is that the subjects could withdraw their consents. Thus the data controllers legal entity require powers that are set out in law even before considering the requirements set out in GDPR.

For departments to use 'Public Task as a function, both parties need to consider whether they have the necessary legal powers' (Home Office, 2015), 'power to share personal data with other departments derive from laws, regulations, polices or its administrative functions' (Wang, 2018).

The public task function can be used in following circumstances:

- In the exercise of official authority. This covers public functions and powers that are set out in law.
- To perform a specific task in the public interest that is set out in law.

The GDPR does not provide a definition of <u>official authority</u> as it is dependent on national law that determines if an entity is public authorities. "The 'exercise of official authority' will likely be based on whether there is a law determining the purpose of the processing and requiring and enabling the processing to take place by the controller" (Carey, 2019).

Official authority is defined by the Data Protection Act 2018 and it states "For the purposes of the GDPR, the following (and only the following) are 'public authorities' and 'public bodies' under the law of the United Kingdom:

(a) a 'public authority as defined by the Freedom of Information Act 2000',
(b) a 'Scottish public authority as defined by the Freedom of Information (Scotland) Act 2002 (asp 13)',
(c) 'an authority or body specified or described by the Secretary of State in regulations, subject to subsections (2), (3) and (4)'" (DPA, 2018).

5.1 Necessity and proportionality test

'Article 26 of the GDPR states where two or more controllers jointly determine the purposes and means of processing (in this case to combat fraud), they shall be joint controllers' (Chapter 4, GDPR, eur-lex-europa.ew). As the sharing of information to detect fraud is going to take place between two parties, joint controllers must fulfil a number of additional obligations under the GDPR. 'Each joint controller needs to fulfil its obligations under the GDPR'.

In addition, the data controllers must demonstrate that sharing personal data is necessary and the data being shared are proportionate in the interest that sharing is balanced against the subjects right to privacy and freedoms rights and the processing fulfils the function specified.

A robust explanation given by the ICO on 'necessity' is as follows:

a. Purpose of data sharing to detect fraud is valid.
b. Such purposes can only be achieved by the processing of personal data.
c. The processing is proportionate to the aim pursued (ICO, necessity test, 2001).

5.2 Purpose limitation

It is important that, when carrying out further processing activities, entities should verify that those operations are compatible with the initial purpose. Otherwise 'the new processing activities will only be lawful by way of renewed consent or by way of a statutory justification in EU Member State law allowing for a change of the data processing purpose'.

5.3 UK legal landscape

At present, there is no general statutory power that permits public bodies to share data, and as such according to the principles of administrative law, public bodies can disclose personal information only if they have been granted the power to do so by statute.

It means reuse of personal data is only lawful given that the authorities carry out these tasks in public interest or in the exercise of official authority vested in it. Legislation may provide that information collected for one purpose may be used for another purpose, for example, Commissioners for Revenue and Customs Act 2005, Section 17 provides that information acquired by the Revenue and Customs in connection with a function may be used by them in connection with any other function.

As discussed in previous section, public sector processing is likely to be justified by and find a stronger legal basis in public task as a legitimate basis enabling them to carry out their functions, that is, for processing in furtherance of legitimate objectives in the public interest to close the fraud gap and as a result better public service delivery.

There are three key primary legislations that allow for data sharing for fraud prevention purposes:

- The Social Security Fraud Act 2001 (referred to as the Fraud Act) introduced powers for authorised Department for Work and Pensions (DWP) and local authority officers to obtain information from listed organisations about their customers, to help combat fraud against the benefit system.
- Local Audit and Accountability Act 2014.
- Serious Crime Act 2007.

5.4 Human Rights Act 1998

As EU laws have direct effect on UK law, under Article 8 of Human Rights Act 1998, Section 1, 'it is unlawful for a public authority to interfere with an individual's privacy unless that interference is authorised by one of the specific exceptions contained in Article 8 (2)' (legislation.gov.uk).

In a report the parliament committee members of Human Rights Act and the Data Protection concluded that the 'Government's approach of including very broad enabling provisions in primary legislation and leaving data protection safeguards to secondary legislation' (p. 7; Data Protection and Human Rights, House of Lords House of Commons Joint Committee on Human Rights).

In practice, this means that in addition to any other rules laid down by UK legislation or case law, any public body that interferes with an individual's privacy must be able to demonstrate that the interference with the obligation to respect private and family life is as follows:

- 'the law and is necessary in a democratic society in the interests of national security',
- 'public safety or the economic well-being of the country',
- 'for the prevention of disorder or crime',
- 'for the protection of health or morals',
- 'for the protection of the rights and freedoms of others'.

5.5 Data sharing powers

The power to collect, use, share or otherwise process information can be derived from common law, as can restrictions on these powers, such as the common-law duty of confidentiality. A breach of confidence can occur when information that one might expect to be confidential is communicated in circumstances entailing an obligation of confidence but later used in an unauthorized way.

Ministry of Justice (2011)

'Government departments headed by a Minister of the Crown may be able to rely on common-law powers to share data where there is no express or implied statutory power to do so. The general position is that the Crown has ordinary common-law powers to do whatever a natural person may do' (unless this power has been taken away by statute) (Ministry of Justice, 2011).

For example, 'the Statistics and Registration Service Act (SRSA) 2007 created the UK Statistics Authority (referred to as the Statistics Board in the Act), with the statutory objective of promoting and safeguarding the production and publication of official statistics that serve the public good; Office for National Statistics is the Authority's executive office and in 2017, the Digital Economy Act amended the SRSA, providing ONS with permissive and mandatory gateways to receive data from all public authorities and Crown bodies, and new powers to mandate data from some UK businesses; in limited circumstances data held by ONS may also be shared with the devolved administrations solely for statistical purposes' (ONS, Data security, governance and legislation policies).

In addition to common-law powers, 'the Crown also has prerogative powers. Although there is no single accepted definition of the prerogative, these powers are often seen as the residual powers of the Crown, allowing the executive to exercise the historic powers of the Crown that are not specifically covered by statute. Residual powers may relate to foreign affairs, defence and mercy, for example. However, Parliament can override and replace prerogative powers with statutory provisions' (Public Sector Data Sharing: Guidance on the Law). To add to the complexity, most of the information gateways are permissive and not mandatory. They leave a discretion to the body with information on whether or not to disclose information. These can result in issues with data sharing as body that holds the information may have no or insufficient incentive to disclose and may not do so, and this may raise issues with data sharing.

Public bodies which are established by statute (e.g. local authorities and HMRC) have only such powers as are conferred upon them by statute. This means that those bodies have no powers under the common law or the Crown prerogative and must rely solely on their express or implied statutory powers.

Ministry of Justice (2011)

And DWP officers who have the Secretary of State's authorisation or local authority officers (where that local authority has responsibility for investigating social security benefit fraud) who have been authorised by their chief executive or chief finance officer may use these powers and can rely on Social Security Fraud Act 2001 (referred to as the Fraud Act 2001) to obtain information from specified persons and organisations about their customers to help detect benefit fraud.

Administrative—or public—law is the body of law governing the activities of government and other public bodies. Before a public body can engage in data sharing, it must first establish whether it has a legal power to share the data in question. 'Where a public body acts outside its powers, the activities can be challenged before the courts by way of a judicial review' (Ministry of Justice, 2011).

The nature of the public body and the rules governing its activities play a crucial part in determining the legal basis upon which it acts and whether its activities are lawful. 'If a public body does not have the power to collect, use, share or otherwise process data, it will be acting unlawfully, and the fact that an individual may have consented will not make the activity lawful' (Ministry of Justice, 2011).

> *Nonministerial departments or those created by statute cannot have prerogative or common law powers. Any data sharing by them must be based on statutory powers (express or implied), while statutory powers can also impose obligations on non-public bodies to share or disclose information. For example, section 52 of the Drug Trafficking Act 1994 makes it an offence to fail to report suspicion of drug money-laundering activities, thereby placing a statutory duty on people and organisations to share relevant personal information with the police.*
>
> *Ministry of Justice (2011)*

Express statutory powers can be enacted to allow the disclosure of data for particular purposes. Such powers may be permissive or mandatory. A permissive statutory power describes legislation that gives an organisation the power to share data, for example, Section 115 of the Crime and Disorder Act 1998. A mandatory statutory power requires an organisation to share data when requested. An example of this is Section 17 of the Criminal Appeals Act 1995 (Ministry of Justice, 2011).

Even where there is no express statutory power to share data, it may still be possible to imply such a power. To this end, 'where the actions or decisions of a public body are incidental to meeting the requirements of an expressed power or obligation, they can be considered to have an implied right or power to act' (Ministry of Justice, 2011).

> *Statutory bodies carry out many activities based on implied statutory powers. This is particularly true of activities such as data collection and sharing, which are not always express statutory functions.*
>
> *Ministry of Justice (2011)*

6 Research findings

The principal objective of this research is to analyse the various strands of legal necessity that must be met to enable effective personal data sharing for fraud prevention purposes. So the obvious place was to start dialogue with data protection and legal professionals in government to get a firsthand opinion on what the key challenges are in data sharing for fraud prevention purposes. Although security remains a key challenge and an assurance factor too, this research focussed on legal aspects of data sharing; therefore the questions were designed to probe legal requirements and ramifications of data shares.

So a targeted approach through a qualitative approach was preferred. The approach was aimed so that selected few in the relevant departments could be targeted and extract value from their experiences. This ensures better understanding of the 'as is' and 'would like to be' assessment.

At the core of this research lied a question whether and what are the legal barriers that hinder personal data sharing to combat fraud in public sector. So, research was conducted in two phases: survey and interview. All ethical consideration where considered through-out the research. The participants were informed in advance that their response would not be used for purposes other than research. Majority of the respondents were from the public sector and bound by the civil service code. To ensure no sensitive information was divulged, respondents were requested not to put in their details or any information that lead to their identification. None of the respondents were forced to participate. The key findings of the research were as follows:

- More need to be done to improve data sharing in government.
- An effective data sharing can help combat fraud in public sector.
- And finally the most important question for this research
  - Privacy and confidentiality concerns (including policies and laws that limit access) were the biggest concern amongst the group.
  - This was closely followed by fear of misinterpretation of data sharing powers.

7 Critical discussions

The core aim was to examine 'perceived' legal barriers that prevent wider data sharing in public sector. Whilst data sharing to improve fraud detection and prevention is the context for the purpose of this research, this can equally apply to other government functions where data sharing is impacted.

Data sharing ad nauseum in public sector have been going on for some considerable time mostly to improve better policy making and statistical purposes.

There are other concerns such as safeguards and security of data, but these are out of the scope in this chapter.

It is worth noting that the government has seen some success in data sharing in public sector. Initiatives such as National Fraud Initiative and CiFAS have gone some way in addressing fraud through data sharing, but the research shows that this has grown piecemeal despite the commitment from the current government and the past government to have a joined-up government to combat fraud.

Based on the this research, it appears that key factors hindering data sharing appear to be the confusion and misunderstanding about the legal framework and how it relates with data protection, human rights and the common law, overlapped with the new privacy legislation, and GDPR. These factors combined together could have contributed to an overly cautious approach.

This issue of confusion is further exacerbated by spates of information misuse highlighted by media, for example, private car clamping company use of the Driver and Vehicle Licensing Agency (DVLA) database to enforce civil parking infringements or misuse of surveillance techniques to establish whether a child was living in the catchment area of a local school.

This research flagged three different strands to data sharing in public sector. This in itself formed part of the critical analysis. These strands are as follows:

- **Administrative power,** data sharing powers that public bodies must have;
- **Common law**, the duty of confidentiality;
- Statutory regulations such as **GDPR** (DPA, 2018) and the **Human Rights Act 1998 (HRA)**.

7.1 Administrative powers

Data sharing must be covered by the specific legislation that govern the service or policy that data sharing supports as there is no general legislative power to disclose data.

Public authorities need to have the administrative power (vires) to share. These powers either drive from primary legislation, for example, HMRC or through common law such as the DWP. Some of these powers also provide information collected for one purpose may be used for a different purpose.

If authorities act outside of the limited statutory powers, it is said to be ultra vires. The receiving body must also have legal powers to receive the data.

The extent of the powers necessary will be determined by the status of the data in question. There are three broad types of power: statutory powers, implied statutory powers, and common law or prerogative powers.

- **Express statutory powers**

Such powers are introduced to enable disclosure of information for particular purposes. Sharing under express statutory powers may be mandatory or permissive.

For example,

Mandatory: *Section 17(3) of the Local Government Act 2003.*
Permissive: *Section 115 of the Crime and Disorder Act 1998.*

These powers are often contained in primary legislation, and they also provide further powers to share information, but there is no obligation to share. This may result in cultural issues of data sharing as the data owners would need to be convinced on why to share. On the other hand, same powers can be applied to share data, for example, disclosure under Part V of the Police Act 1997.

- **Implied statutory powers**

Such powers are dependent on the legal status of the organisation and require interpretation of parliament intention in the legislation. These are also dependent on functions and powers of those organisations, for example, Section 111(1) of the Local Government Act 1972 provides 'Local Authorities shall have power to do anything… to facilitate, or is conducive or incidental to, the discharge of their functions…'.

In other words a public body may be required to share information because of the duty to cooperate. And for this reason, information collected for one purpose may be used for another purpose.

As an example, Paragraph 7, Schedule 5 Tax Credits Act 2002 allows HMRC to disclose information held for the purposes of functions relating to tax credits, child benefits, or guardians allowance to be supplied to authorities responsible for administration of housing benefit or local council tax reduction or to a person authorised to exercise such functions.

- **Common law or prerogative powers**

A department headed by a Minister of the Crown, for example, HMRC, may also be able to establish data sharing powers under the common law and will have the powers to perform functions. This is regulated by the Commissioner for Customs and Revenue Act 2005.

o **The Ram Doctrine**

Data sharing under this exemption can be somewhat unclear. In 1945 Sir Glanville Ram, the first parliamentary counsel, gave legal advice that a minister of crown may, as an agent of the Crown, exercise any powers which the Crown has power to exercise, except in so far as he is precluded from doing so by statute. This basically implies that the crown and therefore the secretary of state have all the necessary powers and therefore do not need to point to any statutory power.

7.2 The law of confidentiality

Law of confidentiality may be waived by consent, or alternatively, disclosure may be lawful if it is necessary in the public interest, that is, disclosing confidential information needs to be balanced with the fact that confidentiality is itself in the public interest. This is the crux.

7.2.1 Human Rights Act 1998

Once the power to share data has been assessed, the next step is to assess whether personal information sharing agenda's breaches the Human Rights Act (HRA). Data sharing gateways must be compatible with the Human Rights Act. It must be noted that this right is not absolute, and the act sees the need for a balance between the society and the individual/s, and interference can be legitimate in certain circumstances:

- national security
- public safety
- protection of the economy
- prevention of crime and disorder
- protection of health or morals
- protection of the rights and freedoms of others

But this interference must be aligned with the law and must be proportionate in both volume and scope.

It is important to demonstrate proportionality in that data sharing has appropriate limitations in both volume and scope. This means that the public bodies must demonstrate that there is no other way in which the purpose of fraud detection and prevention can be achieved through lesser intrusion on individual's privacy rights.

There are numerous instances where the European Court of Human Rights has considered a number of cases involving the disclosure of personal data between public authorities.

In the case of M.S. v Sweden (Application number 00020837/92 dated 27 August 1997) the applicant contested the disclosure of her medical history to the Swedish Social Insurance Office following a claim for industrial injury compensation. The disclosure was made pursuant to relevant provisions in Swedish law, namely, the Secrecy Act and the Insurance Act.

The court found that the disclosure was not in breach of Article 8 of the ECHR because of the following:

(a) There was a legal basis for the interference.
(b) The object of the disclosure was to determine the allocation of public funds and so was in the pursuit of a legitimate aim, namely, the economic well-being of the country.
(c) The disclosure was necessary as the medical records were relevant to the applicant's compensation claim.

In addition, disclosure was subject to effective and adequate safeguards as the relevant legislation provided that duties of confidentiality applied which were subject to criminal and civil penalties if breached. Accordingly the measure was not disproportionate to the aim pursued.

7.3 General Data Protection Regulation (GDPR)

The GDPR does not create statutory gateways for data sharing. The person or organisation must already have the power to share the information before considering any restrictions under the Data Protection Act.

If the sharing involves personal data, which are most likely to be the case for fraud prevention and detection purposes, but it is a requirement that the entire process, starting from collection of the data, the data protection obligations ate fulfilled.

These obligations are primarily on data controllers as the data owner. Whether data controllers are indeed the owners of citizen data is a different question. A very simple definition of data controller is 'a body or an entity that determines the purpose on how personal data will be processed or for what purposes', and this can be a good indication on considering what the most appropriate lawful basis may be.

Although there are six lawful bases for processing of personal data, public task as a lawful basis for sharing of fraud data is the appropriate lawful basis for processing/sharing of personal data for fraud preventions purposes.

The consent of citizens is the gold standard to process their personal data for fraud detection basis. This is not always possible, nor it is feasible because it adds administrative burden on individuals and costly, for example, how the consent will be handled or what form of consent should take place. And consent may fulfil one specific purpose and not cater for further use of citizen data for other purposes. Very rarely is data collected from citizens for fraud purposes unless on few examinations where the subject is undergoing an investigation. This has resulted in citizens contacting relevant departments asking them to stop sharing their data as they have withdrawn consent. But the reality is that government departments have a legal duty to process citizen data, and therefore 'lawful basis' is the most appropriate fit.

In addition, the ICO advises that where personal data are likely to be shared regardless of whether consent has been given or not, it can lead individuals to believe they have a genuine choice. By seeking consent is inherently unfair and likely to breach of the data processing principle which states that information must be used fairly and lawfully.

Common law of confidentiality also needs to be accounted for, and the general rule is that consent should not be sought where there is a statutory obligation or court order to disclose or where the sharing needs to take place regardless of whether the individual consents or not.

Therefore it can be said with sufficient confidence that for almost all sharing for fraud prevention purposes 'carry out a specific task in the public interest which is laid down by law; or exercising official authority (for example, a public body's tasks, functions, duties or powers) which is laid down by law' is appropriate.

So, it would appear that problem does not seem to lie with the regulation itself as it provides a sensitive approach to data sharing because it neither restrict or promote data shares. Instead, it provides a set of principles and circumstances when it can be fair and lawful to process personal information.

So for data sharing and GPDR to work in concert, (a) lawful basis must be established, (b) must be processed fairly, (c) be established and demonstrated 'necessity and proportionality', and (d) be transparent to data subjects through privacy notices on what the purpose is and give data subjects rights not to intrude their rights and freedom.

7.3.1 The Data Protection Act 2018

The GDPR should be read side by side with the Data Protection Act 2018 (the DPA, 2018). It states processing of personal data that is necessary for the following:

(a) 'the administration of justice',
(b) 'the exercise of a function conferred on a person by an enactment or rule of law',
(c) 'the exercise of a function of the Crown, a Minister of the Crown, or a government department'.

8 Digital Economy Act 2017

The Digital Economy Act was introduced to streamline and make data sharing in public sector more efficient in combating fraud, but it is inhibited by the more permissive environment for data sharing across which makes it optional and not mandatory. For example, personal information disclosed by the Revenue and Customs can only be used for purposes other than the purpose for which it was originally disclosed with the Revenue and Customs' consent. This means fraud powers are permissive powers, which mean the persons who are potentially able to share information under them can choose whether to do so. Risk here is that gateways for same purposes are either too narrow or broad, and due to overcautious attitudes, bodies may opt in for the narrower that would restrict the use of efficient and effective use. There is also this fear of unlawful access or error that would result in breach of confidentiality.

9 Conclusions

Timely information sharing can go a long way towards combating fraud in public sector as public authorities hold many databases with rich datasets. This could be exploited to identify patterns of fraud or known fraudsters or highlight frauds which may not yet have come to light or to confirm patterns of fraud.

Most of the data within government is contained in 'silos', and due to complex legal framework, the authorities have found it difficult to understand what information they hold that how this could assist other departments in combating fraud.

Also the recent highly publicised information security incidents by mainstream media has raised eyebrows and cause paranoia amongst citizens whether data provided for one purpose are indeed lawful to use it for a completely different purpose.

As a result the fate of data sharing has often resulted in two outcomes, either defer the decision to share despite the benefit or decision to share is based on what feels right as oppose to what the law says, for example, the recent NHS and Home Office fiasco.

GDPR also has contributed to some of this confusion more recently; although not the fault of GDPR, due to incorrect interpretations, it has left citizens feeling that they have a genuine choice about how their information is processed or shared.

The Digital Economy Act (DEA) goes some way in addressing some of the barriers to data sharing, by establishing 'clear and robust' legal gateways, which enable public authorities to share relevant information more easily. There is a barrier in that most of the information gateways under the DEA are permissive. This means there is no obligation on data holding department to disclose data for the benefit of receiving department. This is more a cultural issue than legal, for example, not pursing such initiatives due to lack of incentives.

Another complexity is around of lawful basis, Article 6.1.(e) of the GDPR for processing of personal data for fraud purposes. Whilst this may sound like a new GDPR requirement, but it is similar to the old condition for processing for functions of a public nature in Schedule 2 of the Data Protection Act 1998. To qualify under this requirement, it must be taken into account whether a legal instrument adopted on the basis thereof foresee a public task in this context (edps.eurpoa.eu, p. 6).

So GDPR principles in themselves are not so much a barrier to effective data sharing as they are neither inhibiting nor promoting. Instead, it only provides framework that balances individual's protection versus resulting benefits that derive from it.

At present, there is no general statutory power that permits public bodies to share data, and every time information is shared, public-sector organisations must go through the process of creating or finding the right legal 'gateway' to enable sharing in a secure way.

Powers statutorily provided enables public bodies to share data within specific circumstances or conditions, and these add significant complexity to the issue of data sharing as there are manifold gateways in place. As an example, there are over 260 for HMRC and more than 60 gateways for the DWP. These gateways spread over 50 odd pieces of legislation.

There needs more awareness of how the current legal framework operates with respect to public bodies' existing powers to collect, use, and share personal data and the interaction of these powers with data protection provisions, and following principles must be complied with to restore public trust:

- adequacy, relevance, and proportionality: 'adequate, relevant, and nonexcessive in relation to the purposes for which they are collected and/or further processed';
- accuracy: 'accurate and, where necessary, kept up to date' and that 'every reasonable step must be taken to ensure that data which are inaccurate or incomplete are erased or rectified';
- fairness and lawfulness: 'processed fairly and lawfully'.

References

Cabinet Office, 2015. Eliminating Public: Sector Fraud (The Counter Fraud Taskforce Interim Report). National Fraud Authority. https://assets.publishing.service.gov.uk/government/uploads/system/uploads/attachment_data/file/61023/eliminating-public-sector-fraud-final.pdf (Accessed 18 September 2019).

Cabinet Office, 2019. Fighting Fraud Together. (Online) Assets.publishing.service.gov.uk (web archive link, 11 September 2019) Available at: https://assets.publishing.service.gov.uk/government/uploads/system/uploads/attachment_data/file/118501/fighting-fraud-together.pdf (Accessed 11 September 2019).

Carey, P., 2019. Practical Law: The Leading Online Legal Know-How Service. https://legalsolutions.thomsonreuters.co.uk/en/products-services/practical-law.html?LastSFDCCampaignID=7011B000001xWK9QAM&utm_campaign=PL-Branded&utm_source=Google%20Adwords&utm_medium=Paid%20Search&gclid=EAIaIQobChMIp96IrfSN6AIVRMjeCh0XMQx1EAAYASAAEgIR2PD_BwE (Accessed 11 September 2019).

Counter Fraud Authority, 2019. Leading the Fight against Fraud. (Online). Available at: https://cfa.nhs.uk/resources/downloads/documents/corporate-publications/Leading%20the%20fight%20against%20NHS%20fraud_NHSCFA%20strategy%202017-20%20V2.1.pdf (Accessed 11 September 2019).

Department of Health, 2013. Information: To Share or Not to Share. Government Response to the Caldicott Review. https://assets.publishing.service.gov.uk/government/uploads/system/uploads/attachment_data/file/251750/9731-2901141-TSO-Caldicott-Government_Response_ACCESSIBLE.PDF (Accessed 9 September 2019).

DPA, 2018. Data Protection Act. http://www.legislation.gov.uk/ukpga/2018/12/contents/enacted (Accessed 15 December 2019).

DPIA, 2018. The Data Protection Act 2018. http://www.legislation.gov.uk/ukpga/2018/12/contents (Accessed 8 August 2019).

Farrell, G., Clark, K., Ellingworth, D., Pease, K., 2005. Of targets and supertargets: a routine activity theory of high crime rates. Internet J. Criminol. 1–25. Retrieved from: http://www.internetjournalofcriminology.com/Farrell,%20Clark,%20Ellingworth%20&%20Pease%20-%20Supertargets.pdf (Accessed 12 July 2019).

Fraud Review, 2019. The Fraud Review. Webarchive.nationalarchives.gov.uk (web archive link, 11 September 2019) (Online). Available at: https://webarchive.nationalarchives.gov.uk/20070222120000/http:/www.lslo.gov.uk/pdf/FraudReview.pdf (Accessed 11 September 2019).

Gee, J., Button, M., 2015. The Financial Cost of Fraud 2015: What the Latest Data from around the World Shows. PKF Littlejohn & University of Portsmouth, London.

Gee, J., Button, M., Brooks, G., 2011. The Financial Cost of UK Public Sector Fraud: A less Painful Way to Reduce Public Expenditure. MacIntyre Hudson, Milton Keynes.

HMICFRS, April 2019. Fraud: Time to Choose, An Inspection of the Police Response to Frauds. https://www.justiceinspectorates.gov.uk/hmicfrs/wp-content/uploads/fraud-time-to-choose-an-inspection-of-the-police-response-to-fraud.pdf ISBN: 978-1-78655-784-1 (Accessed 04 August 2019).

Home Office, 2015. Data Sharing for the Prevention of Fraud Code of Practice for Public Authorities Disclosing Information to a Specified Anti-Fraud Organisation Under Sections 68 to 72 of the Serious Crime Act 2007. https://assets.publishing.service.gov.uk/government/uploads/system/uploads/attachment_data/file/415469/Data_Sharing_for_the_Prevention_of_Fraud_-_Code_of_Practice__web_.pdf (Accessed 11 September 2019).

Hough, L., 2019. Examining the Risks of Fraud and Corruption in Local Government Procurement. https://cipfaannualconference.org.uk/wp-content/uploads/2019/07/Laura-Hough.pdf (Accessed 15 December 2019).

ICO, 2018. https://ico.org.uk/ (Accessed 1 July 2019).

Kemp, G., 2010. Fighting public sector fraud in the 21st century. Comput. Fraud Secur. 11, 16–18.

Ministry of Justice, 2011. Public Sector Data Sharing: Guidance on the Law. https://webarchive.nationalarchives.gov.uk/20150603223548/https://www.justice.gov.uk/downloads/information-access-rights/data-sharing/annex-h-data-sharing.pdf (Accessed 11 September 2019).

National Fraud Authority, 2013. Annual Fraud Indicator. National Fraud Authority, London.

Petraşcu, D., Tieanub, A., 2014. The role of internal audit in fraud prevention and detection, 21st International Economic Conference, IECS 2014. Procedia Econ. Financ. 16 (2014), 489–497.

Pope, L., Blake, P., 2019. Categories: Analysis and Factual Trends, Making Organisations Work Well, Transforming Frontline Services through Better Data Sharing. Blog, 13 February 19Cabinet Office, UK. https://quarterly.blog.gov.uk/2019/02/13/transforming-frontline-services-through-better-data-sharing/ (Accessed 11 September 2019).

Public Finance, 2016. National Fraud Initiative Saves Nearly £200m in Two Years. https://www.publicfinance.co.uk/news/2016/11/national-fraud-initiative-saves-nearly-ps200m-two-years (Accessed 8 July 2019).

Thomas, R., Walport, M., 2008. Data Sharing Review Report; Performance and Innovation Unit, Privacy and Data-Sharing. July 2008 https://amberhawk.typepad.com/files/thomas-walport-datasharingreview2008.pdf (Accessed 8 August 2019).

Wang, F., 2018. Understanding the Dynamic Mechanism of Interagency Government Data Sharing, Government Information Quarterly. vol. 35(4). pp. 536–546 October 2018.

Watson, C., 2019. Information and Intelligence Sharing in the Fight Against Fraud. (Doctoral Thesis) https://researchportal.port.ac.uk/portal/en/theses/information-and-intelligence-sharing-in-the-fight-against-fraud-and-intellectual-property-crime(2ff700ab-e208-4928-b958-3bfc63c08f16).html (Accessed 11 September 2019).

Wells, J., 2011. Corporate Fraud Handbook—Prevention and Detection, third ed. Wiley, New Jersey.

Yang, T., Maxwell, T.A., 2011. Information-sharing in public organizations: a literature review of interpersonal, intra-organizational and inter-organizational success factors. Gov. Inf. Q. 28 (2011), 164–175.

8

Securing the digital witness identity using blockchain and zero-knowledge proofs

Lynton Lourinho[a], Stefan Kendzierskyj[b], and Hamid Jahankhani[a]

[a]NORTHUMBRIA UNIVERSITY, LONDON, UNITED KINGDOM [b]CYFORTIS, SURREY, UNITED KINGDOM

Abbreviations

BC	blockchain
CIA	confidentiality, integrity, and availability
DC	digital custodian
DCoC-IoT	digital chain of custody over Internet of Things
DE	digital evidence
DI	digital identity
DID	decentralised identifier
DLT	distributed ledger technology
DPoS	delegated proof of stake
DW	digital witness
IdM	identity management
IdP	identity provider
IoT	Internet of Things
KYC	know your customer
OCP	official collection point
PI	physical identity
PoS	proof of stake
PoW	proof of work
RP	relying party
SE	secure element
SSI	self-sovereign identity
SSO	single sign-on
TPM	trusted platform modules
ZKP	zero-knowledge proof

1 Introduction

Over 60% of the world's population will be living in cities by the year 2030. Whilst mass urbanisation occurs, city stakeholders at large will become more reliant on smart technologies and will require some form of digital identity to perform online transactions.

Strategy, Leadership, and AI in the Cyber Ecosystem. https://doi.org/10.1016/B978-0-12-821442-8.00010-0
© 2021 Elsevier Inc. All rights reserved.

1.1 Billion people lack formal identification, and with urbanisation on the rise, how will cities be able to validate true identities to justify basic services such as security, education, and healthcare to city dwellers. Identifying users securely is a requirement for Internet-based services though identities shouldn't be restricted to people. Internet of Things (IoT), smart technologies, and nonhuman entities are playing an important role in transacting data and values, therefore governing these entities should be just as crucial.

As service providers rushed to have an online presence in the last 20 years, they have not been able to assure security of customer personal data. The lack of data governance and poor controls has led to some of the largest data breaches in recent years. Many are now realising that the need to be in control of their own personal data is possible as seen with the emergence of combining blockchain with self-sovereign-based technologies. Many research projects are currently in motion to understand the impact of mass urbanisation, some of which have highlighted that large congregations of people living in close proximity may lead to moral and social disorder. Applying preemptive measures by organisations and agencies to maintain urban order is necessary though meeting individuals' privacy and security concerns must be taken into consideration. The digital witness (DW) concept is one approach that may provide digital evidence (DE) to authorised entities via a digital chain of custody (DCoC). The concept may assist urban dwellers in assisting authorities and could meet individual's security concerns in the context of this chapter and research.

1.1 Identity

Identity can be defined as being a specific person or being oneself and not another, and verification of identities can be defined as the act of establishing or recognising a particular person or object. Initially, identification was used in social interaction and was only later used for economic reasons. Characteristics that were sufficient for the purpose of social interaction could be defined as physical appearance and voice recognition which depended on human memory though the need for individuals to exchange more information about one another arose when the complexities of economic transactions developed. Identities in the context of information systems can be defined in two broad categories: physical identity (PI) and digital identity (DI).

1.2 Physical identities

The purpose of identifying an individual is to link the identity to a stream of data to associate the data with an individual. Table 1 can be used as a basis to differentiate between the various characteristics of formal identification.

Acceptable methods such as presenting national identity cards, passports, or driving licences already exist for authenticating personal information (PI), but these methods are susceptible to theft and can be altered and falsified.

Table 1 Characteristics of formal identification.

Definition	Characteristics
Appearance	How individuals' look
Behaviour	How individuals interact with one another
Names	How individuals are referred to by others
Codes	How individuals are referred to by organisations
Knowledge	What an individual knows
Token	What an individual has
Physiology	What an individual is

A study by Toapanta et al. (2016) finds that the Ecuadorian general directorate of civil registry and identification contains a vast sum of database inconsistencies; apparent examples are as follows:

- the altering of birth registration dates,
- issuing of dual identity cards for individual citizens,
- identity cards which contain incorrect parents' names,
- citizens which are reflected as deceased on other public organisation's records but aren't updated in its own database.

Such examples suggest doubts over the country's governance process which results in a lack of confidentiality, integrity, and availability (CIA) of citizen information. Assurance of identity is dependent on the type of information originally captured, transmitted, and stored, and protecting these data comes with privacy, technical, and security challenges. Further challenges to prove citizen's identities in a growing population add pressure to source cost-effective solutions for governments and many global entities. Many nations rely on biometrics for registration, and identity enrolment though biometrics has proven to be fallible due to false-positive and false-negative error rates.

1.3 Enrolment mechanisms

Biometrics are physical security mechanisms which deny any unauthorised access via authentication. This security process is referred to as biometric authentication and is reliant on individuals' unique biological characteristics to identify the individual correctly. These traits can be used instead of passwords to verify and identify individuals as they are bound to the individual. Retina, iris, facial, fingerprint, or palm prints are all unique, but Garcia (2018) states that to preserve privacy, biometrics should never be stored in a public distributed ledger as it's accessible to anyone whether it's in an encrypted or template state. The reason for this is that there are no guarantees that the system will remain safe in future due to advances in quantum computing.

An important part of the process is the method used to compare the information presented versus the information on record as most common used methods still use signature and photo comparisons to perform most transactions. These methods are unreliable, more so when the person who is making the comparison doesn't know the individual.

1.4 Storage of citizen information

A related case study by Toapanta et al. (2018) finds that Ecuadorian citizen information is stored in a master database and is replicated in real time to two separate databases for backup purposes; Fig. 1 demonstrates a similar scenario.

The clear issue with replicating data from the master to the backup databases is that any inconsistencies or compromised data that may exist on the master database will also be distributed to the backup databases. Distributed ledger technology (DLT) prevents these inconsistencies and provides additional benefits such immutability, auditability, transparency, and decentralisation to preserve CIA. DLTs are sometimes confused with blockchain technology (BC) though the two do share a close relationship, but distinct differences exist.

Contract law generally focusses on authenticity of agreements between parties especially in common law jurisdictions (Sullivan, 2018). There is usually the presumption that in face-to-face interactions, each party intends to deal with another who is physically present. However, this can be rebutted if clear, admissible evidence to the contrary is provided.

An example is the antimoney laundering/counterterrorism financing legislation which mandates that financial institutions identify every customer; the requirement is referred to as 'know your customer' (KYC). The KYC process requires an initial in-person interview where the applicant provides a range of original identity documents to fulfil the 100-point identity check. KYC was introduced in 2001 under the USA Patriot Act and was passed shortly after 9/11 to discourage terrorist behaviour.

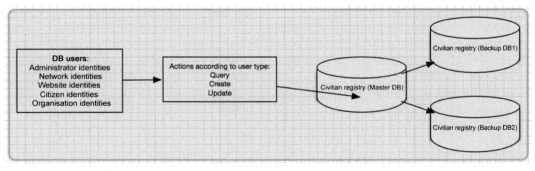

FIG. 1 Enrolment mechanisms.

1.5 Digital identities

A real-life identity can be used in an online environment by means of a digital identity (DI), and the attributes about an entity is usually referred to as a claim. A DI can be used for making agreements and transacting as if physically present in the service provider's office. DIs can be interpreted in different ways, though the simplest way is to understand the three-party model which consists of the following:

- End user—a person who claims to be and use the digital identifier or entity transacting and listed in the claim definition (Singh and Chatterjee, 2015).
- Relying party (RP)—is an entity which is reliant on a third-party identity provider to validate identity and authenticate an end user requesting access to a resource; examples can be a web service or website (Singh and Chatterjee, 2015).
- Identity provider (IdP)—contains information about the end user and translates it into claims (Singh and Chatterjee, 2015).

Identity is a reoccurring requirement for transactions that take place online, especially when there is no physical relationship with online individuals, no face-to-face interaction, and often no human-to-human communication (Sullivan, 2018).

A study on e-services globally by Statista (2018) finds that 'the worldwide revenue of US$135.4billion in 2017 is expected to increase to US$304.8billion by 2022', a substantial increase over the next 4 years. The need to transact using digital identities should come as no surprise given the exponential increase for online transactions over the past 10 years; one can understand why dealings with many governments and private sectors require digital identities of some form.

Financial services have in particular been a driving force of electronic transactions. Being a regulated sector a key requirement is the need for DIs as identified by (Ecb. europa.eu, 2014) where a pretransactional process requires identification, authentication, and authorisation.

Electronic transactions have been around for several years, and the OECD (2001) has defined the phrase as 'the sale or purchase of goods or services, whether between businesses, households, individuals, governments, and other public or private organisations, conducted over computer-mediated networks. The goods and services are ordered over those networks, but the payment and the ultimate delivery of the good or service may be conducted on or off-line'.

1.6 Identity assurance cases

Deceptive activities which include identity fraud are already a massive threat to the current digital community. Technology power users are at greatest risk of identity fraud (2016) found that 'most prolific users of mobile and social technology, who make up 7.7% of the

UK population, accounted for almost a quarter (23%) of all ID fraud victims in 2015'. This group of users happened to be the most technology proficient amongst the UK population and found to be living in more densely populated areas such as cities and surrounding suburbs. The study found that those who embraced online-based technologies were most at risk to identity fraud.

The UK's national reporting centre for fraud and cybercrime has a vast number of listed incidents relating to all types of fraud; many examples of identity fraud are available on the action fraud website. One such statistic illustrates how romance fraud is having a significant impact on society. The statistic shows that this particular approach alone has contributed to the defrauding of £41 million in 2017. Romance fraud is described by Action Fraud (2018) as 'when someone creates a fake identity to enter into a relationship with a victim with intent to steal either funds or personal information'; 3557 romance frauds were reported to action fraud in 2017, an average of 10 reports a day.

Dunphy et al. (2018) finds that $15.3 billion were stolen from 13.1 million US consumers in 2015 in what was recorded as identity fraud-related incidents; a year later, those figures were increased to $16 billion and 15.4 million victims, respectively.

1.7 Authentication

The process of approving an entity via a different entity is known as authentication and is used to determine whether an entity (person or application) has eligible access to what's being requested. In a network environment, the common methods for authenticating are 'log-on credentials, multifactor authentication, third-party authentication, simple text passwords, 3D password objects, graphical passwords, biometric authentication and digital device authentication' as seen in Indu et al. (2018)' research.

All DI transaction schemes essentially depend on two processes to associate an individual to a DI.

o **Identity authentication**: This is done at the time of registration and according to criteria set out by the registration scheme. Information is collected for verification.
o **Identity verification**: This is the process of validation which ensures that the individual is correctly identified. This identifying information could be anything from a simple signature or photograph to enhanced biometric information. In some schemes a combination of these may also be required.

1.8 Zero-knowledge proof

Zero-knowledge proof (ZKP) is the method by where a statement or knowledge can be proved to be true to a verifier without having to reveal any information other than the fact that the knowledge or statement is true.

The notion of ZKP is not novel as it was initially proposed in the 1980s, though in recent years the concept has captured the attention of many blockchain (BC) communities by its ability to address privacy and security concerns. (The subject of blockchain is discussed later in this chapter.) Many industries have hesitated to adopt blockchain, and a study by Assets.ey.com (2019) revealed that security and data privacy were at the forefront of these concerns. However, several highly regulated industries have taken an interest in addressing such concerns by investing in ZKP as a method to tackle privacy, security, and scalability issues. Examples are ING Bank, EY, and JPMorgan Chase as seen by Allison (2018), Ey.com (2019), and GitHub (2018), respectively.

The popular illustration of Ali Baba's cave by Quisquater et al. (1998) explains ZKP in a simple manner, and the example in the succeeding text demonstrates the actions between the prover and verifier.

Fig. 2 describes zero knowledge in a simple manner. The cave has a single entrance near marking **X**; there are two paths (left path and right path) which lead to the secret door on the opposite end of cave. The secret door seals the route between the left path and right path and can only be opened if the prover knows the secret without revealing the secret to the verifier.

The prover enters the cave and selects a random path leading to the secret door. The verifier then enters the cave and stops at marking X. The verifier instructs the prover to come out via a random path towards X. Only if the prover knows the secret will the secret door be opened at random selection of the paths chosen by the verifier each time. However, if the prover doesn't know the secret, there will be 50% probability that the prover comes out via the correct path. This challenge is repeated multiple times until the verifier is convinced that the prover's claims are not based on the probability of luck.

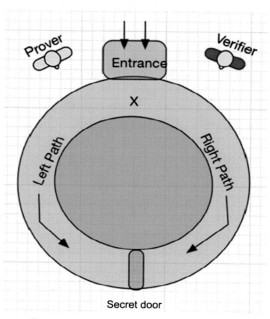

FIG. 2 Zero-knowledge demonstration.

According to Ostrovsky et al. (1999), completeness, soundness, and zero knowledge are the three properties which are necessary to prove correctness.

- **Completeness**—Only if the prover has the secret will, the prover be able to prove it and if the secret is true will the verifier be convinced by that fact.
- **Soundness**—Only if the secret is true will the prover be able to prove, so the more the prover is challenged, and if it's true, then the probability is true, but if there is one lie, then the prover doesn't know the secret.
- **Zero knowledge**—If the secret is true, then the verifier learns nothing else, but the fact that the secret is true.

ZKPs exist in two forms, interactive and noninteractive.

- **Interactive** is where a fact is proven by the prover by carrying out a series of actions to convince the verifier that the fact is known. This method is based on the probability of being able to prove the fact numerous times and is defined by the rules that the verifier has set. If the prover is incorrect during the challenge, the probability of not knowing the fact is increased, and the verifier is not convinced. The process can be time consuming if the verifier isn't convinced, and the series of challenges is restarted.
- **Noninteractive** doesn't require interaction between the prover and verifier. It is a proof which is made available by the prover whereby a verifier can verify for themselves. It targets a large audience of verifiers, and verifying the fact is efficient.

Authentication is one of the primary applications where ZKP can be applied. Due to its design, it mitigates impersonation attacks, replay attacks as seen by its randomness capabilities when challenged, and Man in the Middle (MitM) attacks where zero knowledge is exchanged. It also withstands against reverse engineering attacks which smart card systems are susceptible to though it does have its limitations, such disadvantages are if the secret is not a numerical digit, it may require translation and the proof which is being concealed is only as good as the secret itself.

ZKP is already used in certain blockchain ecosystems; one such example is the cryptocurrency platform called Zcash; it is using a noninteractive iteration called zero-knowledge succinct noninteractive arguments of knowledge (zk-SNARKS). The names within the acronym zk-SNARKS represent the following outcomes and their features:

- **Zero knowledge**—Not revealing any information.
- **Succinct**—The proofs are verified within a few milliseconds, extremely efficient.
- **Noninteractive**—There is no interaction between the prover and verifier as the proof transcript is composed of a single message.
- **Argument of knowledge**—A computational proof which is sound and leverages on polynomial time.

1.9 Identity management (IdM)

IdM is the process of managing infrastructure which supports the functions for creating, managing, and using identities. The majority of IdM schemes are centralised and are controlled and owned by individual entities, though user-centric models offer users control over their identity information. The scope of identities may extend beyond an individual organisation such as national identity cards which are issued by governments and used for multiple organisations (Dunphy and Petitcolas, 2018). IdM schemes need to authenticate citizens correctly to link their online presence to real-world identities, but they assume that IdPs know who the true identities are.

There are no definitive standards to evaluate identity management (IdM) schemes though a widely recognised framework known as the '7 laws of identity' can be used to measure the successes and failures of digital identity systems. The Internet was designed in a way without knowing who and what an individual is connecting to, and although no one can be blamed, the outcome from a security perspective has been damaging. Many people accept prompts whilst conducting business online or just simply accessing the Internet out of habit and unaware of the consequences. Practices such as providing names, passwords, and personal identifying information to unverified parties have led to criminalisation over the Internet, and as a result, many have called for the Internet to have an identity layer.

1.9.1 Federated identity systems

Federated identity systems allow users to establish identity information in a single security domain and gain access to another. Single sign-on (SSO) schemes such as Facebook Connect work in this manner. A user is known to a single organisation which is the registered IdP; this IdP exists within the federation of organisations and has mutual trust agreements between all organisations; Fig. 3 is example of such a model.

SSO protocols are arguably one of the most successful authentication solutions today; they permit users to access a multitude of services via an IdP authentication server, though a major disadvantage is that a single authentication method such as a password may be compromised and grant an attacker access to multiple services. To mitigate this, SSO could be accompanied with multifactor.

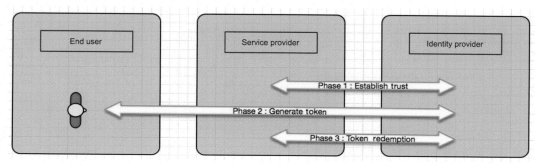

FIG. 3 SSO three-party model.

1.9.2 User-centric identity management systems

User-centric identity management systems hand the responsibility of controlling and administering identity information to the individual, anonymising tools such as Tor and I2P are examples where minimal personal information is disclosed. This solution permits users to store third-party providers' identifiers and credentials on tamper proof hardware devices such as smart cards or portable devices; refer to Fig. 4 for an example.

Regardless of the approaches, one fundamental function which is essential to IdMs is the ability to securely bind an identifier with attributes. An identifier unambiguously distinguishes a user from another within a particular domain, and attributes are the claims such as a name and age of an individual.

1.9.3 Decentralised identifier

A decentralised identifier (DID) is the identity mechanism for binding the identifier to the user. DIDs are data structures which contain unique identifiers and have a related public/private key pair for each identifier. Every DID subject has the ability to issue and sign verifiable claims and puts owners in control of every aspect of their identity such as attributes or claims as opposed to traditional federated IdM systems which are controlled by third-party IdPs. No central registration authority is required as the DID is registered with the DLT and the DID specification strongly recommends that all personally identifiable information (PII) be kept off the ledger and on endpoints which are under the subjects' control.

The W3C community group (Community, 2020) summarises the design goals and principles of DID architecture, and a simple example is demonstrated as 'did:example:123456789:abcdefghi'.

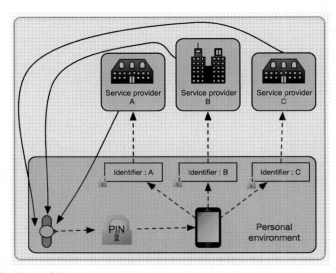

FIG. 4 User-centric identity model.

Many countries are already using DI schemes, with some using the same identity for both private and public sector transactions (Sullivan, 2018). Estonia is well established in its scheme, whilst other countries are on route to implementing its own versions. Estonia's ID card contains an electronic chip which contains information about its holder and can be used online for electronic transactions such as voting, banking, obtaining tickets for public transport, and many more services which the city has to offer. The ID card is secured with two certificates where one authenticates the holder's identity and the other creates a digital signature (Rivera et al., 2017). DI programs are being used by the United States, the United Kingdom, and Australia but face political challenges in trying to establish a formal national identity scheme (Sullivan, 2018).

A major concern for public and business entities is not being able to know the precise identity of users utilising their systems. Many attempts at developing technologies to certify users' basic attributes like names, addresses, and credit records have been created, though existing methods have failed to address citizens' needs sufficiently.

Concerns by Mesnard (2016) around the three-party model are as follows:

- End user
  - User providing false identity information, where a different individual uses the user's credential.
- Relying party
  - Depending on false identity information.
  - Failing to protect an individuals' data.
- Identity provider
  - Identifying and authenticating an individual incorrectly.
  - Failing to protect an individuals' data.
  - Failing to verify or revoke and individual's details.

A study by Holm (2012) finds several practical difficulties with regard to regulating identity-related crimes. The issue of jurisdiction seems to be at the forefront followed by the accuracy of data for both reported and nonreported crime incidences.

Ramalingam and Chinnaiah (2018) conclude that many fake profile detection schemes exist, though no systematic solution for detecting these profiles provides reliable recognition of user information and that these profiles must be detected before they are registered.

An example is when signing up to Facebook; their terms (Facebook, 2019) state that a user needs to 'provide accurate information' about themselves, but when observing their registration page as seen in Fig. 5 (Facebook, 2020), their requirements are dependent on attributes such as name, surname, email address, mobile number, and birthday. These attributes may be associated to functioning email addresses and mobile numbers for completing the registration; however, this doesn't provide any assurance that the person is who they claim to be. RPs that are dependent on SSO solutions need to be aware that many of these services provide authentication mechanisms not verification mechanisms as identities are not verified prior to completing registration.

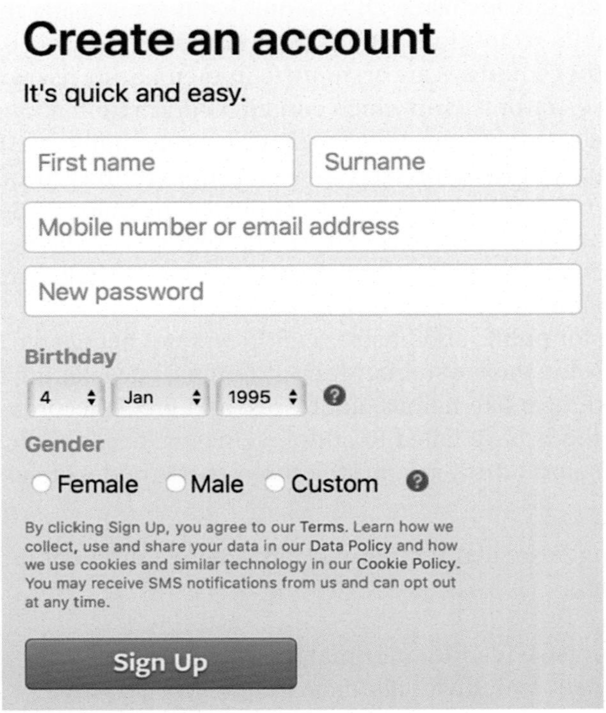

FIG. 5 Facebook registration page.

Globally, governments recognise that their industries need to adopt internet technologies to remain competitive as adoption enables them to adapt to sudden changes. During the last few years, many obstacles have been brought down paving the way for electronic commerce. Examples include the Electronic Signature in Global and National Commerce Act (E-Sign) enacted on 1 October 2000 by the US federal government which legally enforced electronic signatures to provide legal validity for electronic and paper-based agreements (Stern, 2001).

The European Commission also adopted the framework electronic signature directive in 1999 but has since been replaced by Regulation (EU) No. 910/2014 on electronic identification and trust services for electronic transaction in the internal market. The aim is to enhance trust within the EU for cross-border recognition of electronic IDs between its citizens, businesses, and authorities.

2 Blockchain

Blockchain is a decentralised and distributed database technology which initially emerged in 2008 when the Bitcoin cryptocurrency was introduced. The data structure is shared to form a distributed data structure known as a shared ledger. The distributed ledger consists of details for every historical transaction made, and the fundamental unit within the blockchain is referred to as a block; refer to Fig. 6 for a typical block structure. A block could be understood to be an individual bank statement.

BC technology contains a series of blocks which are securely linked in a cryptographic manner, and the order of blocks is governed by an implicit timestamp mechanism which prevents the blocks from being altered unless all successors are modified. This chronological order of the blocks uses cryptographic hashes which prevent the ledger from being tampered with though tamper resistance cannot be guaranteed within a private-based BC environment due to potential meddling that could occur within a closed environment.

Fig. 7 demonstrates the block structure process whereby block N communicates continuously and contains the block hash plus previous block $(N-1)$, timestamp, block version, nonce, and target address with transaction list.

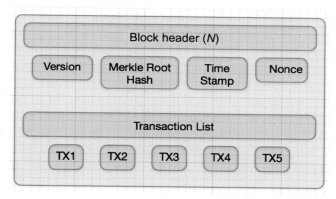

FIG. 6 Block structure.

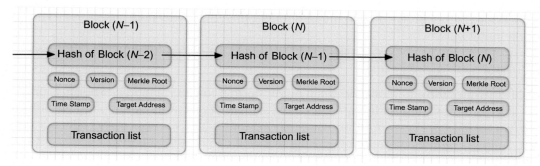

FIG. 7 Block structure process.

2.1 Consensus

All entries that are added on the ledger require some form of consensus prior to being added, and consensus is reached by voting using algorithms amongst the known participants. New blocks are added to the chain via participant consensus, though implementing the consensus protocol differs vastly depending on the BC type. Three types of BC structures exist, namely, public, permissioned, and consortium-based BCs.

The Nakamoto consensus is a method which elects a leader based on a random selection, though this process is vulnerable to attacks. The leader proposes an entry to be appended into the ledger which needs to be checked and validated by all nodes.

Proof of work (PoW) and proof of stake (PoS) are the consensus protocols which validate the work and transactions, respectively, though other approaches, namely, Practical Byzantine Fault Tolerance (BPFT) and Delegated Proof of Stake (DPoS) which are also used to reach consensus.

PoW is based on the first participant to solve the cryptographic puzzle, and this process is known as mining. The winner is then awarded with tokens as an incentive for using computing power, but this method is costly as it consumes a vast amount of electricity and time to generate a new block. A significant level of security is brought on to the chain by being able to withstand up to 50% of malicious nodes.

PoS consumes less energy when compared with PoW as miners need to select nodes based on their account balance; this is an unfair approach as the wealthiest validator will dominate the network, but DPoS a variant of PoS offers a more democratic method.

PoS validators with more tokens have a higher chance of creating the next block, and network attacks are more prone due to the low mining cost. Both DPoS and PoS were created to reduce the energy usage and improve electricity inefficiencies that are associated with PoW. The major difference between DPoS and PoS is that DPoS stakeholders elect their delegates to validate the blocks; therefore dishonest delegates are easily voted outwhile in PoS every stakeholder participates in validating the transactions.

BPFT is a replication algorithm which tolerates arbitrary faulty nodes. Consensus speed is low and is achieved by quorum; the process consists of three phases: preprepared, prepared, and commit. For each phase, every node needs to receive two out of three votes on all nodes before proceeding to the next phase; therefore every node needs to be known on the network.

2.2 Types of blockchain

Fig. 8 illustrates the differences between public permission less and private permissioned-based ledgers, and the later literature elaborates on their properties. In public permissionless ledgers, all members contribute to validating transactions as opposed to selected validator nodes in private permissioned ledgers which can modify the BC.

In a public BC, everyone can participate in the consensus process as all records appear visible; everyone is also permitted to read and write to the ledger without restrictions.

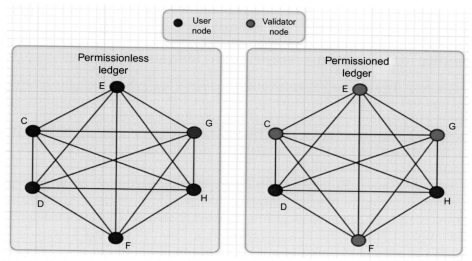

FIG. 8 Permissionless versus permissioned ledgers.

Bitcoin and Ethereum cryptocurrencies are examples that fall within a public ledger environment, and both currently use PoW to reach consensus though Ethereum will support PoS in the near future. Resolving the hash puzzle using PoW means that it's heavy on resources and time consuming as it needs to determine the required predefined hash value.

A consortium BC is constructed by multiple organisations and is partially decentralised since only a group of preselected nodes are permitted to participate in the consensus process. Using preselected nodes saves a significant amount of time and reduces network overhead making it efficient; these can be seen as hybrid BCs which stand between public and private BCs.

Private BCs provide secure and relatively closed business environments but lack transparency and public participation. These permission-based structures form a member only club environment, and only nodes from specific organisations may participate in the consensus process. Private BCs are controlled by a single organisation, and many regard them as a centralised network.

2.3 Advantages and disadvantages

Private and public BCs generate tokens which form the chain of transactions, making BC possible in dealing with double spending problems within a distributed network. This chain-like structure assures security by preventing illegal modification within the network and can easily detect block tampering due to the transparency of data across all members. The use of validation such as PoW accepts only one historical transaction and makes tampering the hash chain impossible; this allows blockchain to adopt and authenticate digital data. Every member of the network contains a copy of all communicated data ruling out any single points of failure rendering the BC reliable.

2.4 Identity management on distributed ledgers

Bitcoin has been the dominating application on BC technology, though the area is being explored and has expanded into other avenues such as healthcare, insurance, and the management of DIs for both governments and private organisations.

A survey by Elsden and Manohar (2018) lists seven classes of BC applications; IdM is listed as one of them where it has the ability to manage and authenticate identities for both organisations and individuals.

End users, RPs, and IdPs may establish trust amongst each other by underpinning a distributed trust model to manage identities, and people in developing countries may be empowered through financial inclusion, asset ownership, and having the ability to recognise identity.

2.4.1 Decentralised and self-sovereign environments

IdMs based on BC fall into two categories, namely, self-sovereign identity (SSI) and decentralised trusted identity frameworks.

SSI management systems are user centric as they grant individuals the right to fully own and manage their own DIs; verifiable claims are central to this concept as the RPs depend on what's being presented. A SSI isn't reliant on any third-party administrative authority, and as a result the identity can't be removed from the controlling individual unlike most IdM systems which are reliant on large IdPs such as Facebook and Google.

Fig. 9 presents the relationship between the various actors of a SSI system.

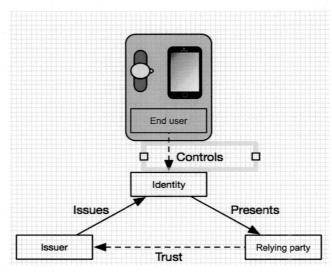

FIG. 9 Self-sovereign identity actors.

Decentralised trusted identity frameworks are centralised services that prove end user's identities based on trusted credentials such as passports. Identity claims are recorded on a DLT which can be validated by third parties.

2.5 Use cases

BC is mostly used in the financial services, IoT, and reputation systems, but all credit is due to Bitcoin for introducing a highly successful Fintech application even though big spikes in volatility indicate that they could be related to hacks and unsuccessful forks.

The Dutch government is piloting blockchain with a variety of applications which include DIs, judicial decisions, managing tourist tax more efficiently, marital status, e-voting, debt counselling, and many more initiatives. Estonia's E-residency program leverages on BC and offers some of its services to e-residents; it has also been innovative in the way that's its used BC to expand its use to identity authentication and verification. Permission-based BCs can coexist within a legal framework. This however can only be accomplished if a government is granted superuser status to modify the content of the said BC database. Due to the distributed nature of BCs, this status would need to be granted by the courts and administrative authorities, thereby permitting the altering of the BC content.

BC in the European Union (EU) could be more challenging in a completely decentralised solution. An example where sensitive information such as price agreements for consumers and commercial service providers must remain confidential in smart contracts which are recorded in the ledger. Solutions for confidentiality, privacy, and IdM need to exist to comply with the General Data Protection Regulation (GDPR)'s legal privacy requirements.

3 Threat model: Digital witness concept

This section focusses on anonymising the digital witness (DW) identity, which leverages on the Sovrin network's design (Foundation, 2016a,b) but relies on personal devices to record and preserve digital evidence (DE). It is a SSI management DLT model which uses ZKP and DIDs to achieve its objectives. The proposed model may provide DWs with an alternative approach to Nieto et al. (2017)'s for anonymising DW identities to assure privacy before transmitting digital evidence (DE) to DW users and digital custodians (DCs).

3.1 Digital witness concept

DWs are personal devices which are effective in identifying and collecting DE. They must have the ability to preserve DE in a secure location and be able to transmit the DE to other authorised DWs for preservation. DWs transmit DE between themselves until reaching the DCs who are responsible for delivering DE to the final destination known as the Official Collection Point (OCP) for processing. The transmission mechanism used is referred to as the digital chain of custody in IoT (DCoC-IoT).

Handling DE via existing practices poses many challenges, and the problematic areas consist of parties which are interacting with the DE, recording and storing of metadata, and accessing and securing the chain of custody. Understanding every detail of how DE is handled throughout the life cycle is crucial for proving the chain of custody.

3.2 Threat model

Threat modelling is the process used to analyse and assess any potential vulnerabilities that may undermine a systems security. The proposed model leverages on a self-sovereign IdM BC approach. As the model is only in a conceptual stage, threat modelling conceptual designs should be done at a high level though the process is essentially the same no matter how granular throughout the life cycle. This model uses the similar approach where the following three high-level steps are initially used as a foundation; these are as follows:

- characterising the system
- identifying assets and access points
- identifying threats

Characterising the system ensures that the designer completely understands the proposed model. This is achieved by the following:

o   Understanding the interconnections for every component within the model. This is evidential in Fig. 13 where the collaboration between the DWs, BC, and the trusted institutions are demonstrated.
o   Demonstrating usage scenarios and can be seen in Figs. 15 and 16 where both scenarios demonstrate two attacks and two offences, respectively.

A crucial step within the threat modelling process is to identify assets and access points which can exploit the system. Assets are the targeted objectives for any adversaries. In this model, DE obtained by the DWs would be considered as a primary asset, though DE dependency on the DW subscriptions would also render owners of DWs as assets to the actual model. If the model is not able to provide DW owners with confidentiality, security, and privacy, then the model's growth numbers in subscriptions will be limited, threatening potential adoption. ZKPs are used to ensure that only authorised DWs exist within the ecosystem and that their identities are cryptographically true. DIDs are the unique identifiers which are used to secure the relationship between the end points.

The access points are areas where attackers are most likely to attempt gaining unauthorised access to the ecosystem. The models' access points are listed in Tables 2 and 3. DWs and IoT transmission signals are potential entry points to the user side of the network, and the trusted institutions are the entry points which are validator nodes on the BC. The BC-type selection is consortium based due to the required permissions that are necessary to host a variety of nonbiased trusted validator nodes. Trust boundaries

Table 2   Actors and DW participants.

Actors or participants	Role
User not digital witness — Vehicle — Person	Regular user which is not classified as a DW
Digital witness (DW) — Vehicle — Person	A DW who may be an offended person or vehicle. This actor may also be a third party to witness a digital offence
Digital witness (DW) custodian — Person — Vehicle	A DC is a DW with elevated privileges for reporting DE to an OCP using the DCoC-IoT approach. The DC may also be a witness and a victim in a digital attack
Cyber hacker (CH) — Person	The cyber hacker (CH) is the offender within the networked ecosystem
DCoC-IoT	DCoC-IoT is the immutable approach to deliver DE to an official OCP
.>>))	The connectivity or transmission used to deliver DE amongst DWs and DCs

are necessary to determine the varied levels of trust, and Table 3 lists the trusted institutions as validators within the blockchain ledger.

Identifying threats is only possible once assets and access points have been identified. This paper doesn't delve into the mitigation strategy, but a classification of threats enables one to map them to the countermeasure to mitigate the relevant risk. Threat classification creates relationships between threats, attacks, and vulnerabilities.

Table 3   DLT-based components.

DLT components	Role
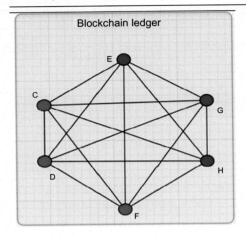	A BC for IdM only which assures • Immutability • Efficiency • Availability • Privacy • Decentralisation
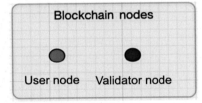	The nodes on the BC are classified as either a user node or validator node
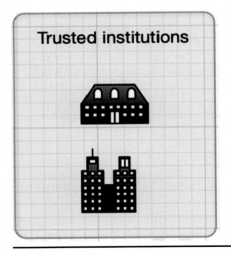	A trusted entity or institution which is authorised to validate nodes on the BC

3.3 Model design

Table 2 contains a list of actors and DW participants to demonstrate various scenarios within the design.

3.4 Self-sovereign DLT-based scheme and consensus

Table 3 lists the DLT-based components which are used in the identity management scheme.

Sovrin is an open-source IdM scheme which is purposely designed for decentralised IdM. It is used to store identity records on DLTs, and users have the choice to store their attributes on the ledger or on their mobile devices.

Consensus is carried out using Plenum which is an implementation of the RBFT protocol (GitHub, 2016) and is achieved by quorum; therefore every node must receive two out of three votes. Traditional Byzantine Fault Tolerant (BFT) protocols tolerate arbitrary faulty nodes, but Aublin et al. (2013) find that a similar performance throughput is achieved when there are no faults when comparing RBFT and BFT; however, degradation in performance whilst under faults for RBFT is below 3% when compared with at least 78% for other robust BFT protocols.

3.5 Trusted institutions

Trusted institutions are defined as Stewards which can participate in the consensus process by validating the identity transactions. These trusted entities are governed by a legal agreement called the Sovrin Trust Framework (Foundation, 2016a,b) which ensures that only reputable Stewards are authorised for consensus participation through means of a web of trust.

Fig. 10 demonstrates the Stewards as validators within the DLT.

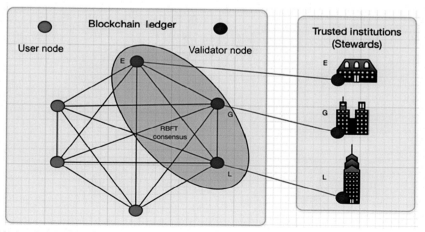

FIG. 10 Validating Stewards within the DLT.

3.6 Authorising the digital witness

All DWs need to be authorised and verified prior to joining the DW ecosystem (Verifier). The ZKP authentication mechanism ensures that the person accountable for the personal device is who they claim to be. The DW ecosystem requires a set of attributes from the applicant (prover) which is then verified using ZKP. The authoritative sources represent the governing offices that issue the person' identity details. Once verification is successful, the DW is authorised and becomes a member of the DW network (Fig. 11).

3.7 Securing point to point (P2P) communications

Table 4 contains a list of features which are used to establish secure P2P communication between DWs.

The mobile devices within the DW ecosystem must contain tamper proof mechanisms such as trusted platform modules (TPM) and secure elements (SE) as for storing DE. The DE is associated to the DW who generated it, and a DID is the identity mechanism for binding the identifier to the user.

The DID can provide the identity owner with privacy by using pairwise unique DIDs for each relationship, for example, between DW and DW or between DW and DC, but this can only be done by establishing an encrypted private channel between their endpoints or mobile devices. These DIDs act as pseudonyms which rely on private software agents that are installed on the mobile devices, but to ensure that the owner is always addressable, an agent can be run on a trusted intermediary or agency which will host the pseudonymous network address.

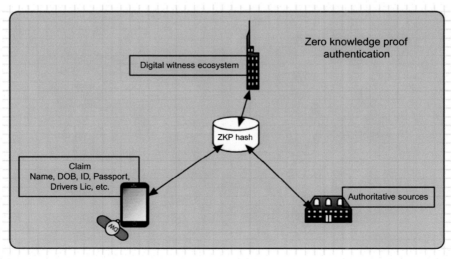

FIG. 11 ZKP verification.

Table 4 Features used to establish secure P2P communication.

Features for securing P2P communications		Role
Mobile devices		A tamper proof mobile device which may contain DE and is bound to the identity owner by means of a decentralised identifier (DID)

Personal IoT enabled devices that are suitable for managing DE. Sovrin currently supports mobile devices, but wearable IoT-based products should be included in future developments which could be used for DW purposes

| Dencentralised identifier/s (DID) | C Identifier: did:leg:123456789:abcdefgh   D Identifier: did:leg:123456789:abcdefgg   F Identifier: did:leg:123456789:abcdefgf   H Identifier: did:leg:123456789:abcdefge | A DID is used for verifiable self-sovereign DIs |
| 3rd party agency | Software agent | Specialised intermediary (cloud provider) which hosts a pseudonymous network address |

In the event of a lost, faulty, or breached mobile device, the DWs have the ability to recover their keys which are stored on their mobile devices. This is done through the mobile application via quorum of appointed trustees that the Stewards on the ledger must verify.

Fig. 12 demonstrates the secure private channel between DW user C and DW custodian F; the chain-like image represents the immutable identifier record in the ledger.

Fig. 13 demonstrates the collaboration between the DWs, BC, and the trusted institutions. The DC in the example shows how one user may have multiple identifiers, that is, 'did:net:123456789:abcdefg' and 'did:leg:0123456789:abcdefzz', and in this case the DC is a regular user in one ledger but holds elevated permissions on another.

3.8 Official collection points

An OCP is a forensics environment for gathering DE that may be used in a court of law depending on the legal frameworks requirements (Fig. 14).

3.9 Collaboration and conceptual demonstration within the digital witness ecosystem

3.9.1 Scenario 1

The scenario in Fig. 15 consists of two cyberattacks, a local attack, and an attack performed from a remote location over the Internet. Every actor within the DW ecosystem has at least one unique DID giving the DW user the selective ability to be anonymous or known as per 2 of the 10 DID principals (Community, 2020).

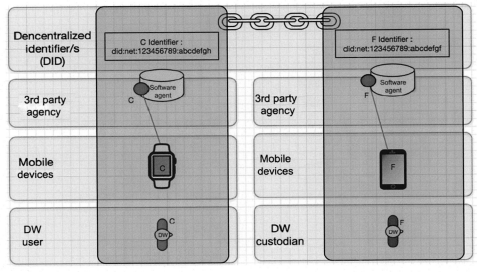

FIG. 12 Secure private channel.

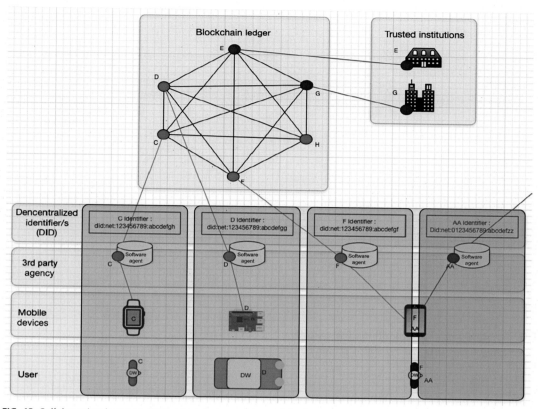

FIG. 13 Collaboration between DWs, blockchain, and trusted institutions.

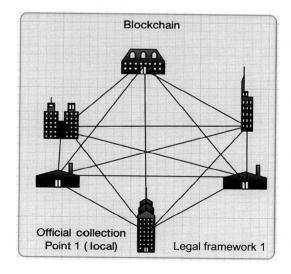

FIG. 14 A local OCP.

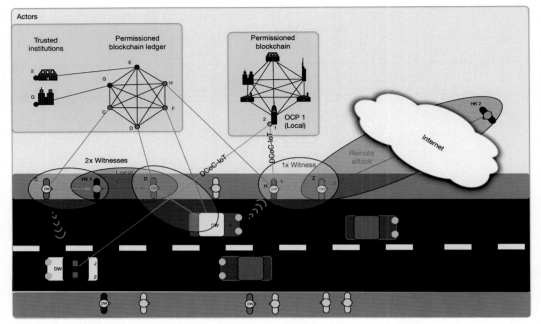

FIG. 15 Various digital attacks within a DW ecosystem.

- Self-sovereignty—'DID architecture should give entities, both human and non-human, the power to directly own and control their digital identifiers without the need to rely on external authorities'.
- Privacy—'DID architecture should enable entities to control the privacy of their information, including minimal, selective, and progressive disclosure of attributes or other data'.

The actors involved in the attacks are listed in Table 5, and all DE transmitted is over IoT and DCoC-IoT connectivity.

Attack 1 (local)

HK1 performs an attack via Bluetooth or via a Wi-Fi hotspot on DW D. All evidence pertaining to the attack includes logs of leaked data and any damage that may have occurred on the victims' device. Key to the investigation are the digital footprints of the attacker that have been stored on the victims TPM- or SE-based device as well as the ability to correlate all digital witnesses.

Should the victim's device no longer function due to the damage caused by the attack, a DW F within range of DW D witnesses the offence and also records the DE locally onto its tamper proof storage. The DE is transmitted anonymously using the DCoC-IoT approach to the nearest available custodian H1. The custodian is authorised on local OCP 1 to

Table 5 Scenario 1 attack actors.

Scene 1 Fig. 15	Attacker	Victim (DW)	Witness/es (DW)	Custodian/s (DW)	
Attack 1	HK 1	D = D Identifier : did:net:123456789:abcdefgg (Known)	C = C Identifier : did:net:123456789:abcdefgh (Anonymous)	H = H Identifier : did:net:123456789:abcdefge (Known) & 1 Identifier : did:leg:0123456789:abcdefgh (Known)	
			DW F = F Identifier : did:net:123456789:abcdefgf (Known)	DW J = J Identifier : did:net:123456789:abcdefj (Known) &	2 Identifier : did:leg:0123456789:abcdefgj (Known)
Attack 2	HK 2	Z = Z Identifier : did:net:11222333:nnnoooppp (Anonymous)	H = H Identifier : did:net:123456789:abcdefge (Known) &	1 Identifier : did:leg:0123456789:abcdefgh (Known)	

deliver DE for investigation, and all records related to this attack have remained immutable throughout the transmission process.

During the same attack a second DW C is also present and is within range of attacker HK1, and DW C also stores the DE securely and transmits the DE via DCoC-IoT to the nearest available custodian J2 who then delivers the DE to OCP 1.

Attack 2 (remote)
HK2 performs an attack via the Internet on DW Z. Similarly, to attack 1, all evidence is stored on the victims' tamper proof device. DW H1 is a custodian which witnesses the attack, securely stores the DE on its tamper proof storage, and then proceeds to transmit the DE via the secure DCoC-IoT link to OCP 1.

3.9.2 Scenario 2
This scenario consists of two vehicular offences in Fig. 16, an offender which has run through a red traffic light and an offender which has violated the traffic speed limit. This approach introduces the use of smart road infrastructure as DWs. Every actor within this DW ecosystem has at least one unique DID, and a known identifier should be preferred over anonymity for correlation purposes within the OCP environment.

According to two of the 10 DID goals and principals (Community, 2020), self-sovereignty also supports nonhuman entities, whilst privacy enables an entity to be anonymous or known in its ecosystem.

- Self-sovereignty—'DID architecture should give entities, both human and non-human, the power to directly own and control their digital identifiers without the need to rely on external authorities'
- Privacy—'DID architecture should enable entities to control the privacy of their information, including minimal, selective, and progressive disclosure of attributes or other data'

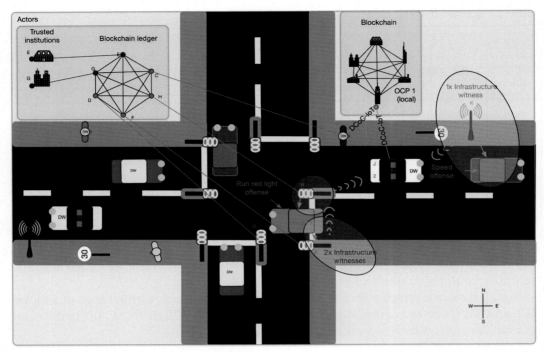

FIG. 16 Vehicular offences within a DW ecosystem.

The actors involved in the attacks are listed in Table 6, and all DE transmitted is over IoT and DCoC-IoT connectivity.

Offence 1
Offender Y is travelling in a westerly direction and doesn't stop at the red signals on traffic light F and H. These traffic lights are also DWs which witness the offence and log the offenders' details on their tamper proof storage.

- F transmits its DE to H.
- H transmits F's DE and its own DE to J2.
- J2 transmits all DE to OCP 1.

Offence 2
Offender Z is travelling in an easterly direction and violates the maximum speed limit of 30 miles per hour. A nearby road side unit (RSU) K not only resides in a vehicular ad hoc network (VANET) but also is a registered DW. DW K witnesses Z violating the speed offence and stores all DE on its tamper proof storage. K then transmits the DE to custodian J2 who transmits all DE to OCP1.

Table 6 Scenario 2 offender actors.

Scene 2 Fig. 16	Offender	Witness/es (DW)	Custodian/s (DW)
Offense 1		F Identifier: did:net:111222333:dddeeefff (Known)	J Identifier: did:net:123456789:abcdefjj (Known) & 2 Identifier: did:leg:0123456789:abcdefgj (Known)
		H Identifier: did:net:111222333:ggghhhjjj (Known)	
Offense 2		K Identifier: did:net:111222333:kkkllmmm (Known)	J Identifier: did:net:123456789:abcdefjj (Known) & 2 Identifier: did:leg:0123456789:abcdefgj (Known)

3.10 Results

The actors in all scenarios are either known or anonymous within their ecosystems. Figs. 17–20 illustrate the flow of DE from the victims and offences to the OCP including the correlation status back to the DW actors.

3.11 Scenario 1

All attacks in scenario 1 demonstrated the following:

- How a self-sovereign IdM scheme which leverages on a DLT-based environment can be used to bind DWs to their owners with the use of DIDs.
- How all DE is associated to the DWs that process it and contains information relating to the acts of crime which also includes identifier throughout the IoT and DCoC-IoT process.
- How an anonymous DW and known DW may contain and deliver the same evidence to the OCP.
- How correlating DE to an anonymous DW may be challenging depending on their selective disclosure of verifiable claims versus a known DW who can be correlated to present themselves and their device to stand as a witness if required.

3.11.1 Attack 1 (local)

Fig. 17 illustrates attack 1 where victim D is a DW which has suffered a data breach by HK1. The DE containing logs to the leaked information has been stored on DW Ds device, though during the attack the status of victim D's devices is unknown and may be damaged. The two DWs F and C have witnessed the same attack as they were in range of capturing

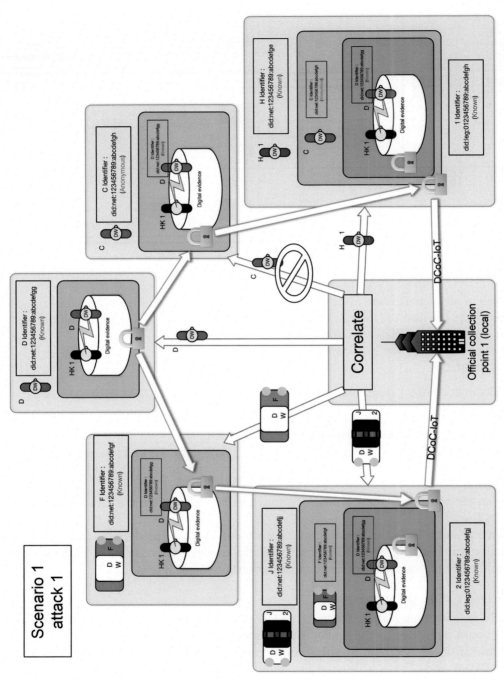

FIG. 17 Scenario 1, attack 1 analysis.

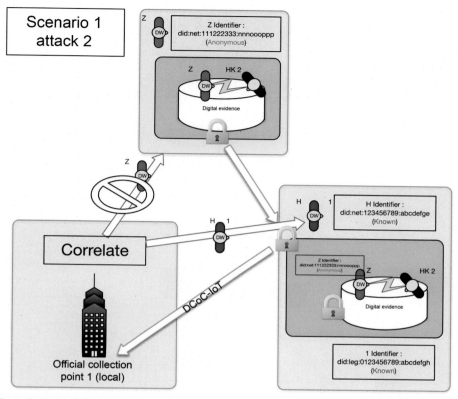

FIG. 18 Scenario 1, attack 2 analysis.

and delivering the DE securely over different routes via DW J2 and DW H1 to the OCP. DW J2 and DW H1 are known DWs within the ecosystem, and because they are DW custodians, they have elevated privileges within the OCP environment.

DW F is known and has disclosed PII about themselves which can be correlated back to the owner in the event of further attesting in the investigation. DW C has decided to remain anonymous and hasn't disclosed any attributes relating to their identity, correlating back to the anonymous DW that is not possible. All evidence is encrypted and securely stored on tamper proof storage which contains DE and identity information.

3.11.2 Attack 2 (remote)

Fig. 18 contains attack 2 where victim Z is a DW and has suffered a remote attack over the Internet by HK2. Victim Z is a DW which contains DE of the attack on its tamper proof storage for further analysis, though the attack has been witnessed by DW H1 who also happens to be a custodian and has elevated privileges to deliver DE to OCP 1. DW Z was anonymous at the time of the attack, and correlating back to Z would be impossible unless the victim decided to come forward and disclose themselves.

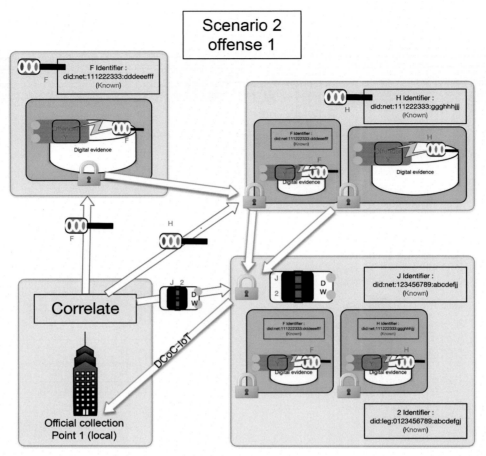

FIG. 19 Scenario 2, offence 1 analysis.

3.12 Scenario 2

All offences in scenario 2 demonstrate the following:

- How a self-sovereign IdM scheme which leverages on a DLT-based environment can use DIDs to bind DWs to their users, though binding DIDs to nonhuman identities such as the smart road infrastructure should be possible as per DID principals.
- How all DE is associated to the DW who processed it and contains information relating to the acts of crime which also includes identifier information throughout the IoT and DCoC-IoT transmission process.
- How multiple known DWs may witness and contain the same DE that will be delivered to OCP 1 via the DCoC-IoT process.
- How correlating DE to the known DWs is possible due to their disclosed attributes.

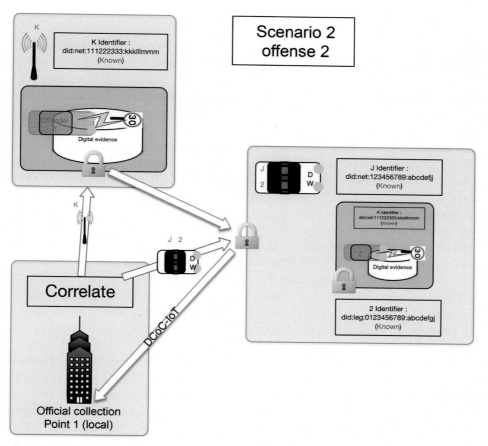

FIG. 20 Scenario 2, offence 2 analysis.

3.12.1 Offence 1

Fig. 19 contains the recorded offence where DW F witnessed offender Y driving through the red traffic light. DW H also witnessed the same offence by offender Y and also recorded and encrypted the DE on its tamper proof storage. Both sets of DE were transmitted to custodian DW J2 who then transmitted the DE via the DCoC-IoT process to OCP 1. All DE was correlated back to the DWs due to their disclosed attributes.

3.12.2 Offence 2

Fig. 20 contains the recorded offence where DW K witnessed offender Z violating the speed limit. The DE was recorded and encrypted on DW J2's tamper proof storage which due to its elevated privilege on OCP 1 transmitted the DE via the DCoC-IoT process. All DE was correlated back to the DW due to its disclosed attributes.

4 Conclusion and future work

This chapter analyses the various mechanisms for proposing an alternative solution to anonymise the DW. The BC-type selection is consortium based as it permits a multitude of preselected institutions to validate transactions in an unbiased manner, and validators are governed by a web of trust. The consensus method satisfies eco-friendly sustainability objectives as it is lightweight and reduces energy demand when compared with other consensus protocols.

A self-sovereign-based IdM meets user's privacy concerns as it puts DW owners in control of their attributes and claims with the use of DIDs. The use of zero-knowledge proof grants the DW and the DW ecosystem the assurance of who the person behind the identity actually is. No user identity data are stored on the decentralised ledger, but instead, users store all details securely on their personal devices. This allows users to conform to the GDPR legislation where a user has the right to be forgotten. The risk of mass identity theft will be mitigated to a large degree in a decentralised self-sovereign environment when compared with centralised third-party providers which have lost millions of user credentials.

The use of DIDs enables anonymity, though when used in a DW ecosystem, DE may not be admissible in a court of law due to the inability to correlate back to the witness; however, correlation is possible if the DW discloses the identity. The use of DIDs may also be used for nonhuman identifiers, and the opportunity to expand the concept of DWs from human to a nonhuman approach may be possible.

Future research may enable smart road infrastructure to act as DWs which could contribute to governing traffic and vehicular-related offences. A challenge when using DWs in a nonhuman environment will be how to determine what unique features to bind witness infrastructure to, in a similar way to how human biometrics have unique characteristics. The vision of a DW is only conceptual, though further research as to how a legal framework may accommodate digital anonymity within the justice system may contribute towards speeding up the DW reality.

References

Action Fraud, 2018. Victims Lost £41 Million to Romance Fraud in 2017. (Online). Available from: https://www.actionfraud.police.uk/news/victims-lost-41-million-to-romance-fraud-in-2017-feb18. (Accessed 27 May 2018).

Allison, I., 2018. Banking Giant ING Is Quietly Becoming a Serious Blockchain Innovator—CoinDesk. (Online). Available from: https://www.coindesk.com/banking-giant-ing-quietly-becoming-serious-blockchain-innovator. (Accessed 4 February 2020).

Assets.ey.com, 2019. Seize the Day: Public Blockchain is on the Horizon. (Online). Available from: https://assets.ey.com/content/dam/ey-sites/ey-com/en_gl/topics/blockchain/ey-public-blockchain-opportunity-snapshot.pdf. (Accessed 9 February 2020).

Aublin, P., Mokhtar, S., Quéma, V., 2013. RBFT: Redundant Byzantine Fault Tolerance. Pakupaku.me. (Online). Available from: http://pakupaku.me/plaublin/rbft/5000a297.pdf. (Accessed 19 October 2018).

Community, W., 2020. Decentralized Identifiers (DIDs) v1.0. W3c-ccg.github.io. (Online). Available from: https://w3c-ccg.github.io/did-spec/#dfn-did-path. (Accessed 21 February 2020).

Dunphy, P., Petitcolas, F., 2018. A First Look at Identity Management Schemes on the Blockchain. (Online). Arxiv.org. Available from: https://arxiv.org/ftp/arxiv/papers/1801/1801.03294.pdf. (Accessed 21 February 2020).

Dunphy, P., Garratt, L., Petitcolas, F., 2018. Decentralizing digital identity: open challenges for distributed ledgers. In: 2018 IEEE European Symposium on Security and Privacy Workshops (EuroS&PW).

Ecb.europa.eu, 2014. Report on the Pan-European Use of Electronic Mandates for SEPA Direct Debit—Issues and the Way Forward. (Online). Available from: https://www.ecb.europa.eu/paym/retpaym/shared/pdf/2nd_eprb_meeting_item4.pdf?27ef4897696839d1e7d0918f6b2dae48. (Accessed 13 October 2018).

Elsden, C., Manohar, A. (2018). Survey and Typology of Blockchain Applications (Sep 2017) (online). https://doi.org/10.6084/m9.figshare.5765502.v1. figshare.com (Accessed 17 December 2019)

Ey.com, 2019. EY Releases Third-Generation Zero-Knowledge Proof Blockchain Technology to the Public Domain. (Online). Available from: https://www.ey.com/en_gl/news/2019/12/ey-releases-third-generation-zero-knowledge-proof-blockchain-technology-to-the-public-domain. (Accessed 3 February 2020).

Facebook, 2019. Terms of Service. (Online). Available from: https://www.facebook.com/legal/terms/update. (Accessed 16 December 2019).

Facebook, 2020. Facebook—Log In or Sign Up. (Online). Available from: https://www.facebook.com/. (Accessed 20 February 2020).

Foundation, S., 2016a. Home—Sovrin. Sovrin. (online). Available from: https://sovrin.org/. (Accessed 5 October 2018).

Foundation, 2016b. Stewards Archive—Sovrin. (Online). Available from: https://sovrin.org/stewards/. (Accessed 10 October 2018).

Garcia, P., 2018. Biometrics on the blockchain. Biom. Technol. Today 2018 (5), 5–7.

GitHub, 2016. hyperledger/indy-plenum. (Online). Available from: https://github.com/hyperledger/indy-plenum/wiki. (Accessed 2 November 2018).

GitHub, 2018. jpmorganchase/quorum. (Online). Available from: https://github.com/jpmorganchase/quorum/wiki/ZSL. (Accessed 11 February 2020).

Holm, E., 2012. Identity crime: the challenges in the regulation of identity crime. In: 2012 International Conference on Cyber Security, Cyber Warfare and Digital Forensic (CyberSec).

Indu, I., Anand, P., Bhaskar, V., 2018. Identity and access management in cloud environment: mechanisms and challenges. Eng. Sci. Technol. 21 (4), 574–588.

Mesnard, C., 2016. Trusted National Identity Schemes. (Online). Eema.org. Available from: https://www.eema.org/wp-content/uploads/mesnard1.pdf. (Accessed 17 January 2019).

Nieto, A., Rios, R., Lopez, J., 2017. Digital witness and privacy in IoT: anonymous witnessing approach. In: 2017 IEEE Trustcom/BigDataSE/ICESS.

OECD. (2001). OECD glossary of statistical terms—electronic transaction definition [online]. Stats.oecd.org. Available from: https://stats.oecd.org/glossary/details.asp?ID=578 (Accessed 15 December 2019).

Ostrovsky, R., Yung, M., Venkatesan, R., 1999. Interactive Hashing Simplifies Zero-Knowledge Protocol Design. (Online). Available from: https://www.researchgate.net/profile/Moti_Yung/publication/2280556_Interactive_Hashing_Simplifies_Zero-Knowledge_Protocol_Design/links/543be2950cf24a6ddb97b948/Interactive-Hashing-Simplifies-Zero-Knowledge-Protocol-Design.pdf. (Accessed 12 February 2020).

Quisquater, J., Guillou, L., Quisquater, M., Quisquater, M., Quisquater, M., Guillou, M., Guillou, G., Guillou, A., Guillou, G., Guillou, S., Berson, T., 1998. How to Explain Zero-Knowledge Protocols to your Children. (Online). Pages.cs.wisc.edu. Available from: http://pages.cs.wisc.edu/~mkowalcz/628.pdf. (Accessed 13 February 2020).

Ramalingam, D., Chinnaiah, V., 2018. Fake profile detection techniques in large-scale online social networks: a comprehensive review. Comput. Electr. Eng. 65, 165–177.

Rivera, R., Robledo, J., Larios, V., Avalos, J., 2017. How digital identity on blockchain can contribute in a smart city environment. In: 2017 International Smart Cities Conference (ISC2).

Singh, A., Chatterjee, K., 2015. Identity management in cloud computing through claim-based solution. In: 2015 Fifth International Conference on Advanced Computing & Communication Technologies.

Statista, 2018. eServices Report 2018. Statista. (Online). Available from: https://www.statista.com/study/42306/eservices-report/. (Accessed 2 June 2018).

Stern, J., 2001. The Electronic Signatures in Global and National Commerce Act. Berkeley Law Scholarship Repository. (Online). Available from: https://doi.org/10.15779/Z38K96S. (Accessed 17 October 2018).

Sullivan, C., 2018. Digital identity—from emergent legal concept to new reality. Comput. Law Secur. Rev. 34 (4), 723–731.

Technology power users are at greatest risk of identity fraud, 2016. Comput. Fraud Secur 2016 (8), 1–3. (Online). Available from: https://www.sciencedirect.com/science/article/pii/S1361372316300574. (Accessed 3 January 2019).

Toapanta, S., Gallegos, L., Trejo, J., 2016. Security analysis of civil registry database of Ecuador. In: 2016 International Conference on Electrical, Electronics, and Optimization Techniques (ICEEOT).

Toapanta, M., Mafla, E., Orizaga, J., 2018. Conceptual model for identity management to mitigate the database security of the registry civil of Ecuador. Mater. Today 5 (1), 636–641.

9

Zero Trust networks, the concepts, the strategies, and the reality

David Allan Eric Haddon

IMPERIAL COLLEGE, LONDON, UNITED KINGDOM

1 Introduction

When Matt Soseman, security architect at Microsoft made the announcement that firewalls were no longer needed (Soseman, 2019) this might have appeared at first sight that Microsoft were throwing caution to the wind and are giving the impression that network security is no longer important.

Following this announcement in April 2019, Microsoft announced that they were dropping the baseline password expiration policy from Windows 10. The direction of travel might appear rash and imply that Microsoft are pandering to the users that hate IT people who disrupt and hinder business by blocking websites and emails with firewalls, web proxies, and email filters and frustrate users by enforcing password changes. The user is king, and any slight inconvenience caused by security is maligned as a nuisance and hindrance to business. Users want security, but they want security to be unobtrusive. The words false positive, quarantine, undeliverable, unavailable, and not found are no longer acceptable, yet at the same time if a spam email gets through an explanation is demanded as to why it was allowed.

Microsoft's view why firewalls are no longer useful as a first line of defence though is based on the following argument:

> *What has made the trusted technology obsolete is the variety of devices employees use to access corporate data from far-flung places outside the corporate offices.*
>
> *Gonsalves (2019)*

Although Microsoft's statements appear rather frivolous, it goes without saying that Microsoft has put considerable thought into how security is evolving. Microsoft see the future with technologies like Windows Hello, authentication using biometrics, facial recognition, and leveraging Azure AD Conditional Access Policies with artificial intelligence checking for user and physical abnormalities and restricting access as needed. AI has long been used in card payment systems, where a suspicious transaction triggers a teleworker to investigate. Tomorrow's network authentication systems like Azure AD Conditional

Strategy, Leadership, and AI in the Cyber Ecosystem. https://doi.org/10.1016/B978-0-12-821442-8.00001-X
© 2021 Elsevier Inc. All rights reserved.

195

Access are already pursuing this approach. Taking this a stage further, Vanickis et al. (2018) have proposed methods whereby firewalls learn rules based on assets and zones.

The world is digital, and banking systems are online, and tax and national insurance submissions are now only accepted in digital format. Validating who, what device, and from what location is connected to a service is essential to reduce fraud.

This chapter will attempt to reconcile the concepts from the latest research from Forrester Research and others and discuss the concepts of a Zero Trust framework.

2 What is Zero Trust?

The Zero Trust model was initially proposed by John Kindervag of Forrester Research in 2010 (Kindervag, 2010). This proposal is very much an academic work considering the network, network zones, the need for central network visibility, and the logging necessary to create a data acquisition network (DAN) for reporting.

The concept of Zero Trust starts with the preposition that everything is untrusted (Vijayan, 2018) and all traffic should be monitored, so that a threat should trigger an alert and be isolated.

Cloud providers who are not responsible for client internal networks may advocate that perimeter firewalls and proxy servers are no longer needed. This is based on the premise that all data is secured in the cloud and that firewalls interfere with access. This though is naive as a rogue keylogger installed on a remote workstation could capture passwords and other information which could then be used to compromise a cloud service.

> *The key element of Zero Trust approach is to treat the internal network as untrusted to the same degree as the internet.*
>
> *Vanickis et al. (2018)*

Where some data are held on the internal network, the model proposes the network be divided into zones based on the assets to be protected by the zone, which implies that traffic between zones should be controlled by firewalls!

Some of the concepts are not new; the age-old practice of least privileged access as extolled in ISO27001 is an example of microsegregation which is a principle of Zero Trust.

3 What are the key principles of a Zero Trust network?

The five core concepts of Zero Trust Networks are as follows (Gilman and Barth, 2017, p. 1):

1. The Network is always assumed to be hostile.
2. External and internal threats exist on the network at all times.
3. Network locality is not sufficient for deciding trust in a network.
4. Every device, user, and network flow are authenticated and authorised.
5. Policies must be dynamic and calculated from as many sources of data as possible.

The other two important elements that John Kindervag includes are:

6. MCAP—'microcore and perimeter'. This is about microsegmentation of networks. Each of the switching zones attached to an interface is referred to as a microcore switch. A physical interface may support multiple MCAPs. Although Kindervag promotes the concept of network segmentation, it must be remembered that there is not a trusted network segment. The rational is that segmentation allows for the isolation of a network segment by software if necessary.

7. DAN—'Data Acquisition Network'. This relates to network visibility of traffic flows. Monitoring network traffic means having access to the traffic on all MCAP's which needs to be planned as part of the implementation strategy.

These two aims, MCAPS and DANS, are clearly slightly at odds because providing greater visibility gets problematic as the network is segregated.

4 Are there variations on the Zero Trust concept?

The Zero Trust model is also known by other names. This is because Zero Trust is a very general concept; when it comes to implementing Zero Trust, choices must be made and implemented in a consistent way. The strategies of Googles BeyondCorp and Cisco Trusted Access (CTA) are different approaches based on the strategies chosen by Google and Cisco, respectively.

Gartner refer their model as Continuous Adaptive Risk and Trust Assessment (CARTA). The concepts focus on software-defined perimeters rather than physical boundaries.

Microsoft's Zero Trust model revolves around Azure conditional access policies and Microsoft Intune which validates connected devices and verifies device-patching state.

Beraud et al. (2019)' technical overview shows how Microsoft interpret how a Zero Trust Network is implemented using Azure Active Directory. Beraud et al. recommend the deployment of at least two Azure conditional access policies.

A sign-in risk policy is a conditional access policy that can be configured based on the level of risk assigned to a connection.

A user risk policy is a conditional access policy that can be configured based on the likelihood that a person has been compromised.

Starting with Windows 2012R2 Data stored on file shares that can be encrypted to protect data in process (Microsoft, 2018). This is another example of a technology that fits the Zero Trust model.

Cisco Trusted Access (Cisco, 2019a) has three themes:

1. workforce—verify the user
2. workplace—verify compliant devices
3. workload—verify app behaviour

This is perhaps a simpler approach but nevertheless is on the same theme as John Kindervag's concepts.

BeyondCorp is the Zero Trust model that Google defined for their own network. Gilman and Barth (2017, p. 197) explain how Google have been moving their internal systems over to this model in a phased approach and how Gmail was rewritten to fit the BeyondCorp project. Google's remote users were migrated from using VPNs to using an access proxy.

> *All applications used at Google are required to work through the Access Proxy. The BeyondCorp initiative examined and qualified all applications.*
>
> *Ward and Beyer (2014)*

The point here is that Google have made sure that all the applications used by the organisation are compatible with the BeyondCorp model. Another example of an Access Proxy is Citrix Netscaler which is a widely for remote access. In Citirx once a remote user is verified access is granted over a TLS tunnel.

5 Let's examine Zero Trust core concepts?

Zero Trust Concept 1—**The network is always assumed to be hostile.** It is assumed that an attacker is already inside a network. If an attacker cannot authenticate either as a user or using a rogue device, then there should be no traffic that the attacker can intercept even if the attacker is connected to the internal network.

Zero Trust Concept 2—**External and internal threats exist on the network at all times**. This argument is partly because so many attacks involve insiders—see Fig. 1. Every device,

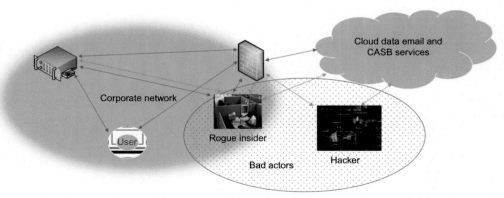

FIG. 1 The blurring of the network perimeter.

user, and network flow should be authenticated and authorised and continuously reauthenticated. In Zero Trust, security is based on authentication and authorisation not network location.

Zero Trust Concept 3—**Network locality is not a good enough reason for deciding trust in a network**. There is no longer a trusted and an untrusted network. Just because a machine is on the internal network is not a valid reason to trust it. 'Hiding information in one part of the network and not another suggests that one is more trusted than the other' (Gilman and Barth, 2017). From a security perspective the subdividing of a network should ensure that if bad actors have access to one network segment, they cannot easily access assets in another segment.

Zero Trust Concept 4—**Every device, user, and network flow are authenticated and authorised**. All network traffic is potentially a threat until authorised, inspected, and secured. Key to a Zero Trust is the principle of continuously verifying users and devices.

Zero trust Concept 5—**Policies must be dynamic and calculated from as many sources of data as possible**. Because network connections are dynamic, the policies that protect the network must be dynamic also. This is where AI and anomaly detection could leveraged threat information from systems like Darktrace, Cognito, a SIEM solution, or Microsoft Cloud App Security.

Zero Trust Concept 6—**Network microsegmentation**. VLANs have been a common way to segregate networks, however because a connection in one VLAN can theoretically monitor the traffic sent on another VLAN because the data travel via the same cable. Also routing between VLANs is often open; so other than pushing different devices into smaller broadcast networks, VLANs often add little to security. Microsegmentation is more common in software-defined networks (SDN's) where more sophisticated management tools exist. In Zero Trust, security starts with the data and service locations and works out from there to the client.

Zero Trust Concept 7—**Network visibility and Zero Trust monitoring solutions**. One of the fundamental principles of Zero Trust networks is to have complete visibility of everything on the network. Monitoring of devices, IP addresses, protocols in use, open ports, and data flows both within the network and from outside and being able to alert on abnormalities is a fundamental principle of securing a Zero Trust network.

6 So what products that can assist with a Zero Trust network monitoring?

Forescout (2018) is a product designed to give visibility of network devices with Zero Trust networks in mind. This is an important point made by Dr. Chase Cunningham, principle researcher at Forrester Research.

Visibility is the key in defending any valuable asset. You can't protect the invisible. The more visibility you have into your network across your business ecosystem, the better the chance you have to quickly detect the tell-tale signs of a breach in progress and to stop it. Zero Trust mandates significant investment in visibility and analytics across the business – regardless of location or hosting model.

Cunningham (2018)

Zeek (aka Bro) is an open-source tool for monitoring network traffic. Zeek separates different traffic types into different logs. Bro emerged in 2001 and can record data at the OSI data-link layer (layer 2) level on all LAN and VLAN traffic (Sommer, 2003). Bro can detect passwords in LDAP traffic, using a Bro script dsniff (Hill, 2016). It has powerful analysis tools like Bro-Cut which, when combined with Linux's awk, allows awesome search capabilities. Connecting mirrored switch ports to a monitoring server is the normal way of gathering visibility of network traffic.

Darktrace and Cognito are based on Bro and use AI and other algorithms to determine a baseline of what is normal on a network and then identify and alert on abnormal network traffic such as unusual traffic between workstations.

Palo Alto (2019) is also backing Zero Trust as the architecture of the future. From Palo Alto's white paper, it is seen that Cortex XDR (Palo Alto's cloud network anomaly detection solution) is the core of the Palo Alto's new strategy. This is supported by endpoint agents and firewalls that pass information to the Cortex XDR platform.

Fortinet has introduced the Fortinet Security fabric as part of their Zero Trust strategy. Forticloud is a cloud-based reporting tool that collects data from an organisations firewalls and gives visibility on network traffic.

Censornet (n.d.), **Netskope (n.d.)**, and **Symantec (2019)** have developed cloud access security broker (CASB) platforms which acts as a cloud-based cloud application, web and email proxy enabling conditional access and reporting on the patching and the antivirus status of an organisations endpoints. Being cloud based, Censornet shares attack information with all other Censornet users real-time, Netscope and Symantec's CloudSOC likewise, providing an advantage over on-premise only solutions. Microsoft Cloud App Security is arguably the most sophisticated CASB solution (Beraud et al., 2019).

For companies not using Office365, Centrify is an example of another Zero Trust framework (Centrify, 2018). In an office environment where all services are delivered by cloud services, the use of Zero-Core clients that have Citrix Receiver, VMWare's Horizon, and Microsoft terminal server client embedded in firmware is an alternative strategy that removes the threat from malware at the endpoints.

Other useful tools are cloud-managed antivirus solutions like Bitdefender MSP and Sophos Cloud, which can alert on devices that are not compliant or have issues so that they can be isolated.

For monitoring networks, several solutions exist including PacketMotion (now owned by VMWare); Lancope, now StealthWatch (Cisco, 2019b); Lumeta (Lumeta, 2019); and SolarWinds.

There are two threads to implementing Zero Trust concepts: The first is the cloud environment, and the other is in a physical environment. These concepts will be addressed in the following sections on Dev-Ops and physical environments.

7 The Cloud, Dev-Ops, and Zero Trust

The Datacentre model has now evolved to DevOps-based, hybrid-cloud environments. In an article in Network Security, Klein (2019) points out that microsegmentation has gone beyond VLANS.

> *These measures are designed to control the flow of traffic in and out of specific areas. However, they are not suited to dynamic, cloud-scale infrastructures in which applications and workloads are provisioned, automated, auto-scaled and migrated back and forth between on-premises and cloud instances or among cloud environments.*

As we can see from the earlier, software-defined networking (SDN) has become very agile and dynamic.

Because application infrastructures are dynamic, Klein goes on to state

> *It is focused on securing the applications themselves, rather than a particular sub-network or domain. In keeping with the zero-Trust model, this approach is intended to reduce the risk of individual applications being compromised by an unauthorised connection.*

In 2014 Google released an open-source system called Kubernetes which has become the de facto Dev-Ops container environment. It has centralised logging and monitoring built in. Google runs all its services now including Gmail, Google Search, and Google Maps in these environments.

> *Zero-downtime deployments are common, because Kubernetes does rolling updates by default (starting containers with the new version, waiting until they become healthy, and then shutting down the old ones).*
>
> *Arundel and Dominique (2019)*

Google provides an open-source email server called MailU, a docker-based mail server which developers can deploy on the Kubernetes platform which provides the monitoring that an organisation requires. This though is reinventing the wheel as Gmail is delivered on much the same platform and is managed and monitored by Google as part of the BeyondCorp framework and not the end user. There is a balance as to what is cost effective for an organisation to monitor and what should be trusted to a third party. This choice is a matter of cost and risk. Full stack monitoring of Kubernetes requires third-party tools such as Data Dog (Datadoghq, 2019), NewRelic (2019), Calico (2019), and Instana (2019).

The Calico project is a solution that enables the security of containers to be scaled providing microsegmentation and security and is commonly used in many Kubernetes deployments (Calico, 2019). In the world of Dev-Ops a Zero Trust Continuous Adaptive Risk and Trust Assessment (CARTA) with anomaly detection can be achieved with Tigera when building a CAAS platform using Kubernetes (Tigera, 2019). IBM have implemented

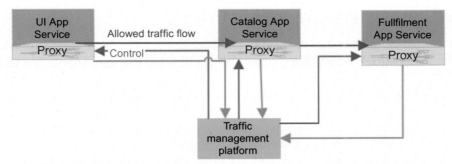

FIG. 2 How a traffic management platform such as Istio Service Mesh controls Sidecar proxies attached to Microservice Apps.

monitoring of Kubernetes with Istio Service Mesh which provides traffic management policy enforcement and telemetry collection (Istio, 2019) using sidecars (proxies) such as Lyft's Envoy which are deployed in each Kubernetes Pod. This is shown in Fig. 2.

It is seen that in the cloud environment the tools to secure microservices are reaching a level of maturity in terms of microsegmentation that has yet to be seen in the on-premise environment.

8 The on-premise environment and Zero Trust

Device-specific private keys based on TPMs allow PKI to be used with encryption keys that are unique for each device. TPMs are a chip embedded in a device that provides keys over secure channels to the operating system. They are used to provide secure boot and device authentication and are now common in notebooks and workstations. Boot security using a virtual TPM is also available in VMWare and Microsoft Hyper-V for virtualised servers. Intel and AMD have introduced TPM support for virtual servers in their processors which can be leveraged in Virtual Servers (Wan and Xiao, 2012). It is interesting to note that most servers including HP Gen 9 and Gen 10 servers are not shipped with TPM modules installed as standard. Since Windows 2016 Microsoft introduced a Host Guardian Service which can be configured to encrypt a virtual machine and manage the keys to start virtual machines.

Network switches are becoming far more intelligent, and quality switches can replicate traffic to a mirroring port which can be used to input data into Bro, Darktrace or Cognito. Although a switch might be described as a layer 2 switch because they pass traffic independent of VLAN tags, many switches are now layer 3 as they operate at the network layer, and some of these are effectively layer 4 as the ports allowed can also be specified. Taking it further, some CISCOs switches can be configured with sticky MACs on ports that lock a port to a specific MAC address. By using a network switch to physically or logically segment, a network provides extra security. A network switch can also be used to restrict the services that are available for communication between workstations and virtual servers; however, switch configurations changes may require switch reboots which may not be practical, so changes to switch configurations are not always the best approach.

Slaymaker (2018) in his comprehensive study on Zero Trust addresses internal threats argues that

> *networks must become more intelligent by moving up the stack to Layer 5, the session layer, where intelligent services reside.*

This provides the state and security functions for lower level functions.

Conran (2017) describes how Zero Trust is all about layer 5 (the session layer) of the ISO network layers. Conran makes the point that security in Zero Trust is end to end and not point to point as it would be with a firewall and a VPN.

9 Authentication mechanisms for Zero Trust networks

To avoid any possibility of a session being highjacked, it is important to verify that the user connection remains consistent and cannot be hijacked. If it is assumed that network traffic can be sniffed, then it is key that credentials are not transferred over the network in plain text.

Authentication mechanisms are various, and the authentication mechanism used for accessing an IMAP email account is different form to that used for connecting to a Windows network. Traditional authentication mechanisms, NTLM, Kerberos, and LDAP, focus on authentication over an internal network. With the evolution of cloud computing authentication, mechanisms have been scaled to support cloud services and internal systems. Microsoft have extended Active Directory to the Azure Cloud, and Google have done this with OpenIAM, but generally speaking, most authentication mechanisms have not changed in years.

Many network protocols including LDAP and RADIUS are decades old, and some commonly used protocols like Telnet, POP3, HTTP, and SMTP were around long before the World Wide Web was conceived by Berners-Lee in 1990, and although these protocols are now used with encrypted channels, the authorisation mechanisms of these protocols have not changed. A characteristic of these protocols is that once a user has been authenticated, access is granted for as long a user needs it. This is at odds with the principle of Zero Trust where reverification of a connection is a requirement. It is the authors view that research into replacing these legacy protocols is needed.

Continuous authentication sounds good, but in an office environment, a program that continually prompts a user for credentials would not be popular. Other methods like a system that checks that a USB key is still connected or that the device in use has not changed are simple mechanisms that solve this. Another approach is to use a session certificate so that once a tunnel is established, it becomes self-verifying. Web authentication protocols addressed these issues a long time ago by using session cookies, which enable wireless web connections to maintain session security even though a wireless internet connection might be flaky. In the future, standard network protocols may need to be improved in a similar manner.

To quote Stallings (2013, p. 439)

> *It is generally assumed that access to physical connection conveys authority to connect to a LAN … In wireless networks 'IEEE 802.11 requires mutually acceptable, successful authentication before a station can establish an association with an AP'.*

IEEE 802.11 also specifies a deauthentication mechanism. One must not forget though that this is the method by which WEP is cracked when a legitimately joined device can be deauthenticated by an attacker causing the retransmission of initialisation vectors. Reauthentication mechanisms must not therefore inadvertently assist an attacker to crack passwords.

As continuous authentication is overlooked in many wired network protocols, a more imaginative approach is required to reauthenticate wired connections. Schiavone et al. (2016) proposes a method of continuous authentication by biometric means. This approach removes the necessity for a user to reenter passwords. Schiavone makes the point that by continuously verifying the user by biometric means provides a mechanism that enforces nonrepudiation as it makes it impossible for users to deny their actions. Ananya and Singh (2018) propose a mechanism of using a user's keystroke dynamics for verifying a user, but this assumes a user is performing the same tasks. A problem with this is when a user switches from writing correspondence to internet banking, the keystroke dynamics will change.

Schaffer (2019) explores the issue of continuous authentication and concludes that smartphones that have several built-in sensors are possible means of continuously authenticating a user.

Using keyboard, fingerprint, and iris biometric methods of authentication results in the same information being used again and again to verify the user. Another novel approach would be to phase out keyboards and mice as these interfaces provide no identity information at the point of input. Speech recognition as a means of data input has much greater possibilities as the data input is modulated with distinguishable voice patterns. Aware (2019) uses two different methods: text independent and text dependent. For text dependent the same passphrases are used in enrolment and for verification. The problem with this is that the phrase would be a recoding which could be used to gain authentication. Text independent ideally would use the same text a user is using with text recognition software. Currently, text recognition software packages like Dragon do not currently authenticate voices, and Aware cannot currently be used for dictation.

Radius Authentication—Radius uses a shared secret to encrypt and a username and a password. Radius is supported by most firewalls and routers and by almost every two-factor authentication vendor and VPN provider. Radius is fast, simple, and secure;

however, its implementation requires the manual input of shared secret passwords which is a challenge for anything other than a small-scale deployment. Radius Authentication uses TCP or UDP port 1812, and to make it usable externally, it is generally proxied over HTTPS.

RSA SecureID—SecureID uses hardware tokens for user authentication. The token requires a passcode to unlock the device and generates a new hardware token every 60 s. SecureID is often integrated with Radius for authentication (Todorov, 2007, p. 24).

Duo Security Authentication—Duo is an example of a radius proxy service that is deployed for two-factor authentication services that uses a radius server that can integrate with active directory. Duo security has championed the cause of Zero Trust with their two-factor authentication system. Duo (2019) in the guide highlights five phases to affect Zero Trust security:

1. Establish user trust
2. Establish device trust
3. Get visibility into devices
4. Ensure secure access to all apps
5. Enforce adaptive policies

This is perhaps like Cisco's approach which is not surprising as Duo is now owned by Cisco.

PKI Authentication—PKI is the chosen method by which Zero Trust Networks should be implemented (Gilman and Barth, 2017). This is because unlike the other authentication mechanisms, it can be used for not only verifying users and servers but also for servers to verify users and connecting devices. This is done with public and private certificates. Although PKI is the chosen method for many Zero Trust implementations, this does not mean that it is the only method, but given the issues with other authentication protocols, it is perhaps the best method that is currently practical to use for implementing Zero Trust at the current time. In implementation a change of method might be needed, for example when it comes to accessing files on a network, rather than using SMB file shares, PKI could be implemented by sharing files using Microsoft SharePoint.

TLS has become a common mechanism for clients to validate a resource; however, TLS is anonymous if the resource just validates the server. Gilman and Barth (2017, p. 155) argue that

> *Mutual Authentication is a requirement for security protocols conforming to the zero-trust model, and TLS is no exception.*

The point being that to prevent man-in-the-middle attacks, the server should also validate the client, so TLS by itself is not satisfactory. Mutual PKI authentication (Sudhakar et al., 2015) therefore provides a means by which once a client has verified a server and a server has verified a client, that data can be transferred over a TLS tunnel. Mutual TLS is now the accepted way to secure and verify SMTP traffic between mail servers.

PKI authentication is also a continuous authentication mechanism and data transferred over a connection protected by PKI does not need to be sent over the internet in a VPN tunnel which means that VPNs are not necessary for external connections. Indeed the concept of a VPN tunnel is contrary to zero trust as it implies that the traffic in the tunnel is not secure.

Implementing PKI is not without its challenges Ferguson and Schneier (2003) state that "PKI's simply do not work in the real world like they do in the dream." PKI ideally needs a trusted certificate authority for certificates to be verified with. There are two options: the first is to use public certificate authorities (CA). The downside of this is that every device needs a public certificate; then this will be costly. Certificate also have an expiration date which may be a few years. Apple Safari and Google Chrome will soon be restricting access to servers with certificates with a validity of more than a year so keeping certificates current is an increasing maintenance task. The alternative is to save money is to use self-certified certificates. The downside of this is that the public certificate generated will need to be enrolled into devices and the network will need to have its own certificate server for generating certificates and rolling out certificates.

Encryption of communications clearly requires processor time which impacts the speed of communication links. RSA is a public-key algorithm based on the difficulty of factoring large prime numbers, however the overhead of RSA is not suitable for very high-speed communications (Schneier, 2015, p. 469). For this reason, DeCusatis et al. (2016) have proposed first-packet inspection based on authentication as a method to defend software-defined networks (SDN) from attack. A steganographic overlay is a theoretical method that embeds network authentication tokens in a TCP request allowing blocking unauthorised traffic. Packets are authorised at the transport layer before any access to the network or servers is granted. This has been tested with a BlackRidge hardware device that implements TAC with first-packet inspection in enforce mode.

An example of improving user verification can be seen in how Facebook have introduced Facebook reauthentication mechanism.

The Facebook auth mechanism introduces the concept of an AUTH nonce – an app generated alphanumeric nonce which can be used to provide replay protection.
Facebook (2019)

When locking a screen on an Android device, the underlying session remains active. Users do not wish to reinput user credentials to unlock a screen. The answer is the use of a nonce (number used once) which is used by the client to validate the session. This process happens in the background and ensures that a session cannot he highjacked. The process is at layer 3, the transport layer, but ideally the process would be at the application layer, but that would require all applications to incorporate a network authentication function which is not likely.

10 Zero Trust and the threat of data theft

Data exfiltration prevention in an organisation very much focusses on detection either at the endpoint (workstation) or at the network perimeter (firewall). In a Zero Trust network where the focus of detection is on the network, however as the attacker can exfiltrate data using encrypted tunnels, the only way to detect the content of the traffic is at the endpoints and not in-between where traffic is encrypted. Examples of endpoint solutions and DLP solutions are Safetica and CoSoSys and is also common in many CASB solutions. Without products like these the network administrator can still have visibility of the traffic flow but not the content.

11 Wireless and mobile networks and Zero Trust

One issue with personal Wi-Fi systems using WPA/WPA2 is the lack of channel isolation in many implementations which allows Wi-Fi devices to attack other devices connected to the same access point. Although enterprise implementations might protect against this, WPA3 better provides channel isolation by default. In 2018 Samsung launched the Samsung 10 and 10+ series of their mobile phones. To improve user privacy, these devices not only support IEEE802.11ax but also resolve domain names using DoH (DNS over HTTPS) as definned in RFC 8484 (Google, 2017). Samsung like other mobile manufacturers are also implementing reauthentication mechanisms (Agarwal, 2016). These are further examples of how Zero Trust concepts are being discretely introduced in the mobile arena though increased privacy provided by DoH is somewhat at the expense of security as when DNS queries are encrypted using DoH in a TLS tunnel, monitoring of DNS queires is no longer possible.

12 DHCP and Zero Trust

DHCP is defined in RFC2131 (Droms, 1997). Hardware validation by MAC address is standard in DHCP, and by specifying option 125, a DHCP server can be configured to service only known MAC addresses; however, user validation is not a standard feature of DHCP and probably never will be because DHCP is really an operating system-independent process. RFC5182 (2008) has options for carrying authentication for network access (PANA). Ideas to add DHCP user authentication are not new, in 1999 RFC 2485 was published (Drach, 1999) The Open group's User Authentication Protocol which proposed using a list of URLs, HTTP, or HTTPS that are capable of processing authentication requests. In 2002 Komori and Saito (2002) also proposed a secure DHCP system with user authentication. Not surprisingly, none of these proposals to improve the security of DHCP using authentication have gained traction.

13 How do network security auditing standards align with Zero Trust?

The statement that firewalls are no longer needed implies a rethinking of security standards which is necessary, and the implication is that the established computer-auditing standards like PCI-DSS, COBIT 5, and ISO27001 that mandate a perimeter firewall are outdated; however, these standards have always promoted defence in depth. One important point when comparing Zero Trust with ISO27001 and Cobit5 is that Zero Trust concepts do not cover physical security, culture, and governance. These are core aspects of ISO27001 and COBIT 5, so Zero Trust must be viewed as an augmentation to these standards not a replacement.

John Kindervag's background is in PCI DSS auditing. Many of the controls specified in PCI-DSS auditing assume that the attacker is already on the inside which is the principle of defence in depth which is perfectly aligned with the Zero Trust model. PCI-DSS focusses on how credit card data are stored and processed. Zero Trust extends these concepts to include all data and processes.

14 Implementing Zero Trust concepts starts with the data

Starting from the data a Zero Trust architecture starts by protecting the data at rest. Encryption of Microsoft SQL data at rest has been possible since SQL 2008R2 using transparent data encryption (TDE). TDE is now also used by Azure SQL and Azure SQL Data Warehouse data files. TDE encrypts SQL log files and data files. Whilst data is in process on the SQL server, the data held in memory is in a decrypted state, so whilst an attack on the data held on the SQL server might be protected, the SQL server could still vulnerable to an attack on data in process or data in memory. If the data to be protected is on-premise and a Cloud CASB solution is deployed then this might not be able to provide the Zero Trust protection to the on-premises assets and an appropriate additional Zero Trust solution might be required to protect these on-premises assets.

15 Developing a Zero Trust network strategy

Palo Alto have published a five-step guide to implementing a Zero Trust network (Balaouras et al., 2019). The stages are as follows:

1. Define your protect Surface. This requires an identification of data assets and assessing their vulnerabilities whilst at rest, in process, and in transit.
2. Map the transaction flows. This involves identifying the data flows to and from the data assets. Palo Alto promote Cortex Data Lake (Palo Alto2, 2019) to do this. This is an AI network traffic collection, analysis, and response solution that integrates with Palo Alto firewalls.

3. Architect a Zero Trust network.
4. Create the Zero Trust Policy.
5. Monitor and maintain the network.

Expanding on this based on the discussion so far, these stages should be considered for developing a 10-point Zero Trust framework in a small on-premise environment.

1. Identify the data assets and services that need to be protected.
2. Map the internal data flows to the data assets and identify the flows and authentication methods in use on the network. Identify any authentication protocols that are unencrypted with the network and secure them, for example, replace LDAP with LDAPS and HTTP with HTTPS. One should even consider replacing printers with ones that do not send printing information over the network to network printers on port 9100 in plain text.
3. Based on the protocols allowed, adjust the desktop and server global firewall policies to only allow the protocols identified in the previous step.
4. Deploy a network monitoring solution such as Zeek on the internal network and determine if any applications are sending network credentials in clear text. https://www.zeek.org/bro-workshop-2011/solutions/incident-response/index.html shows how Zeek can be used to detect user credentials sent in plain text. Other network monitoring solutions that can monitor and record network traffic flows and monitor servers are Nagios and FortiCloud. One must consider how the monitoring tool can be leveraged to enforce policies.
5. Consider creating a secondary network and moving data sets and services one at a time from the legacy network to the Zero Trust network (Palo Alto, 2019).
6. Encrypt the SMB file sharing protocol (Microsoft, 2018).
7. Obtain TPM modules for servers and encrypt all data at rest and encrypt virtual servers and drives with BitLocker and virtual TPM and workstations with TPM and PIN recovery options having been thoroughly evaluated as these must not be diminished due to increase security. This may require extra servers to host server replicas. Once implemented the recovery procedures must be documented and tested.
8. Implement two-factor authentication to validate user authentication, either with a product like Duo, a hardware device or using biometrics.
9. Evaluate loss of recovery options and performance that might arise by implementing encryption on servers and file shares and implement mitigating measures such as real time replication and hardware capable of delivering increased performance.
10. Implement TPM authentication for devices using Conditional Access Policies so that all endpoint connections to the network are validated and deploy conditional access user policies (Beraud et al., 2019).

The ninth point is important as at first sight, it might appear that Zero Trust can be implemented without having to deploy more physical servers; however, having encrypted the servers, the recovery options that a computer engineer has available in the event of a server failure are reduced. This reduction must be compensated for otherwise in the event of a failure the report to the board will state that how recovery was hampered by the increased security. As company boards are focussed on uptime and availability, downtime must be avoided. The performance of servers will also derogate with the increased workload that encryption brings. This situation is not good, and it is therefore advised to invest where possible to improve recovery options and system performance as part of a Zero Trust project. Increased monitoring also means increased costs, though there are several open-source tools that can be used to keep costs down.

16 How a future on-premise Zero Trust network might look

In Fig. 3 the firewall is moved from being a perimeter defence to the heart of the network as a network segregation device that is also a reporting agent linked to a cloud monitoring and reporting service. The ports that are required for communication to the server are specifically set as needed in the same way as outbound ports to the Internet are.

This model also solves the dilemma of microsegmentation in the physical environment as proposed by John Kindervag. Increased segmentation and network monitoring are seemingly incompatible concepts, but making the firewall, the network segmentation and monitoring device, this conundrum is solved. In an ideal world the firewall would leverage AI to dynamically implement policies based on threats as detected by the monitoring service. The policy engine being either built into the firewall or controlling a firewall using a generic firewall control language. A design for a generic policy language and a

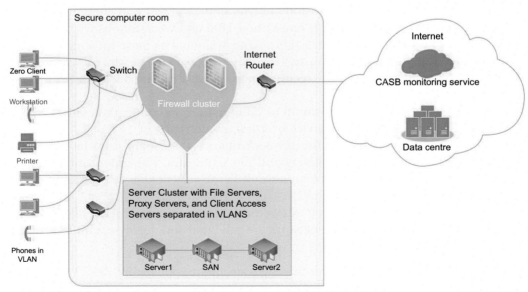

FIG. 3 The Firewall Cluster at the heart of the network rather than at the perimeter.

firewall policy language for Zero Trust networks has been proposed by Vanickis et al. (2018). The concept of a policy engine dynamically implementing policies has now been defined in a National Cyber Centre of Excellence (part of NIST) project as a model for Zero Trust implementations (Kerman et al., 2020).

The minimum ports required for the workstations to access the servers are

Service	Port
DHCP	UDP 67.68
DNS	UDP, TCP 53
SMB	TCP 445
HTTP	TCP 80
HTTPS	TCP 443
KERBEROS	TCP/UDP 88/464
NETBIOS	TCP 143
NTP	TCP 123
SAMBA	TCP 139
WEBPROXY	TCP 8080 (most common)

The minimum ports required for the servers to access the workstations and printers is just TCP 9100 for print queues. In practice, antivirus management and other services will require ports to be open between the servers and workstations.

With a larger network the model might also be a software agent on each workstation controlled by a policy engine and reporting traffic flows to a monitoring server which can alert and act to deal with anomalous traffic. A simple example of this can be achieved using a network switch and Bro as in Fig. 4.

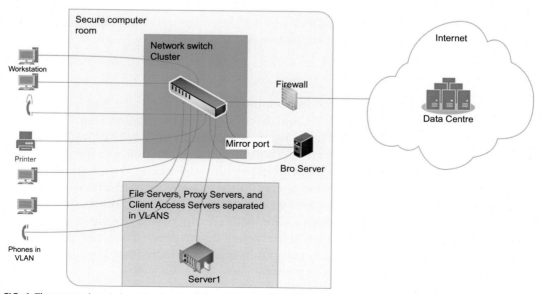

FIG. 4 The network switch at the heart of the network where the policy engine exists on an on-premise server.

Implementing a Zero Trust network is inevitably a staged process. The implementor must be certain having encrypted all devices and connections that encryption keys cannot get lost. If the keys fall into the wrong hands, then the security is broken, or if keys are lost to the implementor, then a company could be locked out of their data.

Zeek Scripts for alerting on large uploads (flow.bro) and large number of DNS queries (dns.bro) are available from the Evernote security team at https://github.com/evernote/bro-scripts/blob/master/exfiltration/scripts/. Another interesting script is bad-share.bro that detects connections to administrative file SMB shares which is available at https://github.com/richiercyrus/Bro-Scripts. These are examples of scripts that can detect anomalies. Zeek can alert on these but cannot by itself dynamically implement policies based on these anomalies.

17 Practical limitations of the Zero Trust model

The Zero Trust model is not without its limitations. As an example, consider a user working on some documents at home on a notebook. The notebook is secure, user access is restricted using restricted privileges, and an antivirus solution is in place; however, the notebook is used to access the Internet. Though access rights will prevent a programme being installed and maintaining persistence, a malicious programme could still be inadvertently loaded into memory and used to give access to workstation resources. If support tools such as TeamViewer QuickSupport can be used without local administrative rights, then so could a malicious key logger or a command and control attack. Zero Trust security concepts do not address physical security, culture, security awareness, policies or governance in an organisation, therefore any audit of Zero Trust implementations will need to assess Zero Trust technologies in the context of an organisations security requirements although ultimately security standards will embrace Zero Trust architectures. The National Cyber Centre of Excellence's Zero Trust implementations project shows how NIST are already heading this way (Kerman et al., 2020).

18 Conclusion

In this chapter, it is seen that as the network perimeter has become a blurred concept, security boundaries are being redefined, and detecting protection against threats is adopting a much more holistic approach. It has been argued that the future of firewalls is could be as a device to facilitate network segmentation, monitoring and policy enforcement as a component of a policy engine rather than as a permiter defence.

If the Zero Trust reality is end-to-end encryption of all network traffic, then servers are going to need to do extra work encrypting data. Ultimately, faster processors will be required in workstations and servers to cope with this increased overhead. Given the power of quantum computing, it goes without saying that to prevent internet traffic being captured and decoded by a quantum computer, then ever-increasing key sizes will be needed requiring ever more processor power.

If organisations are to monitor networks effectively, the cost of implementing a monitoring solution needs to be more affordable. They also need to be easier to deploy. Standard monitoring protocols like SNMP require specialist knowledge to deploy SNMP servers to alert. Hopefully soon, operating systems will have better monitoring and alerting mechanisms built in.

As discussed, many legacy network protocols are at odds with Zero Trust as they exchange user credentials in plaintext. Applications must move to more secured protocols, and further research into more secure network protocols that embrace continuous reauthentication is needed. Enhancements to DHCP which incorporate authentication would improve security, but what is needed is new standards that are vendor independent.

From the discussion, implementing a Zero Trust framework increases cost, and adopting Zero Trust principles is inevitable, and it has been seen that Zero Trust ideology is discretely being introduced, developments in the android platform being examples of that trend. Organisations will no doubt familiarise themselves with the concepts of Zero Trust and devise their own strategies. Just as Google has implemented BeyondCorp in the cloud environment, implementing Zero Trust concepts is now necessary to secure and protect data and services in on-premise environments.

Company Boards are now being constantly being reminded of the risks to their systems, and network security is a fixed topic on many company board meeting agendas.

Boards need to ask IT departments pertinent questions in relation to internal security, for example,

What communications on the internal network are unencrypted?
Are there any application that authenticate in clear text?
What data exist on devices not owned by the company?
Are all new projects, purchases of equipment and applications assessed against the organisations Zero Trust framework for compatibility before being acquired?

The concepts to develop an adhoc Zero Trust solution has been discussed. The Zero Trust framework that will become most popular will no doubt be CASB implementations due to the savings provided by the scale of these solutions and the recognition of the brands promoting these. It is the author's belief that as CEOs begin to realise the vulnerabilities that exist within the corporate network that Zero Trust and its principles will slowly gain adoption using a combination of CASB and other Zero Trust technologies as appropriate for an organisation.

References

Agarwal, L., 2016. Reauthentication Mechanisms for Smartphone. [Online] Available from: https://uwspace.uwaterloo.ca/bitstream/handle/10012/10611/Agarwal_Lalit.pdf?sequence=1&isAllowed=y. (Accessed 7 July 2019).

Ananya, S.S., 2018. Keystroke Dynamics for Continuous Authentication. [Online] Available from: https://ieeexplore.ieee.org/stamp/stamp.jsp?arnumber=8442703. (Accessed 1 August 2019).

Arundel, J., Dominique, J., 2019. Cloud Native DevOps With Kubernetes: Building, Deploying, and Scaling Modern Applications in the Cloud. O'Reilly.

Aware, 2019. Aware Website. [Online] Available from: https://www.aware.com. (Accessed 22 November 2019).

Balaouras, S., Cunningham, C., Cerrato, P., 2019. Five Steps to a Zero Trust Model Forester Research. Available from: http://www.forrester.com/report/Five+Steps+To+A+Zero+Trust+network/-/E-RES120510. (Accessed 8 July 2019).

Beraud, P., Grasset, J., Jumelet, A., 2019. Implementing a Zero Trust Approach With Azure Active Directory. [Online] Available from: https://download.microsoft.com/download/8/2/7/8271584F-A6D6-419A-B262-C37E5FFAB593/Implementing-a-Zero-Trust-approach-with-Azure-Active-Directory.pdf. (Accessed 9 August 2019).

Calico, 2019. Project Calico. https://www.projectcalico.org. (Accessed 8 August 2019).

Censornet, n.d. Cloud Access Security Broker. [Online] Available from: https://www.censornet.com/products/casb/. (Accessed 25 July 2020).

Centrify, 2018. Rethink Security for Zero Trust. [Online] Available from: https://www.centrify.com/zero-trust-security/. (Accessed 19 August 2018).

Cisco, 2019a. Cisco Trusted Access. [Online] Available from: https://www.cisco.com/c/dam/en/us/products/collateral/security/trusted-access-solution-overview.pdf. (Accessed 31 July 2019).

Cisco, 2019b. Stealthwatch. [Online] Available from: https://www.cisco.com/c/en/us/products/security/stealthwatch/index.html. (Accessed 26 July 2019).

Conran, M., 2017. Zero Trust Networking (ZTN): Don't Trust Anything. [Online] Available from: https://www.networkworld.com/article/3307118/zero-trust-networking-ztn-don-t-trust-anything.html. (Accessed 10 June 2019).

Cunningham, C., 2018. The Zero Trust eXtended (ZTX) Ecosystem. [Online] Available from: https://www.cisco.com/c/dam/m/en_sg/solutions/security/pdfs/forrester-ztx.pdf. (Accessed 14 August 2019).

Datadoghq, 2019. Data Monitoring and Analytics. [Online] Available from: https://www.datadoghq.com/. (Accessed 30 July 2019).

DeCusatis, C., Liengtiraphan, P., Sager, A., Pinelli, M., 2016. Implementing Zero Trust Cloud Networks With Transport Access Control and First Packet Authentication. [Online] Available from: https://ieeexplore.ieee.org/document/7796146. (Accessed 20 July 2019).

Drach, S., 1999. DHCP Option for The Open Group's User Authentication Protocol. [Online] Available from: https://tools.ietf.org/html/rfc2485. (Accessed 4 July 2019).

Droms, R., 1997. Dynamic Host Configuration Protocol. [Online] Available from: https://tools.ietf.org/html/rfc2131. (Accessed 10 July 2019).

Duo, 2019. Zero Trust Evaluation Guide for the Workforce. [Online] Available from: https://duo.com/resources/ebooks/zero-trust-evaluation-guide/success. (Accessed 18 June 2019).

Facebook, 2019. Re-Authentication. [Online] Available from: https://developers.facebook.com/docs/facebook-login/reauthentication/. (Accessed 6 July 2019).

Ferguson, N., Schneier, B., 2003. Practical Cryptography. Wiley, Indianapolis, USA, p. 323.

Forescout, 2018. Total Visibility: The Masterkey to Zero Trust Networks. [Online] Available from: https://www.forescout.com/company/resources/total-visibility-the-master-key-to-zero-trust/. (Accessed 9 June 2019).

Gilman, E., Barth, D., 2017. Zero Trust Networks. O'Reilly, Sebastopol, CA.

Google, 2017. Android Is Getting a Feature That Encrypts Website Name Requests. [Online] Available from: https://www.engadget.com/2017/10/23/google-android-dns-tls/. (Accessed 10 June 2019).

Gonsalves, A., 2019. Microsoft Promotes Zero-Trust Security Over Firewalls. [Online] Available from: https://searchsecurity.techtarget.com/news/252459059/Microsoft-promotes-zero-trust-security-over-firewalls. (Accessed 25 June 2019).

Hill, Z., 2016. A Dsniff Project Using Bro. [Online] Available from: https://github.com/rsabir/bro-dsniff. (Accessed 14 June 2019).

Instana, 2019. Instana. [Online] Available from: https://www.instana.com/. (Accessed 30 July 2019).

Istio, 2019. What Is Istio. [Online] Available from: https://istio.io/docs/concepts/what-is-istio/. (Accessed 30 December 2019).

Kerman, A., Borchert, O., Rose S., 2020. Implementing a Zero Trust Architecture. Available from: https://csrc.nist.gov/publications/detail/white-paper/2020/03/17/implementing-a-zero-trust-architecture/draft. (Accessed 24 May 2020).

Kindervag, J., 2010. Build Security Into Your Network's DNA: The Zero Trust Network Architecture. [Online] Available from: http://www.virtualstarmedia.com/downloads/Forrester_zero_trust_DNA.pdf. (Accessed 9 June 2019).

Klein, D., 2019. Micro-Segmentation: Securing Complex Cloud Environments. Available from: https://www.sciencedirect.com/science/article/abs/pii/S1353485819300340. (Accessed 5 September 2019).

Komori, T., Saito, T., 2002. The Secure DHCP System With User Authentication. [Online] Available from: https://ieeexplore.ieee.org/stamp/stamp.jsp?tp=&arnumber=1181774. (Accessed 20 July 2019).

Lumeta, 2019. Lumeta. [Online] Available from: http://www.lumeta.com/. (Accessed 26 July 2019).

Microsoft, 2018. SMB Security Enhancements. [Online] Available from: https://docs.microsoft.com/en-us/windows-server/storage/file-server/smb-security. (Accessed 10 August 2019).

Netskope, n.d. Market Leading CASB. https://www.netskope.com/products/casb. (Accessed 25 July 2020).

NewRelic, 2019. Build Better Software. [Online] Available from: https://www.datadoghq.com/. (Accessed 30 July 2019).

Palo Alto, 2019. 5 Steps to Zero Trust. [Online] Available from: https://start.paloaltonetworks.com/5-steps-to-zero-trust. (Accessed 30 July 2019).

Palo Alto2, 2019. Cortex Data Lake. [Online] Available from: https://www.paloaltonetworks.com/resources/datasheets/cortex-data-lake. (Accessed 10 August 2019).

Schaffer, K.B., 2019. Expanding Continuous Authentication With Mobile Devices. [Online] Available from: https://ieeexplore.ieee.org/stamp/stamp.jsp?arnumber=7328656. (Accessed 29 November 2019).

Schiavone, E., Ceccarelli, A., Bondavalli, A., 2016. Continuous Authentication and Non-repudiation for the Security of Critical Systems. [Online] Available from: https://ieeexplore.ieee.org/document/7794345. (Accessed 31 July 2019).

Schneier, B., 2015. Applied Cryptography. Wiley & Sons, Inc., Indianapolis, USA.

Slaymaker, S., 2018. TechVision Research—Zero Trust Networking. [Online] Available from: https://techvisionresearch.com/wp-content/uploads/2018/07/Zero-Trust-Networking-20180724-final-1.pdf. (Accessed 10 June 2019).

Sommer, R., 2003. Bro: An Open Source Network Intrusion Detection System. [Online] Available from: citeseerx.ist.psu.edu/viewdoc/download?doi=10.1.1.60.5410&rep=rep1&type=pdf. (Accessed 27 July 2019).

Soseman, M., 2019. No More Firewalls! How Zero Trust Networks Are Reshaping Cyber Security. [Online] Available from: https://published-prd.lanyonevents.com/published/rsaus19/sessionsFiles/14208/IDY-W10-No-More-Firewalls-How-Zero-Trust-Networks-Are-Reshaping-Cybersecurity.pdf. (Accessed 8 July 2019).

Stallings, W., 2013. Wireless Communication and Networks. Pearson Education, Harlow GB.

Sudhakar, K., Srikanth, S., Sethuraman, M., 2015. Secured Mutual Authentication Between Two Entities. [Online] Available from: https://ieeexplore.ieee.org/stamp/stamp.jsp?arnumber=7282338. (Accessed 3 August 2019).

Symantec, 2019. CloudSOC Cloud Access Security Broker (CASB). [Online] Available from: https://www.symantec.com/products/cloud-application-security-cloudsoc. (Accessed 15 December 2019).

Tigera, 2019. Zero Trust Security & Kubernetes: Supporting a CARTA Approach With Anomaly Detection. [Online] Available from: https://www.tigera.io/webinars/carta-anomaly-detection. (Accessed 3 August 2019).

Todorov, D., 2007. Mechanics of User Identification and Authentication. Auerbach Publications, New York, USA.

Vanickis, R., Jacob, P., Dehghanzadeh, S., Lee, B., 2018. Access Control Policy Enforcement for Zero-Trust-Networking. Available from: https://ieeexplore.ieee.org/stamp/stamp.jsp?arnumber=8585365. (Accessed 8 June 2020).

Vijayan, J., 2018. What It Takes to Build a Zero Trust Network. [Online] Available from: https://www.csoonline.com/article/3287057/network-security/what-it-takes-to-build-a-zero-trust-network.html. (Accessed 18 August 2018).

Wan, X., Xiao, Z., 2012. Building Trust into Cloud Computing Using Virtualization of TPM. [Online] Available from: https://ieeexplore.ieee.org/document/6405630/references#references. (Accessed 4 August 2019).

Ward, R., Beyer, B., 2014. BeyondCorp: A New Approach to Enterprise Security. [Online] Available at https://research.google/pubs/pub43231/. (Accessed 15 August 2020).

Digital 'hand-shake' of business

10

An analysis of the perceptions of the role of social media marketing in shaping the preferences of the electorate: A case study of the 2018 Colombian presidential election

Natalia Gomez Arteaga[a] and Lillian Clark[b]

[a]NORTHUMBRIA UNIVERSITY, NEWCASTLE UPON TYNE, UNITED KINGDOM [b]QA HIGHER EDUCATION, LONDON, UNITED KINGDOM

1 Introduction

1.1 Objectives

This study intends to research the importance of digital marketing strategies in modern day political campaigns and analyse the role that these strategies played in influencing the decisions and opinions of the electorate during the 2018 Colombian presidential elections. To help explore the study's main theme, a series of subthemes were developed, which intend to do the following:

(1) Identify the theories and current research related to the impact of social media in both political campaigns and the electorate's voting decisions.
(2) Analyse the perceptions about the impact of social media in the 2018 Colombian presidential elections.
(3) Recommend how political parties can improve their use of social media in future political campaigns.

1.2 Topic background

The use of social networks amongst citizens of all ages, cultures, and social statuses has grown exponentially in recent years and has introduced a new form of communication. One that is able to spread messages rapidly not only person to person but also to millions at a time, regardless of borders, with people spending more time using social media platform than reading the news (Satterfield, 2016).

Strategy, Leadership, and AI in the Cyber Ecosystem. https://doi.org/10.1016/B978-0-12-821442-8.00004-5
© 2021 Elsevier Inc. All rights reserved.

Therefore new forms of participation and debate have emerged, as messages can become 'viral' in a short amount of time and can be seen all around the world (Harvey, 2013). As a result, everyone now has the potential to have a voice and have their opinions heard whilst also providing the possibility for two-way communication. In recent years, politicians and political candidates have begun to use these platforms to interact with the general public, especially during political campaigns, to increase their electoral potential and try to influence voter preferences (Ruano et al., 2018). Furthermore, it can be said that every follower or user of social media is an instrument of communication himself with the capacity to influence in the public sphere in a considerable way (Gil, 2017).

2 Literature review

2.1 Overview

This section will analyse and review the extant literature surrounding the topics and themes laid out in the previous section, by establishing a framework of published literature and theories in regard to the use of social media in political marketing and political participation. Through developing an understanding of the literature, a hypothesis will be formulated to answer the problem question. Therefore publications focussing on political marketing, social media in political marketing and political participation, and word of mouth in digital marketing will be the focus of this analysis and review.

2.2 Political marketing

Much like businesses develop marketing strategies to sell their products, political parties and candidates also attempt to promote their policies and beliefs by using marketing strategies to influence public opinion in their favour. This is known as political marketing and can be defined as the application of marketing principles and procedures in political campaigns by various individuals and organisations, including the management and execution of strategic campaigns by candidates and political parties to influence public opinion (Newman, 1999). Political marketing is also a fundamental part of the political world and its structure. Politicians use marketing methods to accomplish their political goals, and political marketing has all the elements that a marketing strategy to sell a product or a service would require. According to Lees-Marshment (2014), in politics, especially in political campaigns, market research is used to understand the electorate's wants and needs, with voter profiling used to identify target segments. Hence, political marketing is about how political elites use marketing tools and strategies to understand and interact with their political market to achieve their goals, the main one being obtaining votes to get elected.

Furthermore, McNair (2017) agrees that political parties have developed communication strategies that belong to the corporate and business world, including marketing techniques, to influence behaviours by stating that "political marketing is similar to commercial marketing to such an extent that political organisations like those in the commercial sector must target audiences using mass communication channels in a competitive environment where the citizen or consumer has more than one choice." Political marketing uses many of the principles applied to the promotion of products and services, such as using forms of communication to differentiate between products, which in this case are political parties and their candidates. Maarek (2008) states that political marketing is considered one of the most demanding applications of political communication, as it takes precedence in the election campaign and influences its strategy, especially in targeting action for resilient voters, and it is also fundamental for a campaign's decision-making process.

Therefore it influences and modifies the contents of politics itself along with the increase of the personalisation of political communications as people tend to focus on the candidate personal features rather than what he/she represents politically.

In terms of the aims of political marketing, Butler et al. (2007) state that it is about creating and maintaining a solid relationship with the voter, as it allows the candidates to meet their goals through a mutual relationship. Having a mutual relationship with the electorate is fundamental in developing a successful political campaign because, as a consequence, the interests and requirements of the voters are clear, and it is easier for the candidates to understand the electorate and offer them what they want in exchange of support in the form of votes. The political marketing process should be done by implementing traditional marketing methods such as market segmentation to target the voters and their needs and preferences for the propose of establishing an effective policy that enable candidates to satisfy the preferences of the electorate (Smith and Saunders, 1990). In the same fashion, Baines et al. (2002) claim that political marketing is the communication process between voters and political bodies to close the gap between the voter's requests and what candidates and political parties have to offer. In addition, there are some indispensable elements in marketing planning that facilitate the creation of a competitive advantage. These include identifying the competition and segmenting the relevant voting groups, allowing parties to approach voters that are likely to change their voting preference, for example, swing voters.

2.3 Social media for political marketing

The rise in popularity of social media platforms has provided a place for political marketing to establish a political marketplace where candidates and political parties can influence and drive public opinion of their convenience and interest (Safiullah et al., 2017). Social media platforms such as Twitter and Facebook have gradually transformed how political campaigns are developed and consequently how politicians share information and citizens learn about politics (Dimitrova and Matthes, 2018). Social networks are new ways of approaching the structure of politics, elections, and some specific elements of the government (Mayorga and Cordova, 2007) as politicians have linked their legitimacy and acceptance on how they manage their governance period on social media platforms (Ruano et al., 2018). Social media, therefore, is a very important element of political communication as it allows Internet users to share information rapidly and to influence opinions through the use of platforms such as Twitter and Facebook and where political actors not only seek to influence and engage with users but also monitor and respond to what they perceive as the views of those users on political affairs. In summary, social media has created a more attractive and effective channel for candidates to communicate their messages during election campaigns (McNair, 2017).

Williams (2017) agrees with this approach, stating that "Facebook, Twitter and Instagram create new ways to market politics through new channels for candidates and voters to interact and it has allowed unaccredited people to register their support or opposition in a campaign phase previously limited to elites." Additionally, the Internet has established a communication platform that is larger and faster than the traditional forms of media and where social media plays a fundamental role. Social media has been gradually integrated as a tool in election campaigns and political communications as political actors use this channel to promote themselves and build an image. Furthermore, communication via social media channels makes for a more personal and direct interaction between candidates and voters and consequently provides personalisation to politics as the main focus of the campaign is the candidate, not the political party (Enli and Skogerbø, 2012). Social media also represents the ideal vehicle and information base for politicians, political parties, and governments to measure public opinion and to build community support for candidates (Zeng et al., 2010).

Social media has drastically changed the way that government and political actors operate and communicate, as well as the manner in which elections are implemented. It informs the public on political matters and allows for political expression and facilitates community building to find solutions for similar interests and needs, providing the possibility for more voices to be heard and to reach the most disinterested of citizens (Owen, 2017). Social media used as a tool for political marketing is a worldwide phenomenon, and according to Puertas et al. (2018), in Latin America, social networks are used to interact with followers and for candidates to be able to influence the electorate's voting preferences. "In Latin America, 63% of the population have active social media accounts and government institutions use social media as a tool for their communication strategy" (Puertas et al., 2018). In 2018 Colombia had around 29 million social media users, with almost half a million following the official account of the presidency and 1 million following the president himself (Facebook, 2018). This strongly supports the idea that social media is a channel of preference for political communication and aspects in Colombia and it is also where a significant amount of political interaction and participation take place.

2.4 Social media and political participation

As Melis and Keating (2017) state, it is widely believed that participation in public affairs through the traditional methods of democratic engagement has declined in many developed countries as citizens look to find more innovative forms to express their political preferences. Social media plays a fundamental role in the forging of new methods of political and civic participation, as it can increase an individual's contact with political information and social movements when other social media users, including friends and family, express their political interests or opinions. This can motivate the individual curiosity for political information by becoming part of political acts or discussions. In the same manner, Skoric et al. (2016) also agree that the use of social media to keep updated with the public affairs has enabled citizens to increase their political participation, defined as "behaviours aimed at influencing formal political institutions and affecting their decisions." Political participation therefore includes the acts of voting, protesting, campaigning, liking candidates on Facebook, and sharing campaign material.

Gil and Shahin (2015) demonstrate that the more people use social networks for obtaining information, the more likely they are to involve themselves in civic activities, including online and offline political participation. From this, it can therefore be stated that social media has a positive impact on political participation. Additionally, informal discussions via online networks about public affairs and sharing interests and opinions about a public affair problem can contribute to civic participation. "More than half of Internet users receive information on current affairs through Facebook, YouTube and Twitter. Social media have been playing a fundamental role for the battle of achieving hegemony, and more than a tool it is the scene itself where this battle develops" (Moreno, 2017). Research conducted by Gil et al. (2014) found that the use of social media as a news source has a direct effect on offline political participation. Nonetheless, it does not have a direct impact on people's engagement with politics, but rather has an indirect effect by means of citizens expressing themselves politically, which could lead to political participation, referring to political expression as opinions and political participation as actions.

2.5 Word of mouth in digital marketing

Word of mouth marketing relates to what people say and tell other people about a product, service, or brand and the reputation that is built around it. It constitutes an important element of marketing communications and strategy as it is a way of attracting more customers and increasing brand reputation and awareness. According to Sernovitz (2012), word of mouth marketing is when a business or brand gives people a reason to talk about the products and services that they offer or about the brand itself, either by communicating to someone face to face or in the form of a comment or review. It is also about facilitating the space and circumstances for that conversation to take place and making the product, service, or brand interesting and attractive enough for consumers or the public in general to repeat the idea based on the business and make it popular. Additionally, it is important to offer good quality and a positive experience to the costumers, and as a consequence, they are more likely to tell other people their good experience, therefore generating more customers. On the other hand, if the experience was negative, the voice will be proliferated, and the reputation will be at risk.

In this way, Trusov et al. (2009) agree that word-of-mouth communication is an effective strategy because it can attract the consumers that have the most resistance and can be done in a low-cost way, especially with the rapid communications and interactions of the Internet and more specifically social media activity. And customers that have been acquired through word of mouth tend to add more long-term value to the company or brand than those acquired through traditional marketing channels. Word of mouth makes the decision-making process of purchasing a product easier as it only takes to ask someone about their experience with that product or service, instead of going through the searching period before of purchasing "what customers want is the best product they can get with the easiest decision-making process" (Silverman, 2011).

2.6 Conclusion

Having reviewed the extant literature, it can be said that political marketing, together with its strategies such as segmentation, targeting, and word of mouth, is a determinant in the decision-making process of the electorate as seen in Section 2.2. With the rise of the Internet and social media platforms, these marketing strategies have only intensified and strengthened the marketing communication and have motivated political participation of citizens referring to Sections 2.3 and 2.4. Word of mouth is the element that has the biggest influence on the decision-making process of the electorate as seen in Section 2.5. This is supported by Nieto et al. (2014), who state that "users generally trust other consumers more than sellers" (Nieto et al., 2014) as people tend to trust other people more and what they say, than adverts or marketing campaigns. Nonetheless, it can be said that there is a lack of research about the literature around word of mouth in political marketing. To develop this study the concepts and theories related to the role of social media in political participation and political marketing and the word of mouth in social media in relationship with political participation will be implemented.

2.7 Conceptual model: Hypothesis and prepositions

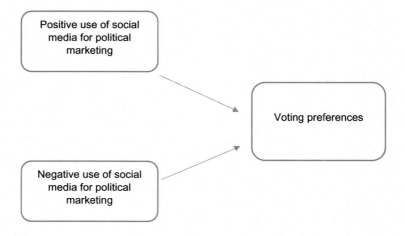

Preposition 1. Social media as a tool of political marketing had a role influencing the decisions of the electorate during political campaigns of presidential elections in Colombia 2018.

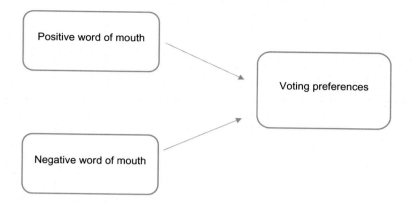

Preposition 2. Word of mouth in social media has a significant role influencing the decisions of the electorate during the political campaigns of presidential elections in Colombia 2018.

Alternative Hypothesis:

H1: Voters perceive social media as having a role influencing the decisions of the electorate during the political campaign of presidential elections in Colombia 2018.
H2: Sharing political-related post on social media had an impact on voting preferences during the 2018 presidential elections in Colombia.

Null Hypothesis:

H1: Voters do not perceive social media as having a role influencing the decisions of the electorate during the political campaign of presidential elections in Colombia 2018.
H2: Sharing political-related post on social media did not have an impact on the voting preferences during the 2018 presidential elections in Colombia.

On review of the literature, political marketing can be summarised as the execution of campaigns by a candidate and political parties, to create a relationship with the electorate and understand their needs and preferences and target with the goal of influencing the public opinion and obtain votes (Newman, 1999; Lees-Marshment, 2014; Maarek, 2008; Butler et al., 2007; Smith and Saunders, 1990). Social media is a fundamental part of political marketing as it allows candidates to establish a political market place where they can promote themselves and influence public opinion in a more effective way (Safiullah et al., 2017; Dimitrova and Matthes, 2018; Williams, 2017; Enli and Skogerbø, 2012; McNair, 2017; Mayorga and Cordova, 2007). Furthermore, social media has enabled citizens to participate more in political matters as it allows access to information and the formation of direct relationships with governments and political actors where they can get involved in political matters and their voices can be heard. Additionally, seeing other people share their opinions in politics can influence users and shape their preferences (Ekstrom and

Shehata, 2016; Melis and Keating, 2017; Skoric et al., 2016; Gil et al., 2014, 2017; Ayankoya et al., 2014; Boulianne, 2015; Chan et al., 2016; Jost et al., 2018; Valeriani and Vaccari, 2015; Uldam and Vestergaard, 2015). Word-of-mouth communication can significantly influence voter preferences as consumers find word of mouth a very attractive source of information (Chowdury and Naheed, 2018; Argan and Argan, 2012; Ozturk and Coban, 2019) and users trust other consumers more than the sellers themselves; in this case the sellers are the political candidates (Nieto et al., 2014).

The purpose of this study is to investigate whether social media marketing influences the preferences and decision-making process of the electorate when voting and to what extent sharing politically related posts on social media effects political preferences. Additionally, this study aims to find out whether word of mouth played a significant role in shaping voter preferences during the 2018 presidential elections in Colombia. As evidenced from the literature review, surveys and case studies are the prevalent research methods used to obtain findings in studies of this nature as demonstrated by (Valeriani and Vaccari, 2015; Ozturk and Coban, 2019; Argan and Argan, 2012; Chowdury and Naheed, 2018) who used surveys and case studies to analyse voting behaviours. However, to obtain a more complete understanding of the case study, interviews will also be conducted as a method of data collection to prove the previously established prepositions and hypotheses.

3 Research methodology

A descriptive study will be conducted around how the role of social media marketing strategies has impacted the preferences of the electorate during political campaigns and voting decisions. This research paradigm is appropriate for this study as "the goal of descriptive research is to describe a phenomenon and its characteristics. This research is more concerned with what rather than why something has happened" (Nassaji, 2015). Its appropriateness is further reinforced by Dulock (1993), who states that it is a "systematic description of something or someone. The something may be an event, phenomena, characteristics such as voting preferences, feelings or attitudes. The something may be an individual, group or community. The research interest may be to determinate whether there is a relationship between two variables" (Dulock, 1993). In the case of this particular study, social media marketing activity is the first variable, and the preferences of the electorate are second variable.

3.1 Research philosophy

To develop the study's research philosophy and approach, the research onion will be implemented as a guide. The research onion was developed by Saunders et al. (2009) in order to describe the different steps that must be followed developing a research study, which includes philosophy, approaches, strategies, choices, time horizons and techniques. To begin with the philosophy of this research is interpretivism that believes that "different people under different circumstances and at different times make different meanings and so create and experience different social realities. The purpose of interpretivist research is to create new, richer understanding and interpretations of social worlds and contexts" (Sanders and Bristow, 2015). Furthermore, qualitative methods tend to be best suited to interpretivist research, and therefore data collection, such as interviews and observations, is part of this philosophy as it brings the researcher close contact with the participants making it more prone to understanding (Thanh and Le Thanh, 2015).

3.2 Research approach

The approach of this research is inductive, which according to Sanders and Bristow (2015) is where data collection is used to explore a phenomenon and identify themes and patterns and to develop a theory from the data analysis. This type of research is likely to depend significantly on the context in which events take place and consequently the study of a small sample might be appropriate. Inductive research tends to work with qualitative data using a variety of data collection methods to establish different perspectives of the phenomenon.

3.3 Data collection methods and strategies

The data for this study will be obtained through primary and secondary research, firstly through the development of a literature review before the completion of field research. Despite the previous subsection stating that it would be convenient to use only qualitative methods for the nature of this study, in this particular case, the study will combine both qualitative and quantitative research. This will provide a greater and more complete understanding of the case study and its findings as it is important to collect data from two different perspectives. Therefore quantitative research will be conducted through the use of surveys targeting the Colombian electorate. This decision is supported by Harwell's (2011) statement that "quantitative research methods attempt to maximize objectivity, replicability, and generalisability of findings, and are typically interested in prediction. Key features of many quantitative studies are the use of instruments such as tests or surveys to collect data." In contrast, qualitative research will be conducted through interviews with experts in the field as "qualitative research methods focus on discovering and understanding the experiences, perspectives, and thoughts of participants allowing a detailed exploration of a topic of interest in which information is collected by a researcher through case studies, ethnographic work and interviews" (Harwell, 2011).

The use of mixed methodology has become ubiquitous amongst social science researchers as instead of seeing qualitative and quantitative methods as opposites, they are seen as complementary methods as the weakness of one can be offset by the strength of the other. As Johnson and Turner (2003) state, the fundamental principle of mixed methods research is that various kinds of data should be collected with different strategies to reflect complementary strengths and not overlapping weakness. Furthermore "the increase of mixed methods research justifies the question of determining the perceived value of mixed methods research compared with a purely quantitative or purely qualitative study" (McKim, 2017). Mixed methods can be defined as "a research where the researcher collects and analyses data using qualitative and quantitative approaches for the same study" (Creswell and Plano, 2007). In this matter the data for this study will be collected through two different methods, to then be able to triangulate the data. This is in reference to a concurrent triangulation strategy, where there are two concurrent data collection phases and each is given equal priority, with the data being integrated during the interpretation or analysis process (Terrell, 2012).

For this study, cross-sectional data will be collected, which involves observations of a sample or cross section of a population or phenomenon that are made at one point in time (Babbie, 2011). The data can either be collected through interviews or through "self-administered questionnaires, of individuals, groups, organizations, countries, or other units of analysis" (Lavrakas, 2008).

3.4 Survey

A survey of Colombian citizens with the right to vote will be conducted to understand their perception of the 2018 Colombian presidential elections. The survey intends to discover how participants felt social media marketing strategies influenced their political preferences and understanding the role these strategies played in their decision-making process of electing a candidate. The main intention of this is to explore their opinions and perspectives on the election's digital campaign; hence the survey will ask questions related to their perception of social media as a tool for politics and political participation and how they feel about the marketing methods that were used and whether it influenced their opinions. Surveys are particularly well suited to the study of public opinion and for measuring attitudes and orientations in a large population and are probably the best method available to the social researcher who is interested in collecting original data for describing a population too large to observe directly (Babbie, 2011). This is certainly the case for this study as over 19 million Colombians voted in the 2018 presidential elections (El Tiempo, 2018).

The survey will include a mixture of closed-ended questions, where the responder is asked to select one answer from a list of options provided by the researcher as it is easier to process these than open-ended ones (Babbie, 2011). A handful of questions will include a comment box and a five-point Likert scale—"these scales range from a group of categories least to most asking people to indicate how much they agree or disagree, approve or disapprove. The most important consideration is to include at least five response categories" (Allen and Seaman, 2007). The survey will be conducted via online methods, using the platform Qualtrics. The reason of using online methods is because the participants are based in Colombia; therefore online methods are the most convenient ways to approach this study. Furthermore, online data collection has the benefit of providing reduced response time, lower cost, ease of data entry, flexibility and control over format, and the ability to obtain additional response-set information (Granello and Wheaton, 2004).

Snowball Sampling will be employed to select survey participants, starting with those close to the researcher before asking participants to send the survey on to other people they know, expanding the sample size and therefore obtaining as many answers as possible. Etikan et al. succinctly summarise snowball sampling as "beginning with a convenience sample of initial subject, this initial subject serve as 'seeds,' through which wave 1 subject is recruited; wave 1 subject in turn recruits wave 2 subjects; and the sample consequently expands wave by wave like a snowball growing in size as it rolls down a hill" (Etikan et al., 2015). The sampling size for a survey must be within an acceptable margin of error, which is between 4% and 8% with a confidence level of 95% (Survey Star, 2008). As the survey sample is of a total population of over 19 million, which is the number of people that voted in the 2018 Colombian presidential elections, there are potential limitations in the collection of the data. Due to the resources and time constraint of the researcher, the margin of error will be at 6%, as this is in the middle of the acceptable margin of error. To achieve this the survey requires a sample size of around 267, which is an achievable target sample given the researchers initial convenience sample of friends and family and the use of the snowball sampling method to expand the sample size further.

3.4.1 Survey questionnaire design

The design of the survey questionnaire was influenced by the topics and findings of the literature review, which primarily focussed on social media in political marketing and participation, word of mouth in digital marketing, and the effect of these strategies on citizens' voting behaviour. The aim of the survey is to prove the hypothesis of this study that social media used as a tool for political marketing plays a significant role in influencing voting behaviour or the decisions of the electorate. In terms of the survey's design, the opening question asks the participant's age to better understand the demographic of the participants. Questions two to six are designed to uncover the participant's political participation and expression via social media channels and how politically active they are. Questions seven and eight concern word of mouth and whether what the participant sees in social media effects their voting preferences. Finally, questions 9 to 11 are directly related to the case study and the role of social media in the election process.

The majority of the questions are designed in a 1–5 Likert scale, with options, for example, '1, never; 2, rarely; 3, sometimes; 4, often; and 5, always'. The questions will be translated into Spanish by the researcher as each of the participants first language is Spanish, and therefore this is considered a necessary step in helping to obtain clear findings.

3.5 Interviews

Semistructured interviews with open-ended questions will be used to collect the necessary data for this research. "Semi-structured interviews are based on open ended questions, and it provides opportunities for the interviewer and interviewee to discuss some topics in more detail, giving the flexibility and the freedom to the interviewer to ask the interviewee to elaborate the answer or give more explanation" (Mathers et al., 2002). Although the interviewer prepares the questions previously, semistructured interviews unfold in a conversational manner, offering the participants the opportunity to explore the topic in the way they consider appropriate and talk about the issues that they consider important (Clifford et al., 2016). Additionally, the questions will vary depending on the interviewee and will be addressed to a small sample, as the semistructured interviews give this flexibility to achieve the desire result. "Semi-structured interviewing is a very flexible technique for small-scale research and is very helpful in mini-studies and case studies" (Drever, 1995).

Two different interviews, containing some similarities, will be conducted with five participants divided into two different groups with open-ended questions including 'what do you think', 'how do you feel', and 'do you consider'. The first set of interviews will be conducted with three political science experts, with the intention to discover their understanding of social media marketing in politics and how this impacts the dynamics of politics and democracy. Additionally, the interviews will ask how they perceive the use of social media as a tool of political communication and what are the consequences of this to current political processes and campaigns. The second set of interviews will be addressed to two people, who are the campaign directors of the two presidential candidates. The intention of these interviews is to discover the role of social media in each of the candidates' campaigns and which marketing strategies were used during these political campaigns and to what extent it impacted the support the candidates received.

3.5.1 Interview questionnaire design

As with the design of the survey's questionnaire, the creation of the interview questions was developed following the review of the existing literature. The questions for the first interview group focus on social media and political participation and the impact of these on the political process and democracy. The questions for the second interview group are mainly concerned with the role of social media in political campaigns and the social media marketing strategies used to shape the preferences of the electorate. The two interviews also share three questions that are directly linked to the case study with the purpose of this being to discover the different perspectives of the participants. It is again important to highlight that these questions will be translated into Spanish for clearer results and to avoid confusion as each of the participants first language is Spanish.

3.6 Data analysis methods

3.6.1 Analysis of methods for quantitative data

According to the findings of the literature review, the data collection results of surveys are analysed using statistical methods such as Poisson regression model (Valeriani and Vaccari, 2015), structural equation modelling (Ozturk and Coban, 2019; Chowdury and Naheed, 2018), and Cronbach's alpha reliability coefficient (Argan and Argan, 2012). SPSS statistical software will be employed to help analyse this study's survey data, and a descriptive analysis of the results will be implemented to summarise the key findings of the survey. Descriptive statistics, as defined by Laerd Statistics, is a method used to analyse and summarise data in a meaningful way where patterns might emerge from the data. This method uses tables, graphs, and charts to organise and summarise the data and to discover the mean, median, and mode of each response (Laerd Statistics, 2018). To aid this study, frequency tables will be used to obtain the percentage and frequencies of each of the responses to help understand them better. "Frequency is a measure of the number of occurrences of a particular score in a set of data, the main advantage of using frequency tables is that data are grouped, therefore is easier to read, it also allows to notice a series of characteristics of the analysed data set that could probably not have been easily seen when looking at the raw data" (Salkind, 2010).

Furthermore, to test the hypothesis, two further methods will be used on the Likert scale and binary yes and no questions. The appropriate method to test the hypothesis for the Likert scale questions is linear correlation, which enable the researcher to discover whether there is a significant relationship between the two variables, as it is a "measure of dependence between two random variables" (Taboga, 2018). In this case the first variable is 'sharing political-related content in social media', and the second variable is 'voting preferences'. For the second hypothesis, as this uses categorical data, the appropriate method is cross tabulation to discover the relationship between the two variables, which is "a technique for examining the relationship between two categorical variables" (IBM, 2019). The hypothesis will be testes using the chi-square method, which "is the primary statistic method used for testing the statistical significance of the cross-tabulation table and determine whether or not the two variables are independent" (Qualtrics, 2018). Question 10, which included a comment box, will be analysed as qualitative data, looking for patterns in the answers as this question has an element that led to an open answer that involve explanation.

3.6.2 Analysis methods for qualitative data

The interviews will be recorded and transcribed, as suggested by (Flick, 2013), to textually analyse the data collected and provide a rich representation of the findings (Roulston, 2013). The data will be divided into categories to organise the data and give it meaning, providing "an inductive exploration of the data to identify recurring themes, patterns, or concepts" (Nassaji, 2015) before then describing and interpreting those categories. As a result a thematic analysis will be implemented, to identify the patterns and themes that are important or interesting within the data and address the research (Maguire and Delahunt, 2017). The data collected from these interviews will then be complemented by the findings of the survey. The main goal of the interviews is to discover from political experts and the people who worked on the candidates' campaigns, their perspectives on the influence of social media in voting preferences, and the role of word of mouth in the elections. Therefore the answers of the interviewees will be analysed to find patterns between the participants and to evaluate whether or not the prepositions established in Section 2.6 are valid.

4 Findings and analysis

4.1 Overview

In this section the results of the quantitative and qualitative research methods laid out in the previous section will be analysed. The findings of these will then be demonstrated to both prove the prepositions and test the hypothesis, as set out in Section 2. A comparative analysis of the results from both research methodologies will also be developed to complement each other's findings and supplement their weaknesses. Initially an in-depth descriptive analysis of the quantitative data will be completed, following by the hypothesis testing, and secondly, for the qualitative data, the results will be analysed using the thematic analysis method.

4.2 Descriptive analysis for quantitative data

A statistical descriptive analysis was initially established to summarise and interpret the features from the raw data. This analysis was carried out on each of the 11 survey questions; however, only the questions and findings that are directly related to the hypothesis will be shown and analysed in this section. The analysis is based on 743 responses of Colombian citizens that voluntary decided to participate in the survey. The total number of participants was somewhat of a surprise as around 267 participants were expected through the use of the snowball sampling method. This sample size would have provided an acceptable margin of error of 6%; however, with the new sample size, the margin of error is 3.5%. The large sample size is a clear demonstration of the importance of this topic amongst the Colombian population and reinforces the idea that this phenomenon requires further investigation.

4.3 Prepositions and thematic analysis for qualitative data

The interviews were conducted during the first and second week of April 2019 by video call as the participants are based in Colombia, with each interview lasting 30 min (Table 1). Ensuring confidentiality and anonymity made participants feel comfortable and allowed them to reveal information more freely. The interviews were recorded and then transcribed before being thematically analysed by interpreting and making sense of the data, following six steps: (1) becoming familiar with the data, (2) generating codes, (3) searching for themes, (4) reviewing themes, (5) defining themes, and (6) writing up (Maguire and Delahunt, 2017). After reading the transcripts several times, codes were identified, and the answers of the participants were categorised into themes, and within the themes, patterns were discovered with similarities between all the participants to obtain findings.

4.4 Discussion of results

This study employed the mixed methodology, as stated previously in Section 3.3. This allowed for the comparison and analysis of the results from both the quantitative and

Table 1 Summary of the five interview participants.

Interview participant	Role
Participant 1	Politics expert
Participant 2	Politics expert
Participant 3	Politics expert
Participant 4	Director of political campaign of presidential candidate
Participant 5	Coordinator of political campaign of presidential candidate

qualitative data, using a triangulation strategy where the two types of data were given the same importance and then integrated (Terrell, 2012).

Beginning with the quantitative results, on the one hand, an analysis of the results supports the preposition "voters perceive social media as having a role influencing the decisions of the electorate during the political campaign of presidential elections in Colombia 2018." However, somewhat paradoxically, survey participants do not believe that social media played a role in influencing their decisions, and as a consequence the hypothesis test accepts the null hypothesis, which is "voters do not perceive social media as having a role influencing the decisions of the electorate during the political campaign of presidential elections in Colombia 2018." Hypothesis 2, which is "sharing political related post on social media had a relationship with voting preferences during the 2018 presidential elections in Colombia" can be accepted. Hypothesis testing shows a positive relationship, and therefore the null hypothesis must be rejected.

On the other hand the qualitative analysis supports the preposition that "social media as a tool of political marketing has a significant role influencing the decisions of the electorate during political campaigns of presidential elections in Colombia 2018." However, according to the interview participants, rather than shaping the preferences and decisions of the electorate, social media instead plays a part in reinforcing preconceived political positions. This strongly supports the reinforcement theory, first proposed by Joseph Klapper in 1960, which states that "media confirms the audience beliefs rather than creating new ones, and it only change opinions if the audience is are predisposed to change, for instance media strengthened political opinion rather than change it" (Harvey, 2012). This could be a possible explanation of the negative results obtained by the quantitative study, which examined the relationship between the two variables social media influence and voting preferences. The findings support the idea that social media strengthens, rather than changes, voting decisions. This idea is further reinforced by the results of the question "do you think that if there were no social media involved, the results of the elections would have been different?" For those respondents who answered 'No', the answer "the electorate have a solid position about politics and their preferences" was the most frequent reason given for this.

Additionally, the qualitative results support the idea that "word of mouth in social media have a significant role influencing the decisions of the electorate during the political campaigns of presidential elections in Colombia 2018." Word of mouth had a significant impact on the candidate's campaign, especially through the use of WhatsApp strategies. However, word of mouth, in a physical and real-life sense, was also very important strategy, which complemented the digital strategy and which supports the findings of the literature review, where "word of mouth communication in political marketing has a positive impact on the voters behaviour" (Ozturk and Coban, 2019). These results can be directly compared with the quantitative findings related to the second hypothesis as there is a relationship between sharing political related posts in social media and influencing the decisions of the electorate. This can be explained by the findings of the literature review, which established that word of mouth is fundamental for marketing campaigns as "people tend to believe in other consumers more than the sellers" (Nieto et al., 2014). For this study, this means that people tend to believe more in what other citizens say on social media about politics than the candidates themselves. This idea can be further reinforced by the results of the question "how often do you forward someone else political commentary or opinion on social media?" The majority of participants revealed they have the habit of sharing someone else's political opinion on social media, but when they were asked "how likely are you to share a political party or candidate's post on social media?," the majority of participants answered "not at all likely" or "not so likely."

Another important finding that arose from the analysis of the results refers to the negative aspect of word of mouth, as the proliferation of fake news is a growing tendency on social media. This is idea is reaffirmed by both the interview participants and the survey participants, who frequently answered 'Yes' and stated 'Fake News' as a reason why, when asked "do you think that if there were not social media involved, the results of the elections would have been different?" This finding supports that of Burkhardt (2017) who states that "social media allows fake news to proliferate and affects what people believe, often without ever having been read beyond the headline or caption." Another important factor uncovered during the cross-analysis of the two data sets is that social media, as a tool and strategy, is important to political campaigns but should be used in conjunction with a variety of other traditional marketing methods. Survey participants believed that the majority of people who vote in the Colombian elections have limited or no access to the Internet, which connects to the interviewees statements that social media should be a complementing strategy in Colombia because Internet coverage is limited.

5 Synthesis and conclusion

5.1 Aims of this study and objectives

The objectives of this study, namely, in identifying the theories and current research relating to the impact of social media on political campaigns and voting preferences as objective 1 and in analysing the impact of social media in the 2018 Colombian presidential elections as objective 2, have been met. This study commenced with a review of the existing literature, which helped identify and analyse the current theories around political marketing, social media as a tool of political marketing as well as word of mouth in digital marketing. The study then detailed the methodical and iterative process of collecting and analysing data through the distribution of a survey and the conduction of interviews, in order to understand the perspectives of both the electorate and also the political and marketing experts involved in the presidential campaigns.

In the extant literature, it was discovered that political marketing and its strategies are fundamental for political campaigns, as it helps to introduce candidates and promotes their proposals before segmenting and ultimately targeting the population. One of the most important elements of political marketing is the implementation of word-of-mouth communications, as this is the strategy with the biggest influence on the decision-making process of the electorate when voting. With the growth of the Internet and the increase in use of social media platforms, political marketing has strengthened, allowing for more direct communication and the establishment of stronger relationships between the candidate and general population.

Political marketing also motivates political participation, not only through suffrage but also through increasing political expression on social media stemming from citizens sharing political content and calls to action for mobilisation and change. Social media has also allowed candidates and political parties to influence the decisions of the undecided 'swing' voters and strengthen the views of those with solid preconceived political positions.

The study's findings support this idea, which found that social media's role in the 2018 presidential elections was to strengthen and reinforce the electorate's solid preconceived political positions, according to the interview results and the analysis of reinforcement theory by Klapper in 1960. Additionally, at this point, it is important to highlight that the study found that survey participants did not believe that social media influenced their voting decisions, which could arise a conflict of self-perception, or there could be the possibility that social media is not actually affecting the voting preferences and the electorate is independent when making their voting decisions; therefore participants may have a false believe about this. Nonetheless the correct reasons behind this remain undiscovered and offer potential for further research. On the other hand the survey participants do believe that social media influenced other people's decisions and the results of the election in general. The study also revealed that there is a relationship between sharing politically related posts on social media and influencing the decisions of the electorate. People are more likely to share their own and other user's political opinions, but they are less likely to forward a post from a political party or candidate, as they tend to believe other consumers, the general public, more than the sellers themselves, the candidates, which support the current literature on word of mouth marketing.

Furthermore, social media can be used to convince swing voters to choose a political side, and this was achieved during the elections through the use of either positive or negative word of mouth. Here, storytelling tactics played a fundamental role, as per the responses of both Participant 2, who stated that "social media networks emerge a feeling that is already there and the tactic was to play with emotions" and Participant 4, who stated that "the strategy was an optimal use of digital tools and combine it with a story telling that was very compelling, that make people think and feel and create strong positive feelings." As a result, it can be posited that word of mouth in social media played a significant role in influencing the decisions of the electorate during the political campaigns, especially through the use of WhatsApp. In parallel to this, it was also found that fake news was used as a negative word of mouth marketing strategy and through the use of social media it is more likely to proliferate and reach a large number of people.

In contrast the results also showed that social media played a significant role in the political campaign from the candidate's own perspectives, as it proved a fundamental communication tool for introducing the candidate, promoting their proposals, and reaching a large audience in a direct way. However, social media does not play a role in the rural area of Colombia as there is limited access to the Internet due to both technology coverage and also wealth levels. As a result, political marketing strategies should be implemented as a complement to traditional marketing strategies.

5.2 Limitations

Time was the main limitation for this study as was developed over a period of 4 months, which restricts how detailed and complete the research study could be. As a consequence of this, some of the topics and findings were only analysed briefly. Secondly the existing literature around the topic of digital word of mouth in political marketing is currently limited, which restricted the researcher in expanding the literature review around the fundamental topic of the study and develop a more complete analysis. In the same way, it was not possible to find any concerning the case study in particular, which therefore was an obstacle in obtaining credible information around the case as the only source of information available was from newspapers articles at the time the event took place.

There were also limitations related to the survey sample size as it was trying to represent a population of over 19 million, which is the number of voters in the elections. Additionally, the convenience sample was obtained through the reliance of the undergraduate contacts of the researcher, who studied politics, and therefore these participants are more likely to have a certain level of political knowledge and be more aware than most of political strategies. For this reason the results of the analysis and findings may not accurately represent the population that is the centre of this research. Furthermore an important limitation in the survey methodology is that the events of the elections happened over 1 year ago, and as a result the participants that answered the questions may not have a strong memory about what really happened. This limited them to recall the exact facts and how they felt about it at the time, meaning the probability that the answers are precise and truthful potentially is lower than had this research been carried out at the time of the elections.

5.3 Recommendations for further research

The main recommendation for further research is to investigate the conflict of self-perception of participants when answering surveys, as the first hypothesis could not be tested properly due to the contradictions in the answers given by the participants. A further research consideration would be to investigate the reasons why survey participants consider that social media strategies did not influence their decisions when voting, but influenced the decisions of others. A further recommendation is to expand the literature review to include other topics such as fake news and the reinforcement theory, which revealed themselves during the course of the study. Additionally, further research would be appropriate in analysing social media marketing and word of mouth as a positive or negative aspect, as in this study the measurement and analysis were carried out at a more general level. The last recommendation for further research is to investigate if social media did actually affect the voting preferences of the electorate and how it was affected and compare the results with this research.

5.4 Recommendations on how political parties can improve their use of social media in their political marketing campaigns

According to the findings from the interviews, a recommendation would be for political parties and candidates to increasingly use social media as a tool for political marketing, but not rely on it as the only strategy, instead complementing it with traditional marketing methods. This is especially true in Colombia and other developing economies as access to the Internet, and therefore social media is currently limited in rural areas. Based on the literature review and survey findings (Sections 2.6), people tend to believe more in what other people say about candidates than what candidates themselves say. This is in line with the findings in commercial marketing, with the same happening with products and sellers. This leads to the suggestion for political campaigns to follow the current commercial marketing trends, which started with 'influencers', or pseudo social media celebrities, advertising products and has now moved to 'microinfluencers', who are normal people with a few hundred to a thousand followers. This is due to the fact that marketers have found, much like the findings of this study, that consumers believe other consumers more than the sellers themselves. A suggestion of this study for future political campaigns would be to follow this path and encourage 'microinfluencers' to share political content with their close circle, reinforcing their voting preferences. This supports the Brown and Fiorella (2013) study that found that "marketers learned the power of word of mouth marketing, when studies showed that such messages were seen as more credible if it was said by the public" and as a consequence, "influencer marketing has become one of the most important approaches for those influencing the purchases decisions" (Brown and Hayes, 2007). Furthermore a last recommendation is for political parties and candidates to realise that the electorate is suspicious about the social media strategies during political campaigns; therefore it would be beneficial to implement strategies to make people less worried and more truthful about the transparency of the campaigns.

References

Allen, E., Seaman, C., 2007. Likert scales and data analyses. In: Qualitative Progress. Retrieved from: http://asq.org/quality-progress/2007/07/statistics/likert-scales-and-data-analyses.html.

Argan, M., Argan, M.T., 2012. Word-of-mouth (WOM): voters originated communications on candidates during. Int. J. Bus. Soc. Sci. 3 (15), 70–75.

Ayankoya, K., Cullen, M., Calitz, A., 2014. Social media marketing in politics. In: International Marketing Trends, Venice.

Babbie, E., 2011. The Basics of Social Research. vol. 5. Wadsworth.

Baines, P.R., Harris, P., Lewis, B.R., 2002. The political marketing planning process: improving image and message in strategic target areas. Mark. Intell. Plan. 20, 6–14.

Boulianne, S., 2015. Social media use and participation: a meta-analysis of current research. Inf. Commun. Soc. 18 (5), 524–538.

Brown, D., Fiorella, S., 2013. Influence Marketing: How to Create, Manage and Measure Brand Influencers in Social Media Marketing. .

Brown, D., Hayes, N., 2007. Influencer Marketing. Routledge, London.

Burkhardt, J.M., 2017. Combating fake news in the digital age. Am. Libr. Assoc. 53 (8), 5–33. https://www.journals.ala.org/index.php/ltr/issue/viewFile/662/423.

Butler, P., Collins, N., Fell, D., 2007. Theory-building in political marketing. J. Polit. Market. 6 (2–3), 91–107.

Chan, M., Chen, H.-T., Lee, F., 2016. Examining the roles of mobile and social media in political participation: a cross-national analysis of three Asian societies using a communication mediation approach. SAGE J. 19 (12), 2003–2021.

Chowdury, T.A., Naheed, S., 2018. Word of mouth communication in political marketing: understanding and managing referrals. J. Mark. Commun. 26 (3), 290–313.

Clifford, N., Cope, M., Gillespie, T., French, S., 2016. Key Methods in Geography. vol. 3. SAGE.

Creswell, J., Plano, C., 2007. Designing and Conducting Mixed Methods Research. Thousand Oaks.

Dimitrova, D.V., Matthes, J., 2018. Social media in political campaigning around the world: theoretical and methodological challenges. J. Mass Commun. Q. 95 (2), 333–342.

Drever, E., 1995. Using Semi-Structured Interviews in Small-Scale Research. A Teacher's Guide. Scottish Council for Research in Education, Edinburgh.

Dulock, H.L., 1993. Research design: descriptive research. J. Pediatr. Oncol. Nurs. 10 (4), 154–155.

Ekstrom, M., Shehata, A., 2016. Social media, porous boundaries, and the development of online political engagement among young citizens. SAGE J. 20 (2), 740–759.

El Tiempo, 2018, June 18. Iván Duque es el nuevo Presidente: Reviva aquí la Jornada. El Tiempo. Retrieved from: https://www.eltiempo.com/elecciones-colombia-2018/presidenciales/resultados-elecciones-presidenciales-2018-colombia-segunda-vuelta-231720.

Enli, G.S., Skogerbø, E., 2012. PERSONALIZED CAMPAIGNS IN PARTY-CENTRED POLITICS: Twitter and Facebook as arenas for political communication. Inf. Commun. Soc. 16, 757–774.

Etikan, I., Alkassim, R., Abubakar, S., 2015. Comparison of snowball sampling and sequential. Biom. Biostat. Int. J.. 3(1).

Facebook, 2018, July. Juan Manuel Santos—Presidente. Facebook. Retrieved from:https://www.facebook.com/JMSantos.Presidente/?ref=br_rs.

Flick, U., 2013. The Sage Handbook of Qualitative Data Analysis. Retrieved from:https://ebookcentral.proquest.com.

Gil, I., 2017. De la 'guerrilla' ciberactivista a las 'brigadas moradas': así manda Podemos en las redes. El Confidencial. Retrieved from: https://www.elconfidencial.com/espana/2017-03-07/guerrilla-brigadas-moradas-podemos-redes-sociales_1343312/.

Gil, H., Shahin, S., 2015, January. Social media and their impact on civic participation. In: Gil, H., Shahin, S. (Eds.), New Technologies and Civic Engagement. Retrieved from Research Gate.

Gil, H., Molyneux, L., Zheng, P., 2014. Social media, political expression, and political participation: panel analysis of lagged and concurrent relationships. J. Commun. 64 (4), 612–634.

Gil, H., Weeks, B., Ardèvol-Abreu, A.-A., 2017. Online influence? Social media use, opinion leadership, and political persuasion. Int. J. Public Opin. Res. 29 (2), 214–239.

Granello, D.H., Wheaton, J., 2004. Online data collection: strategies for research. J. Couns. Dev. 82 (4), 387–393.

Harvey, L., 2012. Reinforcement Theory. Quality Research International. Retrieved from: https://www.qualityresearchinternational.com/socialresearch/reinforcementtheory.htm.

Harvey, K., 2013. Encyclopedia of Social Media and Politics. SAGE Publications.

Harwell, M.R., 2011. Research design in qualitative/quantitative/mixed methods. In: Conrad, C.F., Serlin, R. (Eds.), The SAGE Handbook for Research in Education: Pursuing Ideas as the Keystone of Exemplary Inquiry. (Chapter 10).

IBM, 2019, April 18. Crosstabulation. IBM Knowledge Center. Retrieved from: https://www.ibm.com/support/knowledgecenter/en/SSLVMB_23.0.0/spss/tables/nt_simple_cat_tables_crosstabs.html.

Johnson, R.B., Turner, L., 2003. Data collection strategies in mixed methods research. In: Tashakkori, A., Teddlie, C. (Eds.), Handbook of Mixed Methods in Social and Behavioral Research. SAGE Publications, pp. 297–319.

Jost, J.T., Barberá, P., Bonneau, R., Langer, M., Metzger, M., Nagler, J., … Tucker, J., 2018. How social media facilitates political protest: information, motivation, and social networks. Adv. Polit. Psychol. 39 (S1), 85–118.

Laerd Statistics, 2018. Descriptive and Inferential Statistics. Laerd Statistics. Retrieved from: https://statistics.laerd.com/statistical-guides/descriptive-inferential-statistics.php.

Lavrakas, P.J., 2008. Cross-sectional data. In: Encyclopedia of Survey Research Methods. https://doi.org/10.4135/9781412963947.n119.

Lees-Marshment, J., 2014. Introduction to political marketing. In: Political Marketing: Principles and Applications. Routledge, New York.

Maarek, P.J., 2008. The International Encyclopedia of Communications. Wiley Online Library. Retrieved from:https://onlinelibrary.wiley.com/doi/full/10.1002/9781405186407.wbiecp062.

Maguire, M., Delahunt, B., 2017. Doing a thematic analysis: a practical, step-by-step guide for learning and teaching scholars. All Ireland J. High. Educ. 9 (3) Retrieved from:https://ojs.aishe.org/aishe/index.php/aishe-j/article/view/335.

Mathers, N., Fox, N., Hunn, A., 2002. Using Interviews in a Research Project.

Mayorga, F., Cordova, E., 2007. Gobernabilidad y Gobernanza en America Latina. Ginebra.

McKim, C.A., 2017. The value of mixed methods research: a mixed methods study. J. Mixed Methods Res. 11 (2), 202–222. https://doi.org/10.1177/1558689815607096.

McNair, B., 2017. An Introduction to Political Communication. Routledge, London & New York.

Melis, G., Keating, A., 2017, July 7. Social media and youth political engagement: preaching to the converted or providing a new voice for youth? Br. J. Polit. Int. Rel. 19 (4), 877–894.

Moreno, F., 2017. Use of virtual social networks and citizen participation in Podemos. Teknokultura 14, 351–362.

Nassaji, H., 2015. Qualitative and descriptive research: data type versus data analysis. Lang. Teach. Res. 19 (2), 129–132.

Newman, B.I., 1999. Handbook of Political Marketing. SAGE Publications.

Nieto, J., Muñoz, P., Hernandez, R., 2014. Marketing decisions, customer reviews, and business performance: the use of the Toprural website by Spanish rural lodging establishments. Tour. Manag. 115–123. Retrieved from: https://www.sciencedirect.com/science/article/pii/S0261517714000648.

Owen, D., 2017. The new media's role in politics. In: The Age of Perplexity. Rethinking The World we knew. Madrid. Retrieved from: https://www.bbvaopenmind.com/en/articles/the-new-media-s-role-in-politics/.

Ozturk, R., Coban, C., 2019. Political marketing, word of mouth communication and voter Behaviours interaction. Bus. Econ. Res. J. 10 (1), 245–258.

Puertas, R., Carpio, L., Mora, K., 2018. Facebook as Political Communication 2.0 Tool Subject of Study: Official Accounts of Presidencies in Latin America. Retrieved from: https://ieeexplore.ieee.org/stamp/stamp.jsp?tp=&arnumber=8399448.

Qualtrics, 2018. Cross Tabulation for Researchers. Qualtrics. Retrieved from: https://www.qualtrics.com/uk/experience-management/research/analysis-reporting/cross-tabulation/.

Roulston, K., 2013. Analysing interviews. In: Flick, U. (Ed.), The SAGE Handbook of Qualitative Data Analysis. ProQuest Ebook Central Retrieved from: https://ebookcentral.proquest.com/lib/northumbria/detail.action?docID=1707694.

Ruano, L.E., Lopez, J.C., Mosquera, J., 2018. Dimension politica del discurso en los candidatos presidenciales de Colombia: un analisis de la red social Twitter. vol. 3. pp. 301–309.

Safiullah, M., Pathak, P., Singh, S., Anshul, A., 2017. Social media as an upcoming tool for political marketing effectiveness. Asia Pac. Manag. Rev. 22 (1), 10–15.

Salkind, N.J., 2010. Frequency table. In: Encyclopedia of Research Design. https://doi.org/10.4135/9781412961288.n159.

Sanders, M., Bristow, A., 2015. Understanding research philosophy and approaches to theory development. In: Research Methodology for Business Students. Retrieved from: https://www.academia.edu/13016419/Research_Methods_for_Business_Students_Chapter_4_Understanding_research_philosophy_and_approaches_to_theory_development_.

Satterfield, H., 2016, October 05. How Social Media Affects Politics. Sysomos. Retrieved from: https://sysomos.com/2016/10/05/social-media-affects-politics/.

Saunder, M., Lewis, P., Thornhill, A., 2009. Research Methods for Business Students. Pearson, London.

Sernovitz, A., 2012. Word of Mouth Marketing: How Smart Companies Get People Talking. Greenleaf Book Group Press, Austin, TX.

Silverman, G., 2011. The Secrets of World of Mouth: How to Trigger Exponential Sales Through Runway World of Mouth. Amaco. Retrieved from:http://mnav.com/wp-content/uploads/2011/02/Secrets-of-WOMM-2nd-ed.pdf.

Skoric, M.M., Zhu, Q., Goh, D., Pong, N., 2016. Social media and citizen engagement: a meta analytic review. New Media Soc. 18 (9), 1817–1839.

Smith, G., Saunders, J., 1990. The application of marketing in british politics. J. Mark. Manag. 5 (3), 295–306.

Survey Star, 2008, October. What every Researcher Should Know About Statistical Significance. Survey Star. Retrieved from: http://www.surveystar.com/startips/oct2008.pdf.

Taboga, M., 2018. Linear Correlation. StatLect. Retrieved from: https://www.statlect.com/fundamentals-of-probability/linear-correlation.

Terrell, S.R., 2012. Mixed-methods research methodologies. Qual. Rep. 17 (1), 254–280.

Thanh, N.C., Le Thanh, T., 2015. The interconnection between interpretivist. Am. J. Educ. Res. 1 (2), 24–27.

Trusov, M., Bucklin, R., Pauwels, K., 2009. Effects of word-of-mouth versus traditional marketing: findings from an internet social networking site. J. Mark. 73 (5), 90–102.

Uldam, J., Vestergaard, A., 2015. Civic Engagement and Social Media: Political Participation beyond Protest. Palgrave Macmillan.

Valeriani, A., Vaccari, C., 2015. Accidental exposure to politics on social media as online participation equalizer in Germany, Italy, and the United Kingdom. SAGE J. 18 (9), 1857–1874.

Williams, C.B., 2017. Introduction: social media, political marketing and the 2016 US election. J. Polit. Market. 16 (3–4), 207–211.

Zeng, D.D., Lusch, R., Chen, H.-c., 2010. Social media analytics and intelligence. Int. Underw. Syst. Des. 25 (6), 13–16.

11

Will the new security trends achieve the skin in the game? (Lesson learned from recent IOCs)

Giovanni Bottazzi[a], Gianluigi Me[a], Giuseppe Giulio Rutigliano[b],
Pierluigi Perrone[b], and Luciano Capone[c]
[a]LUISS GUIDO CARLI UNIVERSITY, ROME, ITALY [b]UNIVERSITY OF ROME 'TOR VERGATA',
ROME, ITALY [c]ARMA DEI CARABINIERI, ROME, ITALY

1 Introduction

Looking at the recent reports on IT security, we can observe the almost constant presence of the same threat families. The Internet is always more full of malicious URLs—1 out of 10 (Symantec, 2019); 40% of malicious URLs were found on good domains (Webroot, 2019); emails are still the main infection tool; website is still the main addressed technology to hit the website itself or its users, etc. The purpose remains related and basically motivated by illegal revenues.

Moreover the spread of IoT devices, from a pure technical perspective, has given rise, for some time, to attack techniques that were considered no longer used or completely eradicated (e.g. telnet access with default credentials or living off the land attacks, MS Office macros).

On the other hand the technology market, from the defender's perspective, makes available tools and infrastructures increasingly smart, integrable, interconnected, and, at least theoretically, easy to deploy even in complex and extended architectures.

Does the just mentioned gap depend entirely on the well-known and consolidated paradigms such as "the attacker is getting stronger" or "the end user is the weakest link of the Internet value chain"?

Probably, we should investigate if (and how much) security is considered a crucial component in the product innovation roadmap by all the stakeholders (different from security by checklist), how widespread are the modern cyber defence technologies, how deep is the knowledge of the (security) technologies implemented, if security tools are set and tuned at their best, or what are the reasons of their possible nonimplementation (costs, professional skills, etc.).

The unawareness of the end user not only harms himself, but security designer mistakes imply dramatically concerning negative externalities.

Strategy, Leadership, and AI in the Cyber Ecosystem. https://doi.org/10.1016/B978-0-12-821442-8.00008-2
© 2021 Elsevier Inc. All rights reserved.

In this context, we believe that the future of cybersecurity needs to continue to layer always more on top of technology, people, and processes but with a different polarisation and shape, in particular:

— Technology will be more and more integrated in the software product design, requiring the security professionals to focus more on the integration than to the security itself.
— People will continue to represent the weakest link, although the greatest gap will affect security professionals, instead of end users whose freedom in the device use will be progressively reduced (e.g. nudging security behaviours through 'via negativa').
— Processes should be adapted to the new security by design paradigms and to the progressively adoption of a security aware legal framework, due also to the fact that security and safety will collapse more and more.

All the aforementioned bullet points, supported by facts and current trends, would contribute to the discussion of a better *skin in the game* achievement.

2 Most widespread cybersecurity threats

Currently the most widespread cybersecurity threats are as follows (Carfagno, 2018):

1. *Malware*: Any program or file that is harmful to a computer user. Types of malware can include computer viruses, worms, Trojan horses, and spyware. These malicious programs can perform a variety of different functions such as stealing, encrypting, or deleting sensitive data; altering or hijacking core computing functions; and monitoring users' computer activity without their permission. Today, over 90% of malware is delivered via email, typically hidden in the form of infected attachments or inconspicuous links. One well-intentioned employee, just clicking or downloading a malware, can cross also the best defensive moats. The average cost of a malware attack hovers around $2.4 million, according to research from Accenture. If that figure seems high, remember it considers the nearly 50 needed to identify, address, patch, and repair affected systems.

2. *Phishing*: Uses disguised email as a weapon. The goal is to trick the email receiver into believing that the message is something they want or need—a request from their bank, for instance, or a note from someone in their company—and, thus, to trick the user to click a link or download an attachment. What really distinguishes phishing is the form the message takes: the attackers personify a trusted entity of some kind, often a real or plausibly real person or a company the victim might do business with. In a global survey of IT decision makers, over half stated targeting phishing schemes were the top cybersecurity threat faced by their organisation. A single lost or stolen individual's record costs business $225. Yet, few cyberattacks only target one record. Over 74% of cyberattacked companies who experienced stolen data averaged 1000 files lost during their breaches.

3. *Ransomware*: Is a type of malware that prevents or limits users from accessing their system, either by locking the system's screen or by locking the users' files unless a ransom is paid (Trend Micro (s.d.), n.d.). More modern ransomware families, collectively categorized as cryptoransomware, encrypt certain file types on infected systems and force users to pay the ransom through certain online payment methods to get a decryption key, as already shown in (Me, 2003). Ransomware attacks strike every 14 s. They are amongst the most rapid paced and prevalent of cybersecurity threats lodged at organisations, with the usual intent of shutting down servers or holding data and file hostage until a suitable ransom is paid. Without holistic data backup, ransomware can cause chaos. Between system downtimes, lost data, damaged data, patching systems, and cost to training employees to avoid repeat incidents, ransomware attacks cost businesses approximately $11.5 billion in 2019, without considering the cost of the ransom itself if companies opt to pay.

4. *Fileless attacks* (Carbon Black (s.d.), n.d.): They operate without using traditional executable files as a first level of attack like traditional malware. Rather than using malicious software or downloads of executable files as its primary entry point onto corporate networks, fileless malware often hides in memory or other difficult-to-detect locations. From there, it is written directly to RAM rather than to disk to execute a series of events or is coupled with other attack vectors such as ransomware to accomplish its malicious intent. Because fileless malware doesn't write anything to disk like traditional malware does, it leaves no immediate trace of its existence behind and thus avoids detection by traditional antivirus security. Like ransomware, fileless attacks have seen an uptick in recent years. Nearly 77% of 2017's known attacks were fileless. Fileless attacks cost businesses $5 million when fully executed. Other research indicates fileless attacks' costs can be projected to be $300 per employee.

5. *Human error*: Unintended disclosures, accidental data deletions, or improper disposals of sensitive files all fall under human errors, a common yet under-the-radar enterprise threat. Human errors should focus the attention on terms like cybersecurity awareness and the data-handling policies. Accounting for 27% of data breaches, this type of cybersecurity threat costs businesses around $148 per compromised record and can take up to 196 days to uncover and reconcile.

3 The attackers' perspective

The topic of IT security today needs to give some food for thoughts on what feeds an invisible but always more flourishing industry, which involves many actors. It could be called the 'vulnerability chain' since it is possible to identify phases and structured procedures, according to precise logics. However, over the years, the discovery of new vulnerabilities within software, operating systems, and hardware devices aroused in various ways the interest of companies, criminal organisations, and even governments. We believe it is also true that the attention of industry to the ecosystem of IT has grown, as shown in the following table.

Worldwide IT spending forecast (billions of US dollars).

	2019 Spending	2019 Growth (%)	2020 Spending	2020 Growth (%)	2021 Spending	2021 Growth (%)
Data Centre Systems	205	−2.5	210	2.6	212	1.0
Enterprise software	457	8.8	507	10.9	560	10.5
Devices	675	−5.3	683	1.2	685	0.4
IT services	1031	3.7	1088	5.5	1147	5.5
Communication services	1364	−1.1	1384	1.5	1413	2.1
Overall IT	3732	0.4	3872	3.7	4018	3.8

Source: Gartner Press Release, Gartner Says Global IT Spending to Grow 3.7% in 2020, 23 October 2019. https://www.gartner.com/en/newsroom/press-releases/2019-10-23-gartner-says-global-it-spending-to-grow-3point7-percent-in-2020.

Indeed the age when 'anonymous' hackers, ethically motivated, merely boasting their skills seems far away. They claimed they were able to introduce into some computer systems, breaking what today might seem lightweight protections against abusive access.

In fact, discovering a new vulnerability currently offers the possibility to make some choices: communicating it to the company concerned, trying to monetise it by reselling it to the best bidder, or exploiting it for themselves. Even today's 'bug bounty' programmes, promoted by the software/hardware vendors, are considered obsolete. In fact, it is not difficult to come across companies interested to buy exploits of all kinds and ready to pay much more than any software company would. The most quoted and also the most dangerous vulnerabilities are of course those known exclusively by those who discovered them, followed by the so-called '0-day' which, although known among experts, have not yet been resolved, and therefore there are not feasible countermeasures. It is now known, for example, that '0-day' capable to execute remote code (RCE) on IOS and Android operating systems yield figures of up to 1 million dollars.

Companies specialised to buy and sell vulnerabilities often act as real brokers amongst who have precious technical details necessary to exploit these flaws and the companies that make 'ready-made' products able to take advantage of their use.

In this scenario, state actors are increasingly involved, interested in using this knowledge for espionage activities or for investigative purposes.

Compared with the past, however, the discovery of new vulnerabilities is much more difficult today, thus increasing the level of expertise needed. In fact, *only few expert security IT researchers can find them, supported by companies able to invest huge resources in this type of activity.*

It is clear, therefore, that the interest to search for new '0-day' is mainly based on economic aspects such as to attract the attention of more increasingly selected actors, attracted by the potential offered by this type of vulnerability. However, due to their natural and rapid obsolescence, this particular market tends, on long term, to merge itself with that of low-cost vulnerabilities, because more accessible and less expensive. Thus, for example, the spam and phishing campaigns are commonly used to convey ransomware for extortion purposes, to collect information and personal data to be resold, to steal bank credentials, and to create scams of all kinds. Attacks of this type, by their very nature, are not aimed at individual subjects. Instead, they are broad spectrum or, at the very least, addressed to entire categories of unfortunate people chosen on the basis of common social, cultural, or temporal criteria (ICIT, n.d.).

Many specialised companies in the sector (especially the 'consumer' one) turn their attention to this type of threat, offering increasingly sophisticated hardware and software products, advertised to be able to recognise and contrast actions deemed as malicious.

Over the years, therefore, we have witnessed an evolution of the concept of protection itself, moving from the classic antivirus product, based on the simple recognition of viral signatures of malicious objects, to the more advanced endpoint protection platform (EPP) and endpoint detection and response (EDR) capable of recognising the behaviour of known or in some cases even unknown malware.

In recent years, artificial intelligence algorithms and increasingly refined machine learning techniques have been spreading.

The use of cutting-edge technologies seems, however, not to be sufficient to definitively counter the cyber threats in circulation. To confirm this impression, there are numerous analysis *carried out by important organisations and vendors in the sector*, which have shown a greater frequency in the use of increasingly sophisticated social engineering techniques, as well as tools deemed not only reliable as they are already present in the target systems to be attacked but also usable for other purposes. Therefore the human factor is at the heart of all this, and it represents a variable that cannot be eliminated. In fact, more than 99% of today's cyberattacks are human activated, and most of them, for example, start with a phishing email (Proofpoint, n.d.). These attacks target a specific high-level person and are particularly effective as they appear to come from a trusted source.

To confirm what has just been said about the 'human factor' in general, we can remember the story narrated by the astronomer Clifford Stoll in his book (published in 1989) and titled *The Cuckoo's Egg: Tracking a Spy Through the Maze of Computer Espionage*. He had been hunting for months by a computer hacker who could use the computing resources of the California Lawrence Berkeley National Laboratory (LBNL), for which he was responsible, for free. That episode is considered today amongst the first, if not the very first documented APT attack in history.

Stoll used a printer connected to a modem to transcribe all the commands launched by the attacker and to document the activities carried out by the hacker. The latter sought and sometimes obtained unauthorised access to various systems (including military) in the United States, searched for files containing specific keywords such as 'nuclear' or 'Strategic Defense Initiative' (SDI), copied the files containing passwords (to subsequently carry out dictionary attacks), and made scripts typical of current Trojans to discover new passwords. Even then, Stoll noticed the simplicity with which the hacker obtained access to resources that should have been highly protected, due to the superficiality of many system administrators who never bothered to replace the default passwords or to make the correct configurations of the systems they were supposed to manage (Stoll, 1989).

In light of what has been said so far, it becomes evident how many of the techniques mentioned and used many years ago are still in use today, even if in more refined and sophisticated ways, to obtain the same results.

The 'Threat Report 2019' of SophosLabs (Sophos, n.d.) and in that of ENISA of 2018 (the latest published) (ENISA, n.d.) describe the most frequent threats that it has been possible to census, and at a more careful reading, it is possible, in fact, to evoke a certain 'recursion' in the use of the attack methodologies.

In the last decade, cyber criminals have tried to automate a significant number of attacks to be able to exploit already known vulnerabilities quickly and on a large scale. It is not a coincidence that exploit kits of all kinds spread, easily available on specialised sites; spam and phishing campaigns proliferated through the massive sending of emails containing malicious attachments, and there has been a macroscopic increase in social engineering, often prodromal to the spread of ransomware, spyware, Trojan horses, etc. However, automation suffers from the problem of 'predictability'. For example, once a malicious email message has been identified, it is, in fact, relatively simple to take the necessary countermeasures to prevent similar messages from reaching their destination or carrying any malware.

In this respect, therefore, in recent years, a return to the past has become necessary especially in all those cases in which the attacker tries to carry out a 'targeted attack'. In such cases the activities carried out are mostly manual, and the attacker's behaviour becomes intrinsically unpredictable because, for example, he has the possibility to behave reactively to the actions of contrast possibly undertaken by the protection systems and, therefore, to modify the attack scenario according to different and difficult-to-contrast schemes. It is evident that actions of this type are applicable only to a very limited sample of 'victims', as they are aimed at particularly valuable objectives having completely different purposes and motivations than the spread of large-scale malware.

Another effective indicator that highlights the tendency to reuse already known methods to obtain large-scale attacks is the intensification of techniques such as 'Living off the land', that is, tools natively present in operating systems, which being most often included in the whitelists of the various antivirus and protection software, they lend themselves to being exploitable as attack tools. This, in fact, further demonstrates that the introduction of methodologies that are actually new or capable of using almost unknown technicalities is severely limited by the capabilities available and the objective that is being sought to be achieved.

For instance, we can consider 'CrackMapExec' (hackndo, n.d.), known for being a postexploitation tool that makes use of 'Living off the land' techniques. This tool allows you to authenticate on remote machines through local accounts, domain accounts, passwords, and even hashes. Its modular structure makes it particularly versatile and effective for automating the execution of specific commands on the victim's PC. Once access is obtained, in fact, the attacker has the possibility of executing specific ad hoc modules, including, for example, `Mimikatz`, known for being able to obtain various types of authentication credentials (password, hash, ticket Kerberos, etc.) by extracting them from the allocated image in memory about the process called 'lsass' (Local Security Authority Subsystem). The `Mimikatz` tool is well known today by all the security software on the market, and for this reason, it is easily identifiable. However, the situation changes if we tried to execute the 'Procdump' tool through 'CrackMapExec', included since 2006 within Microsoft's Sysinternal suite. The latter, in fact, contains a series of extremely useful applications for system administrators and developers who are often engaged in trouble-shooting activity.

`Procdump`, in this case, dumps the portion of memory occupied by a running process and brings its contents back to a file. The advantage of using this tool, rather than `Mimikatz`, is that it is digitally signed by Microsoft and therefore is considered a trusted tool by Windows operating systems. In this way, it is therefore possible to memorise the content of the 'lsass' process and subsequently analyse it locally with `Mimikatz` to extract the credentials of interest. Although Microsoft tries to take the necessary precautions to prevent to run this type of tools improperly, the use of `Procdump` just described remains an excellent example of how a 'Living off the land' attack can be conducted.

4 The defenders' perspective

The concepts illustrated in the previous paragraphs must be the technical background of a good defender. But this is still not enough to block cyberattacks. This is where cybersecurity comes into play: cybersecurity is the state or process of protecting and recovering networks, devices, and programmes from any type of cyberattack.

A strong cybersecurity system has multiple layers of protection spread across computers, devices, networks, and programs. But a strong cybersecurity system doesn't rely solely on cyber defence technology; it also relies on people making smart cyber defence choices.

We will try to summarise the defenders' perspective by analysing the different types of cybersecurity defence systems (Toch et al., 2018) associated to the most current widespread threats (as described in the second paragraph).

4.1 Cybersecurity defence systems

It is possible to divide cyberattacks into two different groups:

1. The first group concerns what the attacker wants to obtain:
   - stealing information
   - tracking user information
   - taking control of a system
2. The second group concerns the vector used by the attacker to exploit an existent vulnerability:
   - hardware

- network
- application

Cybersecurity defence systems can be classified in the following four categories (Toch et al., 2018):

1. System architecture

Security systems designed for a specific architecture:

- stand-alone
- centralized client server
- collaborative architectures

2. Type of detection

Security systems that belong to this category operate at the level of the attack vector described earlier (hardware, network, and application). There are two main categories:

- anomaly-based detection, based on modelling normality to identify occurrences of anomalies;
- signature-based detection, based on a database of the signatures that might signal a particular type of attack; they compare incoming traffic to those signatures.

3. Type of data

Security systems can be classified depending on the type of analyzed data:

- application data
- file data
- network data

4. Ecosystems

Security systems can be classified depending on the ecosystem they must protect:

- enterprise
- mobile devices
- IoT

The table (Table 1) reported in Toch et al. (2018) summarizes several cybersecurity solutions according to the classification described earlier. The solutions are differentiated according to the source of the analyzed data:

(a) Network solutions include organisation firewalls and network intrusion detection systems (NIDS).

(b) Content filtering solutions include proxies, web client-side attack detection, and email phishing and spam detection.

(c) Endpoint solutions include host-based intrusion detection systems (HIDS) and host-based intrusion prevention systems (HIPS) that usually monitor a device (system calls, file system integrity, etc.) detecting malware.

4.2 Understanding the true costs and impact of cybersecurity programmes

However, a good defender, as described earlier, not only needs to know the state of the art of cyberattack techniques and technologies but also must be aware of what kind of impact a specific attack can reach on the environment that he aims to protect.

An interesting article of McKinsey & Company (Choi et al., 2017) illustrates that often cybersecurity is a critical but misunderstood aspect of companies' technology infrastructures.

Companies are using all kinds of sophisticated technologies and techniques to protect critical business assets. Surely, it is possible to assure that the most important factor in any cybersecurity context is trust. It should overhang all the decisions executives make about tools, talent, and processes. However, trust is often lacking in many organizations' cybersecurity initiatives. Senior business leaders and the board consider cybersecurity as a priority only when an intrusion occurs, for instance, while the chief security officer and his team view security as an everyday priority, as even the most routine website transactions present potential holes to be exploited.

One issue that continues to arise is the gap between organizations' perceived security strength and their actual security strength. This perception problem emerges because enterprises typically don't establish quantitative metrics to measure security preparedness. Instead, they often use more qualitative, anecdotal experiences to determine security maturity. A common error enterprise makes is to view data security preparedness and maturity as something that can be measured by listing the layers of defence an IT department has in place (two firewalls is better than one firewall). Viewing cybersecurity through this lens means enterprises cannot distinguish between self-perception and reality. One of the key elements of a strong security posture is an organisation's ability to anticipate threats before they happen.

Perceptions become facts, trust erodes further, and cybersecurity programmes end up being less successful than they could be. If incidence of breaches has been light, for instance, business leaders may freeze the cybersecurity budget until the CIO or other cybersecurity leaders prove the need for further investment in controls—perhaps opening themselves up to attack.

Conversely, if threats have been documented frequently, business leaders may reflexively decide to overspend on new technologies without understanding that there are other, nontechnical remedies to keep data and other corporate assets safe.

Also due to the just mentioned perceived security, the world of cybersecurity is full of wrong myths created over time and very resistant to disavowal. The article in Choi et al. (2017) lists four main myths of cybersecurity:

- *Myth 1*—All assets in the organisation must be protected the same way. Obviously, this is a myth because not all data are created with equal value. Companies don't have endless resources to protect all data at any cost. A strong cybersecurity strategy provides differentiated protection of the company's most important assets, utilizing a tiered collection of security measures. For example, is it convenient for a company a full ransomware protection of all the saved data? Probably the company must choose the more convenient asset data to protect.
- *Myth 2*—The more we spend, the more secure we will be. According to Choi et al. (2017), there is no direct correlation between spending on cybersecurity (as a proportion of total IT spending) and success of a company's cybersecurity programme. Companies often don't protect the right assets. A classic example of how this myth is far from reality is the fifth threat described in the second paragraph: human error. A human error can bypass easily all the expensive technologies dedicated to the defence systems.
- *Myth 3*—External hackers are the only threat to corporate assets. The danger of a hacker attack from the outside is certainly high, especially in the case of companies that hold important patents or sensitive data, but there are significant threats inside companies as well. Internal people who are closest to the data or other corporate assets can often be a weak link in a company (e.g. when they share passwords or files over unprotected networks, click on malicious hyperlinks sent from unknown email addresses, or otherwise act in ways that open up corporate networks to attack). Indeed, threats from inside the company account for about 43% of data breaches (Choi et al., 2017).
- *Myth 4*—The more advanced our technology, the more secure we are. It is true that cybersecurity teams often use powerful, cutting-edge technologies to protect data and other corporate assets. But it is also true that many threats can be mitigated using less advanced methods. After all, most companies are not dealing with military-grade hackers. More than 70% of global cyberattacks come from financially motivated criminals who are using technically simple tactics, such as phishing emails (Choi et al., 2017).

We consider this last myth particularly interesting. In fact the Verizon report, about 2019 data breaches (Verizon, 2019), shows changes in threat actions and affected assets from 2013 to 2018. The rise in social engineering is evident in both charts, with the action category 'social' and the related 'person' asset both increasing.

But this phenomenon does involve not only end user weakness in the cybersecurity chain but also the presence of a not negligible weakness in the management of the security infrastructures of the top ranked social networks.

Indeed the mentioned report shows what types of attack patterns are more common to different categories of industry, along with breakouts for threat action categories and affected assets. We want to highlight as in absolute term, incidents, and breaches hit particularly server asset that surely are controlled from expert IT professionals. So the defender weakness does not always rely on the final user.

5 The security frameworks' perspective

We have so far analysed the cyber threat from the perspective of the attackers and defenders. Now, let's see what tools a defender has to tackle a problem that is obviously complex. A complex problem must be approached methodically to be able, with the resources available, to obtain an adequate level of protection for the information or entities to be protected.

As in other areas of science or technology, methodologies for approaching information security have been developed at the international level and organized in the form of frameworks, platforms, or best practices. Later, we illustrate some of these, the best known, and show how they have many points in common, even if they start from different assumptions.

We start from the "Framework for Improving Critical Infrastructure Cybersecurity" (NIST, n.d.) developed by NIST to protect critical infrastructures but applicable, with the appropriate modifications, to any organization. It proposes a modular approach that adapts to realities with different resources and objectives, from the simplest to the most complex situations with challenging objectives.

The framework is a risk-based approach for managing cybersecurity risk and is composed of four parts: introduction, basics, how to use, and cybersecurity self-assessment. Basics are core, implementation tiers, and profiles.

The core lists five concurrent and continuous functions: identify, protect, detect, respond, and recover. These high-level activities are divided into categories and subcategories to refer to simple and well-defined activities. Single activities are also related to informative references that are other standards or best practices that provide details about the implementation.

The Framework Implementation Tiers provide context on how an organisation considers cybersecurity risk and the processes in place to manage that risk. Ranging from partial (Tier 1) to adaptive (Tier 4), tiers describe an increasing degree of rigor and sophistication in cybersecurity risk management practices. Every organisation should decide its tier depending on risks, resources, external constraints or obligations, etc.

The profile is the alignment of the functions, categories, and subcategories with the business requirements, risk tolerance, and resources of the organisation.

The description of the actual profile and of the target profile could be useful to draw a roadmap.

Decision process on tiers and profiles should involve three different levels of people in the organisation that are executive, business/process, and implementation/operations (Fig. 1).

This framework is an excellent guide to tackle the problem of IT security but requires a great commitment in terms of people, economic, and technological resources that increase with increasing security needs.

Network and information system (NIS) (EUR-Lex, n.d.) is a European Union directive and has by definition a very high-level approach. It provides indications on the objectives to be pursued, especially what to protect, to preserve those assets deemed essential for the socioeconomic balance of the countries of the Union. The tools and ways in which to protect these assets are deliberately left to the organizational freedom of individual countries that can adopt national or international frameworks. In Italy, for example, the National Cybersecurity Framework (n.d.) has been developed.

Payment Card Industry Data Security Standard (PCI DSS) (PCI Security Standards, n.d.) is the reference framework for credit card payment services and is widely used by banks and financial operators in general. However, it can be taken as a reference by anyone who

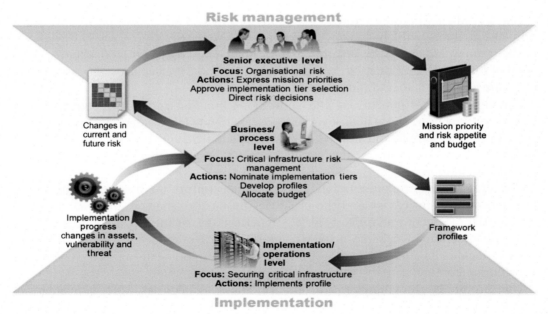

FIG. 1 Risk management implementation according to NIST Framework for Improving Critical Infrastructure Cybersecurity.

wants to guarantee the security of data, transactions, and systems. It is based on a check-list of implementations that aim to obtain the best state-of-the-art cybersecurity systems. For this reason the checklist is constantly updated to cover new or more stringent needs. The approach is high level and is limited to indicating the procedures, activities, or con-trols to be carried out without going into detail on how these actions should be carried out at the implementation/operation level.

COBIT5 (ISACA, n.d.) is a framework that addresses the problem from an organiza-tional point of view. It provides a correct approach that starts from the business to get to protection, also showing how security should be integrated into the business and not considered one of the utilities at its service. It favours the development of more effec-tive relationships between business executives, IT operators, and cybersecurity people.

ISO/IEC 27001 (ISO, n.d.) is an information security standard, part of the ISO/IEC 27000 family of standards. It specifies a management system, a.k.a. information security management system (ISMS), that is intended to bring information security under man-agement control and gives specific requirements. The other central element, besides ISMS, is the continuous control of processes and systems through the plan-do-check-act cycle. This framework also focusses mainly on procedural and organisational aspects and therefore has a high-level perspective, leaving the implementation of the operational/technological level to other standards or frameworks. Organisations that meet the require-ments may be certified by an accredited certification body following successful comple-tion of an audit.

Malware Information Sharing Platform (MISP, n.d.) is an open-source threat intelli-gence platform and open standards for threat information sharing. The platform is optional because the exchange of data can take place through other systems or software that comply with the open standard. The latter consists of a series of data structures (core, object template, taxonomy, and galaxy) represented in JavaScript object notation (JSON). The standardization of data and the use of an object-oriented programming language simplifies the exchange and use of information and the automation of processes, both for the exchange and the use of data.

Implementation requires considerable resources, but correct and widespread use could bring undoubted advantages. The project is cofinanced by the European Commu-nity. Obviously, it is a tool that covers a small part of the needs related to IT security, above all related to the operation of SOCs and CERTs (implementation/operation level of NIST Framework) and not to the overall management of information security.

MITRE ATT&CK (MITRE ATT&CK, n.d.) is a globally accessible knowledge base of adversary tactics and techniques based on real-world observations. The ATT&CK knowl-edge base is used as a foundation for the development of specific threat models and meth-odologies in the private sector, in government, and in the cybersecurity product and service community. The approach is very practical and is based on matrices (enterprises, Windows, MacOS, Android, etc.) that map the known attacks and allow the insight into the details of the various attack techniques. The aim is to make cybersecurity operators aware so that they are able to prepare the appropriate procedural and technological countermeasures.

Even for MITRE ATT&CK the case history is complex and requires a considerable effort of continuous updating. Furthermore, also in this case, the perspective is at technical/operational level and presupposes the existence of an organisational and technical structure capable of optimising the allocation of resources, modifying processes, and implementing countermeasures.

Common aspects found in the various frameworks:

1. The elements of which they are composed—especially at a low level—are common, and in fact, there are mapping matrices between the various frameworks.
2. The high-level ones provide a good perspective from which to start but remain very far from the ultimate goal that is to obtain real safety in practical cases. For this reason, they often refer to other lower-level standards/frameworks.
3. The low-level ones give good indications on how to solve the real cybersecurity problems (low level), but they risk being a very long list of tasks without an overall vision, that is, they lack the big picture. A step forward in this case has been proposed in (Bottazzi et al., 2017) in which authors indicate the most important technical and organisational arrangements that reduce the effects of a security incident and facilitate analysis and recovery operations.
4. The complete ones (e.g. NIST), that is, the synergistic set of multiple frameworks, require large organisational resources, with a dedicated multilevel structure, and the technological ones to cover the large series of attacks (e.g. matrices of the various frameworks).

6 Did we forget anything on the way?

The scenarios just described (considering three different perspectives) can lead to different food for thought. First of all, there is no simple, prepackaged solution. Budgets, shrewdness, and technologies are not enough. The complexity, pervasiveness, and transversality of the problem require a serious and conscious approach, an organizational structure appropriate to the objectives and resources capable of countering the plethora of attacks towards the numerous targets.

With specific reference to the organizational aspects, it would appear that, as with humans, the 'I can change' mantra is false here as well, or at least it is hard to achieve.

It would not be otherwise explained how it is possible that the 38% of the Fortune 500s do not have a CISO and only the 16% of these have another executive who holds the role of responsible for cybersecurity (Bitglass Report, 2019a), even if on the three largest breaches from each of the last 3 years, an average of 257 million individuals had their personal information compromised. The nine publicly traded companies (Bitglass Report, 2019b) all suffered an average of $347 million in legal fees, penalties, remediation costs, and other expenses. On average, they also experienced a steep decrease of 7.5% in stock prices and major declines in overall market capitalisation (an average of $5.4 billion per company).

The shortage of CISOs is only the tip of the iceberg, according to the Cybersecurity Workforce Study 2019 (ISC2, n.d.). This shortage extends to other professionals like IT directors/managers and security architects/engineers/specialists, reaching a global gap estimate of 4.07 million units.

Moreover a global study from ESG and ISSA (Oltsik, 2019) confirmed "that the cyber-security skills shortage is exacerbating the number of data breaches", with the top two con-tributing factors to security incidents being "a lack of adequate training of non-technical employees" (31%) first and "a lack of adequate cybersecurity staff" (22%) second.

Yet, lack of formal education isn't slowing down new recruits to the cybersecurity talent pool. In fact, there is an army of ethical hackers all over the world that won't be hired into traditional full-time roles. In the years to come, there will be over a 1,000,000 ethical hackers. If all these professional skills could also be employed 'on the other side of the fence' (the work of attackers and defenders can be very different especially in extended environments), enterprises should seriously think about how to *recruit and retain individuals*.

Cybersecurity can be a thankless job. Security professionals are on the front lines pro-tecting 'digital societies', yet, they rarely get called out for effectively defending and always get called out when something goes wrong. Thus the skill gap is widening, education is lagging, and society pays the price with data breach after data breach, considering that, as mentioned in the introduction, security and safety will collapse always more.

Computer science programmes struggle to offer adequate cybersecurity courses for the next generation of technologists. Of the top 50 computer science programmes in the United States, only 42% offer three or more information security-specific courses for undergraduates, and this is far more than what was available 5 or 10 years ago.

Today the University of Maryland, College Park, amongst the top computer science programmes in the United States, offers a cybersecurity concentration for computer sci-ence majors. University of California, Berkeley, also offered a Cyberwar class in 2017, teaching 80 students how to hack for good. Northeastern University offers 11 courses that cover some aspect of security, including a class covering laws, ethics, and policy related to digital technologies.

Given the constant rising of data breaches, it is not surprising that 91% of survey respondents (all cybersecurity professionals) believe that most organisations are consid-ered (or felt) either extremely vulnerable or somewhat vulnerable to a significant cyber-attack, that is, one that disrupts business processes or leads to a data breach (Fig. 2).

This heavy lack of cybersecurity professionals impacts organizations in various aspects like hiring and training junior personnel or outsourcing security tasks to service providers, impacting the relationship with the business to align cybersecurity with business pro-cesses, making ineffective use of cybersecurity technologies since organisations don't have the time or personnel to fully learn or utilise some security technologies to their full potential (*a proper approach to cybersecurity should look for the right tool, not more tools*),

In your opinion, how vulnerable are most organisations (other than your own) to a significant cyberattack or data breach (i.e. one that disrupts business processes or leads to theft of sensitive data)? (Percent of respondents, *N* = 267)

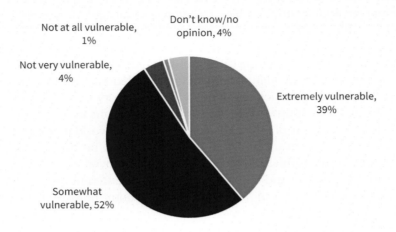

Source: Enterprise Strategy Group

FIG. 2 Vulnerability of most organisations to a significant cyberattack or data breach.

and burdening understaffed cybersecurity teams by manual or made-up-on-the-spot processes.

The key challenge facing security leaders, putting their organizations at risk of breach, is the misplaced confidence that the abundance of technology investments they made strengthened their security posture, according to a study conducted by Forrester Consulting (Cybersecurity, 2019).

The study found that all companies are prioritizing security and risk programmes and investing in security and risk automation. In fact, most companies are using multiple technologies to identify and mitigate enterprise risk, including security analytics; vulnerability management; governance, risk, and compliance (GRC); and vendor risk management platforms.

However, increasing the number of security technologies doesn't translate to improved security, but instead makes it difficult to aggregate risk data for reporting, often requiring manual effort. This, in turn, inhibits them from having insight into their overall risk posture.

The complexity of today's IT infrastructures and the heterogeneity of enterprise security tools perhaps can be considered useful only for taking a traditional reactive approach to cybersecurity.

A proactive cybersecurity programme, instead, requires a real-time visibility of IT assets together with a continuous monitoring of security controls to help identify, prioritise, and remediate risks. The following is a possible shortlist of a set of proactive-oriented capabilities:

- visibility and control over security areas such as inventory gaps, vulnerabilities, endpoint security, privileged access, identity and access, patching, application security, and user awareness;
- a range of security metrics and measures such as key performance indicators, key risk indicators, and service-level agreement metrics aligned to any security framework;
- automating processes;
- unified data processing (e.g. entity resolution, correlation, deduplication, normalization, aggregation, and cleaning);
- data connectors that unify data ingested from various security, IT, and business sources;
- a segmented, categorised, and comprehensive view of inventories (e.g. devices, applications, vulnerabilities, people, databases, and privileges).

Finally the staff currently employed in cybersecurity teams often suffer the frustration caused by the lack of career development (dead-end positions) because, despite a continuous wave of cybersecurity headlines, there is still a large gap between cybersecurity and business priorities (and salaries too).

Thus, again, although the global cybersecurity spending is growing steadily, as reported by the Gartner forecasts shown in Section 3, it seems that technical staff has been completely forgotten, or perhaps, it is not considered neither as a cost nor as an investment.

The cybersecurity professional shortage, as discussed several times in this chapter, is a complex issue to cope with, mostly because it is unclear who ultimately owns the responsibility of this heavy lack of skilled personnel.

First of all, it is fundamental to make it clear that the dynamic nature of cybersecurity is challenging, compounded by work roles differing between organisations (and even departments within) and perspectives (the job of a high skilled ethical hacker could be very different from that of a cybersecurity professional). With the rapidly changing nature of the domain, career pathways and required training must be reviewed and updated regularly. Referring to the medical and legal fields, for example, the necessary skills for those professions have remained relatively consistent, while cybersecurity continuously demands learning brand new concepts. Because of this, curricula can quickly become outdated and less reflective of the current state of cybersecurity at any given time. For instance, artificial intelligence (AI), Internet of Things (IoT), and weaponised psychology are just a few newer priorities in the cyber domain (Cybersecurity Career Paths and Progression, 2019).

This difficulty probably relies on numerous concurrent reasons. In other words the theoretical foundation of skill shortages lies at the intersection of various academic disciplines, including labour economics, human resource management, education, and skills policy. From their intersection, there is a growing body of work that can lead to skill mismatches, which is an umbrella term describing several skill problems, including shortages.

As mentioned before, there are probably some issues on the educational point of view (primary and/or secondary), but the same holds also for higher education, to be understood as master's degrees or specialised trainings and certifications, identified as factors that help professionals progress (De Zan, 2019). Moreover, certifications may not hold the same weight as experience, once a professional has reached a certain point in his career.

Leaving aside what the theory says, the Enterprise Strategy Group (ESG) and the Information Systems Security Association (ISSA) teamed up and initiated a primary research project in 2016 with the goal of capturing the voice and thoughts of cybersecurity professionals on the state of their profession and gaining a perspective on the situational analysis from those closest to the issue. Aiming at this goal, ESG and ISSA surveyed 437 information security professionals (and ISSA members). The survey respondents represented organisations of all sizes and included professionals located in all parts of the world (Oltsik, 2016). The cybersecurity professionals participating in this project were asked a series of questions on a variety of cybersecurity topics, focusing on the life cycle of cybersecurity professional careers. Based upon the data collected, the study concludes the following:

— *Cybersecurity professionals are attracted by a moral imperative.* When asked why they became cybersecurity professionals, 27% said it gave them the chance to use their technical skills to help protect valuable business and IT assets, while 22% claim they were attracted to the morality of the profession. In the mind of many cybersecurity professionals, their jobs equate to a battle between right and wrong.
— *The majority of cybersecurity professionals got their start in IT.* More than three-quarters (78%) of survey respondents say that their career started somewhere in IT and then evolved into cybersecurity. When asked to identify the most helpful skills gained as IT professionals (that can be applied to cybersecurity), respondents listed attributes like experience with different types of technologies, IT operations knowledge and skills, and networking (technology) knowledge and skills. While these were the top selections, responses did vary based upon experience. More senior cybersecurity professionals emphasised lessons learned as part of IT collaboration with the business, while junior cybersecurity professionals highlighted technical training.
— *Most cybersecurity professionals struggle to define their career paths.* Nearly two-thirds (65%) of respondents do not have a clearly defined career path or plans to take their careers to the next level. This is likely due to the diversity of cybersecurity focus areas, the lack of a well-defined professional career development standard and map, and the rapid changes in the cybersecurity field itself. Business, IT, and cybersecurity managers, academics, and public policy leaders should take note of today's cybersecurity career stuck and develop and promote more formal cybersecurity guidelines and frameworks that can guide cybersecurity professionals in their career development in the future.
— *Cybersecurity professionals have solid ideas for skill advancement.* When asked how they improve their knowledge, skills, and abilities, cybersecurity professionals pointed

to activities like attending specific cybersecurity training courses (58%), participating in professional organisations (53%), and engaging in on-the-job tutoring from more experienced cybersecurity professionals (37%). Responses varied by seniority with experienced cybersecurity managers (i.e. CISOs, VPs, and Directors) leaning towards professional organisations, while cybersecurity staff members favoured on-the-job mentoring.

— *Cybersecurity certifications are a mixed bag.* Over half (56%) of survey respondents had received a CISSP and felt it was a valuable certification for getting a job and gaining useful cybersecurity knowledge. Other than the CISSP certification however, cybersecurity professionals appear warm on other types of industry certifications. Based upon these data, it appears that security certifications should be encouraged for specific roles and responsibilities but downplayed as part of a cybersecurity professional's overall career and skill development.

— *Cybersecurity professionals are relatively satisfied with their jobs.* While 41% of respondents claim to be very satisfied with their jobs, 44% are only somewhat satisfied, and 15% are not very satisfied or not at satisfied all. Cybersecurity professionals point to factors like financial compensation (32%), organisational culture that includes cybersecurity (24%), business management's commitment to cybersecurity (23%), and the ability to work with a highly skilled and talented cybersecurity team (22%).

— *Continuous cybersecurity training is lacking.* When asked if their current employer provides the cybersecurity team with the right level of training to keep up with business and IT risk, more than half (56%) of survey respondents answered 'no', suggesting that their organizations needed to provide more or significantly more training for the cybersecurity staff. Organizations that don't provide continuous training to cybersecurity staff will fall further behind adversaries while increasing business and IT risk. This should be an unacceptable situation for all business and technology managers.

— *Many CISOs are not getting enough face time in the boardroom.* While industry rhetoric claims that "cybersecurity is a boardroom issue", 44% of respondents believe that CISO participation with executive management is not at the right level today and should increase somewhat or significantly in the future. This perspective is more common with more experienced cybersecurity managers (who should be working with the business) than cybersecurity staff members.

— *Internal relationships need work.* While many organizations consider the relationship between cybersecurity, business, and IT teams to be good, it is concerning that 20% of cybersecurity professionals say the relationship between cybersecurity and IT is fair or poor and 27% of survey respondents claim the relationship between cybersecurity and the business is fair or poor. The biggest cybersecurity/IT relationship issue selected relates to prioritising tasks between the two groups, while the biggest cybersecurity/ business relationship challenge is aligning goals. The report data reveal that cybersecurity and IT teams are taking steps to improve collaboration but also uncovers that more work is necessary to bridge the gap between cybersecurity and business management.

- *CISO turnover has business and economic roots.* When asked why CISOs tend to seek new jobs after a few short years, cybersecurity professionals responded that CISOs tend to move on when their organisations lack a serious cybersecurity culture (31%), when CISOs are not active participants with executives (30%), and when CISOs are offered higher compensation elsewhere (27%). To retain strong CISOs, organizations must not only provide competitive compensation but also make a serious commitment to cybersecurity executives and comprehensive programmes.

Today's cybersecurity professionals reside on the front line of a perpetual battle, tasked with applying limited resources to defend their organisation against everything from embarrassing website defacement through unseemly ransomware extortion to devastating data breaches. Alarmingly, cybersecurity professionals often accept this challenge even knowing they are understaffed for the fight.

On the other side, cyber adversaries continue to develop creative tactics, techniques, and procedures for attacks. Perhaps, this is the real reason why attackers are getting stronger.

Large and small organizations must recognize risks and priorities and invest in cybersecurity defences and oversight. Recognise risks and priorities should also mean consider the possible externalities when something goes wrong. As mentioned in premise the side effects due to security professional mistakes can be many magnitudes greater than those made by end users.

7 Conclusions

Thus it is likely to suppose that paradigms such as 'the end user is the weak link in the security chain' or 'the attacker is getting stronger' are no longer compatible to justify the current IOCs.

It is equally likely that the increasingly widespread initiatives aimed at 'nudging end-user behaviour through via negativa' will not have any striking results, simply because the consequent externalities, however, important, will be of a minor entity.

Furthermore, it also seems, slightly forcing the assessment, that since the 'Cuckoo's Egg' no step forward has been taken, confirming again that the mantra 'I can change' is false.

Although neither the investments made in cybersecurity nor the scientific results obtained in the last 30 years can be denied, the recent chronicle highlights seem to demonstrate that the endless battle between attackers and defenders is somewhat unfair, or rather the amount of investments in cybersecurity seems to be not coupled with an increased confidence in future results (achieve the *skin of the game*).

Moreover, do the cybersecurity frameworks are really exploited to lower risks and vulnerabilities and increase confidence in an ever-connected world, or do they are just an opportunity (alibi) able to justify a possible data breach (a.k.a. security by checklist)?

As already mentioned earlier, we deeply believe that one or more critical factors have not been taken into proper consideration or have been completely forgotten, amongst which there is certainly the human one. The human factor has been picked up so far almost completely in the set of end users, but little or nothing in the set of people involved in the design and management of IT security systems. These are the people who make technological choices (another technology or the best fitting technology?). These are the people who decide and choose not only technologies but also priorities, implementation, integration and right tuning.

The 'server-side' human factor should include the responsibility of the daily life of a great part of modern societies, which is increasingly IT dependent, and should not consider only how to maximize a business plan.

Finally, what needs to be well focussed and approached is the cybersecurity organization (to be understood as all the staff involved in cybersecurity, not only the CISO), by keeping in strong consideration many critical factors like decision-making processes, training, professional skills, career development, and salaries, whose externalities can have enormous impacts.

References

Bitglass Report, 2019a. "The Cloudfathers". An Analysis of Cybersecurity in the Fortune 500. https://www.bitglass.com/blog/the-cloudfathers-the-latest-cybersecurity-findings-for-fortune-500.

Bitglass Report, 2019b. Monster-Sized Breaches Spell Disaster for the Enterprise. https://www.bitglass.com/blog/monster-sized-breaches-spell-disaster-for-enterprise.

Bottazzi, G., Italiano, G.F., Rutigliano, G.G., 2017. An operational framework for incident handling. In: 2017 Proceedings of ITASEC.

Carbon Black (s.d.). What Is Fileless Malware? Adapted from Carbon Black https://www.carbonblack.com/resources/definitions/what-is-fileless-malware/.

Carfagno, D., 2018. How Much Should Your Company Invest in Cybersecurity? Adapted from Cybershark. https://www.blackstratus.com/how-much-should-your-company-invest-in-cybersecurity/.

Choi, J., Kaplan, J., Krishnamurthy, C., Lung, H., 2017. Understanding the True Costs and Impact of Cybersecurity Programs. Adapted from McKinsey & Company. https://www.mckinsey.it/idee/hit-or-myth-understanding-the-true-costs-and-impact-of-cybersecurity-programs.

Cybersecurity, 2019. Cybersecurity Requires Controls Monitoring to Ensure Complete Asset Protection. Forrester Opportunity Snapshot: A Custom Study Commissioned by Panaseer.

Cybersecurity Career Paths and Progression, February 2019. Sponsored by the Cybersecurity and Infrastructure Security Agency (CISA) of the Department of Homeland Security, and authored by the Software Engineering Institute (SEI) at Carnegie Mellon. https://niccs.us-cert.gov/sites/default/files/documents/pdf/cybersecurity%20career%20paths%20and%20progressionv2.pdf?trackDocs=cybersecurity%20career%20paths%20and%20progressionv2.pdf.

De Zan, T., 2019. Mind the Gap: The Cyber Security Skills Shortage and Public Policy Interventions. Global Cyber Security Center.

ENISA, ENISA Threat Landscape Report 2018. https://www.enisa.europa.eu/publications/enisa-threat-landscape-report-2018/at_download/fullReport.

EUR-Lex, Directive (EU) 2016/1148 of the European Parliament and of the Council of 6 July 2016 concerning measures for a high common level of security of network and information systems across the Union. https://eur-lex.europa.eu/eli/dir/2016/1148/oj.

hackndo, Extract credentials from lsass remotely. https://en.hackndo.com/remote-lsass-dump-passwords/.

ICIT, The ICIT Ransomware Report. https://icitech.org/wp-content/uploads/2016/03/ICIT-Brief-The-Ransomware-Report2.pdf.

ISACA, A Business Framework for the Governance and Management of Enterprise IT. https://www.isaca.org/resources/cobit.

ISC2, ISC2 Cybersecurity Workforce Study 2019. https://www.isc2.org/Research/2019-Cybersecurity-Workforce-Study.

ISO, ISO/IEC 27001 Information Security Management. https://www.iso.org/isoiec-27001-information-security.html.

Me, G., 2003. "Payment security in mobile environment". ACS/IEEE International Conference on Computer Systems and Applications, Book of Abstracts, Tunis, Tunisia, 2003, pp. 34-, https://doi.org/10.1109/AICCSA.2003.1227468.

MISP, Malware Information Sharing Platform. https://www.misp-project.org/.

MITRE ATT&CK, The MITRE ATT&CK™ framework. https://attack.mitre.org/.

National Cybersecurity Framework, https://www.cybersecurityframework.it/en.

NIST, NIST Framework for Improving Critical Infrastructure Cybersecurity. https://www.nist.gov/cyberframework.

Oltsik, J., 2016. The State of Cyber Security Professional Careers: An Annual Research Report (Part I). Research Report. Cooperative Research Project by Enterprise Strategy Group and Information Systems Security Association.

Oltsik, J., 2019. The Life and Times of Cybersecurity Professionals 2018. Research Report. Cooperative Research Project by Enterprise Strategy Group and Information Systems Security Association.

PCI Security Standards, Payment Card Industry Data Security Standard. https://www.pcisecuritystandards.org/.

Proofpoint, Ten Stats That Reveal How Today's Cyber Attacks Target People First, Not Infrastructure. https://www.proofpoint.com/us/corporate-blog/post/ten-stats-reveal-how-todays-cyber-attacks-target-people-first-not-infrastructure.

Sophos, SophosLabs 2019 Threat Report. https://www.sophos.com/en-us/medialibrary/PDFs/technical-papers/sophoslabs-2019-threat-report.pdf.

Stoll, C., 1989. The Cuckoo's Egg: Tracking a Spy Through the Maze of Computer Espionage. Doubleday.

Symantec, February 2019. Symantec Internet Security Threat Report. vol. 24.

Toch, E., Bettini, C., Shmueli, E., Radaelli, L., Lanzi, A., Riboni, D., Lepri, B., 2018. The privacy implications of cyber security systems: a technological survey. ACM Comput. Surv. 51 (2), 1–27 36.

Trend Micro (s.d.) Ransomware. Adapted from Trend Micro https://www.trendmicro.com/vinfo/us/security/definition/ransomware

Verizon, 2019. 2019 Data Breach Investigations Report.

Webroot, 2019. Webroot Threat Report.

12

The role of social media, digitisation of marketing, and AI on brand awareness

Daniel Hagan, Hamid Jahankhani, Lea Broc, and Arshad Jamal
NORTHUMBRIA UNIVERSITY, LONDON, UNITED KINGDOM

1 Introduction

The digital revolution has changed the field of marketing. The world has witnessed new and emerging digital technologies, which have transformed every part of an organisation and disrupted the traditional impersonal marketing communication strategies in recent years. Digital technologies have impacted not only major business areas such as product development, profitability, brand management, customer relationship management, buying, selling, and communication and application of digital technologies (Hudson et al., 2012) but also how organisations relate to their stakeholders, particularly customers, and how these customers interact with companies and their brands.

Digital technologies have had the most substantial impact on marketing and business communication processes due to the major developments in the devices, equipment, and marketing activities (Sheoran, 2012). A marketing activity becomes digital when it relies on a digital means to function (Yasmin et al., 2015). Digital communication seeks to create a direct relationship between a marketer and its stakeholders, particularly customers using digital transmission technology (Bird, 2007). Digital marketing has moved on from channels needing Internet connection to channels needing Internet association (Chaffey, 2020). Offline channels like phones, digital TV, and other digital networks are frequently used by marketers for promoting goods and services, along with online channels like websites, social networking sites, smartphones, email, and online communities (Pandey and Shukla, 2010).

Digital technologies have redefined the communication parlance with their unique capabilities, including interactivity, measurability, customer engagement, customisation, accessibility, and managing large informative sources (Edelman and Heller, 2015). Marketers are resorting to digital marketing communication, as it allows them to deliver real-time personalised services and content to an individual consumer (Holliman and Rowley, 2014). Digital marketing appeals to, notifies, and influences consumers in an attractive yet subtle manner while keeping important customer satisfaction

Strategy, Leadership, and AI in the Cyber Ecosystem. https://doi.org/10.1016/B978-0-12-821442-8.00011-2
© 2021 Elsevier Inc. All rights reserved.

uncompromised. An interactive and targeted communication with an individual customer through digital channels remains at the core of digital marketing communication. However, capability of the digital medium to customise and personalise the individual experience makes it a truly attractive alternative to its traditional counterparts (Hawks, 2015).

Companies around the globe are increasing their digital spending (Maddox, 2015). Conlon (2016) in an article titled 'Winterberry Group predicts increased spending on nearly all marketing channels' noting that it witnessed a growth of 6.4% in spending in comparison with 3.3% growth in TV and 2.6% growth in outdoor media. Magazine and newspapers observed a negative growth of 1.9% and 6%, respectively. Radio spending remained flat and saw no growth in spending (Conlon, 2016). The inbound nature of digital channels is helping marketers to reduce the cost of contacting customers and generating more leads than the traditional marketing with its outbound nature (Angelides, 1997). Hubspot (2013), in its annual study on inbound marketing, revealed that traditional channels of communication are becoming less effective, as 45% of people never open the direct mail, 85% fast forward through TV commercials, 84% don't stay on websites with excessive advertising, and 91% unsubscribe from emails. The study further stated that digital marketing with an inbound focus creates 54% more leads than traditional marketing and costs 61% less than traditional outbound marketing.

In the digital environment nowadays, technological innovation has an influence on the efficiency of marketing improvement and affects changes in consumer behaviour (Oklander et al., 2018). The Internet and social media have played an increasingly important role in accessing information and communication of consumers since it assists them to connect and interact with each other easier and closer, that is, two-way communication. Therefore this benefit of technological advances in social media can be a good opportunity for businesses to promote their products and communicate with target audiences.

2 Social media

Social media became a regular activity for most people following to worldwide Internet accessibility. The unique characteristics and widespread use of social media have transformed the marketing tool from traditional to online, particularly in interaction and promotion such as Facebook, Instagram, Twitter, Blog, and Line due to social media that allows for higher-speed connections and connectivity between firms and customers anywhere without face-to-face meetings (Razak et al., 2016).

Similarly, social media sites are online organisers that allow members of the website to build and maintain a profile, to recognise other people they connect, and to engage by consuming, producing, and connecting with the content created by their connections (Tuten, 2017). Social media is one of the 'best options' for an item to reach potential customers to get in touch with community networking as a tool for social interaction. Besides, social shopping is the active engagement and influence of others in the process of consumer decision making, generally, in the form of perceptions, feedback, and experiences shared through social media.

Social media can commonly categorise users who created the content known as user-generated content as follow:

- Blogs that are considered a form of a content management system that allows users to write posts and broadcast articles quickly in which a blog is created offer an opportunity for people interested in sharing ideas, knowledge, and experience through freewriting. As a result, bloggers are now increasing on the social media platform, which is benefiting online communities to receive content through blogger storytelling. Also, stakeholders can discuss or share ideas as a comment via this channel.
- Twitter and microblog posts are blogs which limit the size of posts to 140 characters in each time. Initially, Twitter designers expected users to write stories about what do you do now? However, companies see it as an opportunity to building brand awareness by creating content which expects to report the content to increase the volume of sales by using it as a marketing tool. Moreover, it is also used to promote articles that are quickly becoming popular.
- Social networking is a network that connects with friends who are becoming an online society in which marketers use social networking to interact with customers. Also, consumers can create and join a group if they like products or services with the same subject. Nevertheless, the main features of social networking are the networking of friends or family, such as Facebook and business networking uses such as LinkedIn.
- Media sharing is a website which allows us to upload pictures or video content to the public. To this reason, marketers can reduce the cost of advertising by using specific electronic devices to convey creative ideas and upload them to websites such as YouTube with the target group that can be shared with society.
- Social news is an Internet website which links the articles and content on the Internet and allows the sender to vote as public and helps filter out which articles and contents are most interesting.
- Online forums are a way for people to discuss topics that they are interested and exchanging ideas and the introduction of various products or services that marketers should be interested in the content discussed in these forums due to it may be a comment about products and services which can understand as well as to build good relationships with customers.

The social media is a new channel of business marketing as it is easy to approach the business's target group with lower cost compares with traditional advertising such as TV or magazine. Similarly, social media marketing uses social media technologies, networks, and software to generate, interact, provide, and exchange services that are of value to stakeholders in an organisation (Tuten, 2017). Besides, Internet media are the main communication channels used by many brands to communicate to the target audience nowadays, because people now live with a mobile phone every day for chatting, coordination, and entertainment.

Furthermore, they use a smart telephone that connects the Internet to various applications, including Instagram, Facebook, and Line, and to its brand website and features that are convenient, fast, and affordable to the Internet. It is also a communication channel, which can contact the target group and receive feedback immediately without passing through an intermediary. Social media are two-way communication platforms that allow users to interact with each other online to share information and opinions. That facilitates communication on the Internet between a brand and customers, such as posting the picture of the product or endorsing the celebrity wearing the brand's clothes to develop a new trend and to stimulate the customer's awareness, which leads to purchasing decision towards purchasing intention. In addition, product inquiries and promotion through social media channels are comfortable for the customer that decides.

Similarly, in the digital era, the online business is becoming more and more popular because it reduces costs and increases customer service and customer satisfaction, for instance, hotel reservations, ticket purchases, payment for goods and services, and food delivery. Therefore the distribution of products and services increases online businesses continuously. Currently, online business is growing in the digital world, which is expanding rapidly around the globe. Besides, e-commerce has integrated a variety of social platform such as Instagram and Facebook and is used to promote products which are accessible to consumers who shop via social media.

For instance, social media marketing tool Instagram is a free mobile application that allows users to share photos and videos. It quickly emerged as a visual medium over the last few years because it offers users a fast way to share their lives with friends through manipulating filter and videos (Manikonda et al., 2014). Many organisations are planning to do marketing via Instagram because it has the capability to create a brand image from the beautiful photos and videos presented. Many researchers point out that Instagram is a marketing tool to endorse customer to raise awareness of the company and get more engaged followers. Businesses can interact with their customers through Instagram by supporting them, for example, connecting them by follow and comment on their post and receiving return an answer (Virtanen et al., 2017). For instance, Topshop, a UK brand-name clothing, also uses 3.8 million Instagram followers by posting images of its new collections and short video clips to use social media as a tool to promote. Furthermore, Burberry used Instagram as part of its marketing in Milan for their fashion runway event titled 'Come Rain or Shine'. Instagram photos were also published by brand marketers to generate enthusiasm and share 'behind the scenes' during the event.

Increasingly, small businesses used Instagram to create brand awareness by uploading images and writing descriptions for their customer base and allowing followers to recognise the appearance and descriptions of the product quickly and to create different imaginations. Due to Instagram's simple Interbrand, 100 brands prefer visual portfolio and brand awareness strategies rather than advertising their campaigns and promotions

(Lazazzera, 2015). Importantly, consumer use of social media sites indicate that Instagram is the brand-following platform that is most popularly used (Virtanen et al., 2017).

Therefore the entrepreneur should be updated all the time. It improves customer perception and might be interested in the content they follow whether they are using bloggers or celebrities to promote the product by presenting a product picture and writing a definite description to make followers realise their desire and to purchase the intention to buy product (Sangthong and Lekchajoen, 2018). The topic of increasing brand awareness to newly established business links to many existing theories. However, the use of social media influencers currently lacks adequate research and generates a more comprehensive understanding in this field.

Traditionally, explanations of consumer behaviour are cast in terms that are rooted in cognitive psychology, which explains consumer's decisions into action. The advertising world today has evolved quickly with the power of media technology. Yet, we are yet to know how effective Instagram is in informing and persuading consumers to a buy a product online. Scott Armstrong (2011) describes advertising an expensive persuasive communication contrivance that reaches broad audiences to connect with the targeted sector and make that sector aware of the product. Consumers select a brand which they are acquainted with, rather than one in which they are unfamiliar. Under those circumstances, how can a new firm create awareness and overcome difficulties in attracting loyal customers?

3 Advertising and the hierarchy of effects

In this postmodern world the way people communicate has developed through technology. Marketers describe a paradigm shift from product orientation to consumer-oriented marketing, which has evolved into understanding and building lasting relationship with costumers. According to McDaniel et al. (2013), advertising impacts on individual's everyday lives, mass information process which influences attitudes and beliefs, and terminates with purchase action. Schmidt and Eisend (2015) state that advertising execution must meet several criteria to be considered effective. Solomon (2016) states that advertising does not change consumers' rooted values towards a specific product, although it may prosper in transforming a negative to a positive outlook in an individual. Traditional hierarchy-of-effect models were used to illustrate that audiences react to communication tools in an ordered way: firstly, cognitively (thinking); secondly, affectively (feeling); and thirdly, conatively (doing) (Barry and Howard, 1990).

However, today, AI, big data, and ad tracking allow marketers to go further to identify and target lot more effectively by learning from past customer behaviours to attract and guide new customers. All these are done through creation of algorithms where tracking and prediction allow marketers to carry out behaviour modifications. Effectively, today, we are seen as a dataset on the spreadsheets, and organisations use this vast joined up datasets to target customers through number of models at their disposal. All these algorithms use artificial intelligence to track and predict. Predictions about consumer behaviour are based on the information the data broker has on that person—credit scores predict the 'likelihood that a person will default on a loan'; 'marketing scores predict how likely the person is to buy a certain product'; fraud scores predict 'how likely a particular transaction is to be fraudulent'; 'stress scores might help organisational customers manage healthcare costs and risks'.

Rathod (2011) reviews and states that the first to successfully portray the effect of advertising was the AIDA model. Originally the model was designed to adopt the steps of persuasive communication (from salesman perspective) stages as followed: attention, interest, desire, and action. The model is considered as a hierarchy-of-effect model meaning consumers are to reach each step before accomplishing the desired action. The theory accentuates that once transiting through the steps, consumers develop emotion towards brand which compels them to act (purchase). Applying this model to marketing corresponds to attracting attention and boosting brand awareness (Rathod, 2011).

The DAGMAR model, which was accepted due to setting communication-oriented objectives (Dutka and Colley, 1995), incorporated elements of awareness, comprehension, conviction, and purchase where the aim to establish an explicit link between ad goals and ad results. Awareness is significantly portrayed as having attributes that elevate audience awareness to follow the next steps, attention and interest are used to convey the advertising message. Comprehension is the step for the target audience to ingest the core message of the advert. Conviction is where the individual realises and believes the intended message (like the desire in AIDA, hence, conviction can lead to a desired purchase). Finally, purchase is the stage where the audience decide to execute the sale through following up his belief from the message pursued by the advert (action in AIDA).

Lavidge and Steiner (1961) demonstrate the hierarchy-of-effect model that associates the theory of advertising justified in seven stages, initiated by a customer being unaware of a product to an eventual purchase. The stages are as follows: unawareness, awareness, knowledge, liking, preference, conviction, and finally purchase. Therefore this model can be used to measure consumers' feelings towards a product/service, as instigated buyers produce an initial impression of a brand in connecting from first brand exposure (Keller, 2009).

4 Customers and smart retail interactions

During the Internet decade, retailing and communication technologies innovated the way of purchasing, allowing consumers to become technology dependent. Retailing has changed due to development and adoption of new technologies in digital channels, specifically mobile and social media, having a very powerful impact on the customers and changing the perspective of shopping behaviour and the business models of the organisations.

Smart retailing changed the consumer behaviour through the decision-making process stages (search, purchase, consumption, and postpurchase) and moved towards an innovative approach for growth of the businesses. Beyond the concept of smart retailing exists a high level of 'smartness' in the application of modern technology being related with deployment of technology.

The perception of smart retailing reflects on the use of technology for companies and consumers. This will recreate and reinforce a new role in economies, by enhancing the quality of customer's shopping experiences. When compared with traditional retail, smart retail brings both flexibility and challenges, as the consumer behaviour evolves due to technological changes and in the future the interface of retail consumers may be completely different from current interactions.

Smart technologies benefit both customers and businesses, which consequently could lead to customer satisfaction and business profitability. Smartphone users worldwide increased from 1.57 billion in 2014 to 2.87 billion in 2020 which will further create the opportunity for companies to invest in smart technologies. Mobile apps, self-checkout, and scan-and-go technologies have impact on consumer's behaviour. However, the development of smartphones has revolutionised how we purchase starting from mobile apps to geographic areas with same interests, creating a continuous connection with online environments which has changed consumer expectations and a firm's ability to connect with consumers.

4.1 Online activities and shopping behaviour

Regarding online activities, more customers use Facebook, YouTube, and Instagram daily to access social media platforms and the preferred method to navigate online through their own smartphone. However, there are other more social media platforms, which customers are using such as Snapchat, LinkedIn, and various blogs. Most preferred posting across social media platforms are lifestyle posts, beauty and personal care on, and fashion products. The social media is used for promotional content adopting promotional articles, product trial, and presentation videos. Similarly, YouTube content includes video products, presentation videos, and vlogs that are preferred. Young consumers often search social media for in-depth information on products or brands and are most likely to recommend the products or brands they have used or seen online via advertisements.

Younger generations are keen on online shopping, as a result of saving time to do other activities. However, on a weekly basis, neighbourhood stores and supermarkets are favourite places to purchase the necessary goods, being more reasonable to have a fast trip to the nearest shop to their locality, whenever they are in need for different goods. Furthermore, from typical e-commerce websites, young consumers purchase clothes, IT&C products, and books, and from foreign websites, women purchase clothing and beauty care products. Young generations when they choose the online retailer, first condition is price followed by terms of delivery. In terms of payment methods, men opt for online payment via the website, and women prefer payment on delivery whether it is cash or card.

5 Categorising social media influencers

The term 'influencer' has been found to become a broad subject that critically it's naïve of brands to be considering a one-size-all approach (Dalstam et al., 2019). Influencers can be categorised into various levels of influence, and some have more impact on their followers than others. They are best used for awareness and positioning. Megainfluencers are those with millions of followers, referred to as 'celebrity influencers', and are generally film stars, sporting icons, TV personalities, singers, etc. A blue tick on their profile can identify their influential status, and their popularity also appears in brand marketing campaign (Mukherjee, 2009). In recent years, there have been a vast growth of a new type 'digital' celebrity: bloggers as 'instafamous'. Caveney (2019) stresses that this category is expensive and is not specifically audience targeted. Microinfluencers give brands the opportunity to disseminate their message more widely, more posts produced, and more thankful the brand reaching out to them.

Moreover, Harmer (2019) suggests that consumers are more enthusiastic and likely follow macroinfluencers due to good quality content and more authentic appreciation towards their feed. It has been argued that macroinfluencers can portray false advertising when posting about a specific item. This is due to being paid regardless of a reaction from their fans, which can in turn demonstrate biasness. Casaló et al. (2018) study found that as influencers' followers rise, the rate of engagement with followers decreases and that SMIs in the 10k–100k follower range offer the best combination of engagement, exceeding SMIs with higher followers. Generally, influencer marketing engagement can be measured through aspect such as fan and follower numbers, engagement rates, relevant links to blogs, other social channels, location, and follower details, particularly demographics like age and gender (Trivedi, 2018).

6 Instagram as the most effective platform/audience

According to Dunlop et al. (2016), 'exposure' is a term to describe public attention or facts of an event, whereas Keller (2009) states "A higher exposure means a higher brand presence and hence more profitability". According to our research through a set of interviews, exposure is significantly important for the growth of a company. According to Keller, intended exposure of the brand on a particular online platform builds a connection between company and the customer. Through our interview, respondent stated that "Building our followers on Instagram is key to driven sales and working with bigger influencers increases our following …" This quotation continues to reveal that influencing marketing is the correct approach as a bigger reach equals more exposure. This found that awareness is achieved through collaborating with macroinfluencers to expose and tag the brand name through an 'Insta story' for 24 h prior sale/event. Accordingly, this reaches out to the macroinfluencer fans, who view the story, visualise the name of the brand, and consequently become new consumers by visiting the brands Insta feed and then exploring the website.

The social media executives interviewed quoted "We collaborate with other clothing brands, beauty brands with a higher following most of the time. So it works as a collaboration on collaboration causing double exposure, reaching out to future consumers". Knoll and Matthes (2016) refer to cross-promoting 'double exposure' as 'cross-promoting' which is designed to be effective in grasping the public's attention, by posting and exposing the same picture on more than one page. This is found to be a great technique to increase their following count and improve their brand awareness amongst the public.

In recent research, Dargaville (2019) expresses that in the last few years, the rise of influencer marketing has revolutionised the way businesses appeal to audiences. The respondent was directly questioned on whether Instagram platform is the most effective method to market. And the response was "… most, 15–35 year old is on Instagram every day and especially the female population, always checking out what others are wearing and trying to get inspiration". Likewise, Clement (2019) reinforces this result by proving through statistical analysis that Instagram reached 1 billion active users in 2018 and concludes with Instagram being the most active social networking site. Moreover, evidence currently stands that Instagram on average increases their active users by a staggering 300 million per month, whereas Facebook is increasing by 228 million to its main service. Marketers state that engagement on Instagram is four times more effective than on Facebook (Holmes, 2019).

Instagram users like any social media funnel tend to assemble themselves together depending on their interests. Consumers follow their desired fashion influencer, which advertise not only the items of clothing but also how to style it in a certain environment (Shin and Lee, 2019). Hence, when brands collaborate with selected SMIs according to their style, this is an opportunity to create brand awareness to the appropriate target audience. Therefore, to maximise benefits, an influencer's followers should be closely linked with a brand's target demographic. Instagram has developed into a vast platform for fashion companies to connect with their audience directly, rather than through a magazine campaign, for example. Wilberg's (2018) research established that 5% of the influencers, which promoted and recommended products, would be pushing 45% of sales by using their Instagram-type social influencing accounts online.

7 Branding

The last three decades are characterised by a growing global competition, and hence companies and especially marketers are seeking for opportunities to strengthen their competitive position. Branding developed as one of these opportunities helps to gain a competitive advantage and therefore has immense importance (Keller et al., 2013; Mudambi, 2001). Over time, companies became aware that their brands are one of their most valuable assets as they enable to create significant customer value (Perrey, 2013). Therefore companies pursue the aim of developing valuable experience and furthermore achieving a powerful relationship with customers (Troiville et al., 2019). Their overall objective is to increase brand equity, which enables an added value to a brand's products (Farquhar, 1989).

Aaker (1991) states that in times of several purchase alternatives, a brand can be the decisive factor for a customer. Consequently, consumers develop the desire to purchase branded products, which suit their lifestyle and hence constitute a status symbol (Lajpatrai, 2016). This makes it necessary for companies to not only offer functional characteristics, but rather, to reinforce their brand image, they must design a unique brand (Ghodeswar, 2008). Consumers have various experiences with brands which they form over a period. These experiences often result in relationships with these brands that have been responsible for the growth of some of the most iconic brands in the world (Cohen, 2012). A significant body of knowledge has explored how consumers form attitudes towards brands, and this has led to the development of various kinds of metrics that assess and help companies to understand these attitudes (Rageh Ismail and Spinelli, 2012). Some of the common metrics that have continued to be used by companies include customer satisfaction, brand loyalty, brand advocacy, and customer experience (Quintal et al., 2016).

A brand is a "name, term, sign, symbol, or a combination of them intended to encourage prospective customers to differentiate a producer's product from those of competitors" (Keller et al., 2013, p. 404). Moreover a brand is an intangible and emotional experience, as it demonstrates the involvement customers have with a company or product. A brand provides a base upon which customers develop a mental structure, as it assists to organise and classify their knowledge and connotations about services and products. This enables a brand to develop a meaningful and positive brand image (Kotler et al., 2016), and hence, consumers view a powerful brand as a type of promise. Consumer's love for the brand has led to the continued purchase of the brand in ways that have continued to enhance the firm's profitability and revenues (Rodrigues and Rodrigues, 2019). A study by Keller and Hoeffler (2003) suggests that marketers pursue two main brand targets: achieving to establish a positive perception and an emotional connection amongst the customers and the brand. Critical scholars articulate the view that companies use branding only for capitalistic value creation. Organisational scholars on the other hand argue that brands provide an important opportunity in terms of sense making and creating an identity (Mumby, 2016). Banet-Weiser (2012) suggests that brands help to solve organisational stakeholder issues related to competing responsibilities, rights, and interests.

The functions of brands can be considered not only from an external, therefore customer view, but also from an internal, employee and company point of view. The internal functions of brands involve delivering a corporate meaning, an internal identity, and symbolic resources; enabling a professional and identity related work; and further offering a guidance for employees (Brannan et al., 2011). Several authors have pointed out that from an external perspective, brands are creating customer value by connecting products and services with certain lifestyle experience (Morandin et al., 2013). Furthermore, Becker-Olsen and Hill (2006) outlines that an important function of brands is that they help to stand out from the competition. Thus brands enable to influence customer purchase behaviour and decision making.

7.1 Brand recognition and image

According to Khurram et al. (2018), brand recognition is a vital impact of brand awareness. This was confirmed from the responses from our interview "We want to become popular on the Instagram, so girls can recognise our brand name and want to buy". This suggests that collaborating with an SMIs is a method for the SMI to represent the brand; when this brand is represented multiple times by the same influencer, it establishes familiarity and recalls customer attention. In addition, customer attention is recalled if, for example, the brand name was initially noticed and forgotten again, the customer will instantly correlate the influencer with that brand upon a second viewing and in turn can recall by visiting the previous uploaded picture and reassess their decision-making process from there.

Selecting specific influencers to collaborate will involve benefitting from their image, which in turn boost brands image and identity. Furthermore the content uploaded onto Instagram reflects upon the boosting brand's reputation regarding style and demographics; Esch's studies reinforce this idea, when argues "a positive brand image elevates brand loyalty, positive word of mouth, purchase intentions" (Esch et al., 2006).

7.2 Quality and consistency

The outcome of the interview revealed that Instagram is consistently growing platform, as the respondent stated, "Since January my growth is on average +8k per month". This suggests that active users are still following and admiring influencers. When asked for the reasons behind the interviewee's influential status, the reply was "Mainly my posts are very consistent and I make sure they are high quality images". Various studies have found that between 65% and 85% of people describe themselves as visual learners, which causes marketers to maximise this by constantly invading social media with images to portray certain messages to their audience (Harmer, 2019; Gregory, 2016).

According to Mizen (2009), 'quality' is defined by what differentiates a 'good' clear photo and a 'bad' one and to what extent these picture qualities do or don't captivate the consumer's attention. Using good quality images when promoting a brand increases engagement with more people appreciating, commenting, and saving the post, which in turn increases its exposure. These factors range from a criterion that is subjective, such as 'quality of content', to highly measurable and objective factors including page views and search engine rank. Harmer (2019) agrees that a good-quality image gives an appealing outlook and relates to the 'need recognition' step in the decision-making process. Harmer (2019) states "an inadequate image will demote your status amongst your competitors … Poor quality images cheapen your brand and communicate to the consumer that your brand is impersonal", which results in detrimental sales outcome.

Harmer's argument concludes that an image must be of good quality to prompt visitors to purchase the products, encourage social shares, which then increases awareness. Therefore a low-quality image won't maximise reach if it lacks interaction. The respondent mentioned that 'posting consistently' is necessary for the influential success. Fahmi Al-Zyoud (2018) deduces that consistently publishing allows the audience to depend on the influencer/brand as a source of information and generates trafficking, maintaining the interest of the audience and giving them a reason to keep returning to the page.

8 Artificial intelligence and brand awareness

The digital revolution has changed marketing communications, for example, smartphones, Internet, and personal computers (PCs). Such advancements have improved the knowledge potential of organisations in identifying customer needs and delivering value offerings and targeting them with the right tools. Furthermore, organisations in a knowledge-based environment create, disseminate, and use knowledge as a key source of competitive advantage. Artificial intelligence (AI) is changing how organisations deliver value to customers. Generally, AI refers to how computers, using software and algorithms, can think and perform tasks like humans. Through personalisation, AI has actively changed human lifestyles in almost every aspect of daily life.

According to Kaplan and Haenlein (2019), AI is a system's ability to interpret external data correctly, to learn from such data, and to use those learnings to achieve specific goals and tasks through flexible adaptation. AI technology operates in the domain of automation and continuous learning, acting as the intelligence that drives data-focussed analytics and decision making. AI automates many of the activities involved in the collection, storage, management, and retrieval of information that can help in the creation and management of firm offerings. By using technologies like deep learning, genetic algorithms, and natural language processing, AI can train machines to recognise patterns in large amounts of data. Widespread AI tools for personal uses include personal assistant (e.g. Alexa, Siri, and Cortana), travel planning (Mezi), music (Pandora), financial planning (Olivia), language translation (Liv), and smart home solutions (Nest). Popular AI tools for business include plug-and-play solutions for business needs (e.g. Fluid AI), e-commerce and digital marketing (Sentient), process automation (Amazon MTurk), face recognition (Haystack), legal language assistant (Legal Robot), and credit scoring (Lenddo).

From marketing perspective, personalisation is often presented and studied alongside customisation as they are related in concept but differ in application. Personalisation occurs when the firm decides, usually based on previously collected customer data, what marketing mix is suitable for the individual, whereas customisation occurs when the customer proactively specifies one or more elements of his or her marketing mix (Arora et al., 2008). A fair amount of consensus prevails in understanding personalisation as a largely firm-controlled process that is powered using customer-level data and customisation as a largely customer-decided process that is focussed on the design and delivery of the offering (Sundar and Marathe, 2010). Personalisation has been shown to work in both digital and nondigital environments (Xu et al., 2011). Classic examples of digital personalisation include 'recommended for you' section in websites such as Amazon, Pandora, and Netflix. In terms of nondigital personalisation, Sprint uses predictive analytics to personalise retention offers to customers who are at risk of churning (Morgan, 2017). Within the service domain, intelligent call routing services also deliver personalisation by matching customers with service representatives with appropriate skills and personality.

Personalisation as a process interlinks customers and marketers and solidifies the relationship between them (Simonson, 2005). Customer relationships also have emotional bonding progress to a state of engagement (Pansari and Kumar, 2017), and positive relationships play a role in influencing customer engagement (CE) behaviours (van Doorn et al., 2010). Accordingly, engagement has been defined as the attitude, behaviour, and the level of connectedness amongst customers, between customers and employees, and of customers and employees within a firm (Kumar and Pansari, 2016). Furthermore the more positive the attitude and behaviour and the higher the level of connectedness, the higher the level of engagement.

The high degree of personalisation in AI is a major factor behind its popularity. AI has shifted the architype from a rule-based expert systems approach to a deep learning-based, data-driven approach (Mullainathan and Spiess, 2017). AI is so unobtrusive that users are mostly unaware that they have interacted with the technology (Steimer and Conick, 2018). When technology works on a personal level, it creates an endearing bond with the users. Furthermore, when marketers tap into such a bond, the potential for customer value creation is enormous. However, the success of personalisation initiatives is constrained by the volume and quality of customer information, the ability of firms to generate insights from customer data, and the effective implementation of insights (Arora et al., 2008). To overcome these three constraints and to go beyond the current level of personalised offerings, companies are now resorting to AI-powered solutions.

Digital curation is defined as "the management and preservation of digital material to ensure accessibility over the long-term" (Abbott, 2008). Curation as a strategy focusses on practices that select, maintain, and manage information in ways that promote future consumption of that information (Whittaker, 2011). Curation of product, price, place, and promotion to individual customers assumes more significance for companies in this digital age where customers are exposed to an information explosion (Beath et al., 2012). For instance, a recent survey found that 48% of consumers moved their purchase to a different provider (online or in-store) because the first company's website was poorly curated (Accenture, 2018). Research has also found that customer engagement improved with curation (Karp, 2016).

In the marketing context, curation refers to the automatic machine-driven selection of products, prices, website content, and advertising messages that fit with an individual customer's preferences. The AI in this case uses data on firm-customer transactions, customers' consumption pattern of offerings, and the communication pattern about firm offerings to customers to automatically predict the type, timing, and purchase of preferred firm offerings. Furthermore, AI can also customise the firm's website content to match customer preferences (e.g. Wix and The Grid), price offerings to align with customer's willingness to pay (pace for hotel room pricing and perfect price for dynamic pricing), and connect the customer interactions across all channels and devices in a seamless and personalised manner (Adobe Sensei and Samsung SmartThings ecosystem). AI tools also learn from customer interactions to improve the accuracy of the predictions about customer preferences, thereby increasing the value from the firm to the customers over the customers' relationship lifecycle.

Within AI, machine learning algorithms (such as collaborative filtering, deep learning, unsupervised clustering, and k-nearest neighbours) have emerged as a preferred method for developing applications that understand consumer preferences (based on their reviews, prior product purchases, and product usage) to find new products or services the consumers are more likely to prefer (Ansari et al., 2018). Recommendation engines are a popular application of machine learning, wherein users are matched with offerings that they liked in the past and/or may be interested in the future. Such curation reduces consumer cognitive load and takes the responsibility of finding the best options for a consumer's choice context to the search platform or the brand. Self-learning neural networks trained on volumes of customer voices have led to the advent of voice as a major interface. In 2016 a tipping point was reached in the ongoing tug of war between human capability and that of machines, specifically in the field of image recognition. As recently as 2010, machine algorithms had an error rate of 30% when attempting to identify images from ImageNet, a large database of over 10 million obscure images, compared with a stagnant human error rate of 5%. By 2016, however, machines had made such strides in image recognition that the error rate had dropped to 4% for the best systems, thus edging out the human eye. In 2017 Google announced the achievement of a 4.9% error rate in speech recognition. This implies that Google now makes a mistake in speech recognition every 20th word (Li, 2017). These developments along with advances in natural language processing technology will make it increasingly possible for buyers to ask 'curation engines' for a narrow set of buying options and even for a buying decision and implementation. These developments in AI algorithms—and devices that interface with consumers in a more cognitive style—pose challenges, opportunities, and threats for brands. Given all this, how should brand managers approach personalisation? Data on consumer interactions with the brand and its competitors are a major requirement for effectively harnessing artificial intelligence technologies for improved CE. Within this premise, we propose an integrative framework to understand the role of AI in personalised engagement marketing and offer predictions on two key strategic firm assets—brands and customers—across developed and developing economies.

9 Customer information processing

Information processing by consumers has travelled through three distinct phases prior to the Internet; curated recommendations have existed as possible buying routes through television, radio, and print media. With these technologies, buyers could rely on the recommendations of celebrities or influencers they like and trust, a brand campaign, or their friends and family. With the advent of the Internet, product configurators or search engines applied fixed 'if-then' rules against a list of preset criteria to narrow the field of product options The abundance of information and frustration amongst consumers to process all the data from a configurator or search engine is reflected in the academic literature as the paradox of choice and the digital cognitive load (Brynjolfsson et al., 2006).

For example, consumers are more likely to click deeper into search results when the keyword is less popular or the consumer is more involved (Jerath et al., 2014).

9.1 Consumer choice and decision making

Nearly all marketing actions address the choice faced by consumers, which is composed of two or more alternatives, conflict amongst the alternatives, and a thought-driven approach to alleviate the conflict (Hansen, 1976). When faced with choices, consumers typically look for information to help them address their dilemma. Although information about the alternatives may be acquired through multiple means (e.g. nondigital sources, such as print media and published reports, and/or digital sources, such as owned media, paid media, and earned media), they all serve an important purpose in avoiding decision regret (Tsiros and Mittal, 2000), thereby helping consumers feel confident about their choices. When consumers face a nonroutine (or less frequent) decision, it is likely that they will seek more information to assuage their concerns. Seeking and processing large amounts of information can lead to 'information fatigue' and an unsatisfactory decision-making process. Customers can suffer from information overload (Jacoby, 1984) and can experience dysfunctional consequences as a result (Malhotra, 1982). How consumers process choices and how they arrive at credible decisions can influence how organisations personalise their offerings.

10 Conclusion

This article is one way to understand the impact of AI on organisation brand image. Specifically, it has explored the role of AI in creating a personalised engagement marketing approach. Firms can leverage individual customer information and AI technology to provide curated products and services. The AI technology can facilitate real-time learning and help managers improve customer value proposition over time. Such a strategy of curated products that provide increasing value to customers will form the basis of customer retention and sustainable competitive advantage. As a start, we have presented here a few predictions on how AI can affect customer management strategies. In doing so, we have also presented the experience and likely varied futures of developed and developing economies. Of course, this is only an early attempt to understand the larger implications of AI in marketing. We expect more such efforts in the future to prepare us better.

References

Aaker, D., 1991. Managing Brand Equity. Free Press, New York.

Abbott, 2008. "What is digital curation?" DCC Briefing Papers: Introduction to Curation, Digital Curation Center, April 2. http://www.dcc.ac.uk/resources/briefing-papers/introduction-curation.

Accenture, 2018. Personalization Pulse Check. https://www.accenture.com/t20180503T034117Z__w__/us-en/_acnmedia/PDF-77/Accenture-Pulse-Survey.pdf%23zoom=50.

Angelides, M.C., 1997. Implementing the Internet for business: a global marketing opportunity. Int. J. Inf. Manage. 17 (6), 405–419.

Ansari, A., Li, Y., Zhang, J., 2018. Probabilistic topic model for hybrid recommender systems: a stochastic variational Bayesian approach. Mark. Sci. 37 (6), 855–1052.

Arora, N., Dreze, X., Ghose, A., Hess, J.D., Iyengar, R., Jing, B., Joshi, Y., Kumar, V., Lurie, N., Neslin, S., Sajeesh, S., Su, M., Syam, N., Thomas, J., Zhang, Z.J., 2008. Putting one-to-one marketing to work: personalization, customization, and choice. Mark. Lett. 19 (3), 305–321.

Banet-Weiser, S., 2012. Authentic: The Politics of Ambivalence in a Brand Culture. New York University Press, New York.

Barry, T., Howard, D., 1990. A review and critique of the hierarchy of effects in advertising. Int. J. Advert. 9 (2), 121–135. https://doi.org/10.1080/02650487.1990.11107138.

Beath, C., Becerra-Fernandez, I., Ross, J., Short, J., 2012. Finding value in the information explosion. MIT Sloan Manage. Rev. 53 (4), 18–20.

Becker-Olsen, K.L., Hill, R.P., 2006. The impact of sponsor fit on brand equity: the case of nonprofit service providers. J. Serv. Res. 9 (73), 73–83.

Bird, D., 2007. Common Sense Direct and Digital Marketing. Kogan Page Publishers, London, UK.

Brannan, M.J., Parsons, E., Priola, V. (Eds.), 2011. Branded Lives: The Production and Consumption of Meaning at Work. Edward Elgar Publishing, Cheltenham.

Brynjolfsson, E., Hu, Y.J., Smith, M.D., 2006. From niches to riches: anatomy of the long tail. MIT Sloan Manage. Rev. 47 (4), 67–71.

Casaló, L., Flavián, C., Ibáñez-Sánchez, S., 2018. Influencers on instagram: antecedents and consequences of opinion leadership. J. Bus. Res. https://doi.org/10.1016/j.jbusres.2018.07.005.

Caveney, L., 2019. How to Find the Right Influencers for Your Brand – Influential. Retrieved 19 September 2019, from: https://www.thisisinfluential.com/how-to-find-the-right-influencers-for-your-brand/.

Chaffey, D., 2020. The Best Digital Marketing Statistics Sources to Inform Your Marketing. Smartinsight. com 05 February.

Clement, J., 2019. Instagram Statistics 2018 | Statista. Retrieved 11 September 2019, from: https://www.statista.com/statistics/253577/number-of-monthly-active-instagram-users/.

Cohen, F., 2012. Evidence-based management. J. Med. Pract. Manage 27 (5), 286–289

Conlon, G., 2016. Winterberry Group predicts increased spending on nearly all marketing channels. February 1https://www.dmnews.com/customer-experience/article/13035858/2016-will-be-a-growth-year-in-marketing-spending (Cited 17 February 2020).

Dalstam, M., Holmgren, D., Nordlöf, H., 2019. The NA-KD Truth About Influencer Marketing. Retrieved 19 September 2019, from: https://pdfs.semanticscholar.org/c609/c7a7177a457b2baf825a0b78a442137a4dd1.pdf.

Dargaville, S., 2019. Why Instagram Is the Best Platform for Influencer Marketing. Retrieved 4 September 2019, from: https://www.digitaldoughnut.com/articles/2019/may/why-instagram-is-the-best-platform-for-influencers.

Dunlop, S., Freeman, B., Perez, D., 2016. Exposure to internet-based tobacco advertising and branding: results from population surveys of Australian youth 2010–2013. J. Med. Internet Res. 18(6), e104. https://doi.org/10.2196/jmir.5595.

Dutka, S., Colley, R., 1995. DAGMAR, Defining Advertising Goals for Measured Advertising Results. ANA, New York.

Edelman, D., Heller, J., 2015. How Digital Marketing Operations Can Transform Business. Insights & Publications. McKinsey & Company. Retrieved from: http://www.mckinsey.com/insights/marketing_sales/how_digital_marketing_operations_can_transform_business.

Esch, F., Langner, T., Schmitt, B., Geus, P., 2006. Are brands forever? How brand knowledge and relationships affect current and future purchases. J. Prod. Brand Manage. 15 (2), 98–105. https://doi.org/10.1108/10610420610658938.

Fahmi Al-Zyoud, M., 2018. Social media marketing, functional branding strategy and intentional branding. Probl. Perspect. Manage. 16 (3), 102–116. https://doi.org/10.21511/ppm.16(3).2018.09.

Farquhar, P.H., 1989. Managing brand equity. Mark. Res. 1 (1), 24–33. 14 October 2019, Retrieved from: https://www.sciencedirect.com.

Ghodeswar, B.M., 2008. Building brand identity in competitive markets: a conceptual mode. J. Prod. Brand Manage. 17 (1), 4–12. 10 October 2019, Retrieved from: https://www.emerald.com.

Gregory, J., 2016. Picture This: Content With Visuals Gets 94% More Views. 7 September 2019, Retrieved from: http://contentmarketing.com/2016/03/08/picture-this-content-with-visuals-gets-94-more-views/.

Hansen, F., 1976. Psychological theories of consumer choice. J. Consum. Res. 3 (3), 117–142.

Harmer, L., 2019. The Importance of Images in Marketing – Solve. Retrieved 7 September 2019, from: https://solve.co.uk/seo-tips/importance-of-images-in-marketing/.

Hawks, M., 2015. Why Digital Marketing Is Really People Marketing? Retrieved from: http://www.huffingtonpost.com/mark-hawks/why-digital-marketingis_b_8186574.html?ir=India&adsSiteOverride=in.

Holliman, G., Rowley, J., 2014. Business to business digital content marketing: marketers' perceptions of best practice. J. Res. Interact. Mark. 8 (4), 269–293.

Holmes, R., 2019. As Facebook shifts, Instagram Emerges as a New Home for Brands. 11 September 2019, Retrieved from: https://www.forbes.com/sites/ryanholmes/2018/02/01/as-facebook-shifts-instagram-emerges-as-a-new-home-for-brands/#46ed2aef7834.

Hubspot, 2013. 2013 State of Inbound Marketing. Retrieved from: http://cdn2.hubspot.net/hub/53/file30889984df/2013_StateofInboundMarketing_FullReport.pdf.

Hudson, S., Roth, M.S., Madden, T.J., 2012. Customer Communications Management in the New Digital Era [Monograph]. Center for Marketing Studies, Darla Moore School of Business, University of South Carolina. Retrieved from: http://moore.sc.edu/UserFiles/moore/Documents/Marketing/Center%20for%20Marketing%20Studies/Customer%20Communications%20Management%20in%20the%20New%20Digital%20Era%20January%202012.pdf.

Jacoby, J., 1984. Perspectives on information overload. J. Consum. Res. 10 (4), 432–435.

Jerath, K., Ma, L., Park, Y.H., 2014. Consumer click behavior at a search engine: the role of keyword popularity. J. Mark. Res. 51 (4), 480–486.

Kaplan, A., Haenlein, M., 2019. Siri, Siri, in my hand: who's the fairest in the land? On the interpretations, illustrations, and implications of artificial intelligence. Bus. Horiz. 62 (1), 15–25.

Karp, P.D., 2016. Can we replace curation with information extraction software? Database (December 2016), baw150. https://doi.org/10.1093/database/baw150.

Keller, K., 2009. Building strong brands in a modern marketing communications environment. J. Mark. Commun. 15 (2–3), 139–155. https://doi.org/10.1080/13527260902757530.

Keller, K.L., Hoeffler, S., 2003. The marketing advantages of strong brands. Brand Manage. 10 (6), 421–445. Retrieved from: https://www.researchgate.net.

Keller, K.L., Apéria, T., Georgson, M., 2013. Strategic Brand Management: A European Perspective, second ed. Pearson, Edinburgh.

Khurram, M., Qadeer, F., Sheeraz, M., 2018. The role of brand recall, brand recognition and price consciousness in understanding actual purchase. J. Res. Soc. Sci. 6 (2), 219–241.

Knoll, J., Matthes, J., 2016. The effectiveness of celebrity endorsements: a meta-analysis. J. Acad. Mark. Sci. 45 (1), 55–75. https://doi.org/10.1007/s11747-016-0503-8.

Kotler, P., Keller, K., Brady, M., Goodman, M., Hansen, T., 2016. Marketing Management, third ed. Pearson, Edinburgh.

Kumar, V., Pansari, A., 2016. Competitive advantage through engagement. J. Mark. Res. 53 (4), 497–514.

Lajpatrai, L., 2016. Brand image and its impact on buying behaviour. Int. J. Res. Manag. Technol. 5 (4), 9–13. 28 October 2019, Retrieved from:https://pdfs.semanticscholar.org.

Lavidge, R., Steiner, G., 1961. A model for predictive measurements of advertising effectiveness. J. Mark. 25 (6), 59. https://doi.org/10.2307/1248516.

Lazazzera, R., 2015. How to build a massive following on Instagram. [Online]. Available from: http://www.shopify.com/blog/14288561-how-to-build-a-massive-following-on-instagram. (Accessed 30 January 2015).

Li, A., 2017. Google's Speech Recognition Is Now Almost as Accurate as Humans. 9to5 Google. https://9to5google.com/2017/06/01/google-speech-recognition-humans/.

Maddox, K., 2015. Study: 80% of Companies Will Increase Digital Marketing Budgets. Advertising Age India. Retrieved from: http://www.adageindia.in/Study-80-of-Companies-Will-Increase-Digital-Marketing-Budgets/articleshow/46033049.cms.

Malhotra, N.K., 1982. Information load and consumer decision making. J. Consum. Res. 8 (4), 419–430.

Manikonda, L., Hu, Y., Kambhampati, S., 2014. Analysing User Activities, Demographics, Social Network Structure and User-Generated Content on Instagram. Retrieved from: http://arxiv.org/abs/1410.8099.

McDaniel, C., Lamb, C., Hair, J., 2013. Introduction to Marketing. South-Western/Cengage Learning, Mason (Ohio, Estados Unidos).

Mizen, M., 2009. The importance of quality in photo gift production. In: International Symposium on Technologies for Digital Photo Fulfillment, 2009 pp. 25–27. https://doi.org/10.2352/issn.2169-4672.2009.2.0.25 (1).

Morandin, G., Bagozzi, R.P., Bergami, M., 2013. Brand community membership and the construction of meaning. Scand. J. Manage. 29 (1), 173–183. 15 October 2019, Retrieved from: https://www.researchgate.net.

Morgan, B., 2017. Five Trends Shaping the Future of Customer Experience in 2018. Forbes. https://www.forbes.com/sites/blakemorgan/2017/12/05/five-trends-shaping-the-future-of-customer-experience-in-2018/#5c1e1aa12d9c.

Mudambi, S., 2001. Branding importance in business-to-business markets – three buyer clusters. Ind. Mark. Manage. 31 (1), 525–533. 11 October 2019, Retrieved from: https://www.sciencedirect.com.

Mukherjee, D., 2009. Impact of celebrity endorsements on brand image. SSRN Electron. J. https://doi.org/10.2139/ssrn.1444814.

Mullainathan, S., Spiess, J., 2017. Machine learning: an applied econometric approach. J. Econ. Perspect. 31 (2), 87–106.

Mumby, D.K., 2016. Organizing beyond organization: branding, discourse and communicative capitalism. Organization 23 (6), 884–907. 07 October 2019, Retrieved from: https://journals.sagepub.com.

Oklander, M., Oklander, T., Yashkina, O., Pedko, I., Chaikovska, M., 2018. Analysis of technological innovations in digital marketing. East. Eur. J. Enterp. Technol. 5 (3–95), 80–91.

Pandey, U.S., Shukla, S., 2010. E-Commerce and Mobile Commerce Technologies. S. Chand & Company Limited, New Delhi, India.

Pansari, A., Kumar, V., 2017. Customer engagement: the construct, antecedents, and consequences. J. Acad. Mark. Sci. 45 (3), 294–311.

Perrey, J., 2013. Retail Marketing and Branding: A Definitive Guide to Maximizing ROI. Wiley, London.

Quintal, V., Phau, I., Sims, D., Cheah, I., 2016. Factors influencing generation Y's purchase intentions of prototypical versus me-too brands'. J. Retail. Consum. Serv. 30, 175–183. [Online]. Available from: https://linkinghub.elsevier.com/retrieve/pii/S0969698916300376> 3 March 2020.

Rageh Ismail, A., Spinelli, G., 2012. Effects of brand love, personality and image on word of mouth. J. Fash. Mark. Manage. 16 (4), 386–398. [Online]. Available from: http://www.emeraldinsight.com/doi/10.1108/13612021211265791 9 October 2019.

Rathod, P., 2011. AIDA model of advertising strategy. Indian J. Appl. Res. 1 (10), 122–125. https://doi.org/10.15373/2249555x/jul2012/39.

Razak, S.A., Azrin, N., Latip, B., 2016. Factors that influence the usage of social media in marketing. J. Res. Bus. Manage. 4 (2), 1–7. Retrieved from: https://s3.amazonaws.com/academia.edu.documents/58717892/Factors_that_influence_the_usage_of_social_media_in_marketing_-_questjournal.pdf?response-content disposition=inline%3Bfilename%3DFactors_That_Influence_The_Usage_of_Soci.pdf&X-Amz-Algorithm=AWS4-H.

Rodrigues, C., Rodrigues, P., 2019. Brand love matters to Millennials: the relevance of mystery, sensuality and intimacy to neo-luxury brands. J. Prod. Brand Manage.. [Online] JPBM-04-2018-1842. Available from: https://www.emerald.com/insight/content/doi/10.1108/JPBM-04-2018-1842/full/html [9 March 2020].

Sangthong, W., Lekchajoen, S., 2018. The Causal Relationship Model of Purchase Intention of Fashion Products on Instagram of Population (Rungsit University). Retrieved from:https://rsujournals.rsu.ac.th/index.php/rgrc/article/view/1048 Accessed 21 July 20.

Schmidt, S., Eisend, M., 2015. Advertising repetition: a meta-analysis on effective frequency in advertising. J. Advert. 44 (4), 415–428. https://doi.org/10.1080/00913367.2015.1018460.

Scott Armstrong, J., 2011. Evidence-based advertising. Int. J. Advert. 30 (5), 743–767. https://doi.org/10.2501/ija-30-5-743-767.

Sheoran, J., 2012. Technological advancement and changing paradigm of organizational communication. Int. J. Sci. Res. Publ. 2 (12), 1–6.

Shin, E., Lee, J., 2019. The effects of product novelty and fashion influencers' socioeconomic status on fashion adoption in social media. In: Global Fashion Management Conference 2019 pp. 407–411. https://doi.org/10.15444/gfmc2019.04.01.04.

Simonson, I., 2005. Determinants of customers' responses to customized offers: conceptual framework and research propositions. J. Mark. 69 (1), 32–45 Wind and Rangaswamy, op. cit.

Solomon, M., 2016. Consumer Behaviour. Pearson Education Limited.

Steimer, S., Conick, H., 2018. What does the future of customer experience look like? Marketing News. August 1 https://www.ama.org/publications/MarketingNews/Pages/what-does-future-customer-experience-look-like.aspx.

Sundar, S.S., Marathe, S.S., 2010. Personalization versus customization: the importance of agency, privacy, and power usage. Hum. Commun. Res. 36 (3), 298–322.

Trivedi, J., 2018. Measuring the comparative efficacy of an attractive celebrity influencer Vis-à-Vis an expert influencer – a fashion industry perspective. Int. J. Electron. Cust. Relat. Manage. 11 (3), 256. https://doi.org/10.1504/ijecrm.2018.093771.

Troiville, J., Hair, J.F., Cliquet, G., 2019. Definition, conceptualization and measurement of consumer-based retailer brand equity. J. Retail. Consum. Serv. 50 (1), 73–84. Retrieved 11 October 2019, from: https://www.sciencedirect.com.

Tsiros, M., Mittal, V., 2000. Regret: a model of its antecedents and consequences in consumer decision making. J. Consum. Res. 26 (4), 401–417.

Tuten, M.R.S., 2017. Social media marketing. J. Grad. Med. Educ. 5 (4), 541–542. Retrieved from: https://books.google.co.th/books?hl=th&lr=&id=XQg_DwAAQBAJ&oi=fnd&pg=PT15&dq=social+media+marketing&ots=tPf2yTZkpK&sig=9JKOh7T6pOIdaV9xr42Ed92FEcc&redir_esc=y#v=onepage&q=social media marketing&f=false Type Scaleshttps://doi.org/10.4300/jgme-5-4-18.

van Doorn, J., Lemon, K.N., Mittal, V., Nass, S., Pick, D., Pirner, P., Verhoef, P.C., 2010. Customer engagement behaviour: theoretical foundations and research directions. J. Serv. Res. 13 (3), 253–266.

Virtanen, H., Björk, P., Sjöström, E., 2017. Follow for follow: marketing of a start-up company on Instagram. J. Small Bus. Enterp. Dev. 24 (3), 468–484. https://doi.org/10.1108/JSBED-12-2016-0202.

Whittaker, S., 2011. Personal information management: from information consumption to curation. Annu. Rev. Inf. Sci. Technol. 45 (1), 1–62.

Wilberg, A., 2018. How Social Media and its Influencers Are Driving Fashion. 4 September 2019, Retrieved from: https://digitalmarketingmagazine.co.uk/social-media-marketing/how-social-media-and-its-influencers-are-driving-fashion/4871.

Xu, H., Luo, X.R., Carroll, J.M., Rosson, M.B., 2011. The personalization privacy paradox: an exploratory study of decision making process for location-aware marketing. Decis. Support Syst. 51 (1), 42–52.

Yasmin, A., Tasneem, S., Fatema, K., 2015. Effectiveness of digital marketing in the challenging age: an empirical study. Int. J. Manage. Sci. Bus. Admin. 1 (5), 69–80.

13

The marketing situation of music public relation agencies in the United Kingdom in relation to client acquisition methods and client search behaviour

Karsyn Robb[a] and Lillian Clark[b]

[a]NORTHUMBRIA UNIVERSITY, NEWCASTLE UPON TYNE, UNITED KINGDOM
[b]QA HIGHER EDUCATION, LONDON, UNITED KINGDOM

1 Introduction

The digital age has generated vast changes within the music industry. Not only do independent (i.e. not contractually obliged to a label or agency) musicians no longer need to rely on record labels to record an album given access to high-quality recording software available on their laptops, but also the marketing of that music has changed as well. While the Internet provides a platform for musicians to be heard by a large amount of new potential fans, it has also increased the level of competition for those fans. This is arguably why the role of music public relations (PR) has never been more critical to the success of independent musicians. As the financial success of a musician requires album, concert ticket, and merchandise revenue, music PR is required to maintain and grow these revenues. The primary marketing method used by music PR agencies has been word-of-mouth (WOM) marketing (Passman, 2015); however, overreliance on WOM has resulted in missed client leads and has become inadequate (Leeflang et al., 2014).

If the key method used by musicians to find music PR companies to work with is through search engines, then music PR companies must adjust their current marketing strategies by applying search engine optimisation (SEO) which has proven to aid companies in competing with fellow agencies online. This chapter will present evidence of the importance of the utilisation of key digital marketing methods such as SEO, examine the extent of their use by music PR agencies through a website evaluation and primary research, and, based upon the results, recommend their use going forward.

Strategy, Leadership, and AI in the Cyber Ecosystem. https://doi.org/10.1016/B978-0-12-821442-8.00016-1
© 2021 Elsevier Inc. All rights reserved.

2 Literature review

2.1 The music industry

As Terrill and Jacob (2015) stated, 'collectively, the music ecosystem generates rich social, cultural, and economic benefits'. The music industry allows for these benefits by playing a key role in the economic growth, job creation, and tourism development for cities worldwide. According to The Economic Contribution of The Core UK Music Industry released by UK Music (2017), in the United Kingdom alone the music industry is responsible for contributing £4.4 bn to the economy and providing 142,208 jobs.

The music industry has faced major changes as technology has advanced, for example, the impact of digital distribution on the economy of the industry (Valencia, 2008). With the emergence of access to digital channels to stream and download music, such as iTunes and Spotify, the music industry has seen a decline in physical sales and a stronger reliance on technology to make up for that loss (Kusek and Leonhard, 2005). Between the years of 1999 and 2014, the global recording industry lost 40% in revenues. It was not until 2015 that the industry began to see a growth again, which was in large part attributed to new technology increasing worldwide access to music through online platforms such as Spotify. By the end of 2016 digital revenues made up 50% of total recorded music industry revenues worldwide and accounted for more than half of revenue in 25 different markets (Global Music Report, 2017).

Before the music industry releases a product, it must rely on the Internet to increase a 'buzz' around the product which will then result in more sales. For example, online chatter through blog posts and social media correspond to increased weekly record sales in the future even prior to a record's release (Dhar and Chang, 2009).

2.2 Music public relations

Music PR is the practice of presenting the public face of a musician or record label while identifying the information needs of a variety of groups and articulating the aims and objectives of the organisation (L'Etang, 2004). The profession accomplishes these tasks to encourage target fans and media to engage with the musician or record label sympathetically at both emotional and intellectual levels. Walenga (2017) argues that PR is a critical piece of the music industry because artists rely on it to sustain and grow their audience. Due to the financial success of a musician relying on the buying behaviour of their audience, there is consequently a large demand for music PR services.

2.3 Music PR and digital marketing

With the invention of the Internet, the opportunities for music PR exploded. While bands can still make appearances on radio and TV, the Internet made it possible for fans to instantly share content, thus introducing the band to previously difficult to reach fans. The same can hold true for other aspects of music PR such as getting artists mentioned in music-related magazines and other periodicals. Ogden et al. (2011) argues that in today's world record, companies are struggling because they have lost control over the industry due to the traditional business models no longer working as effectively as a result of the power of the Internet. However, this can be interpreted as a positive change for independent music PR companies because it allows them to more fairly compete with large record labels' in-house music PR companies. This is because of the large amount of independent musicians no longer relying on a record label to find PR services for them, rather, musicians searching for these services themselves.

The success of a music PR agency largely relies on the acquisition of client leads. When competing with larger in-house PR companies controlled by major record labels, Sahu and Chhabra (2016) argue that digital marketing and search engine optimisation (SEO) are key. By strategically optimising the agency's website, it is possible for independent agencies to appear higher on search engine result pages (SERPs) than their larger competitors. Due to SEO's ability to manage the reputation of brands online, this area of digital marketing is even more relevant to music PR which focusses on image and reputation management.

According to Jones (2008), through the optimisation of quality web pages with relevant information about the music PR agency and the services offered, the reputation can be managed by pushing the quality pages higher on SERPs than any bad reviews of the agency or other competitors. Arguably even more important, SEO will aid in organically putting the agency in front of relevant musicians and managers searching for their services. By utilising the 'most promising field of development for marketing in the upcoming decade' (Okazaki et al., 2007, p. 165), music PR agencies will be able to increase access to potential clients such as independent musicians and their managers.

2.4 Information seeking behaviour

The macromodel for information-seeking behaviour is introduced by Wilson aids in understanding the search behaviour of independent musicians and their managers. Although the model was first introduced in an article published by Wilson (1981), it has continually been modified and has influenced the practice of information research and its theory (Wilson, 1999, 2006; Bawden, 2006). This model examines the process one will go through when seeking information and can be applied to examine what steps a musician takes when searching for a music PR agency.

One of the most important reasons this model is applicable here is because it references information providers, for example, agents and informal systems, which are key to understanding the everyday information-seeking behaviour of individuals such as musicians and managers. Furthermore, Bawden (2006) clarifies the importance of the model's concept of information exchange by explaining how it acknowledges the issue of information most commonly flowing two ways. In the case of music PR agencies and the way musicians or managers search for them, the model recognises that there must be information shared by both parties.

Additionally, this model is particularly relevant because it consists of personal and psychological factors that must also be considered in relation to information-seeking behaviour. This issue of the influence on information-seeking behaviour by personal and psychological factors has also been explored in prior studies by Kostagiolas et al. (2015, 2017) and Hunter (2007), which sought to understand the role personality plays in the way a musician seeks information. The authors concluded that amateur musicians were likely to use the Internet via search engines and social networks to search for information.

In contrast to these studies, Passman (2015) states that artists should 'begin the search for members of their team, including music PR firms, by asking people they know for a recommendation, talking to people they know involved in music, or going onto industry websites such as Broadcast, Music Week, or PR Week to develop a list of leads' (p. 17). While at first glance this contrasts the research presented by Kostagiolas et al. (2015, 2017) and Hunter (2007), it could be argued that asking for recommendations from others in the music industry could occur via social media and lead to a final search on a search engine. Regardless, these differing views will be studied through the examination of data collected through primary research.

2.5 Evaluating SEO effectiveness

An additional model presented by Spais (2010) provides a framework for evaluating the effectiveness of SEO use by music PR agencies. Spais (2010) explains that based on Bendy's perspective of 'activity' theory, a theory used for studying different types of human practices as processes of development, one can expand it to create an 'activity-theoretical approach to information behavior research would provide a framework for the elaboration of SEO contextual issues, for the discovering of parameters that affect information behavior, which can be used to aid the design and analysis of SEO promotion technique investigations' (p. 8). This model provides an overview of the process of evaluating a musician's information-seeking behaviour to identify what a music PR agency's corresponding marketing tactics should be, including use of SEO. This aids in understanding what marketing tactics a music PR agency should be using as a result of a musician's search behaviour. To further evaluate effectiveness of SEO, Solihin (2013) proposes a framework for categorising SEO techniques, enabling researchers to better evaluate the likely ranking of sites.

3 Methodology

The key reason independent musicians were chosen to study is because signed musicians have the support system of their record label and this support system often includes an in-house PR team. On the other hand, independent musicians are working by themselves and are trying to put together a support team on their own. Therefore the first step in this research was to establish the search methods used by these musicians to find PR agencies. This was done through interviews with these musicians about how they search for PR services. Following this the data collected from these interviews were compared with data collected from interviews conducted with music PR agencies. Then existing music PR agency websites were analysed to evaluate the use of SEO and user experience. Twenty-seven independent musicians in the United Kingdom were identified and interviewed, 10 from the pop genre, nine rock, two MOR, two R&B, two dance, one classical, and one hip hop. This distribution was based on the most popular genres of music in the United Kingdom (Statista, 2016).

In addition to the interviews, music PR agency SEO activity was evaluated using ScreamingFrog and WAVE Webaim tools. ScreamingFrog is an industry tool for examining and measuring various aspects of a website's SEO status, while WAVE Webaim, by examining a site's accessibility, can identify potential SEO problems given the impact of accessibility on a sites SERP ranking (Moreno and Martinez, 2013).

The researcher applied the conceptual framework of Wilson's macromodel for information-seeking behaviour to organise the information gathered from musicians into comparable formats. Once this step was completed, this framework was placed into Spais' expansion of Bendy's perspective of 'activity' theory. This step took the information gathered from music PR agencies to identify if effective marketing methods were being applied based on the information search behaviour identified in the interviews with musicians. Finally the framework provided by Solihin was used to categorise SEO tactics.

4 Results and analysis

4.1 Musician interview results and analysis

Twenty-seven musicians with experience working with music PR agencies were selected and contacted to conduct a phone interview with. Upon the conclusion of the interviews, the researcher transcribed the conversations and then used thematic analysis to identify common themes that emerged throughout the interviews.

4.1.1 Theme 1: Musician's experience in the music industry

The first theme identified was experience in the music industry. Eighteen of the interviewees discussed being professionally active in the music industry for over 5 years, with only nine being active in the industry for under that time. Furthermore, it was found that the majority of the artists (regardless of their time working professionally in the music industry) release new music, typically singles, on an average of 3–4 months. These data are supported in an article shared by Leight (2018), in which Leight explains that artists, particularly upcoming artists who are trying to gain attention in the industry, are pushing to release more prealbum singles. The old model for an album rollout of releasing only one or two singles in the time before an album release no longer works because of the 'the breakneck pace of a world driven by streaming and social media' (Leight, 2018).

These pieces of information are important to this study because they reflect how often a musician may need music PR services and, as a result, will be searching for companies to work with. The length of time in the industry is also important to understand to examine if more experienced musicians search for music PR services differently than new entrants to the industry.

The third subsection of this theme was understanding the type of music PR company the musician had worked with in the past to ensure their experience aligned with the type of music PR companies examined in this study. All musicians interviewed had experience working with independent music PR agencies, and only three had additional experience working with an in-house PR company through a record label. This means that all of the musicians interviewed have relevant experience with the subject being studied.

4.1.2 Theme 2: Uses word-of-mouth recommendations

The next theme identified was the use of word-of-mouth recommendations to locate a music PR agency to work with. Of the 27 musicians interviewed, 17 mentioned relying on recommendations to find the company they eventually selected. This supports the argument made by Passman (2015) that artists largely rely on recommendations when putting together their team for a new release.

When this section was further broken down, it was found that there were five main sources for recommendations that musicians would use to gather information about the PR agency they should use.

The most common of these sources was recommendations from other musicians who had used a music PR agency in the past and had a good experience. Following this the second most common source used by four of the musicians interviewed for recommendations was their manager. Two of the musicians referred to recommendations from lawyers, one discussed using their label for advice, and one discussed meeting a music PR agency employee at a gig and then later using their services.

This breakdown reflects an independent artist's reliance on other artists in the industry as reliable sources for information for directing their own career. Waldron (2009) argues that most music communities, regardless of the size of the area, are tight-knit communities. While there is a strong element of competition in these communities, there is also a common theme of supporting other artists in their careers. This can be reflected in this theme identified in the interviews.

One branch of this section worth discussing is that, while all musicians interviewed in this study have been contacted by music PR agencies wanting to work with them, none of the musicians have worked with any PR agencies that reach out to them through social media or email. Furthermore, six musicians stated that they never respond to these agencies because they prefer to do their own research. This may reflect a distrust by musicians of PR company intentions when they contact artists directly.

4.1.3 Theme 3: Uses online search

While there is a large amount of musicians interviewed in this study reporting using word of mouth as a step in their research process to find a music PR agency to work with, 24 of the 27 musicians interviewed discussed using Google first to get a feel of the 'top' music PR agencies in their area. 'Top' is emphasised because it was found from this study that various musicians mentioned perceiving the lead results on their Google searches for music PR agencies to be the top performers in their area.

This coincides with a study done by Smith et al. (2005). Their study found that many online consumers sort the amount of information available during their online search by relying on recommendations. However, it was found that, regardless of the recommender's personal characteristics, the recommendation was used more as a guideline rather than a determining factor. This means that recommendations are highly likely to encourage a choice, but most consumers need more information before making that final purchase decision. This is reflected in the data from these interviews.

4.1.4 Theme 4: SEO keywords used

When the musicians were further questioned on how they search in Google, it was found that key search phrases typically followed the following formats: (1) 'Music PR (location of musician)', (2) 'Music PR Services', (3) 'Music PR (musician's genre)', (4) 'Independent Music PR Company', and (5) 'Best PR For Music'. These search formats are important for music PR agencies to understand to better target these musicians online.

4.1.5 Theme 5: Influences of choice

The next theme identified was the list of factors that influenced the musician's choice in what music PR agency to select.

More than half of the musicians interviewed expressed the importance of the people who work at the agency being friendly and genuinely interested in the artist's music. Additionally, musicians strongly valued seeing examples of where the music PR agency was able to place artists in the past and who they worked with in the past. The third most common subsection of this group was seeing recommendations from artists that the agency had previously worked with encouraging other artists to work with them as well.

The final two factors that were commonly mentioned by musicians were the ability of the musician to set up a first meeting with the agency to speak with them before deciding to use their services and the agency offering a fair price for the musician. These values are also highly important for a music PR agency to note because these are all pieces of information a PR agency could provide on their website.

These data are supported by Bansal and Voyer (2000) examination of service purchase decisions. It was found in their study that noninterpersonal forces were the most influential. This included the consumer's perceived expertise of the service provider, in this case evaluating the PR company's past work.

4.1.6 Information-seeking behaviour

Applying Wilson's (2000) information-seeking behaviour to the research collected from these interviews, a process of search behaviour by independent musicians in the United Kingdom is able to be identified.

Based on the results of this research, it was found that, while it is highly common for musicians to rely on word-of-mouth recommendations from other musicians or managers to get suggestions for what music PR agency to work with, the most active part of a musician's search is through Google and comparing information from different music PR agency websites. This study suggests that online research through Google search is done regardless of whether or not the agency was recommended by word of mouth. While more experienced musicians tended to value recommendations from other musicians more highly than new musicians, both groups conducted a large amount of their search for music PR agencies through Google search.

4.2 Music PR agency interview results and analysis

Applying the same method of evaluation as was used for the interviews with musicians, several common themes were also identified in the interviews with music PR agencies. Again the first theme identified was experience in music PR.

4.2.1 Theme 1: Experience in music PR

On average the representatives interviewed in this study had 6 years of experience, the most experience being 9 years, and the least being 10 months. This range of experience working in music PR is important to note because, as the results demonstrated, the marketing methods used did not appear to be influenced by experience in the field.

4.2.2 Theme 2: Types of clients

The second theme identified was the type of musician the music PR agency typically selects. While all representatives stated that the age of their clients varied, usually the musicians they worked with were in their 20s–30s. While the majority of the agencies mentioned working with artists in the rock genre, each agency typically worked with musicians from three or four different genres. It was found that on average, each music PR agency worked with a variety of levels of artists, ranging from superstars to artists releasing their first single.

What this second theme reflects is a tendency for music PR agencies to not specialise in the type of clients they work with. Rather the majority of agencies appear to work with artists at any stage in their career, regardless of age and genre. Based on articles by McDonald (2017) and Gallant (2013), if a music PR company represents artists from such a mixed background, it may reflect less of a focus on the artist and more of a value on money. McDonald (2017) argues that 'if a company states they work with all genres, this really means they work with anyone that has money'. This could potentially be perceived as a red flag by musicians who, as was found in this study, value PR companies genuinely caring.

However, it was commonly stated in the interviews with music PR agencies that the companies feel it is important to work with music from musicians they believe in even if the genre isn't their personal preference. This nonspecialisation implies that these music

PR agencies do not market themselves to one type of musician, rather all musicians. This dissonance between what artists value when searching for a music PR company and what work music PR companies accept reflects an issue in the way music PR companies market themselves.

4.2.3 Theme 3: Found by clients or search for clients

The third theme identified is the search behaviour of the agencies looking for new clients. Five of the 10 agencies discussed weekly, and in one case, daily, searches for new clients. These searches are reportedly conducted primarily through social media, SoundCloud, or Spotify playlists. Once an artist is found that the agency wishes to work with, the artist is contacted directly through a listed email, phone number, or message on a social platform such as Facebook or Instagram.

This also supports the answers provided by musicians. While most musicians are being contacted in this manner, they do not want to be contacted in this form and are unlikely to give their business to companies who contact them this way. This also reflects an error in music PR marketing tactics because musicians are not being reached in the correct way. Harris and Rae (2009) support this argument by stating that consumers are increasingly demanding an online presence from brands and companies but do not want them to push their business on them.

The other five agencies stated that they do not do any form of search for new clients due to the high volume of musicians contacting them. However, every agency interviewed emphasised the point that whether or not they conducted search for new clients, clients were more likely to find the agency than the agency find them.

4.2.4 Theme 4: Methods agency is found by

This leads to the next theme identified: the methods music PR agencies report being found by.

Six of the agencies interviewed reported being commonly found by word-of-mouth recommendations, one stated a major record label occasionally refers artists to them, and eight of the agencies reported being found online through their website or social accounts.

While there was an overlap with some agencies reporting word of mouth and their website both functioning as sources for client leads, this overlap reflects a theme found in the interviews with musicians. Even musicians that find the PR agencies through word-of-mouth recommendations by other musicians are still likely to research the company online and eventually contact them through either a form submitted on the website or email.

Once again, this mirrors the theme found in musician interviews. While musicians rely on word-of-mouth recommendations, the most active part of a musician's search is through Google and comparing information from different music PR agency websites. This is why music PR companies report getting contacted the most through online forms.

4.2.5 Theme 5: Use of digital marketing

In relation to digital marketing, only four of the agencies interviewed reported using any form of digital marketing. Of the four the most common tool used is social media to post what projects the agency is working on and share general updates. However, even three of the companies using social media discussed the agency issue of not using social media and digital marketing as much as they should.

As for the other agencies interviewed that did not report any use of digital marketing, half stated that the reason for their lack of use was due to the high volume of clients finding them without the agency using digital marketing. The other half of agencies interviewed that do not use digital marketing state that they would like to and know it is important for their business; however, the agency lacks the time to devote to it.

Furthermore, only two of the agencies interviewed reported updating their website frequently, while the others stated that it is very rare for them to work on the company website because it is typically used as a basic information source for their clients and potential clients. Only one agency interviewed discussed actively using SEO on their website and stated that, on average, they receive 70+ submissions from musicians wanting to work with them every week.

When comparing the companies using digital marketing, in particular SEO, to the agencies not using or infrequently using these tactics, there is a clear difference in potential client inquiries.

The companies using SEO and digital marketing methods report such a large amount of inquiries from musicians wanting to work with them that they can only accept a fraction of those inquiries every week.

4.2.6 Spais' expansion of Bendy's perspective of 'activity' theory

Following Wilson's (2000) information-seeking behaviour model established earlier, Spais' (2010) expansion of Bendy's perspective of 'activity' theory allows the information collected from music PR agencies to be applied to evaluate what a music PR agency's marketing tactics should be. Applying the user's information-seeking behaviour, one can see that using online search plays a major role in how musicians approach their search for music PR services. When this is combined with the information collected from the round of interviews with music PR agencies, it was suggested that a suitable marketing approach would include keyword research and implementation, social media marketing, blogging, and other SEO tactics.

4.3 WAVE results and analysis

The PR agency websites were investigated using the web accessibility evaluation tool, WAVE. Using this tool, it was found that there were a total of 557 accessibility errors across all the websites evaluated and an average of 56 errors per website. These errors were broken down into the nine types of errors.

4.3.1 Error 1: Missing alternative text

It was found that there are five types of errors that had an average above 10 errors per website from this sample. The most common of these is a missing alternative text or the presence of an image without alternative text. According to Vaulk (2015), alternative text serves three main purposes for a website: (1) It aids a website's accessibility by allowing visually impaired users using screen readers to better understand the image by being read the alt attribute, (2) alt tags will appear in the place of an image if the image file cannot be found or loaded, and most relevant to this study, (3) alt tags provide search engine crawlers better descriptions to index the image correctly.

This error matters because each image must have an alt attribute. Without alternative text the content of an image will not be available to screen reader users, search engine crawlers, or when the image is unavailable. This issue can be addressed by adding an alt attribute to the image. Ideally the attribute provided should accurately describe the content and function of the image. According to the Missing Alternative Text article on WAVE, if the content of the image is conveyed in the context or surroundings of the image or if the image does not convey content or have a function, it should be given empty/null alternative text (alt=""). What this issue means for this study is that search engine crawlers on average are having a difficult time indexing images on music PR websites, and as a result, these websites may not be appearing high on SERPs.

4.3.2 Error 2: Empty link

Following missing alternative text errors, there was an average of 29 empty link errors per website analysed. This means on average, music PR websites contained multiple links without text to describe the purpose of the link. This is important because, if a link contains no text, the function or purpose of the link will not be presented to the user. As a result, this can cause confusion for keyboard and screen readers in addition to possibly impacting the site's rankability. As Drinkwater (2018) describes, depending on the amount of empty link errors, search engines may take these errors as a signal that the page is no longer relevant and, therefore, may decrease the frequency of crawling the page. Overtime, these types of errors may affect the SERP. This issue can be fixed by either removing the link or adding text within the link that describes the function of the link.

4.3.3 Linked image missing alternative text

The third most common type of error on these music PR websites was a linked image missing alternative text. According to WAVE, this means that there is an image without alternative text which will then result in an empty link. This type of error combines the issues with both of the errors described earlier. Not only will screen readers and search engine crawlers not be able to understand the function of the image, but also it will impact the ability of the page to be correctly indexed which ideally would aid the page to rank higher on SERPs. Again, this error can be fixed by adding the appropriate alternative text that presents the content of the image and/or the function of the link.

4.3.4 Missing form label
Each music PR website from this sample also had an average of 14 missing form labels. What this means is that, while a form label may have been present on the website, it did not contain any content. This is important because a <label> element that is associated to a form control but does not contain text will not present any information about the form control to the user or search engine crawlers (Missing Form, WAVE). Once again, this issue has the potential to impact a website's SERP ranking. However, this error can be fixed by ensuring that the form label contains text that describes the function of the associated form control.

4.3.5 Empty heading
The final common error on the music PR websites sampled was empty headings. The websites analysed had an average of 11 headings without content per website. This is important because, according to Halasz (2018), search engine crawlers need this information to better index the content of the website. Additionally, some users, particularly keyboard and screen reader users, often navigate by heading elements. An empty heading will present no information and may introduce confusion. This error can be fixed by ensuring that all headings contain informative content.

4.3.6 WAVE analysis summary
Accessibility has many SEO implications. On average the homepages of the music PR agencies evaluated contain many accessibility errors, and the most common errors have the potential to directly impact the ranking of the sites on SERPs. The longer these errors persist, the more difficult it is for search engine crawlers to index the pages and have incentive to place the pages higher on SERPs. To explore site accessibility a WAVE analysis was performed on the company's website.

On the homepage alone, WAVE identified 76 errors. In this analysis, there are five missing form labels which impact SEO. When this element does not contain text, it will not present any information about the form control to the user or search engine crawlers.

The proof of these SEO errors impacting SERP is clear when one searches using common search keywords. In this case the agency is located in London, so the researcher searched 'music pr London'. Agency 2 does not appear until the bottom of page 5. This example demonstrates the direct impact these SEO errors have on the ranking of music PR pages and the high competition the company faces when musicians search using this keyword. This example is also worth noting because it further supports the information about keywords including genre discussed in Theme 4.

4.4 SEO analysis

The websites of the music PR agencies interviewed were examined using the SEO analysis software, ScreamingFrog. Although ScreamingFrog tests many different SEO factors of a website, for this research, eight key areas were chosen for examination.

4.4.1 Webpage indexability

The first area examined was the indexability of a website's pages. Across the 1490 pages tested from the 10 websites, only 70% of the pages were indexable. According to Wilson (2018), this means that a Googlebot cannot index these pages and therefore the URLs will not appear in SERPs. As a result, musicians searching for these pages are unable to access any of these 1000+ pages through Google. This is extremely important for music PR agencies to note because of the musicians interviewed who stated they use online search to look for agencies to work with, all of them used Google.

4.4.2 Title 1, meta description, and H1-1 lengths

The next area examined was the length of the Title 1. On average the Title 1 length was 15 characters long for all of the websites analysed. Title tags should be unique to each page on a website, and Patil Swati et al. (2013) state that it is the biggest ranking factor and should be between 60 and 70 characters long. This is a drastic difference in length and is highly likely to be impacting the rank of these pages.

Similar to the importance of the Title 1 length, the meta description length was also examined and had an average of 16 characters for the websites. This is in sharp contrast to the recommended 150–160 character length (Gregurec and Grd, 2012) and again is likely impacting the rank of these pages. Furthermore, according to Nen et al. (2017), the H1-1 length is recommended to contain an average of 50 characters; however, the average for the music PR websites analysed was far below this with only 9 characters. Due to these tags not being optimised, search engine crawlers are unable to understand the content, size, and structure of the site and therefore will not rank the pages.

4.4.3 Inlinks

Visser and Weideman (2011) state that Inlinks, or links from other websites that send traffic to the examined site, aid a webpage's Google ranking and traffic. Google considers these links as 'votes' for a site; however, due to the large-scale buying and selling of links, Google's algorithm subjects these links to analysis before assigning value to them (Visser and Weideman, 2011). The ScreamingFrog analysis found that websites had on average 15 inlinks. Due to the profession of music PR involving connecting with many different publications and artists per year, it could be argued that there should be many more inlinks per website. This could be adjusted by agencies requesting artists they work with linking back to their website when they share an article the agency got them published in.

4.4.4 White hat SEO conceptual framework

The most important takeaway from the ScreamingFrog analysis was the lack of keywords. Across all of the pages analysed by ScreamingFrog for the 10 websites, only 0.07% of pages reportedly contained keywords.

Applying Solihin's (2013) SEO conceptual framework, the websites are analysed by and large lacked keyword research as is required for White Hat SEO that, in turn, results in higher ranking on SERPs.

While the 70% of the webpages were indexable, it still left 30% of the pages that could not be indexed by Google crawlers. This is a problem for SERP ranking as well because, if an important page about the services or reviews of services on a music PR website is unable to be indexed, musicians searching for those services are less likely to find the company.

Given that the character length of the Title 1 tag, meta description, and H1-1 tag is far below recommendation, it is reasonable to assume that there is little to no on-page optimisation as the basic SEO features are not following the standard set for digital marketers. Finally, there is evidence of a lack of off-page optimisation based on the information collected during the interviews with music PR agencies who reported doing minimal digital marketing activity overall, with only a select few working on social media.

The results of these inputs in Solihin's (2013) conceptual framework argue that, on average, the sample of music PR agencies studied in this research will not perform well in search and will not rank well due to the lack of use of important SEO tactics.

5 Conclusions

As the landscape of the music industry more largely relies on technology, the implementation of digital marketing tactics can provide a competitive advantage for music PR agencies. The findings from this study indicate this area of the music industry has generally failed to keep pace with current marketing practices and, as a result, are misunderstanding how musicians are searching for and choosing their services.

5.1 Understanding current search behaviour used by independent musicians to find PR agencies

Through the analysis of the interviews with the musicians, the researcher established the current search behaviour that independent musician's typically exhibit when searching for music PR services, particularly when they are preparing to release a single. Musicians begin this process by asking for recommendations from other musicians who have had prior experience working with music PR agencies or advice from their management team. They then proceed to use Google to research the recommendations they have been given and compare search results for music PR connected to their genre and location. The factors that were found to most influence the musician's final decision on what agency to work with include how the musician feels about the people at the agency, seeing examples of the agency's past work, recommendations, an initial meeting with the agency and, finally, the cost of the service.

5.2 Understanding current marketing methods used by music PR agencies for client acquisition

Through the analysis of interviews with music PR agencies and the results of the WAVE and ScreamingFrog analyses, it was found that music PR agencies typically market themselves to all musicians, regardless of the musician's prior success or genre. It was also found that, due to the high volume of musician's reaching out to music PR agencies for their work, only half of the agencies market themselves directly to musicians by contacting them through social media or email. However, the musicians interviewed reported that they do not want to be contacted in this manner. Furthermore a little less than half of the agencies actively use digital marketing techniques to market themselves online, most commonly through social media (see Section 4.2.5). However, many agencies acknowledge they are not implementing these digital marketing practices as much as they should be.

5.3 Is there a discrepancy between music PR client acquisition methods and the client's search behaviour, and what are the implications?

The outcome of this research did provide evidence of a discrepancy between music PR client acquisition methods and client search behaviour. It was found that, while the majority of music PR agencies do receive client leads through recommendations, many agencies are failing to acknowledge the role their online presence is making in the musician's final decision to work with them. It is clear from this research that musicians are using online search to gather more information on music PR agencies, regardless of whether they have been recommended by a trusted source or not. The lack of implementation of digital marketing tactics, particularly SEO, on the music PR agencies' side reflects a lack of in-depth understanding of how their clients are finding them.

5.4 Recommendations

PR agencies can improve client acquisition through the optimisation of current digital marketing methods as described in the succeeding text.

5.4.1 SEO implementation

As it was found that musicians use the results they find in their online search to determine what agency to work with, music PR agencies should employ SEO tactics to aid the ranking of their website on SERPs. Davis (2006) states that SEO has a direct impact on where a webpage appears in search query results. This means that the more music PR agencies use SEO, the higher on SERPs their website will appear and the more likely the page will be viewed and clicked on. Furthermore, as part of this SEO implementation, PR agencies should include the use of keywords similar to the common searches identified in this research.

In using SEO, it is also recommended for agencies to run accessibility and SEO analysis on the company website to get personalised results on errors that need to be addressed. However, it was found in this study that music PR agencies particularly need to focus on adding alternative text to images, checking to ensure all links have text, and adding form labels and headings. Furthermore, it is recommended that headings are about 50 characters in length, meta descriptions are 150–160 characters in length, and titles are 60–70 characters long. By checking these areas of a website, an agency is able to correct errors and, in turn, rank higher on SERPs.

5.4.2 Additional website sections

PR agencies should also add sections on their websites that address the values identified in this research that have the most influence on a musician's choice. These sections include introductions of all of the team members at the agency, such as a short description of their background and a taste of their personality. Johnson (2013) explains that this section on a website is crucial because it allows potential clients to gain confidence in the team standing behind the business. This area provides a platform for the agency to showcase why they are unique and humanise the agency.

Due to musicians trusting and relying on the recommendations from other musicians more heavily than other source, music PR agencies should request recommendations in written and/or video format to display on a section on their website to reassure new potential clients that other musicians similar to them had a good experience with the agency. In a study done by Hu et al. (2008), it was found that online reviews 'written by previous customers provide information about (a service's) perceived value. These reviews are helpful for making purchase decisions because they provide new customers with indirect experiences and help prospective customers reduce uncertainties' (p. 9). The study further explains that not only the use of reviews on a company's website not only provides more confidence for a potential customer to choose their service but also potential customers are more likely to choose a company that provides reviews than a company that does not. Similarly, it is also recommended that music PR agencies add a section on their websites with examples of previous work and placements.

Another section recommended for agency websites is a form that allows musicians to request an initial meeting. It is acknowledged that many music PR agencies may not have time to meet with every request, which is why it is recommended to offer 30-min Skype meeting/consultations. These meetings may further give a potential client confidence to choose the agency over other options and give the PR agency the opportunity to assess the fit of the musician for the agency. Finally a section that outlines basic prices for various services should be included.

5.4.3 Time allocation

Many agencies in this research also mentioned one of the reasons they did not do more digital marketing is because they do not have the time. One possible solution to this problem is, rather than spending time directly reaching out to musicians the company wants to work with, agencies could invest that time in social media and SEO. This change is recommended based on the interviews with musicians who all reported getting messages from music PR agencies but do not respond to them. Musicians stated that they do not want to be contacted this way, which leads to the conclusion that this method of marketing may not be effective.

5.5 Limitations and future research

One limitation of this study was the sample size of musicians and agencies interviewed. While this research explored the current situation surrounding the marketing methods of music PR agencies in the United Kingdom and the search methods used by musicians, a larger sample of musicians and PR agencies would provide a more accurate understanding of these methods across both sides of the issue.

It is also recommended that future research examines role social media plays on a musician's choice of company to work and how social media is used by music PR companies, why those methods are chosen, the frequency musicians interact with those channels, and the reasons for those interactions.

Finally, it would be recommended for future research to examine the issue of specialisation. While the current research suggests that musicians should be cautious towards music PR agencies that work with musicians from all genres and backgrounds, the implications of nonspecialisation are not clear due to all the companies in this sample not using specialisation. The researcher would recommend further investigating the importance of genre specialisation for musicians and how music PR companies that do specialise in this area perform compared with those that do not specialise their business.

References

Bansal, H.S., Voyer, P.A., 2000. Word-of-mouth processes within a services purchasedecisioncontext. J. Serv. Res. *3* (2), 166–177.

Bawden, D., 2006. Users, user studies and human information behaviour: a three-decade perspective on Tom Wilson's "On user studies and information needs" J. Doc. 62 (6), 671–679.

Davis, H., 2006. Search Engine Optimization. O'Reilly Media, Inc., p. 70.

Dhar, V., Chang, E.A., 2009. Does chatter matter? The impact of user-generated contentonmusicsales. J. Interact. Mark. *23* (4), 300–307.

Drinkwater, A., 2018. Bad Links. *SEMrush*. Retrieved from: https://www.youtube.com/watch?v=PJ6PP61Hwd4.

Gallant, M., 2013. Are You Ready to Work With a Music Publicist. Discmakers. Retrieved from: http://discmakers.com/2013/03/are-you-ready-to-work-with-a-music-publicist/.

Gregurec, I., Grd, P., 2012, June. Search engine optimization (SEO): website analysis of selected faculties in Croatia. In: Proceedings of Central European Conference on Information and Intelligent Systems pp. 211–218.

Halasz, J., 2018. How important is H1 tag for SEO. Search Engine J. Retrieved from: https://www.searchenginejournal.com/how-important-is-h1-tag-for-seo/261547/.

Harris, L., Rae, A., 2009. Social networks: the future of marketing for small business. J. Bus. Strategy 30 (5), 24–31.

Hu, N., Liu, L., Zhang, J.J., 2008. Do online reviews affect product sales? The role of reviewer characteristics and temporal effects. Inf. Technol. Manage. 9 (3), 201–214.

Hunter, B., 2007. A new breed of musicians: the information-seeking needs and behaviors of composers of electroacoustic music. Music. Ref. Serv. Q. *10* (1), 1–15.

IFPI, 2017. Global Music Report. *IFPI*. Retrieved from: https://www.ifpi.org/downloads/GMR2017.pdf.

Johnson, J., 2013. Why About Us Page Is So Important. RocketSpark. Retrieved from: https://www.rocketspark.com/blog/why-about-us-page-so-important/.

Jones, K.B., 2008. Search engine optimization. Your visual blueprint for effective Internet marketing. In: Proc. of the Indianapolis.

Kostagiolas, P.A., Lavranos, C., Korfiatis, N., Papadatos, J., Papavlasopoulos, S., 2015. Music, musicians and information seeking behaviour: a case study on a community concert band. J. Doc. 71 (1), 3–24.

Kostagiolas, P., Lavranos, C., Martzoukou, K., Papadatos, J., 2017. The role of personality in musicians' information seeking for creativity. Inf. Res.: Int. Electron. J. 22 (2), n2.

Kusek, D., Leonhard, G., 2005. The future of music: manifesto for the digital music revolution. Berklee Press, Boston.

Leeflang, P.S., Verhoef, P.C., Dahlström, P., Freundt, T., 2014. Challenges and solutions for marketing in a digital era. Eur. Manage. J. 32 (1), 1–12.

Leight, E., 2018. Why your favorite artist is releasing more singles than ever. Rolling Stone. Retrieved from: https://www.rollingstone.com/music/music-features/why-your-favorite-artist-is-releasing-more-singles-than-ever-629130/.

L'Etang, J., 2004. Public Relations in Britain: A History of Professional Practice in the Twentieth Century. Lawrence Erlbaum, Mahwah, N.J.; London.

McDonald, H., 2017. Questions for Music PR Firm. The Balance Careers. Retrieved from: https://www.thebalancecareers.com/questions-music-pr-firm-2460599.

Moreno, L., Martinez, P., 2013. Overlapping factors in search engine optimization and webaccessibility. Online Inf. Rev. 37 (4), 564–580.

Nen, M., Popa, V., Scurtu, A., Unc, R.L., 2017. The computer management-SEO audit. Rev. Manage. Comp. Int. 18 (3), 297–307.

Ogden, J.R., Ogden, D.T., Long, K., 2011. Music marketing: a history and landscape. J. Retail. Consum. Serv. 18 (2), 120–125.

Okazaki, S., Katsukura, A., Nishiyama, M., 2007. How mobile advertising works: the role of trust in improving attitudes and recall. J. Advert. Res. 47 (2), 165–178.

Passman, D.S., 2015. All You Need to Know About the Music Business. Simon and Schuster, p. 17.

Patil Swati, P., Pawar, B.V., Patil Ajay, S., 2013. Search engine optimization: a study. Res. J. Comput. Inf. Technol. Sci. 1 (1), 10–13.

Sahu, N., Chhabra, R., 2016. Review on search engine optimization. J. Netw. Commun. Emerg. Technol. 6(6) www.jncet.org.

Smith, D., Menon, S., Sivakumar, K., 2005. Online peer and editorial recommendations, trust, and choice in virtual markets. J. Interact. Mark. 19 (3), 15–37.

Solihin, N., 2013. Search Engine Optimization: A Survey of Current Best Practices. Technical Library. Paper 151. Retrieved fromhttps://scholarworks.gvsu.edu/cistechlib/151.

Spais, G., 2010. Search engine optimization (SEO) as a dynamic online promotion technique: the implications of activity theory for promotion managers. Innov. Mark. 6 (1), 7–24.

Statista, 2016. Genre Distribution of Music Album Unit Sales in the UK. Statista. Retrieved from: https://www.statista.com/statistics/276213/genre-distribution-of-music-album-unit-sales-in-the-united-kingdom-uk/.

Terril, A., Jacob, A., 2015. How cities benefit from helping the music industry grow. WIPO Magazine (5), 36–39.

UK Music, 2017. Measuring Music. UK music. Retrieved from: https://www.ukmusic.org/research/measuring-music-2017/.

Valencia, J., 2008. The Impact of Technology on the Music Industry. Florida Atlantic University. Retrieved from: http://fau.digital.flvc.org/islandora/object/fau%3A4299.

Vaulk, J., 2015. Image SEO Alt Tag and Title Tag Optimisation. *Yoast*. Retrieved from: https://yoast.com/image-seo-alt-tag-and-title-tag-optimization/.

Visser, E., Weideman, M., 2011. An empirical study on website usability elements and how they affect search engine optimisation. S. Afr. J. Inf. Manag. 13 (1), 9. https://doi.org/10.4102/sajim.v13i1.428.

Waldron, J., 2009. Exploring a virtual music community of practice: informal music learning on the Internet. J. Music Technol. Educ. *2* (2–3), 97–112.

Walenga, V., August 9, 2017. Public Relations in the Music Industry. Grand PR. https://www.grand-pr.org/blog//public-relations-in-the-music-industry.

Wilson, T.D., 1981. On user studies and information needs. J. Doc. *37* (1), 3–15.

Wilson, T.D., 1999. Models in information behaviour research. J. Doc. 55 (3), 249–270.

Wilson, T.D., 2000. Human information behaviour. Inform. Sci. 3 (2), 49–55.

Wilson, T.D., 2006. Revisiting user studies and information needs. J. Doc. 62 (6), 680–684.

Wilson, O., 2018. Make Sure Your Website Content is Indexable. RYTE. Retrieved from: https://en.ryte.com/magazine/make-sure-your-website-content-is-indexable.

Future digital landscape

14

The application of Industry 4.0 in continuous professional development (CPD)

Eustathios Sainidis and Guy Brown

NORTHUMBRIA UNIVERSITY, LONDON, UNITED KINGDOM

1 Introduction

The first two decades of the 21st century have delivered a volatile, turbulent, and complex environment for organisations to operate. The pursue of globalisation and belief in permanent economic growth have come into question with the arrival of the most persistent financial crisis since the end of World War II, the Great Recession of 2008, and more recently the global pandemic of COVID-19. As with earlier global economic downturns, the Great Recession not only has triggered structural changes to the geopolitical, economic, and social fabric of the developed and emergent economies but has also led to innovations in the application of digital technologies in the workplace. The pandemic of coronavirus (COVID-19) and the introduction of social distancing as a measure to reduce its spread within and across national borders have accelerated the reliance on digital technologies for personal, education, and work communication.

The digitisation of the office space is challenging the current employment skills base of the labour market and urges training providers, universities, educators, academics, business leaders, and policymakers to question their existing practices, processes, and thinking.

The post-Great Recession environment has been defined by high levels of employment and mobility but at the same time with low levels of productivity. Increased activity in reshoring of manufacturing and automation in the service sector will most likely reduce the demand for low-skilled workers (Dophin, 2015). At the same time the ageing workforce is required to keep up to date with increasingly more sophisticated and constantly evolving digital working ecosystems.

The higher education sector has an important role to play in shaping and embedding future technologies and innovation of toolkit of knowledge and skills of young graduates and mature learners, the later in the form of continuous professional development (CPD). Universities are therefore under internal and external pressures to adapt themselves and very quickly adopt and promote the fourth industrial revolution (Industry 4.0) expectations for educators and learners (Abu Mezied, 2016; Feldman, 2018).

At the same time, organisations and their leaders increasingly recognise the importance of CPD as a value-added activity for their human capital which can lead to disruptive innovation opportunities. Using technology which understands how each employee learns and develops professionally calls for transformational leadership qualities of senior managers.

The present chapter seeks to explore these phenomena and in particular offer an insight on how the Industry 4.0 and its digital innovation shapes the workplace, opportunities, and challenges for individuals as lifelong learners and the role of business leaders in supporting a highly productive and fulfilled human resource.

2 Higher education in the Industry 4.0 era

Higher education (HE) institutions are tasked with the development of young adults into employable individuals who will make a valuable contribution to their employer, entrepreneurial ventures, and society at large. Universities have increasingly focussed on the relevance and inspirational teaching provision of their degree programme. Academic staff and student support resources are expected to engage with a number of government-led processes assessing quality of teaching students receive (e.g. teaching excellence framework (TEF) in the United Kingdom). Such metrics have increased the level of accountability by the HE sector and competition amongst universities aiming to offer a student experience which utilises the digital (online and classroom-based) learning technologies.

Graduate employment in the United Kingdom in 2018 was at 87.7% which is substantially higher than for nongraduates at 71.6% (Department of Education, 2018, 2019). The same positive picture is evident in the inactivity rates (graduates at 10% and nongraduates at 24.7%) and median salaries (graduates at £34,000 and nongraduates at £24,000) (Department of Education, 2018, 2019). A similar picture is evident in other developed and even more so for developing economies. Yet despite the financial rewards a university qualification offers to its holder, students' framing ideology is increasingly driven by the notion of 'value for money' of their university experience. A study commissioned by the Quality Assurance Agency (QAA) in British universities identifies students' emphasis on facilities and recourses as central to their perception of 'value for money'. Students see learning technologies as support mechanisms in their learning journey. The same study recommends for a cautious reliance by HE institutions as a substitute to face-to-face learning which student value considerably and see as essential in their academic and professional development (Kandiko and Mawer, 2013).

Popenici and Kerr (2017, p. 4) support the earlier findings and summarise the role of digital technologies in HE and in particular artificial intelligence (AI): "The role of technology in higher learning is to enhance human thinking and to augment the educational process, not to reduce it to a set of procedures for content delivery, control, and assessment". Drawing lessons from AI applications in other sectors (i.e. online search engines, human voice, and command recognition software), digital technologies are seen as tools for the learner and educator in their engagement with an offering of pedagogy. AI offers opportunities for customisation and tailoring education needs. This is achieved by data collection and analysis on the process and progress of learning by each student which is subsequently reported to the educator enabling him/her to focus on individual student needs and tailor learning material and assessment accordingly (Verma, 2018).

However, whilst there is significant evidence to suggest university graduates are acquiring the digital knowledge and skills necessary for success in the workplace, it is recognised that an organisational workforce constitutes a wide range of existing experience, knowledge, and skills. As such, there is a requirement for carefully planned human resource development strategies which recognise employees will be at different stages in their career. To transform and develop the necessary digital skills required to meet contemporary workplace demands, individualised learning plans will be required with strong leadership guiding the way.

3 Career development in emerging technologies: The need for effective and transformational leadership

Cummings and Worley (2001) suggest "a career consists of a sequence of work-related positions occupied by a person for the course of a lifetime". Typically, this will be an evolving process, and as such, knowledge- and skill-based development is crucial for an employee in a fast-moving discipline.

Indeed, there are two primary theoretical approaches when considering the subject of careers: the differential approach and the developmental approach.

The differential approach recognises that people and jobs differ. Some individuals have particular skills and characteristics that make them better suited to certain jobs and roles. In a fast-moving sector, such an approach can be costly and a significantly difficult to resource. Such is the pace of change and need for continually updating skills; an employer adopting a differential resource strategy would be continually seeking new staff to feel new skill needs. Business sectors close to Industry 4.0 markets or supply chain face considerable challenges.

In comparison the developmental approach focusses on the idea that employees continually develop their skills and knowledge as they progress through their careers. This involves the continual development of vocational insight and a commitment to career development.

Writer most associated with this developmental approach to careers is Super (1980). Super extensively engaged with the concept of career readiness and developed a career stage model which noted the main milestone of adult careers. He refers to five stages in a typical employment career journey: growth, exploration, establishment, maintenance, and decline.

The exploration stage is typically the age of leaving education until the age of around 25 when individuals often explore a range of career tracts and roles without much commitment. At this stage, individuals may move from job to job and are confident in developing a wide range of often unrelated skills and knowledge.

From the age of around 25, individuals start to settle down. Super calls this the establishment stage. The establishment stage is characterised by individuals focussing on a single role and continually extending their expertise to progress in the organisation. Often, this result in quite rapid promotions, and there is typically an eagerness to demonstrate self-development to accelerate such a career trajectory.

An individual's upward trajectory will begin to plateau in the maintenance stage. Here, employees are typically highly skilled in their traditional area of employment and have significant levels of experience. These skills and experience, however, may not hold the same degree of currency with new entrants into the organisation.

The maintenance stage will ultimately lead into what Super terms decline. Here the employee is heading towards the end of their career and may be reluctant or unwilling to engage in new development.

For an employer an understanding of these career stages is essential particularly when working in a sector which is characterised by continually updating technologies. Those within the exploration stage will be eager to learn and seek every opportunity for an employer to invest in them. However, recognising the likelihood such individuals will move on in their career during this stage; efforts must be made to align skill development with appropriate other motivation and reward mechanisms. Failure to do so will likely result in the employee leaving the organisation resulting in loss of skill and associated investment.

During the establishment phase the employee is seeking stability. As such, this is an ideal period to invest in development. The employee will be characterised by a desire to show commitment to the organisation with a typically implied expectation that such commitment will be rewarded by career growth such as promotion or other forms of extrinsic reward.

Often, more problematic is the maintenance stage. Here, employees can easily become comfortable with the breath of their existing skills and knowledge. As a result, they may be reluctant to engage in further development often due to a fear that their lack of current skill and knowledge may become exposed. Strong evidence exits of the divide between digital natives (employees at the establishment stage) and digital immigrants (employees at the maintenance stage) (Bennett et al., 2008).

At this stage, employees are also often in positions of responsibility where they have influence over others. As such, their resistance to develop can impact those around them. Leaders within organisations need to carefully manage this group of employees using a range of tools and techniques to ensure their meaningful buy in to emerging technologies. Employers may take advice from the study by Lissitsa et al. (2017, p. 47) who suggest for employees at the maintenance and decline career stage to be catered and empowered by "the acquisition of these skills in late career may weaken negative labelling and serve as a signal to employers regarding the employees' potential productivity, which may be then transformed into extrinsic reward".

4 Career leadership

Northouse (2012, p. 3) suggests that leadership is "a process by which an individual induces a group of individuals to achieve a common goal". In other words, leadership is a way of doing things by which one person is able to focus a group of others towards reaching a shared objective (Hall et al., 2008). As such a leader will have the skills to influence people, by means of their personal attributes and behaviours, to achieve a common goal. This common goal in the context of emerging technology is often about gaining buy in from the leader's followers.

There have been numerous attempts to determine the required personal attributes, behaviours, and competences required to achieve such influence. Dulewicz and Higgs (2005) suggest this would include the following:

- Leadership competences:
  - envision, engage, enable, inquire, and develop
- Leadership characteristics:
  - authenticity, integrity, will, self-belief, and self-awareness

Northouse (2018) provides a further useful guide, suggesting five traits that are common in leaders, namely, determination, self-confidence, integrity, sociability, and intelligence. Determination refers to the desire to fulfil the given job duties and responsibilities and is characterised by initiative, persistence, dominance, and drive. Self-confidence is about the need for leaders to have self-esteem and self-assurance and to be capable to influence others. Integrity refers to the ability of a leader to be reliable and truthful, and sociability is the ability to create social relationships and has a strong relationship with their followers. Finally, Northouse states that "intelligence or intellectual ability is positively related to leadership" (Northouse, 2018, p. 25) suggesting the need for an effective leader to have an ability to solve complex problems and make informed judgements.

Indeed, it is a combination of these competences, characteristics, and traits which, if effectively deployed, can be used to ensure engagement with emerging technology. Specifically, they can draw on these abilities to motivate employees in the exploration stage of their careers to remain loyal to the organisation and use their enthusiasm for skill development to best effect. Similarly, those in the establishment phase often use their leader as a role model and aspire to be similar high achievers. The leader can additionally influence those in the maintenance stage to engage with the direction of travel the organisation is taking and embrace the emerging technology and achieve continual transformation.

5 Transformational leadership

The concept of transformational leadership emerged in the 1970s and is often associated with the work of Downton (1973) and Burns (1978) who discuss the influencing mechanisms this approach to leadership brought in contrast to the more traditional transactional methods which were often more closely aligned with management. At its heart, transformational leadership is focussed on gaining followership and encouraging those following a leader to achieve the common purpose organisations aiming towards.

Whilst Burns work focussed on a political context, Bass and Riggio (2005) transferred the concept of transformational leadership to a business environment. This has subsequently created significant academic and practitioner research to support the potential impact such a leadership approach organisational success.

Bass and Riggio (2005) define transformational leadership as occurring when leaders broaden and elevate the interest of their employees, when they generate awareness and acceptance of the purposes and mission of the group, and when they stir their employees to look beyond their own self-interest for the good of the group. Offering a similar view, Gumusluoglu and Ilsev (2009) note "transformational leaders of those leaders who transform followers' personal values and self-concepts, move them to higher levels of needs and aspirations, and raise the performance expectations of their followers".

Put simply, transformational leadership can be considered a process that changes and transforms individuals and is focussed on treating followers as full human beings. The leader takes a role of influencing back and moves followers to accomplish more than is usually expected of them (Northouse, 2018).

Indeed, Bass and Riggio (2005) suggested that transformational leadership would motivate followers to do more than was expected of them in three ways:

- raising followers' levels of consciousness about the importance and value of specified and idealised goals,
- getting followers to transcend their own self-interest for the sake of the team or organisation,
- moving followers to address higher-level needs.

In doing so, Northouse (2018) notes a range of personality characteristics and behaviours which are essential to enable effective transformation.

Personality characteristics	Behaviours
Dominant	Sets strong role model
Desire to influence	Shows competence
Confident	Articulates goals
Strong values	Communicates high expectations
	Expresses confidence
	Arouses motives

Bass and Riggio (2005) further conceptualised four components of transformational leadership, which include (i) idealised influence, (ii) inspirational motivation, (iii) intellectual stimulation, and (iv) individualised consideration.

Leaders displaying idealised influence have a strong sense of ethical practice and are driven to do the right thing. Indeed, they articulate their values and beliefs in all they do and carefully consider the moral and ethical consequences before making any decisions. In response, their followers admire, respect, and trust them.

Inspirational motivation promotes the role of the leader to provide meaning and challenge to those around them and behave in a way that motivates and inspires followers. In other words, it is the role of the leader to carefully articulate the future state and vision in a meaningful way to their followers. The leader subsequently encourages the development of a shared vision and clearly communicates and mutually agrees expectations to meet the vision. Within the spectrum of artificial intelligence (AI), current (2020) data suggest that only one in five management teams has incorporated some AI process and only one in 20 has extensively incorporated AI in their business model (Ransbotham et al., 2017). This suggests that AI is still at its early development stages to be fully understood and embraced by corporate and middle managers.

The third component, intellectual stimulation, is defined as the ability of transformational leaders to "stimulate their followers' efforts to be innovative and creative by questioning assumptions, reframing problems, and approaching old situations in new ways" (Bass and Riggio, 2005).

As such, transformational leaders encourage shared learning, creativity, and innovation. In particular, leaders and followers are encouraged to pursue their intellectual curiosity and to use their imaginations to generate new ideas and solutions (Shin and Zhou, 2003).

Finally, individualised consideration notes the need for a transformational leader to recognise the individual needs of their followers and make available appropriate developmental support though approaches such as coaching and mentoring. Yukl (2002) aligns such an approach to that of supportive leadership which has been defined as "showing consideration, acceptance, and concern for the needs and feelings of other people" (Yukl, 2002, p. 20).

A supportive leader will demonstrate behaviours including listening carefully, effectively managing the emotions of followers, showing concern for followers' welfare and evidence of caring, and demonstrating consideration for the feelings of others and the provision of sympathy.

In a recent metaanalysis transformational leadership and its impacts, Hoch et al. (2018) report a positive relationship between transformational leadership and affective commitment, increased loyalty and follower satisfaction, trust, empowerment, identification with the leader and group, and goal and value alignment.

Tse and Chiu (2014) and Gilmore et al. (2012) also note a direct correlation between the adoption of transformational leadership with organisational citizenship such as employees going the extra mile. Henker et al. (2015) additionally suggest a link with overall employee motivation.

6 The role of the transformational leader in engaging in continual learning

Goodman et al. (2015) note that the necessity for a leader to engage in strategic workforce planning to ensure an organisation has the skills and competences it needs to compete in a fast pace and highly competitive operating environment.

Furthermore, in the emerging technology industries where demand for staff is typically high, with the additional challenge of limited supply, the importance of leaders taking measures to retain and upskill existing employees becomes even more important. In such a context, Stock-Homburg (2008) notes the need for 'updating training' which she defines as organisational initiatives and actions which serve the retention, expansion, and updating of professional knowledge, skills, and capabilities of human resources and enable professional advancement of organisational members.

Such lifelong learning is a core requirement of today's professional, and an individual's initial professional training is not adequate for the entirety of their working career. However, to be effective, a leader must understand the context of learning and adopt the necessary approaches to facilitate effective learning which will be meaningful and engaging for their individual employees.

The first stage to this process is to understand the preferred learning style of the individual. Scribner and Anderson (2005) note that learning styles have significant importance and influence in terms of learner performance with evidence suggesting individual abilities to attain a specific learning goal can be impacted by their individual learning styles.

Learning styles are a combination of cognitive, affective, and physiological dimensions that indicate a consistent tendency in the way in which individual learners experience, react to, and involve themselves in the learning situation.

As such a leader can use their understanding of individual's preferred learning styles to determine the most appropriate learning tasks and development strategy or method to ensure engagement. Edmondson and Saxberg (2017) highlight the importance of developing a model learning behaviour and invest in the development of learning processes and tools. For learning to succeed within the organisation, it is essential to build a safe atmosphere for employees to engage with such learning interventions.

Indeed, when considering learning style, common models to consider are Honey and Mumford and VARK (Fleming and Mills, 1992).

Honey and Mumford (1982) suggest that learners will typical have learning preferences and approaches should be taken to meet these preferences. They note four preferences: activists, reflectors, theorists, and pragmatists.

- Activists typically prefer to learn by doing and getting involved in learning. In other words, they seek hands on learning and can often engage most when learning interventions are activity based including approaches such as group problem solving, role play, trial and error, live simulation, and learning whilst doing the job. As a leader, it is important that learning activity for activists is varied and includes a significant focus on social activity.
- Reflectors typically prefer learning by observing, thinking, and reflecting. As such, they take time to process information and subsequently reach a solution or learning outcome. Engaging a reflector preference would typically involve learning activities including reading, listening, and then solving problems, often out of the learning environment once they have had an opportunity to absorb what they have learned. As a

leader, it is important that learning activity is designed to allow the reflector to sit back, take in the information, and then have time to think it through and make sense of what has been said.

- Theorists typically prefer learning by knowing the theory that underpins ideas and actions. As such, they prefer learning which allows for significant analysis, synthesis, and absorption of knowledge. This can be achieved through learning which incorporates use of models, theoretical frameworks, underpinning research which has informed these models and frameworks, and subsequent discussion and opportunity for questioning.
- Pragmatists typically prefer learning by putting theory to practice. As such, they learn best when given an opportunity to learn new concepts by experts and then quickly try them out to see how they work in practice. In other words a pragmatist likes learning which allows for continual experimentation and practical activity. This can include interventions such as consultancy projects, problem-based activity, and integrative methods.

The VARK model suggests that learning will have a preference in the way learning is delivered. This can be by means of visual, auditory, read/write, or kinaesthetic methods.

- Visual learners focus on sight and use of visual images to best learn. This can include use of drawings, graphics, diagrams, posters, whiteboard activity, and observation activities.
- Auditory learners focus on listening and sound to best learn. This can include use of discussions, podcasts, web chat, and lectures.
- Kinaesthetic learners focus on touch, feeling, and movement. This can include practical tasks, role play, case studies, and other simulation approaches.

Learners of course can have a number of learning styles/preferences and rarely will an individual learn by only one preferred method.

An understanding of learning styles/preferences will subsequently enable the leader to best identify the method of learning which will exploit the individuals.

The Chartered Institute of Personnel and Development (CIPD, 2020) define learning methods as any interventions deliberately undertaken to help the learning process at individual, team, or organisational level. Alongside learning preference, other considerations a leader should take before determining the choice of learning method should include the following:

- the nature and degree of priority of the learning needs,
- the required expectation and impact on performance postintervention,
- type of occupation and the respective needs and accessibility,
- background of learners,
- organisational culture and budget provision,
- evaluation of the effectiveness of previous learning interventions,
- complexity of knowledge, skill, or behaviour the learning intervention covers.

Learning methods themselves can then be determined to either take place within the workplace or external to the workplace.

6.1 Workplace learning

As the name suggests, workplace learning is delivered within an employee's place of work. This can be by means of one-to-one learning or group-based activities. Such activity can be delivered by fellow employees who are experts in their discipline or other in-house or external training professionals.

The CIPD summarise benefits of such an approach to include the following:

- Learning is relevant and tailored to the specific needs of the organisation and individual.
- Learners are able to practise what they have learned immediately to enhance recall.
- The pace of learning can be specific to the learner.
- The learners existing level of knowledge and skill can be taken into account and used to accelerate the learning.
- The learner can benefit from ongoing positive feedback from their leaders.

These views are further supported by Beevers and Rea (2016) who note the advantages of such learning as the following:

- Very timely—training occurs as it is needed.
- Learners learn the realities of the job.
- Learners tend to learn informally, often from expert colleagues or managers.
- May help engage learner's manager in the training.
- No major reduction in work time.

However, they also recognise limitations of such an approach, including the following:

- Learners may lose out on the bigger picture.
- Learners may not have time to fully reflect on learning or ask questions.
- The pressures of the workplace may detract from the quality of training.
- Leaners may feel uneasy about admitting weaknesses.

Coaching and mentoring approaches can also be used to support learning. These one-to-one learning techniques use discussions to enhance an individual's skills, knowledge, or work performance.

Beevers and Rea (2016) note the advantages of one-to-one coaching as follows:

- Learning can be tailored to individual needs.
- Develops the learner responsibility for own development.

However, they also recognise the limitations of such an approach, including the following:

- Coach or mentor needs to have effective skills to undertake such an approach.
- Coach or mentor must have a rapport with the learner.

6.2 Job rotation, secondment, and shadowing

The CIPD (2020) also note that popular methods of workplace learning are job rotation, secondments, and shadowing. A secondment is typically the temporary loan of an employee to another department or role or sometimes to an external organisation. These individuals would bring specific knowledge or expertise in the area of skills need. They would then use this knowledge or expertise to develop their new colleagues.

Similarly, job rotation and shadowing are interventions whereby employees learn from colleagues in the organisation who have knowledge or expertise from those they currently work with.

6.3 Action learning and learning projects

A further learning approach organisations can initiate it that of action learning. This is a form of collaborative learning where a small group of learners (an 'action learning set') meet regularly to reflect on real work issues. As such, learners learn new skills and knowledge from each other.

Beevers and Rea (2016) note the advantages of action learning as follows:

- Learning emerges from each other's experiences.
- Provides a good outlet for discussing and resolving workplace frustrations.
- Encourages ownership of learning and action.

However, they also recognise the limitations of such an approach, including the following:

- dependent on others wanting the same format,
- takes time away from the workplace,
- requires discipline and commitment and may be difficult to sustain group membership.

7 Off-the-job learning

The challenges of workplace learning can be overcome through investment in off-the-job learning. This typically takes place through formal learning away from the workplace. Indeed, CIPD (2020) note the following benefits of such an approach:

- protected time for learning;
- opportunity to practise, share ideas, and experience in a structured risk-free setting
- the capacity for a course leader to give feedback immediately and in a nonthreatening way;
- the ability to signal what matters to the organisation—essential courses in health and safety, for example, send out a strong signal that this knowledge is important.

Off-the-job learning also enables interaction with people from other organisations which in turn can enable individuals see situations from a fresh perspective and develop skills in a different knowledge-sharing context.

Methods can include tutor input, demonstration, group discussion, expert speakers, lab work, simulations, and a wide of subsequent learner activities such as tests, quizzes, presentations, role plays, skill practice, and reflection. However, prior to investing in any form of off-the-job learning, it is essential that the learning style of the individual is carefully considered, ensuring there is a close fit between methods adopted and learner preference.

Offering formal qualifications or professional recognition is often also associated with off-the-job learning, and as such, this can provide increased motivation for a learner to engage.

7.1 Distance learning and online digital learning

Recognising some of the challenges of off-the-job learning, distance, or online learning involves the use of learning materials delivered through the post or electronically. As such, access is flexible, and typically learners can engage at times which best suit their lifestyle.

Beevers and Rea (2016) note the advantages of online learning as follows:

- Learning is flexible in terms of access.
- Learners can work at their own pace and recap as required.

However, they also recognise the limitations of such an approach, including the following:

- Learners may miss the stimulation of learning from others.
- There may be a need for additional equipment or IT skills to ensure full benefit.

8 Summary

In summary, organisations are increasingly relying on digital technologies to deliver success in the upskilling and lifelong learning initiatives and processed available to their employees. Digital technologies in the form of AI and others have shown a degree of success, but organisations and their leaders have not yet fully appreciated nor utilised the benefits of such resource efficiency tools.

References

Abu Mezied, A., 2016. What Role Will Education Play in the Forth Industrial Revolution? World Economic Forum.

Bass, B.M., Riggio, R.E., 2005. Transformational Leadership, second ed. Lawrence Erlbaum Associates.

Beevers, K., Rea, A., 2016. Learning and Development Practice. CIPD, London.

Bennett, S., Maton, K., Kervin, L., 2008. The 'digital natives' debate: a critical review of the evidence. Br. J. Educ. Technol. 39 (5), 775–786.

Burns, J.M., 1978. Leadership. Harper and Row, New York.

CIPD, 2020. Learning and Skills at Work 2020 – Mind the Gap: Time for Learning in the UK. Chartered Institute of Personnel and Development.

Cummings, T.G., Worley, C.G., 2001. Organization Development and Change, sixth ed. South-Western College, Cincinnati, OH.

Department of Education, 2018. Graduate Labour Market Statistics.

Department of Education, 2019. Graduate Labour Market Statistics.

Dophin, T., 2015. Technology, Globalisation and the Future of Work in Europe – Essays on Employment in a Digitised Economy. Institute for Public Policy Research.

Downton, J.V., 1973. Rebel Leadership: Commitment and Charisma in the Revolutionary Process. Free Press, New York.

Dulewicz, V., Higgs, M.J., 2005. Assessing leadership styles and organizational context. J. Manag. Psychol. 20, 105–123.

Edmondson, A., Saxberg, B., 2017. Putting lifelong learning on the CEO agenda. McKinsey Quarterly (4), 54–61.

Feldman, P., 2018. The potential of Education 4.0 is huge – the UK must take the lead, now. Jisc.

Fleming, N.D., Mills, C., 1992. Not another inventory, rather a catalyst for reflection. To Improve the Academy 11, 137–143.

Gilmore, P., Hu, X., Wei, F., Tetrick, L., Zaccaro, S., 2012. Positive affectivity neutralizes transformational leadership's influence on creative performance and organizational citizenship behaviors. J. Organ. Behav. 34 (8), 1061–1075.

Goodman, D., French, P.E., Battaglio, R.P., 2015. Determinants of local government workforce planning. Am. Rev. Public Adm. 45, 135–152.

Gumusluoglu, L., Ilsev, A., 2009. Transformational leadership, creativity, and organizational innovation. J. Bus. Res. 62, 461–473.

Hall, J., Johnson, S., Wysocki, A., Kepner, K., 2008. Transformational Leadership: The transformation of Managers and Associates. University of Florida, Florida.

Henker, N., Sonnentag, S., Unger, D., 2015. Transformational leadership and employee creativity: the mediating role of promotion focus and creative process engagement. J. Bus. Psychol. 30 (2), 235–247.

Hoch, J.E., Bommer, W.H., Dulebohn, J.H., Wu, D., 2018. Do ethical, authentic, and servant leadership explain variance above and beyond transformational leadership? A meta-analysis. J. Manage. 44, 501–529.

Honey, P., Mumford, A., 1982. The Manual of Learning Styles. Peter Honey, Maidenhead, Berkshire.

Kandiko, C.B., Mawer, M., 2013. Student Expectations and Perceptions of Higher Education. King's Learning Institute, London.

Lissitsa, S., Chachashvili-Bolotin, S., Bokek-Cohen, Y., 2017. Digital skills and extrinsic rewards in late career. Technol. Soc. 51, 46–55.

Northouse, P., 2012. Leadership Theory and Practice, sixth ed. Sage, Thousand Oaks, CA.

Northouse, P., 2018. Leadership Theory and Practice, eighth ed. Sage, Thousand Oaks, CA.

Popenici, S., Kerr, S., 2017. Exploring the impact of artificial intelligence on teaching and learning in higher education. Res. Pract. Technol. Enhanc.Learn. 12(22) https://doi.org/10.1186/s41039-017-0062-8.

Ransbotham, S., Kiron, D., Gerbert, P., Reeves, M., 2017. Reshaping business with artificial intelligence: closing the gap between ambition and action. MIT Sloan Manage. Rev. 59(1).

Scribner, S.A., Anderson, M.A., 2005. Novice drafters' spatial visualization development: influence of instructional methods and individual learning styles. J. Ind. Teach. Educ. 4 (2), 38–60.

Shin, S.J., Zhou, J., 2003. Transformational leadership, conservation, and creativity: evidence from Korea. Acad. Manage. J. 46, 703–714.

Stock-Homburg, R., 2008. Personalmanagement: Theorien-Konzepte-Instrumente. Gabler, Wiesbaden.

Super, D., 1980. A life-spa, life-space approach to career development. J. Vocat. Behav. 16, 282–298.

Tse, H.H.M., Chiu, C.K., 2014. Transformational leadership and job performance. A social identity perspective. J. Bus. Res. 67, 2827–2835.

Verma, M., 2018. Artificial intelligence and its scope in different areas with special reference to the field of education. Int. J. Adv. Educ. Res. 3 (1), 5–10.

Yukl, G., 2002. Leadership in Organizations. Pearson, Upper Saddle, NJ.

A regulatory investigation into the legal and ethical protections for digital citizens in a holographic and mixed reality world

Russell Watkins[a] and Hamid Jahankhani[b]

[a]HISCOX INSURANCE, LONDON, UNITED KINGDOM [b]NORTHUMBRIA UNIVERSITY, LONDON, UNITED KINGDOM

1 Introduction

Our world has always been built on constants: touch, smell, and taste—all tangible, consistent, and measurable. Since humans first emerged from the savannah, the human being has been hardwired with emotions and behaviours that we still exhibit and practice today. For millennia, this has been the case; however, the digital age is now upon us; within just a single generation, the world has advanced towards a hybrid state, mixing the reality we have programmed into our beings with the unreality of digitality. This has happened at such a pace that Darwinism, in which an organism can respond and adapt to new surroundings, has not been allowed to follow its rightful path. Indeed the world is moving towards a state where the extinction of those with no digital footprint is inevitable. The overlap of human psychology and technology is a fascinating area. With such a swift transformation to a hybrid world, it is unknown how this will affect both the *digital native*, the person immersed from a young age in technology, and the *digital immigrant*, those who knew a world before technology.

Regulations seemed lacking, and with the trajectory speeding towards a hybrid reality for all digital citizens, the impact of emerging technologies and the ethical/legal ramifications are at best poorly understood.

> *One day, we believe this kind of immersive, augmented reality will become a part of daily life for billions of people.*
>
> Mark Zuckerberg, Founder and CEO of Facebook Inc.

The analogue age is now over; the digital age is not yet here. Society sits in a hybrid reality that has come about organically yet has little direction and little guidance. Floridi (2018)

Strategy, Leadership, and AI in the Cyber Ecosystem. https://doi.org/10.1016/B978-0-12-821442-8.00018-5
© 2021 Elsevier Inc. All rights reserved.

captures this succinctly when stating that the transition from analogue to digital 'will never happen again in the history of humanity'. Increasingly, society relies on the digital in everyday life, and no area of society seems immune from it.

Augmented reality is a phrase which when used conjures up futuristic style worlds in which reality merges with the virtual. Dictionaries have latched on to the definition as "an enhanced version of reality created by the use of technology to overlay digital information on an image of something being viewed through a device" (Webster, 2019). However, this is only a subset of what has become known as the mixed reality spectrum or as in Milgram's reality-virtuality continuum (Milgram et al., 1994).

This continuum showcases the different stages of interaction between reality and a truly virtual world. Immersion into this spectrum can be at any or various stages of the continuum at any time depending on the technology used. To explain this, consider a subject wearing a VR headset in a building. Each room in the building could have a different virtuality applied to it with seamless connectivity between.

'Augmented reality' as a concept may seem relatively new and however has its beginnings way back in the early 20th century—way before anyone could even comprehend the technology advances and ethical challenges that were to come. To understand this the reader needs to understand the nature of augmented reality and the human dream of 'Star Trek' style worlds, with miniaturised technology supporting human knowledge and advancement (Fourtané, 2019).

Much confusion arises from terms used to discuss different points on Milgrams continuum. Whilst each step on the continuum has different challenges around the CIA triad, for the purposes of this research paper, the terms *mixed reality* and *hybrid reality* will be used interchangeably to describe any point on the scale. The exception to this is the absolutes of the real world and virtual reality. Where there are references relating to specific points on the continuum, then specific terms will be used.

In the 1990s the term *digital divide* was coined to differentiate those with access to computers and the Internet and those that did not. However, this definition only considered the socioeconomic divide rather than that of familiarity with technology. Hargitta (2002) compiled data from EU sources which showed that the level of technological skills and experience is negatively correlated with age; the older the subject, the less skilled in technology. Prensky (2001) goes further in this area by correlating those born of a digital age and those not, the former being digital natives and ergo comfortable in most aspects of technology and the latter classified as digital immigrants with less skills in such areas. These are very broad strokes of society castigated into one of two categories; however, one thing can be agreed on; we are all digital citizens requiring the same protections from harm, whatever the maturity of our information technology knowledge.

The challenge with such terms is that they are binary (Buckleitner, 2009); however, the metrics are constantly evolving; technological and cultural changes mean that evolutions in technology can move the position of an immigrant to a native and vice versa. This research will use the baseline of under 30 years old for digital native and over 30 years old for digital immigrant. The researcher acknowledges that this is a changing waterline which may affect the relevancy of the research in future years (Buckleitner, 2009).

With mixed reality comes a new challenge to how we authenticate and secure our private and personal data. Biometrics are in the mix to become the de facto standard for authentication, and whilst traditional methods of authentication will still be required, they will become a small part of a futuristic and convenient security credential for the foreseeable future.

Many modern technology devices utilise biometrics to control access to personal data and for identification purposes. Ng-Kruelle et al. (2006) and Ng (2006) refer to biometrics as "the automated methods of identifying a person based on their unique physical characteristics". As we will discover in this section, this definition is likely to become blurred due to the addition of behavioural characteristics to complement physical identification. This is a particular concern for mixed reality communications due to the composition of such modalities and the exposing of irreplaceable personal information.

2 Biometrics: The de facto standard

EU consumers on the whole are well versed in the use of biometric devices. According to Yole Développement (2016), 70% of smartphones contain a biometric device (91% of which are fingerprint readers).

Whilst fingerprint biometrics are a mature technology, other physical biometric innovations are also growing in use for identification and access control, with new innovations coming to the fore and gaining market share. Meanwhile, behavioural biometrics—looking at character traits as opposed to physical identifiers—are gaining traction to complement physical biometric techniques. The gold standard in physical biometrics is DNA—whilst this has been limited to government and law enforcement forensics, improvements in technology and cost could bring this technology to consumers. Table 1 summarises the different types of biometrics available today.

Table 1   List of biometric modalities.

Biometric type	Description	Characteristic
Facial recognition	The process of utilising both standard and infrared cameras to map unique points on a person's face for authentication	Physical
Hand geometry/vascular technology	Similar to facial recognition, however using other unique characteristics for authentication	Physical
Voice recognition	The conversion of a person's voice via a digital codec to produce an algorithm unique to the subject	Physical/behavioural
Signature	The recognition of unique points in a subjects handwriting	Physical/behavioural
DNA	The use of a person's unique genetic makeup to provide identification. The most unique of all modalities	Physical
Typing/mouse patterns	Measurement of typing keystrokes and pressure, including mouse movement	Physical/behavioural
Retina/iris	Infrared or photographic scanning of unique optical characteristics	Physical
Finger/palm print	Mapping of the unique characteristics of a fingerprint	Physical
Gait	Measurement of the physical stature of a person and how they walk	Behavioural

As a stand-alone security mechanism, biometrics pose unique challenges over traditional authentication methods. According to Jain and Park (2010), biometrics rely on two key body traits: distinctiveness and permanence. However, the human body biometric markers change throughout the years—biometrics are not constant and can cause false positives over time (Galbally et al., 2018).

The integrity of a fingerprint in consumer devices is key to its success as an authentication mechanism. The premise that fingerprints are unique enough to protect and secure has long been held; however, in an increasingly connected world, this may no longer hold true.

Krisller (2014) was able to create the fingerprint of a German government minister from a high-resolution photograph. The method involved the use of commercial software and photographs—from public media and ones produced by Krisller—to mock up a matching fingerprint. As will be discussed later, the composition of this attack vector with other reconnaissance could leave a user open to attack.

Whilst DNA is unique, there are circumstances where this premise can be disproved which causes an integrity issue for the subject involved. Yunis et al. (2007) discuss the challenges of 'chimerism' whereby through the process of stem cell or bone marrow transplants a person's DNA can be altered. As an authentication challenge/response system, this could pose a catastrophic conundrum if DNA was used to secure data prior to the transplant; such a situation could cause the loss of availability to the data in question with no means of recovery available unless a secondary factor of recovery was maintained. Further publicity to this type of challenge was created recently; the case of a man who had treatment for leukaemia which, after the successful transplant of bone marrow from a donor patient, lost his original DNA identity, which was replaced with that of the donor. In light of this, sections of US law enforcement are reviewing their forensic procedures (Murphy, 2019).

A further challenge centres around confidentiality—secure authentication is built around this tertile without which the person authenticating cannot be verified with any integrity. Additionally, our biometric markers are on show for all to see at all times—unless wearing sunglasses or gloves, a person is open to possible credential theft via something as simple as a high-resolution camera on a smartphone. Considering this further a human can leave behind their credentials in public spaces constantly, just by the process of opening a door and leaving a fingerprint. The simple act of walking past a high-resolution CCTV camera could expose a number of physical and behavioural biometric markers which would then be available for nefarious use. Unfortunately, it is not just technology users who are at risk in this new mixed reality world; a person with no technological presence could have their biometric credentials compromised passively just by being in range of such technology. This may not come to light until much later, when such a person finds that there has been a digital clone in existence of which they had no knowledge (Kugler, 2019).

The leaking of biometric information adds an additional weakness to the combined threat landscape for digital authentication and in some cases could weaken, rather than strengthen authentication mechanisms, leading to a major weakening of the CIA concept.

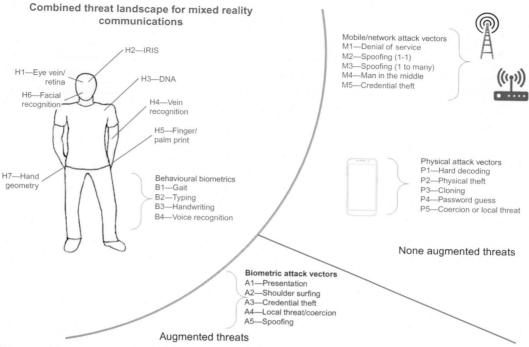

FIG. 1 Combined threat landscape for mixed reality communications.

In the case of mixed reality and holographic communications, overreliance and overconfidence in biometrics could make other forms of attack redundant and increase the chances of a breach of the user's confidentiality and integrity. Furthermore, biometrics are often utilised as single-factor authentication mechanism which, once breached, can give easy access to personal data (Secplicity.org, 2018).

Fig. 1 highlights the biometric threat landscape as described.

DNA biometrics have been used in law enforcement for many years, and for the general public, it is seen as a reliable modality, held up in courtrooms and crime TV shows as the nirvana of identification. Outside of identical twins, DNA is a truly unique biometric method of proving ones identity; however, such a use does have drawbacks; DNA can be stolen or contaminated easily (Delac and Grgic, 2004). Furthermore, there is a danger that public perception of reliability for DNA biometrics could be transferred to other less reliable forms of biometric methods of authentication, leading to a weakness in the authentication chain.

3 Future direction of mixed technologies

To discuss future challenges in relation to mixed reality, it is pertinent to review the trajectory of technologies in this field. Dator (1989) discusses this at length, providing an early commentary and predictions of what we may see in the future. Dator builds on earlier research by Yoneji Masuda and predicts that within decades we will be living in a mixed world of cyborgs, AI, and holographic images. Some of his predictions have not yet come to pass as the technology required for such advances is not yet available. However, Dator intimates at a mixed reality future within decades and "… within a few decades beyond that, humans will live in an environment where there is a large number of such intelligences". Thirty years on from his predictions, humanity is moving to a digital and hybrid reality as was suggested in his writings.

Dator (1989) also intimates at the concept of digital immigrants and digital natives—the premise being that those who currently consume technology will eventually be usurped by future technology users and either adapt or become irrelevant. As mixed reality devices become mainstream, the previous generation will become disadvantaged. This is not a unique situation when the human race invents a revolutionary concept—for instance, those who had access to printed medium in medieval times had an advantage over those who didn't. Similarly, there are other innovations such as the advent of the internal combustion engine, computers, and the television.

4 Holographic reality

Whilst research is ongoing and widespread in the field of augmented reality, there is a dearth of information regarding holographic reality and the potential challenges that this poses in the areas of ethical and legal protection for consumers. Initial hype around the arrival of 5G and the potential of holographic calls has faded away as other closer to market technologies such as virtual reality have taken the limelight. With holographic technologies in their infancy, developers are quietly getting on with what will become a new disruptive area for consumers and businesses (Stoyanchev, 2019).

The nirvana for technology engineers is to build a true 3-D holographic display; however, due to pixel density requirements, motion parallax, and data bandwidth limitations (Suzuki et al., 2012; Verma, 2018), this has not yet being realised. Whilst this technology is not yet available, other novel methods of holographic delivery are in flight. The first holographic smartphone was released in 2018, utilising specific light refraction and led stacking techniques to produce 3-D images (Byford, 2017). Lack of holographic content and mixed reviews regarding the technology have meant that this revolutionary device has not reached mainstream adoption; however, several demonstrations of holographic projections have captured the imagination of the general public.

One of the biggest challenges for holographic phone calls is the requirement for low-latency communication systems with low jitter and bandwidth requirements not seen before for consumer products. The ITU Internet 2030 project (ITU, 2019) highlights data bandwidth as the biggest challenge for holographic communications. The focus is on the correct balance of hologram quality versus resolution. In-development codecs and compression algorithms will help to alleviate bandwidth challenges; however, this can bring its own security challenges. Compressing data can open up the contents to side channel attacks such as Breach and CRIME (Gluck et al., 2013) and will require more sophisticated hardware (and possible impact on battery life) for mobile devices, degrading the experience of the end user.

In an article titled 'The Dawn of Cyber Politicians' (Geiger and Bienaime, 2017), the spectre of sinister use for holographic projections is raised. The article reports on the use of this technology by a French politician to give the illusion of appearing on stage in six different locations in France at once. Whilst the technology used was not a true hologram, the effect was the same in that the politician *appeared* to be present. The technique used is commonly referred to as 'Pepper's Ghost' (Patterson and Zetie, 2017). Attendees reported that after the initial surprise element, the hologram was seen as the real person. "You have the feeling to see the real guy. You just forgot that it's just a hologram" was the comment of one such attendee. This supports Suzuki et al.'s research findings that intimated at the human minds inability to distinguish between differing points on the virtuality continuum.

A holographic interaction in the future could be via disparate mechanisms—mobile device, fixed office or home-based device, or some other method not yet on the horizon of development. In each instance, there will be an initiation of communication by a primary party, synchronisation of the communication between the two parties, and authorisation at the secondary party if one to one. If one-to-many communications are initialised, then this would likely require authorisation from each party.

Holographic interaction adds many challenges to the traditional threat landscape of electronic communication. For true two-way communication to be realised, a sea of sensors will be required to monitor sound, video, and quality. Depending on the circumstances, permissions granted, and environment, each holographic avatar will likely have a requirement for a 360-degree view of the other avatar and its surroundings. Without this a true holographic end-to-end call will be nothing more than an enhanced video call or one-way holographic experience.

5 One-to-many communications

There are three information sharing models which are relevant and common to standard telephony and enhanced holographic communications: one to one (e.g. a conversation with another person), one to many (e.g. a lecturer talking to a classroom of people or a printed newspaper being read by many people), and many to many (e.g. an Internet chat room).

Due to the multimodal data streams involved in a holographic communication, there are various attack vectors introduced which do not apply to current telephony technologies. For example, a telephone call does not need to consider visual spoofing or biometric credential theft as an attack vector. In regard to holographic communications, the integration of voice, data, and video streams introduces a new composition of attacks to the medium.

This research introduces the concept of 'misinformation sharing models' in the arena of holographic calls. Composition of attack vectors in mixed reality could be used to erode the integrity of a holographic communication, ultimately rendering the technology useless as a communication medium.

Consider the following scenario. A holographic communication is initiated and authorised from subject A to subject B, two seemingly known parties. Through the facets of careful reconnaissance, biometric credential theft and deepfake technology subject B are none genuine.

Whilst authenticity has been proven by subject A through various feedback channels, integrity has been compromised. Through a set biometric credential theft experiments in this research, the uninitiated user could be easily coerced in to giving up biometric credentials to complement any attack.

Deepfake cybercrimes—the use of AI to mimic the voice or video of another person— have already been successfully leveraged by threat actors and are only expected to become more prevalent. The malicious use of this technology could be also utilised in such disparate areas as advertising and politics. As this technology relies on access to voice and video data to create the deepfake holographic image, it is currently limited to people already in the public eye. However, as the technology improves, it is expected that alternate data points will allow the mock-up of 'shallow fakes' good enough to fool the uninitiated (Porop, 2019).

6 Privacy challenges for holographic communications

Current video calling technologies for consumers will typically use a static camera mounted on a communication device (typically a smartphone or tablet or utilising a webcam on a personal computer). Most digital citizens will be comfortable with this mature technology which is used through most popular social media and communication applications. As mentioned in the previous chapter, holographic communications will require an array of immersive sensor capability to enable true-to-life interactions. More importantly the field of vision for the third party or third parties will be outside of the current 2-D boundaries, possibly allowing 360-degree views of the first person area.

A further privacy challenge for holographic communications is the loss of control of the viewing area. For a complete immersive holographic experience to take place, each party should have the ability to control the camera and viewing field. Current video communications methods for consumers do not allow for this, giving control of the viewing field to the first party only. If this is maintained, then the holographic experience will be degraded.

Whilst the change from static viewing trajectories to dynamic may be welcome for some communications, there are scenarios where this could threaten the confidentiality of the first party. Consider the example of a cold call or a spoofing call; via a mobile or fixed line telephone call, this has no passive privacy issue. The addition of video to the communications channel introduces a controlled privacy risk within the specified field in; however, for holographic communications, further reconnaissance is possible by the third party as the viewing area is enlarged. Previously hidden information such as the location of keys or written information could be compromised. Corcoran (2017) candidly states the following:

> *many of today's connected devices and associated consumer services rely on the individual consumer surrendering some aspects of personal privacy in return for a corresponding benefit or convenience.*

Whilst Corcoran does not reference this area explicitly, he does refer to 'location and space' as one of the key classifications of personal privacy and the need for protection from harm for such technology users. The creation of 'augmented blackspots' could be a solution to this issue; the first party could delegate areas within the field of vision to be pixelated to ensure privacy; however, this technology is not yet in general use. Additionally, there is currently no standard across augmented reality devices to ensure consistency.

6.1 Legislative challenges

Worldwide, there have been very few initiatives at providing regulation for augmented reality or holographic communications. The reasoning for this is likely to be due to these modalities being in their infancy with very few commercial applications of the technology yet released. Riken (2016) laments regarding Japans regulatory climate "No regulations on VR exist yet, nor does Japan have any government agencies assigned to deal with the potential risks. At this point, it is up to the companies that produce the technologies". Deloitte echo this in their future risks series (Albinson et al., 2016).

Brazil has attempted to bring its data regulation in to the modern age with its newly created General Data Protection Law coming in to effect in February 2020. The LGPD as it is called is similar to EU data protection laws in that it introduces the concepts of data ownership, data classification, the right to be forgotten, and strong punishments for none compliance. However, the LGPD does not reference specifically biometrics or augmented reality except in the broad terms of data subject basic rights.

In the United Kingdom and EU, augmented reality has had no targeted regulation outside of local legislation for wider applications. GDPR (and in the United Kingdom, the Data Protection act 2018) brings data protection and privacy regulations to all consumers in the EU, and biometric data are covered, albeit under 'special categories of personal data' (GDPR, 2018). The regulation states that such data should be processed in a 'lawful and fair' manner.

Augmented reality brings up a myriad of challenges for the consumer. The physical world has rules and boundaries that are easy to navigate, with warnings and protections in place for those who stray outside of the law. The digital world also has such protections in place and is mature with case law to back it up. However, a mixed reality world turns the societal norm on its head. Whilst it is impossible to predict how future case law will legislate for such modalities, common sense would dictate that the mixed reality world will warrant the same protections as would the physical world. However, until the law is tested, this cannot be relied upon. The following sections give some examples of where consumers could fall foul of both civil and criminal laws.

6.1.1 Property rights

Neely (2017) raises important legal challenges around property rights, specifically ownership of the virtual space. Owning a physical property is a common paradigm in the physical world and covered under long-established laws. However, in a mixed reality world, this could be challenged (Bozkir et al., 2019). Consider the owner of a property; in the physical world the colour of the property is red; however, this could present in the mixed world in pink or multicoloured; it could be emblazoned with graffiti—unless the owner enters the mixed reality world, how would they know? Consider further that this is a guest house and a previous customer has daubed an unpleasant review across the virtual space. In current law, there are no protections against this outside of standard civil protections for defamation.

6.1.2 Privacy

Whilst GDPR offers protection from unauthorised collection of information for consumers, current developments in augmented reality applications could have the unsuspecting user overstepping the boundaries of this regulation. Multiple data points for users are already available on social media sites; a smartphone with such applications installed could in the future unintentionally identify the location of users through an augmented display or reveal/collect personally identifiable information. This would be in breach of data protection regulations. If the data collected was for minors, then this could be seen as a more serious offence. Acquisti et al. (2015) created such an application which utilised an augmented application on a smartphone to link a person's picture to an online presence. Such a system could also reveal the pseudonyms or avatars of a person, further breaking the barriers of privacy protection.

Whilst privacy regulations are of paramount importance to protecting subject data, such regulations should not be seen as the nirvana for consumer protection. Whilst a company may receive punitive fines and reputational damage for such a breach, it is the data subject who is left with the burden of such a failing. Some personally identifiable data can be replaced or destroyed; however, biometric credentials in their pure form are irreplaceable. As such, there is a need for technological advancements in protecting irreplaceable personally identifiable data.

7 Research methodology

The experiment was performed at a busy location in London—what3words link 'bumpy. remain.pigs'. The area is a tourist magnet due to the famous Eros statue and hosts street performers and vendors, along with a host of multinational visitors. People in the area are generally at ease and relaxed, often with family members.

A standard mobile smartphone with biometric capabilities was utilised for the experiment. The model used was an LG G8 smartphone which contains the following capabilities which are of interest to this experiment:

- a high-powered Qualcomm Snapdragon processor for image and fingerprint rendering,
- facial ID capabilities,
- screen fingerprint recognition capabilities,
- a high-quality front facing camera with an infrared sensor.

The premise to the experiment is to understand the ease at which a threat actor could steal biometric credentials from the unsuspecting public in a natural environment. With the help of an assistant, the researcher visited the experiment location. The researcher and assistant were dressed casually and blended in with the clientele frequenting the area. Once positioned the experiment was simply to ask members of the public to take a photograph of the researcher and assistant with the Eros statue in the background. This behaviour is common across many tourist attractions whereby two members of the public may want to be framed within the same photograph and need a third party to help.

Prior to conducting the field experiment, the parameters and data points required for measurement were considered and noted. The relevant data points collected were the following:

- date and time of the experiment,
- location,
- gender of subject(s),
- age group of subject(s),
- party size,
- any challenge received from the subject,
- ease of understanding (e.g. language),
- ease of understanding—technical use of smartphone,
- location of phone in relation to body (i.e. held at face height or chest height),
- refusal of request and reason for refusal,
- use of digital or mechanical camera shutter button.

Subjects were chosen at random however to ensure that the key demographics—digital natives and digital immigrants—were captured; an attempt was made to purposely target an even split between the two groups. These were then converted into categorical variables (Salkind, 2010).

The smartphone camera application was already launched, with the subject only being required to aim the smartphone and line up the researcher and assistant in the viewfinder and press the shutter button to take the photo.

There are many ways to steal credentials; biometric credentials, however, by their very nature, are difficult or impossible to replace once compromised. The coercive theft of biometric credentials is not specifically included in the MITRE framework due to being a next-generation attack vector and however is loosely covered under input capture via passive means.

Whilst this exercise was used to prove the ease of credential theft, no credentials were actually recorded. Indeed the smartphone was in its standard form and as such is incapable of recording or storing such credentials.

No personally identifiable data were collected or stored which exempts the data from governance under GDPR rules. Anonymisation is not required as no data could be attributed to any individual person.

Each subject was asked to take a picture and had the opportunity to reject the opportunity. No guidance on smartphone camera usage was given, except to give the choice of utilising the hardware shutter button or clicking the electronic button on the smartphone screen.

To improve the validity of the experiment, the researcher took the decision to repeat the experiment in a different location—what3words location 'fell.cost.elder' on a different day. This area is predominantly retail with little touristic presence, hence enhancing the demographic and scope of the experiment and subsequent results.

The taking of a photograph from a smartphone requires the following physical and cognitive responses:

The smartphone is positioned according to the scene to be photographed; pictures can be taken in a landscape or portrait mode depending on the scene.

The dexterity of the smartphone operator. Depending on the size of the smartphone, this may be a two-handed or single-handed exercise.

The location of the viewfinder. For a portrait picture such as required in the experiment, it would be expected that the subject would hold the smartphone at face height, not only to take the picture from the correct angle but also to ensure visibility of the viewfinder.

Familiarity with the hardware. The camera feature of the hardware utilised in this experiment was chosen for its ease of use and familiarity to any android/IOS users. Fig. 2 shows the viewfinder that was presented to the subjects.

Utilising a smartphone opens up several credential theft possibilities. Front and rear cameras boasting high-definition lens, fingerprint sensors, and infrared and ultrasonic capabilities are all capable components for mounting a passive credential theft campaign without alerting the user of the system. The experimental data points were chosen to test the following premises:

P_1 The smartphone will be held at eye level, exposing the subject to the compromise of the following credentials:
- iris
- eye vein
- facial recognition

FIG. 2 Standard viewfinder of the smartphone used in this experiment.

P_2 The use of a physical button or on-screen button to take the photograph. The use of the on-screen button would expose the subject to the compromise of the following credentials:

- fingerprint biometrics

P_3 The age group of the subjects will be matched to P_1 and P_2.

Additional secondary data points (party size, gender, and ease of understanding) were taken to evaluate any future areas of study or to support the primary data points.

8 Critical discussions

The overall aim of this research was to review the challenges that will be faced by consumers in regard to mixed media communications and augmented reality in general and to decide whether further protections are required to protect consumers from harm.

The principle work undertaken encompassed a range of areas in the field of cybersecurity and the realm of futuristic digital communications.

Whilst reviewing the available literature, this research found a dearth of information regarding privacy and holographic communications. This resulted in various possible case uses being presented alongside the available research in this field.

The work completed in this research clearly shows that the general public are not prepared for a mixed reality world. The human psyche was found to not handle the merger of real world and augmented data very well, and even a competent digital citizen could be fooled by such an environment. Consumers could easily be coerced in to giving away privacy details or personal information under current controls. Augmentation of automotive information systems could be compromised with potentially life-threatening consequences.

The technology companies continue to drive ahead with technological advancements, often with little regard for consumer protections. In the case of holographic communications, it is likely that hardware and software controls will be required to allow users to utilise this technology safely.

While there is a dominance of biometric technology in the authentication and identification space for mobile devices, however, this method of data protection will clearly be utilised in the mixed reality space, with passwords being phased out as a protection mechanism for consumer data. With biometrics often used as a single-factor authentication method, the potential for personal data theft is likely to increase.

Digital consumers often associate biometrics as a forensic 'nirvana', a fool-proof method of assuring both authentication and identification. Both the fieldwork and the literary review showed that there are significant challenges around this thinking, and without further awareness, users are likely to suffer credential theft with ease. The fieldwork in particular highlighted this premise succinctly.

UK and EU legislation give users some protection for biometric information via GDPR; whilst biometrics are not mentioned specifically, they are still covered under 'special situations'. The 2018 regulations are enshrined in law in both economic areas and force companies to treat data with respect. The penalties for none conformance with the regulations are punitive to ensure adherence; however, this would be of little comfort to a digital citizen who has had their biometric data leaked. Whilst a user name or password can be replaced, biometrics are often irreplaceable and require further protections due to their biological and behavioural nature.

The frequency of online fraud is on an upwards trajectory in the United Kingdom; government statistics show that in 2018 there was a 6% increase in such cases in 2018. Importantly, identity fraud is the highest growing type of fraud in this area. Alarmingly, there was a disproportional rise in such crimes against those considered digital immigrants.

The lack of differentials between digital immigrants and natives could be due to the modernity of the technology type—biometrics are a relatively modern form of authentication mechanism on smartphones, and in this scenario, all of the demographics surveyed could be classed as digital immigrants.

There are various recommendations that have been teased out from the research. It is recommended that there is governmental oversight of any mixed reality systems that could be perceived to put the general public in the way of harm. Such oversight could include a regulatory body or mandatory regulations for the design of such devices.

Indeed, in future augmented or holographic communications, there is a risk to privacy due to the passive viewing area of such a communication medium. The technological solution to such a risk with the use of digital 'blackspots' is recommended here. This could be based on a grid system utilising GPS or similar technology; the result being that the owner of the grid area can redact grid squares on demand from the augmented world. This poses many other questions regarding ownership, transfer of ownership, maintenance, and standards. Such a system would provide a solution to a challenging privacy issue regarding such technology.

References

Acquisti, A., Brandimarte, L., Loewenstein, G., 2015. Privacy and human behavior in the age of information. Science 347 (6221), 509–514. Available from: http://www.heinz.cmu.edu/~acquisti/cv.htm. (Accessed 28 November 2019).

Albinson, N., Blau, A., Chu, Y., 2016. The Future of Risk. Available from: https://www2.deloitte.com/us/en/pages/risk/articles/innovation-risk-regulation-response-future-of-risk-trend-six.html. (Accessed 2 December 2019).

Bozkir, E., David Geisler, D., Kasneci, E., 2019. Person Independent, Privacy Preserving, and Real Time Assessment of Cognitive Load Using Eye Tracking in a Virtual RealitySetup. Available from: https://ieeexplore.ieee.org/abstract/document/8797758. (Accessed 24 September 2019).

Buckleitner, W., 2009. Mobile Technology for Children. Available from: https://www.sciencedirect.com/book/9780123749000/mobile-technology-for-children (Accessed 15 December 2019).

Byford, S., 2017. RED Finally Reveals What Its 'Holographic' Phone Screen Actually Is. Available from: https://www.theverge.com/circuitbreaker/2017/9/8/16272838/red-hydrogen-one-holographic-display-leia. (Accessed 22 October 2019).

Corcoran, P.M., 2017. A Privacy Framework for the Internet of Things. Available from: https://ieeexplore.ieee.org/abstract/document/7845505. (Accessed 8 December 2019).

Dator, J., 1989. What Do 'You' Do When Your Robot Bows, as Your Clone Enters Holographic MTV? Available from: https://www.sciencedirect.com/science/article/abs/pii/S0016328789800047. (Accessed 19 May 2019).

Delac, K., Grgic, M., 2004. A Survey of Biometric Recognition Methods. Available from: http://vcl.fer.hr/papers_pdf/A%20Survey%20of%20Biometric%20Recognition%20Methods.pdf. (Accessed 20 November 2019).

Floridi, L., 2018. Soft Ethics and the Governance of the Digital. Available from: https://link.springer.com/article/10.1007/s13347-018-0303-9. (Accessed 1 December 2019).

Fourtané, S., 2019. VR and Holographic Technology Make the Star Trek Holodeck a Reality. Available from: https://interestingengineering.com/vr-and-holographic-technology-make-the-star-trek-holodeck-a-reality. (Accessed 15 October 2019).

Galbally, J., Haraksim, R., Beslay, L., 2018. A Study of Age and Ageing in Fingerprint Biometrics. Available from: https://www.researchgate.net/publication/328526153_A_Study_of_Age_and_Ageing_in_Fingerprint_Biometrics. (Accessed 2 December 2019).

GDPR, 2018. European Data Protection Act Also Known as GDPR. Available from: http://www.legislation.gov.uk/ukpga/2018/12/pdfs/ukpga_20180012_en.pdf. (Accessed 4 December 2019).

Geiger, D., Bienaime, P., 2017. The dawn of cyber politicians. In: Could holograms, as used by France's Melenchon, Turkey's Erdogan and India's Modi be the future of political rallies?, 22 Feb. (Cited 23 April 2020) https://www.aljazeera.com/indepth/features/2017/02/dawn-cyber-politicians-170219104850684.html.

Gluck, Y., Harris, N., Prado, A., 2013. Anatomy of a Cryptographic Oracle – Understanding (and Mitigating) the BREACH Attack. Available from: http://breachattack.com/resources/BREACH%20-%20SSL,%20gone%20in%2030%20seconds_orig.pdf. (Accessed 3 December 2019).

Hargitta, E., 2002. Second-Level Digital Divide: Differences in People's Online Skills. Available from: https://www.firstmonday.org/ojs/index.php/fm/article/view/942/864. (Accessed 5 December 2019).

ITU, 2019. Internet 2030: Towards a New Internet for the Year 2030 and Beyond. ITU Future networks team. Available from: https://www.itu.int/en/ITU-T/studygroups/2017-2020/13/Documents/Internet_2030%20.pdf. (Accessed 3 December 2019).

Jain, A.K., Park, U., 2010. Face Matching and Retrieval Using Soft Biometrics. Available from: https://ieeexplore.ieee.org/document/5471147. (Accessed 20 October 2019).

Krisller, J., 2014. Politician's Fingerprint 'Cloned From Photos' by Hacker. https://www.bbc.co.uk/news/technology-30623611. (Accessed 15 November 2019).

Kugler, M.B., 2019. From Identification to Identity Theft: Public Perceptions of Biometric Privacy Harms. Available from: https://papers.ssrn.com/sol3/papers.cfm?abstract_id=3289850. (Accessed 15 November 2019).

Milgram, P., Takemura, H., Utsumi, A., Kishino, F., 1994. Augmented Reality: A Class of Displays on the Reality-Virtuality Continuum. Available from: http://etclab.mie.utoronto.ca/publication/1994/Milgram_Takemura_SPIE1994.pdf. (Accessed 10 January 2019).

Murphy, H., 2019. When a DNA Test Says You're a Younger Man, Who Lives 5000 Miles Away. Available from: https://www.nytimes.com/2019/12/07/us/dna-bone-marrow-transplant-crime-lab.html. (Accessed 8 December 2019).

Neely, E.L., 2017. Augmented Reality, Augmented Ethics: Who Has the Right to Augment a Particular Physical Space? Available from: https://link.springer.com/article/10.1007%2Fs10676-018-9484-2. (Accessed 4 December 2019).

Ng, R., 2006. Catching Up to Our Biometric Future: Fourth Amendment Privacy Rights and Biometric Identification Technology. Available from: https://heinonline.org/HOL/Page?public=true&handle=hein.journals/hascom28&div=21&start_page=425&&collection=journals. (Accessed 2 October 2019).

Ng-Kruelle, G., Swatman, P.A., Hampe, J.F., Rebne, D.S., 2006. Biometrics and e-identity (e-passport) in the European Union: end-user perspectives on the adoption of a controversial innovation. J. Theor. Appl. Electron. Commer. Res. 1 (2) Universidad de Talca, Chile.

Patterson, S.W., Zetie, K.P., 2017. Exorcising Pepper's Ghost. Available from: https://iopscience.iop.org/article/10.1088/1361-6552/aa589e. (Accessed 7 January 2020).

Porop, J.M., 2019. How and Why Deepfake Videos Work—and What Is at Risk. Available from: https://www.csoonline.com/article/3293002/deepfake-videos-how-and-why-they-work.html. (Accessed 10 January 2020).

Prensky, M., 2001. Digital natives, digital immigrants. On the Horizon. https://books.google.co.uk/books?hl=en&lr=&id=T8aiUYoQvBAC&oi=fnd&pg=PA45&dq=Prensky+2001&ots=YKaUPeasC9&sig=tVVae0TAYKOCkmZ6ZMq3M3ZF11E#v=onepage&q=Prensky%202001&f=false. (Accessed 1 December 2019).

Riken, J., 2016. https://www.riken.jp/en/. (Accessed 16 December 2019).

Salkind, N.J., 2010. SAGE Research Methods: Demographics. Available from: https://methods.sagepub.com/reference/encyc-of-research-design/n108.xml. (Accessed 1 December 2019).

Secplicity.org, 2018. 2019 Security Predictions – Biometrics as Single-Factor Authentication Exploited by Attackers. Available from: https://www.secplicity.org/2018/11/29/2019-security-predictions-biometrics-as-single-factor-authentication-exploited-by-attackers/. (Accessed 16 December 2019).

Stoyanchev, K., 2019. A Holographic Future: Creating and Monetizing the Next Generation of Media Using Blockchain. Media and Entertainment Services Alliance (MESA). https://www.mesalliance.org/2019/02/19/me-journal-a-holographic-future-creating-and-monetizing-the-next-generation-of-media-using-blockchain/. (Accessed 16 December 2019).

Suzuki, K., Wakisaka, S., Fujii, N., 2012. Substitutional Reality System: A Novel Experimental Platform for Experiencing Alternative Reality. Available from: https://www.nature.com/articles/srep00459. (Accessed 20 October 2019).

Verma, S.S., 2018. Holographic Displays: Making Their Way Into Everyday Devices. Available from: https://advance.lexis.com/document/?pdmfid=1519360&crid=6137f8c0-96de-476e-8dea-be193794eecf. (Accessed 20 October 2019).

Webster, M., 2019. Available from: https://www.merriam-webster.com/dictionary/augmented%20reality. (Accessed 10 September 2019).

Yole Développement, 2016. Sensors for Biometry and Recognition 2016 Report. Available from: http://www.yole.fr/Biometrics_ConsumerMarket.aspx#.XZpSU5P0nBJ. (Accessed 3 October 2019).

Yunis, E.J., Zuniga, J., Romero, V., Yunis, E.J., 2007. Chimerism and Tetragametic Chimerism in Humans: Implications in Autoimmunity, Allorecognition and Tolerance. Available from: https://www.ncbi.nlm.nih.gov/pubmed/17917028. (Accessed 8 December 2019).

16

The implication of big data analytics on competitive intelligence: A qualitative case study of a real estate developer in the UAE

Eman Reda AlBahsh and Amin Hosseinian-Far
UNIVERSITY OF NORTHAMPTON, NORTHAMPTON, UNITED KINGDOM

1 Introduction

Considering competition trends in an environment with shorter product life cycles, instant market changes, and marketing strategies thriving to survive, organisations are forced to continuously identify competitors' activities and follow their market insights (Weiss and Naylor, 2010). Business strategies have shifted from knowledge-based status into more optimising added value systems (Drucker, 1998). Managers are changing tools to exploit any market data to support their decision-making cycle (Haataja, 2011). The knowledge of competitors' behaviour supported with evidences (White et al., 2003) has prompted the development of organisational competitive intelligence (CI) systems, helping organisation to prove and strengthen their competitive advantage in the market. Lamont (2002) claims that firms implementing competitive intelligence can achieve 28% higher market growth rate than other firms who do not implement it.

Organisations can gain competitive intelligence either by collecting information to gather raw data about competition and develop insights or by using ready and analysed results (McGonagle and Vella, 2002). Business intelligence specialists use internal and external data to guide the organisation's performance and provide feedback to all employees. Grewal and Tansuhaj (2001) state that organisations have to capitalise in practitioners' capabilities, especially marketing managers; to cope with market viability (Grewal and Tansuhaj, 2001); and to ensure product success. Therefore managers are required to be equipped with advanced tools (Peters and Brush, 1996) so that they can, for instance, visualise all business processes and provide valid strategic input for their organisation (Carrillo and Gaimon, 2000). Knowledge and information are the key for CI (Nonaka, 2009), especially if "connection is created between new product features and consumers preferences" (Joshi and Sharma, 2004, p. 47). However, customer needs

Strategy, Leadership, and AI in the Cyber Ecosystem. https://doi.org/10.1016/B978-0-12-821442-8.00003-3
© 2021 Elsevier Inc. All rights reserved.

and demands can be regularly volatile in competitions (Chen et al., 2005), and therefore information alone will not be helpful to managers to upscale the business; hence, it is vital for the organisations to have this information processed before it is analysed (Kahaner, 1996).

Various CI models were identified in the literature. Generally, CI starts with collecting information and ends with formulating decision-making. Contemporary businesses have raised the need for utilising IT capabilities within the CI process as it can improve forecasting and can dynamically detect competitors' activities (McAfee and Brynjolfsson, 2012) and it will support achieving accurate decision-making (Marshall et al., 2015). One of the recent technological needs of organisations is considered to be big data analytics (Hosseinian-Far et al., 2017; Campbell et al., 2015). Germann et al. (2014) claim that big data analytic (BDA) has recognised a favourable rapport between the deployment of competitor analytics and organisation's performance. Competitor analytics can be descriptive, predictive, exploratory, or prescriptive (Rajaraman, 2016). These results will allow organisations to become more proactive and future promising. Liu (2014) states that BDA will improve decision-making, and it shall decrease customer acquisition costs by an average of 47%. Beyond the downstream effects of big data on CI process, it is important to evaluate how the organisation adapt to feasible BDA implementation approaches to serve their business competitive intelligence. "False correlation results can acquire, if insufficient quality data was incorrectly analyzed" (White, 2012, p. 211). In this paper the evaluation extends to assess factors that contribute to improved organisation's CI process as a result of BDA implementation. The paper provides a comprehensive literature review on the key themes of the subject; Section 3 highlights the methodology to conduct an empirical study, followed by the findings presented in Section 4. Discussion, implications, and conclusions are outlined in Sections 5–7, respectively.

2 Literature review

2.1 Competitive intelligence

There are several definitions for competitive intelligence in literature. Fleisher and Wright (2009) pointed out that CI definitions are similar in terms of CI objective; however, there are differences in terms of semantics and emphasis. According to Brody (2008) the variety of definitions focusses on the constantly changing business environments, making CI a dynamic tool to track competitors' behaviour.

Competitive intelligence can be considered as a tool for filtering, distilling, and analysing information (Kahaner, 1996) to enable managers making informed decision about their competitive market. CI is not market research or a business report (Gilad and Gilad, 1988); it is an actionable information of external competition that adds value to the business (Fair, 1966). Daft and Macintosh (1981) claim competitive intelligence is an examination environmental system that provides unified information for everyone within organisation. Competitive intelligence is an ethical programme of analysing information related to business decisions and operations (SCIP, 2004). Considering the definitions in the literature, one holistic definition is selected that best supports this study. CI is "a process where organizations gather information about competitors and competitive environment, ideally using it in their decision-making and planning process, with the goal of adjusting activities to improve performance" (Wright et al., 2009, p. 942). The definition provides a good match for the critical phases in this research project that are data collection, competitors' analysis, and decision-making.

Muller (2005) claims that CI notifies organisations of any change in the market. The primary objective of CI notifications is to support decision-making by providing the required competitive information (Pellissier and Nenzhelele, 2013). Decision-makers can accordingly develop adequate organisational mechanisms and information utilisation to effectively adapt to major market shifts (Belich and Dubinsky, 1999). Other CI objectives were identified (Cucui, 2009; Peltonieme and Vuori, 2008; Wright et al., 2009) as business development, understanding customers' feedback and requirements; reporting weaknesses, opportunities, and threats and being able to warn an organisation for any environmental changes, competitors' insights, and market predictions; and offering solutions for business obstacles and enriching marketing strategies. Objectives, once achieved, will be provided to management in the shape of product (Gainor and Bouthillier, 2014) of business value added.

Decision-makers should request pertinent information to achieve certain objectives. This information is used to constitute two types of decisions: operational and strategic (Gilad and Gilad, 1988). The difference between both decisions is that strategic decisions place higher influence on the information quality rather than speed by which the information becomes available. Employees who are willing to provide information and achieve targets of competitive intelligence are the CI community (Adeline and Marie, 2004). According to Miller (2000), CI community comprises top management, CI staff, and line manager. Chen (1995) claims that marketing managers are at the centre of CI creation insights. To ensure staff and managers are involved in a CI program, an organisation is recommended to implement incentive plans to encourage participation (Santosus and Surmacz, 2001).

2.2 Process of competitive intelligence

Competitive intelligence is a process of linked phases (Nasri, 2011). The cycle of phases poses a vital influence for decision-making (Wright and Calof, 2006). To create the desired intelligence, it is important to have a structured process of phases (Bose, 2008). Several papers describe the process model; however, each has its own emphasis on the cycle according to the study objectives. In other words, since CI process structure has to fit each organisation's goals, there is no blueprint of CI process model (Adeline and Marie, 2004) that works for all. According to well-established theories and previous empirical studies about competitive intelligence (Herring, 1992; Calof and Dishman, 2002; Badr et al., 2006; Gainor and Bouthillier, 2014), three main aspects have been commonly identified as the process of CI: organised list of required information; system for collecting sourced, stored, analysed, and shared data; and a technique to inform decision-makers of the intelligence results. All studies have identified strength of decision-making to operate CI, highlighting possibilities to improve decision outcomes as the ultimate purpose of intelligence.

Other phases of competitive intelligence were also discussed in the literature; Wright and Calof (2006) propose the process as planning, collection, analysis, and communication. The model omits information storing and feedback aspects. Sawka and Hohhof (2008) introduced the process as an interrelated phase of planning, collection, analysis, production, and dissemination. The model did not emphasise on influential factors and decision-making outcomes. Pellissier and Nenzhelele (2013) highlighted that the CI process entails monitoring, gathering, analysis, and dissemination phases. The model did not incorporate information storage and feedback. Kahaner (1998) proposed a cycle of planning, direction, data collection, analysis, and dissemination. The phases were similarly adapted by Cruywagen (2002) who introduced the CI process as planning, direction, collection, evaluation, analysis, and dissemination. This process has been identified in other papers (Bose, 2008) with the addition of feedback phase after dissemination. Rouach and Santi (2001) proposed a model that aims to audit the organisation's scientific and technical assets whilst comparing them to competitors' assets. The process starts with incubation, conception, implementation, structuration, and evaluation. The model calls for organisation to achieve successful technological choices, bringing value to information with the ability to transmit it. Moreover, Gates (1999) introduced the electronic-based factor within CI process. The study claimed that technology should gather and manage numbers, sounds, photos, and text and then digitalise and disseminate it. Gates stressed on the last phase, claiming that organisations still might fail to achieve competitive intelligence, if employees did not select the right information at the right time.

Informed by the critical evaluation of related models and considering the aims and objectives of this project, Pellissier and Nenzhelele's (2013) model appears more relevant to the context of EK04 case study. This CI process model (Fig. 1) presents a cycle of interrelated phases, investigating output of one phase, as an input for the next one. The model first proposes planning and direction to eliminate ambiguity and provides clear outlines. The model resumes with information collection. This second phase allows this project to highlight on big data utilisation as a main source of CI. Next is the information processing of sorting and storing, which assesses if technology can totally replace human resources. The information analysis phase investigates if decision-making was improved holistically or not by BDA. Finally the information dissemination phase aims to provide the finished 'product' for decision-makers to acquire the actionable intelligence. Whilst dissemination can be achieved through direct communication or by email (Nasri, 2011), this phase can be investigated using qualitative methods to understand what tools the organisation uses for dissemination and why.

Through all CI phases the organisation has to provide clear formal and informal policies and procedures, helping employees to contribute effectively towards CI process, and

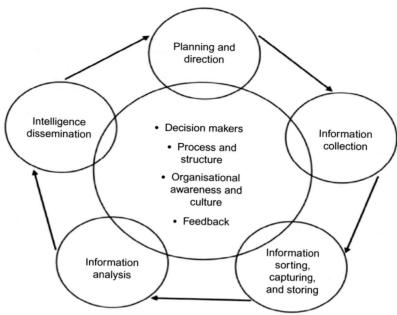

FIG. 1 CI process model by Pellissier and Nenzhelele (2013).

to create an internal appropriate organisational awareness, facilitating feedback for decision-makers.

2.3 Measurement of competitive intelligence

There is a positivist philosophy (Agarwal, 2006; Bon and Merumka, 1999; Chi-Yen, 2018; Heinrichs and Lim, 2008) to measure the competitive intelligence performance. The justification behind quantifying the CI performance was explained by Agarwal (2006), claiming that it gives a holistic view of business performance, provides numeric value of information, supports financial justifications, and offers a better illustration of the competition state for management. On other hand, Gatsoris (2012) emphasises on the importance of collecting in-depth insights to evaluate CI. The main obstacle though is having the intelligence community to agree upon what should be particularly measured and how (Robert, 2010). Nevertheless, practitioners within the field acknowledge that there is a need for measurement and a constant development of CI methods (Gainor and Bouthillier, 2014).

The ultimate CI goal, as discussed in the previous section, is to inform decision-makers (Gainor and Bouthillier, 2014). To achieve the measurement ability whilst improving decision-making outcomes, some requirements are highlighted in the literature:

- adequate staff and appropriate technology to fully function the measurement (Miller, 2000, p. 52),

- strategic funding and cost effectiveness for all CI measurements (McGonagle and Vella, 2002, p. 175),
- linking with other business departments to establish routes of data transfer (Academy of Competitive Intelligence, 1999).

Different metrics for CI measurement were identified by scholars; Buchda (2007) proposed a three-metric method. First metric consists of return on investment (ROI), consisting of process cost ratio to the forecasted financial year. The second metric is the balanced score card (BSC) by Kaplan and Norton (2004), which looks for nonfinancial outcomes of finding intangible problems such as good will. The last metric is the measurement of effectiveness (MOE), which is related to organisational achievement.

A more recent metric seeks 'the right things' in measurement (Robert, 2010). Robert asserts on the importance of conducting personalised practical measurement for the intelligence performance metrics. This approach highlights on the contents more than on the process. It also focusses on providing regular feedback for decision-makers, who in return will add value to enhance the intelligence system activities, and enhancing customer satisfaction.

In summary, CI metrics should measure whether an action has successfully achieved a targeted objective or not. Answering what, why, and how is a key metric of intelligence to evaluate performance, especially when the primary purpose of intelligence is not only to justify productivity but also to inform decision-making.

2.4 Big data analytics

Big data are emerging as a hot topic amongst scholars and practitioners (Hosseinian-Far et al., 2018). Rich (2012) identified 'big data' as a dataset derived from different channels. However, it's a nontypical datasets of database software that capture, store, manage and analyse information (Manyika et al., 2011). It aims to generate actionable insights and help the organisation to sustain their business values (Fosso et al., 2012).

The advent of big data is becoming a global term for the technological complexity which aims to analyse mostly unstructured big volume data, where traditional tools cannot handle it. The notion of 'V' was commonly used in defining 'big data' in the literature. To summarise what the 'V' refers to the following:

- volume: data that require huge storage or contain of substantial number of records (Russom, 2011),
- variety: data that generated from greater variety of sources and formats and contain multidimensional data fields (Russom, 2011; McAfee and Brynjolfsson, 2012),
- velocity: frequency of data generation and/or frequency of data delivery (Russom, 2011),
- veracity: analysis of big data to achieve reliable predictions of smaller samples (Beulke, 2011),
- value: extraction of insights that can help the organisation to save money for the long/short run (Gartner, 2012).

Big data were created by the widespread diffusion and adoption of technology and the 'Internet of Things' related concepts. The importance of big data to a business is derived from the ability to analyse this technology, to provide valuable insights and with a view to improve decision-making, and to reinforce business outcomes through quantifiable and translucent reports (Boyd and Crawford, 2012). Five types of BDA methods (Fig. 2) have been identified in the literature (Sivarajah et al., 2017):

- descriptive analytics: defining the current state of business,
- predictive analytics: forecasting and statistical modelling to determine the future,
- inquisitive analytics: inquiring data to validate/reject business,
- prescriptive analytics: involves both descriptive and predictive analytics,
- preemptive analytics: precautional intelligence on events that may undesirably affect organisational performance.

2.5 Big data analytics

Big data definition had been covered abundantly in the literature. However, a few studies have addressed the impact of BDA on organisational competitive intelligence (Chen et al., 2012a,b; Ram et al., 2016; Marshall et al., 2015). The advent of the Internet and information technology had facilitated the collection of heterogeneous data from multiple sources, providing new opportunities for the organisational competitive intelligence system. BDA is the new tool to handle market and competition data challenges. Bhat and Quadri

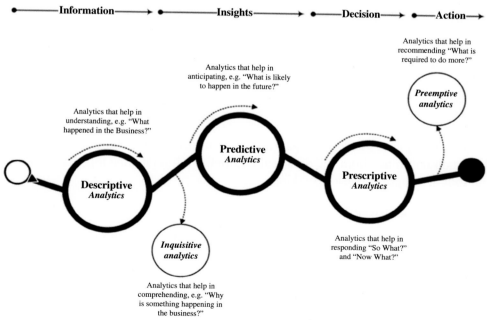

FIG. 2 Types of big data analytics by Sivarajah et al. (2017).

(2015) have listed major advantages of BDA as data visibility and accessibility, improved management performance, and provision of valuable insights for enhanced decision-making. Manyika et al. (2011) assert that organisations will receive new competitive insights that highly improve decision-making, if BDA is used.

Despite that BDA can handle structured, semistructured, and unstructured data (McAfee and Brynjolfsson, 2012), the challenge remains in the ability to utilise the meaning of this information, especially that insufficient skills are expected from many of the involved employees (Zacarias et al., 2017). LaValle (2009) claims that there is one decision-maker amongst three who does not consider the available information as reliable. In addition to this, not pursuing a rational approach for an intelligent decision process is expected considering the emotional influence of technology (Guillemette et al., 2014). To overcome the complexity of data-driven decision-making, machine learning has provided different algorithms to learn from data to create data science platforms (Delen and Zolbanin, 2018). Chen et al. (2012a,b) evaluated some of the top data base suppliers, which are Oracle, IBM, and Microsoft with different technologies of data warehousing, ETL, OLAP, and BPM. Organisations should have an adaptive capability (Day, 2011) to capture all market signals about competitors and consumers, which will create the ability to predict the purchasing trends and thereby foreseeing the future. Chen et al. (2012a,b) claim that the organisational role of handling both BDA and CI ranges between the areas of management, finance, marketing, logistics, and operations.

3 Research methodology

3.1 Scope of research

This paper focusses on evaluating competitive intelligence process performance whilst utilising big data sources and analytics. The evaluation will be conducted within a local real estate developer, in the UAE, Abu Dhabi, hereafter referred as 'EK04'. The organisation has recently adopted Oracle to implement BDA, and this paper will carry out the first evaluation of competitive intelligence process and performance after the first implementation of BDA.

The research plans to fulfil the gap in the literature, by providing a comprehensive model which combines both big data and competitive intelligence together, as an operational tool to support decision-making.

3.2 Research philosophy and approach

The project adopted the philosophy of constructivism, whereby the researcher assumes that reality is constructed intersubjectively through meanings and understandings, developed socially and experimentally (Merriam, 2009). The paper seeks to address complexity and meanings of the variables within a particular situation (Black, 2006), making a detailed explanation and interpretations of collected data that have a myriad meaning (Byrne, 2001, p. 372).

Following a philosophical epistemological approach of interpretivism, the paper will look for subjective and in-depth information, founded in individual intentionality (Husserl, 2012). The knowledge can be generated endogenously and not only exogenously (Packard, 2017). This epistemological philosophy will guide in collecting unique experiences in life from managers and decision-makers and will accordingly provide an eminent picture of reality by which our mental small world representation or model of reality is constructed (Maitland and Sammartino, 2015).

The research rationale is motivated by the research objectives which are exploratory in nature and seeks to gain an in-depth understanding of a certain behaviour. This exploratory type of research often seeks to find out what is happening in a given situation, clarifying and developing better understanding of how things happen (Mansour, 2017, p. 8). It contains a type of questions that are flexible towards a phenomenon to understand the relationship between variables, which means, it will help the authors to clarify how BDA can affect the decision-making within an organisation's competitive intelligence system. Subsequently and once the relationships are demonstrated, a large scale of performance evaluation could be done to determine which components or events are most likely to cause best practices of effective decision-making within the competitive intelligence system.

Through an inductive reasoning the evaluation will begin with a detailed observation of the big data implementation connections with the competitive intelligence system, aiming to move forward an abstract generalisation and statements. In addition, as this research aims to understand the experience of managers, the data intensity is expected to be very high. Therefore the generated knowledge and findings shall be capable to construct a rigid relationship of dynamics and resilience between the variables' components. Whilst the inductive approach can reveal insights about relationships, it is also possible that it will identify other cognitive activities and discover a new phenomenon. Tenenbaum et al. (2007) claim that there are other set regularities associated with an inductive approach which would help in other activities, including categorisation, probability judgement, and decision-making. Moreover, similarity can be a main currency of the inductive approach (Heit and Hayes, 2005).

Given the exploratory nature of the research work, a case study method is selected to reflect the elements of CI and BDA as the central emphasise of the research design and to "stress on developmental factors in relation to environment" (Merriam, 2009, p. 103). Having a bounded system (Merriam, 2009; Stake, 2006) will help the paper to identify how the decision-making fed by BDA will impact the competitive intelligence process. The paper also seeks to investigate relationships between research variables, aiming to provide evidences about reasons for success or failure (Mann, 2006).

3.3 Data collection

The research was carried out based on qualitative approach by using semistructured interviews for data collection to secure rich descriptions supporting the purposes of the research. Interviews will help the research to gain an in-depth understanding of the complexity of the phenomena (Creswell, 2014), and it will establish the meaning of experiences from the perspective of those involved (Merriam, 2009). The questionnaire consists of two areas: the first area used a set of 20 predetermined questions, composed of primary questions, such as "Tell me about the history of the organization", "how usually you propose a new plan to the top management?", and "what materials do you think is best for you to be prepared with? How top management prioritize plans". The second area was the open-ended subquestions or 'probes', which aim to understand the implication of BDA on competitive intelligence; instances include "Can you think of another organization that did this differently than your organization? Why? How?"

The data collection (i.e. the interviews) was conducted in a cautious manner, for example, to pause or prompt appropriately (Ritchie and Lewis, 2003, p. 141), considering the interview guide approach (Patton, 1980) and using an interview schedule prior to conducting the interviews. A pilot study was carried out to test the questionnaire. There were no changes to the data-collection instrument as a result of the pilot study; however, an additional literature review was conducted to include a broader range of theoretical perspectives on big data implementation and competitive intelligence.

A total of seven interviews were conducted at the site of EK04 to fit the research focus, assuring participants are comfortable in their natural setting (Creswell, 2014). Interview duration was between 50 and 60 min and was audiotaped along with important notes taken on a paper. All interviews were conducted by the lead researcher, to limit variation in interview technique. Interviewees were in senior management from five major departments (marketing, sales, operations, finance, and customer service). They all have been nominated by the organisation's CEO who is a key player of decision-making along with the vice chairman (VC).

The experience of participating respondents related to their years of experience and field of work is presented in Table 1.

Ensuring concerns around reliability and validity, full institutional ethics policy was strictly adhered to; the participant information sheets along with the informed consent forms, which have been filled and signed by each interviewee, were gathered prior conducting the interviews. The study was longitudinal in respect that interviewees had insights for the competitive intelligence process before and after the adoption of BDA, and they were able to make comparisons and provide information about the decision-making experience.

3.4 Data analysis

The data analysis process was systematic and iterative, considering Miles et al. (2014), in which we were looking for emerging themes, and comparisons supported by existing literature. After each interview, data were analysed separately and compared with previous interview responses in attempt to identify themes. This was done using a comparative

Table 1 Respondents list (pseudonym), field, and years of experience.

Respondent	Working field	Department	Total years of senior management experience	Years working for EK04
Respondent A	Marketing manager	Marketing	16	3
Respondent B	Branch manager	Sales	15	6
Respondent C	Finance	Finance	20	10
Respondent D	Operating officer	Operation	15	11
Respondent E	Sales manger	Sales	12	9
Respondent F	Customer service manager	Customer service	14	10
Respondent G	IT manger	Operation	10	2

method in which it compared new data with preliminary findings that have been analysed previously. In addition, back and forth actions between interview results and the extant literature were conducted to enable research answering the research questions. The interviews provided patterns and variance in descriptions of how the implementation of BDA supports the process of competitive intelligence; they attempted to also examine the underlying mechanism which links the new implementation to the CI process agility. 'Concept cards' (Glaser and Strauss, 1965) have been used to organise the data and to generate themes. Based on the interview conclusions, grouped and regrouped themes and codes were generated.

For deeper understanding and to improve generalisability (Miles et al., 2014), a comparison between themes and codes across all interviews was made, aiming to find significant information about the CI process and decision-making amongst different departments. The initial conclusions were next shared with respondents and the CEO—who did not participate in the interviews—to assess rationality of results and visualise links of CI's decision-making between the departments. Contrastive explanation theory (Tsang and Ellsaesser, 2011) had guided this meeting, providing suitable contrastive scenarios of why certain process is more important for a certain department.

Finally, emergent themes and group subjects were connected with the extant literature review to explore for possible explanation of the data analysis and enable justification for the proposed process.

4 Findings

According to the narratives of seven managers, four themes emerged. Firstly, CI process has changed after the implementation of BDA. Secondly, BDA has fulfilled the role of data collection, sorting, storing, and analysis. Thus (and thirdly) less decision-makers of CI community are required to run the CI. Lastly, BDA has a great impact on describing and predicting the market.

4.1 Generating competitive intelligence

4.1.1 Before BDA

Planning and direction of CI were observed as a responsibility of the community of the VC, CEO, four branch managers, and five department heads. Every Tuesday the community meet to discuss market feedback and provide decisions and plan accordingly. The questionnaire results found that this phase is integrated and considered as the same phase of information analysis. Following an investigation of data collection, the questionnaire asked managers on how competitive intelligence were regularly created in the organisation. The questionnaire aimed to recognise tactical tools that managers rely on to collect market information.

The tools used to generate competitive intelligence (see Fig. 3) before the implementation of BDA are the following:

- SWOT analysis: It comprises strength, weaknesses, opportunities, and threats of any information in the market, competitors, and/or internal that can affect the organisation. The report is prepared by marketing staff and circulated biweekly by email to senior managers, CEO, and VC.
- Daily press releases: IT staff collect all related published news and put together on daily basis and circulate it through a WhatsApp group to the same concerned management teams.
- Feedback meetings: This has two phases. First a meeting of each branch manager with the concerned sales team. Second a meeting of all senior managers with CEO and VC.

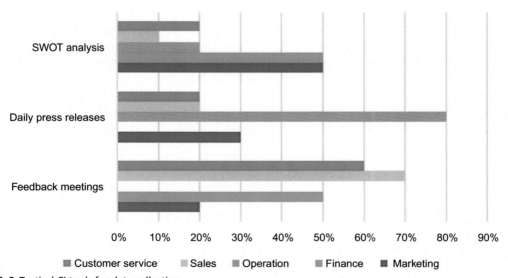

FIG. 3 Tactical CI tools for data collection.

Some managers relied heavily on feedback meetings to gather and collect information; in particular, sales department was found more confident towards collecting data through regular meetings. Respondent B expressed that information are reliable only when it is gathered from his sales team meeting. A sizable fraction had believed in collecting data through the SWOT analyses. Managers considered the market analysis from the marketing department as a trustworthy and valid effort. Remarkably, IT department relied on daily press release reports more than any other tool. Respondent D stated "The daily report contains no sceptical data as they are all published news".

Intelligence dissemination was investigated cautiously using the questionnaire. The analysis showed that dissemination is initiated with management's weekly meetings on Tuesdays. Feedback and solutions are the main topic of these meetings, and decisions are taken and disseminated to all departments.

'Sorting and storing' information was not a recognised phase between the respondents. Respondent F described it as a "phase that doesn't exist in EK04", whilst respondent D found it a responsibility for each manager to manage the concerned information.

4.1.2 After BDA

Respondents were asked about tools utilised so far to generate CI after receiving the first report of BDA (28 April 2019); all answers had overlooked the SWOT analysis. Furthermore, respondents B, C, D, E, and F claimed that data collection phase is a role for respondent A, whilst respondent A considered it as the responsibility of respondent G. Respondent G believed that the data collection phase was a role that no longer exists upon 'Oracle data management software' taking over these tasks. As quoted from respondent G, "don't ask about CI process now, the software is doing the job of collection and analysis based on the criteria we provide".

Daily press that releases news had continued functioning as before, and feedback meetings were not changed nor rescheduled; in fact, respondents B, C, E, and F felt that more meetings are necessary to disseminate the critical insights that BDA can now continuously provide.

Remarkably, BDA has changed the dissemination process, as shown in Fig. 4. Only the IT manager and marketing manager are responsible for it. "Together, we both facilitate the cycle of information between top management and the entire company" said respondent A.

4.2 Role of BDA in CI process

The findings revealed that value of BDA implementation to generate CI is higher in particular processes than others (see Table 2). Moreover, different respondents have appreciated the BDA role towards the CI process differently. Respondents D and G are both in the operations department, and they demonstrated confidence that the BDA can enhance

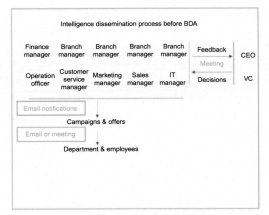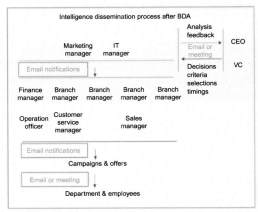

FIG. 4 Intelligence dissemination process: before/after BDA.

Table 2 BDA value for CI process amongst the organisation's departments.

		Assessing value of DBA on CI process within departments				
CI process	Process objectives	Marketing department	Finance department	Operation department	Sales department	Customer service
Planning and direction	Eliminate ambiguity and provide clear outlines	✓	✓	✓		
Information collection	BDA as a main source of information	✓		✓	✓	
Information sorting, capturing, and storing	Replacing human resources	✓	✓	✓	✓	✓
Information analysis	Holistic improvement of decision-making	✓		✓	✓	
Intelligence dissemination	Provide finished product for decision-makers to acquire the actionable intelligence		✓	✓		✓

the CI process through all phases. In contrary, respondent F who presents the customer service department did not greatly acknowledge this impact, and the reason was claimed as "techniques and procedures of creating the intelligence are usually not of priority for customer service department, we ask for solutions according to our interaction feedback with customers".

Marketing, sales, and finance departments have reported BDA value moderately. For instance, respondent E praised the technology that the CI process offers for the actionable insights. However, he went on to add "Collecting and disseminating information is not a great value of BDA". At the same time, respondents were keen to utilise BDA to improve their competitive intelligence output. They are determined for EK04 to outperform competitors in Abu Dhabi. Respondent D stated "Real estate developers in Abu Dhabi are few and customers can recognize price difference so quickly, that's why we are continuously in need to know what competitors are doing every day". Yet the expectation of BDA to describe the market had expanded in the planning phase further to predict seasonal offers that can best suit customers. Respondent C, for instance, stated "our engineering team will appreciate information that helps them while they prepare the master planning for villas and buildings. Determining a size and price is very critical for them; they need to develop a product that the company can sell later".

Respondents emphasised on four common themes that emerged to generate CI process whilst utilising BDA reports (Table 3 illustrates a sample of respondent's quotes):

- The information collection phase through BDA seemed 'descriptive analytics' (Sivarajah et al., 2017), that is why it replaced SWOT analysis. It helped EK04 to know what happened with competitors.
- BDA insights pursue to support 'predictive analytics', as identified in the literature on BDA types by Sivarajah et al. (2017). The prediction analytics allowed EK04 to collect information about consumers' behaviour and future preferences.

Table 3 BDA role in CI process.

Role of BDA in CI process	Illustrating qoutes
BDA replacing SWOT analysis by providing descriptive analytics	'SWOT analysis was used to collect many information and present it together for management to describe what had happened in the market'; respondent A
	'SWOT analysis provided us with competitors presence and had described strength of their campaigns and marketing activities'; respondent E
Additional prediction insights in CI through BDA	'Our CI was about what is currently in the market, but now, we can predict what our consumer will say about each activity or news we would release'; respondent D
	'The process of our CI was going into more tuff routine to acquire intelligence, but now the process looks easier, and also, it catches the attention of CEO for future information related to our market'; respondent B
Sorting information is the most important advantage of BDA	'Probably I can say that now I don't need a human staff to sort out information'; respondent A
	'Seems our CEO is pleased with the ability to adjust and change criteria of information'; respondent G
CI process is shorter with BDA	'We received incredible report in only one week'; respondent E
	'For the report speed comparing to criteria selection, soon we will use it to gain numerical factors of market share figures'; respondent C

- Sorting information is the most important advantage of BDA, it facilitates real-time criteria input according to the management requirements.
- CI process is shorter with BDA implementation.

Finally, questionnaire aimed to assess how organisations measure CI performance during BDA implementation. It seems that keeping decision-makers satisfied was a common answer for all respondents. More prompt questions had followed to clarify on parameters that decision-makers pursue for the organisation's competitive advantage. Market share was the answer of respondents A, B, E, F, and G, whilst respondents C and D stated that it is the ability to integrate new markets.

5 Discussion

The study aimed to understand the experience of decision-makers with regard to BDA utilisation towards CI process. The literature has assisted in framing this case study by highlighting the common phases of CI process to follow. Answering the research question of when BDA can demonstrate as added value for CI, the findings reveal that all respondents realise that BDA will have a significant value if the outcomes demonstrate certain CI objectives. These objectives were introduced earlier in the literature (Cucui, 2009; Peltoniemi and Vuori, 2008; Wright et al., 2009): these objectives are report opportunities, threats, competitors' insights, customers' feedback, and market predictions. Other objectives that were disregarded are business development, weaknesses, environment changes, and solutions for business obstacles. The reason for certain added value objectives is that the management attempted to utilise for the first time.

Results support the literature on having marketing manager at the centre of the CI community (Chen, 1995), only if technology was utilised. Moreover, contribution of other managers (decision-makers) is required when managerial directions and plans are being disseminated Nasri (2011).

The findings provide insights on how big data-driven decision-making creates value for competitive intelligence. Firstly, top decision-makers (CEO and VC) are able to provide pertinent criteria (Gilad and Gilad, 1988) for data collection. Secondly the new CI community has improved the process performance and timings. Thirdly, feedback collection is more accurate and accessible. Fourthly the software (Oracle) had surpassed the expectations by facilitating EK04 with the opportunity to select geographic locations and consumer demographic and, most importantly, to choose between sources of structured and unstructured data which was informed earlier by McAfee and Brynjolfsson (2012). For instance, BDA report consisted of consumer sentiments and likes about competitors' activities was considered more beneficial than gaining insights through a SWOT analysis.

Moreover the study highlights the added value of BDA towards CI through considering the type of insights generated, rather than receiving only descriptive status of the market. BDA had exceeded the expectations of respondents and provided market prediction insights for EK04. For instance, comment analysis had reported customer satisfaction about one-bedroom apartments facing the sea view. This analysis has helped engineers to develop related satisfactory master plans. Nevertheless, in this study, other types of BDA were not assessed: inquisitive, prescriptive, and preemptive (Sivarajah et al., 2017), and this is due to the same reason that BDA was newly implemented, and therefore only the two stated types were appraised.

In attempt to investigate market growth that has been claimed by Lamont (2002) as certain outcome of BDA, the findings reveal that the market share is well maintained after the BDA implementation. Decision-makers were able to develop adequate information utilisation to effectively maintain competitive advantage. Moreover the organisation is currently looking to penetrate new markets through big data utilisation. This means, future market growth is expected within the annual forecast year, if CI is pursued along with BDA.

Finally the findings had led to the proposition of a conceptual model for overarchingly illustrating 'CI process while utilizing BDA' (Fig. 5). The process phases are less, decision-making is clear between two components only, and the cycle is continuous.

6 Implications

The study focusses on actionable intelligence produced by BDA through dedicated CI community. The organisation has to be aware of the technical skills and the knowledge required to demonstrate, run, and understand the analytics. Therefore management has to be cautious when recruiting for BD analysts since these staffs will be solely

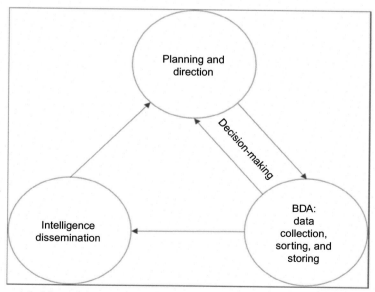

FIG. 5 CI process model whilst utilising BDA.

responsible of transferring accurate and critical data to feed the CI system. The finding of this study revealed that both marketing and IT managers are assigned for this. The extensive experience of marketing manager indicates the good knowledge of market insights and standards, whilst the IT manager possesses strong technical skills to run the analytics with Oracle software implementer.

Another implication is the feedback of other employees about market status. Data collection should not neglect any internal or external feedback and should only rely on BDA. The CI management have to deploy a wider scope for data collection to feed decision-making strategy; strategic information systems could be considered as one of these alternatives (Hosseinian-Far and Chang, 2015).

7 Conclusion

The generation of data has stimulated technology to develop tools to collect, store, and analyse this information. Big data analytics is a new concept of turning the big volume of data into actionable insights. Some companies have realised the value creation of BDA towards their competitive advantage and started to implement BDA solutions. This paper has investigated impact of BDA on organisational competitive intelligence. Planning, data collection, analysis, and dissemination are all phases of CI process that has been enhanced by the implementation of BDA. Organisational intelligence is now reinforced with both descriptive and predictive analytics. The findings highlight that integrating BDA within CI process will generate a new CI structure of feedback and decision-making directions. Future research can benefit from the methodology of this paper and add on a triangulation approach involving both qualitative and quantitative methods. Moreover, further work can provide insights from other industries, rather than real estate only, to enhance the understanding of CI process whilst utilising BDA.

References

Academy of Competitive Intelligence, 1999. [Online]. Available from: http://www.academyci.com/News/IntelligenceAward/motorola.html. (Accessed 1 April 2019).

Adeline, T., Marie, M., 2004. Organizational structure of competitive intelligence activities: a South African case study. S. Afr. J. Inform. Manage. 6 (3), 61–73.

Agarwal, K., 2006. Competitive intelligence in business decisions – an overview. Competition Forum 4 (2), 309–314.

Badr, A., Madden, E., Wright, S., 2006. The contribution of competitive intelligence to the strategic decision-making process: empirical study of the European pharmaceutical industry. J. Compet. Intell. Manage. 3 (4), 15–35.

Belich, J., Dubinsky, J., 1999. Information processing among exporters: an empirical examination of small firms. J. Mark. Theory Pract. 7 (4), 45–58.

Beulke, D., 2011. Big Data Impacts Data Management: The 5 Vs of Big Data. Available at https://davebeulkecom/big-data-impacts-data-management-the-five-vs-of-big-data/. (Accessed 20 July 2020).

Bhat, W.A., Quadri, S.M.K., 2015. Big Data promises value: is hardware technology taken onboard? Ind. Manag. Data Syst. 115 (9), 1577–1595. https://doi.org/10.1108/IMDS-04-2015-0160.

Black, I., 2006. The presentation of interpretivist research. Qual. Mark. Res. Int. J. 9 (4), 319–324.

Bon, J., Merumka, D., 1999. Measuring the competitive intelligence attitude of salespeople: validation of the C.I.A. salesperson scale. In: Conference Proceedings. vol. 10. American Marketing Association, p. 305.

Bose, R., 2008. Competitive intelligence process and tools for intelligence analysis. Indus. Manage. Data Syst. 108 (4), 510–528. https://doi.org/10.1108/02635570810868362.

Boyd, D., Crawford, K., 2012. Critical questions for big data: provocations for a cultural, technological, and scholarly phenomenon. Inf. Commun. Soc. 15 (5), 662–679.

Brody, R., 2008. Issues in defining competitive intelligence: an exploration. J. Compet. Intell. Manage. 4 (3), 3–16.

Buchda, S., 2007. Rulers for business intelligence and competitive intelligence: an overview and evaluation of measurement approaches. J. Compet. Intell. Manage. 4 (2), 22–54.

Byrne, M., 2001. Disseminating and presenting qualitative research findings. AORN J. 74 (5), 731–732.

Calof, J., Dishman, P., 2002. The intelligence process: front end to strategic planning. University of Ottawa, School of Management Working Paper.

Campbell, J., Chang, V., Hosseinian-Far, A., 2015. Philosophising data: a critical reflection on the 'hidden' issues. Int. J. Organ. Collect. Intell. (IJOCI) 5 (1), 302–313.

Carrillo, J., Gaimon, C., 2000. Improving manufacturing performance through process change and knowledge creation. Manage. Sci. 46 (2), 265–288.

Chen, M., 1995. A model-driven approach to accessing managerial information: the development of a repository-based executive information system. J. Manage. Inf. Syst. 11 (4), 33–63.

Chen, J., Reilly, R., Lynn, G., 2005. The impacts of speed-to-market on new product success: the moderating effects of uncertainty. IEEE Trans. Eng. Manage. 52 (2), 199–212.

Chen, H., et al., 2012a. Business intelligence and analytics: from big data to big impact (Special Issue: Business Intelligence Research) (Essay). MIS Quart. 36 (4), 1165–1188.

Chen, H., Chiang, R.H.L., Storey, V.C., 2012b. Business intelligence and analytics from big data to big impact. MIS Quart. 36 (4), 1165–1188.

Chi-Yen, Y., 2018. Measuring organizational impacts by integrating competitive intelligence into executive information system. J. Intell. Manuf. 29 (3), 533–547.

Creswell, W., 2014. Research Design: Qualitative, Quantitative and Mixed Methods Approaches, fourth ed. Sage, Thousand Oaks, CA.

Cruywagen, A., 2002. Establishing the profile of a successful competitive intelligence practitioner. In: Paper presented at the Competitive Intelligence World 2002 Conference, the Conference Park, Midrand, Johannesburg, South Africa, 20 November.

Cucui, A., 2009. A framework for enhancing competitive intelligence capabilities using decision support system based on web mining techniques. Int.J. Comput. Commun. Control 4 (4), 326–334.

Daft, R., Macintosh, N., 1981. Tentative exploration into the amount and equivocality of information processing in organizational work units. Adm. Sci. Q. 26 (2), 207–224.

Day, G., 2011. Closing the marketing capabilities gap. J. Mark. 75 (4), 183–195.

Delen, D., Zolbanin, H.M., 2018. The analytics paradigm in business research. J. Bus. Res. 90, 186–195.

Drucker, P., 1998. The coming of the new organization. In: Drucker, P. (Ed.), Harvard Business Review on Knowledge Management. Harvard Business School Press, Boston, MA, pp. 1–19.

Fair, W., 1966. The corporate CIA: a prediction of things to come. Manage. Sci. 12 (10), B489–B503.

Fleisher, C., Wright, S., 2009. Examining differences in competitive intelligence practice: China, Japan, and the West. Thunderbird Int. Bus. Rev. 51 (3), 249–261. https://doi.org/10.1002/tie.20263.

Fosso, S., Edwards, A., Sharma, R., 2012. 'Big data' as a strategic enabler of superior emergency service management: lessons from the New South Wales State Emergency service. In: Paper presented at the ICIS 2012 MIS Quarterly Executive Workshop, Orlando, USA.

Gainor, R., Bouthillier, F., 2014. Competitive intelligence insights for intelligence measurement. Int. J. Intell. Counterintell. 27 (3), 590–603.

Gartner, Big Data, Available from: https://www.gartner.com/it-glossary/big-data/, 2012, (Accessed 9 March 2019).

Gates, B., 1999. Business at the Speed of Thought. Penguin Books, London.

Gatsoris, L., 2012. Competitive intelligence in Greek furniture retailing: a qualitative approach. EuroMed J. Bus. 7 (3), 224–242.

Germann, F., Lilien, L., Fiedler, L., Kraus, M., 2014. Do retailers benefit from deploying customer analytics? J. Retail. 90, 587–593.

Gilad, B., Gilad, T., 1988. The Business Intelligence System: A New Tool for Competitive Advantage. American Management Association, New York.

Glaser, B., Strauss, A., 1965. The discovery of substantive theory: a basic strategy underlying qualitative research. Am. Behav.Sci. 8 (6), 5–13.

Grewal, R., Tansuhaj, P., 2001. Building organizational capabilities for managing economic crisis: the role of market orientation and strategic flexibility. J. Mark. 65 (2), 67–80.

Guillemette, M., Laroche, M., Cadieux, J., 2014. Defining decision making process performance: conceptualization and validation of an index. Inform. Manage. 51 (6), 618–626.

Haataja, J., 2011. Social Media as a Source of Competitive Intelligence in a Pharmaceutical Corporation. Published Master's ThesisDegree Programme in Industrial Engineering and Management, School of Science, Aalto University, Helsinki.

Heinrichs, J.H., Lim, J.S., 2008. Impact of marketing model application and competitive intelligence utilization on strategic response capability. J. Strateg. Mark. 16 (2), 91–110.

Heit, E., Hayes, B., 2005. Relations among categorization, induction, recognition, and similarity. J. Exp. Psychol. Gen. 134, 596–605.

Herring, J.P., 1992. The role of intelligence in formulating strategy. J. Bus. Strategy 13 (5), 54–60.

Hosseinian-Far, A., Chang, V., 2015. Sustainability of strategic information systems in mergent vs. prescriptive strategic management. Int. J. Organ. Collect. Intell. (IJOCI). 5(4) https://doi.org/10.4018/IJOCI.2015100101.

Hosseinian-Far, A., Ramachandran, M., Sarwar, D., 2017. Strategic Engineering for Cloud Computing and Big Data Analytics. Springer.

Hosseinian-Far, A., Ramachandran, M., Slack, C.L., 2018. Emerging trends in cloud computing, big data, fog computing, IoT and smart living. In: Dastbaz, M., Arabnia, H., Akhgar, B. (Eds.), Technology for Smart Futures. Springer, Cham.

Husserl, E., 2012. Ideas: General Introduction to Pure Phenomenology. Routledge, New York.

Joshi, A., Sharma, S., 2004. Customer knowledge development: antecedents and impact on new product performance. J. Mark. 68 (4), 47–59.

Kahaner, L., 1996. Competitive Intelligence: How to Gather, Analyze, and Use Information to Move Your Business to the Top. Touchstone, New York.

Kahaner, L., 1998. Competitive Intelligence: How to Gather, Analyze, and Use Information to Move Your Business to the Top. Touchstone.

Kaplan, R., Norton, D., 2004. How strategy maps frame an organization's objectives. Financial Executive 20 (2), 40–45.

Lamont, J., 2002. Competitive intelligence: ingredients for success. KMWorld 11 (10), 8.

LaValle, S., 2009. Business Analytics and Optimization for the Intelligent Enterprise. IBM Institute for Business Value, New-York.

Liu, Y., 2014. Big data and predictive business analytics. J. Bus. Forecast. 33, 40–42.

Maitland, E., Sammartino, A., 2015. Decision-making and uncertainty: the role of heuristics and experience in assessing a politically hazardous environment. Strateg. Manag. J. 36 (10), 1554–1578.

Mann, B.L., 2006. Case study research and online learning: types, typologies, and thesis research. In: Mann, B. (Ed.), Selected Styles in Web-Based Educational Research. IGI Global, pp. 70–80. https://doi.org/10.4018/978-1-59140-732-4.ch005.

Mansour, H., 2017. 'Research Methodology and Methods (Overview)', GRA8016-AUTSD: [PowerPoint Presentation]. University of Northampton, UK.

Manyika, J., Chui, M., Brown, B., Bughin, J., Dobbs, R., Roxburgh, C., Byers, A.H., 2011. Big Data: The Next Frontier for Innovation, Competition and Productivity. McKinsey Global Institute.

Marshall, A., Mueck, S., Shockley, R., 2015. How leading organizations use big data and analytics to innovate. Strateg. Leadersh. 43 (5), 32–39.

McAfee, A., Brynjolfsson, E., 2012. Big data: the management revolution. Harv. Bus. Rev. 90 (10), 60–68.

McGonagle, J., Vella, M., 2002. A case for competitive intelligence: 90% of the information a company needs to understand its market and competitors and to make key decisions is already public. Inform. Manage. J. 36 (4), 35–40.

Merriam, B., 2009. Qualitative Research: A Guide to Design and Implementation, second ed. Jossey-Bass, San Francisco, CA.

Miles, M.B., et al., 2014. Qualitative Data Analysis: A Methods Sourcebook. Sage, Thousand Oaks, CA.

Miller, J.P., 2000. Millennium Intelligence: Understanding and Conducting Competitive Intelligence in the Digital Age. Information Today Inc, New Jersey.

Muller, M., 2005. Beyond competitive intelligence-innovation and competitive strategy. S. Afr. J. Inform. Manage.. 7 (1) Art. #244, 6 p.

Nasri, W., 2011. Competitive intelligence in Tunisian companies. J. Enterp. Inform. Manage. 24 (1), 53–67. https://doi.org/10.1108/17410391111097429.

Nonaka, I., 2009. The knowledge-creating company. Harvard Bus. Rev. (November–December), 96–104.

Packard, M.D., 2017. Where did interpretivism go in the theory of entrepreneurship? J. Bus. Ventur. 32, 536–549.

Patton, M., 1980. Qualitative Evaluation Methods. Sage, Beverly Hills, CA.

Pellissier, R., Nenzhelele, T., 2013. Towards a universal competitive intelligence process model. S. Afr. J. Inform. Manage. 15 (2), 1–7.

Peltoniemi, M., Vuori, E., 2008. Competitive intelligence as a driver of co-evolution within an enterprise population. J. Compet. Intell. Manage. 4 (3), 50–62.

Peters, M., Brush, C., 1996. Market information scanning activities and growth in new ventures: a comparison of service and manufacturing businesses. J. Bus. Res. 36 (1), 81–89.

Rajaraman, V., 2016. Big data analytics. Resonance 21 (8), 695–716.

Ram, J., Zhang, C., Koronios, A., 2016. The implications of big data analytics on business intelligence: a qualitative study in China. Procedia Comput. Sci. 87, 221–226.

Rich, S., 2012. Big Data Is a 'New Natural Resource'. Retrieved from: http://www.govtech.com/policy-management/Big-Data-Is-a-New-Natural-Resource-IBM-Says.html.

Ritchie, J., Lewis, J., 2003. Qualitative Research Practice: A Guide for Social Science Students and Researchers. SAGE, London.

Robert, M., 2010. Intelligence Analysis, third ed. CQ Press, Washington, DC.

Rouach, D., Santi, P., 2001. Competitive intelligence adds value: five intelligence attitudes. Eur. Manage. J. 19 (5), 552–559.

Russom, P., 2011. Big data analytics. Transforming Data With Intelligence Best Practices Report. Fourth Quarter 19 (4), 1–34.

Santosus, M., Surmacz, J., 2001. The ABCs of knowledge management. CIO Magazine 23

Sawka, K., Hohhof, B., 2008. Starting a Competitive Intelligent Function. Competitive Intelligence Foundation, Alexandria.

Sivarajah, U., et al., 2017. Critical analysis of Big Data challenges and analytical methods. J. Bus. Res. 70 (C), 263–286.

Society of Competitive Intelligence Professionals (SCIP), 2004. Title what is C. I. www.scip.org. (Accessed 8 March 2019).

Stake, R.E., 2006. Multiple Case Study Analysis. Guilford, New York, NY.

Tenenbaum, J., Kemp, C., Shafto, P., 2007. Theory-based Bayesian models of inductive reasoning. In: Feeney, A., Heit, E. (Eds.), Inductive Reasoning: Experimental, Developmental, and Computational Approaches. Cambridge University Press, Cambridge, pp. 167–204. https://doi.org/10.1017/CBO9780511619304.008.

Tsang, E.W.K., Ellsaesser, F., 2011. How contrastive explanation facilitates theory building. Acad. Manage. Rev. 36 (2), 404–419.

Weiss, A., Naylor, E., 2010. Competitive intelligence: how independent information professionals. Am. Soc. Inform. Sci. Technol. 37 (1), 30–34. https://doi.org/10.1002/bult.2010.1720370114.

White, M., 2012. Digital workplaces: vision and reality. Bus. Inf. Rev. 29 (4), 205–214.

White, J., Varadarajan, P., Dacin, P., 2003. Market situation interpretation and response: the role of cognitive style, organizational culture, and information use. J. Mark. 67 (3), 63–80.

Wright, S., Calof, J., 2006. The quest for competitive, business and marketing intelligence: a country comparison of current practices. Eur. J. Mark. 40 (5/6), 453–465. https://doi.org/10.1108/03090560610657787.

Wright, S., et al., 2009. Competitive intelligence in practice: empirical evidence from the UK retail banking sector. J. Mark. Manage. 25 (9/10), 941–964. https://doi.org/10.1362/026725709X479318.

Zacarias, M., Martins, P.V., Gonçalves, A., 2017. An agile business process and practice meta-model. Procedia Comput. Sci. 121, 170–177.

17

Commodification of consumer privacy and the risk of data mining exposure

John Bridge[a], Stefan Kendzierskyj[b], John McCarthy[c], and Hamid Jahankhani[a]

[a]NORTHUMBRIA UNIVERSITY, LONDON, UNITED KINGDOM [b]CYFORTIS, SURREY, UNITED KINGDOM [c]OXFORD SYSTEMS, BICESTER, UNITED KINGDOM

1 Data brokerage background

Data brokers are described as 'a company or business unit that earns its primary revenue by supplying data or inferences about people gathered mainly from sources other than the data subjects themselves' (Rieke et al., 2016a,b). They collect massive amounts of data on individuals and then create profiles that are traded between other data brokers and then purchased by businesses to better profile and understand consumers' needs. These profiles can contain incredibly sensitive information that most end users have not agreed to share and quite often are completely unaware that it is in the public domain. There are currently over 4000 data brokers operating in an industry worth an estimated $200 billion (WebFX, 2018). Data have become such a commodity that it is considered that it may become the most valuable resource on earth by 2022 (Datareum, 2018). Some of these data brokers are very well-known businesses such as Acxiom, Experian, Epsilon, and more recently Oracle who purchased a number of data brokers, such as Datalogix, to become one of the biggest data brokers on the planet whilst simultaneously one of the world's biggest technology companies. Oracle pulls in feeds from 80 other data brokers who specialise in different areas of brokerage, including online and in-store purchases, social media usage, and financial transactions. Oracle claim to sell data on more than 300 million people globally, with the majority of individuals having over 30,000 data attributes set against them including characteristics such as political views, media usage, net worth, and recent purchases and basic characteristics such as age and gender. They will also track individuals who perform web searches for sensitive criteria such as abortion, gay marriage, legalising drugs, protests, and health matters (Christl and Spiekerman, 2016). Based on this information, Oracle claim to know what consumers do, say, and buy, whilst the majority of individuals have no idea what information is known about them. Wu claims that 'computers' judgments of people's personalities based on their digital footprints are more

Strategy, Leadership, and AI in the Cyber Ecosystem. https://doi.org/10.1016/B978-0-12-821442-8.00009-4
© 2021 Elsevier Inc. All rights reserved.

accurate and valid than judgments made by their close others or acquaintances (friends, family, spouse, colleagues, etc.). Our findings highlight that people's personalities can be predicted automatically and without involving human social-cognitive skills' (Wu et al., 2015). This is achieved through the use of statistical modelling, but quite often, this information can be incorrect. Lucker, Hogan, and Bischoff claim that their review of a 'leading consumer' data broker showed that two-thirds of the 107 people surveyed stated that the data were less than 50% accurate (Lucker et al., 2017).

1.1 Online political microtargeting

The Cambridge Analytica scandal dominated the headlines in 2018, shocking many people who were unaware of the existence and implications of their data. The scandal did, however, raise some awareness, proving exactly how powerful data brokers are through the revelations surrounding their role in influencing numerous global events, such as the US presidential elections and the EU referendum vote in the United Kingdom. Cambridge Analytica built up very detailed psychological profiles of 87 million Facebook users, some of which were targeted with specific communication that helped change the voting outcome for world-changing events, including the aforementioned. The individuals whose personal information was harvested thought they were answering a series of questions from the 'This is Your Digital Life' Facebook application that supposedly judged their online personality. Applications like this are a very common occurrence with Facebook. According to the former Director of Research of Cambridge Analytica and recent whistle-blower Christopher Wylie, the answers were fed into a profiling tool called OCEAN which categorised users on their 'openness', 'conscientiousness', 'extraversion', 'agreeableness', and 'neuroticism', thereby correlating it with their likes and shares resulting in an extremely accurate psychological profile (Wylie, 2019). The individuals would then be microtargeted based on the outcome of the OCEAN scores and sent targeted content based on their psychological profile. Microtargeting exploits personal data without informed consent and has become a demographic crisis. The House of Commons digital, Culture, and Sport Committee (UK) stated that Cambridge Analytica's 'relentless targeting of hyper-partisan views, which play to the fears and the prejudices of people in order to alter their voting plans' is arguably 'more invasive than obviously false information' (DCMS, 2018). Facebook were fined $5 billion in July 2019 for 'deceiving' users about protecting their privacy and their part in the Cambridge Analytica scandal. Facebook argued that the fine was excessive as its consumers were 'not harmed and that they did not suffer personal loss or injury of the company's mishandling of personal information' (Room, 2019).

1.2 Types of data brokerage

Data brokerage is broken down into the three categories:

- marketing
- consumer credit
- fraud prevention/people search

1.2.1 Marketing

This is the largest area which accounts for 50% of the data. Large online businesses such as Facebook, Google, and Amazon work with data brokers to target and optimise adverts for individuals, based on data from their profile such as age, location, interests, and household income. Advertisers will also have access to the consumer's web browsing history, their spending habits and purchases from credit cards (both online and in store) from the data brokers. Supermarkets know exactly when a consumer is likely to visit and how much they are likely to spend and on what products, based on the huge amount of data they have on their customers from shopping history and loyalty programmes. Kirk Grogan highlighted the extent of how much businesses know about consumers at a TEDx Seattle talks recently where he said that supermarkets often know that a woman is pregnant before she does, purely because she buys different products to her normal purchases due to her body's subconscious cravings, such as unscented hand creams and certain vitamins and minerals (Grogan, 2018). Advertising is evolving into a very technical, scientific process and is no longer a case of simply displaying an advert. Now, it is more based on data-driven predictive analytics tailored to the individual, based on their data profile. This marketing profile is constantly changing and being evaluated and is completely different for everyone. Its data profiling use cases and what entities the data is passed through is of a major concern.

1.2.2 Consumer credit/fraud prevention

This accounts for 45% of the data. Well-known credit bureaus such as Equifax, Experian, and TransUnion provide credit reports containing credit history, details on how a person has banked, any borrowed and repaid debts, and any legal judgements, bankruptcy claims, and consumer payment behaviour such as utility bill payments. If any of these data are incorrect, this can cause huge problems for a person when trying to obtain fair and affordable credit. A study showed that 'one in five consumers had an error' in this credit data (Kaplan, 2015). It is incredibly difficult for someone to correct any errors in these data, so the consequences of a bad credit rating can stay with a person for many years. Credit card companies, such as Visa and Mastercard, have made their transaction data available to Oracle (Oracle, 2019) who then combine the demographics with the 'profile' of the consumer. Over $3 trillion US and £522 billion UK worth of card spends from 74 billion Visa transactions alone are fed into Oracle, that outputs spend category, frequency, amount, times, and offline vs online spend, providing valuable data for marketers and credit risk prevention. As an example, the world's largest credit reporting agency, Experian, takes inputs from over 918 million people to provide services to third parties.

1.3 People search

This covers general people searching and government, law enforcement, and health searches. Data brokers provide data to many healthcare providers. One data broker boasts that it holds 'over 85% of the world's prescriptions by sales' (Rieke et al., 2016a,b). Google's

AI Company DeepMind has access to 1.6 million citizens NHS records which include very sensitive information such as details of people who are 'HIV-positive, people who have suffered drug overdoses and people who have abortions' (Hodson, 2016). The patients were not asked for their consent or told how their data were being shared with third parties. It is reported that even a simple web search on specific medical conditions such as diabetes could be added to your data profile (Grauer, 2018), which could then have a detrimental effect when trying to get health insurance or applying for jobs. Bloomberg reported that hospitals are 'mining patients' credit card data to predict who is likely to become sick' based on their spending habits (Pettypiece, 2014). The Executive Director of the World Privacy Forum, Pam Dixon, in her testimony to the US Senate (Dixon, 2013) about 'What Information do Data Brokers have on Consumers' highlighted that data brokers are offering lists of the following:

- people that are suffering from 'mental health problems, cancer, HIV/AIDS, and hundreds of other illnesses';
- a list of police officers home addresses;
- a list of rape sufferers;
- a list of domestic violence shelters;
- a list of people who are suffering from dementia;
- a list of people with addictive behaviour, manifesting in alcohol or drugs;
- a list of people with low credit rating.

This information is all added to the consumer's profile, and a numeric value will be generated that will depict many things, such as the likelihood to become diabetic or dependent on alcohol or drugs. It is possible to buy lists from DMDatabases.com, which is an online source of marketing databases of over 300 million people. (DMDatabases, 2019). One of the databases that DMDatabases offer is of 'expectant parents' which according to their website offers a weekly list of over 70,000 mothers to be which can also be broken down by an 'extensive array of demographics' as shown in Fig. 1.

Acxiom collect data from three different sources—according to their guide to understanding their marketing products (Acxiom, 2019a,b); they collect from government records, public records, and data from commercial entities. They provide data from names and ages of the household to media channel usage; purchasing behaviour; life events, such as new teenage drivers or recently divorced status; household wealth indicators such as estimated net worth; data regarding the age and value of belongings, such as house and vehicles; and if members of the household are heavy social media users. They also score every individual on their likelihood 'to change careers or jobs' and put everyone into one of 13 religious affiliations and 200 'ethnic codes' (Acxiom, 2019a,b).

Predictions about consumer behaviour are based on the following:

- the information the data broker has on that person,
- credit scores that predict the likelihood that a person will default on a loan,
- marketing scores that predict how likely the person is to buy a certain product,

QUALIFY YOUR EXPECTANT PARENT MAILING LIST
You may qualify your parents-to-be mailing list / email list by an extensive array of demographic
*Age of Mother
*Age of Father

AGE PROFILE – PRE-NATAL MAILING LIST
Age 19 to 29: 28%
Age 30 to 39: 61%
Age 40 to 49: 9%
Age 50+: 2%
*You may also select the mothers-to-be mailing list by age of father.

OTHER WAYS TO SEGMENT YOUR EXPECTANT PARENTS MAILING LIST
Marital Status
Education Level of Mother-to-be / Father-to-be
Number of Children in Household
Household Income, Net Worth, Home Value, Home Equity
Millionaires Expectant Parents mailing list
Low Income Households – Expectant Parents
Renters – Expectant Parents mailing list
Spanish Speaking Households Expectant Parents
Single Mothers To Be mailing list

Due Date / Birth Month
Baby's Birth Date
First Child Indicator

FIG. 1 Demographics example.

- fraud scores that predict how likely a particular transaction is to be fraudulent,
- stress scores that might help organisational customers manage healthcare costs and risks (Rieke et al., 2016a,b).

With the vast amount of data these data brokers have on people, they are prime targets for hackers. Many data brokers have had high-profile security breaches such as Equifax (Bloomberg, 2017), Epsilon (Krebs, 2015a,b), and LexisNexis (Leyden, 2007) where many billions of records were leaked and made openly available for download on the Internet. Fig. 2 shows a dump of 200 million records from the Equifax hack, available for free download on the Dark Web Torum.

This downloadable information on individuals contains more than enough data for identities to be cloned, allowing applications for credit cards to be made. There are identities available for sale on the Dark Web for as little as $1 each as shown in Fig. 3 (with sensitive info redacted).

FIG. 2 Downloadable data dump on Dark Web Torum.

Full Name	City	State	ZIP	Year of Birth	Country	Price	
MARSHA	ST. PETERSBURG	FL	33	195		$1	
THEODIS	SPRING HILL	FL	34	197		$1	
HATTIE	PANAMA CITY	FL	32	196		$1	
KAREN C	PALM COAST	FL	32	196		$1	
LAVERNE	ORLANDO	FL	32	196		$1	
LEE ANI	MOLINO	FL	32	196		$1	
STACY G	MILTON	FL	32	196		$1	
JACQUEL	MIAMI GARDENS	FL	33	196		$1	
ALFREDA	MIAMI	FL	33	196		$1	
TURNER	MADISON	FL	32	196		$1	
SANDRA	LEHIGH ACRES	FL	33	196		$1	
LE ROOF	LAKELAND	FL	33	196		$1	

FIG. 3 Dark Web identity sales.

2 Tracking and targeted ads

A person's behaviour gives many data signatures and can be collated through a practice known as website tracking. It's a fairly common understanding regarding the reasons for a cookie that is the small file placed on a visitor's computer, but many may be unaware that cookies can act as back doors for Trojan horses and cause more data extraction via other cookies.

2.1 Online tracking

A tracker collects information about individuals when they search the web. Scripts and tracking pixels are built into webpages that update servers with content such as browsing history which is then linked to the unique identifier of that user that is matched by cookies or fingerprinting, should the user have cookies turned off. Tracking pixels are hidden pixels on a webpage or email that are used to measure how many people are visiting the page, for advertising and integration into social media, and to allow user interaction onto a webpage such as live chat and embedded comments. Over 2000 of the 6000 top websites have more than 10 trackers per page. It is no surprise to find that Google and Facebook have the highest proportion of tracker market share. Google trackers are present on 81% of all web traffic, whilst 27% of the web uses a hidden Facebook tracking pixel. Fig. 4 shows the market share of trackers (whotracks.me, 2019).

2.2 Ad bidding technology

Technology has progressed massively over the past few years, with businesses (aided by Data Brokers) being able to send targeted adverts based on the user's location, likes, preferences, browsing history, etc. Tracking from these data points can be from Facebook like buttons and embedded YouTube videos and the normal tracking cookies. A lot of advertising is based on a real-time online auction where when a person visits a website, metadata containing key information about the user gets sent to the bidding platform with the highest bidding advertiser wins the right to send the advert to the individual. Google has become the market leader in the work of digital advertising, making over $73.8 billion in advertisement sales in 2017 which amounts to 33% of the worlds $223.7 billion in digital advertisement revenue. Facebook came a very distant second earning $36 billion in the same year.

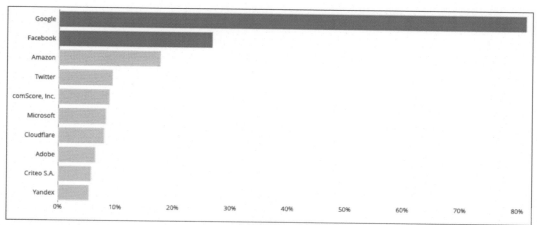

FIG. 4 Tracker market share.

2.3 Behavioural advertising

Behavioural advertising is where an individual is tracked constantly and adverts are delivered to the user, based on their web browsing history, web searches, and general online behaviour. This is where many people will start to see adverts for similar items on their Facebook page to items recently searched for. This has become so sophisticated that the mParticle (mParticle, 2019) platform has the ability to tell if a consumer has recently removed an item from their online shopping cart—this is where they could target the user with ads to 'persuade' them to buy the recently removed product. Having the ability to see if someone has searched other websites for the same product is really important as pricing may need to be adjusted to win the person's business. Moreover the ability to determine the consumer's occupation, income, brand preferences, and interests makes the online store the preferred choice when it comes to what the consumer should pay for a product. Privacy scholar and Harvard Law Professor, Frederik Borgesius, has called for a new regulatory approach for behavioural targeting, describing quite alarmingly how it is possible to single out individuals without actually knowing their names by using relatively simple identification methods including cookies and unique machine codes (Borgesius, 2016).

2.4 Internet of Things and smart devices

The Internet-of-Things (IoT) devices are becoming more mainstream, and although there are benefits in these devices including home automation, there are huge privacy risks around IoT as quite often vast amounts of personal information are sent unencrypted over the Internet to multiple domains. Protecting consumers' privacy is becoming more difficult with the amount and different types of devices connected. Due to the connectivity and lack of security, these devices are vulnerable to the same cyberattacks that the computers used by businesses are today. Many devices are infected with malware such as the Mirai botnet that can be used for distributed denial-of-service (DDoS) attacks to disrupt large businesses and governments. There have been cases where smart devices are becoming a critical aspect of criminal investigations such as where a man's Fitbit location didn't match his alibi when police interviewed him about the murder of his wife (Lartey, 2017). Similarly, police in Arkansas obtained a search warrant for an Amazon Echo as part of a murder enquiry but didn't get the information they wanted; they did however interrogate the smart water metre in the house and discovered that the accused had used 140 gallons of water between 1 am and 3 am which was believed to be used by a garden hose to remove blood from the patio (Roberts, 2016). Amazon Alexa personal assistant devices are one of the most popular 'smart' devices with over 100 million sold worldwide. These devices are always on waiting for instructions for a variety of tasks such as playing music and asking for the weather forecast. Alexa actively listens to and records conversations and then sends them to Amazon servers where they are stored to provide a more 'personalised service'. Many people find adverts for products whilst web browsing soon after these items have been mentioned when Alexa is 'listening' in the same room. Many people now have Internet-connected televisions and over-the-top (OTT) streaming devices such as Roku TV, Apple TV, and Amazon Fire TV that streams content via apps. Moghaddam Hooman performed analysis on these devices and highlighted widespread user tracking and data collection. Eighty-nine percent of Amazon Fire TV channels reported back to known tracking domains and collected data which included video title, SSID details, MAC address, serial number of the streaming device, and the email address and password of the registered owner. It was also discovered that when the researcher selected 'limit ad tracking' in the RokuTV preferences, there was no difference in the amount and type of data that is reported back to the tracking domains (Hooman et al., 2018). Nest was acquired by Google in 2014 and has a range of smart home devices including thermostats, CCTV cameras, doorbells, alarms, locks, and smoke alarms. Harvard Business School Professor Shoshana Zuboff found that for the purchase of just one Nest thermostat, a review of nearly a thousand contracts would be needed. Should the customer not agree to Nest's terms of service, then the thermostat would be deeply compromised (Zuboff, 2019). This really tells us that not many people actually read the terms of service for products.

3 Location tracking

The UK-based security business Pen Test Partners recently discovered a bug in the dating app 3Fun where the app exposed the near real-time location of all its 1.5 million subscribers and personally identifiable data such as date of birth, sexual preferences, private pictures, and their chat data even when privacy was set to high (Lomas, 2019). Fig. 5 shows the location of some users in the United Kingdom and the individual user's location down to a building level.

Augmented reality app Pokémon Go became a hit all over the world in 2016; millions of people downloaded the app and were unaware that when installing it, they gave developers Niantic full access to the users' Google account and permission to collect detailed

FIG. 5 Location map tracking.

location history. This means that Niantic had full access to the user's email's and Google drive documents. The developers also gave permission for third parties to conduct 'research, analysis, and demographic profiling'. Many developers do this, but due to the nature of the game and by its popularity all over the world, it was considered 'one of, if not the most, detailed location-based social graphs ever compiled' (Bernstein, 2016).

Google began the controversial Street View project in 2007. Privacy concerns were raised by the public regarding images being uploaded to Google Maps. It turns out that Google were also collecting Wi-Fi data such as details of the SSIDs (Wi-Fi network names) and MAC address (unique serial numbers) of Internet routers and making it available to third parties (Google, 2010a,b). Upon investigation by consulting firm Stroz Friedberg, Google also admitted to intercepting and storing data from homes and businesses' Wi-Fi transmissions including emails and passwords (Google, 2010a,b). Eighteen months later, Google still hadn't deleted the 600 gigabytes of data it had stolen whilst filming for Street View.

3.1 Social Wi-Fi

Many retail and hospitality outlets offer free Wi-Fi to their visitors. Often when authenticating onto the Wi-Fi, the visitor will be prompted to enter personal information (which is then used for marketing purposes). Recently, there has been a trend in incorporating 'Social Wi-Fi' services such as Purple where a user can simply log in using their social media credentials; this allows for the harvesting of the individuals data. Generally, older people may not have social media accounts but are happy to give their personal details away but don't give rogue details. Younger people are generally happy to log in using their social media accounts as it is quick and easy to gain access to the Wi-Fi. Once logged in, administrators of the portal will have access to the social media account; be able to see likes, friends, and the individual's photos; and even be able to post onto social media accounts on behalf of the user. If the user had read the terms and conditions that they agreed to when logging in, they would know this, but this serves to highlight the vast disparity between those accepting and those actually reading the terms. The Guardian highlighted this when 22,000 people agreed to perform 1000 hours of community service when not reading the T&Cs when logging into Wi-Fi at certain restaurants recently. Marketers will use the demographics of the Wi-Fi users to 'enhance' their stay at the venue by making subtle changes such as changing background music or adverts on screens more suitable to the clientele in the building. The location features will also show how long a person has spent in a certain area and can send eShots offering discounts or preferential services to the user.

3.2 Smart wearables

Smart wearables and fitness trackers have become hugely popular as consumers like to be able to keep track of their fitness and goals. Fitbit is now considered the second largest market leader in wearables (Ubrani, 2018) behind the Apple Watch, having sold over 50 million fitness and activity trackers that constantly monitor steps taken, distance walked, active minutes, floors climbed, sleep tracking, heart rate monitoring, time tracking, call and text notifications, and food logging. There is also the ability to add social networking connectivity that allows the owner to invite and challenge friends. On setup the user is asked to enter sensitive information such as their body size and weight, birthdate, and gender and has the ability to add custom trackers such as moods, blood pressure, and weight loss goals. What many people don't realise, although the idea of fitness tracking is very good, the likes of Fitbit are sending these very personal data to third parties where it is then traded and made available to businesses like health insurances and medical professionals. According to Fitbit's privacy policy (Fitbit, 2018), they 'may share or sell aggregated, de-identified data, personally identifiable information' to third parties. Many large companies offer staff a free Fitbit as part of a corporate wellness programme; this encourages staff to be more active and can then benefit from financial savings such as discounts on health insurance. UnitedHealthcare offered staff up to $1500 to use the devices as they like many other large corporations self-insure their staff's healthcare (Gurdus, 2017).

There are risks around this that include the following:

- **Data security issues**—Over the past 5 years, there have been many data breaches in health insurance, the most notable being the largest in the US Anthem Blue Cross (Anthem, 2015) where 78.8 million people were affected.
- **Data resale threats**—Activity data, location, and personal information such as gender, weigh, and body type could be sold to third parties.
- **Higher premiums/penalties**—People who fail to achieve their targets/goals could be penalised and have to pay higher health insurance or possibly not get treated by healthcare companies.

At this time of writing, it has been announced that Fitbit is about to be acquired by Google for approximately $2.1billion (Fitbit, 2019). Google have stated that the health and wellness data that are currently owned by Fitbit will not be used for Google adverts, but time will only tell with this (Austin, 2019). It must be noted that Google will have a huge amount of additional personal information such as weight, activity, and sleeping habits to add to the list of information they already have on users. StickK, a US-based company that sells white-label software for corporate wellness programmes, encourages punishing users if they don't hit their daily exercise goals or if they smoke or drink too much. Currently, many employers will add a $50 surcharge onto insurance premiums for people who smoke (Olson, 2014). Nudge is a free app that aggregates the fitness data collected from wearables and gives the user an overall health score—insurance companies could use these data when considering premiums. The founders of Nudge have talked to healthcare companies with the aim to make this data available to general practitioners (Olson, 2014).

4 Data leakage

Boyles discovered that '54% of users decided not to install an app onto their phone when they discovered how much PII was required and that 30% of the users deleted the said app when they realised it was collecting PII data' (Boyles et al., 2012).

Barth recently tested the privacy paradox which is the discrepancy between a person's attitude towards privacy and their actual behaviour and highlighted the fact that even for people with a 'higher technical understanding' and had significant awareness around privacy, people still thought that 'privacy aspects did not play a significant role; functionality, app design, and costs appeared to outweigh privacy concerns' (Barth et al., 2019).

Wang discusses data leakage in mobile apps (Wang et al., 2019), and the data leaked normally includes details of location, app usage, call details, and contacts. Due to the size of storage on modern mobile devices, people don't remove apps and therefore have a huge amount of data leaked. The average number of apps installed on smartphones is 80 (Smith, 2019), yet only use on average nine apps on a daily basis (Perez, 2017a,b). Even when apps are unused, they still leak data to third parties. Investigation into how much data are leaked can show some well-known android apps had permissions and trackers that shouldn't be needed.

4.1 Data breaches

The risk around data breach has grown exponentially over the recent years and presents additional issues over the fact that an organisation is breached and extent of PII that goes missing is largely unknown as to what impacts are for individuals.

4.1.1 British Airways
British Airways has been in the press recently due to high-profile data breaches; their app that has had well over 1 million downloads has six trackers built in (Exodus, 2019a,b,c), see Fig. 6.

4.1.2 Spotify
Well-known music streaming service Spotify app has been downloaded over 100 million times and has 12 trackers built in (Exodus, 2019a,b,c).

Leading music streaming service Spotify sells its users data and shares their location, listening preferences and insights on the listeners mood (based on their choice of music) to the advertising giant WPP who has data on over 100 million Spotify users (Newswire, 2019). Fig. 7 indicates Spotify and its practices.

FIG. 6 British Airways trackers.

FIG. 7 Spotify analysing data preferences.

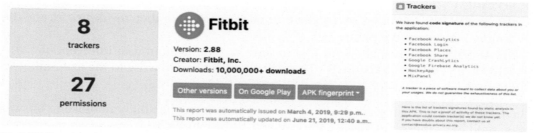

FIG. 8 Fitbit and trackers and permissions.

4.1.3 Fitbit

The latest Fitbit app (version 2.88) has been downloaded over 10 million times and has 8 trackers and 27 permissions in Fig. 8 (Exodus, 2019a,b,c).

4.1.4 3Fun

Analysis of the 3Fun app shows 8 trackers and 17 permissions as in Fig. 9.

> **ACCESS_COARSE_LOCATION**—This will locate you based on mobile cell towers and Wi-Fi networks.
>
> **ACCESS_FINE_LOCATION**—This will locate you based on mobile cell towers, Wi-Fi networks, and GPS.
>
> **ANSWER_PHONE_CALLS**—This will allow the app to answer calls made to your phone.
>
> **CALL_PHONE**—This will allow the app to make calls without user intervention.
>
> **CAMERA**—This will allow the app to take photos or videos at any.
>
> **timeGET_ACCOUNTS**—This allows the app to get any accounts on the phone (includes other app accounts).
>
> **READ_CALL_LOG**—This allows the app to read your call history.
>
> **READ_CONTACTS**—This allows the app to access your contacts and the frequency you call/email/text them.

FIG. 9 3Fun trackers and permissions.

> **READ_EXTERNAL_STORAGE**—This allows the app to read the contents of the external SD card.
> **READ_PHONE_STATE**—This can determine the phone number, the device id, and the remote number of the phone call.
> **SEND_SMS**—This will allow the app to send an SMS without user intervention
> **WRITE_EXTERNAL_STORAGE**—This will allow the app to write to the external SD card.

There indicates no reason for many of these apps to have the ability to make or answer calls, send SMS messages, access the camera, record audio, read and write to external SD cards, read call history, or access to the phone's contacts. This is a massive invasion of privacy that many people do not know about. A real-life example of this invasion of privacy is highlighted in a report from The Superior Court of California against Facebook and shows the extent to which they collect data as Facebook admitted analysing call log data such as duration and frequency of mobile calls and texts which was then be used as Facebook friend suggestions. They also admitted that they were working with manufacturers such as Cisco to identify users whose devices were detected by in-store Wi-Fi and also collecting user data to create 'lookalike audiences' identifying similarities in individuals for the purpose of targeted advertising (County of San Mateo, 2019).

4.2 Browser incognito mode

Many people think that by selecting 'incognito mode' in their web browser, they are not tracked, and their web browsing is hidden. Maris et al. (2019) investigated data leakage and tracking whilst visiting porn websites. Their investigation shows that 30% of all Internet traffic is pornography and that porn websites 'get more visitors each month than Netflix, Amazon, and Twitter combined'. Their stats showed that '93% of pages leak user data to third parties and to an average of seven different domains'. Most alarmingly, only 17% of the websites are encrypted so are very susceptible to credential stealing (Maris et al., 2019). The recent Ashley Maddison data breach of over 30 million logins to the extramarital affair website resulted in suicides (CBC News, 2015), divorces (Griffiths, 2016), sextortions (Krebs, 2015a,b), and the exposure of numerous high-profile names (McCarthy,

2015). Researchers have proven that despite putting a web browser into incognito mode, large companies like Facebook and Google still track activity and that data brokers will add this content to the already very large profile they have on consumers. As these data are sexual data, it is particularly sensitive, which users would prefer to keep private. Data brokers will update profiles with sexual interests, sexual orientation, etc. that could well have a detrimental effect on the individual if these interests are deemed to be abnormal. The knock-on effect to the consumer could be an increase in life insurance premiums or difficulty in applying for certain jobs. These many repercussions of data profiling and other are starting to become more known, and potential behavioural changes are taking place to avoid this type of data exposure, but very likely too late to make an impact to stop this misuse.

5 Conclusion

The review elucidates the process of data brokerage and gives examples of how these issues manifest in real life the impacts to individuals and highlights the major concerns over data profiling and its misuse by third-party organisations. These processes take advantage of inherent flaws in both application and emerging technologies completely unbeknown to the affected users. The size and scale of the industry not only are clear but also highlight the possible security implications that arise upon a breach of a data broker. Once the breach takes place, the data belonging to the individuals enter a different cycle and series of impacts that the individual may not have knowledge that they are now at risk from criminal behaviours or other.

Many people think that adverts appear between applications due to cookies being on the same PC. The concerning thing is that such sensitive personal information will be given to third parties. This reaches into a very personal space that individuals believe to be secure in, but, for example, just this open knowledge that a user had been struggling with addiction could cause many problems when applying for employment or other life-changing events, such as applying for a mortgage. The individual would not have been aware of the third-party access to such profiling data. It's clear a consumer's privacy is compromised on a daily basis and by some of the largest organisations in the world, all of which happens mostly unbeknown to the individuals. Many consumers would not have thought that purchasing a Fitbit to maintain healthy lifestyles actually can increase health and life insurance premiums due to not hitting set goals. Or these devices were given free by their employers but as a way of monitoring who could be a risk. It's also been explained how data brokers work and identify the categories of marketing, credit/fraud prevention, and people search and details the whole concept of tracking and targeted adverts and how these adverts have now become part of a real-time bidding war.

With many consumers bringing IoT devices into their home to make their homes smart/efficient or their lives easier, it distinguishes how many common household devices such as Amazon Alexa or a TV Firestick will pass on huge amounts of personal information to third parties. It is further complicated by many of the vendors making the T&Cs convoluted and complex that many consumers don't actually read them or have choice in rejecting since then that can deny using some or all of the services. Data leakage by well-known smart device apps is another worrying factor, where location and access to camera, storage, and contacts and the ability to make calls and send SMS messages are permissioned by default, again, mostly without many people knowing. Large businesses like Spotify sell their subscribers' data (as well as their location) which gives an insight into the user's mood based on their choice of music, time of day, and location. Based on the fact that there are over 100 million Spotify subscribers, this is a huge amount of data being freely reused!

Likely, one of the most controversial points that this chapter highlights are regarding the Cambridge Analytica scandal. It demonstrated the power of data brokers which alerted many consumers/individuals on raising awareness of the situation, their personal permissions and if they are secure or open to all, etc. Major world changing events have been influenced by political microtargeting of individuals as seen by Cambridge Analytica's involvement in a number of global events. Although Cambridge Analytica is no longer trading, there are many similar businesses out there conducting equivalent services and influencing equally important events but have yet to be exposed. The question mark is since so much data already have been profiled and extent of data known on vast number of consumers, on whether changing habits can make any impact to the individual now. Targeted adverts could even be used for the radicalisation of vulnerable people and if businesses such as Cambridge Analytica have the ability to change one's opinion of politics or marketing companies can make purchase of an item that a consumer hadn't set as an intention of wanting or idea to need it. It goes further to comment what's to stop terrorist groups radicalising people using the same techniques? This is potentially a threat to democracy and its foundations of free and easy access to media and data.

Social Wi-Fi also is flagged as a concern since it can be given a quick and easy way to sign into a store's guest Wi-Fi by a single click, which signs in using an individual's social media account. Although simple for the individual, there is a massive amount of personal data that is given to the store and permissions allowed. The administrators have the ability to track the individual around the store and calculate how long they spend in certain areas. They can also send targeted adverts based on their age/gender/likes/time spent in store or even the number of visits made to the store. The store also has access to the web browsing history whilst the user is on the Wi-Fi so can tell if they are performing pricing comparisons with other stores. Data leakage from smart device apps and how they leak data to third parties by default can show how many trackers are in place and some 'dangerous' permissions such as accessing the users location, contacts, and storage and being able to make calls and send SMS messages on behalf of the user. It is likely a consumer is not aware of the extent of this data leakage and most would not be comfortable knowing this takes place.

In 1890 Warren and Brandeis published 'The Right to Privacy' in the Harvard Law Review, which suggests that everybody has the 'right to be alone' and that it should be protected by law (Brandeis and Warren, 1890). Circa over 100 years later, this is still a topic of consideration! Although there have been some regional attempts such as the California Consumer Privacy Act of 2018, this really needs to be achieved on a more global regulatory framework to protect individuals' data. This framework could be expanded to include an automatic obligation to inform the relevant authorities with their jurisdiction to potential terrorist threats to domestic or international security. The problem is that it is a huge task to regulate and that there are so many 'unknowns' in this rather secretive world. There is also the fact that it is such a lucrative industry and that the largest businesses in the world are all involved, making it a much more difficult task. The fact that the introduction of the European General Data Protection Regulation (GDPR) hasn't made any difference to the industry proves that it's a very difficult area to regulate. Moreover, frameworks such as GDPR fail to tackle these issues as they are regional by nature, and, as stated earlier, a uniform global framework is required to tackle such a multijurisdictional issue. This would be a very interesting further research consideration and setup of global working groups to figure out and take forwards as a global-type framework.

References

Acxiom, 2019a. (Online). Available at: https://www.acxiom.com/wp-content/uploads/2013/09/Acxiom-Marketing-Products.pdf. (Accessed 2 July 2019).

Acxiom, 2019b. Databundles. (Online). Available at: https://developer.myacxiom.com/code/api/data-bundles/bundle/eTechDemographics. (Accessed 2 July 2019).

Anthem, 2015. Statement Regarding Cyber Attack Against Anthem. (Online) Available at: https://www.anthem.com/press/wisconsin/statement-regarding-cyber-attack-against-anthem/. (Accessed 2 July 2019).

Austin, P., 2019. The Real Reason Google is Buying Fitbit. (Online). Available at: https://time.com/5717726/google-fitbit/. (Accessed 12 November 2019).

Barth, S., De Jong, M., Hartel, P., Roppelt, J.C., 2019. Putting the privacy paradox to the test: online privacy and security behaviors among users with technical knowledge, privacy awareness, and financial resources. Telematics Inform, 55–69.

Bernstein, J., 2016. You Should Probably Check Your Pokemon Go Privacy Settings. (Online). Available at: https://www.buzzfeednews.com/article/josephbernstein/heres-all-the-data-pokemon-go-is-collecting-from-your-phone#.coYLRY2EZ. (Accessed 1 October 2019).

Bloomberg, 2017. Equifax Suffered a Hack Almost Five Months Earlier Than the Date It Disclosed. (Online). Available at: https://www.bloomberg.com/news/articles/2017-09-18/equifax-is-said-to-suffer-a-hack-earlier-than-the-date-disclosed. (Accessed 14 August 2019).

Borgesius, F., 2016. Singling out people without knowing their names—behavioural targeting, pseudonymous data, and the new Data Protection Regulation. Comput. Law Secur. Rev. 256–271 (Accessed 14 August 2019).

Boyles, J.L., Smith, A., Madden, M., 2012. (Online). Available at: https://www.pewinternet.org/2012/09/05/privacy-and-data-management-on-mobile-devices/. (Accessed 14 August 2019).

Brandeis, L.D., Warren, D.S., 1890. The right to privacy. Harv. Law Rev. 4(5).

CBC News, 2015. Ashley Madison Hack: 2 Unconfirmed Suicides Linked to Breach, Toronto Police Say. (Online). Available at: https://www.cbc.ca/news/canada/toronto/ashley-madison-hack-2-unconfirmed-suicides-linked-to-breach-toronto-police-say-1.3201432. (Accessed 13 August 2019).

Christl, W., Spiekerman, S., 2016. Networks of Control, first ed. Facultas, Wien.

County of San Mateo, 2019 (Accessed 14 August 2019).

Datareum, 2018. Datareum ICO Review. (Online). Available at: https://icoinrating.com/datareum/. (Accessed 15 October 2019).

DCMS, 2018. Disinformation and Fake News. House of Commons Digital, Culture, Media and Sport Committee, London.

Dixon, P., 2013. What Information Do Data Brokers Have on Consumers, and How Do They Use It? s.l., World Privacy Forum, pp. 7–13.

DMDatabases, 2019. Mailing Lists, Email Lists, Telemarketing Lists. (Online). Available at: https://dmdatabases.com/databases/.

Exodus, 2019a. Exodus. (Online). Available at: https://reports.exodus-privacy.eu.org/en/reports/63421/. (Accessed 2 July 2019).

Exodus, 2019b. Exodus. (Online). Available at: https://reports.exodus-privacy.eu.org/en/reports/3629/. (Accessed 14 August 2019).

Exodus, 2019c. Exodus. (Online). Available at: https://reports.exodus-privacy.eu.org/en/reports/3310/. (Accessed 14 August 2019).

Fitbit, I., 2018. Fitbit Legal—Privacy Policy. (Online). Available at: https://www.fitbit.com/legal/privacy-policy. (Accessed 2 July 2019).

Fitbit, 2019. Fitbit to be Acquired by Google. (Online). Available at: https://investor.fitbit.com/press/press-releases/press-release-details/2019/Fitbit-to-Be-Acquired-by-Google/default.aspx. (Accessed 12 November 2019).

Google, 2010a. (Online). Available at: http://googlepolicyeurope.blogspot.com/2010/04/data-collected-by-google-cars.html. (Accessed 1 October 2019).

Google, 2010b. (Online). Available at: http://googleblog.blogspot.com/2010/05/wifi-data-collection-update.html. (Accessed 1 October 2019).

Grauer, Y., 2018. What Are 'Data Brokers,' and Why Are They Scooping Up Information About You?. (Online). Available at: https://www.vice.com/en_us/article/bjpx3w/what-are-data-brokers-and-how-to-stop-my-private-data-collection. (Accessed 13 August 2019).

Griffiths, J., 2016. The Ashley Madison Hack's Deadly Aftermath. (Online). Available at: https://nypost.com/2016/09/01/the-ashley-madison-hacks-deadly-aftermath/. (Accessed 13 August 2019).

Grogan, K., 2018. The Dark Side of Our Personal Marketing Data. TEDx, Seattle.

Gurdus, L., 2017. UnitedHealthcare and Fitbit to Pay Users Up to $1,500 to Use Devices. (Online). Available at: https://www.cnbc.com/2017/01/05/unitedhealthcare-and-fitbit-to-pay-users-up-to-1500-to-use-devices.html. (Accessed 2 July 2019).

Hodson, H., 2016. Revealed: Google AI Has Access to Huge Haul of NHS Patient Data Read More. (Online). Available at: https://www.newscientist.com/article/2086454-revealed-google-ai-has-access-to-huge-haul-of-nhs-patient-data/. (Accessed 13 August 2019).

Hooman, M.M., et al., 2018. Watching You Watch: The Tracking Ecosystem of Over-the-TopTV Streaming Devices. University of Chicago, Chicago.

Kaplan, P., 2015. FTC Issues Follow-Up Study on Credit Report Accuracy. (Online). Available at: https://www.ftc.gov/news-events/press-releases/2015/01/ftc-issues-follow-study-credit-report-accuracy. (Accessed 13 August 2019).

Krebs, B., 2015a. (Online). Available at: https://krebsonsecurity.com/2015/03/feds-indict-three-in-2011-epsilon-hack/. (Accessed 14 August 2019).

Krebs, B., 2015b. (Online). Available at: https://krebsonsecurity.com/2015/08/extortionists-target-ashley-madison-users/. (Accessed 13 August 2019).

Lartey, J., 2017. The Guardian. (Online). Available at: https://www.theguardian.com/technology/2017/apr/25/fitbit-data-murder-suspect-richard-dabate. (Accessed 29 September 2019).

Leyden, J., 2007. LexisNexis Hacker Jailed and Fined. (Online). Available at: https://www.theregister.co.uk/2007/03/08/lexis_nexis_hacker_jailed/. (Accessed 14 August 2019).

Lomas, A., 2019. Group Sex App Leaks Locations, Pics and Personal Details. Identifies Users in White House and *Supreme Court*. (Online). Available at: https://www.pentestpartners.com/security-blog/group-sex-app-leaks-locations-pictures-and-other-personal-details-identifies-users-in-white-house-and-supreme-court/. (Accessed 14 August 2019).

Lucker, J., Hogan, S.K., Bischoff, T., 2017. Predictably Inaccurate—The Prevalence and Perils of Bad Big Data. (Online). Available at: https://www2.deloitte.com/content/dam/insights/us/articles/3924_Predictably-inaccurate/DUP_Predictably-inaccurate-reprint.pdf. (Accessed 14 August 2019).

Maris, E., Libert, T., Henrichsen, J., 2019. Tracking Sex: The Implications of Widespread Sexual Dataleakage and Tracking on Porn Websites. Cornell University, New York.

McCarthy, T., 2015. Ashley Madison Hack Update: All the High Profile, Celebrity Names Attached to the Private Information Leak From the Cheating Website. (Online). Available at: https://www.ibtimes.com/ashley-madison-hack-update-all-high-profile-celebrity-names-attached-private-2066211. (Accessed 13 August 2019).

mParticle, 2019. mParticle. (Online). Available at: https://docs.mparticle.com/#selecting-data-criteria. (Accessed 13 August 2019).

Newswire, P., 2019. WPP's Data Alliance and Spotify Announce Global Data Partnership. (Online). Available at: https://www.prnewswire.com/news-releases/wpps-data-alliance-and-spotify-announce-global-data-partnership-300362733.html. (Accessed 13 August 2019).

Olson, P., 2014. Wearable Tech Is Plugging into Health Insurance. (Online). Available at: https://www.forbes.com/sites/parmyolson/2014/06/19/wearable-tech-health-insurance/#3fc9aa8c18bd. (Accessed 2 July 2019).

Oracle, 2019. Oracle 2019 Data Directory. (Online). Available at: http://www.oracle.com/us/solutions/cloud/data-directory-2810741.pdf. (Accessed 13 August 2019).

Perez, S., 2017a. Report: Smartphone Owners Are Using 9 Apps per Day, 30 per Month. (Online). Available at: https://techcrunch.com/2017/05/04/report-smartphone-owners-are-using-9-apps-per-day-30-per-month/. (Accessed 14 August 2019).

Perez, S., 2017b. Report: Smartphone Owners Are Using 9 Apps per Day, 30 per Month. (Online). Available at: https://techcrunch.com/2017/05/04/report-smartphone-owners-are-using-9-apps-per-day-30-per-month/. (Accessed 29 September 2019).

Pettypiece, S., 2014. Hospitals Are Mining Patients' Credit Card Data to Predict Who Will Get Sick. (Online). Available at: https://www.bloomberg.com/news/articles/2014-07-03/hospitals-are-mining-patients-credit-card-data-to-predict-who-will-get-sick. (Accessed 13 August 2019).

Rieke, A., Yu, H., Robinson, D., Von Hoboken, J., 2016a. Data Brokers in an Open Society. Open Society Foundations, London. (Online). Available at: https://www.opensocietyfoundations.org/uploads/42d529c7-a351-412e-a065-53770cf1d35e/data-brokers-in-an-open-society-20161121.pdf. (Accessed 1 October 2019).

Rieke, A., Yu, H., Robinson, D., Von Hoboken, J., 2016b. Data Brokers in an Open Society. (Online). Available at: https://www.opensocietyfoundations.org/uploads/42d529c7-a351-412e-a065-53770cf1d35e/data-brokers-in-an-open-society-20161121.pdf. (Accessed 7 November 2019).

Roberts, J.J., 2016. Police Ask for Amazon Echo to Help Solve a Murder. (Online). Available at: https://fortune.com/2016/12/27/amazon-echo-murder/. (Accessed 29 September 2019).

Room, T., 2019. The Washington Post. (Online). Available at: https://www.washingtonpost.com/technology/2019/09/30/unconstitutional-unlawful-unsupported-how-facebook-initially-tried-fight-multi-billion-dollar-us-fine/. (Accessed 1 October 2019).

Smith, C., 2019. 140 Amazing Smartphone Statistics and Facts (2019). (Online). Available at: https://expandedramblings.com/index.php/smartphone-statistics/. (Accessed 14 August 2019).

Ubrani, J., 2018. Global Wearables Market Grows 7.7% in 4Q2017. (Online). Available at: https://www.idc.com/getdoc.jsp?containerId=prUS43598218. (Accessed 3 July 2019).

Wang, Y., Chen, Y., Ye, F., Liu, H., 2019. Implications of smartphones user privacy leakage from the advertiser. Pervasive Mob. Comput. 53, 13–32.

WebFX, 2018. What Are Data Brokers. (Online). Available at: https://www.webfx.com/blog/general/what-are-data-brokers-and-what-is-your-data-worth-infographic/. (Accessed 15 October 2019).

whotracks.me, 2019. Bringing Transparency to Online Tracking. (Online). Available at: https://whotracks.me/. (Accessed 29 September 2019).

Wu, Y., Kosinski, M., Stillwell, D., 2015. Computer-Based Personality Judgments Are More Accurate Than Those Made by Humans. California, PNAS, pp. 1036–1040.

Wylie, C., 2019. Mindf*ck—Inside Cambridge Analytica's Plot to Break the World, first ed. Profile Books, London.

Zuboff, S., 2019. The Age of Surveillance Capitalism. Profile Books, New York.

18

Value of data as a currency and a marketing tool

Sumesh Dadwal, Anwar Haq, Arshad Jamal, and Imad Nawaz

NORTHUMBRIA UNIVERSITY, LONDON, UNITED KINGDOM

1 Introduction

Currency is a medium of exchange that helps us create and exchange economic value across geography and through time. Data has each of these essential characteristics, and already many business transactions involve buying and selling data. So data is a currency. Data is now so useful that it is arguably one of the most valuable assets that a business owns. Globally, during the last decade the top 10 companies in terms of market offered products and services. Today, 50% of the top 10 companies are data-based platforms such as Google, Facebook, Alibaba, and Tencent. This is a fundamental shift in terms of the way the market views the value of data.

Consumers, businesses, and devices (the Internet of Things) create a huge amount of direct data as well as data exhaust, which has latent value. Business organisations harness that Big Data to create and offer value prepositions to their customers and clients. Due to such latent value in data, data is valuable to everyone and is considered an asset. Businesses want to capitalise on Big Data as an asset. Hence, data can be seen as a cashable asset or as a currency.

Data currency is a monetary value assigned to data to identify its financial significance to an organisation, as it can be used as the unit of exchange in a transaction, either as the sole payment or in combination with money.

In a 2013 report, Deloitte argued for data as the new currency and argued for the role that government will—or should—play in establishing data as a currency. The purpose of marketing is to segment the market, target the right customer, and provide specific solutions to customer needs at the right place and right price with effective promotion. All that requires information about consumers and markets. That information lies in the collection of data. Marketers' most common fear about General Data Protection Regulation (GDPR) is their decreased ability to target consumers.

Data-driven marketing (DDM) is at the top of mind for marketers. So, an organisation can be a winner or loser depending upon their access to and use of this 'new oil'. The detected digital transformation has changed the way marketing is executed effectively. The markets need to learn and apply the use of Big Data to develop customer insights. According to Forrester Research in United States, spending on marketing

Strategy, Leadership, and AI in the Cyber Ecosystem. https://doi.org/10.1016/B978-0-12-821442-8.00017-3
© 2021 Elsevier Inc. All rights reserved.

technology, automation in marketing, and services is forecast to increase from $96 billion in 2018 to more than $122 billion by 2022. Consumers assign their data currency value in the form of digital identity and are happy to exchange for money or a customised solution.

2 Concept of data and concept of currency

Data is raw, unorganised facts that need to be processed, organised, structured, and presented in a summary that makes some logical sense of patterns inside the data. The DIKW Pyramid (Data-Information-Knowledge-Wisdom) describes the significance of data as well as its acquisition, processing, retention, and interpretation (Doyle, 2014). This means that any data has a lot of latent value due to data's ability to be converted into information, knowledge, and wisdom for better decision making.

Currency is a medium of exchange for goods and services. The concept of information is evolved over the years. The concept of currency as a medium of exchange has been evolving with human evolution. Over time, it has evolved from barter systems involving stones, seashells, and precious metals to legal tender, what we call hard currency notes. It is still evolving as promissory notes, game coins, plastic currency (credit/debit cards), and contactless currency, Bitcoin and the idea of currency are still evolving in the form of data as currency. The process of developing the concept of currency as a medium of exchange, something that can be cashed out for goods and services, will continue in the future too. Data is seen as currency because data has almost all the characteristics of a medium of exchange.

The common person considers currencies such as coins and currency notes as some kind of legal tender issued by the central bank of a national government. However, as per Nian and Chuen (2015), several currency alternatives have evolved over the years.

Currency with intrinsic utility: This group of currencies includes precious metals, cigarettes, in Berlin after World War II, prepaid phone cards, value smart cards, etc. (Nian and Chuen, 2015).

Token currencies: Token currencies do not have much intrinsic value but are a form of social contact used at the local level. Some examples of these kind of currencies include British tokens from the 17th to the 19th century; the use of Bristol pounds in the United Kingdom; the Berkshares in Massachusetts; and salt spring dollars in Canada (Nian and Chuen, 2015).

2.1 Centralised digital currency

Such currencies as digital promises are centrally governed by a single entity or organisation, and usually that organisation accepts that currency as a medium of exchange for goods and services. Promises with value in exchange in digital form fall in this category. Examples may include loyalty points from national retailers such as Wal-Mart and Tesco; air miles from airlines; and other loyalty-based rewards from financial or welcome companies. Also, Second Life's Linden Dollar or some online game currencies will fall within this type of system. Usually, transactions are limited to a single organisation (Nian and Chuen, 2015).

2.2 Distributed–Decentralised digital currency

These include those media of exchanges that are decentralised, and such digital currencies can be used as a medium of exchange with many players and organisations in transactions of goods and services. A range of cryptocurrencies such as Bitcoin, Litecoin, Dogecoin, Libra from Facebook, etc., fall in the category of distributed digital currency (Nian and Chuen, 2015). Such currencies can be used as a medium of exchange with users outside the governor of that currency, and their governance is decentralised. There is no legal entity regulating it and thus it falls outside the purview of traditional national government regulations for currency.

2.3 Data as currency

A new digital promise as a medium of exchange, which has distributed governance and considers the inherent value of data as a tangible value. This medium can be used as a medium of exchange or could be cashed in by anyone who has some useful monetisable data. The value of the data as currency lies in its latent value of multiple utilities for stakeholders, with data acting as the new oil of the national commerce and economy due to the private ownership of such data.

3 The utility of data and value as a currency

Money or currency has three functions: a medium of exchange, a store of value, and a unit of account (Krugman, 1984, cited in Ogawa and Muto, 2019). The inherent value of currency lies in its marginal utilities for those three functions. Citing the quantity theory of money by George Watson (1880), Thomas (2018) argued that the value of money as bullion is determined by the value of the coin as a monetary unit, and the value of a coin is determined by the number of coins of precious metals such as gold and silver. Data is a scarce entity and has inherent value like any precious metal due to the inherent utility of data in economic activities. Also, any data can be used as a medium of exchange, store of value, and unit of account. National policymakers use data as the source and basis of national planning and allocation of resources. Businesses use databases to manage their internal and external operations. Every function of managing, be it HRM, operations, finance, or marketing, uses data to plan and effectively execute operations. The marketing department of all organisations is always keenly looking for data collection to use data for effective segmenting, targeting, brand posting, and designing a customised marketing mix of product, price, place, and promotion. Social media organisations such as Facebook, Twitter, Instagram, LinkedIn, etc., not only use customers' data for their purposes, but also with other organisations for effective communications and promotions to targeted customers.

4 Why data is currency?

Various people and national economic policymakers have been calling data the 'new oil' (Knowledge@Wharton, 2019). A Deloitte Report in 2013 (Eggers et al., 2013) argued that data will emerge as an instrument of exchange and the national government might need to play some role in this new form of international currency and its management, valuations, etc. There are multiple reasons for such an argument. Analogous to natural oil that runs transportation, plants, and machinery, in the 21st century data is becoming a key to lubricate the economy and let it run and grow. Data aids in reaching target customers, citizens, and institutions as well as exchanging goods and services. In most industries, the face-to-face exchanges of goods and services with currency are being replaced with online exchanges. Thus, it is making much transportation and face-to-face communication superfluous and useless. Thus, data is the new oil. Further, many underdeveloped economies can grow their economies faster due to modern information technology and communications technologies (ICT). All those systems make use of a lot of data. Data is put into use to run economic models. The national governments can reach and deliver various services to their citizens at the bottom of the pyramid using ICT. Many industries in the services sector such as banking, retail, software services, education, public services, and entertainment are essentially on the upward trend of becoming transportless, faceless, and online. All these service deliveries make use of Big Data. Hence data is the new oil of economies and thus data is the new currency. National infrastructure, big projects, national security infrastructure, national strategic plants in the fields of energy production, transport networks, public utilities and services, and so on all rely on Big Data for their efficient and effective operation. This further implies that data has huge value and as per definitions of currency, anything that has value can be used as a medium of exchange and can be called currency.

At the moment, data is used as a one-sided currency, as it is mostly seen as a value to target consumers or reach citizens by organisations and institutions. However, consumers or citizens do not see much value in their data, and they do not exchange data for any value. However, in the coming future, with the rise of awareness and with issues of data security and privacy, consumers will also start seeing the latent value in their personal data and commence considering data as currency. Further, organisations will differentially see value in the personal data of rich versus poor customers from the point of monetisation models such as marketing and advertisements. However, in the future when organisations realise the value of everyone's personal data, they will possibly start considering each unit of data of equal value. Thus, such behaviour will be very close to our behaviour of treating each unit (£) of currency as equal.

Data left by an individual while they are connected to the Internet is treated as 'data exhaust', analogous to transport vehicle exhaust (Knowledge@Wharton, 2019). The difference is that such exhaust is used positively by the organisation, which collects it by tracking all data exhaust. For example, simply by tracking phone locations, it is possible to guess how close two people have been (distance between their mobiles) and the amount of face-to-face communications they had. On a lighter note, it could be possible to determine whether two people had an affair because their phones were technically too close to each other! So, a lot of data is being thrown off as data exhaust and people are not realising its value and implications. Each individual's online behaviour and geolocation are tracked and stored on a data basis as Big Data. Such data is sold and resold by organisations for various monetisation models. Clearly, data is being used as value and currency.

4.1 Marketing data as an asset

There are many examples where data has become the main driver of effective marketing and business process improvement. Netflix uses consumer data about producers, directors, actors, and shows to develop their future products and shows. The success of 'House of Cards' from Netflix has been attributed to smartly utilising customer data. Similarly, the growth of companies such as Amazon, eBay, Alibaba, Google, YouTube, Facebook, Twitter, etc., has been attributed to their decisions on smartly utilising their customer data for future growth.

Data is currency, as data is being used in research and development and innovations. As organisations track online locations and behaviour and come up with offers and solutions. imagine how Amazon knows what else we will buy when we are purchasing something online via their platforms! Organisations related to search engines (Google) and social media Facebook, Instagram) make money by sending and selling our information or behaviour to other industries in education, banking, retail, tourism, transportation, etc. Everyone makes money by claiming that they know a consumer better and such knowledge will be valuable for other product and service marketers. What is traditionally called screen scraping—everything you saw on your screen, whoever you shared the data with could also see it—is a big challenge. The banking industry has realised the challenges of screen scraping, and how fixed passwords as data exhaust can be captured by online systems and fraudsters, then misused. The banking industry has come up with innovations of generating random passwords (chip and on technology in open banking) instead of fixed usernames and passwords.

5 How organisations are monetising data as currency

A business model is a collection of internal and external decisions imposed by an organisation on its employees for the process of production and exchange of values with its customers to create and sustain competitive advantages (Casadesus-Masanell and Heilbron, 2015). A business model includes *a set of activities* (strategic choices, the value network, creating value, and capturing value); *scopes of business pillars* (need, market technology customer interfaces, and financial aspects); *elements* (core capabilities, value configuration, revenue streams, cost structure, value proposition, customer segments, distribution and communication channels, partnerships, customer relationships); and a *range of actions* (who, what, when, why, how, and how much) (Dadwal et al., 2020). A business model helps firms structure their internal constituents (inbound, operations, R&D, marketing, distributions, services, and customer transactions) as well as external alignments with suppliers, customers, distributors, and other external stakeholders (Dadwal et al., 2020).

Smaller and bigger organisations in the public and private sectors have been developing a range of business models to monetise their Big Data and cash out the value of data as currency. The companies have different business models, for example, Apple, Amazon Netflix, and Pandora have different business models around collecting, analysing , and developing customer insight from Big Data to achieve mutually valuable exchanges (Lokitz, 2018). The organisation asks itself, what data do we have? How can we use this data? How can we sell this data? Lokitz (2018) cites the kind of value proposition-based business models of utilising Big Data as currency. As shown in Fig. 1, the main business models of Big Data are: Data as a Service (DaaS), Information as a Service (IaaS), Answers as a Service (AaaS), Data as Sharing Economy-Based Models (DaaSE), and Data as a Currency (DaaC) (Lokitz, 2018).

1. *Data as a Service (DaaS) model*

In the Data as a Service (DaaS) model, the value proposition is to provide processed Big Data and support mechanisms for clients to create their value proposition of revenue streams for monetising the data of their final customers; see Table 2 (Lokitz, 2018). The clients (business organisations) will use their insights and adventures to mine the processed Big Data to find answers or offer suctions to their customers. As the data, in this case, is only valuable as a minor processing, cleaning, and support mechanism for clients to create other value propositions, so the revenue stream is typically quite a bit lower. Most organisations using this kind of business model also make use of the other two kinds of business models. Examples of such companies include government open data sites such as datasf.org, and commercial vendors such as Google, Gnip, Facebook, and Twitter.

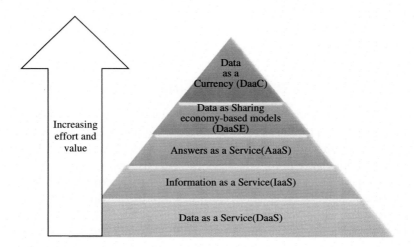

FIG. 1 Different kinds of business models based on Big Data.

2. *Information as a Service (IaaS) model*

The value proposition of this model is to provide information insights based on the analysis of the processed data; see Table 1 (Lokitz, 2018). The targeted clients' job is to come up with their own conclusions or sell an idea based on the information. The clients do not have abilities or resources to analyse the raw data, so the clients are happy to pay for an exchange of analysed data, visuals, and insights (Lokitz, 2018). For example, GIS-based companies such as HERE and TomTom sell their locations and route-related maps to car manufacturing companies. Similarly, companies such as Fitbit can track customer health activities and share the final information with various companies working in healthcare sectors. Facebook and Alphabet/Google use a range of solutions based on the Information as a Service (IaaS) Model, generating $55 billion and $116.3 billion, respectively, from advertising in 2018. In 2018, Amazon generated $123 billion in online sales by collecting, storing, processing, and analysing the personal information of millions of customers (Lokitz, 2019).

3. *Answers as a Service(AaaS) model*

The Answer as a Service business model's value proposition is providing higher-level and specific answers to specific questions or problems. Those specific answers can be directly utilised to make final decisions without the need for any analysis or many interpretations (see Table 1; Lokitz, 2018). As the answers are readymade solutions to customer problems, so such solutions or offerings can trigger instant sales and purchases. For example, Mint, a personal money management app, not only makes specific credit card transaction information to owners of its customers but can also use that customer's information to share with other credit card companies to offer customers better credit card rates.

4. *Data as Sharing Economy-Based Business Models (DaaSE)*

In a sharing economy, 'users share their unused capacities' or untapped resources (e.g. unused capacities, tangible assets, services, money, information, ideas, knowledge) with each other in an on-demand basis (immediately when the need arises). The business models of sharing economy require mutual trust, a sense of giving and sharing, and a motivation for personal and community-based interactions (Dadwal et al., 2020). A sharing economy has enabled customers to turn their physical property into revenue-generating assets through platforms such as Lyft, Airbnb, and Splinter (Lokitz, 2019). The sharing economy allows consumers to access and use the resources completely without having to own or purchase them. A business model of collaborative consumption is based on the distributed networks of connected consumers and communities (as opposed to centralised institutions). Such a distributed system determines how we produce, consume, and learn (Dadwal et al., 2020). The models of the sharing economy use the shared knowledge of communities to develop dynamic capabilities, the organisation's core competencies, and ICT platforms to minimise the transaction costs of the exchange of values. A sharing or

Table 1 Kinds of Big Data-based business models and their element characteristics.

Business model	Key partners	Key activities	Value proposition	Customer targets	Customer relationship	Cost structure	Revenue streams
Data as a Service (DaaS) model	Third-party data sources, online portal service, or publishers	Data processing: aggregation, cleaning, visualisation, marketing, and selling Data expertise and relationship: data, brand, market, niche	Data as a service: clean processed, open, unique, descriptive data	Commercial solution providers and developers	Self-service-online subscription, forum, mail orders, online service	Data processing: visualisation, marketing, sales, website, services, third-party licensing	Free, usage fee, subscriptions
Information as a Service (IaaS) model	Third-party data sources, analytical tools, solution providers	Data analysis and visualisation: aggregation, cleaning, visualisation, marketing, and selling Data analysis expertise and relationship: data, brand, market, niche	Information as a service: make better solutions with accurate, trusted, descriptive, and unique service/ solutions	Commercial solution providers and consumer	Direct contact/ connections: also self-service online community and direct sales in apps online services	Data analysis and visualisation costs: sales, website, services, third-party licensing	Subscription, usage fee, and advertisements
Answers as a Service (AaaS) model	Online platforms, third-party data sources, machine learning and analytical tools, solution providers	Business development and sales: aggregating, cleaning, analysing, and marketing Deep customer insights and market knowledge on brand and products	Answers as a service: valuable offers in no time, contextual presentations, discrete, quality, continents and timely answers and insights	Consumers, third-party advertisers, corporate decision-makers	Direct contact/ connections: also interactive engagement, sales and promotions in apps Online services: direct sales in app service	Marketing and business developments, sales activities, online services, website services, third-party licenses	Advertising, product sales, free and paid value exchanges

Sharing Economy-Based Models (DaaSE)	Platforms, third-party data sources, machine learning and analytical tools, solution providers, banks, clients, customers, and another organisations	Business development and sales based on sharing data: aggregating, cleaning, analysing, and marketing. Deep customer insights and market knowledge on brand and products and exact customer needs, requirements, and orders	Offering shared assets or services based on sharing economy. Valuable offers in no time, contextual presentations, discrete, quality, continents and timely answers and insights and specific products, assets, and services	Clients, banks, asset, product/service providers, customers/users of product or services	Direct contact/connections: also interactive engagement, making sales and promotions in apps. Online services: direct sales or product/services in app service	Marketing and business developments, sales activities, an online offering of products/sales/services, website services, third-party licenses	Sharing of revenue streams among members who exchange assets, products, or services. Product sales, and paid value exchanges and sharing of revenues and profits among platforms, clients, banks, consumers, etc.
Data as a Currency (DaaC) (Lokitz, 2018)	Data aggregators, platforms, third-party data sources, machine learning and analytical tools, solution providers, banks, clients, customers, and other organisations	Business development and sales based on sharing and selling individual's data: aggregating, cleaning, analysing, and marketing. Selling customers data to exact customer needs, requirements, and orders	Offering individual customer data and associated insights to client's ad data-based business model companies	Individual customers as personal data sellers, clients, organisations offering product/service providers, customers/users of product or services	Direct contact/connections: also interactive engagement, making sales and promotions in apps. Online services: offering token/coupons to customers in exchange of data	Customer coupons/token currencies. Data analysis tools, data protection and legality costs. Marketing and business developments, sales activities, an online offering, third-party licenses	Sharing of revenue streams among members, that is, customers, clients, data aggregators, and other organisations that offer products and services. Advertisement and promotions, pay per click, etc.

collaborative economy model is based on the concept of collaborative consumption. This model is somewhat related to traditional systems of bartering, renting, sharing, gigging, trading, and swapping goods/services, but through technology and peer communities. Thus, Data as a Sharing Economy Business Model (Data as a SEBM) may be defined as a strategic process that an organisation uses to create and capture customer value by making use of innovation, technology, online sharing, peer-to-peer sharing, or collaborative consumption to reconstitute organisational internal core competencies, external alignment, and dynamic capabilities, thus achieving sustainable competitive advantages (Dadwal et al., 2020).

5. *Data-as-a-Currency (DAAC) model*

DaaC uses a different multisided platform to offer a value proposition in the form of payments for personal data as currency in the form of digital tokens (Lokitz, 2019). Customers would have more incentive to sign up for new services without spending any hard cash; rather, they would use their data as a cash equivalent (see Table 1).

6 Role of government and public policy in data as currency

The marketplace of data consists of a range of data producers, consumers, and facilitators.

Worldwide national governments are probably the largest producers and users of people's data (Eggers et al., 2013). Also, governments are increasingly playing an important role in regulating the process of data collection, management, privacy, protection, and utilisation. Further, national security agencies have their interests in using so-called private data for national security purposes. Thus, governments are under pressure from different stakeholders to meet the needs of safe data collection, storage, privacy, security, and flow of personal data. Thus, the government's role can be summed up as a data producer, consumer, and facilitator.

The data market has also led other players to participate and play roles as producers, consumers, and facilitators. A range of open data providers is used by national governments and private organisations. There are many data aggregators so, for example, if you have an email address, then aggregator behemoths such as Rapleaf and Acxiom, might know you and your information (Eggers et al., 2013). Data aggregators collect information from public records and consumer transactions along with digital exhaust collected from social media, mobile transmissions, and other sources, thus providing advertisers new insights into target audiences. Customers share their personal information with data for service companies such as Google, Facebook, Yahoo, Twitter, LinkedIn, etc. To help customers with their concerns regarding data protection and privacy, the marketplace now offers data protection products to give individuals control over their personal information. For example, a data locker from Personal.com and other services such as Reputation.com help customers control access to that data and know the flow and utilisation of the data by others.

6.1 Government as data producer

The national government collects data for public policy purposes and that data can be a huge source for other players in the marketplace. In the United States in the initiative Health Arapahoe, the government gave huge amounts of data valued at billions for free to future entrepreneurs (Eggers et al., 2013). The project was managed by CTO, which has been conceded as the nation's 'entrepreneur in chief'. The purpose is to catalyse the development of an entrepreneurial ecosystem—an ecosystem that leverages data to improve health in the United States. The result of such a 'health datapalooza' was multiple entrepreneurial ventures. The result has been that Palantir developed an app that matches patients to clinical trials. The University of Rochester aggregated data from disease incidence and related tweets and developed a map to track the spread of illness. Another app could trace the path of the spread of the salmonella outbreak. Maya Designs developed an app with sources of cheap vegetables (Eggers et al., 2013). Collectively all are trying to improve the US health system. Similar events have focused on GIS (geographic information system), GPS data, energy, and environmental innovation. Energy.datamarket.com is transforming more than 10,000 open energy datasets into useful intelligence for energy companies (Eggers et al., 2013). GIS and GPS data have transformed daily life for many citizens, helping them in natural disasters as well as simplifying travel and saving time, hassles, and energy (Eggers et al., 2013). The governments in different countries such as the United States, Australia, Kenya, the United Kingdom, Denmark, Canada, and India have already signed the Memorandum on Transparency and Open Governments, which will allow the public to access public data through open application programming interfaces (APIs) and use the same for social entrepreneurship.

6.2 Government as data consumer

The government as a player in the public sector collects and uses data in a range of industries and sectors of the national economy. The data is needed in managing public transport, web searches, national IT frameworks, national health systems, demographics, the national census, etc. National governments spend a huge amount of money and time to collect, store, and use citizen data for the effective delivery of public goods and services. Like the other players in the free market (such as credit card companies, banks, Google, Facebook, or some data aggregators) have already got huge data basis of citizens, thus the national government can think about outsourcing data to third parties. Not only will this decrease the burden of cost and timing, but it will release resources for better data analysis and utilisation, Further, such a move will also decrease the costs and liability related to data collection, privacy, security, storage, etc. (Eggers et al., 2013). For example, the US census bureau bus commercial data for address verifications. Police services subscribe to social networking sites such as Facebook and Twitter to monitor online gang activities, track local developments and protests, etc. Similarly, national transport departments have started buying data from TomTom and Google to track and manage traffic and transport networks. The US Department of Health and Human Services has been using data from social network sites or apps to monitor emerging health trends (Eggers et al., 2013). Google Flu and MappyHealth are some examples of social entrepreneurship initiatives in that direction. MappyHealth in the United States analyses groups of 1000 or more tweets on the same topic and in the same area based on keyword matching and location data to predict and monitor disease trends by analysing tweets in real time (Eggers et al., 2013). The useful application of public-private data combinations is huge. For example, by combining census data with data on consumer shopping patterns, one can analyse public health issues such as nutrition and obesity, and then connect the results to other health and social issues such as localised infant mortality rates, school attendance, employee sickness days, or national productivity (Eggers et al., 2013). Some important hurdles could be identifying a unique individual identity number in order to combine such data from different sources and manage the concerns of legality, transparency, privacy, and security.

6.3 Government as facilitator

The third role of the government is to create regulatory parameters for managing data, providing platforms and infrastructure for data exchange, and leading from the front (Eggers et al., 2013). As a regulator, the government can foster an environment that balances the data needs of different stakeholders, respecting the privacy of individual data, promoting national security, and meeting the needs of innovators and organisations using data for commercial or noncommercial purposes. The government develops laws and regulations related to personal data and digital privacy, security, protection, etc. The government also provides platforms to foster thriving data markets. One example is Aadhar, India's Unique Identification (UID) programme that collects and stores biometric and demographic data of every citizen of India (Eggers et al., 2013). The Aadhar data is used by both the private and public sectors in several ways such as issuing a mobile number, owning a bank account, checking credit history, address verifications, national transport toll payments, delivering public sector personal healthcare, financial inclusion, public sector social benefit schemes, social benefits, and subsidy transfers to citizens. The government can also play role in data philanthropy, not only offering their data bases to the public but also persuading private companies to donate their Big Data sets for social good.

Data breaches have been a big issue. For example, in 2018 it was discovered that cyber thieves stole personal data on 500 million customers, including the credit card numbers of 100 million Marriott customers in 2014. This leads to heavy lawsuit costs and the loss brand reputations, such as with Marriott (Lokitz, 2019). Similar data breaches at Facebook involving data analytics have been big media stories that probably affected American elections. As a result of many more such cases and pressure from consumer groups, national governments have come up with legislation such as GDPR (General Data Protection Regulation) and CCPA (California Consumer Privacy Act) in the United States.

7 Data literacy and data value

Data literacy is to extract insights from data and act on them (Knowledge@Wharton, 2019). Data literacy means data user and data producer knowledge, skills, and abilities to understand data, data generation, data exhaust, data privacy and security, data flow, data exchange, data usage, data consumption, and, most importantly, associated value in data. Though the digital literacy of people is increasing, data literacy is still dismally low (Knowledge@Wharton, 2019). Consumers and citizens are creating a huge amount of data voluntarily and involuntarily (data exhaust). Organisations are storing this as Big Data as 'data lakes' without knowing the real worth or mechanisms to develop insights from such data. So for many of them, such data lakes are still data exhaust. The organisations and institutions have to learn the significance and values latent in those data lakes. The citizens and consumers have to learn about the value of their voluntary data as well as about their involuntary data exhaust. The higher the digital data literacy, the more value will be attached to such data.

Data breaches, leakage, frauds, misselling, etc., have been new issues of the modern IT-based economies. Thus, organisations are not only fiduciary stewards for your financial transitions but also for your data transactions and data exhaust. Many lawsuits have been filed by institutions and pressure groups against organisations such as Yahoo, Carphone Warehouse, Facebook, etc., for data breaches. Such data breaches, theft, and frauds have led organisations to hugely invest in data infrastructure. Such a capital investment further increases the value of data, as it has increased the cost of data collection storage and use. So, the issue is not only to limit data sizes, data breaches, and fraud, but also to limit the amount of data exhaust, thus saving the value of data as a valuable currency. Customer data rights and data protection laws such as the Australian Consumer Data Rights law and the European General Data Protection Regulation have focused on ensuring that users know, understand, and consent to the data collected about them and that a person owns their personal data and should be able to access it securely and safely. These laws not only protect individuals against the misuse of data as currency, but also enhance and protect the value of data as a secured currency.

The idea of data stewardship and data fiduciary is still a new concept (Knowledge@Wharton, 2019). Regulators, institutions, and consumer advocacy groups need to work together to enhance the power of the consumers and citizens concerning their personal data and data literacy. This will provide a level playing field for data exchange and data barter. Still, the value of data exchange as a currency is quite unfair and data as a currency is an evolving concept. One has to share huge amounts of personal information on social media to just find a new online friend, see some pictures, or read some ideas. Thus still it is quite unfair, unequal deals of data exchange with another data—in the data barter system. However, as data piracy improves and the concept of data currency evolves further, the exchange value of data will become consistent and uniform, and maybe a universally standardised level playing field among users and providers will become available. Still, many predatory websites continuously scan users who are

Googling for a range of products and services. Such predatory websites than appear on front pages and once the consumer clicks through them, such sites get a huge commission from the sellers for taking consumers to their websites. So ultimately they are making money from consumer data exhaust and without consumer consent to use or share their data. With digital data literacy, the consumer would be able to bargain for such data releases because they would understate the value of data currency and data barter power. As data literacy improves, consumers will also start monetising their personal data by providing or revoking permission to Google or a social media player to use their personal data. Buying things online should be less costly as the customers should get deductions for sharing their data with the product or service providers. The credit card and banking organisations can earn huge dividends by sharing customer data and buying habits with other organisations intending to sell their products and services.

Such consumers can monetise their data in the form of coupons or the like from social media sites or Google or a discount from the seller. This will be the possible starting point of data as currency with a level playing field.

Already, organisations such as BIGtoken have come up with a solution to empower individual customers with their personal data rights. The BIGtoken app uses Blockchain technology to provide transparency and consumer control, where consumers own, manage, verify, and sell their personal data (Lokitz, 2019). The BIGtoken app ensures that the rights of data and the value of data remain in the hands of consumers. This model of agency data as a currency will possibly create a new marketplace in the coming years. For instance, in the future Netflix may work with Facebook to bring users from Facebook to Netflix by enabling customers to pay with 'tokens' garnered from selling their data on BIGtoken (Lokitz, 2019).

8 Models to calculate the monetary value of data as a currency

Data exhibits some unique nature of exchange in value. The normal currency can be exchanged one for one only, that is, one currency note can buy a finite thing at one time only. However, data currency has no such transaction limits. Data currency exhibits a network effect as the data can be used at the same time across multiple uses, thereby increasing its value to the person or organisation who owns the data (Schmarzo and Vantara, 2016). The next sections discuss four models of measuring data value.

8.1 Data value based on data as a goodwill intangible asset

Data has intangible value and could be treated as an intangible asset with values such as 'goodwill' or a 'brand'. In accounting, goodwill is the quantifiable prudent value of an entity over and above the value of its tangible assets (Schmarzo and Vantara, 2016). This prudent value of data as currency can be estimated by knowing how an entity uses data for key business initiatives and decisions to develop and support the overall organisational strategy. The business initiative is the organisational projects that use cross-functional teams to realise SMART objectives, such as to increase market share from 21% to 25% by the end of the year, to disperse customer churn from 50% to 30% within one year, or to increase customer retention. The SMART objectives can be assigned some financial value (sales, margins, profits). Those may not be exact, but could have a range from minimum to maximum value (pessimistic, normal, and optimistic scenarios). Thus such initiatives that use some data to realise organisational objectives can be financially qualified, and thus data as currency can be measured or estimated.

Schmarzo and Vantara (2016) support some steps needed for data currency value estimations, as below:

Step 1: Develop SMART organisational objectives.

Step 2: Convert SMART objectives into some metrics/financial value ranges.

Step 3: Identify individual stage decisions to be taken by different stakeholders and cross-functional departments. The decisions can be in the area of marketing (cosseting, segmentations, promotional effectiveness. targeting, brand loyalty, word of mouth, customer satisfaction, etc.).

Step 4: Quantify the value of individual decisions as rough likely financial value ranges (mean, median mode in pessimistic, normal, and optimistic scenarios) by brainstorming with various stakeholders.

Step 5: Assess value and relative importance/weightage of each data source to support each decision.

Step 6: Aggregate economical value for each data source across all the different business decisions.

8.2 Model of data currency value integration

Another method of estimating data currency value can be a model of data currency value integration. Calculating the value of data as a standard currency value is quite difficult and a multidimensional concept. The total value of data (V_T) depends upon the useful life of the data (Y_i) and on the number of users (N_i) and uses for each organisation (U_i) of that data. In each situation, there will be a number of organisations and institutions (O_i) involved, and each one might assign different monetary value (V_i) to personal data and each organisation would assign a different number of years as the useful data life (Y_i). Mathematically, there can be an infinite number of institutions assigning values ranging from zero to infinite to each data unit and for a time period of years that ranges from zero to infinity. Hence, mathematically the total data value would be equal to the integration of all those variables over a range of zero to infinity:

$$V_T = \int \int \int \int \int_0^\infty V_i \cdot U_i \cdot Y_i \cdot N_i \cdot O_i \cdot dv \cdot du \cdot dy \cdot dn \cdot do$$

8.3 Reverse engineering of market capitalisation model of data as a currency value estimation

One more way to estimate data value is by reverse engineering some successful data company cautions (Walker, 2016). For example, Microsoft acquired LinkedIn at a price of $26.2 billion and some 443 million users, which works out to be a value is $59.14 per user. Similarly, some more examples can be utilised for course value estimations (see Table 2).

Table 2, also illustrates that a user of LinkedIn, Facebook, Twitter, Yahoo, and Google, creates about $93.48 in value from their user data per year.

Table 2 reveals some useful interpretations such as market capitalisation as a portion to several users. However, the relationship is not linear but a polynomial or log-log type, which is analogous to the value of the network effect. The more streams of data usage type, the higher the market caps (e.g., compare Yahoo with Google). The revenue value for most social media or network sites is around $7, yet for Google it is $62.50 per user, that is, almost nine times the other companies.

The average course values are not exact figures, as each user has different values due to user activities, etc. However, this kind of reverse engineering gives a fair way of estimating the value of data currency based on the market capitalisation of the organisations.

8.4 The legality of data as a currency

Any currency is not only a medium of exchange but is also a legal tender of value and that must be owned by parties in an exchange. Thus, any currency must meet certain requirements such as a standardised unit of exchange, legally binding tender, and a unit of measure of economic activity, national income, taxes, etc. There is no doubt that data

Table 2   Market capitulations and market revenue per user.

Market capitalisation, number of users, and per user market cap (2015)	Revenue generated and revenue per user (2015)
LinkedIn: $26.2 B sale price from 443 MM users = $59.14 per user	LinkedIn: $2.99 B from 443 MM users = $6.75 per user in 2015
Facebook: $323 B market cap from 1.65 B users = $195.76 per user	Facebook: $17.93 B from 1.65 B users = $10.85 per user in 2015
Twitter: $11.01 B market cap from 310 MM users = $35.52 per user	Twitter: $2.22 B from 310 MM users = $7.16 per user in 2015
Google: $401 B market cap on 1.2 B searchers = $334.17 per searcher	Google: $75 B from 1.2 B users = $62.50 per user in 2015
Yahoo: $5 B price (recent) offer from 800 MM users = $6.25 per user	Yahoo: $4.98 B from 800 MM users = $6.23 per user in 2015

Source: Walker, R., 2016. What is your data worth? On LinkedIn, Microsoft, and the value of user data. Retrieved 16 February 2020, from KD Nuggets website: https://www.kdnuggets.com/2016/06/walker-linkedin-microsoft-value-user-data.html.

is a new currency. However, there are many logical issues to be addressed before data can become a legal valid tender of international currency. Any national government has to establish systems to value data as a currency unit, validate data as a transaction, bring it in the purview of national tax systems, sort out legal disputes of noncompliance with data as a unit of currency, organisational status and roles of various stakeholders transacting using data as currency, and adjusting monetary and fiscal policies around data as a new currency (Sapovadia, 2015).

9 Conclusion

When converted into information and knowledge, data provides wisdom and value for effective decisions. The future use of automation and artificial intelligence in different spheres of life and economies has raised the value of data, with data being seen as the 'new oil' of business and economies. Data has latent value and hence can be considered an important medium of exchange or barter; so, data is also considered a new currency.

Data currency is a monetary value assigned to data to identify its financial significance to an organisation. It can be considered as currency as it possesses the three essential features of currency: the medium of exchange, the store of value, and the unit of account. The Internet user often releases a lot of data voluntarily and a lot of data exhaust involuntarily. The organisations can make use of both kinds of data for business planning, marketing segmentation, customer targeting, and promotions. The smaller and bigger organisations in the public and private sectors have been developing a range of business models such as Data as a Service (DaaS), Information as a Service (IaaS), Answers as a Service (AaaS), Data as Sharing Economy-Based Models (DaaSE), and Data as a Currency (DaaC) to monetise their Big Data and cash the value of data as currency. The national governments are increasingly playing an important role in regulating the process of data collection, management, privacy, protection, and utilisation. The governments are under pressure from different stakeholders to meet the needs of safe data collection, storage, privacy, security, and the flow of personal data. The issue is how to assign value to data? This chapter has proposed data valuation models such as data as goodwill, data as integrations of values, and data as legal tender. The stakeholders in general and customers in particular need to increase their data literacy to protect and use their data as a currency.

References

Casadesus-Masanell, R., Heilbron, J., 2015. The business model: nature and benefits. Adv. Strateg. Manage. 33, 3–30. https://doi.org/10.1108/S0742-332220150000033002.

Dadwal, S., Jamal, A., Harris, T., Brown, G., Raudhah, S., 2020. Technology and sharing economy-based business models for marketing to connected consumers. In: Dadwal, S. (Ed.), Handbook of Research on Innovations in Technology and Marketing for the Connected Consumer.p. 532. Retrieved from: https://www.igi-global.com/chapter/technology-and-sharing-economy-based-business-models-for-marketing-to-connected-consumers/239497.

Doyle, M., 2014. What Is the Difference Between Data and Information? – Business 2 Community. Retrieved 28 February 2020, from: https://www.business2community.com/strategy/difference-data-information-0967136.

Eggers, W.D., Hamill, R., Ali, A., Hersey, J., 2013. Data as the New Currency Government's Role in Facilitating the Exchange. Retrieved from: https://pdfs.semanticscholar.org/0ce3/553f944710d4dce3dd06eb1bdc2898f1ac66.pdf.

Knowledge@Wharton, 2019. Data as Currency: What Value Are You Getting for It? Retrieved 2 February 2020, from Knowledge@Wharton website: https://knowledge.wharton.upenn.edu/article/barrett-data-as-currency/.

Lokitz, J., 2018. Exploring Big Data Business Models. Business Models Inc. Retrieved 16 February 2020, from: https://www.businessmodelsinc.com/big-data-business-models/.

Lokitz, J., 2019. If Data Is the New Currency, How Might Consumers Have Agency Over Their Value Exchange? Business Models Inc. Retrieved 16 February 2020, from Business Models Inc website: https://www.businessmodelsinc.com/data-is-the-new-currency/.

Nian, L.P., Chuen, D.L.K., 2015. Introduction to bitcoins. In: Chuen, D.L.K. (Ed.), Handbook of Digital Currency: Bitcoin, Innovation, Financial Instruments. Retrieved from: https://books.google.co.uk/books?hl=en&lr=&id=RfWcBAAAQBAJ&oi=fnd&pg=PP1&dq=data+as+a+currency&ots=2MuLPdyfDE&sig=JUukdFTBQBLcKcZqhB4W0RkkEno#v=onepage&q=data as a currency&f=false.

Ogawa, E., Muto, M., 2019. What determines utility of international currencies? J. Risk Financial Manage. 12 (1), 10. https://doi.org/10.3390/jrfm12010010.

Sapovadia, V., 2015. Legal issues in cryptocurrency. In: Chuen, D.L.K. (Ed.), Handbook of Digital Currency: Bitcoin, Innovation, Financial Instruments. Retrieved from: https://books.google.co.uk/books?hl=en&lr=&id=RfWcBAAAQBAJ&oi=fnd&pg=PP1&dq=digital+currency&ots=2MuLPeA9Bz&sig=E0RNOVLirjgztYv7fUs-yTQETvs&redir_esc=y#v=onepage&q=digital currency&f=false.

Schmarzo, W., Vantara, H., 2016. Determining the Economic Value of Data. Retrieved 2 February 2020, from KD Nuggets website: https://www.kdnuggets.com/2016/06/determining-economic-value-data.html.

Thomas, A., 2018. Does the Monetary Unit Determine the Value of Bullion? The Gold Standard Institute International. Retrieved 21 February 2020, from Gold Standard Institute website: https://goldstandardinstitute.net/2019/04/15/monetary-unit-determine-value-bullion/.

Walker, R., 2016. What Is Your Data Worth? On LinkedIn, Microsoft, and the Value of User Data. Retrieved 16 February 2020, from KD Nuggets website: https://www.kdnuggets.com/2016/06/walker-linkedin-microsoft-value-user-data.html.

Index

Note: Page numbers followed by *f* indicate figures, and *t* indicate tables.

A

AaaS. *See* Answers as a Service (AaaS)
Aadhaar, 121–122
ABAC. *See* Attribute-based access control (ABAC)
ACL. *See* Agent communication language (ACL)
Actionable intelligence, 355–356
Activity theory, 288–289, 294
Ad bidding technology, 367
Administrative powers
　common law/prerogative, 151
　express statutory, 150
　implied statutory, 151
　public authorities, 150
　Ram Doctrine, 151
Advertising, 269–270
Agent communication language (ACL), 63
AI. *See* Artificial intelligence (AI)
Aid Transparency Index, 95–96
Android mobiles, 206
Answers as a Service (AaaS), 387
APEC CBPR. *See* Asia Pacific Economic Countries Cross-Border Privacy Rules (APEC CBPR)
API. *See* Application programming interface (API)
APM. *See* Association for Project Management (APM)
Application programming interface (API), 47
ARM. *See* Availability, reliability and maintainability (ARM)
Artificial intelligence (AI)
　brand awareness, 276–278
　definition, 5
　ethics and governance, 11–12
　higher education (HE), 308–309
　human/machine interface, 15
　knowledge representation/language, 6
　machine learning (ML), 6–7
　problem-solving process/search technique, 6
　project management, 13–14
　revolution, 3
　workforce, 8–10
　workplace, 8
Asia Pacific Economic Countries Cross-Border Privacy Rules (APEC CBPR), 113
Association for Project Management (APM), 13–14, 16
Attackers' perspective, 245–249
Attribute-based access control (ABAC), 100
Augmented reality, 322
Authentication, 164
Authentication mechanisms
　IMAP email account, 203
　network protocols, 203
　public certificate authorities (CA), 206
　public key encryption, 206
　reauthenticate wired connections, 204
　session cookies, 203–204
　speech recognition, 204
　text independent and dependent, 204
Availability, reliability and maintainability (ARM), 88

B

Balanced score card (BSC), 344
Baseline password expiration policy, 195
BDA. *See* Big data analytics (BDA)
Behavioural advertising, 368
BeyondCorp, 198
BI. *See* Business intelligence (BI)
Big Data, 3, 7–8, 14, 381, 384, 386, 386*f*, 388–389*t*

Big data analytics (BDA), 340, 344–346, 345*f*, 351–354, 352–353*t*, 356
Biometric authentication, 161
Biometrics, 323–325, 323*t*, 334
Biometric threat landscape, 325, 325*f*
Bitcoin cryptocurrency, 94, 96, 170–171
Blockchain
    advantages and disadvantages, 173–174
    block structure, 171, 171*f*
    case studies, 101–102, 102–104*t*
    conceptual framework, 107, 108*f*
    concerns and smart contract, 99–101
    consensus, 172
    decentralised and distributed database technology, 170–171
    development aid (*see* Development aid)
    effectiveness and relevance, 104–107
    identity management, 174–175
    transparency, 105
    types, 172–173
    use cases, 175
BPFT. *See* Practical Byzantine Fault Tolerance (BPFT)
Brand awareness, 276–278
Branding
    functions, 274
    global competition, 273–274
    purchase branded products, 274
    quality and consistency, 275–276
    recognition and image, 275
    targets, 274
British Airways, 118
Browser incognito mode, 374–375
BSC. *See* Balanced score card (BSC)
Business intelligence (BI), 41–42, 47–48, 339–340

C
CA. *See* Content analysis (CA)
Capital One, 119
Career leadership, 311
CARTA. *See* Continuous Adaptive Risk and Trust Assessment (CARTA)
CASB. *See* Cloud access security broker (CASB)
CCT. *See* Cloud computing technology (CCT)

CDR. *See* Consumer Data Right (CDR)
CE. *See* Customer engagement (CE)
Celebrity influencers, 272
Centralised digital currency, 382–383
Chartered Institute of Personnel and Development (CIPD), 315–316
CI. *See* Competitive intelligence (CI)
CIA. *See* Confidentiality, integrity and availability (CIA)
CIPD. *See* Chartered Institute of Personnel and Development (CIPD)
Cisco Trusted Access, 198
Citizen information, 162
Civic participation, 223
Cloud access security broker (CASB), 200
Cloud-based framework
    conceptual model, 56, 57*f*
    fault identification, 63–66, 64*f*
    multiagent-based manufacturing subsystem, 56–63
    multiagent-based supply chain subsystem, 56, 58*f*
Cloud computing technology (CCT), 42–43, 45–46
COBIT5, 255
COEIA. *See* Combined operational effectiveness and investment appraisal (COEIA)
Cognitive psychology, 269
2018 Colombian presidential elections, 219
Combined operational effectiveness and investment appraisal (COEIA), 84
Combined risk and investment appraisal (CRIA)
    cybersecurity, 84–88
    investment scoring, 84
    risk score, 84
Competitive intelligence (CI)
    big data analytics, 344–346, 345*f*, 351–354, 352–353*t*
    big data-driven decision-making, 354
    definition, 340–341
    generating
        after big data analytics, 351
        before big data analytics, 350–351

implications, 355–356
measurement, 343–344
organisations, 339–340
process, 341–343, 343*f*
research methodology
data analysis, 348–349
data collection, 347–348
philosophy and approach, 346–347
scope of, 346
Computer science programmes, 257
Confidentiality, integrity and availability (CIA), 161
Consent, 24–26
Consumer Data Right (CDR), 32–33
Consumers' privacy. *See* Data mining
Content analysis (CA)
fault and cost implications, 52
faults during warranty, 51–52
text mining, 48–49
word analysis, 48–49, 51, 52*f*
Continual consent, 25
Continual learning
action learning and learning projects, 317
considerations, 315–316
job rotation, secondment and shadowing, 317
learning styles, 314
preferences, 314–315
updating training, 314
VARK model, 315
workplace, 316
Continuous Adaptive Risk and Trust Assessment (CARTA), 197, 201–202
Continuous professional development (CPD). *See also* Continual learning
career development in emerging technologies, 309–310
career leadership, 311
employment skills, 307
higher education (HE), 307–309
off-the-job learning, 317–318
transformational leadership, 311–313
Corporate social responsibility (CSR), 26–27
Counter Fraud Taskforce Interim Report, 140
CPD. *See* Continuous professional development (CPD)

CRIA. *See* Combined risk and investment appraisal (CRIA)
Cronbach's alpha reliability coefficient, 230–231
Cryptocurrency, 96–101
Cryptography, 93, 96–98
CSR. *See* Corporate social responsibility (CSR)
Currency
business transactions, 381
concept, 382–383
economic value, 381
estimation, 396
functions, 383
government and public policy, 390–392
marketing data as an asset, 385
organisations, 385–390
token, 382
utility, 383
Customer engagement (CE), 277
Customer information processing, 278–279
Customers/smart retail interactions
online activities and shopping behaviour, 271
perception, 271
Cyberattacks, 249–250
Cyber criminals, 248
Cyber defence technologies, 243
Cyber effective services
data analysis, 126–129
data breach, identity theft and organisations, 118–124
framework, 129–133
general data protection regulation and data breaches, 113–118
research methodology, 124–125
Cybersecurity, 84–88
effectiveness, 126, 128–129
life cycle, 259
myths, 252
polarisation and shape, 244
threats, 244–245
Cybersecurity defence systems
data types, 250
detection types, 250
ecosystems, 250
system architecture, 250
Cyber threats, 85

D

DA. *See* Discovery agent (DA)

DAAC. *See* Data-as-a-Currency (DAAC)

DaaS. *See* Data as a Service (DaaS)

DaaSE. *See* Data as Sharing Economy-Based Business Models (DaaSE)

DAGMAR model, 270

Damage, Reproducibility, Exploitability, Affected users, Discoverability (DREAD), 86–87

DAN. *See* Data acquisition network (DAN)

Dark Web identity sales, 365, 366*f*

Dark Web Torum, 365, 366*f*

1956 Dartmouth summer research project, 3

Data

concept, 382–383

currencies (*see* Currency)

goodwill intangible asset, 394–395

integration, 395

legality, 396–397

literacy and value, 393–394

Data acquisition network (DAN), 196–197

Data-as-a-Currency (DAAC), 390

Data as a Service (DaaS), 386

Data as currency, 383

Data as Sharing Economy-Based Business Models (DaaSE), 387–390

Data breaches

British Airways, 372, 372*f*

customer retention and satisfaction, 119

definition, 119

encryption, 120

Fitbit, 373, 373*f*

3Fun, 373–374, 374*f*

general data protection regulation (GDPR), 113–118

hackers target information, 120

malicious activities, 120

services of an institution, 127

Spotify, 372, 373*f*

Data Breach Investigations Report (DBIR), 116

Data brokerage

characteristics, 361–362

demographics, 364, 365*f*

description, 361–362

online political microtargeting, 362

types

consumer credit/fraud prevention, 363

marketing, 363

people search, 363–365

Data-driven marketing (DDM), 381–382

Data-Information-Knowledge-Wisdom (DIKW), 382

Data leakage

breaches, 372–374

browser incognito mode, 374–375

Data mining

brokerage, 361–365

leakage, 371–375

location tracking, 369–371

tracking and targeted ads, 366–369

Data privacy, 142

Data sharing

elements, 138

fraud detection, 139–142

legal uncertainty, 137

powers, 147–148

public task, 144–148

regulatory and legal requirements, 138

research, 149

DCoC. *See* Digital chain of custody (DCoC)

DCoC-IoT. *See* Digital chain of custody in IoT (DCoC-IoT)

DDM. *See* Data-driven marketing (DDM)

DDoS. *See* Distributed denial-of-service (DDoS)

DE. *See* Digital evidence (DE)

DEA. *See* Digital Economy Act (DEA)

Decentralised identifier (DID), 168–170, 192

Decentralised technology, 93–94

Decentralised trusted identity frameworks, 175

Defenders' perspective

cybersecurity defence systems, 249–251

true costs and cybersecurity programmes, 251–253

Delegated Proof of Stake (DPoS), 172

Denial of service (DoS), 87

Department for Work and Pensions (DWP), 141–142

Descriptive analysis, 51, 232

Descriptive statistics, 230–231
Design agent (Di), 43, 59–61, 61*f*
Development aid
    budget data evaluation, 95
    contracts, 93
    cryptocurrency and smart contracts,
        96–101
    digital data, 109
    donor politics and economic
        conditionalities, 95
    effectiveness, 105–106
    interactive financial systems, 95
    international development, 93–94
    smart contracts and blockchain, 106–107
Dev-Ops, 201–202
DHCP, 207
DI. *See* Digital identity (DI)
Di. *See* Design agent (Di)
DID. *See* Decentralised identifier (DID)
Digital chain of custody (DCoC), 160
Digital chain of custody in IoT (DCoC-IoT), 175
Digital citizens
    augmented reality, 322
    biometrics, 323–325, 323*t*
    holographic communications, 328–330
    holographic reality, 326–327
    hybrid reality, 321–322
    mixed reality, 322–323, 325–326
    one-to-many communications, 327–328
    research methodology, 330–333
Digital communication, 265
Digital curation, 277
Digital divide, 322
Digital Economy Act (DEA), 144, 154–155
Digital evidence (DE), 160, 175
Digital identity (DI)
    claim, 163
    economic value creation, 124
    electronic transactions, 163
    e-services, 163
    financial services, 163
    security and privacy, 133
    tax returns/government benefits online,
        127–128
    three-party model, 163

Digital identity theft
    carding forum, 121
    payment mechanisms, 121
    schemes, 121–124
Digital immigrants, 10, 321–322, 326, 331, 334
Digital leadership
    attributes, 30
    embrace technology, 29
    information governance, 23
    transformative, 35–36
Digital marketing, 219, 223–224, 286–287, 294
Digital natives, 326, 331, 334
Digital service, 128–129
Digital technologies
    customer satisfaction, 265–266
    impersonal marketing communication
        strategies, 265
    marketing and business communication
        processes, 265
Digital twin (DT), 10–11, 15
Digital witness (DW)
    actors and participants, 176–177, 177*t*
    authorising, 180
    collaboration and conceptual
        demonstration, 182–186
    concept, 175–176
    distributed ledger technology (DLT)-based
        components, 176–177, 178*t*
    model design, 179
    official collection points, 182, 183*f*
    results, 187
    scenario 1, 187–189, 188–189*f*
    scenario 2, 190–191, 190–191*f*
    securing point to point (P2P)
        communications, 180–182, 181*t*
    self-sovereign distributed ledger technology
        (DLT)-based scheme and consensus,
        179
    threat model, 176–178
    trusted institutions, 179
DIKW. *See* Data-Information-Knowledge-
        Wisdom (DIKW)
Discovery agent (DA), 56, 63
Distance learning, 318
Distributed database, 96

Distributed–decentralised digital currency, 383
Distributed denial-of-service (DDoS), 368–369
Distributed ledgers, 174–175
Distributed ledger technology (DLT), 162
Distributed manufacturing, 55
DLT. *See* Distributed ledger technology (DLT)
DoS. *See* Denial of service (DoS)
DPoS. *See* Delegated Proof of Stake (DPoS)
DREAD. *See* Damage, Reproducibility, Exploitability, Affected users, Discoverability (DREAD)
Driver and Vehicle Licensing Agency (DVLA), 150
Driver and Vehicle Standards Agency (DVSA), 41
DT. *See* Digital twin (DT)
Duo security authentication, 205
DVLA. *See* Driver and Vehicle Licensing Agency (DVLA)
DVSA. *See* Driver and Vehicle Standards Agency (DVSA)
DW. *See* Digital witness (DW)
DWP. *See* Department for Work and Pensions (DWP)

E
EDR. *See* Endpoint detection and response (EDR)
Effective leadership
  apply marketing concept, 28
  build on strategic planning, 27
  business ethics and personal integrity, 27
  model military leadership, 28
  motivate in the correct way, 28
Endpoint detection and response (EDR), 247
Endpoint protection platform (EPP), 247
Enrolment mechanisms, 161, 162*f*
Enterprise Strategy Group (ESG), 260–262
EPP. *See* Endpoint protection platform (EPP)
e-privacy, 36–37
ESG. *See* Enterprise Strategy Group (ESG)
Ethical leadership. *See also* Effective leadership
  business ethics, 30
  principle-based, 28–29
  self-constitution, 30

self-knowledge and self-development, 35–36
stakeholder representation/responsible leadership, 35–36
Ethics
  and consent, 24–26
  leadership, 29
  quasi-inviolable principle, 29

F
Fault identification
  analytics framework, 47, 48*f*
  flowchart, 63, 64*f*
  implications, 66
  life cycle, 43–44, 44*f*
  procedure, 65–66
  rectification, 54–55
  social media analytics framework, 47
  steps, 63–65
  substeps, 65
  warranty data analysis, 44–46
Fault learning and rectification agent (FLR), 43, 62–63, 62*f*
Fault *vs.* average cost, 53*t*
Federated identity systems, 167
Federation, 125, 127–128
Fileless attacks, 245
Financial Crimes Enforcement Network, 23
Firewall cluster, 210, 210*f*
FLR. *See* Fault learning and rectification agent (FLR)
Formal identification, 160, 161*t*
Fraudsters, 137, 154

G
GCC. *See* Gulf Cooperation Council (GCC)
General data protection regulation (GDPR)
  compliant services, 126
  data breaches, 113–118
  data controllers, 153
  Data Protection Act 2018, 154
  individuals' consent, 143–144
  lawful basis, 153, 155
  requirements, personal data, 143
  risk and vulnerability assessment, 32–33
  robust governance themes, 12

Governance, risk and compliance
    (GRC), 258
Government
    data consumer, 391–392
    data producer, 391
    facilitator, 392
GRC. *See* Governance, risk and compliance
    (GRC)
Gulf Cooperation Council (GCC), 122–123

H
Harvesting, 370
HIDS. *See* Host-based intrusion detection
    systems (HIDS)
Hierarchy of effects, 269–270
HIPS. *See* Host-based intrusion prevention
    systems (HIPS)
HM Revenue and Customs (HMRC), 137,
    141–142
Holographic communications
    data bandwidth, 326–327
    legislative challenges
        augmented reality, 329–330
        general data protection regulation
            (GDPR), 329
        LGPD, 329
        privacy, 330
        property rights, 330
Holographic reality, 326–327
Host-based intrusion detection systems
    (HIDS), 251
Host-based intrusion prevention systems
    (HIPS), 251
Human error, 245
Human Rights Act 1998, 146, 151–152
Hybrid reality, 321–322

I
IA. *See* Interface agent (IA)
IAG. *See* International Airlines Group (IAG)
ICT. *See* Information and communications
    technologies (ICT)
Idealised influence, 312
Identity
    assurance cases, 163–164

definition, 160
digital, 163
physical, 160–161
Identity management (IdM)
    decentralised and self-sovereign
        environments, 174–175
    decentralised identifier (DID), 168–170
    distributed ledgers, 174–175
    federated identity systems, 167
    user-centric identity management systems,
        168, 168*f*
    user-centric models, 166–167
IdM. *See* Identity management (IdM)
ILS. *See* Integrated logistic support (ILS)
Immutability, 94
Individualised consideration, 313
Industry 4.0
    AI (*see* Artificial intelligence (AI))
    in continuous professional development
        (*see* Continuous professional
        development (CPD))
Influencers, 272
Influencing marketing, 272
Informational engagement, 34–35
Information and communications
    technologies (ICT), 384
Information as a Service (IaaS), 387
Information security management system
    (ISMS), 255
Information seeking behaviour, 287–288
Information Systems Security Association
    (ISSA), 260–262
Infrastructure as a service (IaaS), 42–43
Inspirational motivation, 313
Instagram, 272–273
Integrated logistic support (ILS), 79
Intellectual stimulation, 313
Intelligence dissemination, 352*f*
Intelligence explosion, 3
Intelligence, surveillance, target acquisition
    and reconnaissance (ISTAR), 74
Intelligent Nation Plan, 122
Interface agent (IA), 56, 63
International Airlines Group (IAG), 118
Internet-based services, 159–160

Internet-of-Things (IoT), 368–369
Interoperability (IO), 76–77
IO. *See* Interoperability (IO)
IoT. *See* Internet-of-Things (IoT)
ISMS. *See* Information security management system (ISMS)
ISSA. *See* Information Systems Security Association (ISSA)
ISTAR. *See* Intelligence, surveillance, target acquisition and reconnaissance (ISTAR)

J
JavaScript object notation (JSON), 255

K
Knowledge competence, 13–14, 17
Knowledge discovery databases, 7–8
Know your customer (KYC), 162

L
Law of confidentiality, 151–153
Local Security Authority Subsystem (lsass), 248–249
Location tracking
    augmented reality, 369–370
    smart wearables, 370–371
    social Wi-Fi, 370
Low governance approval model, 72*f*
lsass. *See* Local Security Authority Subsystem (lsass)

M
Machine learning (ML), 3, 6–7, 26
Macroinfluencers, 272
Malware, 244
Malware Information Sharing Platform (MISP), 255
Market capitalisation, 396
Marriott, 118
MAS. *See* Multiagent system (MAS)
MCAP. *See* Microcore and perimeter (MCAP)
MCDA. *See* Multicriteria decision analysis (MCDA)
Measurement of effectiveness (MOE), 344
Microcore and perimeter (MCAP), 197

Microcore switch, 197
Microinfluencers, 237, 272
Milgram's reality-virtuality continuum, 322
Misinformation sharing models, 328
MITRE ATT&CK, 255–256
Mixed methodology, 227–228, 232–233
Mixed reality, 322–323, 325–326
Mixed reality spectrum, 322
ML. *See* Machine learning (ML)
MOE. *See* Measurement of effectiveness (MOE)
Morality, 30, 35–36
Multiagent-based manufacturing subsystem
    agent functionalities, 56–58, 60*t*
    design agent, 59–61, 61*f*
    discovery agent, 63
    fault learning and rectification agent, 62–63, 62*f*
    interface agent, 63
Multiagent-based supply chain subsystem, 56, 58*f*
Multiagent system (MAS), 43
Multicriteria decision analysis (MCDA), 81
Musician interview
    experience in music industry, 289–290
    influences of choice, 291
    information-seeking behaviour, 291–292
    online search, 290–291
    search engine optimisation (SEO) keywords used, 291
    word-of-mouth recommendations, 290
Music industry, 286
Music public relation (PR) agencies
    client acquisition, 298–299
    client's search behaviour, 299
    digital marketing, 286–287
    emotional and intellectual levels, 286
    independent musicians, 298
    interview
        activity theory, 294
        clients types, 292–293
        digital marketing, 294
        experience, 292
        found by clients/search for clients, 293
        methods agency is found by, 293

limitations, 301
methodology, 288–289
recommendations
    search engine optimisation (SEO)
      implementation, 299–300
    time allocation, 300
    website sections, 300
word-of-mouth (WOM), 285

N

National Fraud Authority (NFA), 139–140
National Fraud Initiative (NFI), 141
NATO. *See* North Atlantic Treaty Organisation
    (NATO)
Network and information system (NIS), 254
Network authentication systems, 195–196
Network intrusion detection systems (NIDS),
    250
Network reporting agent, 210, 210*f*
Network switch, 211, 211*f*
NFA. *See* National Fraud Authority (NFA)
NFI. *See* National Fraud Initiative (NFI)
NFR. *See* Nonfunctional requirement (NFR)
NIDS. *See* Network intrusion detection systems
    (NIDS)
NIS. *See* Network and information system
    (NIS)
Nonfunctional requirement (NFR), 74
North Atlantic Treaty Organisation (NATO), 77
Nuclear technology, 12

O

OA/OR. *See* Operational analysis/operational
    research (OA/OR)
Objectives and key result (OKR) framework
    constituent parts, 130*f*
    deliver cybersecurity effectiveness, 131*t*
    economical, 131
    ethical, 132–133
    internal stakeholder/external service user,
      130
    legal, 132
    political, 130–131
    social, 131–132
    technological, 132

OCEAN. *See* Openness, conscientiousness,
    extraversion, agreeableness and
    neuroticism (OCEAN)
Official collection points (OCP), 175, 182, 183*f*
Off-the-job learning
    benefits, 317
    distance learning and online digital learning,
      318
One-to-many communications, 327–328
Online digital learning, 318
Online political microtargeting, 362
Online tracking, 367
Openness, conscientiousness, extraversion,
    agreeableness and neuroticism
    (OCEAN), 362
Operational analysis/operational research
    (OA/OR), 84
Optimism bias, 73
Organisational cultures, 35
Organisation firewalls, 250

P

P3P. *See* Platform for Privacy Preferences (P3P)
PaaS. *See* Platform as a service (PaaS)
Pandemic of COVID-19, 307
Payment Card Industry Data Security Standard
    (PCI DSS), 254–255
'Pepper's Ghost', 327
Permissionless *vs.* permissioned ledgers, 172,
    173*f*
Personalisation
    artificial intelligence (AI), 277
    customer relationships, 277
    digital, 276
    nondigital, 276
Personally identifiable information (PII), 120,
    168, 370–371
Phishing, 244
Physical identity (PI), 160–161
PI. *See* Physical identity (PI)
PII. *See* Personally identifiable information
    (PII)
PKI authentication, 205
Platform as a service (PaaS), 42–43
Platform for Privacy Preferences (P3P), 25–26

PLM. *See* Product lifecycle management (PLM)
PMI. *See* Project Management Institute (PMI)
PMO. *See* Project management office (PMO)
Poisson regression model, 230–231
Political marketing, 220–222, 233, 235
Political participation, 222–223
PoS. *See* Proof of stake (PoS)
Post-Great Recession environment, 307
PoW. *See* Proof of work (PoW)
Practical Byzantine Fault Tolerance (BPFT),
    172
Privacy consent, 25–26, 28, 34–35
Proactive cybersecurity programme, 258–259
Product lifecycle management (PLM), 42
Project management
    government agencies, 13
    human/machine interface, 13
    knowledge competence areas and
        frameworks, 13–14
    services domain, 4
Project Management Institute (PMI),
    13–14, 16
Project management office (PMO), 14
Proof of stake (PoS), 172
Proof of work (PoW), 172
Public bodies, 137
Public services, 138
Public task
    data sharing powers, 147–148
    function, 144–145
    Human Rights Act 1998, 146
    necessity and proportionality test, 145
    purpose limitation, 145
    UK legal landscape, 145–146
Public trust, 155

Q
QAA. *See* Quality Assurance Agency (QAA)
Quality Assurance Agency (QAA), 308

R
Radius authentication, 204–205
Ransomware, 245
Reauthentication mechanisms, 204, 206–207
Reinforcement theory, 233

Reporting of Injuries, Diseases and Dangerous
    Occurrences Regulations (RIDDOR), 79
Reputational risks, 31–32, 36–37
Reverse engineering, 396
RIDDOR. *See* Reporting of Injuries, Diseases
    and Dangerous Occurrences
    Regulations (RIDDOR)
Risk and vulnerability assessment
    challenges, 33–34
    general data protection regulation (GDPR),
        32–33
    reputation, 31–32
Risk-sensing technologies, 31–32
RSA SecureID, 204–205

S
SA. *See* Sentiment analysis (SA)
SaaS. *See* Software as a service (SaaS)
SbD. *See* Security/secure by design (SbD)
Scalable, manageable, achievable, realistic and
    timely (SMART), 72–73
SCF. *See* Supply chain facilitator agent (SCF)
SDGs. *See* Sustainable Development Goals
    (SDGs)
SDI. *See* Strategic Defense Initiative (SDI)
SDN. *See* Software-defined networks (SDN)
SE. *See* Secure elements (SE)
Search engine optimisation (SEO)
    digital marketing, 287
    effectiveness, 288
    implementation, 299–300
    inlinks, 297
    title 1, meta description and H1-1 lengths,
        297
    webpage indexability, 297
    White hat conceptual framework, 297–298
Search engine result pages (SERPs), 287
Secure elements (SE), 180
Secure private channel, 182, 182*f*
Security analytics, 258
Security frameworks' perspective, 253–256
Security professionals, 257
Security/secure by design (SbD), 84
Self-learning neural networks, 278
Self-sovereign identity (SSI), 174, 174*f*

Semistructured interviews, 229–230
Sentiment analysis (SA)
    customer perception
        about dealer competence, 54
        about fault rectification, 52–54, 54f
    structured formatted data, 49
    WordNet dictionary, 49
SEO. See Search engine optimisation (SEO)
SERPs. See Search engine result pages (SERPs)
Service-oriented architecture (SOA), 42–43
Shared ledger, 170–171
Shortage
    academic disciplines, 259
    CISOs, 257
    data breaches, 257
SIG. See Special interest groups (SIG)
Sign-in risk policy, 197
Single sign-on (SSO), 167, 167f
Situational leadership, 30
SMART. See Scalable, manageable, achievable,
        realistic and timely (SMART)
Smart contracts
    atomise contract execution, 98
    big data, 100
    blockchain concerns and, 99–101
    features, 98t
    supply chain management, 98
Smart devices, 368–369
Smart wearables, 370–371
SOA. See Service-oriented architecture (SOA)
Social media
    aims, 234–236
    business marketing, 267–268
    customer perception, 269
    data collection methods and strategies,
        227–228
    data sampling, 50–51
    data sharing, 42
    data usage, 46–49
    fault identification, 42–46
    hypothesis and prepositions, 224–226
    influencers, 272
    Instagram, 268
    Internet accessibility, 266
    interviews, 229–230

    limitations, 236
    online business, 268
    online organisers, 266–267
    for political marketing, 221–222
    and political participation, 222–223
    qualitative data
        data analysis methods, 231
        prepositions and thematic analysis, 232
    quantitative data
        data analysis methods, 230–231
        descriptive analysis, 232
    recommendations
        political parties, 237
        for research, 236–237
    research approach, 227
    research philosophy, 226–227
    research questions and contributions, 46
    survey, 228–229
    two-way communication, 220, 268
    user-generated content, 267
Social networks, 219
Social Wi-Fi, 370, 376
Software as a service (SaaS), 42–43
Software-defined networks (SDN), 201, 206
SoS. See System of systems (SoS)
Special interest groups (SIG), 13
Spoofing, Tampering, Repudiation,
        Information disclosure, Denial of
        service and Elevation of privilege
        (STRIDE), 85, 87–88, 87f
SRSA. See Statistics and Registration Service
        Act (SRSA)
SSI. See Self-sovereign identity (SSI)
SSO. See Single sign-on (SSO)
Statistics and Registration Service Act (SRSA),
        147
Strategic Defense Initiative (SDI), 247–248
Strategic intelligence architecture, 74
STRIDE. See Spoofing, Tampering,
        Repudiation, Information disclosure,
        Denial of service and Elevation of
        privilege (STRIDE)
Structural equation modelling, 230–231
Supply chain facilitator agent (SCF), 43
Supply chain subsystem agents, 59t

SURF. *See* Systems understanding of risk framework (SURF)
Sustainable Development Goals (SDGs), 93
System of systems (SoS), 77
Systems understanding of risk framework (SURF)
  academia, 71
  assessments, 73–74
  assured, 75–76, 75*f*
  combined risk and investment appraisal, 84, 84*f*
  connected, 76, 76*f*
  end user, 71–72
  impact score mapping, 83*f*
  interoperable, 76–77, 76*f*
  likelihood score mapping, 82*f*
  minimal application, 80–81
  risk assessment method, 81–83
  risk score mapping, 83*f*
  safety, 78–79, 78*f*
  secure, 77–78, 77*f*
  supported, 79–80, 79*f*
  timely, 80, 80*f*
  traceability, 72–73

T
TDE. *See* Transparent data encryption (TDE)
Teaching excellence framework (TEF), 308
Technologies and Innovation Futures (TIF), 7
Text mining, 48–49
The Dawn of Cyber Politicians, 327
The Right to Privacy, 376–377
Threat landscape assessment, 86, 86*f*
TIF. *See* Technologies and Innovation Futures (TIF)
TPM. *See* Trusted platform modules (TPM)
Tracker market share, 367, 367*f*
Transformational leadership, 311–313
Transparent data encryption (TDE), 208
Trusted platform modules (TPM), 180
Turing test, 5

U
Unified Modelling Language (UML), 55
Unsupervised machine learning algorithms, 48–49

User-centric identity management systems, 168, 168*f*
User risk policy, 197

V
Vehicle faults, 41
Vendor risk management platforms, 258
Virtual container environment, 201–202
Virtual reality (VR), 322, 326
Virtual residency, 123
Visibility, 199–200
Voting preferences, 221–222, 229, 231
VR. *See* Virtual reality (VR)
Vulnerability chain, 245–246
Vulnerability management, 258

W
Warranty data analysis (WDA), 42, 44–46
WAVE
  analysis, 296
  empty heading, 296
  empty link, 295
  linked image missing alternative text, 295
  missing alternative text, 295
  missing form label, 296
WDA. *See* Warranty data analysis (WDA)
Website tracking, 366
Wireless networks, 207
Word-of-mouth (WOM), 223–224, 233–234, 285, 290

Z
Zero-knowledge proof (ZKP), 164–166, 165*f*, 180, 180*f*
Zero-knowledge succinct noninteractive arguments of knowledge (zk-SNARKS), 166
Zero trust networks
  authentication mechanisms, 203–206
  concept, 196, 198–199
  developing, 208–210
  DHCP, 207
  hardware, 210–212
  implementing, 199–200
  limitations, 212
  monitoring with Bro, 212

network security auditing standards align, 208
physical environment, 202–203
principles, 196–197
threat of data theft, 207
variations, 197–198

virtual container environment, 201–202
wireless networks, 207
ZKP. *See* Zero-knowledge proof (ZKP)
zk-SNARKS. *See* Zero-knowledge succinct noninteractive arguments of knowledge (zk-SNARKS)

Index

Printed in the United States
By Bookmasters